Through Mem'ry's Haze

A PERSONAL MEMOIR

Elizabeth G. Beinecke and William S. Beinecke

Through Mem'ry's Haze

A PERSONAL MEMOIR

William S. Beinecke

with Geoffrey M. Kabaservice

Prospect Hill Press

New York

Prospect Hill Press
99 Park Avenue
New York, New York 10016

Library of Congress Cataloging-in-Publication Data

Beinecke, William Sperry.
    Through mem'ry's haze : a personal memoir / William S. Beinecke with
    Geoffrey M. Kabaservice.
        p. cm.
    Includes index.
    ISBN 0-9676987-0-7
    1. Beinecke, William Sperry. 2. Beinecke family. 3. Businessmen—United
States—Biography. 4. Philanthropists—United States—Biography. 5. Sperry and
Hutchinson Company—History. 6. Trading-stamps—United States—History.
I. Kabaservice, Geoffrey M.   II. Title

HC102.5.B425 A3 2000
658.8'2—dc21
[B]   99-462317

PRINTED IN THE UNITED STATES OF AMERICA

TO BETTY

Who has been with me on this long road every step of the way
through more than sixty years.
Without her love and companionship, there would have been no story.

Contents

List of Illustrations

Foreword

I first heard the name Beinecke in 1961 when, a callow undergraduate newspaper editor, I was asked by Yale President Griswold to delay publishing news of the family's magnificent gift—now the world-famous Beinecke Rare Book Library—until a New Jersey court resolved a dispute concerning S&H Green Stamps, the family's business.

I first met Bill Beinecke in 1971 when, a callow assistant professor at Harvard, I was asked by Yale President Brewster to be a Fellow of the Yale Corporation. I joined that eminent board on the same day as William Sperry Beinecke, chairman of a major corporation, member of important corporate and charitable boards, and scion of a great Yale family.

How can it be that Mr. Beinecke, born the same year as my mother, was the first of my new colleagues whom I felt I could address by his nickname? (Over many years I never achieved the comfort to call John Hay "Jock" Whitney anything but "sir.") And that I was never inhibited from expressing my doubts about whether Yale should inaugurate its School of Organization and Management, an important achievement of Bill Beinecke and undoubtedly the most important expansion of Yale in the past half century? And that when the serendipities of life made me dean of one of Bill's other alma maters, Columbia Law School, we immediately began the most open and helpful dialogue about the needs of this law school and the ways in which those needs could be met?

I have had the good fortune to work with and learn from many remarkable people, especially my first two employers, Justice White and Mayor Lindsay. There is no one—literally no one—with whom I have had more "quality time," from whom I have learned more, or for whom my admiration and affection is greater than Bill. If one accepts the quaint Anglo-American custom of named academic "chairs," then there is no name for which I would trade "William S. Beinecke Professor of Law."

This book comes much closer to a true picture of this very special man than I imagined it would. Bill is modest and self-effacing; I doubted he would communicate how extraordinary his life and his accomplishments have been. But while the words are descriptive, the succession of stories presents a clear and coherent picture. Over eighty-five remarkable years, the same human being has been studying, traveling, engaging with people, and quietly contributing to the public welfare. In this book Bill tells about hundreds of people, but the reader learns most about the story teller.

If this book is even substantially accurate, then Bill has had family relations so warm and supportive that we wish them to everyone we know. His grandparents, his parents, his remarkable spouse, and his fine children and grandchildren all provided positive relationships. (I skip the many uncles, aunts, and cousins in the United States and Germany.) I think Bill is the one who is open and accepting of others. How can he remember the names and descriptions of all the people he knew in school, on foreign trips, and in business relationships? How can he be so understanding and accepting of their vagaries?

The second theme is travel and observation of the environment. Bill remembers the New Jersey of his youth, the Germany and Italy of Hitler and Mussolini, 1930's Shanghai and Singapore, the South Pole, and oh so many golf courses. He is fully aware that as a privileged American he saw only aspects of reality; but he saw a great deal of the whole.

Bill recalls his school-life: Pingry, Madison Academy, Westminster, his eviction from and return to Andover, his time at Yale and at Columbia. Every one of his schools appreciates his lifelong commitment to them.

Like so many in his generation, Bill "won" World War II. (My generation, which "lost" Vietnam, is differently marked.) Though separated from wife and baby, Bill had extraordinary experiences in the navy, and learned from all of them.

Bill was a major business leader. For decades S&H was a key player in the US retail economy. Bill led a quality team and made a series of key strategic decisions, most of them winners.

And Bill, joined by his family, has quietly made a tremendous difference with charitable support. The emphases have been progress for African-Americans, environmentalism, and culture: certainly choices that justify pride.

Living on Central Park West, I must make special note of Bill's founding leadership of the Central Park Conservancy. No single institutional innovation has contributed more to the late-century rebirth of Manhattan as a livable environment for all its residents.

This book tells, quietly, an amazing family story: of German immigrants who achieved remarkably almost from their arrival in the new world; of Bill's father, Frederick W. Beinecke, who lost a great deal in the Depression (so that Bill was the opposite of a rich student when he was a Yale undergraduate) and then built so much more; of Bill's children who are now—each of them—deeply involved in their communities. But the man in the middle, the one telling this story, has been traveling, keeping up with friends, bringing people together, quietly making wise suggestions, and paying attention with an open mind for all of his eighty-five years. So many people love him!

Of the thousand or so vignettes in this book, one is indelibly in my head (perhaps because I am addicted to ice cream and am often on Riverside Drive). Bill describes one fine spring day during his Columbia Law years, when he and a young woman (a fellow law student) "went skipping down Riverside Drive holding hands and eating our ice cream cones. . . . Connie Mittendorf and some of my other dear friends used to tease me to death about that until I was quite fed up." It is a Victorian picture, but it is also an image fully relevant as we enter a new century. All of us who have skipped with Bill, eating ice cream, are grateful for what he has added to our lives.

—LANCE LIEBMAN

Preface

The last stanza of Yale's anthem, "Bright College Years," contains these bittersweet lines:

> *In after-years, should troubles rise*
> *To cloud the blue of sunny skies,*
> *How bright will seem, through mem'ry's haze,*
> *Those happy, golden, by-gone days!*

Any melancholy this verse may produce in the middle-aged or elderly Yale alumnus who sings it at a football game or reunion is quickly dispelled by the climactic last line, accompanied by the traditional waving of napkins and handkerchiefs: "For God, for Country, and for Yale!"

I took the title for my autobiography from my alma mater's anthem for a very simple reason. I do not, fortunately, have many troubles to cloud my sunny skies, nor do I yearn wistfully for happy, golden, by-gone days of yore. But I do undoubtedly look back at my life and times through the scrim of memory's haze. I have tried to recall the people and events in this memoir as accurately as I can, and have done my best to check my recollections against the historical record and other people's impressions. Still, I'm not a professional historian, and I know that memory is a shifting and fallible thing. And I know that sometimes my view of events and the views of others were, to put it mildly, Rashomon-like. This is especially true, I find, with some of the events my shipmates and I shared in World War II.

Most of this autobiography emerged, piece by piece, through a series of conversations. Over the past four years, I was interviewed from time to time by Geoffrey Kabaservice, who started with me when he was a graduate student in history at Yale. He has since earned his Ph.D. and is a lecturer at the university. He asked me innumerable probing questions. My responses were taped and transcribed. Then together we hammered the rough material of my responses into readable prose and narrative shape, a process that entailed more drafts and revisions than either of us could count. Even so, I sense and hope that the book retains the flavor and informality of conversation. We have tried, through reading and rereading every line and double-checking every factual reference, to make this book as free from error as possible. But I fear that errors have a way of creeping in. Those that remain are solely my responsibility.

I could not have put this book together without a great deal of help. My thanks go, first, to my wife, Betty, who has been my companion and love of my life for almost sixty years. Though she has been determined not to look over my shoulder while I have been working on this autobiography, her influence is present on every page. I am also indebted to Robert J. Barletta, who had the idea in the first place that I should write my history, encouraged me to get started on it in the summer of 1994, and has enthusiastically supported the project ever since.

Geoff Kabaservice has been a dedicated and energetic collaborator throughout this enterprise, and has become a friend as well. Russell Till guided me through the publishing process, and deserves the credit for the handsome appearance of this volume. Roslyn Schloss carefully edited the entire manuscript and saved me from many an embarrassing malapropism and grammatical howler. William M. Simpich also read through the whole work and made numerous excellent suggestions, just as he did back in the days when he helped me write speeches at The Sperry and Hutchinson Company. And, thanks to my friend James T. Mills, noted author Robert Carlisle gave this work a careful reading to catch any errors that had crept into the galleys. Paul Stillwell, a historian at the US Naval Institute in Annapolis, examined my chapters on World War II, and my old colleague Eugene Beem went over the chapters on S&H. My shipmates William J. Duddleson and Eugene Somers also read through the chapters on my war service, and together they clarified and corrected much that was vague or misleading. I am grateful to Lance Liebman for doing me the honor of writing the foreword to this book.

The chapters on The Sperry and Hutchinson Company presented particular difficulties, since no complete history of S&H, or of the trading stamp business in general, had previously been written. Much of the information in those chapters comes from interviews with my former colleagues Gene Beem, Walter Beinecke, Jr., Frederick A. Collins, Jr., Peter Cooper, Edward A. Hynes, David Maclay, Jim Mills, Paul Mott, Charles Phillips, Elaine Pitts, Frank Rossi, and Bill Simpich.

Of course their cooperation in no way implies their endorsement of the analysis and conclusions I make, but I deeply appreciate their assistance. Many other people have helped with other parts of this memoir, and I would particularly like to thank Edward A. Ames, Edward G. Beimfohr, Marshall Cleland, Constance Eiseman, Lucinda Geist, Clay Hiles, Peter Johnson, Charles Luce, Wilson Newman, Warren Price, Betsy Barlow Rogers, Ross Sandler, and Deborah Wiley. I would be most remiss if I did not pay special tribute to my hardworking secretary Linda Wool.

And I am indebted, too, to my four children, Rick, Sarah, John, and Frances, for their encouragement and their patience. They supported me and inspired me. Their full involvement in life, and the vigor with which they pursue it, are equaled and sometimes exceeded only by their matchless spouses, Candace Krugman, Gaily Wurtzel, Craig Richardson, and Paul Elston. I cannot overstate how proud they make me and how much I admire all eight of them.

First and last, my thanks go to Betty. This book is dedicated to her.

Chatham, Massachusetts
January 2000

CHAPTER ONE

From the Beginning: Family Background and Early Childhood, 1914–1925

One of my earliest memories is of a fine spring day in Manhattan in 1919, when I was five years old. The First World War had ended the previous November, and the returning veterans of the victorious American Expeditionary Force were marching up Fifth Avenue. I had a splendid view of the parade from my paternal grandparents' suite on the twelfth floor of The Plaza Hotel. Their living room window, which faced Fifth Avenue, opened onto a small balcony, not one that you could really stand on so much as a ledge with a decorative railing of oval-shaped iron rods. It was a warm day, and as I moved near the open window toward the balcony, my grandmother called out, "Be careful, Bubbie." That was a German way of speaking to a child, for my Beinecke grandparents were of German descent. I didn't know it then, but my paternal grandfather, Bernhard Beinecke, was the first owner and proprietor of the magnificent Plaza Hotel, where I stood that day watching the parade outside the window. I didn't grow up with the feeling that The Plaza belonged to my family; it was simply the place where my grandparents lived, where I would go when I came into Manhattan from my parents' home in Cranford, New Jersey, about twenty miles southwest of the city.

Cranford in those days was a small suburban town. When I walked around it as a boy, I used to pass a grand mansion ringed by a great iron fence that overlooked the Rahway River. The house had been built by my great-uncle Thomas Sperry, who was my maternal grandfather's younger brother. I was too young to know that Thomas Sperry had founded The Sperry and Hutchinson Company, the nation's first independent trading stamp company. And I certainly had no inkling that I

1

myself would one day become its president, chairman and CEO and that I would see it grow from a small and marginal concern to a near-billion-dollar business that would become one of America's largest corporations. My association with S&H over the years offered me a wide variety of experiences and insights, introduced me to many remarkable people, allowed me to take part in the creation of several important enterprises, and took me to many different places. But its origins, and my own, go back to the two branches of my family, the Beineckes and the Sperrys, and the connections between the great metropolis of New York City and the small suburb of Cranford, New Jersey.

I was born on May 22, 1914, in my parents' home at 817 West End Avenue at 100th Street in New York City. Within a year, my parents moved from Manhattan to Cranford, my mother's girlhood home. My maternal grandfather, William Miller Sperry, had moved there with several of his siblings around the turn of the century. With his brother Thomas, my grandfather was coproprietor of The Sperry and Hutchinson Company, which had been founded in Michigan in 1896, incorporated in the state of New Jersey in 1900, and headquartered in New York City since the early 1900s. The company gave my grandfather and great-uncle sufficient affluence so that the Sperrys became an important family in Cranford, and the two brothers had a lot to do with the way the town developed. My grandfather was the president of the Cranford National Bank, which he had founded with his brother in 1904. The proprietor of a block of buildings in the downtown area known as the Sperry Buildings, he also owned a number of lots and other properties in Cranford.

By the time I was a boy, my grandfather was living in a house occupying the block between Prospect Street and North Union Avenue. The house faced the Rahway River, with a wide swath of greenery between the river and my grandfather's broad front lawn sloping down the hill. The stretch of land along the river was known as Sperry Park. My grandfather had given the riverfront to the town in 1907, and it was the first park of what eventually became the Union County parks system. My great-uncle Thomas Sperry had lived near my grandfather's, in a rather more imposing mansion across Prospect Street. Both houses overlooked Riverside Drive, which paralleled the river. My other Sperry relatives from that generation included my great-uncle Joseph (who also lived in Cranford), my great-aunt Regina (whom we called Aunt Gene), and my great-uncle Washington Elliott Langley Sperry, who spent most of his time in Florida. The first of the children of that generation, Margaret, had died at age two, and the youngest, Louis, had died in a swimming pool accident in 1886, when he was seventeen years old.

My great-uncle Joe was the oldest of the five Sperry children who survived to adulthood, and I used to visit him at his home in Cranford and talk about Sperry family history. Uncle Joe had a deep interest in his kin, and often visited his cousins in Winchester, Virginia. Sperrys have lived in Winchester since the first member of the family came to this country in the mid-eighteenth century. The family name was originally a German one, variously spelled Spiri or Spirri or Spiry, which was anglicized to Sperry. The first immigrant from the Sperry family was Hanss Peter Spiri, who arrived in Virginia in 1750. His son Jacob Sperry was a soldier in the Revolutionary War, which qualifies me for membership in the Sons of the Revolution. Jacob's grandson was my great-grandfather Jacob Austin Sperry.

When I was very young, I had the good fortune to know my great-grandmother Susan Butler Langley Sperry, who was born in Germantown, Pennsylvania, in 1832. The Langleys were originally from New York but through various circumstances ended up in Michigan (there's a covered bridge named for the Langley family in Centreville, St. Joseph's County, Michigan). My great-grandmother married a Virginian, Jacob Austin Sperry. She lived into her nineties in a house in Cranford that was given to her by her sons. By that time she was the matriarch of all the Sperrys. My brother and I went to see her on occasional mornings after Sunday school. She died when I was eight, and in the last year or so of her life she moved from Cranford to take up residence with my great-aunt Gene (Mrs. August Wiedenbach) in New Rochelle, New York, so I never knew her very well. But I do have a dim recollection of her, and it overwhelmed me even then to think that she had lived her early years at a time when there were many people who could clearly recall the first days of the Republic. For all I knew, an acquaintance or friend of hers might actually have seen George Washington, or even spoken to him. Here, in a way, was a direct link between my life and the founding of the nation. How very fast the process of social change is in terms of human life—only three lives between the founding of the nation and today!

My grandfather William Miller Sperry was born in 1858 in Bristol, Tennessee, his family having moved there from Winchester. Early in 1861, my great-grandfather relocated the family to Knoxville, Tennessee, and set up shop in that growing metropolis as an author and the editor of the local pro-Confederacy newspaper, the *Knoxville Register*. My uncle Joseph Sperry had been born in 1855, and he used to tell me about growing up during the Civil War days. He was too young to be involved in the conflict as a soldier but not too young to sympathize with the "Lost Cause" and help care for the Confederate soldiers' horses. Knoxville changed hands several times during the war. Uncle Joe told me that one day as troops rode through town, he and some other boys ran out in the street and shouted, "Hooray for Jeff Davis and the Southern Confederacy!"—only to discover they were cheering the wrong soldiers! The war caused particular disruption to my grandfather's family as Jacob Sperry was vehement in his support of the Southern cause, writing editorials so fiery that when General Burnside's troops approached Knoxville, he fled back to Bristol. He was publishing his newspaper in Bristol when he was arrested there by Federal troops on December 14, 1864, and remained a prisoner until the end of the war in April 1865. (His diary, which he left in a neat and legible hand, records the experience of Christmas in jail and is good reading even today; it is reproduced as Appendix J in Paul Prindle's *The Ancestry of William Sperry Beinecke*.) Uncle Joe said that the Yankees even smashed his father's printing press, and Jacob Sperry barely avoided execution. My great-grandmother, who was then little more than thirty years old, gathered up young William and the rest of her brood and retreated to her parents' farm in Centreville, Michigan.

After the war, the family was reunited in Little Silver, New Jersey. Jacob Sperry became an itinerant printer and editor and died in 1896 in the Old Printers Home in Colorado Springs. My grandfather grew up in New Jersey, graduated from high school in Plainfield, attended night school in New York City, worked for a time on Wall Street, and went into the hardware business in the 1880s. In 1890, he married my grandmother, Caroline Whitehead, and my mother, Caroline Regina Sperry, was born in February 1891. Sad to relate, my grandmother died in June of that year, at age twenty-two—perhaps of complications from my mother's birth, perhaps of heart problems; I was never told. In 1897, my grandfather married Emily Mooney, who was some eleven years younger than he, and they had three daughters—my aunts Dorothy (Dot), Virginia (Ginnie), and Emily (Emmy Lou). Emily Mooney Sperry was my maternal grandmother in all senses of the words. I always called her Nana. She was a warm, loving grandmother, and I had a wonderful relationship with her.

My grandfather resettled the family in Cranford, New Jersey, in 1898, and soon after became involved in The Sperry and Hutchinson Company with his brother Thomas. He built the beautiful house overlooking the Rahway River, and entered into the social, cultural, and

*William Miller Sperry
(William S. Beinecke's
maternal grandfather),
1858–1927.*

business life of Cranford. I have a portrait of my grandfather painted from an old photograph that probably dates back to a few years after he moved to Cranford. It shows him in his prime: a bright-eyed, good-humored man with a neatly trimmed mustache and beard, wearing a natty bow tie over a high collar, a heavy suit, and an elaborate ornamental waistcoat with a chain.

My mother, Caroline Regina Sperry—known to all as Carrie—was born in Brick Church, New Jersey, but grew up in Cranford, along with her three half sisters. Her uncle Joseph Sperry lived nearby with his wife and children, Lottie and William M. II, as did her uncle Thomas Sperry, his wife, and their four children, Katherine, Thomas Jr., Stuart, and Marjorie. My mother and her sisters all graduated from the Ogontz School, near Philadelphia, an excellent boarding school for girls. (The school no longer exists; it has become part of Pennsylvania State University.) The Ogontz School was intended to foster an appreciation of the arts among the students and did so partly by taking them to the Widener estate across from the school, with its magnificent collection of paintings and other artworks. This experience undoubtedly helped cultivate my mother's lifelong interest in the arts, and she went on to become an opera lover, a ballet enthusiast, and a collector of Impressionist paintings. Perhaps the most unusual aspect of the school was its emphasis on military training—an emphasis that would still be considered unusual at girls' schools today. My family's genealogist, Paul Prindle, writes of the school that "[t]he girls wore uniforms, carried wooden guns, and marched each spring in competition with boys attending military schools in Bordentown and nearby areas, being judged by US Army officers." It would be difficult to say how this training influenced my mother, but she was always a remarkably independent, self-reliant, and disciplined woman.

My mother loved the Ogontz School, and she blossomed there. She was involved in an array of extracurriculars, including academic, athletic and artistic activities. She was class salutatorian at her graduation in 1909, and her classmates voted her "Cleverest" in the class. It was not the custom in those days for women to go on to take an undergraduate degree. But if my mother had gone on to college, she would have made quite an impression. She was warm, witty, and vivacious, and she was also a stunningly beautiful woman. Up until I was in my fifties, she was mistaken many times for my sister. She had a youthful face and appearance, and her whole personality was youthful. She had a young outlook. She would have been a catch for any man, and she was well matched with the man she married—my father, Frederick William Beinecke.

My father was the fifth of the six surviving children of my grandparents Johann Bernhard Georg Beinecke and Johanna Elisabeth Weigle Beinecke. I never got to know my paternal grandparents as well as I knew my maternal grandparents. They were not exactly forbidding, but they were both at least a decade older than my Sperry grandparents, and there was a certain air of Old World formality about them. And since they lived in Manhattan, I didn't see them as often as I did my Cranford relatives. When I was young, I didn't know much about my Beinecke grandparents' backgrounds, and I didn't realize that my grandfather Bernhard Beinecke was one of the titans of American enterprise. His was truly one of the great American success stories. He was born in Elberfeld, Germany, in 1846, and emigrated to New York City in 1865. Ten years later, he married my grandmother, Johanna Weigle. The Weigle family had come to the United States from Germany in the aftermath of the European revolutions of 1848 and operated a business in Manhattan called the Metropolitan Dye Works. My grandfather had started out in America as the driver of a butcher's

*Johann Bernhard Beinecke
(William S. Beinecke's paternal
grandfather), 1846–1932.*

wagon, then had bought out the company and reorganized it as Beinecke & Company; it grew to be one of the largest wholesale meat concerns in New York City. From the meat business, he expanded into shipping cattle abroad, then into banking, becoming one of the early directors of the Germania Bank. In its later incarnation as the Commonwealth Bank, he was its president and, when it was consolidated with the Manufacturer's Trust Company, chairman of the board. Finally he became a pioneer of the modern hotel business, forming one of the first chains in the country. The Hammond Hotel Company, which he organized and ran with several associates, operated the old Plaza and Murray Hill Hotels in New York City and other hotels in Boston, Virginia, and Washington, D.C. He was also the force behind the construction of the Manhattan Hotel in New York and the Copley Plaza Hotel in Boston. The jewel in the crown was the present Plaza Hotel in Manhattan, which he opened in 1907.

Bernhard Beinecke was a man of astounding energy, ability, acumen, and audacity. I have a bust of him by the famous sculptor Gutzon Borglum, well known for having carved the faces of Presidents Washington, Jefferson, Lincoln, and Theodore Roosevelt into Mount Rushmore. In the 1920s, Borglum had been commissioned to do a war memorial in the central square of Newark, New Jersey. My father was a

Newark business leader at the time, and I think he got to know Borglum through that connection. My father and two of his brothers commissioned Borglum to do a bust of their father. Borglum's work is a fine representation of my grandfather, full of power and dignity. Each bust was numbered, and one was given to each of Bernhard Beinecke's six children.

The oldest Beinecke child was Bernhard, named after his father; I always called him Uncle Ben. Born in 1876, he was the first member of the family to go to Yale College, where he graduated with a Ph.B. degree in 1898. I didn't know him well, because he lived in California when I was young. My Aunt Alice, who was born in 1881, was an accomplished musician and a cultivated, artistic individual; since she grew up in a German American household, it was not a great surprise when she married a German named Johann Friedrich Weickert, emigrated, and raised her family in Germany. A second daughter, Johanna, had died in infancy in late 1882. A few months after her death, in August 1883, a third daughter, Theodora, was born. "Theodora" derives from the

Frederick W. Beinecke (William S. Beinecke's father), formal portrait, c. 1952.

Greek meaning "gift of the gods": she was the little girl in place of the one who was gone. Then came Edwin, born in 1886; my father, Frederick, in 1887; and Walter, the youngest, in 1888. Those three youngest brothers were close not only in years but in every other way. They were in business together, they went to school together, they maintained homes in the New York City area, they effectively raised their children together, and they worked as a team throughout their lives. My father and Uncle Walter even married first cousins, Carrie and Katherine Sperry.

The Beineckes were an old-fashioned German family. My father was known to family and friends as Fritz all his life. My Beinecke grandparents spoke German to their children at home, so my father and his siblings were bilingual. (My father, alas, didn't continue that tradition with his own children. I have tried to learn German, but it came much

Edwin J., Frederick W., and Walter Beinecke, c. 1912.

later in my life and I've never been very good at it. I can translate a bit, but I can't speak it worth a hoot and I can't think in it.) My father grew up in a privileged home. Bernhard Beinecke was quite comfortably well off, and the family always had domestic help. When my father and his siblings were growing up in New York City, they lived in a brownstone house on West 76th Street, and at some point they also lived on the East Side. (It was at 47 East 78th Street, just a block from where I live today, that my great-grandmother, who had followed her son to America, died in 1881.) The place my father most often spoke of, however, was the family's country home, Oscawanna, on the Hudson River near Peekskill, New York. It was a large house with a tower, built in the 1880s in the style sometimes called General Grant Gothic. The family had happy times there. My grandparents frequently went to Europe and often took one or two of the older children with them; on those occasions my father and his brothers Edwin and Walter would be left in the care of my grandmother's younger sister Matilde Mittendorf, whom we called Aunt Tilly. The Mittendorfs had a country place in Crugers-on-Hudson, not far from Oscawanna. For several summers a young Princeton graduate was employed as a tutor to look after the Beinecke brothers, though he was really more companion than tutor. One summer about a hundred years ago, he took the boys on a camping trip into the Adirondacks, and on a launch up through the lakes there. The Beinecke family also spent at least one summer on Shelter Island, between the North and South Forks of Long Island. I once had a little silver cup my father's older sister Theo won in the ladies' golf tournament on Shelter Island in the summer of 1898. (I gave it to my cousin Linda Truesdale of San Diego, whose mother, Theo, was named after our mutual aunt.)

Some years ago I decided to try to form an archive of some of the bits and pieces of information I had about my family. I employed a young woman named Patsy Gaskill to organize this material, and she did a superb job. In that archive is some interesting correspondence between Bernhard Beinecke and his daughter Alice, who was living in Germany with her family during the traumatic years after World War I. There was horrendous inflation in Germany, probably the worst in history, when the value of the mark fell so low that a wheelbarrow full of currency wouldn't buy a loaf of bread. It was a revolutionary situation, and Germany very nearly went the way Russia had in 1917. My aunt Alice's family had a difficult time, and she had written something—I don't know what—to her father. He wrote her back a remarkable letter, a reproach of sorts, in which he gently admonished his beloved daughter. What impressed me was that here was a man approaching eighty who had lived most of his adult life in the United States, and yet he wrote with clarity of penmanship and thought about a troubling situation in another part of the world.

My father had a very close relationship with his father, whom he respected and revered. The two of them also had a working relationship; for several years my father was involved in the financial operation of The Plaza. But my father never really told me about going fishing with his father, or going on hunting trips with him, or playing ball with him—though it's possible that they may have done some or all of those things. Neither do I know much about my mother's relationship with her father when she was growing up, although I often saw them together and could tell they were close. And that's a blank in my life that I am sorry for. I hope my children will know more about my relations with my parents than I knew about my father's and mother's relations with their parents.

Dad thought of himself as a New Yorker. He was born and raised in the city. In the late 1890s, when the family was living on West 76th Street, the boys went to the Columbia Grammar School, on Fifth Avenue not far from where the Empire State Building stands today. Every school day morning my father and his brothers would ride their bicycles through Central Park and on down Fifth Avenue to school. After Columbia Grammar, my father went on to Phillips Academy in Andover, Massachusetts and graduated in 1905. Beginning in the 1890s, many of the most established New York families began sending their sons to Yale instead of the local university, Columbia, which may explain why all four Beinecke brothers began their collegiate careers at the home of *lux et veritas*. When my father entered Yale College, he thought he was going to major in the classics. He had studied a lot of Latin and Greek at Andover and kept it up through his freshman year at Yale. Then something awakened his interest in the world of engineering. He shifted over to the Sheffield Scientific School at Yale, studied civil engineering, and in 1909 graduated Sigma Xi (the equivalent, in the sciences, of Phi Beta Kappa) and summa cum laude with a Ph.B., the degree that engineering students got in those days. Dad also played both freshman and varsity football during his undergraduate years, so he appears to have been that rare combination, a scholar-athlete.

After graduation, he went to work as an inspector for the Bethlehem Steel Corporation in South Bethlehem, Pennsylvania. Before long he moved on to work as a rodman (part of a surveyor's team) for the New York Central Railroad. For a while, too, he was a draftsman in the design and engineering department. The railroad was in the process of electrifying its main line into New York City, and Dad was given the mundane task of designing warning signs to be placed along the right of way. He worked up a sign in bold black and yellow that read something like, "Beware 30,000 Volts!" He always had a puckish sense of humor, and true to his training in the classics, he added in smaller letters in the lower right-hand corner the legend: "*Cave Canem.*" The sign was approved by each level of the railroad bureaucracy up to the august level of the general counsel, where it was inspected by someone with sufficient education to wonder why "Beware 30,000 Volts!" was accompanied by the Latin phrase for "Beware of Dog!"

In 1911, Dad became chief engineer of the Red Hook Light and Power Company and was in charge of building a hydroelectric powerhouse on the Roeliff Jansen Kill, a tributary of the Hudson River not far from Poughkeepsie, New York. I once had a book of photographs that belonged to my father that illustrated the project in its various stages. One picture showed my father, on his motorcycle, in front of the dam under construction; others depicted the wooden supports of the dam and the different means by which Dad's team had rerouted the stream until the dam and powerhouse were in place. Finally the company began producing electric power for that little community, as it continued doing until it was absorbed by one of the major power companies, probably Niagara Mohawk or Central Hudson.

Sometime in that period my father invented a power atomizer for industrial oil burners, then in 1914 he became a partner in the Washington Engine Works of New York City, a company that was making experimental oil burners. He and one or two other men were working in New Jersey somewhere, perhaps Bayonne, trying to develop a new kind of oil burner that would enable steamships to shift from coal to oil. Coal-fired burners worked by having a man shovel coal into a very hot firebox; then air was forced into the burner under pressure, which would make the coal burn faster and create more heat for steam. My father and his partners wanted to do something like that with oil-fired furnaces, but in order to have pressurized air work in an oil-fired furnace, you had to find some way of dispersing the oil into small particles. That was where Dad's power atomizer came in. An oil burner is essentially a flame that ignites the continuous stream of atomized particles that are constantly blown from the atomizer into the furnace proper. Later that year he joined the Texas Company (now Texaco) in New York as superintendent of the company's horse-drawn oil and kerosene tank trucks.

A confident and prosperous America was gearing up for the Roaring Twenties, the decade in which the motor car was transformed from a curiosity and a luxury into basic transportation. My father saw the boom coming, and he decided to get in on it by starting a business with two friends. The auto industry included not only Ford and General Motors but many long-forgotten companies with wonderful old names like Auburn, Stutz, Jordan, Locomobile, Pierce-Arrow, Packard, Peerless, Wills Ste. Claire, Overland, Stearns, Willys-Knight, Essex, Marmon, Mercer, Franklin, Hudson, Nash, and Studebaker. In 1919, Dad had run a sales and service station operation in Brooklyn for Studebaker, one of the country's principal manufacturers. Through that connection, he and his partners, Ira Jones and Frank Sholes, were able to organize the Studebaker Sales Company of Newark in the early 1920s. Both Jones and Sholes were friends of the family, Sholes the son of Christopher Sholes, one of the inventors of the typewriter. My father was president of Studebaker Sales Company of Newark, an independent entity; he was not an employee of the Studebaker Corporation of America. Local Studebaker dealerships received their cars from the distributors, not direct from the manufacturing company. Dad's firm was the distributor for Studebakers in northern New Jersey, and the business was very successful. By the time he sold out his interest at the end of 1928, his was the second largest Studebaker distributorship in America, second only to one in Los Angeles. When I was growing up, we always had a new Studebaker (or several Studebakers) in the family garage. Occasionally one of the Newark salesmen would sell one of our cars, telling the customer it was so special that the president of the company himself was driving it. My brother and I learned not to leave anything we cared about in my father's car, because when we got home from school it could be gone for good, along with the car.

My parents were first brought together by my mother's Cranford friend Abby Bourne, who married my father's Yale classmate Wilbur Ruthrauff. I remember my father telling me that when he worked for Bethlehem Steel he used to take the old Lehigh Valley train that ran between Bethlehem and New York, and get off at a stop near Cranford—thus enabling him to carry out his courtship with my mother even though he lived miles away in Pennsylvania. My parents were married on November 14, 1912, in Cranford. Theirs was a union that would endure nearly sixty years, until my father's death in 1971. My wife, Betty, who knew both my parents well, observed that "It was a beautiful marriage. She made a perfect intellectual companion for him since she had herself a remarkably fine mind. She shared his interests while having her own."

Bill Beinecke's boyhood home in Cranford, New Jersey.

We lived in Cranford until I was eleven years old, and it was a marvelous place to grow up. My very earliest memory there is the birth of my brother, Richard Sperry Beinecke, in 1917. I was outside playing in a sandpile that had been put down by workmen who were tarring the streets, and I was told that if I came into the house, I would have a new brother. I was a little more than three years old. Cranford was small enough that I could impose a boyish order of geography on the town, with several fixed points of reference. The first point, obviously, was our home at 401 Prospect Street; our telephone number, I remember, was Cranford 47. Our house was just around the corner from the large, rambling old gray house on Linden Place where my mother lived as a girl. By this time it had been sold to a Mr. and Mrs. Harriet. My parents' friends the Ruthrauffs lived nearby, and I was great friends with their

*Bill Beinecke and friend,
c. 1917.*

son, who was always called by his middle name, Bourne. Two or three
blocks along Prospect Street toward the river was the home my grandfather William Sperry had built. It was large and Victorian, with a turret
on one side. Aunt Dot lived up in the turret, and when she was home
from Wellesley, I would go up there and listen to her read the Oz books
aloud, going through the whole series. My aunt Virginia Sperry lived
with her parents for most of the years when I was in Cranford, and so
did my mother's youngest sister, Emily Louise Sperry. My aunt Emmy
Lou was only six years older than I was! She had a pony and a cart in
which she used to take me for rides. My grandfather's property contained several flourishing gardens, a fountain on the lawn, and a car-
riage house in the back that we always called the "barn." As Granddad
liked to have fresh milk, he always had at least one cow. A hired hand
would walk the cow right up the middle of Prospect Street and graze it
in the lot next door to our house and in the other vacant lots around
town that my grandfather owned. It's interesting that so comparatively

recently you could still see that trace of country living in a suburban town not twenty miles from New York City.

Across Prospect Street from my grandfather's house was the mansion of my great-uncle Thomas Sperry. There was a hotel between my great-uncle's property and the Rahway River, a sort of resort, with a big verandah lined with rocking chairs. I remember that Wilder Breckinridge, the man who married my Aunt Virginia, stayed there a number of times before they were married. My great-uncle Joseph Sperry also lived nearby, at the corner of North Union Avenue and Linden Place. Closer into the town center was the Cranford Presbyterian Church, where my brother and I attended Sunday school. My parents had been married in that church—though I've often wondered why they chose a Presbyterian church, since Granddad was a loyal Episcopalian, my mother's stepmother was a Christian Scientist, and the Beineckes were Lutherans. Perhaps it was because the Presbyterian Church was the largest church in town.

I first started school in Cranford in 1919. It was a nursery school on Holly Street run by Miss Mildred Bourne, the sister of Abby Bourne Ruthrauff. I came across her again when I was elected to the board of the Consolidated Edison Company of New York in 1970. The company sent out the news of my election to its shareholders along with its dividend checks, and much to my pleasure and surprise I received a note from Miss Bourne, who was alive and well and a shareholder of Consolidated Edison. She wrote to me that she had retired, and that she was very pleased to note that the little red-headed boy she knew so many years ago was now on the board of this company in which she had invested. After Miss Bourne's, I went to another school in another house in Cranford. I know exactly where that house is and could go right to it today, but I can't identify the name of the road, if ever I knew it. My brother, who attended preschool several years after me, went to a different school, called Miss McCarter's, only two or three blocks from where we lived.

I then went on to the Grant School, the public school on Holly Street in Cranford, for the first, second, and third grades. My second grade teacher, Miss Almy, had also been my mother's teacher more than twenty years before! In those days, if you didn't behave yourself as you should, the teacher would give you a note to take home to your parents. I once received such a note from Miss Almy, but it never made it home to my parents. I put the note under a loose piece of sidewalk in front of the Christian Science Church, where it may still be today. The Grant School had what I always thought was an excessive emphasis on proper deportment. The teacher of the third grade, Mrs. Lisowski, would bring in something every day for us children to admire. She'd hold it up, and we'd all jump up and run to it—all of us except for one black girl, who would sit at her desk, maintaining perfect posture, with her hands folded neatly in front of her. Mrs. Lisowski would then praise this girl for her perfect deportment, deplore ours, and award her the first view of the object. The funny thing was that this kept up day after day. We never learned to restrain ourselves, and this one girl continued to end up as the privileged person.

After third grade, I went to the Pingry School, which was then in Elizabeth, New Jersey, on Westminster Avenue and Parker Road. Within two weeks of my arrival in the fall of 1923, it was decided that I should bypass fourth grade altogether and go immediately into fifth. The fact that I had come from an ordinary public school to a fine private country day school and almost at once skipped a grade says a lot about the quality of public education in those days. Later on at Andover I repeated the ninth grade, so I ended up finishing school at the same age as my peers.

Coming from Grant to the great Pingry School was like stepping into a new world. The Union County Trust Company had a temporary office right in the lobby of the school and, along with many other Pingry students, I opened a savings account there. The new gymnasium, equipped with everything one could imagine, even an indoor swimming pool, was almost too good to be true. I had never seen an indoor swimming pool or even imagined that such a marvel existed. Likewise, I had never heard of basketball or seen a basket until the first recreation period in the new gym, when I was indoctrinated into the game. I had played baseball, of course, and some football. In football, so far as I knew, the object was to get the ball and hold onto it. I proceeded to do just that with the basketball—to my downfall. I found myself lying on the beautifully polished floor of the gymnasium wrestling around with a couple of other boys for possession of that ball while someone (I suppose it was my hero, Mr. Reese Williams) blew vigorously on a whistle and a host of others yelled, "Jump, jump!" I had no idea what I was to jump at or over. Oh well, such is learning—I believe it is called the empirical method! As for the pool, I don't remember swimming in it much, but I do remember watching in awed admiration an event called "The Plunge." The fatter the plunger, the better—the fatter boys could hold their breath forever, or so it appeared to me.

I don't recall a great deal about my fifth grade experience, but my teacher, Mrs. Wagner, stands out in memory. At that time in Elizabeth, there was a bakery whose delivery vans were a prominent feature of the local scene. Emblazoned with the legend "MRS. WAGNER'S PIES," they were seen all over Elizabeth, and I still remember puzzling over how in the world that lady could bake all those pies and still manage to teach our class at the Pingry School. My sixth grade teacher, Miss Harriet Budd, would read a few pages to us each day as a treat, either from *The Reds of the Midi* or from that stirring Howard Pyle tale *Men of Iron*. Full of knights and squires, valor and honor, like a medieval book of hours come to life, the Pyle book made me think that the finest thing I could possibly grow up to be was a knight in shining armor, with chivalry as my ideal. It also caused me never to forget Miss Budd, who was all that a great teacher could be and a glowing light of Pingry for thirty-five years. Mr. Otho Vars was my seventh grade teacher at Pingry. I marveled at his first name, taken from a Roman emperor who had reigned briefly in 69 A.D., right after Nero and Galba. For more than seventy years now, I have been hoping in vain to meet another man named Otho.

Every afternoon I came home from Elizabeth on the 4:16 train. Now and then I would miss that train and have to trudge home from a little place about a mile and a half from my house called Aldene, where the next train terminated. The walk was a straight shot uphill on Elizabeth Avenue, about three times the distance from the Cranford station. It wasn't terribly far to go, and I used to kick a rock uphill or whack telephone poles with a stick to make the trip more interesting.

One of the other important landmarks in my mental map of Cranford was the sandpit on the edge of what we called the "woods," a couple of blocks down Elizabeth Avenue toward Aldene from our house. A big open pit where builders would get sand for building projects, it was forbidden territory for us children, perhaps because it was used after hours as a lover's lane. But because it was a place where we were always told not to go, of course we went. Another major landmark was the river. The Rahway flows through Cranford into the Arthur Kill, one of the two waterways that separate Staten Island from New Jersey (the other is the Kill Van Kull). I believe that my great-uncle Thomas Sperry had dammed up the lagoon sometime early in the century, which quieted the river for a couple of miles above the dam and made it a splendid place to go canoeing. In those years, Cranford was known as the "Venice of the East," and a canoe pageant called the Venetian Water Carnival would be held on the river around Memorial Day. The town would be decked out in bunting and decorations, and thousands of people would come from all over to see it. The canoes would be lashed together, three or four abreast. Floats would be constructed on them, perhaps with a replica of Notre Dame or the Statue of Liberty or something like that on top, and young ladies would pose on some of the floats. The river was small enough that people could put big cords across the river and suspend Japanese lanterns from them, and the lanterns would burn all evening while this pageant went on below. It was really a very lovely event. In the winters, when the ice was thick enough, we would go skating. A man who lived about a block from us was building an iceboat in his backyard, with a World War I airplane engine and propeller mounted on a sled. His idea was to put the boat on the river when it was frozen over and whiz all around, though I don't know whether he ever went through with his plan.

My grandfather had a canoe that he would let me and my friends use. One time when I was about nine years old, my great friend Ike Lawrence and I took it out for a ride. The river wound through Cranford in a series of meandering loops and bends. Sometimes a street would cross the river in one place, then cross it again two blocks down, which meant that when you canoed along the river you passed under a succession of bridges. Ike and I were caught in a big rainstorm that day, and we took refuge under a bridge, where we unfortunately encountered another canoe full of big boys of fourteen or fifteen. The rainwater from the gutters on the end of the bridge was pouring down like a cataract, inspiring the older boys to wonder whether if it wouldn't be good fun to hold me under the stream. Well, that's what they did, and there wasn't much we could do about it. They tired of that after a while, the rain abated, and Ike Lawrence's father appeared and declared that Ike had to go home for supper. So I was left there, soaking wet, with the canoe, and had to take it all by myself down the loops of the river to get it back to my grandfather's place.

Cranford is west of the port city of Elizabeth, New Jersey, and east of the small town of Garwood. What I remember most vividly about Garwood is not the town itself but the story that when the men who had served in the First World War came home from Europe, Garwood held a parade for its returning heroes and hung a banner over the main street that read, "You done good, Garwood boys!" The dubious usage of "good" as an adverb discomfited one of my mother's dear Cranford friends, Frances Miller. Mrs. Miller was rather a purist with regard to language. Perhaps it was because she was a Smith graduate, as was her daughter, her granddaughter, and her great-granddaughter—there's a wonderful photo of them all together at Smith. When Mrs. Miller played bridge and her partner played the hand well, Mrs. Miller would invariably say, "You done good, Garwood boy." Beyond the fields in back of Cranford was the little town of Kenilworth. When most people hear that name they think of the crenellated castle Sir Walter Scott made famous, and conjure up a vision of grand battlements and towers and banners flying. Kenilworth, New Jersey, however, was a shabby backwash of a town. The name Kenilworth was synonymous with everything second-rate, and this view was shared by the other kids I grew up with in Cranford. There was a livery stable in Kenilworth where my parents and some of their friends stabled their horses, and because Kenilworth was out in the country, there was room enough to ride. The stables were run by the man who took care of the horses, a strict German immigrant named Mr. Witt. When I was nine, my father and mother bought a horse for me from my uncle Edwin, a nice horse that had formerly belonged to my first cousin Sylvia. His name was Greylord, and I loved to ride him. I could ride fairly well and didn't have to be accompanied by anyone.

One Sunday morning I was riding alone up Galloping Hill near Kenilworth. It was an incline with only a slight gradient, so it was indeed a good hill to gallop up. At a certain place on the hill there was a large depression, kind of like a bowl, and you could ride along its rim. On this particular Sunday, I rode up to the edge of the bowl and looked down onto more figures in white gowns and hoods than you could shake a stick at. I had stumbled across a rally of the New Jersey branch of the Ku Klux Klan. Memory plays tricks on you, and it may be that that image stands out sharply because it was so frightening and stark, but I have a clear recollection of that moment. I took one look and thought, "This is no place for me," and I pulled my horse's head around and left in short order. I don't remember how many Klansmen there were or whether they were arranged in rows, standing, sitting, kneeling, or dancing. All I know is that there were a great many of them, that they filled this bowl with their white costumes, and that I was frightened. I didn't know anything about the Klan when I was a boy, although I'd heard of it, and it wasn't until years later that I understood that there was a distinction between the Klan that flourished after the Civil War and the Klan that came into being in the twentieth century and still has some offshoots today in various parts of the country. But in the immediate post-World War I years, the Klan had quite a life in the East and was an important presence in New Jersey. In the early 1920s, the Hall-Mills trial, the "trial of the century," had taken place in the state, receiving the kind of attention that the O. J. Simpson case received in recent times; it was daily front-page news, and even as a little boy I'd heard just about everything about it. I don't think the case was ever solved, but I've read a book on it by the late William Kunstler, the controversial trial lawyer, in which he hypothesizes that the Ku Klux Klan committed the crime because the idea of a minister having an affair with a church choir singer didn't appeal to their sense of morality. A quarterly that we subscribe to, *New Jersey History*, had an article in it some years ago about the Klan and the role it played in New Jersey in the early twenties, and when I read it I thought, "Yes, I can attest to that."

Shortly after my encounter with the Klan, Mr. Witt moved his livery stable three or four miles over from Kenilworth to some other stables across the railroad tracks in Cranford; you had to cross the tracks and go about a block to get to them. Today trains go through Cranford on elevated platforms and the roads run underneath, but in those days trains went through town at grade. One day I was stopped at the gates with half a dozen others riding back to the stables, when an elderly woman with some packages in her arms started to cross the tracks. She must have been deaf, because she didn't seem to hear the train that was bearing down on her at fifty or sixty miles an hour. The little rotund crossing guard had a red disk that he held up as a warning to keep people away when the trains came through, and when he saw this woman crossing the tracks, he flung the disk at her to get her attention. She didn't see it, and she was struck and killed by the train. We crossed over the tracks after the train had passed, and her body lay up against the little fence that separated the westbound from the eastbound tracks. That's a sight that has stayed with me through these years, but it didn't put me off my growing interest in trains.

I was fascinated by all forms of transportation. Even at that young age, I think I had some sense that changes in the means of transportation were an index to changing times. I grew up in an era when the horse was still seen as an important engine of locomotion, and I can remember seeing the horse-drawn fire engines in Cranford responding to alarms. Kenilworth was home to an American Can Company plant that had been a government contractor during World War I, and even several years after the war, truck after truck would pass through Cranford loaded with products from the plant, passing down Elizabeth Avenue to the shipping port at Elizabeth. Those were the primitive kind of Mack trucks that had chain drives instead of crankshafts. Once when I was five or six, one of these trucks broke down about half a block from my house, where I was playing with two other boys. The driver asked us to watch his truck while he went somewhere for assistance, so we three very proudly sat in the truck until he returned.

I was most interested in trains, however, perhaps because trains were the primary means of travel between Cranford and New York City. The metropolis cast a long shadow on Cranford even then. It was an important presence because most of the professional people in town commuted to New York. Even after my father moved to New Jersey in 1915, there were ties of business and family that drew him into the city. His parents and closest brothers were there, and he was associated with Edwin and Walter in business in New York. They had a controlling interest in The Plaza Hotel, and from 1923 on, they controlled The Sperry and Hutchinson Company, which was headquartered in Manhattan.

If you go to the upper floors of a downtown Manhattan skyscraper and look toward New Jersey, you can see a little building on a point of land jutting out into the harbor, just north of Bayonne and very close to Ellis Island. The building, which is now part of Liberty State Park, was once the terminal of the Central Railroad of New Jersey. When I was a boy, that terminal building was the midpoint of my journeys between Cranford and New York. My mother took me to the city on the Central Railroad of New Jersey, or the Jersey Central, as everyone called it. High-speed express trains from Philadelphia to New York, operated by the Philadelphia & Reading Railroad and the Baltimore & Ohio Railroad, also operated on that line. The Jersey Central trains ran to the old terminal in Jersey City, on the river, and ferryboats crossed from there to lower Manhattan, passing Ellis Island and the Statue of Liberty and docking at Liberty Street. After my family moved from Cranford in 1925, I didn't visit that terminal for a long time. Then in about 1990, the New Jersey Conservation Foundation took over the building, and my wife, Betty, our daughter Frances, and I drove down there for an event. I hadn't seen the inside of the building for more than sixty years. I wondered whether anyone else at that gathering had seen it in those happy golden bygone days, when the trains pulling in would cough out great bursts of steam that would escape through the vents in the train sheds. That was the tail end of the Age of Steam, and all the terminals catering to steam engines needed that way of releasing smoke and steam; otherwise the stations would have been unbearable. The tracks in those days had platforms on either side and a roof over the platforms as shelter from the rain, but there was always a little vent all the way along the top of those sheds for the smoke and steam.

As a kid, I always thought that the Jersey Central was a big, important railroad, on a par with the New York Central Railroad my father once worked for. I didn't understand that the New York Central was one of the giants of American railroading and the Jersey Central nothing but a little spur that carried commuters into the city. It did furnish a right of way for some through expresses and freights, but it was a minor railroad with a comparatively small railroad yard. But to me the railroad yard was big, and it was right there where Cranford met Aldene, a town that has probably since been incorporated into either Cranford or Roselle, the next town over. There was a small local railroad (long since defunct) called the Rahway Valley Railroad that connected the Jersey Central with the Lackawanna. It went from the Aldene train yard through Kenilworth and across the eight or ten miles of countryside to Summit, where the Lackawanna right of way was. The Baltimore & Ohio Railroad operated the railroads on Staten Island—in effect the local rapid-transit system—and ran across bridges over the Arthur Kill and the Kill Van Kull, so the great B&O had a link into this little yard at Aldene. The Lehigh Valley Railroad, running from the Hudson River to the region where Bethlehem Steel and the Allentown mining companies were located, did as well. It was fun for a boy to see these trains go through Aldene transporting coal from the anthracite fields of Pennsylvania, and freight and passengers from all across the country, into New York. When I was about seven, one of the anthracite trains suffered a derailment just west of town, near Garwood. My father took me out to see it. We walked up and down along the right of way, looking at the amazing jumble of piled-up coal cars.

Even before I was ten, I would often go to the Aldene rail yard to look at the steam engines in the roundhouse. The yard was small, so this particular roundhouse was only half round—it was a semicircle—but it served the needs of the locomotives that came there. There was a circular table out front, big enough to put a locomotive on, that would be made to revolve slowly until the tracks would align and the locomotive could be backed into the roundhouse to be worked on. All that stuff fascinated me; I grew up in a railroad era. Railroads were important. Curiously, even though the Aldene terminal was nothing, the railroad yard was a fairly important junction; some trains went only as far as Aldene, and then you'd have to change trains there.

Even as a boy I was often taken to New York City. Not only were my Beinecke grandparents there, but in the mid-1920s, when my Sperry grandparents sold their house in Cranford, they had an apartment in the city for a number of years before my grandfather's death. As a youngster I went to some of the Saturday programs at the American Museum of Natural History. My mother occasionally took me to a matinee, and once in a while, when I got a little older, I was taken to a store like De Pinna or Rogers Peet to buy clothes.

Once you got to the Jersey Central terminal, it was still a rather long trip by ferry to New York. It's strange to recall how jammed with waterborne traffic the Hudson River and lower harbor were in those days. There were all the ferries from the railroad lines, and the ferries carrying people back and forth to Staten Island. There were also the railroad car ferries. The freight trains would terminate in New Jersey at the freight terminals, which were either adjacent to or a part of the passenger terminals, and then the freight cars were put on lighters and taken to different places in Manhattan and Brooklyn. There were railroads—the J Street Connecting Railroad and the Brooklyn Eastern District Terminal in Brooklyn—where a lot of the tugs would deliver these lighters laden with freight cars. In addition to that, there were incoming and outgoing ocean liners and ocean freighters. All of that is gone today. The ferries are gone, the train car lighters are gone, and the ocean liners don't come in anymore, except for an occasional cruise liner that docks at 54th Street. The container ships operate over in the Port of Newark and to some extent in Brooklyn. But Manhattan and the Jersey shore facing Manhattan no longer have any seagoing traffic to speak of. The Hudson estuary no longer serves as the great highway that it once did.

When the ferry deposited you in New York, you had to make your way from lower Manhattan to other parts of the city. You could get out of the ferry at either of two levels. On the upper level there was an inside passenger cabin and an outside deck, with seats all round. When the ferry made the landing, it connected with a bridge at the upper level, so passengers could enter the terminal from the upper level or the automobile level down below. It was really better to get off at the upper level, because when you emerged on the New York side you were facing a vast street, thronged with traffic, that was so wide it was overwhelming—at least in the recollection of someone who was a small boy in those days! But it must be remembered that the West Side Highway didn't then exist, and neither did the Holland and Lincoln Tunnels; the only way to get back and forth from New Jersey was by ferry. So all the traffic along the west side of New York was moving at right angles to all the people pouring off the ferries, not only from the Jersey Central and the Lackawanna ferries but from the Erie ferries, the Pennsylvania

William M. Sperry and Carrie Sperry Beinecke in Jupiter, Florida, c. 1922.

Railroad ferries, and all the other ferries delivering commuters to New York.

When I was in the city with my father, he would often tell me what it had been like to grow up there in the last years of the nineteenth century, in the days when New York Central steam engines came down Park Avenue, an open railroad cut at that time. Park Avenue today has six lanes—three lanes northbound, three lanes southbound—and the so-called park in the center is very narrow. But shortly after the railroad cut was filled in, when the street traffic was only two lanes on each side, the park was much wider. With the development of the automobile and more traffic, the park area was compressed to its present size. My father and I shared an interest in railroads. He, too, had been interested in them from the time he was a boy, and had worked for the New York Central when he was young. When we moved from Cranford to Madison, New Jersey, my father (who was always a great hobbyist) built a small-gauge model railroad in the basement, and later on he actually built larger-scale, working model locomotives.

Those trips to New York weren't the only journeys I made when I was young. I have particularly vivid recollections of traveling south to Florida to visit my Sperry grandparents. William Miller Sperry had a home on the Loxahatchee River in Jupiter, on the southeast coast of Florida, where he would go every winter for several weeks of fishing, boating, golf, and offering hospitality to family and friends. His place was directly across the river from the famous red Jupiter lighthouse, even in the 1920s a long-time landmark in that part of Florida. It was there in 1898, during the Spanish-American War, when the battleship *Oregon* triumphantly reported for duty at Jupiter, having come all the way around South America through the Strait of Magellan from the West Coast, a long journey in those pre-Panama Canal days. I visited my grandfather in his lovely home three times before I was ten years old. It was a wonderful place for a small boy to visit, and my mother and I would stay there for a few weeks each time we went. My father would usually spend three or four days with us, then go back. It took nearly thirty-six hours to get there by train. We would get on the train at Elizabeth, New Jersey at five or six o'clock on a winter's afternoon and travel all night, all day, and then all night again to arrive at Jupiter around six or seven in the morning. (The train would pull into Palm Beach at a more civilized hour, sometime after eight.)

When my grandfather acquired his property around 1910 or before, it was on an island, and the only way to get there from the railroad station was by boat. By the time I visited ten years later, there was access by a yellow dirt road that went from the railroad station over a small bridge and onto my grandfather's property. I was told that my grandfather's place had belonged to the Western Union Company. If so, it probably was the location for the Western Union cable over to Nassau in the Bahama Islands, only a few miles east of Jupiter. His place wasn't an elaborate mansion but rather a collection of cottages and bungalows. There was a one-story house on a little hill that we called the Main House, which consisted of his and my grandmother's bedroom and a nice living room with books and a card table. There was a separate building housing the kitchen and dining room where we ate, served by the Chinese people my grandfather employed as cook, butler, and waiter. When they first acquired the property, my grandparents, their family, and guests would eat next door at a boardinghouse for fishermen run by "Mother" Carlin, but by the time I came along, they had their own kitchen and cooking staff. There were two or three other cottages on the site, and another building that was the light plant. As there was no publicly supplied electricity, my grandfather had to make his own. The light plant probably wasn't as large as I thought it was when I was a small boy, but it was a substantial building with machinery, rotating belts, and so on. The generating plant provided electricity not only for the buildings but also for the fancy iron lamp posts that illuminated the outside walkway and the stairs leading downhill from the main house to the boathouse. The boathouse was quite elaborate, with three riverside doors for the boat slips and a deck around two sides of it. My grandfather had a speedboat called the *Dorothy*, named after my aunt; his principal fishing boat, the *Virginia*; and a very quiet, slow-moving electric boat, the *Carrie*, named after my mother (I was told that it had been purchased from President Taft). Later on my grandfather got a fishing skiff that he was kind enough to call the *Billy B*, after me.

Florida in those days was a natural paradise. My grandfather's property extended over about eighty acres. The main house, boathouse, lawn, and cottages occupied twenty or more acres, so some fifty or sixty acres were undeveloped. We used to call that area the "jungle," and there was a path into the jungle that was kept clear. It was fun to walk into the wilderness, out to a tremendous banyan tree, and back. Sometimes we took the electric boat three or four miles up the Loxahatchee River into another junglelike area. Because it moved so slowly and quietly, you could see water snakes sunning themselves, alligators slipping into the river, manatees, and other wild creatures. Years later, when Betty and I stayed in the caretaker's cottage there on our honeymoon, we went up the Loxahatchee to see Trapper Nelson, a man who had caught a lot of animals in that area and kept them in cages. I realized then that much of the Florida countryside is really quite wide and open and that it isn't all jungle overhanging rivers, the way I remembered it from my boyhood days.

Florida has changed drastically since that time. The beach was nearly undeveloped then, and there were only a few establishments on the riverbanks. Everything east to the inlet from where the railroad bridge crossed the Loxahatchee River was still undeveloped, and the lighthouse stood in stark isolation. The lighthouse is still there today, but surrounded by so many high-rise buildings that you can hardly see it. There was nothing but mangrove trees on the north shore of the Loxahatchee from the lighthouse to the sea until you got farther north, to the development now known as Hobe Sound. It was called Olympia at that time, perhaps because the developers thought it sounded more chic; it later went back to the old name, Hobe Sound. There were a few houses in Olympia in those days, and my grandfather would take us in his boat up the Indian River from the confluence with the Loxahatchee. There was a public park and gazebo and a few wood-frame houses, nice houses with big sloping lawns, and Granddad knew many of the people residing there. But there were few people living in what is now the rather elaborate Hobe Sound colony.

At the time I first went to visit my grandparents in Jupiter, the Loxahatchee River had no exit to the sea. The Jupiter Inlet, where all maps of Florida today show the Loxahatchee River exiting to the sea, had ceased to exist. The United States government dug a canal, now part of Florida's Intracoastal Waterway, that changed the natural flow of water so that the hydraulic courses of the sea built up a dune all the way across what had been the mouth of the Loxahatchee. I remember seeing the big sand dredges at work, sucking up the sand and blowing it out through long tubes onto mounds on either side of the river near where the mouth had been. Finally there was only a narrow trench, not more than about six feet wide, between the freshwater side and the sea. I stood there at low tide with my mother and my grandfather, looking at this last little bit of sand between the Loxahatchee River and the sea, and they said, "See this, Billy? Tomorrow this will all be gone." The next day when I looked out, there was the sea, and the dune was gone. The incoming tide had surged through and ripped out the rest of the little trench, and the Army Corps of Engineers had placed great rock jetties on the northern and southern sides of the inlet to prevent the silting up again of the mouth of the river.

Granddad took me fishing with him on that first visit. I remember how important it made me feel when he designated one of the fishing poles as "Billy's rod." Another time he took me for a long walk through an orange grove, explaining how the trees were planted as we sampled the different varieties that grew on them. After a while my young legs gave out, and Granddad hoisted me on his shoulders and carried me all the way back to the grove's entrance, where a car awaited.

Besides the visits to Florida, my family made several expeditions to some pleasant summer resorts when I was young. One of my very earliest summer recollections is of going to 'Sconset on the island of Nantucket. The town's real name is Siasconset, but it's always been abbreviated to 'Sconset; it was first a fishermen's village and then an artists' colony. My uncle Walter Beinecke eventually bought a home in 'Sconset and summered there until his death in 1958. His two children, my cousins Betsy and Walter Beinecke, Jr., also summered in Nantucket and owned homes there; their children have acquired homes in Nantucket now. My parents were never Nantucketers, but when I was very young, in the first or second summer after the Great War, we had a small cottage in 'Sconset. I don't remember much about it, but thanks to my early fascination with railroads, I did find out that there had once been a train that went from Nantucket town out to Siasconset. I don't know whether it just went back and forth or whether it made a loop around the edge of the island and came back into Nantucket town from another direction. It had gone out of business long before that first summer, but I did see the old railroad depot that was once in 'Sconset.

In 1920, we went up to New Hampshire for the summer and stayed at an inn in Sugar Hill, not far from Franconia. My mother was there, along with the nurse who had been brought along to look after my brother and me. That was a long trip in those days, and I recall that it took two days to drive from New Hampshire to Cranford. My father can't have spent much time with us there, since he was then only about thirty-five years old and busy working, and it was such a long drive home. I do not remember if he came up by train occasionally on weekends, or whether we just went there for his two week vacation.

We were there two summers, and then in 1922 we summered on Fisher's Island, off New London, Connecticut in Block Island Sound, and stayed in what was called the Mansion House. Just before we went to Fisher's Island, I burned myself rather severely. I had a bag of sparklers in my lap, and somehow or other I managed to ignite the bag and all the sparklers. I was still in my short-pants days, of course, and so I severely burned the inside of my right thigh. When we got to Fisher's Island, my mother took me to see the hotel doctor, but not much good came of it. The leg was festering and sore, and my mother must have been quite concerned. The army had a base at Fisher's Island called Fort Wright, where they were still practicing coastal defense and protecting the navy submarine base in Groton (New London), Connecticut. They had these big guns they called disappearing guns. The gun would be loaded below the parapet, then raised on a big hydraulic lift until the muzzle protruded across the top of the parapet. The gun was fired, recoiled, and then lowered again. And we could hear this booming as they did their practicing. I think someone must have told my mother that the army doctors were very good at treating burns, because she took me to the army medical dispensary at Fort Wright, and my terrible burn healed quickly.

For the next three summers, I went away to camp. The first summer, 1923, when I was nine years old, I went to a place on Cape Cod near Buzzards Bay called Camp Wampanoag, named after some old Indian who was there when the Pilgrims arrived. That was not a very profitable venture for me. The only successful part of it was my passing the swimming test; if you were able to stay afloat twelve minutes, you were permitted to go out in a rowboat by yourself. While I was at camp, President Harding died in San Francisco and was succeeded by Calvin Coolidge. It's interesting how you can remember something like that from your boyhood. We lived in tents, under some kind of military discipline, or so it seemed to me. The camp authorities would inspect the tents for cleanliness—how neatly your bed was made, whether your shoes were lined up properly, and so on. If you did very well in the inspection, your tent got a dinky little American flag that you hung from the top of the tent pole, signifying what a nice tent you lived in. If you didn't quite measure up, you didn't get anything. But if you were at the other end of the scale, they stuck a little black pig on your tent pole. My tent had a black pig on it for most of the summer, and that shamed me. I didn't like the notoriety, but more than that, I didn't like the idea behind it. I remember that stigma very well, and I didn't care for that camp.

The following two summers I went to a camp in New Hampshire called Mishe Mokwa. It was on an island in Lake Winnipesaukee, not far from Wolfeboro. That was a more successful experience. There was a paddle wheel steamboat called the *Mount Washington* that plied the lake, and once a summer the people who ran the camp would take us boys on it. The big revolving beam that held the paddles passed through the steamboat and through each of the two passages, fore and aft. The beam was thickly padded and moved slowly above your head, and it was fun to jump on it and revolve along with the paddle wheels. We lived in cabins in that camp, not in tents. The cabins had six cots down each side, twelve boys to a cabin. There was an outbreak of mumps late in the first summer I was there. The camp had a small cabin at the other side of the island that was used as an infirmary in case a boy didn't feel well, but everybody had been exposed to the mumps, so by the end of the summer that small cabin was not adequate and at least two regular cabins had been designated as mumps cabins. Unfortunately for me, I didn't get the mumps until the end of July, so I had to be quarantined for two weeks after camp was over until the disease ran its course.

A surprising number of our counselors were prominent Yale men and football players. One was Raymond "Ducky" Pond, who was a football standout at Yale and later became its football coach. Another was Pond's great friend Phil Bunnell, who was captain of the team in the mid-1920s. Stuart Scott, another counselor, and Charlie Williamson, a fellow camper, were also connected with the football team at Yale. Scott played end, and Williamson was the manager in the 1930s. He actually went in for one play against Harvard and thus won a letter. These fellows would throw passes to one another and talk about the team, so we boys were exposed to Yale football early on.

In 1924, during the first summer I was at Camp Mishe Mokwa, my mother and her close friend Gladys Mathey Banker (later Mrs. Chalmers Bryce) came up to see their two sons. There were several boys from Cranford at Mishe Mokwa, including Bourne Ruthrauff, Barclay Morrison, Bobby Elser (whose father, Frank Elser, a war correspondent, wrote some highly interesting dispatches about General Pershing's pursuit of Pancho Villa in Mexico), and Gladys Banker's son, Dean. While my mother and Mrs. Banker were visiting, a barnstorming aircraft with pontoons landed in Lake Winnipesaukee and taxied up to the camp landing, and the pilots offered to take people up for four or five dollars. We boys encouraged our mothers to do this, but I guess Dean Banker was more encouraging than I was, because to his great delight his mother made one of these flights. The pilot circled around the lake and came down in about ten minutes. I wasn't persuasive enough to get my mother to do that, but I remember that as one of the highlights of my Camp Mishe Mokwa experience.

An incident occurred that summer that still strikes me as an example of how badly young boys can behave, and I remember it with great clarity and unhappiness. I was ten at the time, one of the younger boys in camp. Fifteen or twenty boys went on a camping trip with a few counselors, down on the shore of the lake. One day the boys decided to go for a hike. We came upon an unoccupied house and barn; looking back on it, I guess that it was someone's summer home. We completely vandalized the place. We just went crazy. We went into the barn and threw stuff down from the top floor; we went into the house and chopped up the banisters with our hatchets. When we had finished this terrible act, we were filled with excitement, and we marched in a line back to the shore singing the only song we knew, "Onward Christian Soldiers." Of course the owners of the house and barn knew where the vandals had come from, and they reported what had happened to L. Theodore Wallis, a Dartmouth alumnus who ran the camp. A couple of days later some of the senior boys came to us and said, "You know, Mr. Wallis is in a bad spot. He is going to have to pay for that work, and we should help him." Someone had put out a Dartmouth banner on a table in the rec hall, and we all put some money on it. We didn't have much money—I suppose if I had three or four dollars I thought I had a lot—so when I saw all the money on the Dartmouth banner, I thought, "Boy, we've really given Mr. Wallis many times more than is needed to fix up that damage." Little did I know. I never heard another word about it, and I've often wondered how the matter was resolved. I know that if Mr. Wallis had told my father that I had been involved in this act, that the damage was considerable, and that he needed financial help to fix it up, my father would have contributed, and I suspect that other fathers would have also. Perhaps that's what happened. I doubt that Mr. Wallis ever told the parents what had taken place, though, because had he done so, it would have become very apparent to them that their boys did not have adequate supervision.

In 1925, when I was eleven, my family moved from Cranford approximately ten miles northwest to Madison, New Jersey. I was sorry to leave behind my boyhood home and its deep-rooted associations, but I was excited by what promised to be the opening of another chapter in my youth.

CHAPTER TWO

Family Life, School, and Youthful Years in Madison, New Jersey, 1925–1931

y parents moved to a large home on Green Avenue. I think we moved because my parents wanted to upgrade our lifestyle; my father's Studebaker distributorship had been doing extraordinarily well. Ours was a lovely house, set on five or six acres, with an expansive front yard and a side lawn leading to a garden. The backyard sloped down into a valley, then rose up a hill to the back fence in a kind of wasteland that we referred to as the "orchard." When my parents acquired the property, that whole rear area was barren; nothing grew there. My father speculated that the topsoil had been taken away for use by the numerous greenhouses in Madison that supplied New York City florists—that's why Madison was called the "Rose City" of the Garden State. My father planted a number of fruit trees in the back to make it less sterile. The trees never really grew much and never bore any fruit, but they did change the appearance of that area, so that the back hillside looked more like an orchard than a desert.

The house had been acquired from a Mr. Davidson, who had built it some ten years before we bought it. The house had no garage, perhaps because automobiles were still rare in 1915, so my father built one. The garage was actually quite an impressive building, housing three cars on the ground level. An apartment upstairs contained a bedroom, living room, kitchen, and bath for the succession of live-in chauffeurs we had all the years we lived on Green Avenue. There was a furnace room downstairs and a room for my mother's pots, spades, and gardening paraphernalia, which we called the flower room.

The house had wings on either side of the main entrance, beyond the living room on the right and the dining room on the left. The first-

Bill Beinecke's home in Madison, New Jersey.

floor room in the right-hand wing was enclosed with floor-length windows and French doors; we called that the sun porch. People would relax out there, and my mother, who loved to play bridge, would frequently have her games there. A comparable wing on the left side featured a large room that at first we called the billiard room, and indeed in our early years in Madison there was a fine pool table there, with balls and cues racked up on the walls. My twelve-year-old friends and I just loved that pool table and used it all the time. My parents, however, decided that their plans for their new home did not include operating a juvenile pool hall, and so within two or three years the pool table was banished to the third floor, and the so-called billiard room was converted to a library. Floor-to-ceiling bookshelves replaced the cue racks. A lovely working fireplace was located at one end of the room, and a great overstuffed couch was brought in, which made a very comfortable place to sit and read. The pool table that had been banished to the third floor did not serve as a pool table for long. It was placed on a rubber mat there, and when I and some of the other boys played pool there, we extinguished cigarettes on the mat with our heels. When my father discovered what we were doing, he took us to task in a way that I will never forget. I came home from school to discover that the pool room had been turned into a storage area for my mother's linens, curtains, and drapes. The pool table itself was now no more than a level surface on which to pile all that stuff. We were out of business.

My mother ran our Madison home remarkably. When I was growing up, the operations of the house seemed to proceed effortlessly, but I know better now. My mother provided for all of us—my dad, my brother Dick, and me—probably too well. My brother and I were brought up in a lifestyle that was much too good for us, and we were taken care of in a way that is probably regarded as old-fashioned today. My mother's top priorities were always her home and her family, and she devoted herself to her role with serene self-confidence. Mother exhibited enormous managerial competence. She had to run a household enterprise that included a cook, a waitress, a chambermaid, a gardener, a couple of gardening assistants, and a chauffeur. She did it all quietly, with poise and grace. I grew up in a home where my mother was sincerely and compassionately interested in what my brother and I were doing. Mother would sit and read poetry to Dick and me as children. I can still remember the haunting refrains of Matthew Arnold's

Carrie Sperry Beinecke, May 1941.

"The Forsaken Merman," and a favorite poem whose every stanza ended, "with Billy and me." My mother even wrote a special poem about me, one of many expressions of her love and devotion to her children. My mother was also an active gardener, and while I don't have a sufficient grasp of botany to recall the specific plants and flowers in her garden, I know it was a thing of beauty.

Our family led a very happy life in Madison. Ours was a relaxed household, filled with fun. Once my father, Dick, and I raised a fuss about the absence of some dish or other at dinner. We held a protest march around the table, improvising placards and all. Dad liked to do outrageous things like that. Sometimes Mother would respond by acting shocked, but on that occasion she just sat there quietly and smiled, and the dish did appear! My father had a Great Dane named Helios, and it was a firm rule that Helios was not, under any circumstances, to enter the dining room during meals. Time and again, the dog, flat on his belly, would creep inch by inch into the dining room toward the table. Without fail, when the dog had nearly approached the table, my father would lift his head, glare at him, and roar, "Back to the mines, Helios!"—whereupon the offender would promptly scuttle back to the library, and the process began again. This was a regularly recurring event, and the scenario never varied.

Domesticity had worked some changes on my father. As a young man at Yale, he had been very athletic. He was a big man, tall and loose-jointed, who walked with an athlete's grace. He was always physically strong and used to swim and play tennis and golf, but when we got to Madison, he stopped doing most of those things. Dad remained a devoted outdoorsman, though, becoming more involved in fishing and hunting and bird shooting and boating. For years he and his brother Edwin and some of their friends used to go salmon fishing in New Brunswick on the Miramichi and Restigouche Rivers. Every Fourth of July in the early years of our marriage, my wife, Betty, and I would receive a salmon through the mail or by railway express, packed in salt and ice, sent down from my father's June expeditions in New Brunswick. My dad liked to go deep-sea fishing with my brother Dick, who loved the sport. He would go duck shooting in North Carolina at Currituck Sound, and soon after we moved to Madison, he took up bird watching, seeking to find how many different species he could identify on that relatively small property.

In or about 1930, my father bought a lovely, slim, fifty-foot cruising yacht called the *Innisfree*, after William Butler Yeats's beautiful poem, "The Lake Isle of Innisfree," one of my mother's favorites. It was an elegant boat. My parents had a professional captain and took the yacht on cruises around Long Island, up through the Great Peconic Bay to the Sound, and they went up to Martha's Vineyard and Nantucket a couple of times. My father loved yachting, for it gave him a chance to pursue another of his hobbies, navigation. Franklin Roosevelt, while he was governor of New York, once borrowed the *Innisfree* to make an inspection trip of outer Long Island, passing through Shinnecock Canal and Peconic Bay. I once saw FDR's note thanking my father, but it disappeared somewhere along the way.

My father was also a first-class bridge player. He was not in the world champion class of his brother Walter but was still good enough to go with Walter and Edwin to the Whist Club in New York City, where they frequently played at the end of the day. I recall one of his hands being featured in the bridge column of the *New York Times*.

My father had gravitated away from engineering toward business when he went to work for Studebaker, but throughout his life he retained an engineer's ability to fix anything—and I do mean anything. He had a deep-seated compulsion to take automobiles apart, and no car was safe when he was around. In the 1920s, when I was a boy, cars were always breaking down. Fritz Beinecke could make them run. He would open the hood, emerge from the bowels of the car with grease up to his elbows, and casually ask my mother or some other lady present for a hairpin. One of them would reach into her hair and hand him a hairpin, he would disappear into the insides of the car, manipulate something, and to everyone's amazement and relief the engine would start up and purr along beautifully. I never knew what my father did with those hairpins, and I used to wonder why he didn't carry his own supply. When I grew a little older, I realized how much more dashing and stylish it was that my father did the repairs in his own way.

He was marvelously clever with his hands. Besides tinkering with automobiles, he also built intricate and delicate replicas of clipper ships, whaling vessels, and other ships. He had a strong creative and inventive bent, and there was no end to his ingenuity. One time a severe winter storm hit northern New Jersey and the power went out all over our part of the state. Without power, none of the houses in our area had heat, because it takes electrical power to make an oil burner work. My father, undaunted, descended into the cellar, called on his earlier engineering experience, and somehow connected the belt drive of the oil burner to our gasoline-powered lawn mower, propped up in a stationary position. Remarkably, the lawn mower kept the oil burner working throughout the storm, and for several days, until the emergency passed, our house was the only one for miles around that remained warm and cozy in one of the worst recorded blizzards in our region.

My father's mechanical turn of mind was in sharp contrast to his brothers. Edwin Beinecke, for example, never learned to drive a car. But my father, from early on, was highly interested in new technology. I think this age of electronics would have fascinated him. Once when I was about seven, I was home from school with a cold, and my father came in and strung wires all around the room and clapped a pair of earphones on my head. It was my first experience of radio, probably five years before the public had even heard of it. My father used to assemble radios from the ground up. He built a crystal radio set in the early 1920s, and later an early tube set called a superheterodyne.

In the 1930s, my father became an early aficionado of color photography. Color film was nonexistent sixty-five years ago, and my father had to use some sort of laborious bath process that took up an entire bathroom in our Boston apartment at 176 Beacon Street. It says much for my mother's patience and goodwill that she was willing to put up with the clutter from my father's hobbies, and I suspect it was at her insistence that he later constructed an elaborate darkroom in Madison. My father's color prints were quite sophisticated for their time, and I still have a remarkable color photograph, a still life, that my father took in the mid-1930s. He also owned one of the earliest Polaroid cameras and had an extensive file of travel slides that he loved to exhibit. He even built a television set in the late 1930s that incorporated a revolutionary scanning technique for capturing images on a screen. There weren't any television programs at that time, of course, and all that a TV receiver could pick up was an experimental telecast from the top of the Empire State Building. My father set up his television in our sun porch in Madison, where we strained to view a few wavering images. Even so, for years we were one of the few families in the world, really, to have a television. That was the start of a whole new era, and my father was absorbed by it from the beginning. He was a "firster," a real innovator.

My father's hobbies were a necessary part of his life. The business world could not contain or sustain his broad intellectual range and boundless enthusiasms, and his hobbies provided him with an escape. They also were an outlet for his energies, his relentless curiosity, and his scientific inclinations. Many of his hobbies also brought us closer together, even when I was very young. For example, when we lived in Cranford, my father had become interested in the set of Lionel trains I liked to play with. When we moved to Madison, his interest became a full-blown enthusiasm, and he constructed an intricate scale-model network of trains and tracks in the basement, with controls and box signals and allied equipment. It was truly a wonderful creation. I don't think it was supposed to be a replica of any particular railroad, but it was a beautiful and complex system, designated as going from New York to Chicago. It was the wonder of all in the neighborhood, and even of people from farther afield. The entire system was eventually given to the Bonnie Brae Farm, a home for boys in the Basking Ridge area of New Jersey.

In my parents' later years, when they lived in Great Barrington, Massachusetts, my father oversaw the construction of an elaborate machine shop, a copy of one of the buildings in colonial Williamsburg; it was an architectural gem. He laid out a treadmill in it on which he ran scale-model locomotives that he had built out of miniature parts he'd fabricated himself. The treadmill would start, the whistle would blow, the wheels would turn, the place would fill up with smoke—and how he loved it! Unfortunately, one day one of his engines got a little too fired up, and the beautiful machine shop burned to the ground. My father by then was nearly eighty years old, and this was a terrible blow. But his

Fritz Beinecke working on a model train in his Tredinnock machine shop at Great Barrington, Massachusetts, c. 1956.

was a thoroughly uncrushable spirit, and he rebuilt the machine shop. Still, he also became more cautious, and thereafter his locomotives operated on compressed air.

With all his energies and enthusiasms, my father had an impetuous side. In that sense, my mother was the perfect complement for my father, because she was able to provide him with both encouragement and balance. She had a quiet command and composure, and I think she brought him a sense of serenity. My parents also derived some of their equilibrium from their extraordinarily close circle of friends. The friendships they had established in their early years in Cranford endured through the years wherever they lived. There were the Ruthrauffs, the Ira Jones family, the Blakes, the Coadys, the Biglows, the Elsers, the Kepners, the Carnahans, the Morrisons, the Millers, the Wassons, the Donnellys, and the Ryans—especially the Ryans. My parents and these couples had an intimate and friendly relationship and did everything together. My parents were always going to dinner at the homes of the other couples, and the others would come to dinner at our home. They would play bridge together, and sometimes poker. It was a wonderful set. They had all originally come from Cranford, and they all moved away over time. The Ruthrauffs moved to Rumson on the Jersey shore, the Ryans to Short Hills, the Joneses to Short Hills and then to Summit, the Coadys to New York City, and we to Madison. But all the families continued to keep in touch, and at some point in the mid-1920s, someone in the group—I believe it was Mrs. Coady—said, "We ought to go to Long Island for the summer." She had just heard about the Townsend Cottages that had been newly built on the shore at Westhampton Beach. So the Coadys, the Joneses, the Ryans, the Beineckes, and perhaps one or two of the other families rented these cottages year after year. We stopped going in 1931 due to the Great Depression. All those cottages were blown away by the great hurricane of 1938. I was recently in Westhampton Beach, for only the second time in about sixty years, to attend the funeral of our good friend Mrs. Standish Hope Medina. After the burial we went to the old Medina home, situated right across Moriches Bay from the site of the old Townsend Cottages.

When we first started summering in Westhampton in 1926, Dad thought that it would be wise to employ a tutor for his boys, just as his parents had hired a young Princeton graduate to be a companion to their sons during the summers. My parents hired Wilfred Wingebach, a medical student at Cornell who had graduated from the City College of New York, and he came down to Westhampton and spent three summers with Dick and me.

My brother was about my size and had very red hair. He radiated good spirits and good fellowship. I suppose there is always some element of competition between siblings, especially when there are only two in the family, but we were quite different people and we each followed a different star. My brother was at a certain disadvantage in the kinds of games we played, because although he was stronger, I was physically more adept. He had a muscular stiffness in the back of his legs that caused him to walk in a strange manner. It didn't prevent him from taking part in sports, but he was never really an active participant in ones where you had to run a lot, like football and baseball. Wilfred Wingebach went swimming with us, taught us to sail the catboat we rented, and helped us with our developing interests in those important years. Even as boys, however, Dick and I pursued different activities. I was beginning to take up golf, but Dick was more interested in boats.

A few years later, Dick began to be drawn more and more to the West and became passionately devoted to the ranching life. During the early 1930s he spent his summers at the Lazy K Bar Ranch in Melville, Montana, owned and operated by the Van Cleve family. There was a Beinecke connection there. Uncle Ben Beinecke, my father's oldest brother, worked in my grandfather's hotels for a few years after his graduation from Yale in 1898, then went out to Melville, a little town about forty miles north of the railroad junction in Big Timber, and opened a general store. Ninety years ago, Montana still had frontier characteristics. It had been an unincorporated territory until 1889, and cattle ranching was king. Uncle Ben married Agnes Van Cleve, whose father had homesteaded that part of Montana in the 1880s and had established the Lazy K Bar Ranch. The Van Cleves had money problems during the Depression, so my father and his brothers helped them finance a conversion of the ranch: where once it had emphasized cattle-raising alone, now it welcomed urban visitors and vacationers from the rest of the country—known as "dudes"—who wanted to experience ranching life in the West. These operations are now known by the more dignified name of guest ranches, but in those days they were called dude ranches. By that time Ben Beinecke had decided that the Montana climate was too tough, and he and my aunt Agnes had moved to San Marino in southern California. We continued to have good relations with the Van Cleves, though, and Dick began going out to the Lazy K Bar Ranch to work as a ranch hand over the summers. He was always very much interested in farming, the great outdoors, and life on the range, and he went out there summer after summer during his late teens and early twenties.

After we moved to Madison, we continued to take the train into New York to see my relatives, but now we went on the Lackawanna Railroad. Its proper name was the Delaware, Lackawanna & Western Railroad, or the D, L & W—often referred to as the Delay, Linger & Wait! The Lackawanna ran its own ferries across the river, from the Hoboken terminal to Barclay Street, and also a more northerly line straight across to Christopher Street. But while the Lackawanna terminal was built in more or less the same way as the Liberty Street terminal, the Lackawanna Railroad was electrified, so the steam vents that I had observed at the Jersey Central terminal were no longer functional. (Later, when I lived in Summit, New Jersey, I commuted on the same railroad to that same Lackawanna terminal for thirty years. I continued to take the ferries until they were discontinued and thereafter crossed the Hudson via the Hudson Tubes, now known as the PATH trains, short for Port Authority Trans-Hudson.)

My grandfather William Miller Sperry and Nana spent part of the year in a rented apartment in the Chatham Hotel in Manhattan. Sometimes we would visit them there, and sometimes they would see us in Madison. Occasionally when some time had passed between visits, Granddad would write me letters. In one I remember that he declared that his Eversharp mechanical pencil had run out of lead, and he would be forced to spend as much as fifteen cents to get it going again. He died of cancer in May 1927, when I was thirteen. I didn't know that he had cancer, or even what cancer was; I'm not certain that he knew himself. He spent the weekend at our house in Madison just before going into the hospital for what proved to be his final operation. I had just started learning to play golf—a game I'm still learning. The Madison Golf Club, sporting nine holes, was just across the street from where we lived, and on that Sunday afternoon I walked around it with my grandfather, explaining the layout of the holes, my club selection, and other fine points of the kind that golfers like to dwell on. Granddad listened to me gravely and at the end placed his hand on my shoulder and told me that when he got back from New York we were going to have a game there together, just the two of us. That was the last time I saw him.

Throughout the 1920s, my Beinecke grandparents lived in Apartment 1235 in The Plaza Hotel, in a suite of rooms on the twelfth floor facing Fifth Avenue. The suite ran north to south. The door opened onto the living room. There was a small room to the left of the living room that was used principally for sewing and domestic chores. The next room to the south was my grandparents' large bedroom, and next to that was a very narrow space, a tiny room where my grandfather kept his great rolltop desk. He would often be sitting at it doing his personal work when I'd come to see him. My grandfather was always very happy to see me, and when I got to be thirteen or fourteen, he would give me and my cousins twenty dollars apiece when we visited. He was a generous man, and twenty dollars to a thirteen-year-old boy in 1927 was a magnificent sum of money. Even today, when I think of giving some money to my grandsons, twenty dollars seems almost too much. My grandfather had a bit of a German accent, though not a particularly noticeable one. When I saw him, he was always formally dressed. He was more distant with me than I am with my grandchildren, but that may have been because he was European or because he was in his advanced years. I have a photograph of Bernhard Beinecke and his wife, Johanna, on the balcony of their room in the Axelmamistein Hotel in Reichenhall, Germany. It was taken in 1925, on one of their trips, by my first cousin Bernhard Weickert, who grew up in Germany. My grandfather was seventy-nine at the time. The photograph shows him very much as I remember him, somewhat sedentary in appearance, wearing glasses and a hat, and very formally dressed in a dark suit. My grandfather was not then an active man, and I believe that by that point he was no longer significantly involved in the management of The Plaza, though he remained chairman of the board until his death in 1932. But he was a chess aficionado, and well into his eighties he continued to play chess every afternoon at the Manhattan Chess Club.

It wasn't until I was older that I had a sense of my grandfather's tremendously successful career. I didn't have any idea of the extent of the Beinecke family's equity interest in The Plaza until much later. But the hotel was familiar territory to me from the time I was quite small, and I was at home there. So, too, were my other Beinecke cousins who were about my age; in fact, it is alleged that my cousin Betsy was the model for the heroine of Kate Thompson's popular children's book *Eloise*. Certainly long before the Eloise series came into being, Betsy was rampaging through the hallways, teasing the doorman, and running the elevators up and down. I was more interested in the elevators themselves. They were the old-fashioned plunger types that have long since been replaced by cable-suspended ones. The plunger elevators were hydraulically driven and rested on columns, and when the cars went down, those columns descended into the earth. I can remember looking through the elevator door and seeing the columns shimmering as they ascended and descended.

I went to The Plaza often enough so that I knew some of the permanent staff by name. I remember Hugo, the head waiter, and Ralph, who

was the doorman for thirty-five years. Back in those days, it was customary to hire doormen who looked like Russian nobility. They had to be at
least 6' 4" and handsome, and were dressed in uniforms and high-
plumed hats that made them look even taller. Ralph definitely fit the
part. According to my cousin Bud (Walter Beinecke, Jr.), Ralph had a
twin brother who was the doorman at the Pierre Hotel. Bud loves to tell
the story that the standard solution for dealing with drunkenness at
The Plaza was to have Ralph usher out the offending party, put them in
a taxi, and send them to the Pierre two blocks away. Apparently it was a
source of amazement to a considerable number of high-class New York
drunks that the big man who put them into the cab was there to help
them out of it as well! Perhaps apocryphal, but still a good story.

My grandfather took his meals in what is now called the Edwardian
Room. He always sat at the window table in the northwest corner, and if
my father and I went to the dining room when my grandfather wasn't
there, we would sit at that table, too. One time when we were visiting,
my father told me that any time I was hungry, I should just go into the
dining room and the head waiter would get me something to eat.
"That's a wonderful thing," I thought, "I'll try that sometime." Once
when I was about sixteen and was in The Plaza all by myself, I went into
the dining room to find out if this scheme would really work. Hugo recognized me, asked me to sit down, and asked what I would like. I looked
at the menu and saw "Salisbury steak," so I ordered that, not knowing
that Salisbury steak was a fancy term for hamburger. Instead of getting
the good rare steak I expected, I got a piece of hamburger, though I'm
sure it was wonderful hamburger. That was part of my education.

My grandfather Bernhard Beinecke died in 1932 at age eighty-six.
My grandmother continued to live in Apartment 1235 until she died,
but the suite was reduced by a room or so; I think that the study was surrendered to the hotel. I can say very little about what my grandmother
Johanna Weigle Beinecke was like, although I remember her well. She
was never unkind. She died in 1938, when I was twenty-four. I have
recently come across the last letter my mother received from her, dated
May 21, 1937, when our family group was motoring through Europe in
my father's Cadillac. Oma, as I called her, remembered traveling over
many of the same roads for several weeks in 1893 in a horse-drawn
stagecoach hired by "Father." When I was in law school, my grandmother and Aunt Theo (who was widowed by that time and was living
on the same floor of The Plaza with her mother) would come to see us in
Madison. They would be brought out by a car and driver, and I would
drive them back into New York. We'd have conversations as we were

going into the city, but I can't for the life of me recall them today. Aunt Theo's was a very sad story. Her husband had died in 1931, and her daughter, Elizabeth, their only child, died three weeks later. When her mother died, Aunt Theo was desolate; I don't think any of us realized how lonely she was. She committed suicide by jumping out the window of her apartment in The Plaza in 1940.

When I first came to know The Plaza during the twenties, Prohibition was in effect and the ground-floor bar on 59th Street, just off the Oak Room, was closed and leased out as a brokerage office. Coupled with the Depression of the early thirties, Prohibition meant that hotels had a difficult time financially. With its end and the economic recovery that accompanied our participation in World War II, though, they began to be profitable once again, and so my father and Uncle Edwin sold The Plaza to Conrad Hilton during the war years. I don't know what the price was, but it seemed like a very good deal to them. The Plaza has since gone through various owners, at one point passing through the hands of the famous New York real estate man Donald Trump. I don't know exactly who owns it now. Since the time it was sold during the war, the Beinecke family has not had any connection with The Plaza, except of course for a sentimental connection.

I was going to the Pingry School in Elizabeth, New Jersey at the time my family moved to Madison in 1925. When our family lived in Cranford, my father would drop me off in his Studebaker each morning on his way to work in Newark. In the afternoon, I would take the train home. The fare—or, rather, the half fare, as I was entitled to the "junior-citizen discount"—was nine cents. Our move to Madison presented transportation difficulties as there was no sophisticated bus system—only railroads, family transportation, or shank's mare. During the first year we lived in Madison, my morning routine remained the same. To get home, however, I had to take a rather complicated route that included being driven to Summit by Mr. George W. King, Jr., the Latin teacher, boarding the Lackawanna train and taking it to Madison. When I got to Madison, I had a long walk up the hill to our home. It was quite a stiff journey for a young boy.

Finally, it was decided that the afternoon commute from Pingry was just too much. Furthermore, the fare on the Lackawanna from Summit was *eleven* cents. So in the fall of 1926 my parents, having removed me from Pingry, entered me in the Madison Academy in town, a school much closer to our new home. At the outset, of course, my thoughts kept drifting back to Parker Road. I conceived the idea of a football game between my new eighth-grade friends at Madison and my old eighth-grade friends at Pingry. Arrangements were made, the encounter took place—and Pingry murdered us. To make it even worse, the chief assassin was my own cousin, "Kim" Whitehead, later the football captain at Pingry and somewhat later football captain at Yale, too. He ran through us like green corn through the new maid. When the game was over, our team left the field in defeat, only to find that our clothes had been tied in knots and strewn all over the locker room. That day's events cured my nostalgia. Pingry soon faded from my attention until it was no larger than the object referred to in the first Latin phrase taught us by Mr. King: *mica, mica, parva stella*.

I attended Madison Academy for two years. It wasn't a large school. It had only one building, which has since been torn down and replaced by homes. It was surrounded by a large lawn, with a walk leading up to the building. There was an athletic field of sorts, much smaller than regulation size. We could practice there, but we had to play our games elsewhere; even for baseball, we didn't have the proper accommodations. We had only eleven boys in the top two grades, so all the boys played on the football team—and on the baseball team, too, for that matter. Once we had to play a football game against another private school when one of our boys was sick. We had to borrow a boy from the public school in Madison.

I have a picture of the Madison Academy football team in 1927 that shows the eleven boys, with the headmaster standing at one end and our football coach at the other. The coach was a man named Lloyd "Red" Krug, a student at Drew Theological Seminary (now Drew University) in Madison. In the 1920s, the seminary was a very small school engaged solely in theological teaching; it probably had no more than three or four hundred students. Krug had been a football player at Dickinson College in Pennsylvania—as was confirmed for me much later when the Dickinson College alumni office sent me a photocopy of his entry in the yearbook—and when he was our coach he was about twenty-four years old. The Madison Academy headmaster was Joseph Pooley, a Pennsylvanian of Pennsylvania Dutch origin, a graduate of Harvard College, and a contemporary of my parents.

My friend and football teammate Dean Speir introduced me to the Madison YMCA. It was a modest affair, with a dinky swimming pool and a basketball court that was square. The players who made up the adult basketball team, mostly divinity students from Drew Seminary, could easily throw the ball from one end of the court to the other. It occurs to me, looking back with a 1990s sensibility, that all the boys who went to that YMCA were white. There was a place called the Settlement

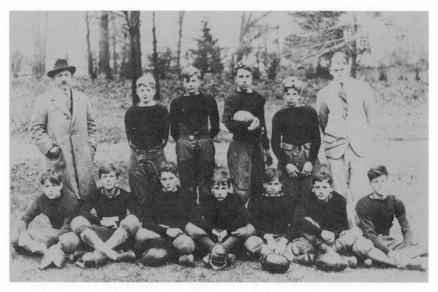

Madison Academy Football Team, 1927.
Front row (left to right): William S. Beinecke, Radcliffe Cheesman, Jack Noe,
Sam Kopper, Lamson Scoville, Owen Davis, Alan Day;
Back row (left to right): Joseph E. Pooley (headmaster), Harry Wilkinson, L. Dean
Speir, Otto Schundler, Alan "Buddy" Mills, Lloyd L. "Red" Krug (coach)

House, only a block or two from the YMCA, where the black boys of Madison went for basketball, physical training, and other sports and activities. So whether intentionally or just by happenstance, there was a segregated relationship between the blacks and whites who lived in that town. On the other hand, the public schools in Madison were not segregated, and there were black boys playing on the public school football team. I joined the Madison YMCA swimming team and swam the breaststroke in dual meets against Summit and Morristown. Once when I went down to the Oranges for a regional championship of several YMCAs, I won the breaststroke competition and was awarded a little gold medal that my mother wore on a charm bracelet for many years. When the announcer declared me the winner of the event, he somehow garbled "Beinecke" into "Barnycagle," one of the more classic mispronunciations of my frequently mispronounced name. Perhaps he was thinking of Chris Cagle, who was then the big star on the Army football team. For years afterwards, when my friend Ben Moyer felt like kidding me, he would call me Barnycagle.

At Madison Academy, I took the regular school courses you would take in the eighth and ninth grades. One year the school put on a pro-

duction of Dickens's *A Christmas Carol* for the benefit of the parents. My
responsibility had to do with lighting and making sure that the electric
"fire" in Scrooge's office glowed properly. I managed to blow out all the
lights in the schoolhouse an hour or two before the event was supposed
to take place. In panic I called the headmaster; he called the local electrician, and the whole problem was quickly corrected. I had some good
friends at Madison Academy, and one of my closest friends there, Dean
Speir, remains one of my closest friends today.

I made a number of other friends through my interest in horseback
riding. When we moved from Cranford to Madison, my horse,
Greylord, was moved to the livery stable in Madison. The stable was,
oddly enough, right in the middle of town, not far from where the trolley cars ran; I think there's a filling station there today. My parents stabled their horses there, too. My friend Alan Day from the Madison
Academy and some of his friends also had horses, but they all rode
Western saddles while I had been taught to ride English. In order to
ride with them, I had to shift from the more traditional type of horse-
show riding I had been taught to the type these other boys did. In the
spring of 1927, we put together a rodeo in Chatham, New Jersey, on
the banks of the Passaic River. We didn't have wild steers or bull riding,
but some boys did stunts, like bending down from the saddle at a gallop
to pick up a hat from the ground. We also brought out a stagecoach,
mounted an attack on it by some boys dressed up as Indians, and staged
a stirring rescue by other boys dressed up as cowboys. We charged
admission to this rodeo, and it was a complete success. My recollection
is that it coincided with Charles Lindbergh's famous nonstop solo flight
to Paris.

In the fall of 1928, when I was fourteen, I went to boarding school
at Phillips Academy in Andover, Massachusetts, following in the foot-
steps of my father and his brothers, Edwin and Walter, who had been
students there at the turn of the century. I roomed by myself in Williams Hall, the special dormitory for entering boys whom Andover
called "juniors," or, less formally, "preps." (New boys of any year were
also called "preps.") First-year students were at the bottom of the
Andover social hierarchy and were basically at the beck and call of the
older boys. In my first letter to my parents, I wrote that "when I come
home, I will have my degree Mo.D. (Doctor of Moving). I've had to
move trunks, desks, tables, beds and big packing boxes loaded with
junk, to say nothing of a lot of small things. I'll be walking along and
then some fellow will yell, 'Hey, prep, I've got three or four trunks for
you to move!' And I say, 'O.K., be right there.'"

If Andover had given a prize to the student with the worst performance on record, I would have won it hands down in my first year at the school. I failed every course I took except English, and I passed that by the skin of my teeth. I even managed to fail Latin, though it was the same old Latin I'd been studying for years. I left at the end of the school year and in the summer of 1929 began summer school at the Westminster School in Simsbury, Connecticut.

Despite my abysmal academic performance, I got a lot out of that year at Andover. That was a time of new insights and awakenings. Just living at Andover was a lesson in aesthetics. The campus is situated on a hill, and as you approach it you see the chapel and several venerable brick buildings on the left, and the library on the right. At the crest of the hill, framed by a line of elm trees, is Samuel Phillips Hall with its ancient blue clock. It's a glorious vista, one of the grand American scenes, and it made me very conscious that I was following in the line of an old tradition. Indeed, my father and uncles were still remembered by many of the teachers at Andover, and I once got into a fight over an incident from Uncle Edwin's student days. Edwin Beinecke was in the Class of 1903 and had lived in one of the large Victorian rooming houses along Main Street. A student in that house named Leeds was given a pistol as a gift from his father, and as Leeds was looking at his new present, he said to my uncle, "You know, I bet you I could hit you with this." My uncle replied, "I bet you fifty dollars you can't." Fifty dollars was a fortune in those days, particularly for a boy. "All right," said Leeds, "let's go out in the driveway." Uncle Edwin went outside, put his hands on his hips, and said, "Go ahead and shoot." Fortunately Leeds didn't dare but fired three shots in the air instead, and Uncle Edwin collected the fifty dollars. My father used to shake his head when he told that story, because Leeds might very well have tried to wing Uncle Edwin's ear and shot him in the head by mistake. It was an early indication of Uncle Edwin's iron daring and steely nerve—qualities that would be amply displayed in his business career.

At any rate, at the end of the 1929 Andover spring term, I was in the railroad station heading home, resplendent in a new vanilla ice cream-colored suit, when I got into a fight with a kid who had heard this story and was ribbing me about my uncle being such a damn fool as to stand out in the driveway and let another student shoot at him. I got in lots of fights when I was young, partly because I had red hair in those days and used to be called things like "redheaded woodpecker" and so on. They say that all redheaded kids have bad tempers, but the reason they have bad tempers is because of the way they get teased! The fight in the railroad station ended as my fights usually did, with me getting a bloody nose, and that was also the end of my nice vanilla ice cream-colored suit. My dear friend Shorty Greenwood had a ringside seat for the bout, and in later years he used to laugh and laugh as he told how I yelled at my opponent, "You can say anything you want about me, but you can't criticize my uncle!"

After I flunked out of Andover, my father asked me whether there was any other school I might like to attend. I was only fifteen and didn't know much about any other schools, and my father didn't offer any suggestions. I did remember, however, that the outstanding boys at Camp Mishe Mokwa, the Williamsons—Clem, Mac, and Charlie—had gone to the Westminster School, though I think all of them also spent a final year at Andover as well. My father drove me up to Westminster and I was interviewed by the headmaster, Raymond McOrmand, who had graduated from Yale in 1907 and had also taught at Choate. He told my father that I could start summer school right away, and I was immediately assigned a room in the Main Building. I had no clothes with me, so my father drove me to Hartford to buy some shirts and other articles that would tide me over until I could return home for a weekend. Instead of guiding my choice of clothes, however, as my mother would have done, he let me pick my own. My floundering taste in clothing at that time ran toward items like ridiculous vanilla ice cream-colored suits, and alas, I selected a half dozen green shirts. By the end of my first week at Westminster, the other boys thought I was wearing the same green shirt all the time. This monotonous sartorial behavior rankled them, so one day they wrestled my shirt off me and ran it up the flagpole. Fortunately I was soon able to go home and return to Westminster with a broader repertoire of more tasteful clothing, and the rest of the summer passed without incident.

Westminster in the late 1920s was a third-rate school. It was in bad financial shape then and declined even further as the Depression deepened, and it nearly went under in the mid-1930s. Nonetheless, I enjoyed a much more productive academic experience there than I'd had at Andover, and I passed all my classes, perhaps because Westminster had supervised study and exercised more discipline than Andover did. Certainly there were rules and regulations at Andover, but its approach was to teach independence and self-reliance by setting students free to stand or fall. I needed more discipline, in those early years at least, and I did better in Westminster's more structured environment.

After summer school I was able to enter Westminster in the fourth form, or sophomore year. I went out for football, and although I was still only fifteen and too small to get on the varsity, I made a letter that fall. The team was coached by Ronald Michelini, who had graduated from Dartmouth only a year or so before. (He stayed on at the school, and was a senior master when my son John attended Westminster; he was a good teacher and in a way was a mentor for John. I became good friends with Mr. Michelini then, and played a round of golf with him at his club.) In the winter of 1929-30, I went out for swimming and had no trouble making the team. I excelled at the breaststroke, and I also swam freestyle on the relay team. For two years I was the school's leading breaststroker and even set the pool record. In the spring the track coach tried to interest me in throwing the hammer, but I was no good at it. In my second year at Westminster I played baseball on the third team, sort of the equivalent of JV. Once when we were playing the Loomis School, I tagged out Winthrop Rockefeller at first base—my first contact with a Rockefeller, so to speak.

The senior master of Westminster was a mathematics teacher named Lemuel Pettee. On the faculty for half a century, from 1899 to 1949, he was a real Mr. Chips figure, much beloved. My favorite teacher was John Gow, who taught physics and geology and was the tennis coach as well. I earned a College Board credit for taking his course on physical geography (a sort of introduction to geology) in the summer of 1930. One day late in the summer of 1932 when I was driving back from Canada with my friends Ben Moyer and John Wight, I passed near Simsbury and noticed Mr. Gow driving his distinctive Whippet car, which always seemed too small for him. I hailed him, and I remember he said to me, "I hear you got in down there," meaning Yale—in a tone that indicated congratulations rather than surprise.

Simsbury was a pleasant little town in an attractive part of north-central Connecticut. We sometimes had dinner with parents and friends at the Pettibone Tavern in town, where we also saw the girls from the Ethel Walker School with their parents—though they were not allowed to talk to us, of course. Some of the farms around Westminster grew leaf tobacco, and on Sunday mornings we were permitted to walk a mile or so through the tobacco fields to the house of a woman who served delicious made-to-order waffles. Those Sunday breakfasts were quite a treat, and even now my mouth waters to think of those waffles.

I was friendly with many of the other boys at Westminster, but I didn't make many close friends. I remember Burrall Barnum, who was killed in the war and whose letters home were later collected and make good and poignant reading. Several of my Westminster acquaintances ended up at Yale more or less when I did, including Robert Ebling '37 (who was my roommate in my second summer at Westminster) and my classmate Fred Houghton. Fred was a superb piano player and would always perform all the popular songs of the day for us. Fred came from Stamford and was a friend of my late brother-in-law Richard Gillespie; he later served as a trustee of Westminster. My years at the school also overlapped with George Vaill, who graduated from Yale in 1935 and went on to become the associate secretary of the university. He was a great wit and a colorful character, and once won the National Limerick Contest with an inspired rhyme about the bustard, a bird who "escapes what would be/ Illegitimacy/ By grace of a singular vowel." He married Pinky McOrmand, the headmaster's daughter. I was also friends with Bob Farrell, Tim Gibson, and Bob Baxter.

In the summer of 1930, Tim Gibson and Bob Baxter invited me to visit them at their homes in the Midwest. Tim lived in Middletown, Ohio (near Cincinnati), and Bob in Grand Rapids, Michigan. It was the first time in my life that I had been away from the East Coast, and I wouldn't travel west again until after I had graduated from college. I took the Ohio State Limited, an overnight train from New York to Cincinnati. I got off in Middletown and stayed with Tim for three or four days. We had some good times, and played a little golf on the Verity family's private course out by the Miami River. Tim introduced me to some of his friends, and one night we drove to Cincinnati with some dates and danced the night away on the roof of one of the hotels, where a popular swing band was playing. From there I took another train to Grand Rapids and stayed a few days with Bob Baxter. That was my first sight of the Great Lakes. Bob's father had a good-sized boat that he'd acquired as World War I surplus from the navy. One day we took the boat onto Lake Michigan. It was hot on the deck, and Lake Michigan looked awfully inviting, so I said to Mr. Baxter, "Would it be all right if I went swimming?" He said, "Sure." I dove off that boat into the coldest water I'd ever felt in my life. I got out of Lake Michigan as fast as I could. Had it been possible to make a reverse dive, the way a movie of a dive might look if you ran it backwards, I would have done so.

In the fall of 1930, I was sixteen and a little bigger than I'd been in my first year at Westminster, and this time I made it onto the varsity football squad. We played against schools like Suffield, Loomis, Salisbury, and Taft. The previous season we had been murdered by Kingswood, a country day school in Hartford, so when we beat them by the nominal score of 8-0 in my junior year, it was sweet revenge. At the conclusion of that season, my friend Bob Farrell, by far the best player, was elected captain by me and the other teammates. He came from Hartford, Connecticut, where he had starred on his high school team. One day I went with Bob to his home, which provided another of my awakenings as a young boy. Bob's was a very modest home in a working-class neighborhood. All of the houses were shotgun houses—neat enough, but all the same size, all in a row. I'd never had any experience with that type of environment. I'd passed houses like that, but I'd never been inside them. After Bob was elected captain, Raymond McOrmand, the headmaster, declared that a scholarship boy was not eligible to be captain of a Westminster team. That was nonsense, of course; McOrmand had personally recruited Bob to be on the football team and had created an athletic scholarship for that purpose. But in those days the school was a sole proprietorship—it wasn't operated by a board of trustees the way it is today—and so Mr. McOrmand could do anything he wanted. He told me that I was going to be captain of the football team, not Bob Farrell. I thought it was an unconscionable act. The whole thing upset me so much that I decided that I would try to rejoin my class at Andover.

Looking back, I think Mr. McOrmand was trying to do a hard job amidst difficult circumstances. He and his wife, who had some means, had purchased Westminster in the early 1920s from the estate of George Cushing, the school's founder. He wanted to make Westminster competitive with the good private schools in Connecticut—Choate, Hotchkiss, Taft, Loomis, and the like—but the school had no endowment, no annual giving fund, or anything like the kind of support that financially well-managed schools have today. I think that helps explain his ambivalent behavior regarding Bob Farrell. Not long after I left Westminster, the full impact of the Depression flooded in on the McOrmands, and they had to dispose of the school. I doubt if Mr. McOrmand and his wife got much if anything for their interest, for the school was in bad shape at that point. Shortly thereafter McOrmand died under odd circumstances, when his car ran off the road into a river somewhere in the Midwest and he drowned. There are those who think that the car did not run off the road accidentally. Westminster was subsequently reorganized and rescued in the mid-1930s by a group of men under Robert Darling, Jr. (the uncle of my friend Fred Houghton) who bought it and organized themselves as the board of trustees. They began to run Westminster as a not-for-profit secondary school and gradually acquired the necessary background knowledge and administrative infrastructure. They hired "Prof" Milliken as headmaster, and he set the school on its feet and pointed it in the right direction. It has been running successfully ever since and is now one of the most highly regarded independent schools in New England.

I had done all right academically in my second year at Westminster, but in order to return to Andover I had to attend summer school yet again at Westminster between my junior and senior years. I remember very little about the courses I took. I do have a vivid recollection of playing a couple of rounds of golf that summer at Wampanoag in West Hartford. Wampanoag was designed by Donald Ross, a Scot from Dornoch who was the principal course designer in America in the 1920s and one of the outstanding golf architects of this century. That summer I also went with some other boys to Tumble Brook in West Hartford to watch an exhibition between the golf pros Billy Burke and George Von Elm. Not long before, they had tied for the US Open after seventy-two holes, and had to play another seventy-two holes to decide the winner. Billy Burke finally took the prize after a total of one hundred forty-four holes. Nothing like that had happened before—or will ever happen again, since the rules have been changed to prevent a disastrous recurrence. But the event made such a splash that Burke and Von Elm were able to capitalize on it by barnstorming around the country and restaging their duel. Those were the Depression days, before the PGA tour, and money was hard to come by for even the best golfers. I remember that Billy Burke shot sixty-four at Tumble Brook—an absolutely superb round!

I got the necessary academic preparation at Westminster that summer and was allowed to return as a senior with my class at Andover in the fall of 1931. Westminster designated another boy, Donald Dunham, as captain of the football team. Even though Bob Farrell wasn't captain, he came back and played, so my absence probably didn't make much difference to the team; I wasn't a star. It would be pleasant for me to believe that the captainship episode revealed some innate sense of justice within my schoolboy self, but there's another episode I'm ashamed of that counteracts that idea. There was a student at Westminster named Friedman. He was Jewish, but at that time I didn't know the difference between Jews and non-Jews; that was an awakening that came later when I was at Andover. Friedman reported somebody's infraction to the powers that be, as he was supposed to do under the honor system—but I and some of the other guys thought that that wasn't the way things should be done. I told him as much, then challenged him to go out behind a building and have a fight. We fought and I won, but he really had more courage than I, because we both knew he couldn't fight as well as I could. It was an unfair thing for me to do, and I should not have done it. I have been ashamed of it ever since.

CHAPTER THREE

Andover and Yale, 1931–1936

9 had flunked out of Andover in 1929, but after two years at the Westminster School, I rejoined my class at Andover for senior year in the fall of 1931. I still couldn't master my nemesis, solid geometry, and so even though I went on to Yale College in the fall of 1932, I exited Andover without sufficient credits to receive my diploma. I never graduated from any high school anywhere, which is somewhat ironic in view of my later service on the boards of trustees at several preparatory schools, including Andover.

I very much enjoyed my return to Andover, because the school continued to offer me new insights and awakenings. I talked about Andover with my father and Uncle Edwin and learned more about the school in their time. The Andover campus in the early 1930s looked different in certain respects from the way it did when my father and uncles had attended around the turn of the century. In their day, Bartlett Hall and Foxcroft Hall, the two old dormitories that flank and in a sense frame Samuel Phillips Hall, had been part of the Andover Theological Seminary. Sometime between my father's graduation and my arrival at Andover, the seminary was moved lock, stock, and Bible to Harvard University, where it was absorbed into the divinity school. Phillips Academy acquired the former seminary's land and buildings. Then in the early 1920s, Thomas Cochran, a partner at J. P. Morgan, gave money to support a complete rebuilding. Cochran might not even have been an Andover alumnus, for all I know, but he certainly fell in love with the school, and it still bears his stamp. A considerable amount of money has been spent on Andover since Cochran's donation, but the general physical concept that was established has remained the same. A third building, Pearson Hall, which had stood between Bartlett and Foxcroft, obscured the vista extending up to Samuel Phillips Hall, so it was moved to a different location. For similar aesthetic reasons, Bancroft Hall, a big dormitory, was also physically moved during my first stint at Andover, and I remember seeing the building up on railroad ties for most of that year as it was inched from one location to another by workmen using giant jacks.

My father used to tell me stories about life at Andover in his time and some of his doings as a student. Even as a boy, my father excelled at tinkering. At Andover, he hooked up a telegraph line from his room to a classmate's in another dormitory so they could send each other messages in Morse code. My father loved to tell the story of the time he was nearly caught downtown, off limits, by Dr. Page, the school physician. Figuring he was in serious trouble, he ran all the way back to the dormitory and dropped on his bed. Dr. Page came into his room shortly thereafter and found him lying in his bed perspiring from head to foot from his run. Instead of punishing him, the good doctor pronounced him "feverish" and bundled him off to the infirmary. Another favorite story was of the occasion when Edwin was in his dormitory room, and my father shouted up to him that one of their friends had turned in a false alarm, a misdemeanor that carried a serious penalty. As the sound of the fire engine could be heard approaching the dormitory, Edwin legitimized the alarm by setting fire to his wastebasket and holding it up to the window! All three boys congratulated themselves on their alertness and presence of mind. I have always wondered what happened when the firemen arrived.

One of the ways that my experience at Andover was similar to that of the previous generation was that it offered a space in which to grow up. It seems that young people today become adults all too quickly, while in my time the process of growing up was slower and more extended. When I was at Andover, I still had a boy's enthusiasms and limited horizons. Students were allowed three free weekends away each semester. Although usually I would go home, I decided one time that I would seize the chance to do something different, something daring. About a half dozen miles from Andover is the city of Lawrence, Massachusetts. Lawrence is a mill town, and even in those days it was no queen of the bright lights. But some of the boys in Paul Revere Hall, where I lived, claimed that at night they would sneak out and go to Lawrence for wild times; they assured us that there was nothing like it in this world. I think now that these stories must have been the figments of our collective imaginations or that some of the fellows made up these stories for the entertainment of the rest of us. In those days, though, I was determined that I, too, would go over to Lawrence, to enjoy the bustling entertainment and see some of the seamy side of life. I didn't dare sneak out at night after hours, but on one of those precious weekends away from Andover, instead of going to Boston or New York, I and another fellow checked into a hotel in Lawrence. We went out in search of excitement, but of course there was no excitement to be seen, and we wasted our free weekend walking fruitlessly up and down the streets of Lawrence. It was one of the most disappointing and disillusioning experiences of my life!

I did acquire one adult vice during my time in boarding school: the habit of smoking. You could smoke in certain areas at Andover—in your fraternity house, for example. You were also permitted to smoke at the Grill, a building some distance from the dining hall where you could buy a hamburger. The place was blue with smoke, and cigarette butts and ashes were strewn all around. Smoking was de rigeur, an accepted part of growing up. Seniors had special smoking privileges, though even they were not supposed to smoke in the fall if they were in training for football.

Once in a while several other boys and I would rent horses from a nearby stable and ride them up a particular hill in Andover. There was a tall metal fire tower atop the hill, with nice views from the "summit." One day as we were riding our horses near this hill, we saw a troop of girls from Abbott, the girls' school in Andover, out for a walk. We decided to show off. We galloped up the hill, tethered our horses to the base of the tower, and raced up to the top on foot. But we made such a racket running up the steps that the horses became alarmed, broke their reins, and ran off. Fortunately some of the Abbott girls, who were much more experienced riders than we were, got hold of them, repaired the reins, and returned the horses to us. It was really quite embarrassing.

I was a member of the Phi Beta Chi fraternity—PBX for short. Andover had two kinds of fraternities in those days, the secret, "closed" fraternities and the more social, "open" ones. PBX was an open fraternity, and you could invite friends into the house to visit and play pool. It was nicknamed the Andover AC because a large proportion of its members were athletes, and there was some good-humored ribbing on that score. Of the "closed" fraternities, the most secretive was the Knights of Andover, also known as KOA; it was the Skull and Bones of Andover. My cousin Kim Whitehead, who took a year at Andover after graduating from Pingry and of course was a star on the Andover football team, was a member of KOA. A school newspaperman—perhaps it was Ring Lardner—broke into KOA and took some flash pictures, which were published in the paper, the *Phillipian*. The pictures didn't show much more than a fireplace and a table with some books and magazines on it, but there was a big outcry.

Both Kim and I had only arrived at Andover in the fall of 1931—I had been away for two years, so I was practically as much a new boy as Kim was. Since the fraternities didn't tap new initiates until the end of the fall semester, our fraternity experience was limited to about half an academic year. Fraternities have long since been abolished at Andover, and their houses have been absorbed into the overall physical plant— and a good thing, too. When I was a student there, of course, I thought it was great to belong to a fraternity, but the system was not good for the school or for class unity. Andover was supposed to be democratically organized, yet it had fraternities that were run on an exclusive basis and catered to only a limited number of boys.

Andover was also where I first realized that the academic subjects I groaned and sweated over might be something more than infernal punishment for my sins. When I came home for Christmas in 1931, I had just finished a biography of William Jennings Bryan, the silver-tongued "Boy Orator of the Platte." I had never before read a biography of a historical figure, and for me it was an awakening into a world I didn't know anything about. One day during the vacation while I was having dinner with my parents, I happened to mention that I had read this Bryan biography, and I gave them a little summary and said that I had found reading it very interesting. My parents were astounded. They took me from the dining room into the library and said, "If you're interested in biography, take a look." And there were shelves and shelves of biographies about statesmen, literary figures, explorers, adventurers. I had never before known anything about the books that my parents possessed, but I began to realize that they had wide-ranging interests and were widely read people. And I remember how pleased my parents were that this ne'er-do-well son of theirs, who'd had such a terrible time in school so far, seemed all of a sudden to show some small glimmer of intelligence.

During my senior year at Andover, I made friends with a boy in my dormitory named Herbie Stern. If I had known anything about Jews, I would have known that his was a Jewish name, but all I knew about Jews came from occasional overheard references (usually pejorative) by other boys at Andover or from characters in literature like the usurer in *Ivanhoe*. I'm sure that when I was growing up I must have had some contact with Jews, but I was never aware of it. And I honestly believed they were a different breed of people, perhaps with tails and horns or something like that. Herbie Stern and I used to talk for hours about politics and the Depression, which was an inescapable, indisputable fact of American life by 1931–32. We both knew all about economics (or thought we did) and were both going on to Yale, where we would study it and no doubt solve the economic problems of the world. One evening in that senior year, we had a conversation about Rasputin and the last days of the Russian tsar's court. It seemed to me that somebody who had played a malign role in that story was Jewish, and I made a comment to that effect to Herbie Stern. "But I'm a Jew," Herbie said to me. I looked at him. "Herbie," I said, half as a question and half as a statement, "you're a Jew?" This was actually the first time in my life that I had ever had the experience of knowing that I was talking to someone who was Jewish.

Could you go through life today, growing up in New Jersey and going to Andover as I did, and have no idea of who or what a Jew was until you were seventeen years old? I doubt it. The whole concept of race and ethnicity is something that young Americans learn about much earlier today. They also quickly become aware that minority groups can be offended—and rightfully so—by expressions that were once commonly used. When I was growing up in Madison, the town movie theater did not have a balcony; instead, the orchestra was separated by a transverse corridor about two-thirds of the way back, and from there the seats angled up severely toward the ceiling. The black people in Madison sat in the top third of those seats, and I and the other boys in town referred to the section as "nigger heaven." We saw nothing wrong with that situation or that designation. Unbelievable as it sounds, we thought that black people sat there by choice, and we didn't quarrel with that. It wasn't until some time later that I learned not to use pejorative and highly offensive words like the "n-word." The fact that I did once use that odious term, although out of innocence and ignorance rather than malice, indicates that I grew up in a homogeneous, insulated, and even somewhat segregated environment.

It was during my senior year at Andover, when I was seventeen, that I really became awakened to the problems of the world. I think it was my conversations with Herbie Stern, as much as anything, that made me aware of the Nazis' coming to power in Germany and the deepening of the Depression in this country. By the summer of 1932, I was very conscious that something was wrong with the American system and that there was a need for change. Herbie Stern and I agreed that the economic system had fallen flat on its face. It was apparent to me that capitalism was finished, and I thought that the cure for this terrible international economic predicament lay with socialism. Socialism described how society would function for the benefit of everyone, not just of the few, and that seemed to me to be a fair and logical arrangement. Socialism made philosophic, if not economic, sense. I wasn't thinking about communism. I didn't know much about Russia. I didn't know the finer points of difference between communism and socialism, and to the extent that I contrasted socialism with communism (if I did at all), I contrasted it with communism with a small "c," not the Communism represented by the political regime in Russia. I didn't know much about Franklin Roosevelt—or Herbert Hoover either, for that matter. I was an adolescent making new discoveries and being inspired by new ideals. I thought socialism was the answer to the economic and social ills of the society. It was the political movement that was going somewhere, and I wanted to get involved. Norman Thomas was running for president on the Socialist ticket, so I spent the summer of 1932 in his campaign headquarters in New York City. It was my first job.

I drove into Manhattan in early June with my closest friends, Dean Speir and Ben Moyer, to call on Thomas's office on East 19th Street and ask for summer employment with the Socialist cause. I went into the office and spoke with Norman Thomas himself. He was tall, good look-

Dean Speir, Ben Moyer, and me many years later (c. 1974) in Summit, New Jersey.

ing, and wore a dark suit. He was well-educated, well-spoken, and very personable—a Princeton man through and through. I was most impressed. I got the job, and I spent the rest of the summer as a clerk under the supervision of Mary Fox, the woman who ran the place. The campaign covered my expenses, which consisted of my meals and my railroad fare from Madison into New York, but I was essentially a volunteer. The job was a nothing, really. I was one of several people helping to send out mailings, typing up envelopes and churning out administrative paperwork. Office jobs in those days were not machine-driven or electronically operated, so another pair of hands was useful. I remember being impressed by some pamphlets written for the campaign by Reinhold Niebuhr, later a famous theologian. I also remember sending out mailings for something called the Committee of 10,000, which was soon changed to the Committee of 100,000. The committee was a way of enlisting people in the Norman Thomas campaign. You wouldn't ask people to join the Socialist Party, you'd ask them to commit to Norman Thomas for the election with a small cash donation to the committee. The campaign was presented as an adjunct of the Socialist Party, not the party itself. I think its organizers were smart enough to realize how the country still felt about socialism, and they knew that they needed more than simply to wave the hammer and sickle. I don't remember whether I actually joined the Socialist Party, but I don't think I did.

People who know about my Norman Thomas interlude tend to overemphasize my youthful flirtation with socialism, which I suppose is natural when you consider that my grandfather Bernhard Beinecke was such a capitalist hero and that I ended up as a corporate CEO. Still, this particular chapter in my life lasted only a couple of months in the summer of 1932, when the United States was in the deepest trough of the Depression. Perhaps the people at the Norman Thomas headquarters didn't quite know what to make of me, either. At eighteen years old, I was the youngest worker there by a considerable margin. I remember having a conversation with one of the men in the campaign who asked me what I was going to do when I got up to college. I said, "Well, I guess I'm going to go out for football," because I had loved to play football as a boy and all through my school years. And he laughed and said that he thought it was quite strange for a socialist to play football for Yale.

I'm not sure that I ever thought about why I wanted to go to Yale. My father had gone there, my uncles and many of my father's friends had gone as well, so Yale was very much a part of my growing up. When I was a boy, my parents occasionally took me to the Yale-Princeton football game when it was played in New Jersey. I remember driving down to Princeton from Cranford in the early 1920s in an open touring car, Yale banners fluttering from the sides. When I was very young, Princeton had a certain attraction because I lived in New Jersey, because it was the only college I had any awareness of, and because when I went down there I saw how beautiful it was. I was also very much interested in the United States Naval Academy. I had an early fascination with naval warships, and there was a section in the Sunday paper that published sepia-tinted pictures of horses, mansions, and always a warship or two. When I was in grade school, I would cut these pictures of warships out of the Sunday paper and stick them up on my wall.

In the end, my father helped direct me toward Yale. He never aimed persuasive speeches at me or bombarded me with Eli propaganda. Still, the memorabilia around the house, the comings and goings of my father's college friends, and my father's attendance at class reunions and so forth meant that there was a Yale presence in our home. It made me aware, even if unconsciously, that Yale was there. Andover also helped point me to Yale, because most everybody who went to Andover in those days went on to Yale. Our class at Yale numbered not quite a thousand, and over a hundred of us—more than a tenth of the class—had gone to Andover at some point. Neither was it terribly difficult to be admitted to Yale in those days, and I managed to get in without having actually graduated from Andover. Yale's glorious football tradition made it an attractive place for Andover boys, and I'd first heard about Yale's football from my counselors at Camp Mishe Mokwa. When I was a senior at Andover, I saw the great 1931 Yale-Harvard football game, which ended in a 3-0 Yale victory when Albie Booth broke a scoreless tie with a drop kick from the 14-yard line.

Before matriculating at Yale as a freshman, and after I had completed my work with the Norman Thomas campaign, I went on a brief trip to Canada with my friends Ben Moyer and John Wight in early September 1932. I had known Ben for just about as long as I had lived in Madison, and John, who lived in nearby Summit, was another old friend. We decided that we would take John's Model A Ford touring car, which had a backseat and a folding top, and camp out. We didn't know anything about campsites, and I'm not sure we even had a tent. We just figured that we'd sleep out in fields and that it wouldn't rain— and it didn't! It's amazing to me to think back on how little money we had when we set out. I don't think any one of us started off with more than twenty-five dollars. But it was the nadir of the Depression, and our expenses were absurdly low by today's standards. Gas cost fifteen cents a gallon or less, food was almost nothing, and we never paid for overnight accommodations.

Our first stop was Buffalo, where some of my mother's Whitehead cousins lived. Of course, since we were all eighteen years old, it never occurred to us to let the Whiteheads know in advance that we were coming, and they weren't home when we arrived. Fortunately, their next-door neighbor befriended us and let us know when they would return. Ben and John and I went into town, killed some time at a burlesque show (of the tame vaudevillian variety), and eventually met up with my second cousins later that evening. From Buffalo we pushed on up to Niagara Falls, where we had a wonderful time at the falls and a nearby amusement park. We went into a sideshow where, for ten cents, we saw a fellow and his big rubber ball, ten feet in diameter, in which he had ridden over the falls some years earlier; when we saw it, it was in rather shabby shape. We crossed over into Canada and stopped at a beach at Saint Catharines, on Lake Ontario, where we met a number of young Canadians cavorting on the beach. A bit further on, after we'd passed through Toronto, we went out to the beach at Oshawa, on the northern shore of Lake Ontario. There we met another group of Canadians our own age having a cookout. They were roasting fresh, delicious corn on the cob, and gave us as much as we could eat. Later that evening, after our new friends had gone home, we three boys slept on the beach.

When we arrived at Montreal, we called on Tom Brainerd, whom I had been friends with at Andover. I hadn't known it before, but the Brainerds were among the more affluent families in Montreal. They lived in a magnificent townhouse, complete with a butler in tails, and Tom and his parents kindly invited us to stay. Indeed, they invited us to stay on in their townhouse even though they were leaving the next day for their summer home on Martha's Vineyard. (I was puzzled why Canadians would want to go to Martha's Vineyard for a seaside holiday and eventually decided that it was because the beaches east to the sea from Montreal are rocky and forbidding, while there are plenty of nice beaches to the southeast.) John, Ben, and I remained in Montreal for a couple of days. We met some of Tom's friends, who invited us to the Laurentian Mountains, north of Montreal, to spend a day or two. We went to Saint Adele, and it was glorious, so much so that I later went to Saint Sauveur des Monts for three months with Betty and our two-and-a-half-year-old son, Rick, after I returned from the war.

From Montreal, we headed east down the Saint Lawrence River to Quebec City, camping along the way near a town called Trois Rivières. We wanted to go to Quebec not because it is a fascinating and historic city or even because my great-great-great-grandfather Jacob Sperry was taken prisoner there when the forces of Benedict Arnold assaulted it in 1775—no, we went to Quebec because one of John Wight's friends had a summer job as a bellboy at the Chateau Frontenac. When we arrived in town, we saw John's friend (who was too busy to do more than say hello) and did some sightseeing. I was impressed by the city's battlements on the heights over the Saint Lawrence and by the city itself.

It was time to head home. On the outskirts of Quebec, in a heavily French area, we stopped at a garage for gas, and in the back we encountered several young men gathered around a great cask of wine. I didn't know as much French as I was supposed to have learned in school, but I knew enough to get by, and we stayed at that garage for several hours, making friends and drinking too much wine. The next day we crossed a wonderful bridge over the Saint Lawrence, and soon we were back in the United States. Since we were in the vicinity of the White Mountains, we dropped in on our friend Corbin Moister, whose parents had a summer place in New Hampshire. We were all quite tired by this point, and John in particular was thoroughly worn out. Mrs. Moister took us under her wing, gave us a good meal, and put us up for the night. We left for home the next morning with all dispatch, and it was while traveling through Connecticut near Simsbury that we encountered my old Westminster teacher Mr. John Gow, who congratulated me on being accepted at Yale. That ten-day trip was a marvelous experience, and it put me in a jubilant state of mind as I prepared for the start of my freshman year.

My career as a Yale undergraduate was not distinguished, but neither was it particularly undistinguished. I was in the great middle. I made lifelong friends with whom I still keep up, and I had a busy and satisfying social life. But I was also interested in my studies. Despite the woes of my high school years, Yale was easy for me academically. Although I wasn't Phi Beta Kappa, I was on the Dean's List the last couple of years. Nevertheless there were times when I got fed up with college, if not with Yale. I remember once calling my father and saying, "Dad, I think I'd better come home." I felt that I was wasting my time and costing my father money he could ill afford, and that maybe I'd be better off going to work. My father, being a wise man, persuaded me to stay a little longer. I suppose that any adolescent goes through periods of self-doubt, but my time at Yale was generally quite happy.

The class of 1936 has been called "Yale's Greatest Class"—at least that's what we've been calling ourselves for the past sixty years. John

Hersey and his friend Andy McBurney came up with the label as a way of creating excitement and enthusiasm for our junior prom, and somehow they managed to make the name stick. Yale has had a lot of great classes, but ours is the only one to have gotten away with this crazy boast. We've taken a lot of ribbing about it from other classes, but we've claimed it for so long that now it's just the way we naturally think of ourselves. And it is true that there were quite a number of illustrious individuals in our class, men like John Hersey, Lloyd Cutler, Brendan Gill, S. Dillon Ripley, J. Peter Grace, and Jonathan Brewster Bingham. Those men were not a part of my inner circle at college, but I was acquainted with them all. I knew Jack Bingham fairly well. He became an eminent lawyer, an adviser and counsel to Governor Herbert Lehman of New York, and then served in the House of Representatives, where he had a long and distinguished career. He lived in Riverdale, not far from where my daughter Frances lives today. I was good friends with John Hersey, who later became a celebrated writer. I got to know him when we were freshmen on the fall football squad. Not everybody knows that John earned a football "Y" at Yale along with his literary honors, but he did. He played end, and he was good, but he was playing at a time when the Yale team had two extraordinary ends. One was Larry Kelley, an All-American and Heisman Trophy winner, and the other was the great Bob Train, whom we nicknamed "Choo-choo." Those were the glory days of the Yale football team. The 1934 Yale-Princeton game, which was played in New Jersey in the fall of my junior year, was the famous "iron man game," where the same eleven men played the whole sixty minutes. Clint Frank, another Heisman Trophy winner, was also on the team in the thirties, but not early enough for the famous 1934 game.

Yale was small enough in those days that you could get to know quite a lot of your classmates—but only up to a point. I find that even today I'm still meeting men in my class whom I did not know. I was the cochairman of the Class of '36's sixtieth reunion, and we had a joint meeting of the class executive committee and the reunion committee in 1995 at which I met one fellow who was completely new to me, even though our numbers are shrinking all the time. We're now down to a little over three hundred survivors, and only a fraction of them are in good enough shape to participate in class functions. I'm in fairly good physical shape and have a pretty good mental grasp of things, which is great good luck. So many of my classmates have fallen on hard times mentally; Alzheimer's hasn't got me yet.

In my freshman year, I lived in Vanderbilt Hall on the Old Campus, way over on Chapel Street. My Andover friend Robert A. "Butch" Schultz and I shared a room on the fourth floor. When I first came to Yale in the fall of 1932, I was fresh from my summer activity working for Norman Thomas. The political campaign went on all that fall, and I was determined to find out what Socialist activism(if any) was going on at Yale. Then as now, political activity at Yale covered the whole spectrum, from very conservative to very radical and everything in between, and there was indeed an active Socialist group on campus. The Socialists had an office, with a few typewriters and desks, in the basement of the Methodist church on the corner of Elm and College Streets, diagonally across from Battell Chapel. When I made contact with them, they invited me to take part in the intercollegiate Model League of Nations, which was scheduled to meet later that fall at Smith College.

I don't know how the official Yale representation to this event had ended up in the hands of the Socialists, but I decided that I would accept their invitation. There were only four of us in the delegation. I had arranged to rent a car in New Haven to get to Northampton. There weren't any established rental businesses at that time, but I found someone who agreed to rent me a car for the weekend. It cost fifteen dollars, but like a damn fool I gave him a twenty-dollar bill, and he said he would give me the five dollars' change when he had it. He never did have it, so that was an early lesson in Depression-era economics. I got the car and drove the delegation to and from Northampton. I knew a girl at Smith, and I think I paid more attention to her that weekend than I did to upholding Yale's role in the League of Nations. All the different countries in the intercollegiate League of Nations were represented by different colleges, and the Yale delegation represented the government of South Africa, which was called the Union of South Africa at that time. The Union of South Africa was at odds with the rest of the world over some issue and had threatened to walk out of the League of Nations meeting in Geneva. The Yale upperclassmen leading our delegation chose a propitious moment and walked out of the assembly to protest whatever the delegation in Geneva was protesting.

The League of Nations was in a way the predecessor of today's United Nations. I didn't know much about the League, other than that it was an instrument to try to prevent war. Later on, as I studied more American history and took Charles Seymour's course on the Great War, I began to think that the League of Nations was a good thing, but even then I realized that it didn't have enough power to preserve peace. Even now the United Nations lacks sufficient power. One hears plans today for the UN to have its own army, with greater capability than its present force of peacekeepers. The League of Nations didn't even have peacekeepers and finally went out of business when World War II erupted. But I thought well of the idea of the League of Nations, just as I later supported world federalism, the movement for more of a world government that emerged during World War II.

Upon returning from Northampton, I never saw the Socialists again or went near their office. I didn't abandon my support for Norman Thomas, though, and I actually voted for him in the presidential election of 1940, when he was running against Roosevelt and Willkie. But I was so caught up in other undergraduate activities that I had no time for politics, and my trip to Northampton with the Socialist delegation was the last connection I had with that sort of activism.

Our time at Yale was essentially happy and carefree, as college life usually is for most undergraduates, but our years were also shadowed by the omnipresent Depression. Some of my college memories illustrate the depth of the Depression, how it really affected values. One lazy spring day, six or eight of us were sitting out on the lawn of my residential college. We were all reasonably well dressed, as usual, in jackets and ties. Quite a contrast with the way students dress today! But students today have money, and perhaps we tried to dress well because we didn't have any. We heard the bell of the Good Humor man coming along Elm Street. A Good Humor bar cost ten cents, but if you were fortunate enough to get a stick that had "lucky stick" written on it, you could return it and get another ice cream bar free. Someone in our group asked, "Has anybody got a dime?" One fellow said, "Well, I think there's a dime on my bureau. I'm in room so-and-so. You can have that dime if you want to go up there and get it. But," he warned, shaking his finger, "if you get a lucky stick, it's mine." So the first fellow got up, retrieved the dime, and bought a Good Humor. But then he went back and got a second Good Humor. My friend who had advanced the dime was furious. A trivial trick like that took on much greater importance in the Depression, even in an easygoing college environment.

How did the Depression affect me personally? It affected me materially and substantively, and perhaps beneficially. I was at the Westminster School in October 1929 when I heard about the stock market crash. Only a few months earlier, my father had sold his interest in the thriving Studebaker dealership to his colleagues and, with his friend Charles Coady, had formed the stock brokerage firm of Coady, Beinecke & Company. I'm not sure why my father had wanted to leave the automobile business, but I think that since he was already a successful man at age forty-one, he was casting about for something more challenging. He set up his business on Wall Street, bought a seat on the New York Stock Exchange in April of 1929—and six months later came the crash. The horrific economic events that followed, and America's plunge into the Depression, didn't immediately seem to affect my family's lifestyle. We continued to live well. We returned to Westhampton in the summers of 1930 and 1931, and my father continued to cruise in the *Innisfree*. We still had help looking after everything, and we seemed to have all that we needed.

I saw enough of the men of my father's generation to know that the experience of the Depression affected them in a way that is hard to describe. In 1933, I was nineteen and my father and mother and I were spending the weekend with my parents' friends the Blakes down at the New Jersey Shore. One afternoon that weekend, my father told me to go downtown and get the evening papers. You could listen to the news on the radio in 1933, but people didn't do that as much as they do today; we got the news from newspapers. So I went down to pick up the *World Telegram* or the *Sun*, or probably both; they were the two evening papers. I saw in the headlines that Albert R. Erskine, the chairman of the board of the Studebaker Corporation of America, had committed suicide. The Studebaker Corporation had taken such a nosedive financially that he just couldn't face it, and took his own life. I brought that paper home, and as I handed it to my father, I said, "There's some bad news here," or words to that effect. My father had worked for Studebaker all during the 1920s, when Albert Erskine had headed that highly successful company. This man had been an idol to my father, and four years after the crash, he took his own life. I'll never forget my father's reaction upon reading of Mr. Erskine's death. Never. He was deeply shocked.

My father's stock brokerage firm failed in 1933. I have a tangible reminder of Coady, Beinecke & Company, in the form of a beautiful marine painting that now hangs in my office in New York. In 1934, when I was twenty and home for a weekend in Madison, my father asked me to borrow Mr. Blake's station wagon and drive to a certain address in Westchester County to get a picture. I ended up at a house in some pleasant suburban town, knocked on the door, and said to the lady who answered, "I've come for the picture." She said, "I was expecting you," and she sadly took the painting down from over the mantelpiece and gave it to me. I laid it on a blanket in the station wagon and drove it home. This painting was one of the last assets remaining to Coady, Beinecke & Company after it went belly-up in the Depression.

My father and mother hung the painting in their home in Madison, and when they moved in 1949, my father had it over the mantelpiece in his beautiful book-lined office in New York. It's the work of Karl Theodor Boehme, and is a remarkably alive painting, highly naturalistic. The sunlight on the waves follows your eye no matter where you stand. It's not a Renoir or a Rembrandt, but I like to tell visitors that it was one of the most expensive paintings of its era. And it was, when you consider that it was all that remained to my father from the large amount of money he had invested in his brokerage business.

The failure of Coady, Beinecke & Company finally made the Depression hit home—quite literally. My parents had to change their lifestyle substantially, and that was very hard on them. We had become accustomed to living in a grand manner in our beautiful home in Madison, with in-house help, a chauffeur, a gardener, and others. We even took three of the household help with us to the so-called cottage in Westhampton for the summers, so even that was quite elaborate. When my father's brokerage firm collapsed, I was still in college and my brother, Dick, was about to start. The Sperry and Hutchinson Company, which had come under the control of the Beinecke family in the 1920s, stopped paying dividends and was struggling to remain solvent. My father had no income, and had to borrow money from friends to meet the bills and keep the wolf from the door.

Over the years, S&H had become interested in some of the department stores to which it sold trading stamps. Among its properties was a company called Houghton & Dutton, an old department store in Boston. The important thing about the store, from my uncle Edwin's point of view, was that it was a wholly owned subsidiary of The Sperry and Hutchinson Company and paid S&H substantial money for the use of its stamps. So in 1934, Uncle Edwin said to my father that it would be helpful to the family if he would go up to Boston, take over the management of the Houghton & Dutton department store, and untangle its financial affairs, and he did. My father was not an experienced merchandiser, so while he was the president, the principal operator was a man named Ullman, who had made a career in department stores. During those years, my parents and the Ullmans had a close relationship, and they helped the store survive a little longer, I think, than it otherwise would have. Houghton & Dutton was located in a hodgepodge of buildings on Tremont Street, catty-corner from the Parker House Hotel. It had some clientele, but it was a block away from the principal Boston department stores such as Filene's and Gilchrest's on Washington Street. It went out of business at about the time I finished college. The building has since been razed and replaced by something modern.

For a while, my father lived alone in Boston in the Copley Plaza Hotel. At that point he could not have afforded such an expensive hotel, but because it was still part of the Beinecke family business he got complimentary rooms. My mother was living by herself in Madison, unhappy and alone, and I'd come back from Yale to see her. My father would come home occasionally on the train; I remember meeting him one day at Grand Central and taking him back to Madison. Sometime after that, my parents closed and shuttered our lovely Madison house, and both of them took up residence in a modest apartment at 1 Primus Avenue in Boston. That was a curious address. Primus Avenue was an alleyway on Beacon Hill, about a block or so from the intersection of West Cedar and Charles Streets. They were there for about a year, and then they got a small second-story apartment in a converted brownstone at 176 Beacon Street. When I would visit them in my college years, I found Beacon Street interesting because its cross-streets, named for English lords, are in alphabetical order: first Arlington Street, then Berkeley, Clarendon, Dartmouth, Exeter, Fairfield, Gloucester, and Hereford. My parents' building on Beacon Street was somewhere between Dartmouth and Exeter on the river side, with an expansive view from the back windows over the Charles River basin. My parents were in that apartment for another year.

The yacht *Innisfree* had to be sold, the summers in Westhampton became a thing of the past, the servants were dismissed, and now that my parents were in Boston, they rarely saw their old friends. My father was still a young man, only in his forties, and the experience of being unable to provide for his family was seriously wounding. He maintained an outward facade of cheerfulness, but his inner mood was one of profound despair. It was a searing ordeal, for people who had been successful to that point, to see everything that they had built up fall into shambles around them. Up to that time my father, while not enormously wealthy, had been far from poor. He had known no particular want as a boy or young man. Indeed, he had known nothing, really, but success in anything he had ever turned his hand and mind to. Failure was a stranger, and then suddenly, like some awesome physical cataclysm, an event larger than himself and beyond his control had seized his life and, in effect, obliterated a successful career.

My father recovered, but he never forgot what he had been through, and it left a deep scar. The experience made him think deeply about economics. He read a number of works on the subject, and thought he saw some ways to reform the system. He wrote a book called "Liberty and Wealth," describing some of his ideas on economics. It was never published, but I have a copy of it in typescript. "Liberty and Wealth" is an indication that in a sense my father was always a student. By the 1930s, he had long since ceased to work as an engineer, but he was still a curious man, interested in how and why things worked. He tried to study the Great Depression, learn from it, and contribute something toward understanding it. My father believed that the Depression had come about because of some of the contradictions of our economic system, contradictions that resulted in needless suffering. He emerged from the Depression with a continuing concern for the welfare of mankind.

The Depression also had the salutary effect of bringing my father and mother closer together. It always seemed to me that my mother's own sense of fulfillment came very importantly from helping others. She was at her most magnificent when my father was so badly hurt in the Depression, the period when she and Dad moved up to Boston and lived in a modest apartment that was in such sharp contrast to our home in Madison. My mother sensed that my father needed her, and she was at his side. She seemed to find strength and self-realization in the process of being helpful. My parents were already very close, but the privations they were compelled to put up with, and the fact that my father had to borrow money, meant they had to rely on each other to a greater extent than ever before. If anything could have bonded them more closely than they were already, it was the experience of the Depression.

Perhaps the Depression also helped bring the whole family closer together. I visited my parents as often as I was able, particularly during the period when my mother was living by herself in Madison. My parents came to see me fairly regularly, and my mother, especially, tried to show her interest in whatever Dick or I happened to be doing, including our athletic efforts. She would go to a lot of trouble. One time during my Yale days, my mother was coming down from Boston to New York, and we arranged that she would get off the train in New Haven and visit with me. I planned for her visit by inviting some friends, looking up instructions for making a martini, and serving her a God-awful concoction when she arrived at my room. She never batted an eye. She drank the "martini," had a happy visit with us, and got back on the train. Dick also came to New Haven to see me a few times when I was at Yale, and I once went up to visit him at his boarding school during my freshman year. After his years at Madison Academy, Dick had gone away to the Raymond Riordon School in Highland, New York, across

the river from Poughkeepsie. There was never a question of his going
to Andover and then someplace like Yale; he didn't have the same academic interests that I had. The Riordon School appealed to Dick, in
part, because he could take his horse with him. In March 1933, Mr.
Riordon, the proprietor and director of the school, took his students
down to Washington, D.C., to attend the first inauguration of Franklin
Roosevelt, so Dick was there on that historic occasion. At some point
early in my Yale career, my roommate Butch Schultz and I had agreed
to drive our friend John Whiting's Ford from New Haven to Pittsfield,
Massachusetts, where John was teaching at a school nearby after having
graduated from Yale. When we went past Poughkeepsie, we crossed the
river and called on my brother at his school, then drove on to our destination, arriving in the middle of the night. I remember the bus ride
back because there was a passenger covered with dirt and coal dust,
coughing like a consumptive, who kept telling us, "I've trimmed eighteen tons of coal today." It was many years before I learned that "trim-
ming" means loading coal onto a truck by hand, so lifting eighteen tons
of coal in a day must have been quite a feat.

With the failure of my father's business in 1933, I had no money to
speak of from sophomore year on. I was broke all the damn time. I
worked for two years in the YWCA cafeteria on Howe Street for two
meals a day, breakfast and dinner; lunch was catch as catch can. I could
not afford membership in a fraternity or society, even if I'd had any
interest in it. Though it sounds something of a cliché, the Depression
taught me the value of a dollar, and I think that's true of all of us who
went through those years. We have much more reluctance to spend
money than people in the generations after us. There was a cartoonist
in the *New York Herald Tribune*, H. T. Webster, whose one-panel cartoon
usually bore captions like "The Thrill That Comes but Once in a Lifetime" or "Life's Darkest Moment." Webster was a trout-fishing aficionado, so quite often life's darkest moment would be the fish that got
away, but one panel he used to illustrate life's most thrilling moment
showed a young boy in a restaurant enjoying the fifty-cent blue plate
special, where every meal you could possibly eat would cost only fifty
cents. That's the way it was during the Depression years; those were the
prices. I recently received a photocopy of the V-E Day issue of the *New
York Daily News*, and I noticed that the paper sold for two cents and a
plate of fresh vegetables at the Horn & Hardart automat cost ten cents.
A high-quality lady's coat cost $16.95. Even when I was in law school
before the war and I ate meals in New York restaurants, I paid only
forty cents for breakfast at a drugstore, forty-five cents for lunch, and

sixty-five cents for dinner at a Japanese restaurant. That was how I ate for three years. I think that the great contrast in prices today is something that someone who lived through those years never gets over, not if they had to scrabble for money to put food on the table. If you've had that experience, you just don't forget it.

So to that extent I think the Depression was beneficial to me, making me appreciate and understand the importance of having some money to spend, and the value of what it meant to have money, and the pain of being without. I had been brought up in very comfortable circumstances and had seen them vanish, but I never, of course, had it as hard as many did. I had that job at the New Haven YWCA. I was broke but not hungry. I didn't have much clothing, but what I had was warm and well-made. I was furious when my overcoat was stolen, because it had been brought back from Bermuda for me by a friend of my mother's, but that was a shame, not a disaster. Still, the Depression was an education.

The Depression also made me see the necessity of summer employment. At some point in my sophomore year, I was on the train from Grand Central up to New Haven, and I happened to be sitting next to a man who introduced himself as Mr. Norcross. Somehow I ascertained that he was assistant treasurer of the International Paper Company, and then something impelled me to write him a letter to ask if there was a possibility of summer employment with his company. I had no idea what an assistant treasurer did, but it turned out that he had major responsibility for running the accounting department. He wrote back to say that he thought something could be arranged, and so I worked in the accounting department of the International Paper Company for the summers of 1934 and 1935. The International Paper Company used to sell newsprint—that is, the paper on which newspapers are printed—to the newspapers by the ton, and in 1934 newsprint was selling at around forty dollars a ton. A lot of newspapers didn't have the money to pay their bills (which was normal in the Depression years), so the company would charge interest, and my principal job was figuring the interest on the unpaid bills. I still wonder how much of that interest was ever collected.

The head office of International Paper in those days was at 220 East 42nd Street, which was then the nearly brand-new art deco building created to house the *New York Daily News*. It was a fabulous building to work in. The lobby positively glowed. The *Daily News* ran an information service in the lobby comparable to the information services that public libraries provide today, and you could ask those people practically any question and they would supply the answers. The *Daily News* flourished during the Depression years. This was before the days of television advertising, and the *Daily News* carried the advertising for the masses, much more so than the *New York Times* or the *New York Herald Tribune*. The *Daily News* had the largest circulation in New York City and the largest amount of revenue, so it was an extremely profitable concern during a period when almost everybody else was experiencing adverse circumstances. Benton Moyer, the father of my good friend Ben Moyer, Jr., was then advertising manager of the paper, a very important job. I sometimes caddied for him at the Madison Golf Club across the street from our home in Madison.

The Depression was also partly responsible for leading me to major in economics. My father had suggested that I ought to study the subject, and I was concerned about the Depression and the direction the economy was going. I thought maybe I could find some answers. I did at least learn that the economy is a very complicated thing. I also took a number of courses in sociology and history. I took only one English course, in my freshman year, and I regret that I didn't take more.

The best course I took at Yale was a lecture series on American history taught by A. Whitney Griswold, who later became president of the university. He was a vibrant, moving lecturer, and the readings he assigned were excellent. I would hold him up to anybody as an exemplar of a good teacher. I was already interested in history, but my passion for the subject may have been kindled by Griswold's course. My friend Cole Oehler helped me get through the worst course I ever took, The Financial History of the United States, in which the professor would start each class with a fifteen-minute quiz on the readings we were supposed to have done the night before. Cole and I worked out a system where we alternated the assignments. We both did all the reading, but one of us would type out a summary. We realized that merely reading the whole assignment didn't do you much good; you had to go through the drudgery of picking out and memorizing the main points, which consisted largely of the names and provisions of the various tariffs of the nineteenth century. Even though we started out miserably, we ended up doing pretty well because of the system we devised for committing a lot of useless facts to memory.

I have a clear recollection of some of the economics courses I took at Yale. The subject matter in Money and Banking, taught by Ray Westerfield, was interesting, and I think Mr. Westerfield probably knew his subject, but his presentation was unbearably boring. It was more than your life was worth to sit and listen to him. And yet I guess we

learned something. In junior year I took a full-year course called Public
Control of Business, taught by Irston R. Barnes. Most of the people who
took it disliked it intensely, since Barnes was a tough taskmaster. I found,
however, that I enjoyed the course and the professor. Barnes was also
somewhat on the liberal side, which naturally appealed to me at that
time. The first semester we studied the regulation of public utilities,
public control of business, and that kind of thing. We had to go over to
the Law School library to read public utility regulatory cases, and then we
each wrote a paper on the regulation of a particular utility. I wrote mine
on a utility in the Northampton, Massachusetts area, and Jean Palmer, a
girl I knew at Smith, did me a big favor by going to the company's office
to get some information on a case that was not fully covered in the collected reports in the Yale Law School. The second semester of Barnes's
course had to do with the regulatory legislation introduced by Franklin
Roosevelt's administration and the New Deal; although this was only a
year or so into the New Deal, there was a lot for us to study.

Professor Barnes was also one of my patrons when I worked at the
YWCA, and I used to see him there with some other professors almost
every day when I was serving breakfast in the cafeteria. Years and years
later, when I was general counsel at The Sperry and Hutchinson Company, I had occasion to go down to Washington when we had a squabble
with the Federal Trade Commission. I was walking down one of the
long corridors in the immense FTC building when I saw a sign on one
of the doors, "Irston R. Barnes." It's an unusual name, so I looked in,
and sure enough, it was this man who had been my professor at Yale so
many years before. I stopped in and had a short visit with him. He told
me about why he'd left Yale, for reasons that had to do with the oral
examination of a graduate student in economics. He didn't feel that the
questions he asked this student were unfair, but apparently his colleagues on the Yale faculty did, and he was asked to go elsewhere. He
told me one of the questions he had asked, and I must say that I would
have sided with the graduate student, because it seemed quite narrow
and abstruse. But what astonished me was how Professor Barnes unbur-
dened himself to me, even though I had only been an undergraduate
student in one of his classes.

Although I worked hard, there seemed to be considerable room for
fun. I know I went to the movies an awful lot. There were four major
first-run movie theaters in New Haven, and the shows changed weekly.
Each theater had a new movie on Thursday, and by Saturday night, it
seems to me, we'd seen all of them. One of my classmates was so stuck
on movies that he'd go to theaters where they showed old ones all day

for fifteen cents. Somebody once showed me how to take two tickets and fold them together so that when the ticket taker tore them apart, he would tear along the perforated edge and hand you back one folded complete ticket instead of two half tickets. A friend and I pulled this trick at the Fox Poli once, and I was about thirty feet past the ticket taker when he looked at what he had in his hand and realized how we had tricked him. He took off after me, but I ran into the theater, disappeared into the upper balcony, and lost him.

On football Saturdays in the fall, everyone would ride out to the Yale Bowl in old-fashioned yellow streetcars that ran along Chapel Street. These were antiques, really, out of service except for game days. The cars were completely open to the air all along the side facing the sidewalk, with long wooden benches and a running board along the bottom of the car. Streetcars also ran along Elm Street, and it was a popular prank for students to disengage the metal rod that connected the streetcar to the electric wire above, shutting off the power to the streetcar and immobilizing it. One time in the fall of my first year at Yale, when the freshman football team had no Saturday game, I was riding to the Bowl along Chapel Street in one of these streetcars. We came to an intersection where a policeman was standing, and one of my friends suggested that I reach out and tip the policeman's hat off. Why he ever suggested this to me I don't know, nor do I know why I did what he told me to, but I did. The policeman started around to the front of the streetcar. One of my friends said, "Hell, Bill, you'd better get going!" I was in the middle of the streetcar on the side facing the street, and the policeman had to go around the front of the streetcar to get his hands on me, so I scrambled over the people on the other side of the seat, jumped out, and took off down the street. The policeman chased after me, but he was older than I was, and I could run pretty fast.

In my sophomore year, I roomed in Wright Hall on the Old Campus with Butch Schultz again and with Jonathan Woodworth Pine of Baltimore, whom I'd met during my freshman year. He had gone to the Hill School in Pottstown, Pennsylvania. We became good friends at Yale and remained friends until he died in 1987. Wright Hall is across the street from Berkeley College, which was then under construction. The site where Berkeley College and the Cross Campus Library now stand had, during my freshman year, been occupied by the Berkeley Oval, a five- or six-story red sandstone building in the shape of an oval, which ran the length of the block. It was an enormous structure, closed in at the Wall Street end, open at the Elm Street end. The early thirties saw the dawn of Yale's residential college system. The old Berkeley

Oval was demolished at the end of my freshman year, and Butch Schultz and I were able to move into Berkeley College at the beginning of junior year—that was a marvelously rapid piece of construction. The two lions that flanked the big clock of the Berkeley Oval now guard the entrance to the university power plant.

Butch Schultz left college after junior year. I'm not sure when he really left, because I remember him saying to me one day, "George V. King is dead." "Who is George V. King?" I asked. He was playing a joke on me, because he was telling me that George V, King of England, had died. I was recently looking through an old almanac, doing research for a class reunion, and I was surprised to see that George V died in January 1936. I thought that Butch Schultz had already left Yale by then, but he may have been up visiting us. In senior year I rejoined Jonathan Pine, who had lived with some other people at the far end of Berkeley in our junior year, and we roomed with John VanBenschoten Dean, who had been my friend all through college. We had a good association of friends together in Berkeley College during our senior year. We were friends with the fellows next door to us, so we propped open the fire door between our suites and lived together in a string of rooms running across the top of our two entryways. On one side were my roommates and I, and through the fire door were Cole Oehler and his roommate, Mac Stringer. Across the hall from them were Willard "Wid" Cates (whose brother Jack was in Timothy Dwight College) and Dick Herold, who was a star on the football team. That was a terrific group. Mac Stringer and the Cates brothers are dead now, and Butch Schultz and Dick Herold unfortunately have developed Alzheimer's, so age seems to have taken its toll on our little group, as it has on our class as a whole.

One of my roommates in senior year had difficulty with a course he needed to get a certain grade in to graduate. One day as I was sitting in our room in Berkeley College, the professor came by and told me that my roommate hadn't done very well on the final examination. "But," he said, "I don't want to stand in the way of his graduating. I'll give him another examination." He asked me whether I remembered the three or four basic principles that had been taught in the course, and I was in fact able to rattle them off. The professor said, "That's right, but your roommate doesn't seem to understand them properly. Why don't you make sure that he gets those, and then I'll give him another exam." I agreed, and we had it all cooked up so that my roommate, properly tutored by me, would pass the examination. It wasn't cheating, it was just a question of making sure that he knew what he was supposed to have learned in the course, and I thought that I could teach him that in practically no time. The trouble was, the professor had left by the time my roommate came back, and I had the devil of a time convincing him that I was telling the truth. Neither was he enthusiastic about the idea of being tutored by me, because he didn't think I was that smart anyway! I did finally persuade him that the professor had been in our room, that he meant what he said, and that if my roommate would sit down with me for about an hour, we'd get him in shape for the exam. In the end, he did take it, he did pass, and he did graduate.

I was never a standout in athletics at college. I played a lot of recreational squash, and recreational golf in the spring, but I wasn't proficient enough to play on the golf team. I used to play at the Yale golf course with my classmate Thomas "Shanty" Ward, whom I had known at Andover. I went out for the freshman football team, and although I didn't make it, I was at least good enough and big enough to be on the squad and eat at the team's special training table in the Freshman Commons dining hall. There was a wonderful camaraderie among the freshman football players, and many of the people I met through the program have remained my friends. I never got my numerals as a freshman, and I never got onto the varsity squad in football. I was on the junior varsity and played in just about every position there is, but I wasn't high enough on the roster to get to play against the JVs of any other college. Walter Levering '33, who had been a star halfback when he was at Yale, was coach of the JV team. I still see him occasionally at the Yale Club, and Walt likes to tell a story about the time the Yale JVs went over to West Point to play Army. According to Walt, there was one player on the field of combat that day who was a real standout, who played the most inspired, aggressive, and heads-up football—a certain Bill Beinecke. The only problem with Walt's recollection is that I didn't even make the trip to West Point that weekend, let alone get a chance to play. Walt is a good guy, and I haven't the heart to tell him he's all wet.

The JV team would put on practice plays for the varsity, plays that our scouts had identified from the repertoire of our opposing teams. One day we were walking through one such play, and I was lined up in the position of offensive tackle, on the opposite side and four yards down from Larry Kelley '37, the All-American, Heisman Trophy-winning end. Kelley, who was the star and didn't have to practice all this stuff, didn't want to take the two or three steps from his regular position to meet the new play. So he reached out, grabbed me by the shoulders, lifted me up off my feet, and moved me three or four yards to the right. He plopped me down and said, "Stand over here, son." I was a year older and a class ahead of Kelley, and the seniority should have been the other way around, but I had to laugh because he was a good guy, as well as a strong and headstrong football player.

Since I was on the JV squad, I had tickets to sit on the bench for each football game, whether or not I dressed for the game. The "bench" in those days was a series of about seventy graduated seats in the front of the grandstand. I attended the 1934 Yale-Princeton game in my junior year, the famous "iron man game," but I wanted to go with Jean Palmer, my Smith College girlfriend, so I sat with her in the stands on the Yale side instead of on the bench. I gave my bench ticket to my dear friend Dean Speir, who never went to any college, and he sat next to my roommate Butch Schultz, who did dress for the game. That was one of the most exciting games of that great era of Yale football, and those of us who saw it have never forgotten it. Ivy League football back in those days was really big business. Professional football had not yet come to prominence, and the athletic programs of the state universities were still fairly undeveloped. Yale and Harvard and Princeton fielded nationally ranked football teams, their games were lavishly covered in all the Sunday sports papers, and the major games in the Yale Bowl drew crowds of up to eighty thousand. In the fall of 1934, Princeton was undefeated when it faced Yale and the Tigers were favored by a wide margin, but Larry Kelley put on a star performance and Yale won 7-0. Yale scored in the first quarter with a pass from my classmate Jerry Roscoe to Kelley. Kelley tipped the pass up in the air with one hand, caught it when it came down, spun around, stiff-armed one Princeton defender, evaded another, and crossed the goal line for a touchdown. Yale kicked the point after and managed to defend that small margin for the rest of the game. The same eleven Yale men played the entire game, on both offense and defense, and so they were dubbed the "iron men." I've seen photos of that immortal eleven at Mory's and in the bar of the Yale Club of New York.

By senior year, I had gone out for football for three years, and while I enjoyed it and had made many good friends through it, I hadn't achieved anything. So instead I played intramural football on the Berkeley College team for my final year. Berkeley College won the Yale intramural college championship and then played against the winning Harvard house team. I played the whole game, because in those days you didn't have separate offensive and defensive squads. It was my own "iron man" performance, so to speak. The game ended in a 0-0 tie, but it was a great day for me.

Yale has given up boxing as a collegiate sport, but in my day it had a boxing team and a boxing room up in the tower of the Payne Whitney

Gymnasium. I used to go up there occasionally and work out, punching the bags and occasionally putting on a pair of sixteen-ounce gloves and sparring in the ring with someone who didn't know much more about boxing than I did. One day I was there with Ogden Brouwer, better known as Oggie, who was captain of the Yale boxing team and a good friend. He asked me if I'd like to work out a little with him in the ring. I said, "Sure, Oggie, but I don't tap myself as any kind of a boxer, so I don't know whether I ought to get in the ring with you." He replied, "Don't worry, Bill, I just need some exercise. Rest assured, I won't smack you." We climbed into the ring and began to spar. I think I must have inadvertently hit Oggie on the nose, because the next thing I knew, the world went black and I was sagging up against the ropes. Oggie had his arms around me and was saying, "Gee, Bill, I'm sorry. I hadn't meant to do that. It all happened so fast, I don't know exactly what happened." I had just blacked out momentarily, and I accepted his apology. But I came to my senses—in more ways than one!—and ended my boxing career.

The sport that I was probably best at was swimming. But after being on the teams at Andover and Westminster, I was tired of the drudgery of practice and did not try out at Yale. I don't know that I could have made the team, because in that era Yale had the best collegiate swimming team in the United States and compiled an unparalleled record of victories. But if I had gone out and been coached by the legendary Robert Kiphuth, I would certainly have become a much better swimmer. My classmate Larry Hart, who swam on the Yale water polo team and was cochairman of our sixtieth reunion with me, continues to swim in international competition even now that he's in his eighties. He comes home from these events with a trunkful of medals. He's remarkable, and of course he is a product of Bob Kiphuth's Yale swimming program.

Twice during my college years I went to Florida at Christmastime to stay with my Sperry grandmother. In my sophomore year, I drove down to her winter home in Jupiter with Ben Moyer, and two years later Ben and I took my mother's youngest sister, Emmy Lou, to my grandmother's place in Hobe Sound. In those days Hobe Sound was still a vestigial community, and Ben and I played on what was then its brand-new golf course. My grandmother had moved for reasons that went back to the highway department's 1925 decision to run Route 1 down the east coast of Florida. The through highway before that was called the Dixie Highway, parts of which still exist; it was a winding road that ran north-south, to the west of the railroad line. The new Route 1 bisected my grandfather's property, so it wasn't as attractive as it had been. He sold his property to developers and bought himself a place in what is now known as Hobe Sound. The developers who bought the place offered my grandfather a considerable sum for the property, but they didn't have any cash. They anticipated being able to sell off the property in individual lots, and so my grandfather took what was called a purchase money mortgage. He died in 1927; the developers never paid for the property, so it reverted to my grandmother, and she was living there in the winter of 1933–34 when Ben Moyer and I visited her the first time. Then the Depression collapsed the Florida land boom, and my grandmother, who by this time was wintering in Hobe Sound, was unable to sell the property for any money at all, let alone for the large sum my grandfather had been offered several years earlier. My grandmother finally sold the Jupiter property after World War II, but it was still in her possession in 1941 when Betty and I were married, and we spent our honeymoon in the caretaker's cottage there.

The sale and consumption of alcoholic beverages had been banned during all the years that I was growing up, and Prohibition was still in effect when I entered Yale in 1932 at the age of eighteen. I had been exposed to some drinking before that, though not much. My parents patronized bootleggers, as did all their friends, and they had cocktails in their home. During my first year or two at Yale, I learned about speakeasies, and it was considered very daring to visit the speakeasies in New York City. I vaguely remember having to sidle up to the little grilled windows and identify myself by saying, "I'm a friend of Eddie's," or "Mike sent me," or something of that sort. It was all part of the code of those days, but I don't think it made much difference whether you said those things or not; those establishments were looking for business. When I was nineteen or twenty, somebody would usually have a bottle in the parking lot at country club dances. I also remember going to a large speakeasy in the Oranges, not far from the Edison Electrical Works; we called it "Mike's by Edison's." In New Haven there was a speakeasy called the York AC, located near Oak Street down by the hospital, where we went quite often on Saturday nights. I don't remember much about it other than that they served liquor and it wasn't very attractive. Prohibition was repealed in late 1933, so my experience with speakeasies didn't last long. Prohibition was set up by the Eighteenth Amendment, which prohibited the manufacture, sale, or transportation of intoxicating liquors, but the definition of "intoxicating liquors" was provided by the Volstead Act. The repeal of the Eighteenth Amendment was under way all during 1933, but the process of

William S. Beinecke, photo portrait, Madison, New Jersey, 1936.

unamending the Constitution is as cumbersome as amending it, so the end of Prohibition proceeded in stages. While the Twenty-first Amendment, repealing the Eighteenth, was making its way through all the state legislatures, the Volstead Act was repealed or amended to permit the legal distribution of beer with the very modest alcoholic content of 3.2%. Ultimately the Eighteenth Amendment was repealed, and whiskeys, wines, liqueurs, and everything else flowed freely in 1934.

In the fall of 1935, in my senior year, my roommates and I decided we'd hold a big bash in our rooms following the Yale-Princeton game, invite a lot of people, and have some drinks. My roommates assigned me the job of getting fruit for mixed drinks; the old-fashioned was a particularly popular drink in those days. I had to get several dozen oranges and lemons, and I decided that the least expensive thing to do was to buy them wholesale. I found a fruit wholesaler in the telephone directory, called him up and said that I wanted four dozen oranges and four dozen lemons. He and I had a very strange conversation until I realized that he was talking about carloads of oranges and lemons rather than quantities you could carry home in a grocery bag. When I finally caught on that I was about to order a couple of trainloads of fruit, I hung up without identifying myself and went to the grocery store. It was a wonderful party.

Although it says in my yearbook that I wanted to teach after graduation, by the time I actually graduated from Yale that was no longer one of my plans. I did think that teaching in private secondary schools was a good job—at least that's what I thought when the people who were getting out the yearbook asked me what I wanted to do—but that idea lasted only a few months. I certainly had no interest in teaching economics, which would have meant getting a Ph.D. degree and becoming sufficiently knowledgeable to teach at the college level. That's not what I had in mind.

By the time I graduated from Yale in the spring of 1936, my parents were back home in New Jersey. I can place that date with some precision, because my father had a very serious ruptured appendix that almost took him from us and he couldn't come to my graduation. My mother couldn't come either, since she was attending him, so I borrowed a car from a friend of mine in New Haven and drove down to see them. I missed the college's Class Day events, but I came back for the graduation ceremonies themselves. I took my degree, said goodbye to my college friends, returned to my parents' home in New Jersey, and prepared to travel around the world.

CHAPTER FOUR

Around the World, 1936–1937

The Depression had knocked my father out of his Wall Street business, but the Beinecke family still controlled The Sperry and Hutchinson Company, and by 1936 S&H was recovering and had begun to pay dividends again. My parents were beginning to live a little better than they had for the previous two years, though they hadn't yet returned to their former affluence. The country was slowly moving out of the Depression, and my father was better off financially and could afford to offer me some sort of post-graduation opportunity. He very much wanted me to go abroad. Since he came from a German background, he wanted me to go to Heidelberg or some other German university to learn the language and absorb some of the culture. He suggested to me several times in the spring of 1936 that I ought to spend a year in Heidelberg, but although it probably would have been a good idea, his suggestion didn't really sink in.

I did know, however, that he thought it would be useful for me to go abroad. I had never been out of the country, except for the visit to Canada when I was eighteen. At Yale I had made friends with a couple of graduate students who were studying for Ph.D.'s in anthropology. One was John Whiting, whose car I'd driven to Pittsfield when he was teaching there; he was a short, powerful guy who had been captain of the Yale wrestling team as an undergraduate. The other was John "Doppel" Ellsworth, who came from Simsbury, Connecticut, near Hartford. I got to know Whiting through Butch Schultz—they both came from the small town of West Tisbury on Martha's Vineyard—and through Whiting, I also became good friends with Ellsworth. When I told them that I was thinking of traveling abroad, they asked me to come along with them to New Guinea, where they were going to pursue their studies. I took the idea up with my father and mother, and although New Guinea was very far off in 1936, they permitted me to go. I bought a two-year around-the-world ticket, which allowed me to travel west, with unlimited stopovers, on various steamship and railroad lines. A second-class ticket of this sort cost $750, which was quite a lot of money then, but it did include meals on the steamships. So that's how I embarked on my trip around the world, and it was a strange deviation from my father's original hope that I would study at Heidelberg University. I arranged to meet Whiting and Ellsworth in Vancouver and travel across the Pacific with them to New Guinea. Then I set off alone for the West Coast.

I began with a three- or four-day stop at my Yale classmate Cole Oehler's house in Saint Paul, Minnesota. At the railroad station when I left to continue my trip, he arranged for a sign saying "Around the World" and a German oom-pah band to send me off. From the Twin Cities I took a Canadian Pacific train to Vancouver. The train went across the prairies, crossed the border into Canada at Portal, North Dakota, and continued on through the magnificent Canadian Rockies. The Canadian Pacific trains passing through the mountains in those days had open observation cars (instead of the dome cars used today), and one beautiful July afternoon as I was sitting back watching the mountains go by, I started talking to the two people in the seat adjacent to mine. They turned out to be New Zealanders, John Bull and Bill Rathbone. We discovered that we were going to be boarding the same steamship at Vancouver. Later they suggested that I continue on past Hawaii and visit them at their sheep farms in New Zealand. I thanked them for the invitation and promised to keep it in mind.

In Vancouver, I met up with Messrs. Whiting and Ellsworth, and we boarded a Canadian-Australasian line steamship called the *Aorangi*, the Maori name for the big mountain in the South Island of New Zealand called Mount Cook. The Canadian-Australasian line had two ships, the *Aorangi* and the *Niagara*. They took about a month to go across the Pacific, and their captains arranged their courses so that when they crossed the midpoint of their journeys in the mid-Pacific, they'd pass close by each other, whistles tooting and passengers enthusiastically waving. We had a pleasant voyage to Hawaii. Also on board was a group of British Columbian schoolteachers on a low-priced excursion that took them on the *Aorangi* to Honolulu for three or four days, then back to Vancouver on the *Niagara*. My New Zealand friend Bill Rathbone took a liking to one of these schoolteachers, a young woman named Elizabeth Locke, and when the ship got to Honolulu he asked her out to dinner every night of her stay.

When the *Aorangi* put in at Hawaii, I bailed out of the anthropological expedition to New Guinea. I told Whiting and Ellsworth that I had decided I didn't know anything about anthropology, I had no training for it, and I wouldn't be any good on a scientific assignment. I don't think they were surprised. They were graduate students on a mission. So they continued on to New Guinea when the *Aorangi* departed Honolulu, and I remained in Hawaii. I stayed there for about a month, doing all the things a young man could do in Honolulu. I played some golf and went on a few dates. I knew some people there, and I got to know more. I tried surfboarding, and perhaps because I was twenty-two and athletic, it wasn't long before I was able to stand up on the board and even balance on one foot as I rode a wave into the shore. When I had satisfied myself that I could do it, I quit surfing. I spent too much time sitting on the board waiting for a wave, and I got a bad sunburn. It was more fun just to go swimming.

I decided that I would take my friends Rathbone and Bull up on their offer and visit them in New Zealand. Boarding the *Niagara*, I arrived in Auckland in September, the beginning of spring in the Southern Hemisphere, and stayed for a couple of months. I visited John Bull at his farm in Ngaruawahia, which he had inherited from his father. It was hilly country, lush and fertile, quite different from the arid Australian outback. They used to say in those days that in New Zealand they ran seven sheep to the acre versus one sheep to seven acres in Australia, and there was a considerable concentration of animals on small farms in New Zealand as compared to the tremendous sheep stations on many thousands of acres in Australia. The early spring was lambing time at Mr. Bull's farm, when the lambs were born. The farmers were also "docking" the lambs, which meant cutting off their tails and castrating them. The castrating was rather shocking the first time you saw it, because a man would take a knife, make an incision in the lamb's sensitive parts, then bite off the testicles and spit them out. I don't think the farmers do it that way anymore; I'd like to believe that they have since developed a more efficient or at least a more antiseptic method. I didn't dock any sheep, but I did help with the regular daily patrolling of the sheep in the fields, which they called paddocks. We think of a paddock as a small enclosure for a couple of horses outside a barn, but to New Zealanders a paddock is a large tract of land, which might be measured in hundreds of acres, enclosed by a fence so the sheep couldn't get out. And they would say, "Today we'll go out and check the sheep in the southeast paddock," or something like that, and we'd put some sandwiches in a saddlebag, get on a horse, and be gone all day long. I found that fun and interesting work.

John Bull had several helpers on his farm, including a cook, three or four hired hands, and an occasional visitor like me. John also introduced me to his fiancée, whom he soon married. A few years later they had a daughter, and whether because it looked like the Japanese might invade New Zealand or just because they thought it a nice idea, they asked me if I would be the child's godfather. I agreed. My goddaughter is now a charming young lady named Penelope "Penny" Davies, who recently visited us here in New York. John Bull's first wife, Beatrix "Trix" Monckton, Penny's mother, died at an early age, and he has since remarried. He's still alive, although not well, and we occasionally exchange communications. Penny and her husband, Pete Davies, operate a sheep farm near Rotorua, New Zealand, and we keep up good relations with them, too.

On that first visit to New Zealand, I also spent time with Bill Rathbone on his sheep farm and found that he had stayed in contact with the young Canadian schoolteacher he'd met on the *Aorangi*. He had continued on to New Zealand from Honolulu with the *Aorangi*, and Elizabeth "Lockie" Locke had taken the *Niagara* back to Vancouver, but they wrote to each other. Eventually he asked her to marry him and move to New Zealand—and she agreed. They're both gone now, but they lived happily together in New Zealand and had a very good marriage. I made a trip to the South Pole in 1968, and while I was going from New Zealand to Antarctica my wife, Betty, stayed in New Zealand and visited Bill and Elizabeth. Their son Buzz married the second daughter of the Bulls, Patsy, the sister of my goddaughter Penny.

After a few weeks in New Zealand, I was thinking of heading west to Australia. My New Zealand friends said to me, "As long as you're here, you should really go to the South Island," and so I went. I saw the Southern Alps and Mount Cook (or Aorangi). I went skiing there, for the first time in my life. I didn't really have proper boots, but I was able to rent skis and do a little downhill. I stayed in a pleasant lodge not far from the Franz Josef Glacier. Today you can fly up to the glacier, but in those days you had to take a covered wagon on skis that was pulled by a tractor. That was quite an experience.

There were no airplanes from New Zealand to Australia, so I got a passage on the Union Steamship's *Awatea*, a big, high-speed modern ship. It didn't go as fast as the *Queen Mary*, but it probably cruised at twenty knots or more, which meant you could cross the Tasman Sea from New Zealand to Australia in about two days. Not many years later, I served in the navy in World War II on the destroyer USS *Buck*. The *Buck* was lost to a German torpedo in 1943, but it was almost lost in the summer of 1942, when it was escorting a convoy of transports and freighters and collided with the *Awatea*, of all ships. When war broke out, the British commandeered every ship they could lay their hands on, so the *Awatea* was carrying troops across the Atlantic when it collided with my destroyer. I was attending torpedo school in Newport at the time, but I was officially attached to the *Buck*. Several men were lost in the collision, and the *Buck* was out of business for some time while it was repaired in the Boston Navy Yard.

I arrived in Sydney in November 1936, did some sightseeing, then went south. In Honolulu I had met a man a few years older than I named Jack Manton, who said that if I ever came to Australia I should visit him in Melbourne. It turned out that the Manton family operated one of the major department stores in Melbourne and were pretty well off, and I had a nice visit with them. They took me to the big horse race in town, the Melbourne Cup. They said, "Bill, you ought to see what this country is really like. Take one of those automobile trips from Brisbane to Sydney." I returned to Sydney and took the train ride of almost twenty-four hours up to Brisbane, changing trains a couple of times because of the different gauges of the railroads in the different Australian states. Once I reached Brisbane, the automobile trip back to Sydney began. We would call it a bus trip today, but they didn't have buses then; it was really a caravan of two or three cars. The countryside was quite undeveloped. Once in a while we'd pass big wagons full of logs, pulled by teams of two, four, and sometimes as many as six bullocks. Rivers had to be crossed by ferry, each car going across the river in turn. It took three or four days to get back to Sydney, with stops at little inns along the way.

From Sydney I went to Singapore aboard an old single-stack steamer that had been a German ship prior to World War I and was now transporting freight and passengers between Sydney and Singapore and intervening points. One of the rewarding things about traveling by commercial ship is that it takes so long to get where you're going that you've got nothing else to do but meet your fellow passengers. I made a few friends on the steamer, including two girls who played violin and piano in the ship's orchestra—indeed, they *were* the ship's orchestra— and a Dutchman named Peter Cellarius from Surabaya in the Dutch East Indies, now Indonesia. We went north through the islands by the Great Barrier Reef, off the east coast of Australia. We stopped at Brisbane, Townsville, and Thursday Island, a little speck of land north of Australia's Cape York, just south of New Guinea. From there the ship crossed the Gulf of Carpentaria to Darwin, very much a frontier town, consisting of a few small houses with corrugated iron roofs. This was the extreme northern end of anything in Australia, and the only contact the town had with the rest of the world was through the occasional ships like ours that came there. Peter Cellarius and I went ashore at Darwin, where we drank a lot of lemon squash and went hunting. As soon as you were two or three hundred yards out of town, you were in the bush, and there was nothing in front of you but wilderness and desert for hundreds of miles. Peter Cellarius had a gun and shot a bird or two. We saw lots of kangaroos and wallabies, those small animals much like kangaroos. It certainly felt to me that I was in an extremely remote part of the world.

The ship continued on to Java and stopped in Surabaya (where Peter Cellarius got off), Semarang, and Batavia, then the capital of the Dutch East Indies, now known as Jakarta. I disembarked at Batavia and took another cross-country trip by car, visiting the magnificent Buddhist temple Borobudur along the way and returning through the highlands to Surabaya. I was impressed by the beauty of the country and the density of the population. I was aware that the country was governed by the Dutch, but I had no particular impressions of colonialism one way or the other. I spent a day or two in Surabaya with Peter Cellarius and his wife, then boarded another vessel for Singapore.

On the long voyage up from Sydney to Batavia I had met a young lady named Ruth Mabin, about my age, who came from a town on the South Island of New Zealand, just south of the Cook Strait. She was on her way up to Malacca on the Malayan Peninsula to visit her uncle, who was the Number Two (British shorthand for second-in-command) in the British colonial government there. At that time, the administration of the Malayan Peninsula was divided into two parts. One, consisting of Singapore, Malacca, and Penang was called the Straits Settlements; the other was the Malay States Federated and Unfederated (I never quite understood the difference between the federated and unfederated states). Kuala Lumpur was the capital of the Federated Malay States, and is today the capital of the very prosperous country of Malaysia. The Straits Settlements were direct British colonies, but the Malay States were protectorates, each with their individual sultans. The sultans were loyal to the British Crown, but they were also independent, at least to a certain extent. The Sultan of Johore, for example, was an important person, and the seat of his government was just across the bridge outside of Singapore.

In any case, Ruth Mabin was on her way to visit her uncle in Malacca, and she invited me there for Christmas. And so, after a few days in Singapore, I went up to Malacca, and we had quite a house party. I met the Number Two, who was an affable bachelor. Ruth called him "Nunkie," her affectionate term for uncle, so we all called him that too. He was the lieutenant-governor there, the assistant to the man in charge, who was known as the Resident. In the old British colonial tradition, he wasn't paid handsomely, but the people who worked for him were paid a great deal less, so he was able to have a large staff and live well. Also at this Christmas gathering were three young officers from the Royal Air Force (one South African, the other two English), and two young sisters named Shakespeare, who were the daughters of a brigadier general attached to the British army in Singapore. I've often wondered what happened to those bright young people during the war. This wonderful house party went on three or four days, and we had a happy and vibrant time. Then the army and air force people had to return to their bases, and I took the bus service back to Singapore. Although it was called a bus service, you actually traveled in an ordinary Ford car quite some distance from Malacca to Singapore. I was in Singapore on New Year's Day, 1937, and was part of a group invited to the Singapore Club for luncheon that day by a Dane in his late forties who was there on business. Afterwards we all piled into rickshaws, and I remember feeling uncomfortable because it was a hot day and the rickshaws were pulled by men running barefooted through the streets. I was reminded of this when my wife, Betty, and I were in Madagascar in 1995 and saw men pulling rickshaws as they had in Singapore in the 1930s. I wasn't aware that the practice still existed anywhere in the world.

I had little sense of the politics of what we now know to have been the twilight of the imperial powers in Southeast Asia. The British and Dutch seemed to have matters running smoothly, and there was nothing to indicate that their rule would be less than permanent. I remember meeting one young man in Malacca who had trained as a lawyer in Britain and landed a job in the colonial government as a magistrate, and he assured me that his career in that part of the world was quite secure. There was no feeling whatsoever that Japan would be moving in soon, although there was a sense that the Chinese were becoming increasingly important businesspeople in the Singapore area. I was aware of the several different populations in the area. For example, the original Western settlement in Malacca had been founded by the Portuguese in the sixteenth century, and in the 1930s there was a remnant of the old Portuguese colony still in place. Of course, its members were at a different social level from the British, who dominated the social, political, and governmental structures, and many of them had inter-married, but nevertheless they remained a presence. A small colony of White Russians lived there and kept largely to themselves. I learned about these populations in part by going to a dance hall. The girls you'd dance with were from these different groups, and they clustered together, the Russian girls here, the Malaysian girls there, the Portu-guese and Chinese in another corner, and so on.

But as a young man, I didn't know anything about political struc-tures. My travels didn't bring up the kinds of feelings and reflections that I have today when I look at the governments and social structures of different countries. I was having a good time, and I enjoyed the com-panionship of other people my own age, male and female. I kept run-ning into people, meeting people—not so many Americans, but people from all over the world. And we did what you would do at that age: we went out, we drank, we danced, we engaged in athletic activities, and we didn't think about the great events of the world. I was not so different from the young people you see today backpacking around the world with other young people and having a good time. It wasn't that I wasn't thinking or reading—I was. I would read whatever I could get my hands on. I soaked up a lot of information and experiences. I felt bad that I didn't vote in the 1936 United States presidential election, which was the first election in which I was eligible to vote. I was too far away to get an absentee ballot, so I merely witnessed that election from afar. But I was a young man just out of college, footloose and free, and enjoying life on a day-to-day basis.

I had a passport, in which I collected an interesting set of stamps from the governments of the places I visited. Perhaps before the First World War you could go around the world with just your business card, but the routines of passports and visas were becoming much more common by the 1930s. Getting money posed a different set of prob-lems. I didn't have severe money worries. I had my around-the-world ticket, so I didn't have to concern myself about transportation. I was staying in places that were first-class but not the very top level; they were quite comfortable but inexpensive. When I was in Singapore, for example, I didn't stay at Raffles, the hotel with the beautiful porch and verandah that was then *the* place to stay in Singapore. I stayed at the Adelphi, a block or two away. Still, by the time I got to Singapore, I was almost out of money. There weren't credit cards in those days, and although traveler's checks existed, I wasn't using them. I had what was called a traveler's letter of credit, a very formally written letter in old-fashioned English from a major bank addressed to its correspondent banks throughout the world. My bank was the Manufacturers Trust Company in New York, and I had a mile-long list of its corresponding banks across the globe. You would present the letter of credit at the office of one of these correspondent banks and draw as much money as you wanted, up to the limit of the letter of credit. My letter of credit was good for $1,000, and I ran out in Singapore, so I cabled my father and told him that I was halfway around the world and out of money. He had the Manufacturer's Trust Company in New York cable the bank in Singapore authorizing an increase of another $1,000 to my letter of credit, thus revalidating it and making me solvent once again. I've used the traveler's letter of credit two or three times since, once when we were abroad with our children in the sixties and again when we made our first trip to Africa in 1971. I think that with the development of traveler's checks and credit cards, that form of travelers' funding has fallen into disuse.

The around-the-world ticket that I had was a one-way ticket. You were supposed to keep going in the same direction, and having once gone from A to B and from B to C, you couldn't go back to B or A. When I was in Java, I debated going to Bali, which is just off the eastern end of Java. But I had already passed west of Bali, and in order to go there I would have had to buy a round-trip ticket and pay for a hotel and all the rest, and I didn't want to spend the extra money. Besides, I thought, I'll always be able to visit there another time. Well, I've still never been to Bali, and Bali has acquired a certain symbolism for me now. Betty Beinecke and I were booked to go to Bali in 1977, but we never got there because we got caught in a strike of air traffic controllers in Australia. So my experience has given me what I call my "Bali Principle": Don't miss out on doing something when you get the chance.

One of the people I met in Singapore told me I ought to go to China. I told him that I had ample time and no deadlines to meet but had already passed China. "Well," he said, "it really doesn't cost anything to get up to China. There are these P&O ships that run all the way from London or Southampton to Japan, carrying passengers through the Indian Ocean to India, Ceylon, Singapore, and Hong Kong. By the time they get here they're practically empty, and they have special rates for their run up to Shanghai and over to Japan." So I set off for China. My friend's information was accurate. The round-trip ticket from Singapore to Shanghai cost less than fifty dollars, meals included, so I went first class. I went from Singapore to Shanghai on the *Rawalpindi* and returned on the *Ranpura*. En route I stopped off in Hong Kong, where I looked up the Shakespeare sisters, whom I had met in Malacca. Since they were British army dependents, they were able to take a British troopship to Hong Kong for free or for a negligible fee, and they had asked me to call them when I got into town. I did, and I was invited to a dinner party in the home of a Mr. Wodehouse, the brother of the famous author P. G. Wodehouse. It was a fine dinner, with somewhere around a dozen guests. At the conclusion of dinner, the men stayed in the dining room, and brandy and cigars were passed around. I don't remember the postprandial conversation, but I reveled in the feeling of soaking up life in the old British tradition. At the conclusion of the evening I returned to the *Rawalpindi*, which sailed in the morning for Shanghai.

The *Rawalpindi* deposited me at the docks in Shanghai one cold January morning in 1937, and I took my suitcase and handbag and checked into a first-class hotel. From there I planned side trips to Nanking and Peking (now Beijing). I took the train from Shanghai to Nanking. Nanking was at that time the official capital of China; the embassies of the Western nations were still located in Peking, but the capital was Nanking. Nanking was a walled city; outside its walls was a large watery area. I don't think it was really a moat, though it was hard to conceive of it as a lake. A guide arranged for me to be rowed around this watery expanse by a boatman who was also a fisherman. It was cold, a shimmering of ice was beginning to form on the water, and the boat made crinkling and crackling noises as it went along. The boatman had brought along a large wicker basket that was narrow in the center and open at each end; one end had a relatively small aperture, the other end a wide one. He peered down into the shallow water from the bow, suddenly plunged the wicker basket through the water into the mud below, and then dived into the basket, disappearing except for his feet sticking out over the edge. I wondered what the devil he was doing, but soon realized that he had imprisoned a fish in the narrow end of the basket, and when he up-ended himself into the wide end, he was simply going down to grab the fish in one hand. In the course of three hours or so, he put quite a few fish into the bottom of that boat.

I had to pay for some transportation and hotels, so I decided that I needed to get some Chinese currency. I didn't have any idea about Chinese money, so I went to a bank in Nanking, presented my traveler's letter of credit, and told them how much I wanted to draw. When the equivalent in Chinese currency was shoved at me through the window, I had a mountain of it, and there was no way I could carry it or stow it. I told the banker it was just too much for me to handle, and that I would like to cancel the transaction. He took the money back, but charged me a transaction cost each way. That was another learning experience. There was no reason to have any more than a dinky amount of Chinese money, and a dinky amount of American money would get you all the Chinese money you would need.

In due course I returned to Shanghai. I had only about a week to spend in China, because the terms of my round-trip ticket from Singapore meant that I had to catch the P&O line steamer on its return leg. I inquired about transportation to Peking and learned that there was an airline operating, the Chinese National Aviation Corporation. It was either a subsidiary of Pan American Airways or operated by Pan Am, and knowing how some of those cultures worked and still work, I suspect that the airline was operated by Pan American but more than half owned by the Chinese government. The airline had few aircraft—perhaps only one Stinson propeller plane—and only two fixed routes, north and west. On Mondays it would fly west over the Yangtze River to Changsha and back to Shanghai, on Tuesdays it would fly up to Peking and spend the night, and on Wednesdays it would come back to Shanghai. Then it would repeat the cycle. On Tuesdays and Wednesdays it would also stop in Tientsin, but Tientsin was only a hundred miles or so from Peking. I took the airline north to Peking and planned to stay there three days, take the train to Tientsin, and catch the plane back to Peking.

I checked into the Grand Hotel in Peking. The Grand Hotel in 1937 was hardly grand, but it was the best hotel in town. I employed a Chinese guide who spoke some English, and did some sightseeing. The city of Peking still had walls around it, although even then it had sprawled beyond the walls. The walls are now long gone, but I remember standing by them, watching camel trains from the north come into the city. They were the two-humped Bactrian camels, rather than the one-humped dromedaries of Egypt, and as they came into the city loaded with cargo, Chinese women would run along the streets behind them, sweeping up the droppings for fertilizer and fuel. I visited the Forbidden City and the Summer Palace but not the Great Wall, because I was told that it was nothing but a ruin, and what was the use of going out to look at a ruin? And in fact this meandering, serpentine wall was just a crumbling heap at the time, and most of it still is. The part of the wall where tourists and dignitaries ever since Nixon have been going is a tiny and fully restored segment. I did visit a Taoist monastery and had some conversation with the monks through my guide. I purchased two little jade elephants in town that I tucked away in my luggage and brought home to my mother. Betty has those little jade elephants today in her collection of elephants at our home in New York.

While I was in Peking, a young United States marine approached me at the Grand Hotel. What were the marines doing in Peking, particularly when the capital was in Nanking? After the xenophobic Boxer Uprising in 1900, the United States (like all the rest of the Western countries) had brought in the marines to protect its diplomatic staff. Thereafter a series of treaties was imposed on the Chinese that gave the Western powers certain extraterritorial rights, like the right to station troops in Peking and the right to have Western citizens tried by their own nationals instead of in a Chinese court. These treaties stipulated, however, that the Western powers could station troops only in Peking, so when the Chinese capital was moved to Nanking, the US embassy remained in Peking, behind walls topped with broken bottles and protected by a contingent of marines. The young marine who came over to visit me was just about my own age, and he was from Brooklyn. He would periodically scan the hotel registers to see if anybody had checked in from his part of the world. He invited me to the enlisted men's mess at the marine barracks in the embassy, and we had a few beers and an amiable conversation. I had been traveling by myself since Singapore and was very lonely in Peking, so I welcomed the chance to talk with him.

I wanted to go to Tientsin, at least in part because I knew that my Yale classmate John Hersey had been born there of American missionaries and had lived there during his boyhood. So I took the train from Peking to Tientsin, did some sightseeing, and spent the night in a hotel. The next morning when I went to check out, the man at the desk told me that the airplane was not running, that the airplane was out of business. I was supposed to take this plane to Shanghai and was scheduled to board the *Ranpura* the next day for the return voyage to Singapore, so now I was in a quandary. Nobody had any idea as to when or whether this plane was likely to turn up. I found out that I could take a train to Shanghai, but that would take about thirty-six hours, and the ship would be long gone by the time I arrived. But then I learned that there was another airplane, a seaplane, which flew between Shanghai and Hong Kong, so I could overtake the *Ranpura* in Hong Kong. I decided to try that.

I met some people in the dining car of the train to Shanghai, some of them American, and we played bridge almost continuously from Tientsin to Shanghai. This was a period of turmoil in China, when the country was in the grip of various warlords, and there were Chinese soldiers all over the place, on the roof of the train and in the vestibules between the cars. The war between China and Japan hadn't really started in earnest, although a few years before, the Japanese had invaded Manchuria and created the puppet state of Manchukuo. At Yale I had entered the freshman history essay contest with a paper entitled "Manchukuo: The Problem and a Suggested Solution." I had plagiarized the title from something my father had written about economics, and the suggested solution was lifted in its entirety from a plan that a British commission had developed to solve a political problem somewhere else in the world, but I was quite interested in the subject. I've always thought that World War II really began in July 1937 with the incident at the Marco Polo Bridge outside of Peking. I've never managed to get to the Marco Polo Bridge on my two or three visits to Peking, and I guess it's not a very prepossessing landmark, but the clash between Chinese and Japanese forces there was the spark that led to the World War, or so I have always believed. China was in a seriously unsettled condition in early 1937, and you felt that anything might happen.

When we arrived in Shanghai, I immediately went to the airport. I had telegraphed from the hotel in Tientsin to reserve a spot on the small Curtiss Dolphin flying boat. It came down into the river with a swish, then taxied alongside the dock. I was a little nervous as I boarded the plane—not about the flight but about a logistical problem. I had been traveling around the world for six months by this point. When I left New Jersey in July of the preceding year, my mother (who always took very good care of me) saw to it that I started out with an adequate amount of clothing and good luggage. I had quite a lot of stuff along with me, including a portable typewriter that I wrote some notes on occasionally. People can't travel that way anymore; you have to travel light because you're traveling in airplanes instead of ships and trains. When I went on my excursion to China, I left most of my luggage in the baggage room at the hotel in Singapore. By the time I got to Shanghai, the suitcase I had with me was pretty battered, the hinges were broken, and it needed repair. I took the matter up with the porter in the hotel in Shanghai, and he said yes, he'd send it out and have it fixed. I went up to Peking with only my toilet kit, a pair of pajamas, and some clean socks. The problem was that I had to make a quick connection from the train in Shanghai to the seaplane if I wanted to make it to Hong Kong, and the railroad terminal and the airport were quite some distance from the hotel downtown. I had also sent all my laundry out in Shanghai and had expected to pick it up along with my suitcase when I got back to the hotel. And so, in the midst of China's turmoil and trouble, I sent a telegram to the hotel in Shanghai requesting it to put my suitcase and laundry on board the *Ranpura*; then I crossed my fingers. When I eventually got on board the *Ranpura* in Hong Kong, my suitcase was standing in my stateroom, fixed, cleaned, and glistening, and my laundry was neatly folded and spread across the bunk. I'd like to see even the best American hotel duplicate that feat today.

Aside from my flight to Peking, I had flown only once commercially, when I was seventeen and at Andover and flew home from Boston to Newark Airport. But I had been an airplane enthusiast since I was a boy. The seaplane that was to fly us to Hong Kong was small, with only one row of seats on either side of the aisle and room for about twelve passengers. One of those passengers was a middle-aged woman, the only woman on the trip. Another was a man from Cleveland, who was wearing a camel's hair polo coat. He had decided that what he wanted to do on his vacation was to go as far from Cleveland as he could by air and then return. He had flown all the way to China, and now he was on his way back. Not long before, Pan American had established its transpacific flights by Clippers, which were great big flying boats, and this man had taken these Clippers across the Pacific from Midway to Wake Island to Manila. As there was no air link between Manila and Hong Kong, though, he'd had to go by ship until he reached Hong Kong and had then flown as far into China as he could. So he spent his entire vacation flying in airplanes or waiting for airplanes, except for the time when he was on the ship between Manila and Hong Kong. I thought that was a little crazy.

The seaplane taxied along the Whangpoo River, built up speed, and then became airborne. The plane never flew very high, and when we went from one valley to another we flew up through passes rather than over the tops of the mountains. After we had been flying for about an hour, the plane descended. I said to myself, This is interesting, we're making our first stop already. Well, it was certainly our first stop, but it was the same stop—we were back in Shanghai. It was overcast, and these planes did not have the instrumentation available today. Moreover, they couldn't go very high, so most of the flying was visual. I began to wonder whether we were actually going to beat the *Ranpura* to Hong Kong. After a while the plane took off again, and we stopped at a succession of places along the coast of China—not to pick up or discharge passengers but to refuel. It took us almost two full days to get from Shanghai to Hong Kong. First we stopped at Wenchow, then at Amoy. The plane landed in the river and taxied up to a floating gasoline barge to refuel. The pilot and the local agent in Amoy decided that we couldn't go any farther that day, so we were escorted ashore to stay the night.

There were no accommodations and we slept on chairs or the floor in the local airline office, but we were taken out to dinner at a Chinese restaurant in town. We got going again the next morning, made at least one more stop, and eventually swooped into the Hong Kong harbor. I could see the *Ranpura* from the air, because it was the only big passenger liner in the harbor. I went aboard and was elated to find all my gear in place. The ship sailed a few hours later.

The *Ranpura* took me back to Singapore. On board I met Jane Foster, a young lady about my age from Lincoln, Nebraska, who was traveling around the world with her mother. She was on her way up to Kuala Lumpur to see a classmate of hers, someone she had known at the University of Nebraska, who was married to a man in the oil business. I took a train to Kuala Lumpur from Singapore to see her and spent a couple of days there. I met a lot of young people at a club in K-L (as we called it), including one fellow who had been an Olympic diver on the British team.

I returned to Singapore from Kuala Lumpur, then embarked on a Dutch steamship called the *Indrapoera*, bound for Europe; I would get off at Suez, at the eastern end of the Suez Canal. I had been in touch with my parents throughout all this time. We would write letters back and forth, and I would get my mail periodically at Thomas Cook's in the cities I visited. I let them know where I was going a month or so in advance, so they knew my itinerary fairly well. By the time I had gotten way out in the Far East, they decided they wanted to go on a trip, too, and we agreed to meet in Alexandria. My voyage on the *Indrapoera* was uneventful. I met an Englishman on board named Sam Hughes, a young man of about thirty who was an art or antiques dealer in London. He was on his way to Petra, and that was the first I ever heard of the "rose red city half as old as time." I also met the Reifels, a well-to-do family from Vancouver. Mr. Reifel operated a brewery business, and he and his wife had a very attractive daughter, Audrey, who was about my age. Having just circumnavigated the globe, the family was headed for London to attend the coronation of George VI. I managed to keep in contact with Audrey Reifel until the war years, and she came to New York once or twice. She died an untimely death.

It took us about two weeks to travel from Singapore to Suez, a relatively long ship voyage. I'd wake up in the morning, walk along the deck in my bathing trunks, wave to the Reifel family (who were usually having breakfast in the dining room at about that time), and climb up to the open deck, where there was a swimming pool about as big as my stateroom, round and made of canvas, with seawater pumped into it through a hose. It was refreshing to dunk yourself in that pool as you were crossing the hot Indian Ocean. I'd plunge in, swim up and down a couple of times, then go back, get dressed, and have breakfast. There was one other man on board whom I remember, an obnoxious middle-aged captain in the British army. Once he found out I was an American, he never let me hear the end of the glories of the British Empire. He would march up and down the deck incessantly, and every time we'd pass a speck of sand above high tide, he'd point it out to me and announce, "That's British territory!" I got sick and tired of learning about all these tiny British outposts in the Indian Ocean.

The *Indrapoera* eventually got to the Suez Canal sometime in February. There are two ports, Port Said and Suez, at opposite ends of the Canal. I disembarked at Suez. I still had two weeks before my family was to arrive at Alexandria, so I decided to do some traveling. I went up to Cairo and got a room—not at the famous Shephard's hotel but at the less expensive Savoy. I had done some sightseeing in Cairo when someone advised me that I ought not to miss the opportunity to go to Palestine. I took a train to Jerusalem, crossing the Suez Canal, and checked into the King David Hotel. With a native guide, I visited the city walls and the Church of the Holy Sepulchre, which is supposed to stand on the place where the stone was rolled away after Jesus arose from dead. To what extent you think any of this actually happened depends, I suppose, on your degree of belief. My guide, who was an Arab Mohammedan and didn't believe any of it, told me there was a squabble between the various Christian sects as to who should look after the church. Indeed, the Roman Catholics, Greek and Russian Orthodox adherents, and various Protestants seemed to have set up rival camps within the church, and it was never clear whether one group had primary responsibility or whether they had achieved a compromise. I was also told that the Copts (then in some kind of relationship with the Church of Abyssinia, since dissolved) were not permitted in the church, and had to do their worshiping on the roof. I believe this prohibition continues to the present time.

I went to the little town of Bethlehem—at least it was a little town sixty-some years ago. I noticed a group playing backgammon at tables outside a drinking establishment, and since I thought I was pretty good at the game, I asked my Arab guide whether I could get into one of these matches. He told me they'd be delighted to have me, and indeed they were. I never won. I finally realized that the dice were not thrown from a cup and the roll did not rely on luck. My opponents rolled the dice in their hands, and if they needed a 5 and a 2, then by God, they would roll a 5 and a 2. I endured this for a limited number of games and then withdrew, poorer but wiser. While I was in Bethlehem, I also went into the little church that stands on the site of the stable where Jesus was born; it was very dark and very low. On my way back to Egypt after two or three days, I passed a railroad station where they were selling immense, beautiful Jaffa oranges on the platform; the Palestine citrus industry was flourishing even at that time, before the modern revolution in agriculture.

My family was coming into Alexandria on the American Export Line steamer *Excambion*, which went from New York to various ports in the Mediterranean. I sat on the dock in Alexandria on a warm and clear winter's day and watched the *Excambion* come in and tie up. My father, my mother, and Dick came off the ship, and we had a wonderful reunion. While we were on the dock, I asked my father what had happened to the Cadillac. I had known that my father was bringing a new Cadillac on board the *Excambion*, which he was planning to disembark at Naples. I had told one of my Arab guides in Palestine, and he had enthusiastically recommended that my father bring the Cadillac to Egypt, where Bedouins could guide us east across the desert to Trans-Jordan (as it was called then) and perhaps to Iran. I had wired this suggestion to my father, but fortunately he paid it no mind, the car stayed behind in Naples, and that was the end of that. We all went to Cairo and checked into the Shephard's Hotel. Dick introduced me to two young ladies whom he had met on board the *Excambion*; my trip seemed to be full of young ladies that I met here and there around the world. One of Dick's new friends was Lisa Spillman, a West Virginian whom I had known as an undergraduate at Smith. (Now she is Lisa Sutphin, the widow of Sam Sutphin, Yale '34.) The other was her cousin Trudy Brown from Tennessee. They were accompanied by Trudy's parents; the Browns and my family had become friends aboard the ship. We all dined together in Cairo, along with the captain of the *Excambion*, on the evening of their arrival; we had a wonderful time.

The next day we hired an Egyptian guide named Missouri and went out to see the pyramids and the Sphinx. My brother thought it would be a good idea to invite the young ladies for a camel ride, and so we did. I must say that camel riding is not a very comfortable mode of transportation. My father, who was an amateur photographer among other things, took a slew of pictures and even some home movies. His penchant for studying and doing new things showed itself again in Cairo, because it wasn't long before he became quite proficient in reading hieroglyphs. (The Rosetta Stone had furnished the key a little over a hundred years earlier.) My father bought a dictionary of hieroglyphs and was able to translate the inscriptions in the museum in Cairo, much to the amazement of everyone there. Later on in the visit, we hired a car and driver, and were traveling through a squalid village outside Cairo when the driver struck and injured some livestock animal, perhaps a goat. People came out of their huts yelling with clenched fists raised in the air, and my father suggested that we stop and pay for the loss of the animal. Missouri said that was not the thing to do, and urged the driver to move on. I know my father felt bad, but Missouri was a local citizen and knew something about local conditions.

After a few days in Cairo, my family and I, together with yet another young lady, a very attractive American girl about my age, took the overnight train up to Luxor. Our guide there was also named Missouri; I suppose Egyptian guides looking to attract Americans found Missouri a good name for that purpose. My father decided to take us all for a ride on the Nile in a dhow. When we got to the water's edge, we saw a man sitting beside the skipper in the dhow. Missouri told us that he was a snake charmer who would perform for twenty pounds. The pound in those days was fixed at $4.86, so that was a lot of money. My father said that he didn't want to bother with any snakes or snake charmers, and he stayed resolute even when the price was reduced to ten pounds, then five pounds, then one pound, and finally five shillings, so we never did find out whether the man was any good at the business of charming snakes. We were three or four hundred miles south of Cairo, and the Nile was freshwater at that point. It was a warm day in the sun, so some of us went for a satisfying swim.

The banks of the Nile were green for a few hundred yards out, and then the green stopped and the desert began, as abruptly as if you had drawn a line in the sand. Irrigation was a primitive and labor-intensive process. A man would dip a bucket on a sweep down into the Nile, lift it up, and empty it into a reservoir on a ledge cut into the riverbank. Then a man on the level above would use another long lever to dip the water up to a reservoir at the top, and the water would drain out through ditches to irrigate the fields. I saw the operation proceeding in as many as three stages, and I wouldn't be surprised if they're continuing to get water out of the Nile by this method even today.

The one Arabic word that I learned on my travels was "emshee," which means "go away, get out of here." I learned the word when I was standing on a street corner in Cairo and a fellow with a shoe shine box said to me, "Look at your shoe. Wouldn't you like to have a shoe shine?" I looked down and saw that one of my shoes was smeared with mud and filth, and I realized that this fellow had dirtied my shoe on purpose. Later I asked our Cairo guide Missouri what to do in that situation, and he told me, "You should say 'emshee' to these people." Apparently it's a very stern way of saying "get out of here," because every once in a while today I'll get an Egyptian taxi driver in New York and I'll tell him that I know how to speak Arabic. He'll say, "What do you know how to say?" I'll say, "Well, I know the word 'emshee,'" and he'll laugh uproariously.

In a way, all of us in the Beinecke family were at transitional points in our lives as we toured around together. My brother had finished up at the Raymond Riordon School and was thinking about college, although not with great enthusiasm. I had no clear vision of the future, and still hadn't committed myself to a decision about what to do after Yale. My parents were in a transition, too. They had been weathering the Depression up in Boston, and when they had returned to Madison in early 1936, they had had to reopen our house and pick up their life there again. My father hadn't yet gone back into the business world after the terrible experience of the Depression. He had lost his brokerage firm, and his presidency of Houghton & Dutton in Boston had terminated. The Sperry and Hutchinson Company was beginning to pay dividends again, so we could live all right. But although my father was bright, able, and effective, and only a little past his fiftieth birthday— still a comparatively young man—he had been spiritually injured by the Depression. I think the reason my father so heavily immersed himself in the model railroad train he built in the basement of our home in Madison, complete with signal lights, switching, and multiple platforms, was that he desperately needed something to fill the time. He enjoyed working on that model railroad, but it probably was something he would not have done if he had been operating a business.

And then in the winter of 1937, a few months after our return from Europe, my father would go to work at The Sperry and Hutchinson Company. I think I know why. The Beinecke family controlled the Company—indeed, they not only controlled it, they owned it 100 percent. None of the brothers, however, played a direct role in its daily operations. My uncle Walter had his own business to run, an insurance brokerage firm called John C. Paige on lower Broadway. My uncle Edwin was chairman of the board not only of The Sperry and Hutchinson Company but also of the George A. Fuller Company. He participated in important decisions about the Company, but he did not operate the business day in and day out. That was the job of Vernon C. Brown—or V. C., as everyone called him—who was president and general manager of The Sperry and Hutchinson Company. Sometime in the winter of 1937, V. C. Brown fell ill; he was seventy years old and would die the next year. My father and Uncle Ed must have decided that this was a good time for my father to begin to manage the operations of the company in a way my uncle Ed could not. I don't know whether my father spent those five months in Europe with us in the first half of 1937 because he was still without a compelling nine-to-five job or because he knew that he was going to go to work for The Sperry and Hutchinson Company and saw the trip as a chance to spend time with the family. I wish I knew the answer. I think it could have been a little of both. Certainly my mother and father kept hearing from me, and it was natural for them to want to see me again. And then Dick was between school and college, and they wanted to take him along. It was an open-ended trip—none of us had any fixed date of return.

We took an Italian ship from Alexandria sometime in late February. There were some members of the Mussolini family on board, perhaps the dictator's son and his family, and they were much fawned over. Mussolini had just won what the Italians considered a great victory over the Abyssinians led by King Haile Selassie. We disembarked at Naples, where we spent a couple of days. Our small family group took a side trip to Pompeii, which was much the same as it is today. At that time, however, women were forbidden to view the famous erotic wall paintings. From Naples, we crossed the bay to the famous little island of Capri. Because of a popular song, "The Isle of Capri," we pronounced it ca-PREE, but the Italians call it CAP-ree. We went up to San Michele, the home atop Capri that was the subject of a fascinating book called *The Story of San Michele*, an autobiographical account by a Swedish doctor named Axel Munthe of how he built his home as a vacation retreat and over the years filled it with various artifacts and sculptures; I believe I had read the book before our visit there. In ancient times, there was a large villa on Capri built by the Roman emperor Tiberius, who was notorious even in an age when Roman emperors seemed to vie with one another for brutality. The present-day inhabitants of Capri seemed to remember Tiberius very well, and without affection. To have a memory like that obtain for over two thousand years, I thought, was remarkable.

While on Capri, we also visited the Blue Grotto, famous in travel lore and literature. It's a cave where the sea sweeps in and out, and the reflected sunlight on the water and the sides of the cave gives it an almost mystical blue color. Getting in and out of the Blue Grotto was not easy, since the entrance was submerged every time a wave came through. Local inhabitants swam in and out the narrow passage between the bay and the cave, but visitors had to go in a boat, crouching to keep their heads from hitting the top of the passage. The boatman would hover outside the mouth of the Grotto, and then at just the right moment, when the wave had subsided, the boat would dart in.

We continued our journey through Italy in my father's Cadillac, driving from Naples to Rome. Early one morning in our hotel in Rome, I heard a high, passionate voice outside singing "Ave Maria"—it was Easter Sunday, 1937. My father had some connections that enabled us to get tickets for the service at Saint Peter's Cathedral in the Vatican. I remember seeing Pope Pius XI come in, borne aloft in a sedan chair, blessing the people right and left all the way down the long, long center aisle of the cathedral. I was surprised by the exuberance of the Italian worshipers, all calling out, "Viva il Pape! Viva il Pape!" In the Protestant tradition in which I'd been brought up there was no yelling in church, and the service was always subdued and quiet and reverent. But in Saint Peter's Cathedral on the occasion of the Pope's visit, it was different. There was excitement and enthusiasm, and he was a hero to the people in the church. "Viva il Pape!"—I can still hear them today.

In Rome, my parents were disgusted to see how enthralled I had become with a new best-seller they had brought with them called *Gone with the Wind*. I couldn't take my nose out of it. One day when the rest of the family was going out for a walk in the Eternal City, I said, "Nope, I'm going to stay here in the hotel room and read." When they came back, they said, "Bill, we went to the place where Mussolini lives, and he came out on the balcony and made a speech to the cheering multitude. We experienced history, and where were you? Here in the hotel room, reading a book that you can read any time!" We made the usual stops in Rome. Sites like the Colosseum and the old Forum and the remnants of the Appian Way had been cleaned up for tourists but were nonetheless in their modern state of decrepitude. After Rome fell to the Visigoths and Vandals in the fifth century, it ceased to exist as a seat of government, and by the Middle Ages the Eternal City had become nothing but an overgrown village. All the old Roman places of significance had been buried, marked only by a couple of toppled columns, and people used the Colosseum as a quarry. By the fifteenth century, sheep and goats grazed in fields over what had been the Roman Forum. This history of decline, rather than the ravages of time, really accounts for the ruined condition of the monuments of ancient Rome.

We soon set off for Florence along the divided highways called the autostrada. By 1937 Mussolini had started to copy the autobahns of Germany, so you could make good speed between major cities in the more urbanized and industrialized parts of northern Italy. We stopped for a meal at a restaurant between Rome and Florence, and when Betty, my parents, and I ate in the same place in 1963, we found that the old register recorded that the Beinecke family had lunched there in 1937. In Florence, we stayed at a little pension at 32 Via Montebello run by a vivid man, Signor Leone. My mother and father had a double room, and my brother and I had another. The ceilings were covered with painted angels and other figures, perhaps not rivaling the Sistine Chapel but still quite charming. We were in Florence for nearly a month, and had a grand time visiting the Uffizi and other galleries and museums and simply walking around the city. We took a side excursion of five or six days to the walled medieval town of San Gimignano and a few other towns in that part of Italy. When the time came to leave our pension in Florence, my father looked at the bill and said to Signor Leone, "This total isn't right." Signor Leone raised his hands, threw his palms outward, and shrugged his shoulders in his characteristic gesture of perplexity and shock. My father said to him, "You didn't charge us for those five or six days we weren't here." "But no," replied Signor Leone, "I could not charge you. You were not here." My father said, "Yes, but you couldn't rent the rooms because they were filled with all our things." "But no," said Signor Leone again, "you were not here." In the end, of course, my father insisted on paying for the period that we weren't there. He had been in the hotel business himself, and he knew that Signor Leone's generosity wasn't a very good business policy.

In 1963 I returned to Florence with my parents and my wife Betty, and we stayed in the same pension, still run by Signor Leone. On that occasion we were captivated by the Boar Fountain in one of the squares in Florence. The central statue is a gigantic male pig, and water flows out of his mouth and trickles down into a pool below. We found a full-scale working replica of the fountain for sale in one of the sculpture shops along the banks of the Arno. We didn't buy it, but I learned later that it was purchased and now stands in front of the Children's Hospital in Kansas City, Missouri. But my father, remembering that I liked the fountain so much, ordered a smaller reproduction of the boar from that shop, had it shipped to the United States, and gave it to me for Christmas. The boar is now in my office, and his nose is quite shiny because I invite people to rub it for good luck. My friend and fellow Columbia law graduate John Bainbridge sent me some information about the origin and history of the fountain, including the fact that the boar was the creation of a sculptor named Tacca. I'm glad to have that statue in my office as a reminder of what a kind and generous man my father was.

I had another interesting experience in Florence in 1937. My father and my two uncles held an interest in a business called the Patent Scaffolding Company. It was a subsidiary of George A. Fuller Construction, the company that had built The Plaza Hotel and for which my uncle Ed went to work when he left Yale at the end of his junior year. At the time of our visit to Italy, the Patent Scaffolding Company was headed by a man named Eugene (Gene) Pitou, and since Mr. Pitou knew that my father was going to Italy, he asked if my father would look into the whereabouts of a number of scaffolding machines that the company had sold to an Italian contracting firm in Milan and for which they had not been paid. My father wasn't all that enthusiastic about poking around in the warehouses of Milan, and asked me if I would do it. I agreed, but pointed out that I'd had no business experience. I'd only graduated from college the year before and had spent my time since then going around the world having a good time. I had no idea how to go about ascertaining the whereabouts of these missing scaffolding machines or finding out why they hadn't been paid for. Indeed, I didn't even know what a scaffolding machine was. I soon learned that it was a windlass and ratchet affair on either end of a scaffold that hoisted the scaffold up the side of a tall building or let it down. The Patent Scaffolding Company had in the mid-1930s developed and patented a new machine for lowering and raising scaffolds efficiently and safely. Before I went to Milan, my father decided that the first thing to do was to make me a vice president of the company, so we went to a printer in Florence and had some cards made up that read, "William S. Beinecke, Vice President, Patent Scaffolding Company, Long Island City, New York."

I thought it was ridiculous, but I put on the only suit of clothes I had, stashed the cards in my pocket, got on the train, and went to Milan. Somehow or other I located the contractor there and presented my card. The contractor was indeed most impressed at having this twenty-two-year-old vice president of the Patent Scaffolding Company appear on the scene. He showed me the machines, which were lined up against the wall of the warehouse. They looked in good shape to me—that is, they were clean, well-oiled, and not rusty—and they were all there. The contractor also assured me that he intended to pay for them. I got back on the train to Florence and reported all this to my father, who directed me to send the information along in a letter to Mr. Pitou. Several months later, when I had returned to New York, Mr. Pitou invited me to lunch at the University Club. I recapitulated my report, and it seems to me now that Mr. Pitou was quite interested in whether I thought the contractor was going to pay. I don't know if I answered the questions to his satisfaction, but I did get a very fine lunch, and that was the first time I'd ever seen that impressive dining room at the University Club. I had no further encounters of any importance with Mr. Pitou or the Patent Scaffolding Company, and I have no idea whether the Patent Scaffolding Company was ever paid anything for the machines they had shipped to Italy. I do wish that I had saved one of those phony vice president's cards.

I did not see much evidence of Fascism at work in Italy in 1937. We were enjoying the Italian art collections, the museums, the good food, and the pleasant lifestyle, and there was nothing to indicate that Italy was soon to be involved in a terrible war. Of course, everyone knew that Italy was building up its military forces. I remember that the Italian air general Italo Balbo led a large flight of Italian warplanes to Chicago in those years, and everybody marveled at this great flying feat. In 1936, the year before our trip, the Italians had invaded Ethiopia and absorbed it into the New Roman Empire. Many in the United States deplored Italy as a big bully for this action, and yet we didn't do much about it. In the spring of 1937, the Italians were warm and cordial to us Americans, and seemed delighted to have us as guests in their country. My father's Cadillac drew a lot of attention. It was much larger than European cars, and cars of any sort were rare in Italy then. Whenever we'd stop in a town or village, people would gather around this big luxury Cadillac and goggle in awe.

I have been to Europe many times since, and sometimes it's hard for me to keep straight what I saw on which visit. In 1954 Betty and I made our first trip to Europe as tourists after the war. We spent two weeks in Italy and retraced some of the steps my parents and I had taken in 1937. We rented a small Fiat in Rome—renting a car was much more difficult then than it is today—and drove up to Florence. There were still vestiges of the German occupation of Italy in the form of hand-painted signs in German on some street corners: one pointed in the direction of "Florenz," for example, rather than "Firenze." Those signs had been painted on the sides of buildings as directional aids for German occupation forces ten years before. By 1963, when I next returned to Florence, such evidence of the war was long gone. On that trip, as I was on my way to catch up with my parents in Spain, I visited Milan again and went to see Leonardo DaVinci's "Last Supper." I'm glad that I saw it then, because it is fading badly, despite efforts to preserve it.

After my family's stay in Florence in 1937, we drove to Venice—or, rather, we drove to a garage on the outskirts of the city, since you couldn't take a car into Venice. We entered Venice in a vaporetto, one of those motor-propelled launches that serve as water buses on the city canals. I remember feeding the pigeons in Saint Mark's Square, and I remember also the statues of the horses on top of Saint Mark's Cathedral. The horses had been taken from Venice by Napoleon to be displayed in Paris and been returned to Venice by the French only about twenty years before our visit. This was not the first time the statues had been stolen, for they had been brought to Venice following the sack of Constantinople in 1204, during the Fourth Crusade.

From Venice we headed north through the Dolomites, up precipitous roads and perilous switchbacks, until we reached the Brenner Pass, which for many years was the principal way through the Alps; it's not as high and forbidding as some of the other passes. We crossed over into Innsbruck in the spring. On May 6, 1937, I was on my way from our

Feeding the pigeons in Saint Mark's Square, Venice, 1937

hotel lobby up to our room when the elevator operator asked me if I knew about the *Hindenburg*. I said that of course I knew of that famous airship, and he responded, "Alles kaputt!" When I got upstairs I asked my father what that meant, and he said, "It means 'All broken.' Why do you ask?" I said, "Well, the elevator operator said that the *Hindenburg* was 'Alles kaputt.'" That was our first knowledge of the disaster that befell the *Hindenburg* when it arrived at Lakehurst, New Jersey. It was particularly chilling to us because Uncle Ed and Aunt Linda had traveled from Europe to the United States on the *Hindenburg* not long before. I later learned that my Yale classmate Peter Belin miraculously survived the fire. How he escaped I have no idea. I do know that he ran around in the parking area giving out a family whistle to alert his father, who was there to meet him, that he was on the ground and not in the *Hindenburg*. They met and fell into each other's arms.

From Innsbruck we went to Munich, staying at the Bayerische Hof, a fine hotel even today. Shortly after we arrived, my mother became ill. I believe she had some kind of feminine problem, but because of the puritanical outlook that affected such matters in those days, I wasn't told the nature of her illness. I don't think she was in danger of her life, but she was seriously indisposed and uncomfortable, so she went to a hospital in Munich for two weeks. She had a spacious room in the hospital, with several chairs and a table, almost like a hotel room. I'd go there and play chess with my father. My father's older sister Alice was living in Leipzig, and at my father's request she jumped on a train and came down to Munich, conferred with the doctors, and was the greatest aid to my parents. When we weren't with my mother, Dick and I would go to a tennis court in Munich and volley back and forth for exercise. My brother was not very good at tennis, so there was no point playing a competitive game.

We were visited in Munich by my father's first cousin, Martha Ihl. She was the daughter of my father's aunt, Caroline Weigle Ihl, the younger sister of his mother, Johanna Weigle Beinecke. Martha married Richard Rettich, who became the first violinist of the Munich Symphony Orchestra, one of the top symphony orchestras in Germany. I remember that he was a diabetic and had to have insulin from time to time. Paul Prindle's genealogy, *The Ancestry of William Sperry Beinecke*, makes a reference to that visit with Martha Ihl. One evening Aunt Alice, my father, my brother, and I drove to a restaurant some distance out in the country, and I had quite a lot of beer with dinner. I was very uncomfortable on the drive back, and I remember how wonderful I thought my Aunt Alice was because she recognized my discomfort and said to her brother, "Fritz, stop the car and let your son out to relieve himself. He can't stand it any longer." She was right—I couldn't. You can imagine how much agony I was in if I can remember that for more than sixty years!

One of the events in Hitler's ascendancy was an incident at a place called the Brown House in Munich, and there was always a sentry or two on watch outside. There were also ceremonial Nazi guards at a couple of big sarcophagi in the Königsplatz. The guards in both locations were rigidly at attention. They could not move anything other than their eyes, and they had to hold that position for quite a stretch, two hours, I think. I hadn't picked up much of a sense of Fascism in Italy, but you certainly had a frightening sense of Hitler in Germany. I was more interested in Germany's past history than its present, though. I remember the sign we passed commemorating the Battle of Leipzig in October 1813, a three-day battle that ended in a decisive victory for the Austrian, Russian, and Prussian forces over Napoleon. I'd like to see that sign again.

After my mother had recovered, we left Munich and visited my aunt Alice at the Weickerts' big brick house in a little suburb of Leipzig called Eutritsch. It was spring, and the weather was warm and delightful. Aunt Alice had a beautiful garden behind her house, with a small pond crowned by a little bridge. The grass was green, the daffodils were starting to bloom, and other spring flowers were beginning to appear. We had dinner at Aunt Alice's house one night, and she was very proud to serve us fresh water prawns, which she said was a favorite dish of her brother, my uncle Edwin. He used to visit Germany more often than the other members of the family, and he saw Aunt Alice more frequently. Aunt Alice's husband, Johann Friedrich Weickert, had died in 1929. I have no recollection of ever having met him, and yet I have a reel of film that my father took that shows Aunt Alice and Uncle Fritz Weickert at our home in Madison. They must have come over for a visit when I was away in school. My father took a lot of 16-millimeter amateur movies back in the 1920s and 1930s. They are now very brittle, but when I threatened to throw them out, my four children protested. My daughter Sarah took twenty or thirty of these reels to a professional and had them transferred to two videotapes. I sat down to watch one of the tapes and was surprised to see how closely Uncle Fritz resembles my first cousin Bernhard (Berni) Weickert, who is two years older than I am. Berni was the youngest of their four children, and he emigrated from Germany to the United States in 1954. He was in Leipzig in 1937, as was his older brother, Edwin, and his two sisters, Alice, known as

"Alli" for short, and Irmgard, or "Putti." Putti was about thirty years old, and was living with her husband, a doctor, somewhere in Leipzig. Alli was living at home. Berni was in the *Hochtechnische*, the technical high school, which was more like a graduate school. He was studying artificial fibers and the like, thinking that would be useful to him in the family business, but his training was actually more useful to him when he came to the United States. With his special technical skills, he had no difficulty finding a job with Du Pont in its experimental laboratory in Wilmington, Delaware, studying the new processes that the company was developing. He worked for Du Pont from 1954 until he retired twenty-five years later, and he still lives in Wilmington. His wife, Alex, died in 1999. They had two daughters whom they brought over to the United States in 1954. Renate lives in the Jacksonville/Ponte Vedra area and is married to a Yale man named Joe Hixon. Steffi went to Smith and also married a Yale man, Robert Reponen, who unfortunately died of a heart attack at an early age and left two young boys for Steffi to bring up, which she has done very well. Edwin Weickert and Putti have since died. Alli lives in the Black Forest region of Germany and celebrated her ninetieth birthday in 1998.

Edwin Weickert, the oldest son, was more or less running the family business while we were there in 1937. The Weickerts had a felt-making factory in Wurzen, a smaller town on the banks of the Elbe not far from Leipzig. The family had owned the Weickert Felzen Fabrik, as it was called, since 1783, and held onto it through the Napoleonic Wars, the revolutions of 1848, the Franco-Prussian War, and the First World War, until the Communists took it all away after World War II. The company began making piano felts in 1841, and its best customer was Steinweg und Söhne; when that firm moved to New York City in 1853, it became known as Steinway & Sons. I always thought that the J. D. Weickert company's major product was piano felts, but in fact the bulk of the business was the sale of felt to Swedish paper factories for industrial use. Pulp would be liquefied, heated, and spread on long rolls of felt, and when the moisture evaporated, what was left was paper. I don't know whether that process is still used today, but the rolls of felt came from the Weickert Felzen Fabrik. Edwin was about thirty-five years old then and lived in a small house next to the factory.

While we were in Leipzig, we met up with my cousin Walter "Bud" Beinecke, Jr. What was he doing there? He had gone to Saint George's School in Newport, Rhode Island, and then to sea for a while in the United States Merchant Marine. His father, like my father, thought it would be useful for his son to go to Germany and learn something about the country of his ancestors, and so Uncle Walter arranged with his sister Alice for Bud to spend a year working for the Weickert Felzen Fabrik. My father and mother invited him to join us for a portion of our trip, and we headed east. One hot day as we were crossing the border into Czechoslovakia, something went seriously wrong with our Cadillac. We didn't pay much attention, though, because we knew that whenever anything went wrong in a car, no matter what the problem was, my father would be able to fix it. Mother sat in the back of the car reading her book, Dick and Bud and I whiled away our time walking around and talking, and my father took off his coat and tie and began to take the engine apart. Some curious border guards came up, and my father had a fine time explaining to them in German what he was doing with the car. A glass compartment in the carburetor had cracked, and fuel and air were not being mixed in the proper ratio in the engine. Somehow or other my father improvised a repair and put the car back together again. It ran like a charm for the rest of the trip all the way to Paris.

On we went into Czechoslovakia, where we paid a visit to Marienbad, a warm-springs resort where my Beinecke grandparents had gone to take the waters during their own visits to Europe. From Marienbad, we headed south in the direction of Vienna. My father wanted to take us through the Grossglockner Pass not far from the Italian border in Austria, one of the high passes through the Alps, much higher than the Brenner. While we shimmied up a series of switchbacks on the mountain road leading to the pass, it started to snow, and it snowed and it snowed. The road became slippery and then impassable, until the only thing to do was to retrace our way down. But how to turn the car around? Dick, Bud, and I got out and put our shoulders to the Cadillac, and when my father backed the car to the edge of the switchback, we pushed so it wouldn't go over the side. (My mother had sense enough to get out and watch this procedure.) Then my father inched the car forward again as far as it could go, turned the wheels, and backed up again. We did this repeatedly until we got the car turned around. Part of the way down we stopped at a small official building along the road and saw a tour bus of Hollanders in the same predicament. My father made an inquiry and discovered that we could spend the night at an inn nearby and put the Cadillac on a train and take a tunnel through the Alps the next morning. So we spent the night in a tiny inn full of Dutch people, and the next morning took the train to the other side of the Grossglockner. In the summer of 1965 when Betty and I and our four children were in Bavaria for a month, I remembered that incident of twenty-four years before and thought it might be fun to make a trip over the Grossglockner. Our trip failed for a different reason: the gear-shift lever in our rental car came right out of its socket and up into the air as I was shifting gears. So I've never managed to get over the Grossglockner Pass. In 1937, our family group continued east through Austria to Vienna, and then to Budapest. I was impressed by the enor-mous swimming pool, complete with artificial waves, in one of Buda-pest's hotels and by the fact that the city's top night spot was improba-bly called the Arizona Club.

From Budapest we returned Bud to Leipzig, then drove on to Paris. I remember seeing a grand fireworks display from our hotel window in Paris, but I think it was too early for Bastille Day; perhaps there was some kind of world's fair or major exposition in Paris in June that year. Dick had to return home to file an application for the Univer-sity of Vermont. This posed a problem, because although I, of course, had been traveling around the world on my own passport, my mother and father and Dick had a family passport, issued in all their names and with three photographs. The joint passport meant that Dick couldn't travel on his own. So we went to the American embassy, the family pass-port was severed, and a separate passport was issued to Dick. After a few days in Paris, my parents and I crossed the Channel.

In London I went on several dates with a young lady named Joy Swinton-Browne, whom I had met when she and her mother were stay-ing at Signor Leone's with us in Florence. Her late father had been a col-onel in the British army and had served as some kind of special overseer to the Clarks, the Singer sewing machine family, when they lived in upstate New York. I spent a couple of days in London with Joy Swinton-Browne, maneuvering my father's big American Cadillac through traffic on the wrong side of the road. Joy and her mother invited me to accom-pany them to the Lake Country, and so we spent a few days in a country inn in Ullswater. I thought it was marvelous that there were still isolated rural places where you could take long, rambling country walks. I would hike through the hills in the afternoon with Joy, returning for tea with her mother, and then every evening I would have to put on a tuxedo for dinner. It's amazing to me, as I look back on it, that even in the country-side one had to dress for dinner, but that was the custom. From the Lake Country I took a train to Liverpool, where I rejoined my parents and embarked on a one-week passage to New York via Boston.

Thus ended the trip around the world. I had been away so long, and had had so many experiences, that when I returned home to Madi-son, New Jersey, it seemed to me that time had stood still. My friends were in the same place as when I'd left, our house was the same, and, to my surprise, nothing had changed.

I took only a few notes about my travels, and those have long since vanished. Even if I had made a more extensive record of my trip, I don't know that it would make good reading, for it would have been the observations of my callow and less observant younger self. But a trip like that helps take away some of the callowness. There was once a tradition that after a student had finished up at a university, he embarked on a journey of a year or more—the Grand Tour—and this was thought to be a significant learning experience. I was very fortunate that my parents availed me the opportunity to make that trip around the world, and I learned a lot. Those few days in China, for example, have been with me all my life. Those who have never been to China know that China is there and that China is big and important. But to see it! Once you've seen it, you have something in your background and consciousness that's there for all your life. There is no substitute for direct experience.

CHAPTER FIVE

Columbia Law School, 1937–1940

I returned home in July 1937 and had to figure out what to do with the rest of my life. The country was just beginning to crawl up from the Depression, and there were no clear signposts to indicate which road a young man should travel. Like everyone else, I had read in the papers about the Hall-Mills case, the Scopes trial, and the Sacco-Vanzetti case, and I had given the law some passing thought, but I didn't know much about it. I went to see V. C. Brown, the president of The Sperry and Hutchinson Company, to see what he thought of my going to law school as opposed to joining the family business. He told me it would be better for me to study law, but I suspect that what he really thought was that it would be better for him to have me in law school and out of his hair for three years. I don't think he particularly wanted to have a young product of the Beinecke family come aboard. If that had to be, he much preferred my cousin Ed, the son of Uncle Edwin, who was the head of the company. V. C. Brown was visibly relieved when I told him that I was considering law school.

In any case, I did decide to apply to law school. I was guided in my decision by the advice of three men. The first was my father. The second was Horace Corbin, who was the leading banker in New Jersey, a great friend of my father's, and a man I had known for a long time. I got to know him fairly well because I used to take his daughter out, and I was around their house quite a bit when I was in my late teens. The third was Harold Medina, a professor at Columbia who was later a distinguished United States appeals judge in the Second Circuit in New York. I first came to know him during my parents' summers at Westhampton, when I sailed, golfed, and played tennis with his two sons. I also went sailing with the professor, and when I played hearts with him at the Medina home, I learned that he was quite an unconventional man. His version of the game was to administer a wallop on the head with a stuffed sock every time someone drew a heart, or thirteen wallops for the queen of spades. I distinctly remember Professor Medina drawing the queen of spades and biting his cigar in two!

I applied to the Harvard and Columbia law schools. If Harvard had accepted me, I would have gone there. I never even thought about the Yale Law School. The Harvard Law School was the citadel of legal learning at that time, up and above the rest. In college we had all heard of it, and most of us hadn't heard of any other law school. I knew a little bit about Columbia through Harold Medina and a couple of neighbors who had gone there. I can't remember how I applied to Harvard, but I took the subway up to Columbia to file my application there. I knew Columbia was at 116th Street, but I didn't know enough about the New York subway system to realize that it branches at 96th Street; one line goes north and the other goes northeast through Harlem. I got off the train at 116th Street and Lenox Avenue, and Columbia was to the west on Morningside Heights. So I walked right through Morningside Park, something you would be fearful of doing today. It was a very hot day, and by the time I got to Columbia, I was disheveled and perspiring. But I never again made the same mistake on that subway line. It was August 1937, and I was seeking admission to the September class. Harvard said I was too late. They didn't say I wasn't qualified, they just told me I was too late. Columbia said that they did have a place for me. So I went to Columbia, and I never regretted it.

I didn't know anyone who was a student there. My friends in the Yale class of '36 who had gone on to law school had already completed their first year at Yale, Harvard, or the other places they went. I later discovered that Bob Case, who was in my class at Andover and at Yale, was also at Columbia, but I didn't know he was there until I arrived. He was an interesting fellow. His father was a founding partner in a famous New York law firm, White & Case, so Bob had a real heritage in the law. Unfortunately, he had hemophilia, and it eventually got him. He graduated from law school and went to work as a lawyer, but I don't think he lived long after that. I had a high regard for him. Another of my former Yale classmates who attended Columbia was Bill Burt, who left Yale at the end of our junior year and entered Columbia Law School under its "professional option." An undergraduate who had finished up his third year at Columbia College could, if he qualified, enter Columbia Law School during his senior year, and when he graduated from the law school he would get a degree from both institutions. Bill Burt learned about that, persuaded the faculty at Columbia to extend this privilege to a Yale man, and went through his first year at Columbia Law School during our senior year at Yale. Then he left to serve in the air force as an aide to General Hoyt Vandenberg, whom he admired, and went on to be a colonel during the war. He returned to finish his law degree at Columbia after the war, so he was both ahead of me and after me at Columbia, but we were never contemporaneous.

Also in my class at Columbia, unbeknownst to me when I entered, was my cousin Constantine (Connie) Mittendorf. He was the son of my father's cousin George Mittendorf, who had been a companion of my father and his brothers in their early days when they summered at Oscawanna and Crugers-on-Hudson. George Mittendorf went on to graduate from Yale College in 1900 and Columbia Law School a few years later, and became a lawyer in New York. His son Connie had graduated with the class of '37 at Yale, where he had rowed on the crew. Columbia was part of his heritage, and he always knew that he wanted to be a lawyer. Connie simply followed his father's path into the law. Although we were cousins, I didn't know Connie well, but I got to know him much better during our years at Columbia.

I rented an apartment near Columbia, but was only there for about a week when I met a pair of Harvard graduates, Edward Bennett and Harry Stimpson, who invited me to room with them. We got a set of rooms at an apartment house called the Kingscote on 119th Street and lived there for our first year. Harry didn't like Columbia, and after a year he transferred to the University of Virginia Law School. Ed Bennett and I continued to be good friends and roommates throughout our three-year Columbia experience, and he was best man at my wedding in 1941.

I immediately became totally absorbed in the life of the Columbia Law School, and I was scared to death. The grading system was terrifying. The only grade you received was the one you got on the final examination, so you really didn't know how you were faring until after the exam. And some of the required courses—Torts, for example, and Contracts—were two-semester courses, so your entire grade rested on only one examination at the end of a whole year. What a prospect! Young Berryman Smith, the dean of the school, taught Torts. He didn't make it particularly interesting, but it was a mandatory course, so we had to put up with it. Karl Llewelyn taught Contracts. He was a strange man, who I believe had won an Iron Cross fighting for the Germans back in World War I. I took a course in Evidence, which was taught by Jerome Michael and was way above my head. And then there was Julius Goebel's course on the Development of Legal Institutions, called DLI for short. That frightened the daylights out of everyone. Most of the legal events that we considered in that course happened back in the twelfth and thirteenth centuries—the fourteenth century was about as modern as we ever got. To me it was totally incomprehensible, and yet somehow I passed the examination, perhaps because it didn't seem to have anything to do with the subject matter of the course. I also took a first-year course on Legislation, taught by Walter Gellhorn, who continued to teach on the Columbia faculty until he died in the winter of 1995. He was one of two very young men on the faculty at that time; the other was Herbert Wechsler, whom I particularly remember from that first-year experience.

Professor Wechsler's course was quite unexciting, but Herb was a very interesting man and so near to us in age; I don't think he was more than four or five years older than I was. He had graduated from CCNY when he was fifteen or sixteen and finished Columbia Law School three years later, with one of the highest records anyone ever achieved there. He clerked for Harlan Fisk Stone, who had been dean of the Columbia Law School and was one of the great jurists on the United States Supreme Court. During World War II, Professor Wechsler worked in the office of the alien property custodian, which was under the jurisdiction of the attorney general, and later he participated in the Nuremburg Trials. He continued to teach at Columbia until he finally retired in the 1990s. I hadn't seen much of Herb for a number of years until one day I realized that we were both members of the Eastward Ho! Country Club in Chatham on Cape Cod. Herb's health no longer permits him to play golf, and the Wechslers sold their summer home on the Cape a few years ago. Up until that time, however, Betty and I occasionally played golf with Herb and his wife, Doris, at Eastward Ho! and quite often dined with them there. The Wechslers live not far from us in New York, and we continue to have a warm and friendly relationship. One day a few years ago, just as Herb and I were about to begin a friendly game of golf, I asked at the pro shop whether there was any kind of a competition that day. I was informed that the Senior pairs championship was being played, and I said, "Go ahead and enter Professor Wechsler and me." I returned to the tee and communicated this development to Herb, who expressed shock and trepidation and said that he never played in competitions. I had my best round of the summer that day, and we won the championship. Herb—who is nonathletic, to put it mildly—made a real contribution to our great win and was very much on hand in the early fall when the prizes for the summer were handed out.

In the beginning of my law student career, I was told to go buy a certain case book and read so many pages, and having read those pages, I went to class quaking in my boots. I found out that some people knew what they were supposed to have learned from those pages, and I did not. Indeed, the first time I went to class, I marveled at all the Phi Beta Kappa keys my fellow law students displayed on their watch chains. The professors knew that those students were out to impress, so right away they called on the fellows with the Phi Beta Kappa keys and made them appear to be very stupid. I never saw the Phi Beta Kappa keys again until we went looking for jobs in our third year. After a while, even non-Phi Beta Kappa students like myself began to catch on, and things began to fall into place.

I was taking these courses in an area that was completely new to me: the language was new, and so was the subject matter, the method of studying, the case system, and the method of instruction. At college you would listen to lectures and take notes, and then study your notes and the text in order to spout them back on an exam. Law school teaching was entirely different. You were to read the cases, and then in class they would be taken apart in minute detail. That meant you had to study the cases before each recitation and try to dissect each one while you were studying it, so that in class you could have some concept of what was important to the case, and how it fit into the development of the law. Each case and all its predecessors were building blocks, parts of a system that you had to try to understand. I think I understood this theory pretty well, but I was not as good at it as some of my classmates, who were really competing with one another to see how well everyone would do. I was in the middle of the class.

We had a moot court system at Columbia Law School, where each court had about twelve members and tried mock cases against other student courts. Each court would be given a case, and you had to take a side, write a brief, and then argue your side against an opposing court before a panel of judges, who were upperclassmen or teachers at Columbia, until the final round of competition, when real judges from the New York courts were brought in to adjudicate. Each of these moot courts was named after a famous figure in the law: there was a Blackstone court, a Stone court, a Holmes court and so forth—as many courts as were needed to take care of all the students. In my first year I became a member of the Kent Moot Court, named for Chancellor James Kent, an important New York jurist and the real creator of the Columbia Law School. The Kent Moot Court was for the most part made up of young men from Harvard, Princeton, and Yale, although it also included my good friend Jim Casey, later my law partner, who had been captain of the basketball team at Columbia College. My cousin

Connie Mittendorf, who had graduated from Yale, was in the Kent Moot Court, and so were my roommates, both Harvard grads. The second- and third-year students above us in Kent were also Ivy Leaguers. Another moot court was made up of graduates of New York City schools like CCNY, NYU, and Brooklyn College, another was made up of graduates from colleges in the South, and so forth. This created a clublike atmosphere in the moot court system, and I suppose you could say it was somewhat elitist. Indeed, some people said that democracy should prevail at all costs and that membership in the moot courts should be chosen by lot. A few people in the Kent Moot Court decided that this plan would cause the club to lose its identity, and I believe they actually incorporated Kent so that its integrity as a separate club would be preserved even if it were taken out of the moot court system. In retrospect, the whole affair seems silly. We did maintain our identity as the Kent Moot Court and argued cases against other moot courts in the competition, but eventually the system was broken up and the faculty controlled the assignments, so that it was no longer a group of insiders asking other insiders to join their club. The controversy didn't greatly affect my day-to-day life as a Columbia Law student.

Each of the moot courts had a faculty adviser, and Professor Julius Goebel, who taught the course in the Development of Legal Institutions that I didn't understand, was the faculty advisor to the Kent Moot Court. It was a good thing I got to know him that way, because it turned out that he was a very human person even though his course was inhuman. He lived on Riverside Drive with his wife, Dorothy, who wrote a biography of William Henry Harrison; they had no children. He was very much of a conservative politically, at a time when the Columbia student body was very liberal. Columbia was quite a political place in the late 1930s. There were some German Jews at the law school who had been members of the bar in Germany, but they could see what was going to happen to them there and they had enrolled in American law schools so that they could practice in this country. There weren't many of them at Columbia, but they were noticeable. One was Max Goldman, who became a very successful lawyer in Puerto Rico; another was Walter Pond, who became a prominent lawyer in the office of the general counsel of AT&T. There were two or three others whose names I can't remember. These Germans were older than most of us, in their early thirties, and were more mature and seasoned. They had also learned civil law, whereas American law was based on Anglo-American common law. It was an interesting experience to be rubbing elbows with them. The civil war in Spain was going on, pitting the Communists and

Nationalists against the Fascists under Franco. The Communists and Nationalists were supported by more-liberal American students, but the lines were fuzzy. The Communists had maltreated priests and nuns and had desecrated churches, so Roman Catholics were alienated from the Nationalist side and tended to sympathize with Franco. Several Columbia Law students were veterans of the Lincoln Brigade, Americans who had fought in the Spanish civil war on the side of the Nationalists. There was considerable tension on campus about the Spanish civil war, and people were always arguing about it. I was more an observer than a participant in these debates. I deplored the war, but it didn't move me as it did some others. I think that was because I was too preoccupied with my academic work, and practically everything else was extraneous. In fact, though I had been a devoted moviegoer at Yale, I hardly went to the movies at all when I was a law student. I rarely even went home, although my family was nearby in New Jersey. It was a time of intense study.

I'm extremely glad that I went to law school. It taught me how to think. Does that mean that Yale College hadn't? Yale taught me a lot, but I don't believe that I learned how to think critically there. I don't know whether any college teaches undergraduates to think critically. At Columbia I quickly moved into a routine where I was studying for many hours a night, hitting the books really hard. That was the expectation: you were plunged into an environment where you had to do that. It was an all-encompassing, all-engrossing experience. My friends and I used to do most of our studying in the law school library. In those days the law school was housed in one building, Kent Hall, which embraced the library, classrooms, and offices. You entered the building through two glass doors and walked into the rotunda, which had a marble floor, a stairway at one end, and the entrance to the library straight ahead. We would study in the library every afternoon and night, and once an hour, with great regularity, we'd stop studying and go out to the rotunda to have a cigarette and talk. Back we would go for another hour of study, out again for a cigarette, and back into the library again. I was working to the limit of my ability, stretching to keep up. I think I was changed for the better. I don't want to denigrate Yale, but my Columbia experience taught me to demand more of myself than I had before.

I don't know exactly what it was that made the law compelling for me, but I thought that the philosophy of the law brought home to us certain aspects of the human condition. Human conduct is not regulated solely by the law as handed down by the highest authority in the nation, be it the dictator, czar, president, or king. Neither is it determined only by the enacted statutes of the legislature or parliament, although those are part of the regulating medium in the society in which we live. There are many other things that regulate our lives: manners, customs, morals, family interactions, the rules of the company that we work for, and so on. All these regulatory mechanisms are the fabric of the cocoon in which we live. Even dealing with the telephone requires knowing and complying with the rules that have been imposed in connection with its use, and that's a form of governance. The realization of how these mechanisms are interconnected and interwoven, and thus control the lives of all of us, seems self-evident when you state it, but when I was a young and callow kid embarking on law school, this revelation had a major impact.

In the fall of 1937, when I was getting associated with Kent Moot Court, the upperclassmen of the club invited the new members to dinner at Lüchow's, the famous German restaurant and beer hall on 14th Street. They had a big room upstairs, and we had dinner there accompanied by lots of beer. The upperclassmen asked us first-year students to argue with one another a case having to do with false imprisonment. In civilian life, if someone has detained you improperly, you've been falsely imprisoned and you can sue for damages. The classic case used to exemplify that tort rule is *Talcott* v. *National Exhibition Company*. The National Exhibition Company was the company that ran the New York Giants baseball team. Talcott was attending a game at the Polo Grounds, where the Giants played, and wanted to get out of the stadium for some reason but couldn't because of all the people streaming in through the turnstiles. It took him an hour or two to get out, and he sued the National Exhibition Company on the grounds that he had been falsely imprisoned. The upperclassmen knew that we had studied that case, so they made up a hypothetical case on the same subject. A fellow was taken to an island that was separated from the mainland by a strait, and he wanted to get off the island. The water in the strait was only two feet deep, so he could have walked across it, but he didn't know that. The upperclassmen's question to us was whether this man was falsely imprisoned, since he could have gotten out. We argued for a couple of hours in that upper room at Lüchow's, then we drank more beer and had a hilarious time.

At the conclusion of our first semester, we had a break of about a week. Connie Mittendorf and I, together with a Kent Moot Court member named Jim McDonnell, decided we should go skiing. I had put on a pair of skis a year or so before when I was on the southern island of New Zealand, but it was more tramping around in the snow than real downhill skiing. So I had zero experience, and I don't think Connie Mittendorf had much either. I asked my good friend Ben Moyer for advice. He was working in the advertising business in New York, and since he'd gone to Dartmouth I figured he knew everything about skiing. He recommended that we get some gear at a ski shop over on Third Avenue and suggested that we go to a ski resort in Vermont near Manchester called Johnny Seesaw's.

We got our equipment together and took the overnight train from New York to Montreal that would run over the Rutland Railroad right of way as it passed through Vermont. (While the Rutland Railroad passenger service has long since ceased to exist, freight trains continue to operate on the old Rutland right of way.) We boarded a Pullman car that would be detached at Manchester in the middle of the night. You could stay on it until seven in the morning, though, and the car was heated throughout the night. So early one morning in January 1938, Messrs. McDonnell, Mittendorf, and Beinecke emerged from that Pullman car in Manchester with our newly purchased skis. We took a taxi to Johnny Seesaw's, which was on Bromley Mountain, five or six miles up the hill from the railroad station. We got there and found the proprietor, Bill Parrish. He looked at us and we looked at him, and we said, "We'd like to rent some rooms here and learn about skiing." He said, "Well, do you fellows have a reservation?" We hadn't thought about a reservation, so this set us back somewhat. Then Bill Parrish squinted at Constantine Mittendorf and said, "You know, you look to me just like Fred Mittendorf." "Well," said Connie, "Fred Mittendorf is my brother." To which Bill Parrish exclaimed, "Fred and I were classmates at Yale!" That solved the reservation problem. We stayed at Johnny Seesaw's for several days. We had a learning experience on the ski slopes and a roaring good time, and we returned to law school refreshed and invigorated for the second semester. Connie Mittendorf and I often went for a quick weekend's skiing during the rest of our law school years, and after the war I returned to Johnny Seesaw's over and over again with my wife and children. It's a low, rambling building with some cottages behind, and people stay there not only in ski season but year-round. It had been built as a roadhouse, before skiing got to be popular, and it was presided over by a man with a Polish name that no one could pronounce. The nearest pronunciation of his name was Johnny Seesaw, and the moniker has stuck ever since.

In the spring of 1938, at the end of my first year at Columbia, Connie Mittendorf suggested that we take a trip to Europe. It was a very interesting experience to see Europe again, especially Germany, as the

Kent Moot Court group after first year final exams, at Coney Island, 1938. Left to right: Constantine Mittendorf, Thomas Crosby, James McDonald, James J. Casey, Edward H. Bennett, Standish Medina, Charles Sloan, Harry Stimpson, William S. Beinecke

continent was increasingly affected by the rising tide of Nazism. Connie and I had booked passage on a German steamship called the SS *New York*. Just before we were set to leave, I got a message from my New Zealand friend John Bull. He and his wife, the former Beatrice Monckton (known to us all as Trix), had taken a trip to England and were returning home across the United States. Unfortunately, they arrived in New York the day after I left for Europe. My mother, however, knowing how kind they had been to me when I was in New Zealand and being the wonderful person she was, knew that they shouldn't be neglected just because her thoughtless son was going off to Europe. She got in touch with them, had them out to our house in New Jersey when they arrived, and arranged for her younger sister Emmy Lou and Emmy Lou's husband, Paul Liston, to have a nice visit with John Bull and Trix. I was gratified that my mother did that, because I couldn't really change my travel plans. The *New York* was full of young people, so we had a happy time during the week it took to get to Hamburg. There was a group of girls on board, mostly from the South, who were touring Europe under the wing of a lady who took groups of young women there every year. Our paths crossed from time to time during our travels in Europe that summer.

The book that was on my mind that summer was *The Way of a Transgressor*, a personal recollection by a newspaper reporter named Negley

Farson, who was a contemporary of my father's at Andover. Farson had been a reporter during World War I and had traveled around Europe a great deal in the postwar years. He made an extraordinary trip in the 1920s from the North Sea to the Black Sea by sailboat. It's possible to do that today, since a new canal link has recently been opened through Germany that passes right through Nuremburg. But at that time, Farson had to take the old Ludwig's Canal, which had been begun by Charlemagne and by the 1920s was totally disused and overgrown with weeds. Farson and his wife sailed the boat from Holland up the Rhine to the abandoned canal, where they unstepped the mast and Farson had to haul the boat through the locks over the Frankischer Jura mountains. They emerged at Ratisbon in southern Germany onto the upper Danube, and as they came downstream, people gathered on the bridges to see them and were amazed. This was the first time in decades, perhaps centuries, that anyone had come from upstream in a sailboat. Farson and his wife rerigged the boat and then went all the way down the Danube to the Black Sea. The Danube is the boundary between Serbia, Romania, and Bulgaria, and they were periodically shot at by hostile forces on one shore who thought they belonged to hostile forces on the other shore. I've always thought that Farson's trip across Europe by sailboat was one of the greatest adventures I ever read about.

Connie and I were not about to duplicate Farson's feat, but we did plan to rent a car and travel around Central Europe and Germany, revisiting some of the places I'd been with my parents the year before. Connie knew German pretty well, and he also knew about Aunt Alice. So we went right to Leipzig, where we stayed with her and renewed our friendships with our cousins. Living conditions in Leipzig at that time were acceptable, but there were some privations. Aunt Alice wanted to serve eggs to us, which she knew we liked, but eggs were in short supply. She had to send somebody around town to various places to purchase eggs.

While we were in Leipzig, Connie and I rented a Horch, a German car comparable to an American Packard or Pierce Arrow. It wasn't quite of the quality of a Mercedes Benz or a Daimler, but it was a good touring car, open at the sides with no windows. We had arranged to meet up with Billy Leake and his sister Virginia, whom we had met on board the *New York*, and we recruited our cousin Alli to come along. So we traveled around Germany, three young men and two young women, along with our baggage, in this big old-fashioned touring car.

In Munich, we went to a restaurant called the Schwarzwälder, which was superb. (I remembered it so well that when Betty and I

returned to Munich in 1991 on a Yale trip, we had dinner there once
again. It's down a side street just a little way from the Bayerischer Hof.)
While in Munich, we intercepted the group of southern girls we had
met on board the *New York*, and one evening Connie and I and three of
these young ladies went to the Hofbrau House. That was, and still is, a
cavernous beer-drinking place frequented by young people, and there
were a number of swaggering young German military personnel there
in uniform. They'd had a couple of beers, as we had, and one of them
came up to our table and said that we had one too many young women
in our party and that one of the girls should go with the Germans.
These young American girls were not inclined to go anywhere with
those Nazi soldiers, and so both Connie Mittendorf and I rose to our
feet and told them that they shouldn't come around and make any such
suggestions. The young ladies were out with us and they were going to
stay with us. I told the Germans to go away and gave one of them a push
in his chest for emphasis. That produced a tempest, to put it mildly.
The soldier reared up and pulled a dagger from his belt. He said that
my pushing him was equivalent to pushing the Führer, an insult to
Hitler, and he'd meet me behind the Hofbrau House, where we could
attend to each other. I wasn't about to do any such thing, and discretion
proved the better part of valor. Connie, the three young ladies, and I
eventually went home without any further interactions with the soldiers.

There were a lot of young men in uniform in Germany in the
summer of 1938. A great many of these people were very truculent, full
of feelings of anger and resentment about people to the west of them. I
could understand that they would feel that way about the French or the
English, but I was surprised that they resented Americans, too. There
was a violent and belligerent feeling in the air in Germany in those
days, so different from the Germany of today. Germans today in my
experience are polite, warm-spirited, and welcoming to visitors. On the
other hand, we read in the newspapers about how they can't stand the
Turks and Eastern Europeans living there, or that at best they tolerate
them as temporary visiting workers. We live in a country that has managed to integrate so many different peoples of so many different ethnic
and cultural backgrounds that we find it difficult to visualize a nation
that is so homogeneous.

The five of us continued our trip around Central Europe in the
Horch. According to our rental terms, we could not take the car outside
the Reich. Austria had not long before become part of the Reich under
the Anschluss, so we were allowed to drive there, but we had to leave the

car in Vienna and take a train in order to visit Budapest. In Budapest, we stayed at the Pension Grimm, an inexpensive guest house that was a step up from a youth hostel. It was filled with young people, including many Americans and Western Europeans, who found Budapest an exceedingly pleasant place to spend the summer holidays. Our time together there was convivial and lots of fun.

We returned to Vienna and headed for Switzerland, but we left the car, along with most of our luggage, in Freiburg, not far from the Swiss-German border. We boarded a train there, and in Switzerland we rented a smaller car and drove through the Alps. Once while driving through the mountains, we stopped by a roadside meadow for a picnic lunch. There was a little stream nearby, and after we had finished lunch, Connie took a nap on the grass and the two girls and I went down to the stream. We were wading in the water when we heard a commotion up by the roadside. We came running up carrying our shoes and socks, and saw Connie confronting a furious Swiss farmer. The farmer had come along while Connie was sleeping and had woken him up, told him that he was ruining the grass where the farmer's herds grazed, and demanded that he get up and get away from there. To emphasize his point, he struck Connie a couple of blows with the stick he was carrying. Connie didn't like that much, so he took the stick away from the farmer and broke it across his knee, which enraged the farmer. At that point the girls and I reappeared, and we decided that we should drive off before this very annoyed Swiss farmer rallied his friends to his side.

We didn't stay in Switzerland long, and upon returning to Freiburg we continued on to Leipzig, where we turned in the Horch. Connie Mittendorf's skill in dealing with the world was on full display on that occasion. The Horch had come with tires made of ersatz rubber, an unreliable synthetic material that was easily punctured. Every time we got a flat, we had to take the luggage out of the car, get out the old-fashioned jack, and change the tire, which was a lot of work. Eventually Connie became so annoyed that he bought a new set of tires. As we were turning the car in, Connie told the renter the sad story of the ersatz tires, pointed out that he had been forced to purchase new tires that were right there on the car, and offered to make them available to the renter in exchange for a credit against the cost of renting the Horch. The car renter refused to pay for the tires, but he didn't realize what a resourceful fellow this Mittendorf was. Connie said, "Well, that's all right. The car will stay here, but those tires belong to me, and I'm going to take them with me." And he got out the jack and began to take the tires off. You can imagine what happened. A compromise was reached, and Connie extracted a credit.

Connie and Alli and I returned to Aunt Alice's home in Leipzig, and we said goodbye to Bill and Virginia Leake. We didn't see them again, although we corresponded with them for a while after they had returned to Tacoma, Washington. It was while we were in Leipzig that Aunt Alice and her eldest child, Edwin, came to a parting of ways. I couldn't help but overhear a strong argument between them, though I don't know what they said because it was in rapid German and I didn't want to hear it anyway. Edwin went out of Aunt Alice's life and her business at that time. I don't know what he went on to do, nor do I have any idea what he did in the war. I know nothing about him, and I had no knowledge of him from the last time I saw him in 1938 until I learned of his death ten years or so ago. I think his brother, Berni, whom I have kept in touch with and see from time to time, knew where Edwin was and what he was up to. But Berni was not about to tell me anything about him. It was an unfortunate family rift, and I think it might well have involved the political situation in Germany. Edwin Weickert was the kind of person who would have been very pro-Hitler. I knew Edwin, and I could see why people wouldn't like him. He tried to be too domineering for his own good.

We were all in a strange family situation, where part of our family was German at a time when the Nazis were taking over Germany and America and Germany were headed for war. The separation would bear tragic fruit, and in December 1943 cousin Putti's young daughter Ursula would be killed in an Allied bombing raid that destroyed her family apartment in Leipzig, the hospital and clinic that Putti ran with her husband, and most of the city. I can't now reconstruct how I felt about the growing tension between Germany and America in the late 1930s or how my family felt about it. Perhaps the older people in my family in America felt that we were heading for war. I don't believe that I thought that. In that summer of 1938, we knew that Hitler had taken over Austria, had remilitarized the Rhineland, and was threatening to dismember Czechoslovakia. There was definitely a feeling of menace and tension in Germany, but I don't think any of us knew that there was going to be a war in another year's time or had any inkling of how horrific it would be.

My aunt Alice had led an interesting life. Born and raised in New York, she had emigrated in 1901, when she was about twenty. She was a rarity in having been accepted into the tight German social circle in which her husband moved—owning a business at that time conferred privileged status—while remaining an independent American woman. She was fluent in English, German, and French. After her husband died in 1929, and she became president of J. D. Weickert, she showed her great administrative talents, and when the company was incorporated in 1938, just about the time when Edwin was separated from it, she became the sole owner. My grandfather had asked her to come back to America when her husband died, but she said that she couldn't do it. Her four children had no background other than German, and she wanted to continue the family business. In the 1920s, at least, Aunt Alice also believed that World War I had been "the war to end all wars" and that there would be no more hostilities between the Germans and the Americans. I'm not sure she still thought that by the time I visited her in 1938. Once or twice when I was with her alone, she indicated that she didn't have much sympathy with the Nazis. But she was very careful in expressing herself even then, and she never said such things in the presence of her children. While Edwin may have been the only true Nazi sympathizer in the family, the other children had also been affected by growing up in Hitler's Germany. Once during that summer, when we were in Switzerland and stood gazing at the Alps, my cousin Alli said, "You know, this country will all be Germany's soon. The Führer will make it happen." I knew that was a thoughtless statement, so I didn't react, but Connie Mittendorf absolutely blew his top. He told Alli she was crazy, that Switzerland had been a neutral country for centuries. He was furious. Alli didn't argue. I think she was amazed at the virulence of Connie's reaction to what she thought was an innocent comment.

Edwin Weickert kept bees, and when my father had visited Aunt Alice in the course of our family visit the year before, he had immediately become enchanted by the unique German beehives. Back in the States, my father read every apian book he could find and placed an order for a shipment of beehives to be sent from Germany to America. When I visited Germany in 1938, my father instructed me to bring back the shipment. The crate was formidable; it must have been an eight-foot cube. I remember the US customs inspector looking at me as if he thought I was crazy when I told him the crate contained beehives. My father was delighted. He acquired all the proper beekeeping gear: the gown, the masks, and the gloves. The project was a great success. At one point my father had twenty-four hives going in Madison, and by experimenting with different kinds of pollen, he was able to create some very exotically flavored honey. He gave a lot of the honey to hospitals in the area, especially to the Morristown Memorial Hospital. Eventually he passed on his entire beehive collection to my friend Barclay Morrison, who was then living in Morristown, New Jersey. Barclay in turn eventually gave it to friend nearby, and it may still be going today.

In the fall of 1938, after I had returned home from Germany, Chamberlain went to Munich and capitulated to Hitler, and Czechoslovakia was partitioned. At the time of the deal, much of the United States was preoccupied with a hurricane that was devastating the East Coast, with great loss of life. The hurricane swept across Long Island and the Sound, ravaging the Hamptons and flooding downtown Providence, putting streets, stores, and powerhouses out of business. It marched on through New England, knocking down trees and power lines, before it finally petered out. In those days before satellites, our communication across the Atlantic was by radio and wireless, and the storm knocked those communications out. As a result, much of what was happening with the takeover of Czechoslovakia was not reported in real time. I don't think that Americans, even had they known what was happening, would have taken any action to stop it. Most people considered each act of capitulation to be a step toward peace. I think the people who were running things thought we were heading toward peace. I didn't think in those terms; I was preoccupied with my life as a law student, trying to do what I had to do.

Connie and I remained in Leipzig for a few days, then continued on through Europe. He wanted to go to Paris and I wanted to go to Berlin, so we arranged to split up, spend a few days in our separate cities, and rendezvous in Copenhagen. I have been to Berlin twice in more recent years, once on a very special Council on Foreign Relations trip and then with Betty on a trip through Central Europe with the New York Philharmonic. I remember those visits more clearly than my first visit to Berlin in 1938. I do recall taking the train from Berlin to Copenhagen, because I was worried about getting into trouble when I purchased my ticket. In those days you could buy "Reisemarks" in New York for about half the regular rate of exchange of the German mark. "Reise" is the German word for travel, and this was a way for the Germans to build international credit; by selling their currency at less than the going rate, they could promote tourist travel to Germany and thus boost their foreign exchange. It was stamped in your passport how many Reisemarks you had ordered in New York, and you could obtain the marks by presenting your passport to a bank in Germany. The Germans had to be sure that these marks didn't compete with the normal currency, so they were to be used solely for hotel accommodations and tourist expenses of that sort and there was a daily quota on them. But the travel marks were ordinary German currency—it was just that you could obtain them at half the usual rate of exchange. I had some of these travel marks when I went to buy my railroad ticket to Copenhagen, and I knew that they weren't supposed to be used for that purpose. So I was a little apprehensive, but I needn't have been, because the man behind the counter never thought to examine my passport when I paid for my ticket with what was, after all, regular German currency.

The train took me north out of Berlin, onto a ferry over part of the Baltic, and then to Copenhagen. I got there a day or two ahead of the projected arrival of Connie Mittendorf. We hadn't arranged to rendezvous at any specific place in Copenhagen. We just said we would meet at a hotel—but there were many hotels in the city. Up to this point Connie had subjected us to various privations, like insisting that we stay in third-class hotels, so I thought, "Now that I'm on my own, I'll make sure that we stay in a really first-class hotel." For years afterward, Connie would hilariously recall that he began his search for me in Copenhagen by going to the best hotel in town—and there I was! That was the only time I've been in Copenhagen, and I've always meant to return. It's a beautiful city, and our hotel was directly across from the Tivoli Gardens. From Copenhagen, Connie and I went down the Belgian coast to the little town of Le Zoute, where we met up with Joy Swinton-Browne, the young English lady whom I had last seen in the Lake Country the year before. She and her mother were staying at the Golf Hotel in Le Zoute, so Connie and I spent a couple of days there, exploring the town and walking on the beach. The highlight of our visit was our trip to the medieval city of Bruges. We floated along its canals in little rowboats, looking at the old buildings and churches. There was some kind of a pageant going in the city square, and I was interested to hear people there speak Flemish, which sounded more like Dutch or German than the French that many Belgians speak. From there we went to Zeebrugge, famous as a German U-boat base in World War I. A museum in town depicted the activities that took place in Zeebrugge during the war, and told the stirring story of a British seaborne commando raid on the submarine base.

After our visit to Zeebrugge, we went to London, where we met up with Connie's older brother, Fred, who was working there. Fred and his first wife, Marie, were kind enough to take us in, and we stayed in their spare room for a few days. Fred had a few copies of a new picture magazine called *Life*. It was put out by Henry Luce, the cofounder of *Time* magazine, who had graduated from Yale fifteen years or so before I did. I had never heard of *Life* before, although it had been out since

1936, and I thought it was fascinating. Fred had access to a golf course not far from London, and we played a round there. By then it was well past the middle of August, and we had been away from New York since the end of June, and so before long we made our way to our ship in Southampton and returned to the United States.

I did not work in the summers during law school, as I had in my college years. I finished my second year at Columbia in May of 1939. I worked harder in those law school years than I ever had in college, so when the term ended, I enjoyed the summer. I played golf and visited friends here and there. Toward the middle of the summer, I went to stay with my cousin Betsy Beinecke at 'Sconset on Nantucket Island, along with my good friends Ed Bennett and Harry Stimpson, playing golf at the Sankaty Head Golf Club almost every day. Ed had read in the paper about the opening of a highway from Laredo, Texas, all the way down to Mexico City, and he decided that the three of us ought to drive down to Mexico in Harry's Ford. Off we went.

Those were the days before the big divided interstate highways. The roads we traveled were blacktop, two-way US routes, some of which still exist. Most of those routes went directly through towns, and you would have to stop for traffic lights and stop signs, though occasionally an alternate route would bypass the town. The route we took south in 1939 led us directly through Bristol, Tennessee, just across the street from Bristol, Virginia. Virginia is on the northern side of Main Street, Tennessee on the southern side. This stop was of particular interest to me because Bristol, Tennessee, was the birthplace of my maternal grandfather, William Miller Sperry. We proceeded south to Gulfport, Mississippi, a beach resort not far from Biloxi. A certain class of racing yacht was built down there, and Harry Stimpson wanted very much to see the port.

Harry loved sailing, and he also loved to run for exercise. He was a runner long before the great modern fad of jogging came along. Indeed, Harry ran several times in the Boston Marathon and continued to run in it until just a few years ago. As we were driving through the rolling hills of Mississippi, Harry said, "You know, I haven't run for a long time, and I feel like running a mile. Give me a few minutes' start, then go ahead and clock a mile exactly on the odometer, and wait for me there." So Ed and I sat in the car for a few minutes while Harry got out and started jogging along the road. When we drove ahead we caught up to him in no time at all. It didn't seem to us that he'd gone very far, and we told him so! But the road went uphill and down, uphill and down. Since my son Rick later got seriously into running, I know that sort of terrain isn't the easiest to run, so maybe we shouldn't have teased Harry. At any rate, he finally jogged up to our car, in good spirits and in good shape.

We drove on to New Orleans and stayed a night or two in a hotel there, then went through Texas. As we were heading for Laredo, we paid a visit on Barclay Morrison, who was living in Houston. Barclay, who has since died, was about a year older than me. He went to the Pingry School and Andover at the same time as I did but was two grades ahead of me. He studied engineering at Princeton and, when he graduated with the class of '34, got a job with the Shell Oil Company. He had been married in May of 1939 to Polly O'Gorman of Montclair, New Jersey, and I was one of the ushers at his immense wedding. In the summer of 1939, Polly and Barclay had just moved to Houston, and they didn't have a stick of furniture in their new house. We slept on mattresses in their spare room. They introduced us to some of their friends in town, and I played tennis with them at the Houston Country Club. Houston in August is a hot place, and that's where I first learned to take salt tablets if you have been perspiring a good deal. There were little salt tablet dispensing machines right there on the tennis courts, next to the water coolers.

From Houston, we went directly to the border, crossed into Mexico at Laredo, and drove along the well-engineered highway which had just opened that summer. I don't think it had been possible until then to drive a car from the Texas border to Mexico City, although I'm sure the journey had been made by some adventurers who went equipped with spare tires and great supplies of gasoline. The route was the first installment of the Pan American Highway, which was supposed to link the top of North America to the end of South America. The plan never came to be. There are parts of Panama south of the canal that are still not traversable by automobile today, and certainly there are parts of Central America where it would be unwise for a casual traveler to drive. My recollection is that it was about 750 miles from the border crossing to Mexico City, and it took perhaps three days for us to cover that distance. As you crossed the Rio Grande into northern Mexico, the terrain was mostly desert, but then came a very mountainous stretch. The road twisted through many grades and curves and cuts. It had clearly taken a major engineering feat to build the road through this desolate and forbidding landscape. You had to plan your fueling stops very carefully as you traveled this highway. We rarely encountered another car, and the fueling stops were often the only sign of human civilization. Filling stations were still in their infancy in 1939, even in the United States. You got your gasoline at garages, though the gas you pumped was usually distributed by the major oil companies. The fueling stops in Mexico were much more primitive. They were practically the only places to get food as well, and the two places where we stayed overnight were also fueling stops. Often there would be a line of cars at those places, because the gas pumps were hand-cranked and slow, as they were back in the days when my father was running the Studebaker dealership and we had a fuel pump in our garage. By 1939, when we were traveling, most American garages had the power-operated pumps with the big glass tops.

In Mexico City, we toured the buildings and monuments downtown, and saw the famous Xochimilco flower garden. I remember the vendors traveling about in canoes, loaded down with piles of vegetables and flowers. Then we went out to the pyramids that the Aztecs had created, and climbed to the top of the largest one. Harry Stimpson's older brother Eddie, one of the great golfers of his generation, had visited Egypt not long before and had hit a golf ball off the top of the Great Pyramid at Giza. And so Harry carried a golf ball and driver to the Aztec site, and he drove the golf ball off the top of the pyramid in emulation of his brother. Eddie Stimpson had been captain of the Harvard Golf team in the mid-1920s and was good enough to attempt to compete in the national championship, though I don't know whether he ever qualified for match play. He achieved golf immortality by inventing something called the Stimpmeter that is used every day by the people who run the major golf tournaments. It's a very simple device, consisting of a board with a groove in it. You elevate the board to a certain height and let a golf ball roll down it. The distance the ball rolls along the flat part of the green before it stops gives you a Stimpmeter reading, and that tells you the speed of the green. Eddie Stimpson was also a revered member of the Bay State Seniors Golf Association, an organization of which I am a member and in which I participate as a player from time to time. Eddie was one of the heroes of that association throughout his more senior life as a golfer. I never played golf with him, since I wasn't in his class or his age group. He died several years ago. He had three sons, all of whom are good golfers and all of whom I know.

Harry, Ed, and I learned that it was possible to travel farther south to Acapulco on the Pacific side of Mexico, and so we did. Acapulco today is an internationally famous resort, and you can fly there directly from New York. In 1939, Acapulco was an obscure and undeveloped locale that wasn't so easy to reach. The changes that took place in Acapulco between my first visit in 1939 and my next in 1959 were immense. There were only a few hotels in 1939, and they didn't amount to much. In 1959, hotels ran all the way along the beach, and new resorts were being created and expanding up and down the Pacific coast. I can hardly imagine what it must be like there today.

In the late 1930s, resorts like Mazatlán were also smaller and largely undiscovered, and current popular destinations like Cozumel didn't even exist. The reason for the change is not only that people have more vacation time today, but also that modern transportation allows them to go to exotic locales and return in a very short time. Jets have made possible the expansion of these resorts and their ability to attract visitors. When such places had to be reached by sea, vacations there were something only the affluent could afford, both financially and in terms of time. Bermuda was a popular destination before World War II because you could arrive there after a day and a night's travel by ship, spend four or five days in Bermuda, and get back on the ship and come home, all within the space of a week. But you couldn't do that if you wanted to go much farther south. In early 1952, when I was leaving one job and was about to start another, Betty and I decided to take a lengthy vacation in Barbados, a Caribbean island we had heard much about. We flew to Puerto Rico and spent the night in San Juan. On the second day, we flew to Trinidad, stopping at Antigua and a number of other islands on the way. We stayed the night in Trinidad in a small and attractive hotel operated by Pan American Airlines, one of the many guest houses that Pan Am created at airfields all over the world for people temporarily stranded while waiting for the next day's flight to their eventual destinations. The next morning, we got on another propeller plane and flew the short distance to Barbados. The whole journey had taken two days and a fraction of a third. Today when Betty and I go from New York down to Barbados, as we did every January for about a dozen years, we get in a jet and fly directly to Bridgetown, and it takes about five hours. In 1952, it simply took too long to reach Barbados by plane to make it a viable vacation spot for most tourists from the mainland. It was also too far away for most cruise ships, and American tourists there were considerably outnumbered by Venezuelans. Barbados as an important travel spot is a product of the jet age, and the same is true of most other Caribbean islands and resorts like Acapulco.

In 1939, the beaches at Acapulco were not at all crowded, and we went swimming in the Pacific. I was used to the waters of the Atlantic along the Long Island shore, where one dove through the waves without much difficulty, but the Pacific was different. The ocean was calm, but the waves that rolled in to break on the shore were huge and you had to be careful. Not far from the beach was a high cliff overlooking a narrow, rocky inlet. Some of the local boys would dive off the cliff for a small fee, perhaps a peso. It was a high and dangerous dive, but these boys performed the feat with great skill.

We chartered a boat in Acapulco and went deep-sea fishing. We caught a few sailfish, and watched as our Mexican guide caught a sea turtle, a horrible sight. He stood up on the bow as a sea turtle floated by on the water's surface, and drove a harpoon through the turtle's back. The turtle was hauled aboard, wriggling and struggling, kicking his legs as it lay upside down on the deck. The fisherman said with a deep Spanish accent, "Give me a chance, give me a chance," meaning that he wanted everybody to get out of the way so that he could give the turtle the coup de grace, probably the kindest thing to do at that point. It was a cruel process, but turtle meat was a delicacy and brought a good price in the market. We made port and paid off the fisherman, and I don't think we kept any of the fish. I went deep-sea fishing in Mexico again some years later with Betty and good friends Joe and Barbara Jayne, off Cabo San Lucas down at the southern end of the Baja Peninsula. Joe was Dartmouth '36, a friend of his classmate Ben Moyer, and a pitcher on the Dartmouth baseball team.

Harry, Ed, and I drove back to Mexico City, and one Sunday we bought tickets to a bullfight. It was the only bullfight I have ever witnessed, and I found it cruel but interesting. When the bull was led into the arena, picadors on horses stuck daggers into his neck to goad and enrage him. Then the matador entered and played the bull with his red cloak, while the crowd applauded enthusiastically. I remember thousands of people cheering "Olé!" in unison, something that one doesn't forget easily. Eventually the matador gave the bull his coup de grace, just as the fisherman in Acapulco had to the turtle. Horses were brought in, ropes were tied to the dead bull, and the horses dragged the carcass out of the arena. Seven bulls were brought on and killed in the course of the afternoon. I have since read some of Ernest Hemingway's writings about bullfights, but I can't muster up his enthusiasm for them.

I enjoyed Mexico very much. I liked the food and the tequila, which I tried for the first time on my visit, and the whole culture and landscape. I found Mexico less strange than either Ed Bennett or Harry Stimpson did, probably because I had completed my trip around the world only two years before and memories of that trip were still very fresh. Ed had not traveled much at all, and both he and Harry were put off by some of the third-world aspects of Mexico, while I was not.

One night in early September 1939, Harry, Ed and I were having dinner at a restaurant in Mexico City when the news appeared in the evening papers that war had broken out in Europe. There had been one European crisis after another for several years; war was not totally unexpected. Even considering all the events leading up to it, however, the start of the war still came as a shock. We didn't know much Spanish, but we knew enough to understand what "la guerra" meant in the headlines. A middle-aged American couple was sitting at a table nearby, and when they heard the news they were overjoyed. The woman cried out in jubilation, "God be blessed, the British have at last decided to make a stand against those vile Germans," or words to that effect. Ed Bennett overheard that, and he turned to her and frowned and said that she shouldn't be so elated. He told them very solemnly, in typical Ed Bennett fashion, that young men like us would have to fight the war. That dampened their enthusiasm somewhat. The three of us looked upon the start of fighting in Europe with a certain amount of foreboding, because although the United States was not yet involved, if it did enter the war all of us most likely would have to go. And indeed, when America got into the war two years later, all three of us went, and fortunately we all returned. The news of the war sobered us considerably and brought to an end our boyish adventures in Mexico. We decided that we ought to get home and see what was happening. We drove back through Mexico and the American South, and eventually Ed and Harry dropped me off in Madison and continued on home to Massachusetts. I returned to law school a week or two later and was caught up in the events of my third and final year at Columbia.

Ed Bennett returned to Massachusetts after the war to practice law in a famous Boston law firm. He became a judge in one of the trial courts in Massachusetts and served for a long time with distinction. He retired to live in Marblehead, Massachusetts with his wife, Barbara. He fathered three children, two of whom have become lawyers. Harry Stimpson married into the Byrd family of Virginia. He transferred from Columbia Law School to the University of Virginia Law School, which he preferred to Columbia. He became interested in the Foreign Service of the United States and worked as a personal assistant to Secretary of State Christian Herter. In 1960, he ran for Congress on the Republican ticket in Massachusetts, but almost any Republican running for office in Massachusetts at a time when Jack Kennedy was running for president was bound to lose, and Harry was indeed defeated. Eisenhower, before leaving office, named Harry the United States ambassador to Paraguay in 1961. After his return to this country, Harry became an adopted Virginian, participating in the Byrd family apple orchard business as well as the Stimpson family real estate business, which he ran with his brother Eddie after their father passed on. Harry and I still play golf occasionally. He recently had a stroke but has recovered from it very well.

Until my third year, most of my courses were large classes where a professor guided the students' analysis of the assigned cases through Socratic-style questioning. Our curriculum was fixed, and the entire first-year class attended courses as a unit. We were all in one enormous room in the shape of a great amphitheater, with seats rising steeply all around, and way down in the well was the professor who conducted the course. And it was an extraordinary thing to have 180 or 190 people in the same course, working hard and getting something out of it—quite a contrast with some articles I've read lately where teachers lament that they can't control a high school class of forty. Classes of nearly two hundred worked well at Columbia, and we moved together through Torts, Contracts, Criminal Law, Legislation, and DLI. The first year had a sledgehammer impact. I can remember all the courses, professors, the structure of the classroom, and so on. My recollections of the courses I took in my second and third years are less clear. I took a course on New York Civil Practice with Professor Medina and another in the Conflict of Laws with Elliott Cheatham, who also taught Constitutional Law. I also remember a course in Taxation given by Roswell McGill, who was quite a famous professor at that time. I can actually remember more of my professors at Columbia than of those at Yale. Those men were very impressive. One course called Trust and Estates was taught by Richard Powell, an extraordinary man. He had written a textbook that he seemed to know by heart, down to every page reference and footnote. At one point he went around the room asking students where they intended to practice. Most answered New York, New Jersey, Connecticut, Pennsylvania, or the like. Professor Powell would then ask if the student had familiarized himself or herself with a certain case on a certain page that was relevant to the state where he or she wanted to practice. When he posed the question to Connie Mittendorf, Connie replied, "Hawaii," having fond memories of his visits there. Hawaii was then still a territory. This did not faze Professor Powell, who immediately inquired if Mr. Mittendorf was familiar with the case referred to in footnote zilch on page zap. This *did* faze Connie.

There was a young lady in the class ahead of us named Isabel Basanta who always used to study in the same part of the library as my friends and I, so one spring day as we were hunched over our books, I said to her, "Let's go get an ice cream cone." I was in my early twenties, it was spring, and Isabel Basanta and I went skipping down Riverside Drive holding hands and eating our ice cream cones. But, of course, one of those damned classmates of mine spied us, and for the rest of my law school career I was constantly asked whether I was busy taking Isabel Basanta out for ice cream cones on Riverside Drive. Connie Mittendorf and some of my other dear friends used to tease me to death about that until I was quite fed up.

By the time you finished the first semester of the third year, you wanted to get out and put the bar examination behind you. In other words, the last part of the senior year was a bore. You still had to keep working, but you weren't fired up. You felt that you knew pretty well how to work the cases, and they began to seem repetitive. In the sixty years since I graduated, the people teaching law must have figured out some way to make the last part of the final year more interesting for the students. Toward the end of our third year, a group of us went down to the Stork Club, a well-known nightclub. The group included Jim Casey, Standish Medina (the son of the professor), and Dick Keresey, who was a class behind me. We had along with us two young ladies from Worcester, Frances Dresser and Nan Morse, who shared an apartment next door to Ed Bennett and me and were taking extension courses at Columbia University. It was a very warm and happy evening. The proprietor of the Stork Club used to run around with Ethel Merman, the singer; she was at his table that night. Someone challenged me to invite Ethel Merman to dance, and Medina said, "I'll bet you five dollars you won't invite her to dance." "Oh yes I will," I said, and I walked over to her table. The next thing I knew, I was being escorted to the street by a phalanx of Stork Club waiters. My classmates tried to argue the waiters into letting me stay, but this resulted in all of us being escorted to the street—which doesn't say much for my law classmates' early skill in forensic argument! I have often told Standish Medina that he's never paid the five dollars he owes me, and his response is that I vowed to dance with Ethel Merman and didn't, so therefore he's off the hook!

At the end of law school I took a cram course for the bar examination given by that very same Harold Medina, who was a practicing lawyer as well as a professor. Perhaps as many as a thousand people took the New York Bar Association examination each year, and it seemed like almost all of them took the Medina cram course. I do not remember the cost, but with so many students it was a very lucrative enterprise for him. The course was given in an auditorium on 39th Street between Fifth and Sixth Avenues, and it took place at five in the evening because Professor Medina would come directly from work. The course consisted of a two-hour lecture on the materials that you were supposed to be studying during the day before you went. Well, this was at the end of three years of studying all the time in law school, so my friends and I were going out every night, and sometimes I was out so late that I would have difficulty getting up in time to go to the cram course at five o'clock! During the course of the lecture series, one of Professor Medina's two daughters-in-law had a baby. As I was on my way to the lecture just after that happy event, I stopped at a print shop in Times Square with another of the fellows in the course, and we had a headline made up on a newspaper that said, "Stork Visits Medinas, New York Bar Rejoices," and we put it up on the lectern before he came in. When he saw it, he was so delighted that he turned it around and held it up so that all five hundred or so people in this colossal auditorium could see it.

After the lecture was over, I was talking with Professor Medina, along with two or three friends, and he thanked us for our little tribute. "Now," he said, "you fellows have all been studying very hard"—little did he know—"and you need to have a break in this routine. You fellows know how to get a date. Mrs. Medina's down in the country, so grab a date tomorrow night and let's all go out and have dinner. You meet me up at my apartment." His son Standish exclaimed, "Oh boy!" His father said, "You're married, you can't come." I don't know why Standish was so intimidated; he should have gathered up his young wife, Hope, and come along too. The next evening all eight of us arrived: Connie Mittendorf, Jim Casey, another fellow, and I, and our four dates, including the two young ladies from Worcester. Professor Medina said, "I'm so worn out after these lectures"—and he was, since he put so much into it that he worked himself into a sweat—"that I have to go and take a shower and put on a clean shirt." So the eight of us waited in the lobby of his apartment with two taxicabs idling outside, and when Professor Medina came down, he swept the four girls into the taxicab, and off he went! We followed him to a place in the Bronx called Ben Riley's Arrowhead Inn. He gave me a hundred-dollar bill—the first time I'd ever seen or held one—and said, "Here, Bill, you take care of all the expenses." And indeed, in 1940, a hundred dollars was nearly enough to pay for dinner for the nine of us and the cab rides there and back. It was a grand evening.

About two weeks later I took the New York State bar examination, administered in Washington Square in one of the buildings of New York University. The examination lasted several hours, and I came out of it literally in a daze. I got on a bus in Washington Square and rode all the way up to my apartment at 121st Street and Amsterdam Avenue, still in a daze. I had committed myself totally, and I was completely done in. A few days later I closed up the apartment—Ed Bennett had already gone back to Massachusetts—and went home to New Jersey, and that was the end of my experience as a student. I was one of the fortunate ones who passed on the first try. Some people have to take the bar examination a second time and a third time, and some people never do succeed in passing it; I've known a few. In those days you found out whether you had passed from the *New York Times*. That was your official notification. I opened the *Times* one day to the list of all the people who had passed, and there I was. In due course, you had to go through the necessary formalities to get admitted to the bar. It was not automatic. You had to file documents with the Committee on Character and Fitness, demonstrating to them that you had not been convicted of a felony and things of that sort. I was admitted to the Bar of the State of New York in the early part of 1941.

CHAPTER SIX

Early Employment, the V-7 Program, and Marriage, 1940–1941

I had graduated from Columbia Law School somewhere around the middle of the class. I was not an A student, and I doubt if I was really a B student. I was maybe a low B-minus or high C-plus student. I received one A and one D, but all my other grades were in the B to C range. So I was not the most outstanding candidate Columbia had to offer when it came time to look for a job. In those days, employers did not come to the law schools and business schools to interview students. Instead, it was up to the students to call on the law firms. All through the spring of 1940, I would go down to the major Wall Street firms like White & Case, or Davis, Polk, or Cravath, Swaine, only to find a number of my classmates and several students from Harvard and other law schools also waiting to be interviewed. No one had briefed me on how to be interviewed, and I didn't have anything resembling a résumé. I simply went around from law firm to law firm, and while I was always cordially received, no job came out of my visits. I soon realized that the job offers were being made to the people who were on the law reviews. I learned that the hard way, by the empirical method, in the spring of 1940.

I had another plan in mind. I had gone skiing in Vermont at the end of each first semester at Columbia and had fallen in love with the state. So after I was unsuccessful in getting a job in New York, I thought I might like to be a country lawyer. Through Ed Bennett's father I got a number of introductions to lawyers in Vermont, and I spent several days in late June and early July 1940 driving around the state calling on lawyers. As it turned out, a number of them said they'd be glad to have me work for them if I would work for free. Those Vermont lawyers didn't have very much money, or if they had it they weren't interested in spending it on a young law clerk. Perhaps they thought that if I wanted to come to Vermont that badly, I would do it just for the experience. That didn't appeal to me, so I abandoned the notion. But it was part of my growing awareness that I was facing some difficulties at that point in my life.

After I got back from my trip to Vermont, I went to visit my cousin Betsy Beinecke at 'Sconset. It happened that her close friend Elizabeth Barrett Gillespie was also summering on Nantucket. The Gillespies were regular summer visitors, and in the summer of 1940 they were renting a cottage in Nantucket town, which was a good thing as far as I was concerned. I had met Betty Gillespie in September 1939, when she was visiting Betsy at Walter Beinecke's home in the East 70s in Manhattan. I was just back from Mexico, though I don't think I had much of a tan. Betty was a beautiful young lady with long blonde hair, and I think that for some reason she was not wearing shoes when I first saw her! She was nineteen years old, and she and Betsy Beinecke had graduated from high school a year or so before. They were classmates at the Greenwood School, a good boarding school for girls in Baltimore that has since gone out of business. She was studying music. She was a fine singer and had a marvelous voice—and still has, although she won't reveal it to anyone. I don't know whether she had a real desire to become a professional singer, but she took lessons from a Madame Rio, and one of her heroines was the opera singer Madame Melba.

I was attracted to Betty on first sight, and not long after we met I asked her out to lunch. I asked her to meet me at The Plaza, simply because I thought that was a convenient place to meet, but I think that maybe she misinterpreted the invitation and thought that I was going to take her to The Plaza for lunch. Instead I took her down the street to a Child's restaurant. The Child's restaurant chain in New York no longer exists, but it was the most inexpensive place you could go. Taking someone to Child's after The Plaza would be like inviting some-body to meet you at the Ritz today and then taking them to lunch at McDonald's. I don't think Betty and I had another date for a long time after that. We went out occasionally during my last year at Columbia, but she lived in Stamford, Connecticut, and I was sharing an apartment in New York City with Ed Bennett, so we didn't see each other very often. But in that summer of 1940 on Nantucket, something fell into place and our courtship began. We spent our days together in the sun, we walked along the beach at night, we spent more or less all our time together, and we continued to see each other throughout the fall and winter.

At about the same time, an opportunity to join the navy presented itself. I'm not saying that I seized on it because I'd had difficulty finding a job in the legal profession. But I was in fact unemployed, I was only twenty-six, and the navy was something that I was interested in. I had liked the navy ever since I was a boy. When I was a teenager, I tried to impress girls by telling them what the different ranks in the navy corresponded to in the army: a navy captain was equivalent to an army colonel, a navy commander to an army lieutenant colonel, and so on. Contemporary world events also figured in my considerations. The Germans had made mincemeat of Poland in very short order in the fall of 1939, but things were fairly quiet for the next seven or eight months of "the phony war," as it was called at the time. I knew some people my age who were actually enjoying life in "gay Paree" during the winter of 1939 and 1940, when France was technically at war with Germany. They felt safe behind the Maginot Line, and Paris was still a comfortable place. Then in April of 1940, the Germans launched their blitzkrieg assault on Scandinavia, the Low Countries, and France, bypassed the Maginot Line, and brought France to its knees. I remember the front pages of the *New York Times* each day showing maps with arrowheads indicating the advance of the German armies, how they went all the way to the Channel in no time at all, forcing the evacuation of the British troops from Dunkirk. That evacuation was played up as heroic, but it was simply a military disaster. With all these things happening, it was not unusual for those of us of military age to think about going into the American military.

As a law student I had been caught up in my day-to-day activities and hadn't participated in the bigger political questions. I read the newspapers, though, and was well aware of the burning issue of American intervention versus nonintervention in the European conflict. I knew about the Neutrality Act, and I remember the agitation of the Future Gold Star Mothers of America, an antiwar group founded at Vassar College, and of the America First Committee, the isolationist organization that Kingman Brewster had helped start as an undergraduate at Yale. A future colleague of mine at S&H, Patrick McGee, was a student at St. John's University in New York City in the early 1940s, and he participated in America First activities there. He remembered the prominent role Brewster had played in organizing East Coast universities like St. John's on behalf of the committee. I did not join American First, but neither did I oppose it.

By 1940, however, it was obvious that whether or not the United States would be involved in the war, it needed a much expanded military force. The V-7 program was a crash course created in 1940 to get more officers into the United States Navy. You had to be older than nineteen but younger than twenty-seven to be accepted, and you had to have finished high school and two years of college. I had just passed my twenty-sixth birthday in May of 1940, so I was one of the older enlistees. I signed up for the V-7 program in the summer of 1940, and was informed that on August 19 I would embark on a cruise aboard the battleship USS *New York*.

I knew that if it came to fighting and America was involved, I would go, but beyond that I didn't think about it very deeply. I never thought the plans I was contemplating could come crashing down because I'd have to go and fight in the war. And yet I did think that war was likely. I had the confidence of youth. Even though intellectually I knew that wars take lives, I didn't think war would take my life. Not long ago my grandson and I watched a video about the Civil War, and when I thought about Pickett's Charge at Gettysburg, where the Confederate troops were slaughtered in their unprotected assault across the wheat fields on that hot July day, I wondered whether they knew they were all going to be killed. My own experience is that you don't really think that war is going to get you.

The battleship *New York* (by coincidence the name of the Hamburg-America Steamship Line vessel I traveled to Europe on in the summer of 1938) was moored in the Hudson River, along with the USS *Arkansas* and the USS *Wyoming*, off the New York Naval Militia dock on 135th Street. The USS *Illinois* was berthed at that dock, and sailors took boats from the *Illinois* out to the other ships in the middle of the river. The *Wyoming* looked like a full-fledged man-of-war, but it had been decommissioned for use as a training ship. The gun had been removed from one of its turrets, and the turret had been converted into a small auditorium where students would be seated in a semicircle to listen to a lecture. The *Illinois* was a hulk that had been commissioned in 1901, decommissioned in 1920, then turned into a training vessel for the Naval Militia of New York, a now-defunct naval equivalent of the National Guard. In 1924 she was completely disarmed and rendered unfit for war service under the terms of the Washington Treaty and was turned into a floating armory in the Navy Yard in Brooklyn. In July 1940, preparations were made to use the *Illinois* as a school ship for the training of naval reserve midshipmen, and as I was entering the V-7 program in August, the first class of five hundred V-7 enlistees was returning from its thirty-day cruise aboard the *Wyoming* and starting midshipmen's school on the *Illinois*.

Our V-7 class consisted of fifteen hundred inexperienced kids, mostly recent college grads, who embarked on our naval careers as apprentice seamen, which is a lower rank than private in the army. We were divided into groups of five hundred. My group was assigned to the USS *New York*. The remaining thousand apprentice seamen were assigned to the *Wyoming* and the *Arkansas*, and would accompany us on our cruise at sea. We were additions to the regular crews of those ships, but we were equally part of the navy and subject to military discipline. If we successfully completed our thirty-day training cruise, we would go on to a ninety-day program at a midshipmen's training school, and would emerge as navy officers—the "ninety-day wonders," as graduates of the program were somewhat scoffingly referred to. As it turned out, we were among the last V-7 enlistees to have our thirty-day training cruise at sea. After the bombing of Pearl Harbor, all navy ships were employed in wartime activities and none could be spared for cruising activities. Nor would it have been wise to put a ship at risk in hostile waters by adding a complement of scraggly college students to its regular crew. The thirty-day training period as apprentice seamen continued, but on land, with drills and tasks and duties to attune recruits to the military life.

Once on board the USS *New York*, we were relieved of our civilian clothes, which were stored in a container, to be returned to us at the conclusion of the cruise. We were each issued a number (mine was 295), our navy uniforms, and a small locker in which to keep them. Our naval attire consisted of three sets of white trousers and white T-shirts. One set had to be kept spotlessly clean for Friday inspections, and so was carefully folded up in your locker. The second set you wore every day and washed every night. You had to wash it in one of the vast men's rooms. Those places were hot and steamy, and there we all were, stark naked, vigorously scrubbing our trousers and shirts against the men's room floor so that they would be clean for the next day. We used the third set on the three or four occasions when we went ashore.

We were also issued a little notebook, in which we were supposed to keep a record of the trip and of anything we learned, and a hammock. The hammock consisted of a piece of canvas with holes at either end that we had to rig with ropes, connect to a series of hooks in the "overhead" (the naval term for ceiling), hang up, and sleep in. Few of us had any idea how to rig a hammock, and it wasn't easy. Some of our number weren't as lost as the rest of us because they had spent time at Annapolis or West Point. Either they had washed out because they didn't keep up academically or didn't satisfy the physical requirements or they had left because they didn't like the military program. But they still had had some preliminary training, knew what to expect on the battleship, and knew how to do small but challenging things like rig a hammock. Most of us did not, and it took a while to learn how to do the things that become instinctive to regular sailors. Eventually the rest of us mastered the subtleties of hammock drill. At five o'clock in the morning, you were awakened, and you rolled the hammock up and stowed it in a big pile. At night you had to find your hammock in that pile and hang it up. The early wakeup meant that I was often very tired. I found out that if you climbed up over the top of the hammocks later in the day, you could make a little nest behind the pile and catch a half hour's nap. A few of us did that on occasion.

The navy was not prepared to take five hundred absolutely green college kids aboard a ship, and there was a series of small but significant glitches. After we'd been issued the clothing, the locker, the makings of the hammock, and the notebook, we were assigned mess numbers and mess locations. The mess tables on the *New York* were all hung from the overhead, and at mealtimes they were pulled down and secured to the deck, and the enlisted men sat around the tables to eat. The trouble was that the navy had assigned mess locations to only about four hundred fifty of us. Those poor souls who were not issued mess locations had no place to get anything to eat, and so for several days they had to scrounge food from their luckier friends until the problem was resolved. I remember this because I was one of them.

Another indication that the navy wasn't fully prepared for us was that they had problems keeping us all occupied, and they had us do make-work things like scrubbing decks that were already spotlessly clean. On one of the very first nights out, as the ship headed south, I was assigned to stand watch on the starboard side near the running light. One of the naval officers who had been put aboard to give us some training said, "Beinecke, it is very important that this ship show its running light at all times. You stand here and keep observing this running light to make sure it is burning bright and then report on it to the bridge." He explained to me that I was to pull a flap at the bottom of the speaking tube and yell into it, "Bridge," and a voice at the other end of the tube would say, "Bridge aye." That meant that somebody on the bridge was now in communication with me. I was to say to him, "Starboard running light burning brightly," and he would respond by saying, "Report received." And then half an hour later, I would have to make the same report. The person who would receive this report on the bridge was another clerk like myself who had nothing else to do, and so they put him to work receiving these rather humdrum reports from different places on the ship. I rather doubt that after receiving my half-hourly update he then reported to the officer of the deck that the starboard running light was still burning brightly.

The *New York* was powered by reciprocating engines, with big pistons churning up and down and a lot of visible moving parts. As the high-temperature steam came out of the boiler, it passed through three chambers, each at a different pressure. When the steam in the first chamber was exhausted, it would enter the second and then the third chambers and give a new propulsive shot to the engine. When the steam was finally exhausted, it was condensed, conserved, and reused. I found it interesting to watch the *New York*'s engines in operation. Because I was not an engineer, I didn't realize that what I was looking at was an anachronism. When I returned home and talked about the cruise with my father, who *was* an engineer, he was somewhat skeptical when I told him that the *New York* was powered in this way. As steamships were modernized, the propulsive plant changed over to steam-powered turbines, which were more efficient, could handle super-heated steam at higher temperatures, and could therefore drive faster and also provide electric power as needed. My father had a hard time believing that any naval warship could still be powered by old-fashioned reciprocating engines. But as a matter of fact, the *New York* was not a modern naval warship. It was a vintage 1914 ship, and so was one of the very few in the navy to have this outmoded type of power plant. It occurs to me now that the ferry boats I used to take across the Hudson when I was a boy and the steamer *Mount Washington* I took around Lake Winnipesaukee also had reciprocating engines, with enormous steel pistons moving rhythmically up and down. I was able to persuade my father that I wasn't completely out of my mind when I described how the *New York*'s engines worked.

The first stop on our cruise was Panama, where we received permission to go ashore. There was not a great deal to do there in the few hours that we were allowed. A railroad excursion ran across the isthmus and back, but I can't remember whether or not I took it. We mainly visited places where we could drink, and the sailor's drink of choice in Panama in 1940 was something called rum, gum, and lime. From Panama we sailed to Guantánamo Bay, the American naval base on Cuba. By this time, the routine had become more established. Our training officers, who had been assigned as adjunct members of the crew, were becoming more proficient at what they were supposed to be doing, and our days were better occupied. For example, we had more interesting watches. We got to see the engines in operation and visit the bridge to find out what was really happening. I learned that a battleship is a vast place. The five hundred scraggly college kids aboard were in addition to the regular complement of the battleship, which consisted of about fifteen hundred seamen and a hundred or so regular officers. One night after I had washed my clothing, I left it in a bucket outside my locker and was taken to task by one of the officers. He knew that we didn't know anything, but he had to impose some kind of discipline on me for this infraction. He assigned me to spend the evening assisting in the cleanup of one of the firerooms. The ship had a number of oil-burning boilers that created the steam. This particular fireroom was one that was not operating, so it was called a "dark" fireroom. I made my way there to help clean up, but by the time I arrived the regular ship's crew had matters well in hand, and they were very nice to me and didn't inflict any great hardship. That was interesting, because while the V-7 apprentice seamen intermingled with the regular ship's company in the close quarters of shipboard life, we didn't really interact in any sense. We mostly were kept to ourselves. Another day I was running up a "ladder," the naval term for a ship's staircase, when I ran smack into the captain of the *New York* himself. Of course I was covered with embarrassment and apologized profusely. The captain, who I thought was a very old man—he was maybe in his late forties—said to me, "Son, that's all right, but don't do that to an ensign." I thought that was very amusing and an indication that the captain was a good-tempered man.

The next port of call was Norfolk, Virginia, and then in mid-September we returned to New York, where we disembarked at the naval base on Staten Island, not far from the Narrows. (This base was shut down in the recent downsizing of military installations.) We were handed back the containers with our civilian clothing, I was given a little money to cover my transportation back to Madison, and I made my way to the Staten Island Ferry and back home.

I was told that the navy would call me up for midshipmen's school when I was needed. Another complement of apprentice seamen was embarking on their cruise as we returned. The navy didn't have the infrastructure in place to absorb fifteen hundred V-7 trainees into the midshipmen's schools every ninety days. (Once the war began, of course, they didn't have anywhere near enough officers even though the V-7 program was vastly expanded, and they had to commission people into the navy directly without giving them any training at all.) I was subject to recall by the navy, but I was in civilian life.

I was still jobless, so I had discussions about my career with a couple of my relatives. Austin Dohrman was married to my mother's first cousin and was one of the top officers of the Anaconda Copper Company. He offered to help me find a job with the law firm that represented Anaconda Copper. My uncle Walter Beinecke was in the insurance business, and his principal client was the American Tobacco Company. He said that he would ask his friend George Washington Hill, who was the chairman of the ATC, if he could help me get a job with the law firm that represented American Tobacco. As it happened, the firm that represented both the Anaconda Copper Company and the American Tobacco Company was Chadbourne, Wallace, Parke & Whiteside, and I received an employment offer in late September. By the beginning of October I was at work in the firm, which still exists today as Chadbourne & Parke, and I worked there until May 1941. Its office was way downtown in the Cunard Building (which also housed the offices of the Cunard Steamship Line) at 25 Broadway, facing Bowling Green, right by the Bowling Green stop of the IRT line.

I was paid $1,800 a year as a new associate, $300 a year less than the salary earned by law graduates who were fortunate enough to have loftier credentials. Practically all my salary went to rent and food, and there wasn't anything left over. My father's financial position had improved to the point where he was comfortable again, but I was not relying on him for money. I had rented a room in the Shelton, a hotel on Lexington Avenue and 47th Street, a block or two from the back door of the Waldorf. My room was at the rear of the building on the twentieth floor, pretty high up, but I could still hear every rumble and scrape of the Third Avenue elevated trains as they went rattling by below. I don't miss the Els. The city is well rid of them. They were unsightly structures, and blocked up the street with their support towers, much like the remnants of a railroad that you can see today on the West Side down below the Javits Center.

I was interested in litigation, and so I was put to work under the supervision of Leonard P. Moore, a Columbia Law School graduate, a wonderful man, an excellent litigator, and an excellent person for me to be exposed to. He was quiet, thoughtful, and unflappable. He was my mentor during that first year of my legal career, and I worked on a number of cases under his direction. Leonard Moore eventually became a judge of the United States District Court of New York. He lived in Brooklyn, so I suppose he was first appointed to the Eastern District, but then he became a judge of the Second Circuit Court of Appeals. For years after I returned from the war, I would go down to the Federal Courthouse on Foley Square in lower Manhattan, and Leonard Moore and I would have lunch at an Italian restaurant on Mulberry Street and talk about old times. We became particularly close in the later years of his life, and he and his wife, Patty, were good friends with Betty and me.

I spent much of that year learning my way around the legal profession. One of my first cases involved the Towers Hotel on Willow Street in Brooklyn. Leonard Moore told me to check our office files and prepare a complaint against the transfer agent. I had no idea what he was talking about. All we ever did in law school was read the decisions of the great judges and learn the legal principles that were reported in the casebooks and the collected reports. I knew how to look up cases and read reports, but the practical, workaday stuff that lawyers deal with all the time—preparations of motions, filing documents, and so on—was never taught in law school. So here I was, completely at sea all over again, just as I had been three years before when I started out as a law student! That was another comeuppance. Mr. Moore was very patient and explained that a complaint is the thing that initiates a lawsuit, and a transfer agent in securities law is the body charged with recording the shares of stock in a company. Somehow or other I managed to do what was needed in the Towers Hotel case, and I continued my slow and painful learning process. I learned where the courts were, and how to file briefs. It was an interesting experience, even exciting, and eventually I came to the startling but satisfying conclusion that I was able to do what was needed. But I was really an apprentice. That's one of the things that baffles me about the high salaries that young men and women command today when they come out of law school, because they're still in training in that first year when they're earning $80,000 or $90,000.

Chadbourne, Wallace, Parke & Whiteside was a medium-sized corporate law firm, a fine firm but in the second tier as measured by its number of lawyers, partners, and associates. Its clients included not only the Anaconda Copper Company and the American Tobacco Company, but the two major airlines, Eastern and Trans World. Another client was the company that owned Madison Square Garden, and I remember working on some of its cases. Yet another client for whom I did some work was the Manufacturers Trust Company, one of the constituent banks in the gigantic banking enterprise now known as the Chase Bank. Unknown to me at the time, there was a Beinecke connection to the Manufacturers Trust. My grandfather Bernhard Beinecke was one of the founders of the Germania Bank, which in the anti-German hysteria of World War I changed its name to the Commonwealth Bank and then became one of the constituent banks of Manufacturers Trust. My uncle Ed was actually a director of the Manufacturers

Trust at the time when I was working on some of their securities cases. I was also engaged in a Federal Trade Commission proceeding with the American Tobacco Company.

My work with the American Tobacco Company led indirectly to my giving up smoking cigarettes. In those days before television was of any importance, radio was a major advertising outlet. The American Tobacco Company's advertising slogan was "LSMFT," short for "Lucky Strike Means Fine Tobacco." It had become a household phrase. In one of the "LSMFT" radio commercials, you could hear what purported to be an auctioneer selling a bundle of tobacco in a warehouse down South, running all his words together: "Three-dollar, four-dollar, five-dollar, ten-dollar, fifteen-dollar—sold, American." As a young lawyer I did a lot of work in the office of the American Tobacco Company, and of course when you were there you had to smoke Lucky Strikes. You couldn't smoke Camels or Chesterfields, the two competing brands, because Camels were put out by R. J. Reynolds and Chesterfields by Liggett & Myers. The Philip Morris Company distributed a brand of cigarette called Philip Morris, which probably wasn't even in fourth place. Their ad featured a little page boy who would repeat, "Call for Philip Morris, call for Philip Morris, call for Philip Morris." There was a Federal Trade Commission proceeding brought against all the tobacco companies—or perhaps it was only brought against the American Tobacco Company—and the FTC proceeding was checking out the advertising. My job was to examine the language of these radio commercials to see whether they said anything that came within the limiting areas of the FTC complaint. I had piled up on the floor stacks and stacks of scripts of the commercials for the preceding two or three years. I read one after another, and I had to be liberal in my interpretation as to what met the embracing language of the complaint or whatever the legal document was that we were going to answer. One night I was working late at the office of the American Tobacco Company. I went across the street to a Schrafft's restaurant, came back to the office, and prepared to open a new package of cigarettes. I looked at the scripts of these commercials and looked back at the cigarettes. I said to myself, "What nonsense!" and threw the pack of cigarettes across the room. The next morning I went out and bought a pipe. It wasn't the idea of health or anything else that caused me to give up cigarettes but the nonsense in the advertising that I was supposed to be supporting. I smoked a pipe for the next several years.

All of us young lawyers were expected to work overtime and at night. I got to work at 9:30, worked through the day, had dinner at

Schrafft's or some other restaurant in the neighborhood, then went back to work for two or three hours. I worked a minimum of ten hours a day, five days a week, and that was the standard pattern for rising young lawyers in that era. There was time to do things outside of work, but work came first. I shared an office with a man whose name I can't remember. I was one of five recent law school graduates who were hired at Chadbourne that year. Another was Sid Thaxter, whose father was a distinguished lawyer and judge in Maine. Sid served on submarines during the war, then went into his family's law firm in Portland. Later, when I was the head of S&H, Sid Thaxter became our Maine counsel and took care of some problems we had there, and I visited him at his lovely summer home on Cushing Island in Casco Bay. On another occasion, Sid was skiing with me in Alta, Utah, when I was rammed from behind by a wild young skier. Sid kept me from assaulting the out-of-control skier and assisted me down the mountain. The other recent law graduates working at Chadbourne in the early 1940s were Gordon Bickert from Minnesota, Bob Meisenholder, and Bill Cann. They were all assigned to different departments and I never worked with them, but because we were all juniors in there together, I knew them in a social sense. I also knew one of my superiors, Bill Harnisch, fairly well. He was in litigation and I was assigned to assist him on some of his cases. I got along with everybody at the firm, although I didn't make any longtime friends that year other than Sid.

I had continued to see Betty Gillespie throughout the fall of 1940, and I was invited to stay at the Gillespies' in Stamford on many occasions. Their family home still stands on Newfield Avenue, not far from the Merritt Parkway. I would often drive up to Stamford on the Merritt in my Mercury, and occasionally Betty and I would go out dining and dancing in New York at the Stork Club and LaRue and a few other places. Sometimes I would take the train, and there were many Monday mornings when Betty's father, Richard H. Gillespie, would drive me to the station in Stamford, so I could catch an early train and make it to my office by 9:30. Mr. Gillespie was a clean-shaven man of medium height and good physical presence, who was always well turned out. He was an active man and had been commodore of the Stamford Yacht Club. He sailed his boat on cruises up the New England coast and often took along his son, Richard, Betty, and her sister, Jean. He ran the family business, Gillespie Brothers, Inc., which owned the business acquired by his uncle William Gillespie in 1867. Gillespie Brothers published the two principal newspapers in that area, the *Stamford Advocate* and the *Greenwich Time*. He was editor and publisher of the *Advo-*

cate. The Gillespie family was a prominent family in Stamford and still is. Stamford in 1940 was an industrial city, but it didn't have all the glass high-rise buildings that it now has. It had an active downtown area, with shops and businesses, in contrast to the gargantuan office buildings of today and the downtown that empties out like a ghost town at night.

There came a day when I asked Betty if she would be willing to marry me. How did I decide that she was the one? I don't know. I didn't go through any rational process. I suppose that in something as important as a marriage, I really should have gone through a rational process and examined all the pros and cons, marshaled the facts, and prepared a brief as I had been taught to do as a lawyer. But I didn't do any of that. It sort of came upon me, and it came upon Betty, and we were swept along. It was around Christmastime in 1940, and we were driving from her house to a party in Greenwich. I thought it was as good a time as any to pop the question, and besides, I had her captive in my car, so she couldn't escape. She didn't say yes right away, but she gave it some thought and finally she agreed. We announced our engagement in February 1941, set the date for May 24, and had a little party in Stamford when we made the news known to the world.

In the spring of 1941, I went down to Lexington, Kentucky, with some of the other younger lawyers in Chadbourne, Wallace, Parke & Whiteside to represent the American Tobacco Company in a proceeding brought by the US Department of Justice against several of the tobacco-processing companies. The reason the proceedings were held in Kentucky, I'm sure, was that the government felt that they would do better against the tobacco-processing companies in the area where the tobacco was actually grown. If a jury was to be selected, it would presumably be more favorably disposed toward the tobacco growers than toward the industrial giants that processed tobacco into consumable products. The government had issued a subpoena duces tecum, a document requiring a person to appear with the papers and documents to be employed in what is called a discovery proceeding. It fell upon the young lawyers of our office to examine the relevant letters and other documents to see whether they had to be produced for the government's inspection in compliance with the subpoena duces tecum. So I and a half dozen of my colleagues went to a tobacco warehouse in Lexington, and there we saw hundreds and perhaps thousands of manila file boxes full of old letters and documents of the American Tobacco Company. There was no way we could have examined all those documents within the amount of time we had available, so the more senior lawyer in charge of our activity devised a program. A large group of clerks and other employees of the ATC went through the files with information sheets we had prepared that outlined in very clear but broad terms the papers that should be produced. After they had culled those particular needles from the haystacks, we went through the papers to see how many of them were needed to comply with the somewhat narrower subpoena duces tecum. While I was in Lexington, I received word from home that I had received my orders to go into the

Bill and Betty Beinecke coming down the aisle after their wedding in Noroton, Connecticut, 1941.

navy, and so I informed my employers that I had to sever my relationship with them to go on active service.

On May 24, not many days after I returned from Kentucky, Betty and I were married in a small Presbyterian church in Noroton, Connecticut. It was a wonderful spring day, and the reception was held on the grounds of the Gillespie home. My best man was my law school friend Ed Bennett, and the ushers included my brother, Richard, my boyhood friends Ben Moyer and Dean Speir, and my college roommate John Dean. Betty's attendants included her sister, Jean, her cousin Jane (Babbie) Gillespie, my cousin Betsy Beinecke, with whom she had gone to Greenwood, and two other school friends, Ann Teall and Bobbie McDowell. My parents and many of my relatives were there, and so was Betty's family. Alas, her father was not among us. In January, some time before we announced our engagement, Mr. Gillespie had had a heart attack and died. He was sixty-four years of age and had appeared to everyone to be in good health. That was a sad and completely unexpected event.

The wedding party. Left to right: Jane Gillespie (Babbie), Margaret McDowell (Bobbie), Jean Gillespie, Edward H. Bennett, Elizabeth Gillespie Beinecke, William Sperry Beinecke, Sally Gillespie, Anne Teall, Betsy Beinecke Shirley.

Betty and I spent our wedding night at The Plaza Hotel, which seemed an appropriate place, and then set out on our honeymoon by taking a train to my Sperry grandmother's home in Jupiter, Florida. That was the beginning of a happy and durable marriage. There have been ups and downs, as there are in any relationship, but we have grown together over the years. The fact that our marriage has endured as well as it has says a great deal for Betty, because she has had to put up with a lot, but somehow we've come out of it successfully. Betty and I spent our honeymoon in the caretaker's cottage of my grandmother's place since I didn't have enough money to take us to a resort or a nice hotel. We swam from the dock and in the ocean and went boating along the Loxahatchee River. It was the last time I visited the old Sperry site in Jupiter, because my grandmother finally sold the property after World War II. I occasionally go to that part of Florida today, and we have driven by the site of my grandparents' property. There's a fish restaurant right there by the bridge as it crosses the Loxahatchee River on Route 1, and the rest of the property has been converted into trailer camps. The only building of my grandfather's that's still standing is the boathouse. If you look sharp, you can spy it from the bridge crossing the Loxahatchee River, southeast from the northern shore.

Neither Betty nor I had been to Key West, so we borrowed a car, stayed a night in Miami, and drove over the long series of bridges that connect the mainland of Florida to the Keys. The highway was relatively new. Mr. Flagler's Florida East Coast Railroad, which had once run Pullman cars all the way from New York to Key West, had been blown out by the hurricane of 1926. The highway was built a few years later on the railroad bridges and structures that remained. We had a pleasurable time in Key West, then drove back to Jupiter, said our goodbyes, and took a train back to the Northeast.

Betty had the good sense to realize that now that we were married we were a family, even if only a two-person family, and we ought to have a home. There was a small cottage on the Gillespie family property in Stamford that she turned into a home for us that summer. It was a two-story structure not far from the barn, across from the garden, and it served as a very nice home of sorts during the early days of our marriage.

CHAPTER SEVEN

Midshipmen's School on the USS *Prairie State* and Service Aboard the USS *Buck*, 1941–1943

he next step in the naval parade took me from apprentice seaman status to midshipmen's school. I had received orders to report to the former USS *Illinois*, now renamed the USS *Prairie State*, on June 12, and so that morning my bride of two-and-a-half weeks drove me to the dock at 135th Street. On the way we picked up my dear friend John Bainbridge at his apartment in Gramercy Square, and John and I started the next stage in our training to become naval officers. We were processed immediately and issued our uniforms. As it was summer, we wore sailor suits—white blouses and white trousers—and round midshipman's caps, which differed from the regular sailor's cap in having dark blue edging all the way around. The conditions of the V-7 program had stipulated that it would accept only single men, but there was nothing in the regulations that said that you had to remain single until you were commissioned. By this point I was no longer single, and I thought I owed the navy an explanation. So when I went aboard, I sought out the executive officer of the *Prairie State* and told him the facts of my case. He remonstrated with me and told me that I should not have gotten married, but finally he said, "All right then, but don't expect any special consideration." I didn't expect any, and I didn't get any.

The *Prairie State* was an old hulk moored to the banks of the Hudson at 135th Street, where a major sewage disposal plant now stands. The hull had a deck with a gray shed over the top of it, and it didn't have any guns or other arms. The navy had done a considerable amount of work to make it a place where five hundred young men could eat and sleep and be trained. Space was limited, which meant sleeping

161

in three- or four-tier bunks, where your head was very close to someone else's feet. There were not enough classrooms on board the *Prairie State* to accommodate everybody, so the navy took over the New York Central freight warehouse as an adjunct classroom. The warehouse stood next to an old railroad line that still carries trains north out of Penn Station, passing underneath and alongside the West Side Highway. The navy had refurbished the building and had classrooms on two floors, but there were no corridors, so in order to get to the back of the building you had to go through all the other classrooms on that floor. That would have been inconvenient if the school had not operated under military discipline, but the navy simply marched its midshipmen through the building until they had reached their assigned classrooms, and at the end of the period everyone lined up and marched back out again. Our drilling ground was the yard outside the warehouse, and we had room enough to do only a left face, right face, and about face. Our other facility was a dock just to the south of the *Prairie State*, on the site of the Department of Sanitation dock today. It was called the *Sylph* dock because the training ship berthed there was a yacht called the USS *Sylph*, which the navy had acquired from its civilian owner. We were marched out to the *Sylph* dock to do calisthenics. Periodically a few midshipmen went out on the *Sylph*, which was manned by a regular navy crew, for a cruise down to the neighborhood of Sandy Hook and back.

Classes aboard the *Prairie State* began as soon as everyone was processed and assigned their bunks and lockers, and ran on a rigorous schedule from then until the fall. In ninety days, the navy couldn't possibly cover what it spent four years teaching the midshipmen at the Naval Academy, so it tried to approximate half the standard midshipman course. All the officers who graduated from the Naval Academy's regular four-year course had some background as both engineering officers and deck officers, but the accelerated V-7 course trained midshipmen in one discipline or the other. An engineering officer is concerned with the machinery that powers a ship while the deck officers maneuver the ship and direct other activities, such as firing the guns, communicating (including signal flags as well as wireless and radio), and performing celestial navigation. The *Prairie State*'s assignment was to commission 250 EVGs, for Engineering Volunteer General, and 250 DVGs, for Deck Volunteer General. Since not enough people had volunteered to be engineering officers, the balance was made up by arbitrarily directing certain midshipmen to engineering. I was one of those selected to be an EVG, and that presented a problem because engineering was absolutely foreign to me. I'd been trained as a lawyer, and I had no training in engineering or mathematics or anything like that. I inquired about changing my designation, but was told that I didn't have any choice. The midshipmen who were candidates to be deck officers studied navigation, seamanship, and communications. I, on the other hand, had to take courses in electrical engineering, boilers (which had to do with the operation of steam turbines aboard ship), and damage control or some other beastly subject. The electrical engineering was the worst, and I found it completely incomprehensible.

The five hundred men aboard the *Prairie State* constituted a regiment of two battalions, each consisting of two companies, half of them engineers and half deck officers. The companies were subdivided into platoons and squads, and the people in your squad were the ones you went to class with. Our squads were arranged alphabetically, so I was in class with a fellow named Wallace Borker, who had graduated with highest honors in engineering from Cornell University, though he ended up as a lawyer. My friend Wally never seemed to be paying any attention in class. He would have his notebook at any angle in front of him, and he'd just sort of scrawl something diagonally across the page. But of course he always got a perfect score on his tests, because he

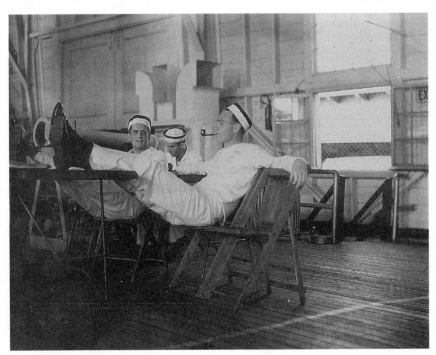

Aboard the Prairie State, *with a pipe.*

already knew all this stuff better than the instructor, who was only a young ensign who had graduated from the preceding ninety-day training session.

You had classes and exercises during the day, study hall in the evening, and were supposed to be in bed at ten o'clock at night. There were frequent quizzes, and if your grades were unsatisfactory you were put on something called the "tree." Normally you had every weekend free except the fourth weekend of the month, when you had a special watch duty. But you wouldn't get the weekends off if you were on the tree, and I was in danger of being forever there because engineering was completely mystifying to me. Of course I wanted to get off the *Prairie State* as often as I could to see my bride. It was a crazy way to start off on a marriage—to be married barely two weeks and then be cooped up on a training ship. I saw Betty on our free Wednesday afternoons (which for some obscure reason were called Ropeyarn Sundays), and sometimes we'd drive up the parkway and get a sundae. The prospect of losing my free weekends drove me into a frenzy. So I had to request special permission to stay up after hours each night and do late study. I received permission and damn near every night I stayed up for hours laboring over this awful stuff that I shouldn't have been studying in the first place. And perhaps because the power of matrimony was compelling me, somehow I managed to get off the tree.

Sargent Shriver, a Yale graduate in the class of 1938, was in my class on the *Prairie State*. He had not yet married John F. Kennedy's sister Eunice, but he was already pretty much of a politician. He was highly regarded and was singled out for a prominent role. Another of my *Prairie State* classmates was Robert Morgenthau. Once on one of my free Wednesday afternoons, Betty was visiting. I was standing on the deck talking with her and some other midshipmen. Suddenly Betty said to me, "What's that fellow doing there behind you?" I looked down over my shoulder, and there was someone kneeling on the deck with matches, trying to give me a hotfoot. His plan was to stick the sulfur tip of a match into my shoe just above the sole, then light the other end. The match would burn slowly until it hit the sulfur tip, and then all of sudden it would burst into flame and I would be hopping around like mad with a scorched foot. I saw a fellow get a hotfoot one time, and he ended up with a serious blister. So I looked down and I saw this person sticking a match in my shoe, and I stamped my foot and said, "What the hell are you doing there?" I knew, of course, that he was trying to give me a hotfoot. That midshipman's name was Bob Morgenthau, who is now the district attorney of New York. I have told that story many times over the years to people who live in New York, and they always say, "I can't imagine Robert Morgenthau doing anything like that." Well, Bob Morgenthau did do that. We've remained good friends, although we don't see each other often. Shortly after I became president of my company I got a letter from him that said, "I guess that hotfoot got you going!" So he remembered the incident as I did. I didn't make many friends on the *Prairie State*. We were brought together for such a short time, and the military organization and atmosphere of intense study were not conducive to making friends.

We graduated on September 16, 1941. Treasury Secretary Henry Morgenthau, Jr., Bob's father, was at our graduation, though I can't remember whether he actually handed out our commissions. We had a postgraduation dance at the Terrace Cascades, the roof restaurant of the now-defunct Biltmore Hotel, which stood a block or two south of where the Roosevelt Hotel is today. We all wore white uniforms, with our ensign's shoulder boards proudly displayed.

As we were about to graduate from the *Prairie State*, we were all given the opportunity to ask for the type of duty we wanted. I couldn't indicate that I wanted some duty other than engineering; I was stuck with that. But I could choose to go with the fleet in the Atlantic or the Pacific, and I could indicate the type of ship I wanted to go on. Some people in our class who had very high standing, like Wally Borker, were selected to go to advanced technical schools. Some of them went to England to study the latest development in navigational technology, which, although none of us knew it, was radar. I recently read about a $15 billion submarine-detection installation on the ocean floor that the navy is now allowing to be put to civilian uses such as tracking blue whales and things of that sort. The navy today is technologically alert, and it was in 1941 as well, though not to the same degree. I opted for destroyers in the Atlantic, and I got my wish. When my orders came through, I was told to report for duty to Newport, Rhode Island, in two weeks.

Betty and I packed up the car and drove to Conifer, a small resort in Maine a little to the west of Portland. It had cottages, a lake, and a few boats. We went boating and canoeing, we played tennis and golf, and I think we may have done some fishing. On our way down to Newport, we stopped off to see Andover play its first football game of the season. It was a lovely, clear fall day. As Betty and I were sitting in the stands, I saw one of the oldest Andover faculty members nearby, and I said hello. He replied, "Hello, Beinecke." I was amazed that he had recognized me. Then he asked, "How are your brothers?" He had confused me with my father and my uncles, who had been at Andover in the early years of the century. There had been several Beinecke boys at Andover over the years, and we had all run together in this old master's mind, even though a generation separated my father and his two brothers from me.

Betty and I arrived in Newport, and I checked in with the naval authorities there. The Newport base was a collection point for the East Coast, where sailors would go to wait until Washington assigned them to a ship. The ship went about its duties, and the people who were assigned to it had to find it, wherever it was. I asked about my assignment at the naval headquarters every day, and they kept saying, "Come back tomorrow." Betty and I got a room at the Viking Hotel for a day or two, then arranged to move into a less expensive boardinghouse where a lot of young naval officers and their wives were staying. There wasn't much to do but wait, and we whiled away the time with the other officers. Finally the authorities told me that my ship was at Norfolk, Virginia, and they arranged for me to take a boat up Narragansett Bay to Quonset Point and then a PBY patrol plane to Norfolk. I was reporting aboard ship for what could be quite a long time, and I had a substantial amount of gear. By that point, I had the summer white uniform I had worn at the *Prairie State* graduation, the several blue officer's uniforms I had purchased upon graduation, some khaki uniforms, the shirts and black ties that went with the uniforms, appropriate shoes, and the rest of it. I cannot for the life of me remember how I got it all to Norfolk.

In October 1941, I reported to my ship, the USS *Buck*, in Norfolk. The *Buck* was a destroyer, and a rather new ship. It had gone into commission in mid-May 1940 and had been moved from the Pacific Fleet to the Atlantic Fleet not long before I met up with it. A destroyer is a relatively small class of combatant ship. The ships that made up the navy's fighting fleet in those days included aircraft carriers, battleships, cruisers, destroyers, and submarines. There were light and heavy cruisers; the distinction had to do with the size of the guns (six-inch versus eight-inch) rather than with tonnage. Destroyers were escort and combat vessels. Submarines were used to prey on enemy warships and merchant shipping, carry out surveillance, and perform occasional special missions, as when they evacuated some nuns from Bougainville in the Solomon Islands. The navy had lots of support ships, including supply ships, repair ships, tankers (which the navy called oilers), and hospital ships. Then there were various kinds of patrol craft, including the PY class of yachts (such as the *Sylph*) that the navy had taken over, and the destroyer escorts, which were smaller than destroyers and didn't have the same speed or combat capability. The destroyer-escort classification was DE, while DD was the designation for destroyer; the *Buck*'s identification was DD420. Other types of patrol craft included the SCs and PCs, very small ships created to guard against submarines, and the small, shallow-draft, speedy PT torpedo boats. The most famous of the PT boats, of course, was PT109, the one John F. Kennedy commanded, which was rammed and sunk by a Japanese destroyer down in the Solomon Islands. When Betty and I traveled to the Solomons in 1983, we visited Plum Pudding Island on which Kennedy and ten or eleven other survivors of PT109 took refuge. Richard E. Keresey, a law school friend of mine, has recently written a small book telling the exciting story of his boat, PT105, especially its activities in the Solomons. PTs 105 and 109 operated together on a number of occasions. A PT boat was about forty feet long. A World War II destroyer was three hundred or so feet long with a displacement of 1,650 to 2,100 tons. Cruisers had displacements of between ten and twelve thousand tons, while a battleship's displacement was about that of an ocean liner, between forty and fifty thousand tons, and an aircraft carrier was larger still.

When I arrived at the *Buck* in Norfolk, I reported to Captain Horace Robison and George Peckham, the executive officer. I also reported to Engineering Officer John S. Reese, my immediate superior. He was a nice man, with a rather receding personality. He was an extremely effective engineering officer and knew his business. I did not. I was assigned to be an assistant engineering officer, a job about which I knew absolutely nothing. Even though I had taken the engineering course on the *Prairie State*, I was no more qualified to be an engineering officer on a destroyer than I was to fly an airplane. When Reese realized that I didn't know anything about engineering and there was no way that I could be turned into an effective engineer, he pretty much gave up on me and didn't really bother to force the issue. He thought that I would be succeeded by somebody who knew more than I did, and that was my hope as well. In the meantime, I did what I was told. There was an engineering course for assistant engineering officers that had been designed by some methodical pedant. It required you to jot down statistics related to the engineering plant on the ship. It was a matter not so much of learning anything as of making notes of details relating to the boilers, steam turbines, electric generating plants, wiring, and so on. It was an exceedingly dull task.

I asked Captain Robison about applying to transfer from the EVG classification to a DVG classification, so that I could learn how to become a deck officer, which is what I really wanted to be. In order to get your designation changed, you had to make a formal application to the powers in the personnel department of the navy; it was then called the Bureau of Navigation and was in 1942 renamed the Bureau of Personnel. I could write to the bureau only through the commanding officer of my ship. The procedure was for him to forward my request along with his recommendation. That was the difficulty. After many tedious winter months in the North Atlantic, the captain agreed that he would do me the favor of endorsing my application if I first completed the destroyer engineering officer's course. That requirement didn't seem to make much sense, since I was going to get out of engineering altogether, but he regarded it as a necessary part of the whole affair. I perforce had to complete the engineering course before my application was forwarded with his recommendation and the explanation that I had been trained as a lawyer and not as an engineer. My application was approved by headquarters, but with an odd development. Instead of my becoming a DVG, as distinguished from an EVG, they simply added the "D" and didn't drop the "E." So now I was a DEVG, which so far as I know was a unique designation. I laboriously went about the task of getting the "E" removed from my list of qualifications so I wouldn't be faced with the possibility of having to do engineering duty. I eventually succeeded when my request was forwarded by the captain of my next ship. I chafed a great deal under that kind of bureaucracy.

As a newcomer to the *Buck*, I not only had to complete that awful engineering course but also got all the unwanted jobs that are automatically dumped in the lap of the most junior officer. For example, I immediately became the laundry officer, which meant that I was in charge of running the ship's laundry. I also was the ship's service-store officer, which entailed overseeing the little store where the two hundred seventy or so men aboard could buy toiletries, cigarettes, and candy. Every month, I had to prepare a report on the operations of the store and balance the books. It was a boring job, but I had taken a course in accounting in civilian life and that was something I could do without having to worry about it. As a matter of fact, I knew more about accounting than the captain did, and I had the devil of a time trying to explain the concept of a simple debit to him.

My primary duty, however, was as the assistant engineering officer. For the first several months on the *Buck*, I stood watches in the engine room and tried to learn something about how the engines operated. I had to stand watch for four hours, then had eight hours off before going back on watch for four hours. You were supposed to do other things in between watches. The engines were big turbines that were made to revolve very rapidly by superheated, high-pressured steam. The steam was at a pressure of 600 pounds per square inch (PSI) and at a temperature of 850 degrees, or some remarkably high numbers of that sort. If the steam line burst and you had the bad luck to be around, an invisible jet of steam would go right through you. But you needed to have steam like that to make the turbines operate efficiently. There was something called a reduction gear that reduced the revolutions of the turbines so that the shaft of the propeller would revolve at a more sensible speed; it wasn't a direct hookup. When I finally got my designation changed, the captain saw fit to let me stand some watches up on the bridge as a deck officer in training. I didn't accumulate enough experience on the *Buck* to become a qualified deck watch officer.

As time went on, I began to make friends of the other officers on the *Buck*. One of my closest friends was Robert K. Irvine, known as "Rab." He was in the class of 1938 at the Naval Academy, and thus a "regular" naval officer—as distinguished from we reservists. He is living today in a retirement home in Annapolis, and we remain good friends. Another dear and delightful friend of mine was George H. "Gabby" Harrington, of Somerville, Massachusetts. He had gone to the Massachusetts School Ship, which was operated by the state, and when he graduated he received a commission in the merchant marine and a reserve commission in the navy. He went to sea in the late 1930s aboard United Fruit Company liners, hauling bananas and other fruit up from Central America. He was ordered to active duty in the navy not long before I came aboard. He was about my age but was already a professional mariner and extremely proficient in taking celestial sights and in all other aspects of shipboard life. He was the best seaman aboard. I loved and admired him, and he taught me much. Gabby didn't like serving on the *Buck* at all. He wanted to get into almost any other branch of the naval service, but his applications for transfer to lighter-than-air or submarine duty were unsuccessful. He was on board the *Buck* when it was torpedoed in 1943 and went down with the ship. In 1963 when my father and I visited the US military cemetery in Italy at Anzio, there was inscribed on the wall a list of all those who fell at Anzio and another list of the soldiers whose bodies had never been found and the sailors who had been lost at sea. And I remember finding Gabby Harrington's name on that memorial.

My roommate on board the *Buck* was another ensign, Eugene Somers. I was five years older than Gene, but he was in the class of '41 at the Naval Academy and had been commissioned in February while I got my ensign's bars in September. So he was senior to me, and as a result he got the lower bunk. He was, among other duties, the ship's morale officer. One time in December, I noticed two identical boxes sliding back and forth on the metal deck in our stateroom, and Gene informed me that the boxes contained the ship's Christmas candy. "I'll tell you what," he said, "we'll make an equal division. That box will be for the crew, and this box will be for us officers." We laughed at that, since the boxes were the same size and there were only about twenty officers compared to two hundred fifty or so members of the crew, and of course he didn't mean it. The officers and crew joked back and forth like that a fair amount, but you tended to make your friendships on board with your fellow officers and not with the enlisted men. It wasn't that you disliked them, you were just in a different living and working environment.

After I reported to the *Buck*, the first place we went was right back to Newport, to replace a torpedo that had been lost at sea. The torpedoes on submarines, as everybody knows from the movies, are carried in tubes located down on the lower decks, but the torpedo tubes on destroyers are located on an upper deck: five (sometimes four) horizontal tubes on a rotating mount that can be trained out to starboard or port. The tubes can be fired one at a time, or simultaneously. The torpedo is fired with sufficient force so that it flies through the air for about ten or twenty yards before it enters the water. The forward thrust activates the starting mechanism of an engine inside the torpedo, and it then runs under its own power toward the target, which can be several miles away. The explosive warhead is the forepart of the torpedo. When we would fire a torpedo in practice, we would replace the warhead with a "dummy head," so that it would just bump into the target without an explosion. The practice head would then eject its water ballast, giving it positive buoyancy. It had an eye in the front, so that when it had completed its run, it would float with its tail hanging down in the water, and you could hook the eye with a gaff and recover the torpedo. Torpedoes were expensive, and there was no point in losing one in practice. You could practice torpedo attacks without firing them by entering computations like speed, course, and range of the target into a torpedo director and training the tubes out to simulate the actual bearing indicated by the director solution. The *Buck* had been doing this exercise before I came aboard. Once, when the ship had rolled, an improperly secured torpedo had slipped from its tube and fallen overboard. It had sunk in deep water, so we had to stop in at Newport to pick up a new one.

The ship had a disciplinary proceeding that charged an enlisted man in the gunnery department with dereliction of duty for losing the torpedo. There was a hearing, a kind of minor court martial. Three officers sat at the head of the wardroom table to hear the evidence and decide the case. As the most junior officer—but also because I was a lawyer—I was designated to represent the enlisted man. I snooped around in the torpedo shop, the area where the men whose responsibility it was to take care of the torpedoes did their work. On a shelf in the shop, I found two plates with instructions on how to secure the torpedoes. During the ship's building process, the plates had not been hung up, as they should have been, where they could be seen by the men handling the torpedoes. I produced one of these plates in the hearing and argued before the trial court that others had been negligent in failing to put these notices up. The sailor couldn't have seen the notices, and I argued that he should therefore not be faulted for losing the torpedo. It was probable that anybody who was handling the torpedoes already knew what was supposed to be done, whether or not the notices were posted, but my arguments apparently were persuasive and the court let the man off. The officer who bore the ultimate responsibility was my friend Rab Irvine, and they issued him a letter of admonition because he had failed to put up the plaques. I felt bad about that, because of course that letter of admonition became a part of his permanent record. Rab was then an ensign and hadn't yet been promoted to lieutenant junior grade. Promotions in the navy were considerably slower before Pearl Harbor than after the United States declared war, when an officer would not remain an ensign for long. I worried that the letter of admonition would slow Rab's promotion, though in the event it did not. In any case, I felt that I had to do the best I could for the young enlisted man whom I was supposed to represent. I later heard that he was lost at sea.

When we arrived at Newport, I noticed that several other ensigns were saluting Executive Officer Peckham and going ashore. I wanted to go telephone Betty, so I saluted him, too, and headed for shore. All of a sudden, wham, he put a hand on my chest and said, "Where the hell do you think you're going?" I learned then and there that the proper procedure for going ashore was to say to the executive officer, "Sir, I request permission to go ashore." And then he would give you permission if he thought you had completed your duties satisfactorily. The other people who were going ashore with only a perfunctory salute had been there longer and were on better terms with George Peckham than I was. But after all, I'd been there only a few days and I didn't know the procedures at all. He explained the situation to me and eventually gave me permission to go ashore. It was another one of an almost constant

series of learning experiences. It was amazing to me how little indoctrination you received before shipping out. It almost seemed that you
were supposed to learn everything the hard way.

In 1941, the *Buck* was assigned to convoy duty, escorting ships
crossing the North Atlantic, bound for Great Britain. The United States
was supposedly neutral in the fighting between Britain and the Axis
powers, but since early that year we had been escorting convoys all the
way to Iceland, where we had a military base. We were assisting the British, and so by 1941 we were already engaged in a shooting war with the
Germans in the North Atlantic. Many people have forgotten this. The
destroyer USS *Greer* was engaged in an incident with a German submarine in the North Atlantic in early September when I was on the *Prairie
State*. President Roosevelt claimed that the *Greer* had been attacked
without provocation, though it had actually been tracking submarines
for the British, and after that American naval vessels were authorized to
attack hostile submarines on sight. In early October, the USS *Kearney*
was hit and badly damaged by a German torpedo while on convoy duty
in the Atlantic. I saw it in the Boston Navy Yard and pointed out the
hole in the hull to Betty and my parents when they came up to see me
one time that fall. And not long afterward, the destroyer USS *Reuben
James* was sunk and over a hundred American sailors were lost. So we
were in fact involved in a shooting war with the Germans by the time I
was aboard the *Buck* in the North Atlantic, and it would have just been a
matter of time before we went to a declared war had the Japanese not
cinched the issue by bombing Pearl Harbor. I don't know whether the
Buck ever encountered a submarine during the months I was aboard.
We fired depth charges at what we thought were submarines picked up
on our sonar, but I suspect what we actually had were schools of fish.

It was extremely, fiercely rough in the North Atlantic. For the ships
caught up in the waves, it was like being swept up a mountain of water
and down into a valley, then back up and down again. While I was off
watch and laboring over that doggone engineering course, the ship
rolled and heaved so much that my papers went scattering this way and
that, and I could hardly hold onto the desk. I was lucky that I never got
seasick. Many people are extremely susceptible to seasickness. The
waves in the North Atlantic were enormous and powerful, and it was a
particularly rough experience for a relatively small ship like the *Buck*.
The chief commissary steward aboard the *Buck* had previously been
assigned to a much larger and more stable ship, a carrier or battleship,
and he got so seasick aboard our destroyer that he couldn't do his job
and had to be transferred away to some other duty.

The destroyers were always rolling, even in what appeared to be calm seas. We used to say on the *Buck*, just as they had on old sailing vessels, "One hand for yourself, one hand for the ship." That meant that whenever you were going from one place to another aboard a destroyer, even in a calm sea, you always held on to something stable. I used to retain that habit even when I went ashore, though I think it faded when I left the navy after the war. You also had to have a catlike response to being rolled off your bunk. One time as we were coming down from Iceland, we ran into another of those terrible winter storms, and the ship began to be thrown about by the waves. It was the practice in the navy in those years that whenever a ship was going from one place to another, its captain would tell the port director's office whether there was room to transport anyone needing to go in that direction. Just as there were people always hanging around receiving stations like Newport waiting for their assignments, so there were always people waiting in one port trying to get to another on whatever government transportation was going. Once we had aboard a lieutenant colonel in the army air forces who was catching a lift back to the States, and one evening he was asleep on the wardroom transom, a big sofa with leather cushions that was bolted to the deck. I was in the wardroom at the time, sitting at the table drinking coffee. Suddenly the ship rolled. If any of the *Buck*'s officers had been sleeping on the transom, we would reflexively have fallen to the deck, but this army air forces officer hadn't had our training and didn't know what to do in that situation. He was thrown up into the air and caught his ribs against the sharp point of the wardroom table, which was bolted in place. He was seriously injured, and after reaching port he died as a result of the internal damage he had suffered when the ship made that violent heave.

We had a ship's doctor, a young man not long out of his residency. Once when we were just off Iceland in terrible weather, one of the ship's company had a serious case of appendicitis, and in those conditions there was no way we could transfer him to a ship that had the proper facilities. So the doctor and the Captain conferred, some lights were rigged, and the poor fellow was laid on the table in the wardroom. The pharmacist's mate served as the anesthetist and administered whatever anesthetic was available. Gabby Harrington stood next to the doctor and tried to hand him the instruments he asked for. My job was to stand at the foot of the table and hold the patient's feet down, so that when the ship rolled the patient remained on the table. At one point the patient cried out, "Oh, doctor, you're cutting me!" The doctor said, "No, I'm not," but he was, and they had to get more morphine from one of the battle-dressing stations and administer a stronger dose. Then the ship made a violent lurch, and all the surgical instruments fell on the deck. That meant they had to be resterilized, a procedure that seemed endless. The patient had already been opened up, and the doctor kept looking at his watch and saying, "Not yet, not yet." Finally the operation was completed, and we carried the patient to one of the nearby officer's staterooms and put him in a bunk, where he stayed until we got to Boston ten days later. In retrospect, I think that the doctor, while he was an experienced physician, was an inexperienced naval officer. He had no idea what he was getting into in trying to perform an appendectomy on a small ship that was pitching and heaving in stormy seas. That was a night I'll never forget.

I never did go ashore in Iceland. Most of the American destroyers that escorted convoys across the North Atlantic had only a short stay there, and most of that time was spent moored in the Hvalfjord, a fingerlike fiord in the shadow of the hills, not far from the capital, Reykjavik. It was part of Roosevelt's plan to assist Britain that American destroyers would escort the convoys to a point called the Mid-Ocean Meeting Place. The British navy would escort them the rest of the way. After turning the convoy over to the British, the US destroyers would peel off, flash a few signal lights to the British saying goodbye and good luck, and go up to Iceland. MOMP, as we called it, was not always in the same place. It had to be changed every four hours so that the German submarines would not lie in wait there, and we communicated with the British in code to tell them when we would arrive. After a few days in Iceland, a group of US destroyers would come down to MOMP (wherever it was), pick up a westbound convoy from the British, and take it back to Boston via Newfoundland or Halifax. One time we were in the harbor just outside Reykjavik, and I was detailed to go with our ship's boat to pick up something at the dock. The ship's boat was a small, covered whaleboat, manned by the coxswain, the engineer, and the bow hook, whose job was to secure the boat to the dock when it came alongside. It was one of these terribly rough December nights, and the boat was tossed on the waves like a toy. I was sure we were going to sink. That wasn't a combat experience, but it was one of the scariest moments of my naval career.

The winter storms in the North Atlantic brought not only huge waves but extreme cold. Several times as we were rounding Cape Ann south of Nova Scotia on our way back from Iceland, the waters would spray over the ship and freeze. The ship would come into port in Boston covered with ice, encrusted with icicles hanging from the bridge and railings. The watch on those cold, stormy nights was terrible. The waters of the North Atlantic were blackish gray, and anyone who had to be exposed to the elements was thoroughly miserable.

The nature of convoy duty meant that the *Buck* returned to Boston every month or six weeks, and I was in Boston on December 7, 1941. There are only a few events that are so significant that everyone remembers where they were when they heard the news. I have a vivid memory of May 21, 1927, when Lindbergh landed in France; November 22, 1963, when Kennedy was assassinated; and December 7, 1941. I had Sunday dinner that day at a hotel on Commonwealth Avenue, along with Betty and our good friends Eddie Bennett and Harry Stimpson, who were working as lawyers in town. I could bring guests aboard the *Buck* when the ship was in port, so I invited everyone back to the Boston Navy Yard. We went up to the gate, and the marine on duty said, "No guests today," and he told us why. That's how I learned that the Japanese had launched a sneak attack on the US Pacific Fleet at Pearl Harbor. We were dumbfounded. We tried to find out what we could from newspapers and radio, but information about the extent of the damage was being withheld. Betty and I returned to our room at the Copley Plaza, and later in the day I telephoned my parents in New Jersey and we speculated about the attack, what it meant, and whether I would now be headed for the Pacific. Nobody really knew. The crew of the *Buck* was equally stunned, particularly since practically the whole ship's company had been with the ship in Pearl Harbor in May before it was transferred to the Atlantic.

All the time we had been training and performing convoy duty in the North Atlantic, we had been gearing up for war with the Germans. I had never given a thought to going to war with the Japanese. Indeed, I believe that the *Buck* had been transferred from the Pacific in the belief that war with Germany was coming in the Atlantic. On the other hand, I was told that in early 1941 the *Buck* had stopped at the Revilla Gigedos island group off the west coast of Central America to check that there was no Japanese activity in that part of the Pacific. They found nothing on uninhabited Clipperton Island, and only a herd of sea elephants and a detachment of goats from the huge resident goat population on Clarion Island. It is interesting but pointless to speculate about what might have happened if Germany had not declared war on the United States after the Japanese attack. I also wonder when my term of enlistment would have concluded if the Japanese had not attacked Pearl Harbor; after December 7 it was extended for the duration. At any rate, from then on we were engaged in two wars, one against the Germans and one against the Japanese.

After war was declared, the *Buck* didn't go to MOMP again. We delivered the convoys all the way to Great Britain, to a place called Greenock near Glasgow on the river Clyde. Once we were cruising along the coast of Scotland on a misty day, and through the foggy mist you could see a town on the Scottish shore. I was standing a watch on the bridge under the tutelage of my friend Rab Irvine, and he said to me, "See that town over there, Bill? That's an important town. You should really look up the name of that town on the chart." Believe it or not, the name of the town was Irvine, and we had a good laugh out of that. Not long afterwards, Rab and I got overnight leave, and we spent the night of June 2, 1942 in the Central Hotel in Glasgow, near the railroad station. We had a fine dinner in the company of some Canadian naval officers we met that night, and our dinner bill came to eight pounds, six shillings, and six pence. It wasn't much compared with modern prices, but Rab and I were so impressed with the amount of money we spent that we saved the account bill, which I still have. While I was in Scotland I bought some tweed fabric that I took home to Betty, and she turned it into a very attractive skirt.

Early in 1942, the great historian and Harvard professor Samuel Eliot Morison, who wrote the magisterial history of the US Navy in World War II, came aboard the *Buck* at Newfoundland. I don't believe that I knew then what an illustrious man he was. We were told that he had the rank of lieutenant commander, that his role was to record some of the history of the navy, and that the *Buck* was giving him passage across the Atlantic. I saw him at meals in the wardroom occasionally and rather admired his stern Yankee profile, but I don't recall that we had any conversation of substance. I have by now read many of his magnificent works, including his histories of Columbus and Commodore Perry, and his naval history of World War II is something I couldn't live without. I later wrote him a letter about the *Murray*'s role in the Pacific war and sent him a painting of the *Buck*.

After we had delivered our convoys to Scotland, the destroyers would sometimes proceed to a small base at Lisahally, down the river a bit from Londonderry in Northern Ireland. We went ashore, and since the Captain thought the crew had been cooped up in the ship for too long and needed to get some exercise, he asked me to lead them in some calisthenics. I was young, fit, and full of energy, and I wanted to show off, so I led the crew through some very rigorous calisthenics, which was probably unfair.

One fine spring day, I went for a walk through the countryside with Gene Somers and a few other young officers, and in one of the fields we came across a downed sheep. When I had visited New Zealand a few years before, I had learned from my farmer friend John Bull that a sheep rests on the ground with its legs folded underneath it and gets up by extending its legs. But if a sheep in full fleece is thrown off balance onto its side with its legs extended out sideways, it can't get up. Worse yet, circulation to the front and rear legs underneath the sheep is cut off, much the way that your leg goes to sleep if you have it in the wrong position. The sheep will remain downed until someone grabs it by its fleece and turns it right side up. But if you don't hold the sheep upright on its legs for a minute or two so that circulation can be restored to its legs, it will fall right down again. So I saw this downed sheep across a stone wall, and I explained the situation to my fellow officers. I picked up the sheep, held it upright, and in due course released it, and the sheep trotted away. I remember how amazed those fellows were that I knew how to do that. In the half century plus since that episode, I've never again been called upon to demonstrate my ability to right a downed sheep.

Later that spring, after we had put to sea again, several of the ship's company decided that we needed some recreation, and so they decided to set up a little target in the bow and practice shooting the pistols that we had on board. Before we could practice we needed permission from the captain, but when he heard the request he looked around and said, "Permission not granted. We're too close to Ireland." I think we were several hundred miles from Ireland at that point. I had realized not long after joining the *Buck* that Captain Robison, while he was a perfectly decent person, was not really a good captain or naval officer. He didn't have the confidence of the junior officers. Of course, I was so junior that not having my confidence was meaningless, but the morale aboard the *Buck* often flagged, among both the officers and the enlisted men, and it was partly because of incidents like that one.

When we got back to the East Coast of the United States early that summer, we got a new commanding officer, Captain L. R. Miller. Captain Miller was ordered to send those junior officers who needed instruction to the schools that the navy operated. I was still one of the most junior officers on the ship (though I think that another engineering officer had come along to replace me after I "graduated" to deck), and so I could be most easily spared. The commanding officer also recognized that I had been trained at midshipmen's school as an engineering rather than as a deck officer, and I needed more instruction. Those two factors coincided to send me back to school. I never went on another extended cruise aboard the *Buck*, and I was transferred from the ship in March 1943.

The first of the schools I went to in the summer of 1942 was in Key West. Betty and I went back for the second year in a row and found lodging in a big, old-fashioned house with a verandah on the first floor. We had a nice room overlooking Duvall Street, Key West's main street, and it was almost like a second honeymoon. Betty and I actually spent more time with each other that summer than all the other time put together between our marriage and the end of the war. The navy had sent me down there to attend sonar school—or "sound school," as we called it. The sonar instruments would send a sound wave through the water to strike the hull of an enemy submarine, or so you hoped, and the echo and its timing would indicate the range and depth of the sub. The summer of 1942 was a time of great success for German submarines and great calamity for British and American merchant shipping. Ships were being lost all over the Atlantic all the time; it was a disaster the Allies could not cope with. While we were in Key West, I saw survivors of torpedoed ships being brought ashore in pajamas and nightshirts.

As part of my training, I took a dive in an O-boat, a World War I-era submarine. The O-boats had been superseded by the more modern S-class submarines and by the much more modern fleet boats, but the O-boats the navy kept in Key West could submerge, and you could echo a sound wave off the hull. The navy also had some strange ships called Eagle boats. They had been built by the Ford Motor Company at the same time the company was building Model T Fords. An Eagle boat looked a lot like a Model T, because it was a square-ended triangle, with a sharp point and a square back, and it didn't have anything like ship lines. Ford turned out great numbers of Eagle boats for the navy in World War I, and some of them had been used on the Great Lakes for training purposes between the wars. When World War II came on, the navy used the Eagle boats to train people to use sonar, because the Eagles could carry sonar as well as any other vessel, and the good ships could not be spared from active duty. One day I was out on an Eagle boat practicing sonar detection with several other students, and just as we were about to come into port we got word that there was a real live German submarine at large in the waters around Key West. The ship's company had to take over everything, and we schoolboys were thrust aside while the ship went into its operating phase. Betty and the other brides ashore became very anxious when we didn't come home that afternoon, but fortunately nothing happened and we finally drifted in some time in the wee hours.

The sonar school at Key West lasted about two weeks. The students in my class came from all over the United States, one of them from Key

West itself. He lived in the Southernmost House, on the part of the island closest to Cuba. He got married near the end of our class, and he invited his classmates to attend. After the ceremony, all of us junior officers stood outside the church and our classmate and his bride walked out under an arch of our crossed swords. I had received my ceremonial sword when I was commissioned, but I'd never had any use for it and had left it at home. I had to scrounge around and borrow a sword from one of the Eagle boat officers, who turned out to be the older brother of my Yale classmate Ogden Brouwer, the captain of the boxing team. I never did use my ceremonial naval officer's sword, and it reposed in my attic for years and years after the war. When my son Rick, who had been in Vietnam, got out of the Marine Corps, he donated some of his equipment to the marines to be given to people who were still on active duty. I thought that was a good example, and I knew that the graduating class of midshipmen at the Naval Academy had to purchase that expensive ceremonial sword as they began their careers as officers. So I had my sword cleaned and the scabbard repaired, and offered it to the Naval Academy, where it was accepted with alacrity. I got a nice note from one of the faculty members, who expressed his appreciation for the gift and told me the name of the young man to whom the sword had been given. The young ensign who had received the sword never wrote me. I didn't count that as very important, since I doubted that he'd had the old indoctrination in his upbringing that said you were supposed to thank everyone for everything. But my secretary at S&H, Mrs. Fran Abatemarco, thought otherwise, and was much put out.

After the sonar class had concluded, Betty and I took a bus to Miami, where we stayed the night with my old Yale roommate Jonathan Pine, who was also on active duty in the navy and was stationed in Miami. We flew back to New York the next morning. Immediately after returning to my ship from Key West, I was sent away to school again, this time to radar school in the Brooklyn Navy Yard. Betty was with me in New York, of course, and we got a room at the Grovesnor Hotel on lower Fifth Avenue. Every day that I had class, I took the subway to the Brooklyn Bridge, and then I took a trolley car across the bridge, went underneath the Manhattan Bridge, and ended up at the gate of the Brooklyn Navy Yard. Most of my classes were held in the yard, although one time we went out on a ship down in the lower harbor to see how the radar operated on a destroyer. New York was not a very different place because of the war. I don't remember that there were security blackouts at night in the city, though places on Long Island and the Jersey shore were subject to them. New York City did have dimouts, when illumination was reduced. One aspect of life in the city that was visibly different was that the streets were filled with young men in uniform. We all wore uniforms all the time.

My brother Dick was also doing something around the Brooklyn Navy Yard at that time, so I saw him once or twice. In the fall of 1937, when I had entered Columbia Law School, Dick had entered the University of Vermont in Burlington. His career there was limited to one year. He didn't do well in college—or perhaps he didn't choose to do well. He went into the farming business in New Jersey with Alan Day, a friend of mine from Madison Academy who had also been one of the performers in the great Madison rodeo. Alan Day was raising milk cows on a shoestring. He didn't have any land of his own and had leased some barns in Livingston. Alan, Dick, and a third partner would buy used-up brewer's grains from the breweries in Newark for cattle feed. This wasn't much of a business, though, and it wasn't well capitalized. My father was very much interested in dairy farming and offered to finance the acquisition of the Coppergate Farm in Basking Ridge, New Jersey, and its good stock of Guernsey dairy cows if Alan and my brother would operate it. I'm sure that my father suggested quite forcefully to Dick that he ought to do it, but I think it also fit well with Dick's own interests in farming and the outdoors that he had developed during his summers at the Lazy K Bar Ranch. Dick and Alan Day went into business at the Coppergate Farm in 1940.

Almost immediately after Pearl Harbor was bombed, my brother left the farm and volunteered for service in the Marine Corps. He was in the marines at the same time I was in the navy, and our paths diverged. I remember seeing him only in the early summer of 1942, when we met near the Brooklyn Navy Yard. Later that year, Dick was part of the marine attack on Guadalcanal in the Solomon Islands, a decisive turning point in the Pacific war that marked the end of the Japanese surge forward.

I caught up with the *Buck* when it was doing training exercises in Casco Bay, Maine, outside of Portland. A tug was out on the bay towing a piece of iron behind it, and the *Buck* was trying out its own sonar on this piece of iron. The *Buck* happened that day to be entertaining an admiral, the commander of all the destroyers in the Atlantic, who was on the *Buck* to see how well the sonar worked. Unfortunately, the sonar wasn't working well at all; it just could not get an echo from the sheet of iron that the tug was towing. I'd just come back from sonar school in Key West, so I was supposed to be an expert. The captain called me over, introduced me and said, "Now, this here ensign, he knows everything about sonar. He's just been to sound school down in Key West, Admiral." The admiral took off his hat, banged it down on the chart table, and yelled at me, "Goddammit, son, get an echo off that thing!" Well, of course, I was terrified. I didn't know what to say to an admiral, and I couldn't make the sonar work, either. The sonar sound wave doesn't always go out at the same gradient. The temperature varies from the water surface to deeper levels, and a sonar wave is bent as it passes through different temperature layers. The water in Casco Bay was very cold that day, and it bent the sonar sound wave so that it probably went underneath its target. Sonar didn't work over great distances, anyway. I don't think you could detect a submarine if it was more than half a mile away, and in any case it was hit or miss.

My roommate, Gene Somers, was also married, and one afternoon when we were in Portland we got off early and went looking for our wives. We couldn't find them where they had said they would be, but we knew damn well that they had gone to the movies. There were only four or five movie theaters in Portland, so we went up to each one, explained that we were looking for our wives, went inside, and had to wait until our eyes got accustomed to the darkness. We found them in the third theater and managed to extricate them from the movie.

The third school I was sent to that summer was torpedo school in Newport. Betty and I rented a room in a small private home in town. The torpedo school was on a little island just a couple of hundred yards off the shore in the harbor. A causeway now connects the island to the mainland, but no such bridge existed in the summer of 1942, and so I took a little ferry to class. I learned all about the innards of a torpedo, and how to take it apart and put it together. School ended late in the afternoon, and Betty and I would swim in the bay or, since there was gas rationing and you couldn't drive a car, we would go biking. We had a grand time during those couple of weeks in Newport.

The *Buck* was once again engaged in Atlantic convoys by that time, and one night in August, while Betty and I were in Newport, a tragic event occurred. The *Buck* was escorting a convoy across the North Atlantic on a dark, foggy night. Radar was not then in universal use, and no ships displayed lights. In order to prevent collisions, the convoy traveled in columns, and each ship would trail a spar a certain distance from its stern. The next ship in line would keep an eye on that spar in the water even if it couldn't see the ship ahead. On this particular night, the commander of the convoy saw a light on one of the ships in the convoy and directed the *Ingraham*, another destroyer escorting the convoy, to go over and tell the ship to put out its light. The *Ingraham* tried to go between the columns, and it cut right across the bows of the *Chemung*, a big naval oiler. The *Ingraham* was cut in two and sank with a loss of almost all hands. The *Buck* was directed to go look for another ship, the *Letitia*, and in turn it cut across the bow of a high-speed troop transport called the *Awatea*, which coincidentally I had traveled on from New Zealand to Australia in 1936, when it was a commercial steamship. The *Buck* was luckier than the *Ingraham*. It was hit in the stern, and ten or a dozen men who were in the rear living compartment were killed. At least one of the propeller shafts was thrown out of kilter, so the ship could no longer move forward under its own power. A German submarine skipper would have been awarded the Iron Cross with oak-leaf clusters for inflicting the damage the American navy inflicted on itself that night. The *Buck* had to be taken in tow, presumably with an escort, back to Boston to be repaired. Indeed, when the *Buck* came near the Navy Yard, it got stuck on the bottom of the harbor because its propeller shaft was bent down at such a steep angle. When I reported back to the *Buck* after torpedo school in Newport, it was still in the Boston Navy Yard under repair, and remained there for most of the fall.

By this time, Betty was pregnant with our first child, Rick. We decided that she would be better off at home than hanging around Boston while I was on the *Buck*, so she returned to Stamford in early November. Betty had the good sense to realize that the cottage she was living in behind her mother's house was inadequate for the family she was now in the process of creating, so she found an apartment nearer the center of town. It was in the Knollwood apartment complex at 70 Strawberry Hill Avenue in Stamford. It was a first-floor apartment with a living room, kitchen, and a couple of bedrooms; it was a comfortable place.

After Betty left Boston, I was ordered to take a group of enlisted men over to Newport for training at machine gun school there. When I reported with my crew, I had a chill, and the officer in charge ordered me to sick bay. The next thing I knew, I was diagnosed as having a bad case of viral pneumonia, and was transferred to the naval hospital in Newport. I remained there from early November until February 1943. I don't recall anything about Thanksgiving, but I remember that Betty managed to get some gas for the car, and she drove up from Stamford to Newport at Christmastime. She took me and the fellow in the bed next to me, a dentist named Steigerwald, out to Christmas dinner. We were both in bad shape. My normal weight was 180 pounds, and I had dropped down to about 150. We went to a restaurant in the Munchener

King Hotel, near the Viking Hotel. Neither I nor this other fellow could walk by ourselves, and Betty, who was well along in her pregnancy by this time, had to take each of us by the arm and propel us up to the front door of the Munchener King. It's interesting that the restaurant had retained that name, considering the vehemence of anti-German feeling during World War I. Sauerkraut was renamed "victory cabbage," the study of the German language was forbidden in schools and universities, and my grandfather Beinecke changed the name of the Germania Bank. Even with the country at war with Hitler in the 1940s, I don't think there was the same kind of anti-German hysteria. After a very enjoyable Christmas dinner, Betty took my friend and me back to the hospital, then returned to Stamford.

I recovered by January, but the navy didn't have anything like a convalescent period. You were kept in the hospital until you were 100 percent fit for duty. So it wasn't until February 1943 that I was released from the hospital and set out, once again, to find the USS *Buck*. I had a short interlude before I met the *Buck* when I was sent to be a teacher at the Lido receiving station. The Lido is a resort area out on Long Island, and the hotel there had been taken over by the navy. It was my first experience as a teacher—just me, a blackboard, and a room full of seamen. I would give an hour's lecture on depth charges or torpedoes or similar subjects. I tried to be interesting and to keep my class awake. I tried stunts like walking up the aisle, picking some guy in the middle row of the big classroom who looked like he was half asleep, and asking him how the detonation mechanism on a particular torpedo worked. Since he actually *was* asleep, he wouldn't know, and everybody would laugh.

By this time, the *Buck* had participated in the North Africa landings and activities on the Mediterranean front. I finally caught up with the ship when it reappeared at the Brooklyn Navy Yard. I was standing on the dock as it came into port, and I went aboard and said hello to my friends. They told me how lucky I was to have missed the North Africa landings. Then I was summoned by the executive officer, who told me that some time ago they had received new orders for me. I was directed to join the crew of the USS *Murray*, then under construction in Texas. So my hellos turned into goodbyes, and that was the end of my tour on the *Buck*.

On March 11, 1943, Betty's twenty-third birthday, I flew to Texas to report to the *Murray*. I left from the old airline terminal across the street from Grand Central, where the Philip Morris building now stands. The small plane was headed for Houston with a stop in New

Orleans, but we made an unscheduled stop in Greensboro, North Carolina, since the plane couldn't fly over the Appalachians in bad weather. We spent the night there, then flew to Houston the next morning. From there I took a train to Orange and to my new assignment on the USS *Murray*.

CHAPTER EIGHT

War Service with the USS *Murray*, 1943–1944

Eternal Father, strong to save,
Whose arm hath bound the restless wave,
Who bidd'st the mighty ocean deep
Its own appointed limits keep;
Oh, hear us when we cry to Thee,
For those in peril on the sea!

—NAVY HYMN

O range, Texas lies on the banks of the Sabine River, the border between Texas and Louisiana. It's north of Beaumont, a port city of some substance. Orange was just a little East Texas town that probably had a population of less than ten thousand in the late 1930s. But a local shipyard, the Consolidated Shipbuilding Company, got a sizable contract with the federal government to build twelve destroyers and a larger number of DEs, and Orange became a hive of activity. From then on, there were always three or four ships being worked on simultaneously, ranging from skeletal form to nearly complete. When I arrived in March, the finishing touches were being put on the *Murray* (DD576) and the *McKee* (DD575), which had been under construction for somewhere between six and nine months. Consolidated Shipbuilding had begun to employ hundreds or perhaps thousands of workers, including a lot of women of Rosie the Riveter fame. People came from all over the South, from as far north as Tennessee, to work on these war orders. The population of Orange tripled or quadrupled almost overnight, and there were nowhere near enough facilities in the little town to accommodate the influx. The navy created a bachelor officers' quarters (BOQ) for single officers and appropriate facilities for single enlisted men, but those who had brought their wives with them had to find rooms in places like the New Holland Hotel, which was undoubtedly among a select number of the world's very worst hotels. I stayed in the BOQ, since Betty was pregnant and couldn't make the journey to Texas.

The crew of the *Murray* was slowly assembled in Orange from the time the ship began to be built until it was finally commissioned. We were sent there piecemeal, from hither and yon, by the Bureau of Personnel in Washington, whose job it was, among others, to furnish crews for naval vessels under construction. I was one of the early arrivals—one of the "plank owners," to use the navy term for people who put their ship in commission. But there were already a few other future *Murray* officers on hand by then, and quite a few enlisted men. Our duties were to attend to a myriad of precommissioning details. At about that time I was promoted from ensign, the lowest officer rank in the navy, to lieutenant junior grade, which would be equivalent to being promoted from second lieutenant to first lieutenant in the army. Lieutenant junior grade was an in-between rank, and it never seemed that there were many of us around. Lieutenants were the officers with responsibility, and the ensigns and j.g.s worked for the lieutenants. I was assigned to the gunnery department of the *Murray* as an assistant gunnery officer and began to do administrative tasks in an office provided for us by the shipyard. My principal responsibility was to see that the gunnery department had the necessary supplies and that all the equipment met specifications. The five-inch guns aboard the *Murray* were very heavy, and you could rotate them only with power machinery. The guns rested on a revolving support surface, and one day as we were testing one of the guns, one of our men rested his hand up on that surface and lost part of his hand and several fingers when the gun turned. Injuries were a major worry in that industrial setting, and of course there are always injuries in the armed services, even today, just because of the hazards of the equipment and of military life. It's a dangerous activity to be part of, even in peacetime.

After I'd been at work for two or three weeks, some of the other officers with whom I would serve began to arrive. I met Robert White, the engineering officer, who later became executive officer. Bob was a graduate of the Naval Academy in the class of 1940. He and his wife rented a room from an old retired sea captain, who had a second career piloting the new hulls around the river for the shipyard. In early April, the gunnery officer James Boyd arrived in town, and I worked under him after that. Jim Boyd came from the little town of Willows, in northern California, where he still lives today.

The only social gathering place in town was the Orange Athletic Club, better known as the Orange AC. It was not in fact an athletic club but a third-rate bar with sawdust on the floor and a couple of nickel pin-ball machines. It served food, and one sign of the segregation that pre-vailed in the South in 1943 was that blacks were forbidden to order or eat food inside the Orange AC. They had to order from a side window and eat in the alley behind the bar. When Jim Boyd arrived at the *Murray*, he asked what we did at the end of the day for amusement, and we replied that we always went down to the Orange Athletic Club for a workout. Jim didn't want any more exercise at the end of his first tiring day, but he was a good sport and agreed to come along. He was very relieved when he saw that the Orange AC was a place where the princi-pal exercise was lifting glasses of beer.

The Orange AC was practically the only place where the naval per-sonnel came into contact with the workmen who were building the ships. We lived in separate worlds, even within the small town of Orange, and we didn't mingle much. One afternoon when I was playing pinball, a man in a hard hat came over to me and said in a southern accent, "Ah'd like to play the pinball machine." I said, "Sure, just as soon as I get through with my turn." Then he kind of leaned on me, and I noticed that although I was six feet tall, he was looking down at me from a height of what appeared to be ten feet. He said, "Ah mean Ah'd like to play the pinball machine right now." I was no fool. I said, "Yes, sir," and surrendered the pinball machine and my unexpended turn right away. There wasn't much else in the way of recreation in Orange, although I once played a round of golf at the Orange Golf Club. Up until then, I had always played golf hatless, but the sun beat down on my head that afternoon, even in early April, and I believe that was the last time I ever played golf without a hat.

The *Murray* was noticeably more technologically advanced than a destroyer in the Sims class such as the *Buck*. It was larger than the *Buck*, at 2,100 tons, with heavier armament. The Sims-class destroyer was designed with an eye toward achieving certain economies that, in retro-spect, were probably mistakes. A flush deck destroyer of the type built in World War I had an engine room linked to a boiler room, followed by another engine room linked to another boiler room, so that a ship could operate even if one of its engineering spaces was hit. The fumes from the boilers went up through four smokestacks, which gave those vessels a handsome silhouette. I saw some of those World War I destroy-ers in operation as high-speed troop transports during World War II. The Sims-class destroyers, which were built in the late 1930s, had only one smokestack. The two boiler rooms were next to each other, and the two engine rooms were connected to each other, so you had to pass the

USS Murray *(DD576).*

steam pipes from boiler room number one through boiler room
number two in order to get steam to the engine rooms. It was a strange
hookup from an engineering standpoint, and I think the navy realized
that, because they built only ten or twelve ships in the Sims class before
they created another class that returned to the old sequential arrangement of engine and boiler rooms and had two smokestacks. That
design continued with the Fletcher class, which was the standard class
of destroyers through World War II, although slightly larger destroyers
were produced near the end of the war. The *Murray* was an attractive
ship. While many American naval ships had once been painted white—
as with Theodore Roosevelt's Great White Fleet—during World War II
all combatant ships were painted gray, or in different patterns of black,
white, gray, and blue, to try to camouflage them. That disguise was
more effective in the foggy Atlantic than it was in the Pacific.

The *Murray* had been launched sometime before I got there, and it
was afloat in the river while the shipyard was finishing up work on it.
The ship was worked on around the clock, because it was only through
the operation of the three-shift system that the United States could
hope to meet the material demands of the war. The navy people
assigned to the *Murray* would check ship specifications during the day,
and at night we took turns manning a security patrol on board the ship.
One night when I was on patrol with a couple of enlisted men, I came
across a shipyard worker who was sound asleep. It wasn't any of my
responsibility, but I felt put out by that, so I woke him up. Those work-

ers made decent wages, and it was important to the nation that they do their jobs properly. I had the next night off, and some friends and I went across the river to one of the honky-tonk gambling houses in Louisiana. I got into a poker game upstairs, and as I was putting some chips on the table, I looked up and saw that the fellow playing poker directly across the table from me was the very same one whom I had found asleep on the job. It was a surprise to both of us, but we tried to keep poker faces.

Meals were served in the BOQ dining room both to the officers who were in residence and to those who were living in rented quarters elsewhere with their wives. Most of us were junior officers, and we came from the several ships being built in Orange at that time. The senior officer present was a Commander Smythe, the designated captain of one of the other ships under construction. He insisted that whenever he came into the dining room, all the officers (and their wives, too) should stand at attention until he had seated himself. This practice evidently was a mark of office he felt entitled to. It went on for ten days or so until the arrival of the captain of the *Murray*, Richard F. Stout. He, too, was a commander in rank, but he was called captain since the commanding officer of a ship is always called captain regardless of his rank. The first time Captain Stout went into the dining room and everybody stood up, he asked to know the reason and was told that we all had to stand up by order of Commander Smythe. Captain Stout said, "That's a lot of nonsense." He was senior to Smythe, and he said, "I don't want anybody to have to stand up anymore when the senior officer enters the dining hall." Captain Stout endeared himself to a lot of people very quickly by that action.

Richard Stout was one of the best naval officers I ever met. The *Murray*'s initial commanding officer took the ship through its commissioning and its shakedown cruise before he was transferred to another post just after we transited the Panama Canal. Despite the brief duration of his captaincy, he left his mark on the *Murray*, and a good deal of the ship's success was the result of what he had achieved in the short time he had the command. He insisted upon obedience to all sensible regulations, but he didn't manufacture regulations just to gratify his ego, as officers like Commander Smythe did. He was exacting in terms of shipboard discipline, and he paid meticulous attention to the things that had to be done. You knew that what he was demanding was sensible and fair, even though it took a great deal of effort to comply with his orders.

Captain Stout had just come from the Solomon Islands, an area of savage fighting between the Japanese and the Americans from the time the Americans made their initial landing at Guadalcanal in the late summer of 1942. Captain Stout had commanded a destroyer that had been sunk or severely damaged, and he wanted to make sure that all the equipment aboard the *Murray* was working properly. Since I had been to radar school, one of my first assignments on the *Murray* was to be the radar officer. The upkeep of the radar system was a task for specialized technicians, but I was responsible for the system's operation. Radar was brand-new, and something we were still learning to use. Captain Stout knew better than we did that it needed to function continuously twenty-four hours a day, and you weren't going to make the radar last longer by turning it off when you didn't need it. Captain Stout insisted that we test the hell out of our radar, and indeed in the course of testing we discovered that part of the system was faulty and had to be repaired. Suppliers of equipment to the Navy provided personnel attached to the construction site who would see to it that the equipment functioned as it was supposed to and that glitches were fixed. I later found that the manufacturing companies had engineers in Guantánamo Bay, Cuba, who corrected some difficulties the *Murray* had developed during its shakedown cruise. So after our radar malfunctioned, technicians from the Raytheon Company and Western Electric came aboard and repaired the system. If we had subjected our radar to less rigorous testing, it might not have worked when we needed it and we easily could have been in a situation where it would have been very difficult to replace the system. Captain Stout made sure that all the *Murray*'s equipment was so thoroughly tested that when we finally went to war, we had none of the malfunctions that might have landed us in the soup.

The qualities that made Captain Stout a superb naval officer included thoroughness, attention to detail, an understanding of the equipment on which we relied, and personal involvement. He didn't live in the BOQ, although he came there for meals a few times. He and his wife had an apartment down in Beaumont, and he commuted the twenty miles or so to Orange. One afternoon he invited the officers of the ship down to his apartment for cocktails, where he demonstrated his ability to concoct high-quality, high-octane martinis. He was in the class of 1927 at the Naval Academy and was in his late thirties or early forties when we met. He went on to become at least a rear admiral, and may have attained an even higher rank. For a few years after the war, we exchanged Christmas cards, and after he died his widow lived on for a number of years in Carmel, California.

As the senior officers in the gunnery department, Jim Boyd and I had the responsibility of loading the ammunition onto the *Murray*. The bulk of it was semifixed ammunition, which meant that the charge and primer came in a brass cartridge separate from the projectile. To fire the 5-inch/38-caliber guns aboard the *Murray*, you would first load an explosive projectile into the gun, then put a two-foot-long brass cartridge into the breech, close the breech, and fire. Orange didn't have an ammunition depot, and the ammo arrived by train, along a railroad siding running by the dock. It was closely packed into an enormous boxcar, which appeared to be almost empty when you first peered into it, because the ammunition could not be stacked. The boxcar had been left on the siding about fifty feet from the unloading point, which wasn't too handy. So Jim Boyd had fifty or sixty sailors push the car from behind and sent a couple of fellows who had worked on railroads up to the roof of the boxcar to work the brakes. Then we lined up and manhandled the ammunition aboard, passing the cartridges and fifty-four-pound projectiles from one man to another all the way from the boxcar to the ship's magazine, where the ammunition was properly stowed. You couldn't have done that on a battleship, where the great fourteen- or sixteen-inch guns fired projectiles that weighed about a ton, but the *Murray*'s five-inch (in diameter) ammunition was just the right size to be handled by strong young men.

The *Murray* headed down the river into the Gulf of Mexico for testing. First came firing trials to ensure that the supports of the gun mounts could handle the strong recoil of the guns. Then came the speed trials where the ship was run at flank speed, thirty-five knots, to be sure the parts wouldn't fly apart and the turbines could function at maximum pressure. The turbines gave off a high-pitched whine and the ship went shooting through the water; it was quite exciting.

After the *Murray* had passed its trials, it was accepted by the navy in a commissioning ceremony on board the ship while it was at the dock in Orange, in late April. The crew lined up at attention, with the enlisted men in white uniforms and the officers in khaki uniforms. The Captain was informed by the man in charge of the yard that the ship was now ready to be turned over to the navy, and the Captain accepted command. The commissioning pennant was hoisted to the top of the mast, and there was a speech or two. The USS *Murray* was now an active warship in the United States Navy. Then the Captain said, "Set the watch." From that point, watch followed watch until after the war, when the ship was decommissioned in Charleston, South Carolina.

We cleared our belongings out of the BOQ, packed them aboard ship, and put to sea. Our first port of call was Galveston, not far from Orange along the Gulf Coast. The ship was immediately dry-docked so that its bottom, which had been floating in the Sabine River ever since its launching, could be cleaned and certain structural details inspected. There was a pier in Galveston that extended some distance out into the Gulf, with a gambling establishment at the end. To get access to the pier, you had to show identification to a guard at the entrance gate. When the guard looked at my navy ID card, he asked me if I was the son of Fritz Beinecke. It turned out that he had known my father at Andover. I have no idea what he had done at Andover or how he had ended up as a guard at a gaming house. I think that gambling was illegal in that part of Texas, because the Galveston casino was set up so the gambling equipment was either disguised—we played craps on an old pool table—or could be thrown out into the sea.

From Galveston we traveled up the Mississippi River to a naval base at Algiers, Louisiana, a bit downstream and across the river from New Orleans, so that the *Murray* could be equipped with its degaussing apparatus. Mines were a major danger for ships at sea during World War II. Contact mines detonated when a ship bumped into them, and all you could do was hope to avoid them. Magnetic mines, however, detonated when ships came near their lines of magnetic force, and a physicist at Princeton named Karl F. Gauss had discovered a way for ships to be protected from them by means of a cable around the hull of the ship that would neutralize the ship's magnetic field. So all American ships that put to sea, including ours, were equipped with degaussing gear.

After leaving New Orleans, we began a vigorous training period. Both crew and officers had widely varied levels of experience. A lot of the enlisted men had come directly from boot camp and had never been on board a ship. There was, however, a group of about thirty enlisted men who had previously served on the old and honorable destroyer USS *Worden* , which had survived the hazards of 1942 including the battles of the Coral Sea and Midway, until it was wrecked on the rocks during a landing in the Aleutian Islands in January 1943. The Department of Personnel should not have sent that large group of *Worden* survivors to one ship, because they constituted an appreciable fraction of the *Murray*'s crew of three hundred, and they remained a cohesive unit. Any order or new procedure was met by a growl of protest from this group, and they were forever grumbling, "Things were never like this on the *Worden*." No matter what the business, be it air bedding at 0600, "Sweepers man your brooms," or movies for all hands at 1900, it had always been done differently on the *Worden*, and this gang lost no time in telling us about it. It took a year for the *Worden* sailors to become *Murray* sailors.

The *Murray* had a nucleus of experienced petty officers—the chief gunner's mate, the chief machinist's mate, the chief electrician's mate, the chief quartermaster and so on—who had come from different ships and were proficient at their jobs. And then we had an essential coterie of experienced officers, including Captain Stout, gunnery department head Lieutenant James Boyd, and chief engineer Lieutenant Bob White. The executive officer, Lieutenant Posey Hooper, had served with Captain Stout in the Pacific. Captain Stout had a high regard for Hooper and had asked the navy department to assign him to the *Murray*. This was a good thing, because Hooper was another professional naval officer who knew his business, and he also knew the standards Captain Stout insisted upon. Ensign Sid Legg was head of the deck department, responsible for the lines and anchors and other marine gear, and thus he was in charge of the deck forces, known familiarly as "deck apes." The communications department was headed by Lieutenant Walter Scott Martin, who was also in charge of the navigation equipment; nearly everything on the bridge fell under his supervision. Scott Martin, who has since died, became a great friend. Scott and Jim Boyd were both in the class of '38 at the University of California at Berkeley. Before coming to the *Murray*, Scott had been in a naval armed-guard unit. After the sinking of the *Reuben James*, naval gun crews like his had traveled on our merchant ships with authorization to fire on hostile vessels on sight. I'd be curious to know how effective they were. I was not as experienced as many of the officers, but I had been to sea on another ship and by now had held my commission for eighteen months, and there were ensigns on the *Murray* who had just graduated from midshipmen's school and were junior to me.

I got to know the crew fairly well, particularly the people in my own department, but there was very little social or recreational mixing of officers and enlisted men. I think wartime service was not the great democratizing experience that people sometimes claim. It was, of course, a segregated navy, in which very few of the blacks that I saw were ever given anything but the lowest jobs. The steward's mates, the people who waited on the officers, were either blacks or Filipinos. I remember one black man on the *Murray* who was much dissatisfied with his role as a steward's mate. He was a graduate of Montclair High School in New Jersey. His attitude toward his place in society was therefore much different from that of some of the blacks who came from humble circumstances and a segregated environment in the South and were none too surprised to find themselves in a segregated navy. This particular fellow was a good-sized young man, and the part of naval service that he liked was going to general quarters, which meant going to action stations and preparing for battle. He had an important job as "first loader" of a gun crew because of his size, and he may have been one of the few people on the ship who looked forward to going to general quarters, because then he was no longer in a servile position.

But the navy was not really a democratizing experience. The officers were not exactly a higher class, but they were in a different position from everyone else. The captain had his own nice cabin with his own bed, and a "sea cabin" up on the bridge where he spent most of his time when we were at sea. The officers had little staterooms, with from two to four bunks to a room. The crew, on the other hand, lived in cramped quarters with bunks stacked up three high and little lockers underneath where they kept their limited personal belongings. Most of the crew had not been through high school, and a good many of them had not gone beyond the eighth grade. Some had minimal reading skills at best. A lot of them would call me "sir" because they couldn't pronounce "Beinecke." If anyone had been to college and got into the navy with the status of an enlisted man, he was sure to be selected pretty soon to go to Officer Candidate School. The difference between the college-educated and the non-college-educated people was clear. The chief petty officers were mostly high school graduates who had not gone on to college, and they were mechanics in the sense that a carpenter or a plumber or a radio repairman is a mechanic. These people were dealing with technical equipment, and they had to have sufficient technical education. They invariably knew their specialty well and were extremely competent. But navy officers are not specialists, they're generalists. An officer will move from one role to another, whereas the chief petty officers remained specialists in their particular tasks. I got along with everyone regardless of their class or rank, and I still do, but I think that has more to do with my personality than with the navy experience.

After leaving New Orleans, our shakedown cruise began in earnest as soon as we arrived in Guantánamo Bay. Every morning we practiced firing all the weapons in our repertoire, though we used practice torpedoes and loaded only one torpedo into the middle tube instead of firing all five. We also dropped simulated depth charges on an actual submarine, an exercise I had practiced when I was attending sonar school in Key West. And, again, we had engineers from the radar manufacturing companies on board, making sure the radar system was working.

On the fifth of June, I received a telegram from Betty in Stamford informing me that I had become a father two days earlier. I told Posey

Hooper and requested permission to go ashore and send congratulations to my wife of a little more than two years. He was kind enough to assign a ship's boat to take me over to the main base, I sent my message to Betty, and when I returned all of the officers congratulated me. Betty and I had decided to name our son after my father, and so he became Frederick William Beinecke II. For the first few months of his life, we called him Fritz, as my father was also called. But my father, while he was flattered that we had named our firstborn son after him, remembered how Americans had felt about the Germans during the previous world war, and he said, "You really shouldn't call that baby Fritz when we're engaged in another war against the Germans." And so we started to call him Ricky. When he was old enough to decide for himself, he preferred to be called Rick, and that is the name he has been known by ever since.

From Guantánamo we went to Charleston for what was called the postshakedown overhaul. Once the naval architects had settled on the design for the Fletcher class of destroyers, they sent out blueprints to shipyards and factories, where the ships were produced by the dozens. While the ships were under construction and at sea in their first service, the naval architects had thought up ways to improve the existing design, often based on problems that ships in combat had reported to the Bureau of Ships. Rather than send out new instructions to all the shipyards engaged in building the destroyers, they would bring the ships to Charleston and a few other navy yards after their shakedown cruises, then take the ships apart again and install the new alterations. Since this process would take several weeks, Betty found a sitter for our new son and joined me in Charleston. We took a nice room at the Francis Marion Hotel in town. One night when we were ashore, Jim Boyd went out with Betty and me, and when we returned to the hotel, he said, "I don't feel like going back to the ship. I'll just curl up on that sofa in the corner of your bedroom, and don't you mind me." I was a young bridegroom who hadn't seen his wife for months. Jim Boyd did indeed spend the night on that sofa, and he's never forgotten it—because I'm not going to let him forget it! I remind him every time I see him, and ask him how he enjoyed that evening.

After staying at the Francis Marion for two or three days, Betty and I looked around for something a little more homey, and we found a couple of very attractive rooms down on the Battery in what would today be called a bed and breakfast. It was an old-fashioned white house at 2 Meeting Street, right on the seawall at the edge of the harbor, in the heart of the loveliest part of Charleston. I had not seen Betty since

March, when I was still getting over a bad case of pneumonia, and I was overjoyed to see her again. The weather was beautiful, and we spent an idyllic few weeks together. I would go down to the ship in the morning, put in a day's work, and go ashore at about four o'clock, except every four or five days when I had the nighttime watch. My parents came down one weekend, which was wonderful, and we went out to dinner with Captain Stout. We were in Charleston on the Fourth of July, and Betty and I went with Jim Boyd and a couple of others to Folly Beach, a resort area near Charleston; we had a picnic lunch and some beers. Charleston was an interesting and gracious city even in wartime. I enjoyed sitting on the joggling boards, an article of furniture unique to Charleston, and jouncing gently up and down, with something between a bouncing and a rocking motion. While we were in Charleston, the *Murray* officers went to a jeweler in town and had him make a nice silver baby cup, which they presented to Betty and me. That cup is inscribed to Fritz, since that is what Rick was called at that time.

After the *Murray* left Charleston, we went down to Trinidad, from there to Norfolk, on to Boston, then back to Norfolk. Bill Duddleson and Marshall Cleland were two young ensigns serving in Norfolk that summer when they saw the *Murray* come into port. A brand-new Fletcher-class destroyer! Just what they wanted, rather than the four more months of schooling that they'd just learned was to be their next assignment. Besides, Marshall said, he recognized the ship's camouflage pattern and hues as "Med camouflage," designed for Mediterranean weather conditions. They hitched a ride out to the *Murray* as it was riding at anchor in the harbor, saluted everyone in sight, and were invited to join Captain Stout in the wardroom for a cup of coffee. He asked them whether they spoke Italian. They didn't and they admitted it, but they inferred from his question that the *Murray* was indeed going to the Mediterranean, maybe even to the Isle of Capri. They told the Captain that they figured the war in Europe would end before the war in the Pacific, and they wanted to be in both. They requested duty aboard the ship, and a few days later received orders to report to the *Murray*. Were they ever surprised when the ship transited the Panama Canal not long after that and went into the far Pacific!

While we were in Norfolk, we were engaged in various training activities, and so Betty took yet another southbound train from New York to see me. After the *Murray* had tied up in port, I raced over to the hotel where we had arranged for Betty to stay, and I found that she had been put in a women's dormitory, from which men were forbidden. I complained to the desk clerk, who said, "Don't you know there's a war on?" I did indeed know there was a war on, and that was one of the reasons I wanted to change Betty's room assignment. Didn't the clerk know that my wife and I might never see each other again? My argument did not prevail. Betty and I held hands on the porch until it was late, then she went up to her room and I went back to the ship. The next day we found space in a private home that rented to naval personnel, in a room that was so small that if one person wanted to stand up, the other person had to sit on the bed. After we had been there for two or three days, Betty woke up one morning with a bedbug bite. It was a bad omen. I headed down to the ship and told Betty I would see her later in the afternoon, but instead the *Murray* sailed south to the Panama Canal on that July day, bound for the war in the Pacific. I couldn't even send a message telling her that we had gone. But it was not a totally unexpected departure, and that sudden separation was one of the things you got used to in those days. The next time I saw Betty was a year and a half later, when the *Murray* arrived in San Francisco the day after Thanksgiving in 1944.

In the first half of 1943, the United States was encountering serious losses in the Pacific, and victory was far from certain. One might suppose that the navy would have wanted to get the *Murray* out to the Pacific as rapidly as possible, and yet here we had spent several months in testing, training, and design modification. There are two explanations for this apparent delay. First, the navy had learned through the empirical method that their ships were better off if they were subjected to rigorous training before they were exposed to the enemy. Second, ships were being built not only at Orange, Texas but at the Brooklyn Navy Yard; Camden, New Jersey; Bath, Maine; Newport News, Virginia; and at many other shipyards. Ships were being produced around the clock, and the *Murray* was but a drop in the torrential outpouring of the mighty American industrial machine. We could afford to test and train because there were so many ships in the pipeline.

American films about the United States's participation in the war often give the impression that the reason we won was that we had braver and better troops. I'm skeptical of that view. There was heroism on all sides, and cowardice too, and the German military was second to none. What beat the Germans and Japanese was America's technological innovation and our sheer ability to outproduce our enemies. During the American Civil War, Robert E. Lee out-generaled the North time and again, and the North lost battle after battle. But the North ultimately won the war on the strength of its reservoir of immigrant manpower and its industrial capacity. The Confederate soldiers' heroism and gallantry could not overcome the larger economic factors that were arrayed against the South. So it is in all wars. Mettle is no match for metal, so to speak.

After the *Murray* transited the canal, just as we emerged into the Pacific, we had a change-of-command ceremony when Captain Stout turned the ship over to Paul R. Anderson, a North Carolinian who had graduated from the Naval Academy in 1930. Commander Anderson, known to some of us as Captain Andy, was our commanding officer for over a year. He was relieved by Paul L. de Vos, known as Pablo, as we returned to the Mare Island Navy Yard near San Francisco in November 1944. Our fourth commanding officer, Lt. Comdr. Frederick M. Radel, took over on August 29, 1945, just as the war was ending. I didn't get to know him well because I left the ship and went off active duty soon after that.

From the Panama Canal, we set a course for Pearl Harbor, escorting the new cruiser USS *Birmingham*. We held a number of practice exercises en route, including a simulated nighttime gunfire attack on the *Birmingham*. We fired "star shells," phosphorus-filled shells that lit up the night when they ignited. Somehow or other we managed to whistle a star shell right between the *Birmingham*'s masts, a major screwup of the sort we called a "rhubarb." I was in charge of the fire-control room at the time, and when I tried to find out why the switch had not been thrown that would have prevented this rhubarb, I was told that it had been thrown and something must have been wrong with the circuit. All the circuits later checked out perfectly, and I realized I'd been had by my men, but I was too green to appreciate that. Fortunately the star shell merely made a great racket as it tore harmlessly through the cruiser's rigging, and no damage was done. Needless to say, we heard plenty from the *Birmingham*.

We arrived at Pearl Harbor, better known to us as Pearl, and the *Murray* made a quick escort mission to Howland Island and back. I didn't accompany the ship, because I had been sent to a destroyer officers gunnery school at a camp in the hills a few miles from Pearl. The course lasted only two weeks or less, but it was a necessity for anyone who was going to be involved heavily with the gunnery department of a destroyer. It involved a lot of reading and writing, and we went out on some ships to do firing exercises at sea. When the *Murray* returned to Pearl, we set out for Wake Island and our first combat assignment.

We didn't know it, but the assault on Wake Island marked the beginning of the operations of the fast-carrier striking force, which by spring 1945 became the largest and most formidable fleet ever assem-

Tribute to Commander Paul R. Anderson "Captain Andy" from the crew of the Murray *upon his departure from the ship. Published in the "Fantail Gazette" (see page 202), November 15, 1944.*

bled. Throughout the war, the *Murray* was usually a tiny part of much larger operations. Sometimes we were part of the Seventh Fleet, which was Douglas MacArthur's navy in the southwest Pacific. At other times we were part of the Third or Fifth Fleets, which were actually identical except that their commanding admirals and staffs rotated, and which contained Task Force 38 (58), the principal high-speed carrier assault force. The numbering of the fleet and task force changed depending on whether Admiral William Halsey or Admiral Raymond Spruance, "the quiet warrior," was in command; Halsey was Commander 3rd Fleet, Spruance Commander 5th Fleet. The *Murray* also moved in and out of two of the three command areas in the Pacific. We were never in the Southeast Pacific area, but we saw plenty of action in the Southwest Pacific area (which included the Philippines, what is now Indonesia, New Guinea, the Solomon Islands, and Australia) and the Pacific Ocean area, which was Chester Nimitz's command. The Pacific Ocean area was further divided into the North Pacific area (mainly Alaska and the Aleutian Islands), the Central Pacific area (which extended from 42° N down to the equator and included the Hawaiian, Gilbert, Marshall, Caroline, and Marianas Islands), and the South Pacific area (which extended from the equator to the South Pole, and took in New Zealand, Fiji, and the Ellice, New Hebrides, and Marquesas Islands). I didn't understand the delimitation of the command areas when I was actually involved in the war. We had no sense aboard the *Murray* of the full extent of the grand scale of US naval operations and the dimensions of the battle zone. We had a mole-sized picture of what was happening, and our horizon was limited to the view from the ship's deck.

The *Murray* was part of a squadron of eight destroyers, organized into two divisions of four each. We were attached to the same squadron through the whole war, though we were often operating independently a long way from the other ships. The USS *McKee*, which had been built alongside our ship in Orange, was part of our squadron. We used to see people from the other destroyers in our squadron—not often, but more frequently than we would see people from other ships. Once in a while the gunnery officers of the squadron would be called to a preoperation conference, where our targets would be identified and pointed out on a blackboard. Thirty or forty ships might be participating in the operation, so you'd have a fairly large group assembled for these skull sessions. Sometimes the squadron was commanded by one of the destroyer captains, who then was called by the honorary title of commodore. There is a wartime naval rank of commodore, equivalent to brigadier general in the army, but a man who is in command of a group of ships is generally called a commodore, regardless of rank. Sometimes we actually had a squadron commander, a captain who traveled with a small staff and usually rode in the *John Rodgers*.

On October 6, 1943, the *Murray* took part in a raid on Wake Island, which brought together six aircraft carriers plus a host of battleships, cruisers, and destroyers. The destroyers escorted the larger ships, ran patrol, and used sonar to guard against submarine attack, while the carrier-borne aircraft attacked the Japanese positions and the big guns of the battleships and cruisers bombarded the shore. The *Murray*'s role was not central, but it was my first exposure to combat. We returned to Pearl after the raid, and from there we were sent to the New Hebrides, which was the staging area for the Gilbert Islands operation.

War is mostly boredom punctuated by moments of sheer terror. The great bulk of the *Murray*'s wartime activity was endless patrol across the blue Pacific, moving from one operation to another. We saw some action, a lot of water, and a lot of one another. There was usually very little to do on board other than try to stay alert, do your assigned tasks, and play your part in the watch system. The schedule over the course of a twenty-four-hour period was four hours on watch and eight hours off, four hours on and eight hours off, with the schedules arranged so that someone was on watch at all hours of day and night. That was the theory, at any rate. The problem was that no one wanted to end up with the uncomfortable night watches all the time, so we would "dog" the more desirable afternoon watch, shortening it and rotating the watches so that everybody got a fair shake. That meant that every third day it was your turn to stand the mid-watch from midnight to four in the morning. We also went to general quarters an hour before sunrise, because that was supposedly the time when the enemy was most likely to attack.

Then there was the regular, everyday maintenance and administrative work that had to be done aboard ship during the hours when you were not standing watch or sleeping. The gunnery officer oversaw the administrative details of running the ordnance department. He kept track of all the ammunition and ordered replacements for the 40-mm and 20-mm guns as well as the five-inch guns. He kept track of the torpedoes, depth charges, and ammunition for small arms like rifles and pistols. It even fell to the gunnery officer to look after the gun that fired the small projectile that threw the messenger line out. He had to keep track of how many rounds had been fired through the guns, because after a certain number of firings the gun barrels had to be relined when the ship put into the navy yard. I could delegate some administrative detail—Jim Boyd had two or three assistants, and so did I later on when I became gunnery officer—but it was a lot of work. The officers also had to keep an eye on the crew's duties and run training activities to keep the crew alert and ready to fight at a split second's warning.

Consequently, we were tired all the time and were always looking for a place to lie down and take a nap when we were off watch and not working. The constant heat and humidity of the South Pacific made it even harder to stay awake. I was a grown man and could handle the serious lack of sleep pretty well, but some of the younger sailors who were still more boys than men had a hard time of it. They were always sleepy and frequently had to be awakened to attend to what they were doing. They performed their duties admirably, but they were also more likely to be asleep than those of us who were older.

There wasn't much time for recreation, and there wasn't much you could do. We bet on cards a lot. There usually weren't enough people around to have a four-handed bridge game, but we played the two-handed game. We played poker, cribbage, and acey-deucey, which was the navy version of backgammon. Our radiomen used to copy the official navy Morse Code broadcast of world news headlines, translate it, then put it out as a three- or four-page mimeographed newspaper every morning. Chief quartermaster J. C. Clay and sonarman David Bailey, who were pretty good artists, used to draw an illustration for the first page of the "Fantail Gazette," and that was a nice thing to have. We read magazines, especially *Time* and the *New Yorker*, reproduced in special pocket-sized armed forces editions, without advertising. We also read lots of books, not only books that people had donated but paperbacks that were printed specifically for the boys in the armed services. We used to get crates of reissued classics and best-sellers, printed in double-column format, two columns to the page. I particularly remember Jack London's *The Cruise of the Snark*, because he was writing about sailing to islands in the Pacific that we visited aboard the *Murray*. Jack London went to Pearl Harbor before it was a naval installation, and he even traveled to the Solomon Islands. When we were in the South Pacific, we would sometimes come across an island that was several miles off the position indicated on our chart. On one of those occasions I looked at the chart and saw that it was dated 1841, with corrections added in 1865. It occurred to me that we were even then using the same navigation charts that Jack London had used on his cruise aboard the *Snark* in the first decade of the twentieth century. All our South Pacific charts initially were based on nineteenth-century surveys, and more accurate and up-to-date information on the ocean depths, location of reefs, and shapes of shorelines had to wait until the US Navy had captured that territory from the Japanese. The navy survey ships immediately moved in, and it wasn't long before we had up-to-date, accurate charts.

We had mail call whenever we got into port, though "port" was usually no more than some godforsaken atoll in the Pacific where the mail

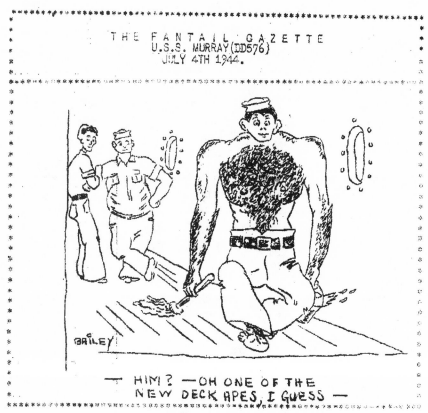

First page illustration from the "Fantail Gazette," July 4, 1944.

had been flown in by military air transport. We also received mail at sea, from time to time, via ship-to-ship high-line. Mail call was really for the enlisted men, since officers' mail was deposited in the wardroom. Sometimes you'd go two or three weeks without any mail, and then there would be a great accumulation of it. Betty was my most frequent correspondent, and I got regular letters from my mother and occasional letters from my father. I didn't hear much from my friends, since they were scattered all over the world in the various military services. They didn't know where I was, and I didn't know where they were. Someone serving in the Pacific theater had a thoroughly anonymous address. Mail was addressed to you in care of your ship, Fleet Post Office, San Francisco. Mail was important for keeping up morale, so the military went to great lengths to get mail to the boys as promptly as possible.

I didn't mind life at sea, but I can't say that I particularly enjoyed it. It was hard to shake the feeling that, in spite of your tasks and the diversions available to you, there was absolutely nothing to do and no escape from the weariness of it all. The biggest problem with shipboard life, obviously, was lack of feminine companionship. Aside from that, I missed less about civilian life than you might expect. The whole nation was caught up in the war, and we haven't had an experience like that since. The draft had taken most of the nation's physically competent young men into the armed forces. The United States had been converted to a wartime economy, and not only luxuries but even many consumer goods were no longer available. Just to take one example, there were no automobiles produced in America until the war was over. Whether I was in the navy or somewhere else, I was bound to be caught up in the nation's wartime activity, and service with the navy was my preferred means of involvement.

Indeed, while I had been quite dissatisfied with life aboard the *Buck*, once I got my designation changed to deck officer and began to have a responsible role to play aboard the *Murray*, I no longer thought about escaping from destroyer duty but recognized it as a way of life that I was now fitted for. I learned a lot about the experience of command and what it takes to run an enterprise, and that was useful when I became head of The Sperry and Hutchinson Company. The navy style is something that you retain, along with a sense of what the navy calls loyalty up and loyalty down. You're supposed to be responsible and look out for your juniors, just as you're supposed to be loyal and obedient to your superiors. One example of that was the relationship of the officers to the boat crew. The *Murray* had a couple of small boats that plied back and forth between ships or between the ship and shore. The boats transported messages, supplies, and personnel when the ship was in port. The boat crew consisted of an engineer, a coxswain, and a bow hook. They went around at all times and in all weather, and frequently they were away from the ship at the mess call that summoned the crew to their meals. It was the responsibility of the deck officers to make sure that when the boat crew returned, there would be a hot meal ready for them.

In October 1943, as the *Murray* was steaming toward the island of Efate in the New Hebrides, I read in the ship's newspaper that the USS *Buck* had been sunk on October 9 by a German submarine at Salerno, off the coast of Italy. Navy people would always report to one another when a ship was lost. The German torpedo hit the magazine underneath the *Buck*'s number 2 gun, causing a massive explosion and destroying that whole portion of the ship. Coincidentally, my Yale classmate Dick Pinkham was aboard an SC or PC nearby, and he saw the destroyer blow up and sink. There were few survivors, and almost all the *Buck*'s officers were lost. When a destroyer went to general quarters, the captain and the officer of the deck would be stationed on the bridge. Directly above the bridge was the rotating gunfire director, a conning tower known as Control, which controlled the main battery of five-inch guns. Directly underneath the bridge was the wardroom, and adjacent to the wardroom was the Combat Information Center, known as CIC, where radio, radar, and sonar information was collected and relayed to the bridge and the guns. The torpedo that hit the *Buck* destroyed the bridge, Control, wardroom, and CIC, the locations where most of the deck officers were stationed, and blew up the engine rooms where the engineering officers were on duty. The only surviving officers were the junior officers in the damage control party, who were stationed far aft.

The survivors of the *Buck* never held reunions, because there weren't enough of them, but about ten years ago the veterans of the *Buck* went to a reunion in Norfolk of all the ships in their squadron. They wore hats embroidered with the name of the USS *Buck*, and as they were sightseeing around the harbor one day, a German immigrant employed in Norfolk saw their hats and introduced himself as a former member of the German submarine service. He knew about the *Buck*, and he put the ship's survivors in touch with Siegfried Koitschka, the captain of the U-boat that had sunk the *Buck*. Captain Koitschka was still living in Germany, and he wrote the survivors a letter about the sinking of the *Buck* (reprinted on the next page). It turned out to have been sort of a fluke occurrence. He said his submarine found itself directly in the path of the *Buck*, and was unable to maneuver out of the way. The only weapon that was in a position to stop the oncoming destroyer was an experimental torpedo that had been put aboard the sub at the last moment. The Germans fired the torpedo and scored a direct hit, and the *Buck* immediately exploded, burst into flames, and sank.

I was greatly saddened when I learned of the *Buck*'s sinking. I had so many friends aboard, including Gabby Harrington and Robin Scully. One of the enlisted men who perished was the son of the well-known band leader Meyer Davis, whose orchestra played dance music at many debutante parties and college proms around New York. I went to a dance twenty-five years later where Meyer Davis was conducting, and although it was supposed to be a festive occasion, since so many years had elapsed I thought it would not be inappropriate to mention

Königsbergerstraße 7   Löhra   11, November, 1988
3554 Löhra

Dear Mr. Brooks,

Fred Geils told me that he stumbled upon some members of the
destroyer *Buck*. It is 45 years ago that we had a rendezvous in the Salerno
Bay. But I remember the October 9, 1943 very well. At that time I got my
first T-5 (acoustic torpedo, Gnat, Zaunkönig). We had to leave for patrol
and it was too late for an instruction in Gotenhafen, We did not know
very much about this kind of torpedo and put it into the stern torpedo
tube without having much confidence into this fish. One night on October 9, 1943, 0036 we sailed in the Salerno Bay. Our position was
39°57' N, 14°28' E. The weather was a little misty and the mist lay like a
screen on the surface. Suddenly the radio-room reported a radar contact
by a surface craft. After a little while we observed a one funnel destroyer
which approached in a high speed. We found ourselves in a very miserable situation. The destroyer had got radar contact and there was no
chance to attack her in the usual way. The only thing we could do was to
submerge and wait for the depth-charges. In this moment the T-5 came
into my head. We had no confidence in that fish but there was no alternative. In the meanwhile the destroyer increased her speed and black steam
came out of her funnel. I think we steered in a northern direction. In our
wake steamed the destroyer in full speed ahead and armed her depth-
charges in order to try to kill us. It was a goddamned situation. When she
was in a distance of 2½ nautical miles we fired the Gnat out of the stern
torpedo tube. If you believe it or not we did not feel very well. After a few
minutes we observed and heard a huge detonation. The destroyer
became very small and then she disappeared. May be that the destroyer
depth-charges detonated too. There were other destroyers in the neigh-
bourhood and we had to make off. We shot only that single T-5. We did
not release aphrodites. The captain of the destroyer could not know that
we fired a T-5. He had to think that the sub could not do any harm to his
ship in this situation. I am sorry that so many sailors had to cross the bars.
But what should I do? The *Buck* intended to kill me by all means. Weeks
ago the *Buck* sank the Italian submarine *Argento*. The captain of the
Argento, Conde Brizzi, told me this when we met during an international
submarine congress. In autumn 1989 I take part in the reunions of
Ellyson and *Rodman*. Maybe we shall meet on such an occasion.

   All the best,

      Yours

      Dr. Siegfried Koitschka

Letter from the commander of the German submarine that sank the Buck.

to the old band leader that I knew his son and had served with him on board the *Buck*. And I think that he was pleased to hear that.

When I heard that the *Buck* had been lost, I also thought, "There but for the grace of God go I," since I had left the *Buck* only six months before and would have been in its CIC if I had not been transferred off the ship. My friends Gene Somers and Rab Irvine had also been transferred from the *Buck* before the sinking, and we have continued to see one another from time to time. We have never really talked about the quirk of fate that took us off the *Buck* before it was sunk.

From Wake Island in the Central Pacific area, the *Murray* traveled to the New Hebrides in the South Pacific area. Our journey took us across the equator, and as we passed 0° latitude the crew held the traditional ceremonies in which "pollywogs," those who had never crossed the equator, were initiated into the realm of Neptunus Rex. I had crossed the equator some years before on my trip around the world, and I foolishly thought that I didn't need to go through the ceremonies that were imposed on the pollywogs by the "shellbacks" who had already made the trip. I had already taken part in the gentlemanly frolic that marked the passing of the equator on a passenger liner. I had no particular urge to go through the rougher naval ceremony, where the shellbacks threw fuel oil on you, banged on you as you crawled through a tightly constricted canvas chute, and finally doused you in a pool of saltwater brought up from the sea. So I got my father to supply me with a rather elaborate certificate from the S&H advertising department, which attested that I had already crossed the equator in a passenger liner, and I produced this when the *Murray* crossed the equator for the first time. The enlisted men of the ship took this in bad faith. We had a row, and they said (in suitable naval language) that I was avoiding something that every proper sailor ought to experience.

In the end, I didn't participate in the ceremony, but I recognized later that I really ought to have. I was about the third officer in seniority on the ship, and I worried that my lack of proper shellback status might cost me some of the respect of the crew. So the next time the *Murray* shipped back from Pearl Harbor with some new pollywogs aboard, I came forward as we approached the equator and said that I had avoided the previous ceremony through a subterfuge and that I now ought to be properly initiated. Well, this was the crew's opportunity to take it out on me for having evaded the gauntlet the first time around, and they really let me have it. It was a grueling experience, and I just had to take it. I looked up at one point in the ordeal, and I saw the captain watching from the bridge. When it was over, I went to the head and began the arduous task of trying to get the fuel oil off my body and out of my hair and the rest of it. When I was finally more or less cleaned up, I saw the captain and he complimented me for having gone through this really difficult initiation, knowing that I would get it worse than anyone else, and he told me how well I had borne it.

While the *Murray* was in the New Hebrides, she was loaned out to the Southwest Pacific forces for support operations, all in preparation for the great fleet assault on the Gilbert Islands. We arrived at Espiritu Santo in the New Hebrides on November 4, 1943, and promptly loaded up a deck cargo of five-inch projectiles, to be delivered to the ammunition barges at Guadalcanal a couple of days' run to the north. This deck cargo got in the way and loaded us down and prevented the *Murray* from traveling at its top speed, so we were very relieved when we unloaded the cargo upon arrival in Purvis Bay.

Guadalcanal is one of the main islands in the Solomons group. It had been the scene of vicious fighting between Americans and Japanese in 1942 and early 1943, and its place names had passed into the consciousness of many Americans. Nearby were the sites of the sea battles of Tassafaronga, Cape Esperance, and Savo Island, where the ocean floor was clogged with Japanese and American ship remains; the Metanikau and Lunga rivers, which ran red with blood at the height of the fighting; Edson's Ridge, where a contingent of marines turned back a determined Japanese effort to retake the landing strip at Henderson Field; and Point Cruz, where my friend Paul Moore, later New York's Episcopal Bishop and a fellow member of the Yale Corporation, was wounded and almost died. My brother Dick did not participate in the initial landings on Guadalcanal in August 1942, but he was part of the action from the early fall of 1942. When his unit was relieved, he participated in the marine landings at Cape Gloucester at the western end of the island of New Britain in the Bismarck Sea, just across the strait from New Guinea. The landings at Cape Gloucester were not heavily resisted, fortunately for the marines, because they had to go ashore in waist-deep water, and each man had to hold his rifle—his weapon, as my brother always referred to it—up above his shoulders to keep it dry. They dug in quickly on the beach, and the Japanese assault came shortly thereafter. Then my brother came down with a bad case of malaria and skin diseases as a result of living, working, and fighting in those jungles and was sent to a rest and recuperation area near Melbourne, Australia, where he spent the better part of a year.

My brother had been married in August 1942 to Margaret Buckwald, a Sarah Lawrence girl. I met her only once or twice. The two of them were married in New York just before my brother shipped out to Guadalcanal. Like many other wartime unions, their marriage didn't last long, and it terminated while Dick was still out in the far reaches of the vast Pacific Ocean. While he was recuperating down in the Melbourne area, he met a young Australian woman whom he became quite close to. I remember that she and my mother had a warm correspondence, even though they never met. My mother was delighted that there was someone to take a loving interest in her son when he was ill and halfway around the world from home.

By autumn 1943 the tide of war had moved northward, and Guadalcanal and the surrounding islands had become a support area. Purvis Bay, where we unloaded the projectiles, is on the south shore of Florida Island, down the coast a bit from Tulagi Island and across Iron Bottom Bay from Guadalcanal. It was formerly the seat of the bishop of Melanesia, and the bishop's house, dock, and front yard had become the Iron Bottom Bay officers' club, in which I spent many happy hours.

We had no sooner unloaded our ammunition cargo than we were sent up the Slot, the channel that runs through the Solomons group, to deliver reinforcing troops at Empress Augusta Bay on Bougainville. On the night of November 8, our engineering officer, Larry Armstrong, hearing a lot of noise and commotion, poked his head out of the engine room to find out what was going on. He was surprised to see flares drifting down out of the night sky and hear ships firing their guns in all directions. "Just like the navy," he remarked, "to hold a practice at this time of night." Upon being informed that this was no practice, he dived back into the more congenial surroundings of the engine room. The Bougainville engagement was the *Murray*'s first important combat experience, and it was brief, hectic, and educational. We escaped without a mishap, but our old friend, the cruiser *Birmingham*, which we had escorted from the Panama Canal, was hit with two bombs and a torpedo.

Three days later, the *Murray* and the *McKee* steamed out of Purvis Bay as the sun rose gloriously over the Coral Sea. We joined Halsey's carrier task force for an assault on Rabaul, at the northeastern tip of the island of New Britain, off the coast of Papua New Guinea, less than eight hundred miles from Australia's Great Barrier Reef. My brother Dick landed with the marines that December at Cape Gloucester, on the extreme western end of New Britain. Rabaul, on the other side of the island, was the Japanese headquarters and major base in the South Pacific. It was heavily fortified, lined with concrete bunkers, and honeycombed with over four hundred miles of tunnels in which supplies were hidden, so that Japanese submarines could come right up to shore for secret nighttime fueling and provisioning. The Japanese did not intend to lose Rabaul, and they didn't. Eventually the Americans bypassed it, but the place was leveled by thousands of tons of bombs in the last couple of years of the war. Simpson Harbor at Rabaul, as I discovered when I visited there in 1983, is a landlocked bay amidst steep volcanic cones lush with tropical greenery. Not only is it one of the most beautiful harbors in the world, it can easily accommodate vast numbers of ships, and it did for the Japanese in the war.

On that morning of November 11, 1943, the carriers' planes flew out to bomb the shipping in Simpson Harbor. When they returned they were followed by a flock of Japanese planes, perhaps as many as a hundred and fifty. I couldn't say what it was like to be attacked by that many planes, because when they were bearing down on us I was in the depths of the Plotting Room (or "Plot"), and I might as well have been in a submarine. The Plotting Room contained the Mark I (Ford) computer and the Sperry stable element, a large gyroscope. Plotting rooms were way below decks near the center of rotation of the ship, so that the gyros could minimize the ship's rolls and make them less violent. The Combat Information Center (or CIC), on the other hand, was located in close proximity to the bridge. That was the place where the CIC gang tried to put together information from the Plot and the radars and to keep track of what was happening for the benefit of the captain on the bridge. Officers and men with headsets put marks on plexiglass plotting boards, each X indicating the probable location of a Japanese ship or plane, with an arrow indicating direction. The CIC was a response to the need for a data-correlation room when radar became a reliable tool; it was a sign of the growing complexity and technological nature of the war. Thanks to our radar, by 1945 we also served as a fighter-director ship and guided our carrier-based aircraft to intercept incoming enemy planes. The work was complicated, which is why the officers often referred to the CIC as "Christ, I'm Confused." The *Murray* did not have a CIC until one was installed at its first major navy yard availability at Mare Island.

As assistant gunnery officer, I dealt with the data received in the Plotting Room and directed the fire-controlmen who operated the large mechanical computer there, a big gray monster about the size of a pool table. All the information on enemy targets was processed in the computer, which calculated the ballistics of where to aim the main-battery guns so that projectiles would intersect the target. After it had ground away for a while, a buzzer would go off and the word "solution" would light up. We would send the firing solution to the guns and up to

Jim Boyd in the director, and he would swivel around and take the planes under fire as quickly as we could give him the target information. He could see the planes coming in even if we couldn't, and he shot down four or five planes during the attack on Rabaul. He even had a sufficient sense of the occasion to reach down and make a chalk mark on the side of the director when he scored a hit. He could do that because the planes didn't come in one after another on top of him, as they do in the movies. It didn't happen that fast, and he had time to look around and see how the situation was unfolding. After the battle, our signalmen painted a small Japanese flag up on the outside of the bridge for each Japanese plane we had shot down. The *McKee* always felt it was in competition with us, and there was a friendly rivalry to see who could put up the most little Rising Sun flags.

The Rabaul strike was a major event for the sailors on board the carrier *Bunker Hill,* who for years afterward held a reunion every November 11 to commemorate the event. For the *Murray,* however, it was a one-day diversion. Destroyers were in short supply at that stage of the war, so the *Murray* was shuttled about from one operation to the next. After the Rabaul strike, we were immediately dispatched to Espiritu Santo and attached to the Tarawa Attack Force for the assault on the Gilbert Islands. The battle for the atoll of Tarawa and the islet of Betio was famous for its savagery, but the *Murray's* role was minor compared with that of the marines. We spent most of our time steaming back and forth along the so-called ping lines screening the transports from submarine attack.

Three days after the initial landing, on a cloudless and perfect day as we were on patrol several miles from Tarawa, we came upon the bodies of three marines who had been killed in the assault. They were horribly bloated and discolored by then, and one was missing a head. Our doctor got the names, ranks, and serial numbers of those who still had dogtags, and we wrapped them in heavy green canvas weighted down with shells, held a brief naval religious ceremony, and buried them at sea. Alton R. Pruit, our ship's doctor, wrote a letter to his sister describing the scene and his emotions. He was a man of great sensitivity, and his sister showed the letter to a friend on the staff of *Time* magazine, which published it. Shortly after the incident, we received peremptory orders forbidding us from recovering any more bodies until Tarawa was secured—because while we stopped or slowed to launch or retrieve a whaleboat, we were more vulnerable to submarine torpedo attack. We had to stand and watch as twenty-five dead marines quietly floated by us on their way out to sea. It was a beautiful day, with

"WHEN THE SEA SHALL GIVE UP HER DEAD . . ."

The U.S. had taken another island in the Pacific. Aboard a destroyer a young Navy surgeon was actor and spectator in one of the thousands of throat-tightening epilogues that follow the thundering drama of battle. He described it in this letter to his sister:

WHAT THE DOCTOR SAW

The names aren't real, the rest is.

It was three days after the major part of the battle had ended and we were out a few miles from the island patrolling our little sector of ocean, swinging back and forth in huge figures of eight. The noise and colors of battle were gone. The bombing had ceased and the big guns on the ships were silent.

Now there was only a little smoke on the island and though we could see occasional puffs from the guns of the one destroyer which was still firing, the sound didn't carry to us. It was altogether quiet. The sun was shining; the sky was a clear blue and even the water was so still that there were only ripples, like it is on a lake at home on a quiet day.

Most of the men not on watch were sprawled around topside trying to relax and cool off in the little breeze the ship's movement made. A few of us were standing by the rail thinking our own thoughts when someone called attention to some objects in the water. We began to watch them.

There were three of them, a hundred yards or more apart, and as we came closer we could see that they were men and that they were dead. They were bobbing up and down in the water with their arms stretched out ridiculously straight and stiff. We could see a V of white undershirt at their necks and the ripples breaking over the toes of their brogans.

Lower Away. The order came down from the bridge to lower away the boat, go to them, determine their identity and, if they were ours, to bring them back to the ship.

They were so horribly bloated and discolored that even their race was indeterminate but the uniform was that of our

that they would stay decently buried. Then the Captain came down from the bridge and the ceremony began. . . .

What would you have said, Thomas or Wilson, or Nobody-at-all, had you the words? What reason for being here? What regrets? I think I know. I think the words were said for us long ago in a language simpler than you or I could choose. I will say them for you.

*"Here dead lie we because we did not choose
To live and shame the land from which we sprung.
Life, to be sure, is nothing much to lose;
But young men think it is, and we were young."*

A simple reason. A single profound regret. That's right, isn't it?

I heard the last words of the ritual . . . "We therefore commit these bodies to the deep, to be turned into corruption, looking for the resurrection of the body, when the sea shall give up her dead. . . ."

The stretchers tilted. The flags fell away. There were three dull splashes in the water.

WHAT THE DOCTOR FELT

To those of us who were not so unfortunate as Thomas or Wilson, the emotions I could not feel at the time later take on an added significance. Too often it is a bitter significance, because so many of the things we hear from home make all this seem so hopelessly fruitless, so terribly futile.

I wish there were words adequate enough to explain how deeply most of us feel about being out here; how much it means to us to win completely and unequivocally so that our sons and our sons' sons, and those of our enemy need not know this again; how much it hurts to be forced to the realization that so many of our hopes are empty.

I wish there were words adequate enough to explain the bitterness, the scorn, the unrest and the lack of faith most of us have for so many things at home:

own men. When we tried to take hold of their arms and legs and lift them up and over into the boat, the skin would slip away in our hands. One of our boys was sick from the odor.

As we got each one in the boat we'd empty his pockets and search for identification. One was named Thomas. He had a canteen on his belt and a map in his pocket, both with that name on it. John Thomas. Wilson, H.W., had an identification tag around his neck. He also had a billfold with a picture of a girl, some foreign coins, a wrist watch, and a bottle opener.

The third had a knife and some coins in his pocket but there was no name. If he ever had an identification tag around his neck, it would have been gone. He had no head or neck. He was and would continue to be an unknown—a nobody-at-all. We put them, one on the other, in the bottom of the boat, covered them with a canvas and started back. It was a long ride back.

The Cunning Brethren. Perhaps I should have felt more emotions than I did, riding back with them in that boat: a fierce anger at the "thing" which allows nations and peoples to do this to each other; an urgent personal desire for retaliation; bitterness because they had given their all and reaped this, while some of their more cunning but less conscientious brethren at home were giving nothing and reaping all; horror because of the added indignities they had suffered even after death; sorrow for their parents, for their girls, and for the many people who must grieve and forget as best they can.

If I did feel any one of these, I put it all aside as being relatively unimportant. These were brave men and they were dead. Bravery and death were linked together in a natural and inevitable sequence. It seemed as simple as that.

We brought them aboard and began preparing them for a proper burial at sea. The men were crowded around in close, curious bunches. They were quiet for once and there was a queer, hard look on their faces.

Each was wrapped in a heavy canvas (it was green, I remember) and weighted with heavy shells from our big guns so

For the ineffective, bumbling legislature; for all the political devices and stratagems which are so obviously for the gain and glory of a few politicians though clothed in the sanctity of the words, "For the men in the service."

How bitterly we resent the strikes. (How can we be 100% for something that they're only 75% behind at home?)

How we feel about the stupid racial prejudices that are fostered and festered by some of our "great democratic" Senators while many of the same races they so denounce are out here risking their necks to give those same Senators the right to go on fostering their hatred. What a sordid story! How we feel to have even our right to vote fashioned into a political football.

How much we scorn the little crumbs that are thrown our way, such as the $300 mustering-out pay and all such meaningless tommyrot.

First Things. The thing that is important to us is first to win the war and then to set about rehabilitating not only ourselves but the people in India and China and Japan and Germany so that we can live together and call each other friends. It seems to me that that is what we set out to do. Even though few of us ever expected to attain that much, it is bitter knowledge indeed to see how infinitely little we are likely to attain at all.

The plain and simple truth is, I'm afraid, that we, as a people have not yet grown big enough, tolerant enough, wise enough, nor just enough, to manage our own affairs with honor and justice, let alone those of the world. We are still trying to delude ourselves with the idea that we are a democracy instead of accepting the truth that we are not, and planning ways and means of becoming one some day.

Still, had Thomas or Wilson or I or any of us the same choice to make again, knowing all this, we would not change our decision. We may be denied and shamed by the things which happen at home but we cannot shame ourselves by denying the things we personally believe in.

white specks of cloud in the blue sky. The awful irony of looking down at the bodies of those young men, as they drifted in the clean, clear water on the long, lazy swells of the Pacific, was almost too much to bear.

We spent Christmas of '43 at Funafuti in the Ellice Islands, which today is the capital island of the tiny nation of Tuvalu (population 10,000). Funafuti is such a low-lying island that as we approached it from the sea it looked like a forest of ships' masts. As we drew closer we could see coconut trees and finally the beach. We passed a week of idleness there, painting the ship, replenishing supplies, and swimming over the side in the gin-clear Funafuti Lagoon. On Christmas Sunday, December 26, the welcome news appeared on the *Murray*'s bulletin board that for the first time since we had arrived in the Pacific, church services would be held on the tender (the supply ship for the destroyers present) for those members of the starboard section who wished to attend. The more devout (or *Murray*-weary) of the crew put on their cleanest white uniforms, washed up, and climbed into the boats to go to the tender. There were general high spirits aboard as everyone looked forward to a morning of religion, ice cream, goofing off, and seeing friends from other ships. The men laughed and called to one another, "No work today!"

As the religious services began, our supply officer/paymaster, Ensign Hugh "Pay" Hall, stopped in at the tender's supply office. The *Murray* had been at sea for a month, and Pay was going to replenish our food supplies, Christmas Sunday or no. Pay's mission was successful, and soon he stood on the tender's deck amid a mountain of packing cases. Alongside the tender bobbed the boat that would transport the mountain to the *Murray*. Now for a working party. Why not let the *Murray*'s church party already aboard the tender volunteer its services? As the religious ceremonies ended, the tender's loudspeaker boomed, "All *Murray* men lay down to the port quarterdeck." There stood pink-cheeked, twenty-two-year-old Pay, fresh out of the University of Texas, amid his mountain of packing cases. He drew himself up to his full six feet two inches and pleaded, "Come on, fellas, bear a hand with these stores, will ya?" The supply officer was not an officer with authority over the enlisted men who had been summoned. They grumbled, "We didn't come to church to be on no working party." It so happened that the *Murray*'s chief boatswain's mate, who had near-unlimited authority over those men, was among the churchgoers. The supplies moved into the boat. The white uniforms were soiled, and spirits dampened. Church call had a limited response after that.

We were in Funafuti for a week, then returned to Pearl Harbor for a few days and had a chance to get away from the *Murray* for the first time since the Wake Island raid. I swam at the officers' clubs in Pearl and Makalapa, went to the beach at Waikiki, and saw friends on Oahu. I paid a visit on my parents' friends Bill and Frank Jefferson, the sons of the well-known nineteenth-century actor Joseph Jefferson. Bill Jefferson and his wife lived in a small beach house near Diamond Head, and Frank Jefferson lived alone in a couple of rooms at the Halekalani Hotel at Waikiki. I also went a few times to Kailua with Jim Boyd to see a woman who had been one of Jim's classmates at the University of California. She lived with her children in a small house near the beach. We took the bus from Honolulu, which made a scenic and rather hazardous trip over the mountains, with many switchbacks; nowadays you go through a tunnel instead.

The Hawaii interlude was a welcome break, for once we set out again, we would not see civilization or get off the ship for an extended period until almost the end of 1944. From the time we left Pearl Harbor in January until we arrived in San Francisco eleven months later, I never had a night away from the ship. By the end of January, we were off for the Marshall Islands with Task Force 52. We were part of a two-pronged campaign to take the island of Kwajalein, our wing attacking from the south, another from the north. I saw one of our planes attack a Japanese ammo depot on Ebbeye, one of the southern islets. The pilot went in for a dive-bomb attack and scored a direct hit, but he flew too low. As the depot went up in a great mushroom-topped cloud, the plane was blown this way and that, like a falling leaf in a strong breeze, and crashed on the island. The main Marshall islands of Kwajalein, Eniwetok, and Majuro were secured, but some of the others were bypassed, and the Japanese troops who hid out on those islands would fire at passing ships for months or even years afterwards. There were some Japanese holdouts hiding in the jungles of Guam as late as 1960, as E. J. Kahn relates in his book *The Stragglers.*

We returned to Espiritu Santo in the New Hebrides archipelago, which is today the nation of Vanuatu but was then a "condominium" jointly administered by France and Great Britain. We parked alongside the tender while one of the guns was dismantled to see if we could figure out why counterrecoil fluid was leaking over the outer housing, a potentially serious problem. Fortunately no crack was discovered, only a small leak in a fitting that could be plugged with a little packing and the tightening of a closure screw. This incident inspired me to write a letter to the Bureau of Ordnance, submitting my one and only idea for improved gun design. I suggested that they include a hole in the outer housing that would enable the ship's gunner's mates to inspect and pack the leaky fitting without taking the whole gun apart. Much to my amazement and great personal pleasure, a reply came back that this problem had cropped up so often that corrective action had already been taken. The suggested peephole would be installed on new guns, and those already in service would be altered when ships put in for overhauls.

Even in 1944, I thought that Espiritu Santo was one of the very few Pacific islands to which I might like to return, and I did return in 1983. It was surely Espiritu Santo that inspired the musical *South Pacific*. It is a lush, verdant, heavily wooded island, full of dense jungle, creepers, and vines. Pretty red-roofed houses march right up to the shore. Coconut trees fringe the black sand beaches, stepping off into the distance in long, orderly rows. I remember visiting one of those beaches with Captain Anderson and Dr. Pruit, swimming through the warm, clear water looking for cat's-eye seashells. In 1944, the main port of Santo was a major naval support base, with a harbor full of ships and a shore establishment of almost a hundred thousand men. When I returned years later, I found it strange to see the anchorage nearly empty and to realize that the population of the island was only one-tenth of what it had been during the war. Many of the buildings in town were the Quonset huts that had been put up all over the place in the 1940s and that by 1983 were corroded and rusting away in the hot tropical sun. The natives had made fences out of the metal mats that the Seabees used all over the Pacific to surface airstrips. In the spring of 1944, hundreds of us sailors sat one rainy evening on the jagged edges of one such unfinished airfield to watch Bob Hope, Frances Langford, and Jerry Colona do their stuff in a big USO show. And it was great!

In February 1944, we joined our squadron at Efate, further south in the New Hebrides. The *Murray* anchored at the naval base in Havannah Harbor, a large sheltered roadstead formed by the tiny islands of Lelepa and Moso off the northwest coast of Efate. Captain Anderson went fishing for the multicolored fish that lazed in the lacy, convoluted forms of the live coral. The crew played baseball near the town of Port Vila and adopted a friendly native dog. We all watched *Dumbo* one evening in a driving downpour. After one memorable evening at the Havannah Harbor officers' club, a stuffy old admiral sent around a directive to all ships expressing dismay at the behavior of some "tin horn drunks" at the club, especially their "loud and obscene language, feet on the table, and other ungentlemanly conduct." The officer who had so behaved would surely recognize himself, said the admiral (and he did!), and there would be no more of that. This directive was produced at a hilarious, beer-drinking court martial at our Cape Cod *Murray* officers' reunion years later and was key evidence in my conviction for "conduct unbecoming"! All told, we spent nearly two relatively quiet months there in the New Hebrides. Dr. Pruit, who was an obstetrician and gynecologist by training, assiduously polished his cat's-eyes and complained about the dearth of pregnancies among the ship's crew.

In March, we had a week's diversion from our New Hebridean idyll to take part in the bombardment of Kavieng, at the northern tip of New Ireland, to the north of Rabaul on New Britain. It had originally been planned to take Kavieng in order to complete the neutralization of Rabaul. This operation was later canceled as unnecessary, and the marines instead seized beautiful little Emirau in the Bismarck Sea. On March 20, we went with our dog, several other tin cans, and four old battleships to shoot up the Kavieng airfield and prevent the Japanese from interfering with the marines' landing at Emirau. It was my first operation as gunnery officer. Not a plane from Kavieng turned up at Emirau. Success! But the poor dog... I know no noise harder on the eardrums than the sharp, ringing crack of the 5-inch/38, which probably has a lot to do with my present hearing problems. During the occasional lulls in the firing, we heard our dog howling below. Needless to say, he was promptly disembarked upon our return to Efate.

Our two-month idyll was at an end. We now joined the Seventh Fleet, the MacArthur navy. Our destroyer squadron left Efate, and we crossed the Coral Sea, traveling at high speed in column formation through the treacherous shoals and currents of the China Strait. We called at Milne Bay and eventually dropped anchor at Cape Sudest, on the northeast coast of the Papuan peninsula of Papua New Guinea, where there was a large American base with thousands of troops. There were a few American Red Cross girls at Cape Sudest, one of whom had known our shipmate Scott Martin in San Francisco. Scott promised to make contact with the girls. Eagerly looking forward to a picnic and a little feminine companionship on the New Guinea strand, we cooked up a turkey, complete with all the fixings, and put forth in the whaleboat. Scott's Red Cross contact took the turkey, all right, and then she said to us, "Scott wouldn't dance with me in San Francisco. I'm not going to go on any picnic with him in New Guinea." Our hopes were shattered. We had to settle for beer, a little whiskey, and some baseball.

MacArthur ordered a simultaneous assault on the Japanese positions on the north coast of New Guinea on April 22, 1944. The attacks, in accordance with MacArthur's leapfrog technique, were made on Tanahmerah Bay to the west, Aitape to the east, and Hollandia in the middle. The *Murray* was part of the Aitape attack. Aitape was nothing more than a small spot on the north coast of New Guinea, lacking even a harbor, but although this was a relatively small operation, it was a mighty big one for us. The *Murray* and another destroyer stayed on after the initial landing and subsequent unloading, steaming back and forth on anti-sub and anti-aircraft patrol in the "roadstead" area between Aitape and the three or four small islands a few miles offshore. It was a dull task. Then one night—bong! bong! bong! bong! bong!— our general-quarters alarm went off. In a single movement, I woke up and went racing to my general-quarters station. From the main-battery director high above the bridge, I could see that the ship lay conspicuously in the midst of a small illuminated circle, with flares drifting down around us. Jim Hawco, staring at the edges of the circle of light, said to me, "I can hear them, but I can't see them." At that instant a Japanese plane roared in from the wall of darkness, barely as high as the masthead, like a thing out of a nightmare. The *Murray* was lit up in a terrifying burst of light from the flares dropped by the plane. It came directly for us and launched a torpedo. To our great good fortune, the depth setting was too deep and the torpedo passed harmlessly underneath the ship. The *Etamin*, one of the two Liberty ships in the area, was hit by another Japanese plane. (Liberties were small ships built speedily and in great quantity during the war by the Henry Kaiser shipyards.) Our skipper took the *Murray* into a protective rain squall, and we got off a few rounds at a radar image once or twice before the night was over.

I can say with real feeling that for the *Murray*'s sailors the next morning's sunrise was a beautiful one indeed. At mid-morning we came across the wing of a downed Japanese torpedo bomber. We never knew whether it was one of our unwelcome guests of the night before, nor could we be sure that our few rounds had brought it down. Nonetheless, we hauled it aboard, and all hands cut souvenirs. Before nightfall we departed Aitape screening the two Liberties, one towing the other. Before long, we were escorting a group of dock landing ships (LSDs) back to Purvis Bay in the Solomons. We didn't know it that April evening, but we were on our way out of MacArthur land, this time to participate in the next great push of the Central Pacific force: the Marianas.

CHAPTER NINE

Combat in the Pacific with the USS *Murray* and the End of the War, 1944–1945

ay 1944 found the *Murray* once again in Purvis Bay, her officers enjoying the pleasures of the Iron Bottom Bay Club. According to the scuttlebutt, Guam was to be our next assignment. It didn't make sense. The Marianas were beyond Truk, a major Japanese base, on the direct line from Japan to the Carolines. Obviously somebody was crazy. As it turned out, the rumor was right, and we were indeed bound for Guam. The powers that be had decided to bypass Truk, just as they had decided to cancel the Kavieng operation.

Preparations for the amphibious operation were meticulous. The experiences and lessons of the Gilberts and Marshalls were toted up and applied. After a conference aboard the flagship, all ships put to sea. We practiced our Guam assault at Cape Esperance on Guadalcanal, using a local chart with a map of Guam superimposed on it. The landing beaches were designated, fire-support sectors were assigned, and there was even simulated gunfire. The *Murray* had a fire-support mission covering one of the beaches near Agat Village, south of Orote Peninsula. D-day at Saipan was set for June 15 and at Guam three days later. As it turned out, the Guam landing was postponed a month, for a number of reasons. The carrier force then at sea, scheduled to furnish air support at Guam, was required first to meet the challenge of the Japanese fleet in the great battle of the Philippine Sea. Moreover, as a result of the Saipan experience, the preliminary estimate that two divisions would be sufficient to take Guam was upgraded to three. This meant that a reserve division then at Oahu had to be embarked and given time to catch up. For nearly two weeks our group of ships steamed back and forth over a large chunk of Pacific Ocean designated

My thirtieth birthday, Solomon Islands, Iron Bottom Bay Club, 1944. Front: William S. Beinecke; rear, left to right: William J. Duddleston, Commander Paul R. Anderson, Lawrence (Larry) Armstrong, Hamilton, Edward M. Cleland, Follansbee.

Area Nebraska. On one course, the breeze from astern was barely greater than our own speed, just sufficient to keep those of us on watch in the director choking and gasping as the stack gases were blown lazily over us.

Eventually the whole shebang was sent back to Eniwetok in the Marshall Islands to wait out the situation. The *Murray* fueled immediately after we arrived at the island, which was always our first responsibility upon making port. The rest of the stay was given over to necessary ship's work, under ideal conditions. At its advance bases, the navy provided immense floating dry docks, amazing in their size and capacity, and the *Murray* entered dry dock for the first time since leaving Charleston over a year before. Cleaning and painting the hull was an easy task when all hands turned to at once. Moreover, it was different enough from the established routine as to be sort of a lark. The entire crew swam every afternoon in the beautiful clear waters of the lagoon, and there were occasional shore trips to a palm-studded islet. The ten days or so at Eniwetok must have been miserable for the marines, who had already been combat-loaded in the transports for over a month, but for us it was a pleasant interlude.

The *Murray* arrived at Guam early in the morning of July 21 and took up her fire-support mission three or four hours before H-hour. As chief gunnery officer, I was up in the director, above the bridge. Also in the tower with me was the pointer, who operated the gun sights in the vertical dimension, and on his right the trainer, who tracked the target in the horizontal dimension. They operated the gun sights by rotating their sighting handles vertically and horizontally, and between them they kept the guns fixed on the target.

The main battery of a Fletcher-class destroyer consisted of five five-inch guns: the number 1 gun in the bow, the number 2 gun aft and above it, the number 3 gun amidship, and the number 4 and 5 guns back astern. These five main guns operated in unison, so that when the pointer and the trainer sighted on a target, all five guns were aimed at the same target. This information, together with the range, was electrically conveyed to the CIC, where the computer calculated the correct elevation to enable the guns to hit the target. Also in the director, behind the trainer and the pointer, were two men whose job it was to get the range to the target. There were two devices used to determine how far away a target was. The older contraption was a big piece of optical equipment known as the range finder, which used lenses mounted a little bit to either side of the director. The man who operated it had to adjust the optics so that they were both fixed on the target, and then, through triangulation, he could determine the range to the target. The newer piece of equipment was radar, which was faster and more accurate, but radar had not yet completely superseded the old range finders. All this information was also transmitted down below, both through the electrical system and by voice phone. Everybody wore a headset, and the operator of the optical range finder was constantly reporting the range down to his colleague in the CIC.

As the boats landed that morning on Guam, the *Murray* and our sister destroyer the *Dashiell* fired a barrage of rapid fire ahead of the initial landings. Then we slowly moved the curtain of gunfire inland to sweep the beach clear of enemies who resisted the advance of our marines. I don't think our barrage was all that effective, because the Japanese were so well entrenched that they were able to give the poor marines a terrible struggle. But we did what we could. Hardly had the marines landed before an ammunition barge appeared alongside to replenish our needs. It was this sort of logistics support, successfully evolved over the vast distances of the Pacific, that made the American navy so formidable. We ceased firing at H + 10 minutes, at which point our shells were falling two hundred yards inland, and stood by awaiting specific fire-support missions. A fire-control party would locate pockets of Japanese resistance, determine their coordinates on a map, and radio that information to us. We would then pour gunfire onto those targets. While we were cruising back and forth waiting for the fire-control party to call up and give us a target, I had a pair of binoculars trained on an American tank up in the hills that was heading into a Japanese-held area. Contrary to everything I had seen in the movies, it was not rolling along hell for high water, firing its guns off in every direction. It was moseying forward, proceeding in the most careful and methodical manner imaginable, moving about five yards and then swiveling its gun left and right before advancing another five yards. So it would appear that the movie version of tank warfare is no more accurate than the movie version of air warfare at sea.

The Guam mission lasted about a week. At night we fired star shells and white phosphorous to shake up the Japanese and keep them awake. One day we were given a target high on Mount Alafan, which rose to an altitude of 868 feet just behind the southern beaches. While such a target would pose no serious problem for army field artillery, it did for our destroyer gunnery. Our 5-inch/38s were designed to shoot either at airplanes or at ships and shore installations at or near sea level, so to shoot at a target at such an altitude was unusual. There was a sort of rule-of-thumb table that permitted the quick introduction of the proper correction. It amounted to shooting at a theoretical sea-level target, at a range that would place the high point of the trajectory through Mount Alafan at the target's altitude. We must have been delivering the mail pretty well, for we were soon told to cease fire.

The *Murray* left Guam toward the end of July to rejoin the Seventh Fleet in the Southwest Pacific. Hollandia on New Guinea was home port for the next several months. In 1944 there was an officers' club of sorts there, the so-called Platform Club. It was just that, a thatch-roofed platform standing on stilts in the harbor, inherited from the Dutch, its original purpose a mystery. Sometimes we would also go ashore to walk along the beach and go swimming. Most of the time the *Murray* swung on her hook near the eastern entrance of Humboldt Bay, where a small cape pushed out into the Bismarck Sea. A good swimming beach lay on the other side of the point, accessible only via a little trail up and over the spine. Here once more we sought and found Pacific cat's-eyes— inferior, however, in quality and quantity to the New Hebrides variety. We developed our own private landing there, and our crew laboriously erected an amateurish floating dock supported by gasoline drums. They were disappointed when, upon our return from the Philippines, they found that it had been completely washed away.

First page illustration from the "Fantail Gazette," August 23, 1944.

Soon we were off to Morotai, escorting some of the ships scheduled to arrive there a day or two after D-day. Morotai is remote, to put it mildly. It lies a couple of degrees north of the equator between the 128th and the 129th east meridians. The voyage from Hollandia crossed about 13° of longitude but only about 4° of latitude, or about a thousand miles almost entirely on the equator. One windless day when the sea was smooth and glassy, we passed the little Asia Islands, which sit fairly astride the equator. I have often wondered what it would be like to live there. The landings at Morotai were unopposed. Few Japanese troops were on the island, and those who were took to the hills.

Nine of them managed to hide out there, with arms intact, until 1956. For the better part of a week following our arrival, we patrolled the narrow strait between Halmahera and Morotai, watching the constantly changing cloud of steam and smoke that rose in the southern sky from Halmahera's volcano.

A few natives came to trade with us at Morotai. I have forgotten what they offered, but I remember that they wanted white cloth. Our bluejackets were soon in business. Regular USN-issue white mattress covers served as a grand medium of exchange. We rarely encountered natives in the South Pacific. The islands we fought over, patrolled, and landed on were not deserted, but they were sparsely populated. The inhabitants were peaceful, primitive people. The violent technological war between the Americans and Japanese that erupted in their homelands and that had no connection with them at all, was very upsetting for them. The American authorities did what they could to isolate the natives so that they would have minimal contact with the American military, and I think that was a good thing. Too much contact would have overwhelmed them and ruined their state of life. The rise of the cargo cults that sprang up in the islands after the war was one way the natives tried to make sense of what had happened and put it to their own use. Years later, when I was traveling in the New Guinea highlands, I saw a tribe of Melanesians living in a massive gold dredge, 120 feet long by 70 feet wide, which had been flown in piecemeal by the Dutch during the 1930s, assembled there, and then abandoned. That, too, was symbolic of the collision of the Stone Age culture of that area with the modern industrial development of the West. When I returned to Guadalcanal in 1983, I spoke with a young Solomon Islander who was very concerned and upset about the eyeball-to-eyeball Cold War confrontation between the United States and the Soviet Union. After all, if nuclear war broke out, for all he knew it might take place right there in his islands all over again.

We were soon back at Hollandia, and before long the *Murray* was one of three destroyers escorting the HMS *Ariadne*, the only Royal Navy vessel around. She was a high-speed mine layer about the size of a small cruiser. We stopped off at Aitape to pick up the latest dope on bypassed Wewak Harbor from the PT boats based there. That night the *Ariadne* and her escorts swept into the harbor, delivered *Ariadne*'s mines, and swept out again. There was not a sign of life from the beach, a welcome development considering the shivering, shaking, and general consternation the mission had evoked among all hands.

Our next assignment turned out to be the battle of Leyte Gulf. The *Murray*'s task in the great Philippines operation was a tiny one. She had an assigned shore-bombardment mission, plus a postlanding responsibility to work with a shore-bombardment party not far from the village of Tacloban. October 20 was designated A-day. At one point I was given a coordinate by a fire-control party at Tacloban, and I was just about to open up on the position when I realized that I had been given the wrong coordinates and was about to fire on a group of Americans standing on the beach. Fortunately, I didn't fire, and we got the error corrected, but things like that happened. "Friendly fire" was an awful reality in wartime.

All our men were extremely fatigued that night, after more than forty-eight hours at general quarters. One man at a time was permitted to go below to relieve himself. Early the following morning bogeys were reported. The pointer sitting next to me in the fire-control director chose that instant to request permission to go below. Permission denied. A moment or two later the bogey, identified as a Japanese plane, came in low overhead. We got the guns on. The order to "commence firing" was given. Nothing happened. Our pointer, who was supposed to pull the trigger, refused to shoot. Although one of the auxiliary firing keys was immediately used, there was a moment or two's delay, in which time the plane passed overhead and crashed into the bridge structure of HMAS *Australia*, killing the skipper and nineteen others and wounding half a hundred, including the senior Australian flag officer present. Maybe there was nothing we could have done to prevent this tragedy, but I have long been plagued by the thought that too much of it was due to a man who refused to shoot at the enemy on account of his aching loins.

There was a sort of collective knowledge at work among the troops that was part grapevine gossip, part covert intelligence system, and part plain old irreverence. You've heard many times that when MacArthur landed in the Philippines again in 1944, he said, "I have returned." But somehow we sailors knew in advance that he was going to say that. Two weeks before Leyte, as we were slowly cruising up towards the Philippines, I asked one of my colleagues on the ship, "Who said, 'Fire when ready, Gridley'?" He responded that that was surely Admiral Dewey's command at the Battle of Manila Bay. And which famous naval commander made the statement, "We have met the enemy and they are ours"? "That would be Oliver Hazard Perry, after the Battle of Lake Erie," he replied. And then I asked, "Who will say, 'I have returned'?" My friend answered, "Douglas MacArthur at the Battle of the Philippines," and we both cracked up. I don't know how we knew that two weeks in advance, but we did.

By this point the *Murray* had been more than fifteen months away from home and was long overdue for a navy yard overhaul. As a result, we were among the first ships away from Leyte Gulf, escorting the first empty tank landing ships (LSTs) and Liberties back to Hollandia. While we were en route, the battle of Surigao Strait took place. Destroyer after destroyer in our group went alongside one of the Liberties and refueled, making ready for an immediate return to the Philippines. There were a lot of crossed fingers on board, and in the end we were not recalled. We set our course to the northeast, flying a homeward-bound pennant. My Yale classmate John Herold rode the *Murray* as a passenger from Hollandia back to San Francisco. As a high-ranking guest (captain of his own ship), he occupied the captain's cabin just off the wardroom. From time to time when I had the mid-watch, I had an irresistible compulsion to telephone John to report "all's well!"

One morning as we were somewhere off Manus in the Admiralties, our engineering officer, Larry Armstrong, had made one of his rare ventures outside the engine room and was sunning himself near the bow. Through half-closed eyes, he saw what appeared to be a mine right in the path of the ship. "It can't be," he decided, and went back to sleep. I was on the bridge at the time, about to complete the morning watch and go below for lunch, when I, too, spotted this little stranger right against the port bow wave of the ship. The wave kept it off as it passed down the entire three hundred fifty or so feet of the hull. I grabbed the TBS and informed the destroyer five hundred yards directly behind us that we had a mine in our wake. The captain heard this on our monitor loudspeaker while he was eating lunch below, and he came galloping onto the bridge just as I was reaching for the wardroom phone. Our sister astern veered off, commenced shooting, and soon exploded the mine. That woke Larry up! He arrived for lunch about the same time as I, declaring that the morning activities had certainly enhanced his regard for the engine room.

We called at Manus, Majuro, and Pearl. As the four destroyers sortied from Pearl, the main channel was blocked by an inward-bound freighter. One ship in our group veered off too much into shallower water, shearing off her sound dome. Fearing that a report of this accident to Comdespac (Commander Destroyers Pacific) at Pearl would have brought orders to return to port, this ship (carrying the squadron commander) continued on her way homeward bound to San Francisco. The war was far to the west; this was the last leg of a long journey across the Pacific. Nothing unusual could happen. We took screening positions on either bow of our now-deaf sister, as we would with a merchantman or larger combatant vessel. We were no more than a day at sea when a message came in announcing that a freighter had reported an enemy submarine off the coast of Mexico, and our group of destroyers was directed to investigate. A frigate was standing by. After a day or two's hard steaming, we found the frigate, which had discovered nothing. We set about the box search. Our squadron flagship was helpless for this purpose and had to keep station directly astern of one of the pinging destroyers, like a baby elephant holding his mother's tail. Some of our passengers who had boarded us for a passage home from New Guinea were now most enthusiastic. At last they would see at first-hand the vaunted destroyer hunter-killer tactics! These consisted of starting at the point of supposed contact and carefully making ever-widening circles searching for the alleged sub. It was a painstaking, time-consuming, unexciting process. No submarine was found. Our passengers soon returned to their acey-deucey and wardroom coffee. After the standard prescribed period, the search was abandoned and course resumed for San Francisco.

We finally arrived in San Francisco the day after Thanksgiving 1944, in time for a delayed Thanksgiving dinner. It was wonderful to be back. We had a six-week overhaul in the Mare Island Navy Yard, which included a three-week leave for all hands. Betty came across the country to meet me, and we had a joyous reunion. That was also the first time I saw my son Rick, even though he was born in June 1943. Although he was already about a year and a half old, I was expecting him to be a babe in my wife's arms, so I didn't immediately notice the little boy who was with Betty in San Francisco. Betty asked, "Aren't you going to say hello to your son?" I looked left and right, up and down. "Where?" She pointed to the young boy walking along the sidewalk and said, "There he is." "That's my son?" I asked. She nodded. That was my first meeting with my first child.

One day in May 1944, I had made the acquaintance of a certain Burleigh B. Brunson, one of the enlisted men aboard the *Murray*. He came to me and said, "The chief tells me you're a lawyer." I admitted I was but pointed out that it had been some time since I had practiced. What was his problem? It seemed that Burleigh had contacted a lawyer in San Diego concerning his divorce but hadn't heard from him. I undertook to write to the lawyer, and in due course I received affidavit forms and a few other legal odds and ends. Over the next several months, Burleigh and I worked pretty hard on his divorce. Meanwhile, Burleigh continued to receive strange letters from his spouse: "Dear Burleigh.... You s.o.b., I love you," and so on. In any event, when we arrived in San Francisco, Burleigh took off in the first leave party to attend court in San Diego. Toward the end of his time on shore, I received a telegram from him requesting a three-day extension of leave because the court had not yet reached his case. I approved the extension request by return wire and then shoved off on my own. I didn't see Burleigh again for three weeks. Then on the night before we were to sail out into the Pacific once more, Burleigh came by requesting special liberty for the evening. I asked him how he was, how he had enjoyed his leave, and whether he had successfully obtained his divorce. He told me that everything had gone very well, but now, the night before sailing, it was necessary for him to go over and see his wife. "You don't mean to tell me you got married again?" Indeed he had. "I hope to a better woman this time?" "The same one!" he said. "Permission denied," said I. And that was the last time I ever laid eyes on Burleigh B. Brunson, for over the hill he did go.

Our overhaul at the Mare Island Navy Yard came to an end, and the *Murray* again headed west across the Pacific. Twenty-four hours or so out of San Francisco, I stepped out onto the wing of the bridge and into a gale on a dark and stormy night. Solid water poured down over the main decks as the ship dipped its bow into the waves and the wind lifted the crests of the waves high into the air. It looked like a scene from the movie *Action in the North Atlantic*, starring Humphrey Bogart, which had come out not long before and was a Hollywood version of what they thought life at sea was like in wartime. "Good evening," I said to the young lookout, "nice night, isn't it?" Then came the classic reply: "Mr. Beinecke, Humphrey Bogart ought to be doing this, not us."

After calling briefly at Pearl Harbor, the *Murray* arrived at her berth in the vast lagoon at Ulithi in the Caroline Islands, nine hundred miles north of New Guinea and a thousand miles east of the Philippines. The war seemed to have changed since we had left it in November. It had speeded up considerably, and the American forces had grown tremendously. Prior to this time, the European theater had gotten the highest priority. There were relatively few army divisions operating in the Pacific theater, and ships, too, were assigned when they could be spared from the Atlantic. Even in 1944, the Pacific war still had some of the quality of a milk run. One got to know the people on the accompanying ships, on the tenders, and at the bases. The number of ships engaged was limited, and the waiting period between operations permitted the kind of poking around we had done at Espiritu Santo, Hollandia, and Purvis Bay. By 1945, all this was behind us. It was to be practically one continuous operation from then on until the end of the war.

Mogmog, one of the fringe islets at Ulithi, served as the northern anchorage recreation area. The SOPA instructions informed us that the recreation facilities were "limited" at Mogmog, surely one of the great understatements of the war. The destroyers used the southern anchorage at Feitabul. At least Mogmog had a baseball field. Feitabul did not. The recreation facilities at Feitabul consisted of a sandy beach, a few palm trees, and such beer and sandwiches as we could transport. The recreation that was "enjoyed" at Feitabul always terminated at dusk. This was involuntarily modified one evening when, just as the boats had set about ferrying everyone back to their ships, a great flame shot up away off in the distance. A kamikaze had crashed into one of the carriers. All ships present went to general quarters and recalled their boats, leaving a good many of us beer drinkers marooned on Feitabul. It so happened that my old Columbia Law School friend Jim Casey, who later became my law partner, was ashore that afternoon from his destroyer, the USS *Richard P. Leary*. We had a reunion that, thanks to the visit of the kamikaze, was somewhat extended.

As we were outward bound to Ulithi one calm, clear day in January 1945, just as I was about to conclude the morning watch, I happened to have my glasses trained on the brand-new carrier, the *Bennington*, our guide. Two men could be seen swinging on a scaffold well forward on the carrier, painting the hull. The ships were ticking off some twenty-two knots, a decent speed, and were dipping a little into the long, high Pacific swells. Suddenly the two men were dipped off into the sea. Those Essex-class carriers had crews of over thirty-four hundred men. Not all of those on the *Bennington* sought to succor their two shipmates—not more than half, I would say. As the ship slipped past, a great assortment of life rafts, life jackets, and other odds and ends were heaved over the side to the two swimming bluejackets. I had the pleasure of telling the carrier *Belleau Wood*, directly astern of the *Bennington*, to keep clear. Normal operating procedure was for destroyers to keep clear of the larger ships, so as we speeded to the rescue, the *Murray* sailors had the unaccustomed thrill of watching the *Belleau Wood* veer off quickly to keep out of our way. The two men were duly picked up and transferred by high line to their home ship. Before nightfall, the skipper received a commendatory message from the *Bennington* CO thanking him for saving the two men and complimenting him on his fine seamanship, copy to screen commander and other interested parties. The very next day, while fueling alongside the *Bennington*, we parted a fuel hose, spraying a good deal of black oil on the *Bennington*'s decks. Another message came through forthwith, this time commenting on the poor seamanship displayed, copy to screen commander and so forth.

Early in February 1945, Task Force 58, the fast-carrier force, left Ulithi for an extended cruise that included air strikes at Japan, support of the Iwo Jima assault, and strikes against Okinawa. A track chart of this cruise appears in the fourteenth volume of Morison's history, graphically illustrating how the great fleet kept at sea from February 10 to March 4, destroying nearly six hundred fifty enemy planes en route. During the night of February 25-26, the *Murray* shot up a small craft of some sort. Of this Morison says, "En route (Nagoya) destroyers *Hazelwood* and *Murray* sank three small craft that were too tiny to be mentioned in postwar assessments." Since I was directing the *Murray*'s gunfire and had a good look at this "small craft" during the flashes, I can certify that she was tiny indeed. I have some doubts as to whether this craft was a Japanese naval vessel at all. We were close to Japan, and it must have been Japanese, but it looked to me a lot more like a harmless fishing boat than a naval ship. Morison added, "During that night both wind and sea came up and speed had to be reduced to 12 knots to avoid damage to the destroyers." Since we had stopped to shoot at the little Japanese vessel and were forced to stop again to clear a hangfire, we were far behind and had to catch up at a speed a good deal more than twelve knots. We suffered for it, too.

A hangfire is a charge that does not go off. We fired the number 1 gun the night that we were shooting at the little Japanese craft, and nothing happened. We hit the firing pin repeatedly, but the firing mechanism in the back of the cartridge didn't go off. The projectile and cartridge remained in the gun, and there was no way to know if the cartridge was going to explode or not. The only proper way to unload a gun is to fire the projectile, and if you can't do that, you physically have to remove the projectile and the cartridge from the gun. Clearing a hangfire is the specific responsibility of the gunnery officer, and a nerve-racking task under any circumstances. It was even worse with the deck heaving up and down in those rough seas and the skipper impatient to catch up with our task group, which had disappeared into the night. The chief gunner's mate and I soaked down the gun with a hose, trying to keep our footing while the seas coming over the bow pounded at our little enclosure. When everything was in readiness, we phoned the bridge, the ship slowed down, and we gingerly opened the breech. I took the thirty-pound brass cartridge out of the gun, and as quickly as I could, I handed it down to two men on the deck, who rushed to the side and dropped it into the ocean. Then we did the same with the projectile, and we were safe. It may not sound like it, but I think those were the scariest moments of the war for me. We surged forward at high speed and caught up with our task group, but with the gun shield around Gun 1 stove in and all electrical and fire-control circuits in that area knocked out. The damage was not properly repaired until we visited the Pearl Harbor Navy Yard in May.

It was also on that cruise that we learned about the charms of picket duty and "Tomcat." Each task group always sent out destroyers as pickets some fifteen miles or so ahead to serve as early-warning ships to alert the carriers when an enemy attack was coming in. That was a lonely spot, but not as lonely as Tomcat, which was a task-force rather than a task-group responsibility. Three destroyers were positioned fifty miles away from the task force, in the direction of Japan. The planes that took off from the carriers to bomb Japan were gone for several hours, in which interval the task force might have covered a good bit of ground. Tomcat was a point on which the returning planes could "home" and from which they could be quickly directed to their home carriers. This traffic cop's role was vital, since sometimes those planes were low on gas or damaged. The Japanese planes knew about this arrangement, of course, so they would follow the American planes and attack these Tomcat destroyers.

We were on just such a Tomcat mission in July, about a month before the war's end. We started shooting at a straggler following a group of our returning planes. Thinking it was a friendly plane, I rang the cease-firing gong and called over the phone, "Cease firing! Cease firing! That is a friendly plane." Back over the phone came the voice of Morris, our tough gun captain way aft in gun 5: "That 'friendly plane' just dropped a bomb a hundred yards south of my ass!" I twisted around for a look, and sure enough, there was a great column of water rising in our wake.

It wasn't always an easy thing to make a positive identification of an enemy plane. One of our targets was the "snooper," a high-flying Japanese plane that appeared to be only a tiny speck glinting in the sunlight. Those planes flew so high they were well out of range, but we would shoot a couple rounds in their direction anyway to encourage them to stay away. One morning I fired at what I thought was a Japanese snooper plane, but it turned out to be the planet Venus, which is sometimes visible during daylight hours. It was a little out of range. Another set of targets were what we called "Bettys," Japanese patrol planes with high tails. The planes flew close to the water to stay out of sight, but from the high superstructures of our ships, we could see their high tails cutting back and forth like sharks' fins over the arc of the horizon.

In mid-March 1945, TF 58 sortied once again from Ulithi lagoon, this time to support the Okinawa operation. First air strikes were gotten off against the Kyushu airfields and against enemy shipping in the Inland Sea and in the ports of Kure and Kobe. On March 19, *Murray* sailors had their first glimpse of Japan, and the carrier *Franklin* was hit by bombs from a Japanese plane, with a loss of over seven hundred killed or missing and over two hundred wounded. Although she was not of our task group, we saw the smoke and flames from miles away. The *Santa Fe* took off some eight hundred of the *Franklin*'s survivors, and the carrier was towed clear of the battle area by the *Pittsburgh*. Eventually the *Franklin* regained power and, with only one stop at Pearl Harbor, steamed all the way to New York, making the *Franklin* probably the most severely damaged carrier to be saved.

TF 58 continued its prelanding support activity, and on March 24 our task group launched 112 planes to strike a convoy northwest of Okinawa. An entire eight-ship convoy was destroyed. That same day, the *Massachusetts*, the *Indiana*, and several destroyers, including ourselves, began softening-up bombardments of the Okinawa coast.

On the morning of March 27, the *Murray* was at Tomcat position off Okinawa. I was up in the director. Suddenly, the fellow sitting next to me called my name and pointed. I turned to starboard and saw a Japanese plane right on top of us. It was much too close for us to get the main battery of five-inch guns turned on it, but our six 40-mm dual-purpose guns took the plane under fire. I believe that the starboard 40-mm mount managed to hit the plane, but by then it had already dropped its aerial bomb. The bomb fell and shot forward, and as it came toward me at eye level, I momentarily thought, That thing is going to hit me right in the face. It happened so quickly, I don't know whether I was actually scared or not. The bomb fell and penetrated the starboard side of the ship just above the waterline, shot through an ammunition hoist and crew living compartment, then exited the port side and exploded. Fourteen sailors were wounded, and one man— Orval Knox by name, a big, strapping twenty-year-old farmboy—was killed. He was our only fatality in the thirty months that I spent on the *Murray*. We buried him at sea.

If there had been a "luckiest ship of the year" award, we would have won it going away. Why didn't the bomb explode inside the ship? The enemy wanted those bombs to penetrate a certain distance into a ship and then go off. I think that the delayed-detonation fuse for that bomb was set for a big ship such as a battleship or a carrier, which turned out to be a very good thing for our smaller destroyer. Fragments of the bomb had exploded in all directions, and I later noticed that the metal plate above the radar screen in the director was pockmarked with shrapnel, which meant that shards of the bomb had passed a few inches above my head.

I have in my apartment in Florida a photograph of the *Murray* that shows the hole the bomb made in the side of the ship. As the bomb went through the *Murray*, it hit the shaft holding lots of the ship's electrical circuits, knocked out the loading hoist that brought the ammunition up from the number 2 magazine, destroyed the cold-storage area that we had loaded up just a few days before, and cut off all the control circuits to our two five-inch guns and two twin 40-mm guns forward. Meanwhile, the sea was gurgling in and out of the holes drilled by the bomb. There still were men in the magazine, which was below the waterline. They were safe and dry, because they were protected by a watertight hatch, but they could hear water sloshing around on the deck above, and they wanted to get out. Bob White, the executive officer, called down to them, "Now, I'm going to open this hatch, and you fellows come out—but remember, there's a lot of water up here." He reached down through two or three feet of water and undid the hatch. He said later that these three or four or five men came popping up like so many jacks-in-the-box through the water cascading down on them.

We didn't have enough facilities to treat our wounded. We had only the emergency dressing facilities and the ship's doctor's small sick bay. The admiral ordered us to go alongside the carrier USS *Hornet* and transfer our wounded to it. We connected a high line between our ships, one after another of our wounded young men were transferred in a stretcher that was pulled back and forth, and not one was dropped into the sea. Several years ago, Bill Duddleson went to the National Archives in Washington and found several photographs of this particular operation in the *Hornet*'s photograph collection. He blew them up and brought them to our 1993 *Murray* reunion in Kerrville, Texas. One picture of this episode is especially dramatic, showing part of the *Hornet*'s side and many of her crew looking on attentively as our wounded are transferred from the *Murray*. I thought this was a wonderful picture, and Bill was kind enough to give it to me. I had it framed, and now it is hanging in our apartment in Florida.

The *Murray* headed off with a group of fleet oilers to Ulithi, where temporary plates were welded over the holes in the ship's sides. We

Wounded man on stretcher hanging from wire being transferred from Murray *to* Hornet, *March 27, 1945.*

arrived in Pearl Harbor by May, and the ship put into the navy yard for repairs. Break of breaks, after the *Murray* was mended we caught a month's duty as a Despac school ship. This meant taking classes from the Camp Catlin gunnery and torpedo school every morning at six, back to the mooring buoy at four, and off to the night spots by six. We were reminded of how lucky we were by seeing our sister destroyers arriving almost daily from Okinawa, minus bow, minus stern, minus bridge structure, sometimes holed forward, sometimes aft. The *Murray* was a lucky ship, just as the *Buck* was an unlucky ship. Luck, in the naval world, is not just that. The fact that the bomb didn't explode until after it exited the *Murray* was pure good fortune, but luck also has to do with the quality of how you conduct yourself. I think that a lot of the good fortune of the *Murray* had to do with standards that had been set by Captain Stout. That beginning made it a happy ship, which in turn had a lot to do with making it a lucky ship.

Early in June 1945, the *Murray* put to sea once again to rejoin TF 38, by then rampaging off the coast of Japan. Together with another destroyer, we were escorting the older battleship *Idaho* to Saipan. The battleship skipper thought that a little live bombardment practice would be a good exercise, so en route we headed in close to the bypassed Marshalls' island of Jaluit. We came in column: first the

Murray, then the *Idaho*, then the other destroyer. Some flashes on the beach greeted us immediately. There were splashes to port, splashes to starboard—a straddle on the very first salvo. It didn't take much to figure out that there were two or three more on their way in the air. We got the range and silenced that battery in short order. My friend Mark Hall—then a lieutenant on the *Idaho*, later a distinguished Episcopal minister—told me later over lunch at Saipan that all on the *Idaho* were greatly impressed at how fast we went to work that day at Jaluit.

Scarcely had we delivered our charge at Saipan than we were under way again, this time in a strange direction—east—right back over the track we had just covered. We returned to Eniwetok to take aboard fuel and two Japanese-language officers, then on July 2, on orders from Admiral Nimitz, headed northward to Wake Island. Our patrol planes had spotted what appeared to be a Japanese hospital ship en route to Wake Island, presumably to evacuate the starving garrison there. Our task was to intercept and inspect: to determine whether this was in fact a hospital ship carrying no contraband (such as guns or ammunition), according to agreements the United States and Japan had signed at The Hague after World War I. Early in the evening of July 3, we intercepted the ship, painted white with an illuminated red cross on the stack, just off Wake Island. We sent over a boarding party. Just as the first of our two whaleboats was shoving off, the skipper handed over a Very signal pistol, saying, "If they try any monkey business, shoot this thing and I'll blow them out of the water." One of the crew asked the officer with the pistol, "Sir, are you really going to shoot that thing?" Response: "Do you think I'm crazy?" Reply: "I'm not sure, you're an officer." Our boys looked like pirates: unshaven, red bandannas on their heads, pistols in holsters, tommy guns in hands, all remembering Pearl Harbor. Our inspection found that the Japanese hospital ship, the *Takasago Maru*, was on a legitimate mission to take the starving Japanese from that tiny, lonely, bypassed sand-spit. Three and a half years had gone by since the Japanese overwhelmed the small United States Marine garrison on Wake. The war had moved westward. Few supply ships had got through to them, and for a long time none. They had been living on rats and gooney birds.

We let the *Takasago Maru* pass, and steamed back and forth just over the horizon from Wake, every now and then closing sufficiently to see her masthead. We boarded her again two days later, after she had taken off nearly one thousand patients. Our ship's doctor reported that many had tuberculosis, and many more were suffering from malnutrition. He estimated that fifteen to twenty percent would not survive the voyage home to Japan (see Appendix).

The two language officers we had brought along helped solve the communication problem. Our meeting with this Japanese ship was unique. Here, for once, Americans and Japanese were not seeking to exterminate each other. The Japanese captain gave our boarding party some beer and *sake* as "a gift for your captain." We gave them some American cigarettes and news magazines. They wanted to know whether Babe Ruth was still playing for the Yankees. All the way back to Guam, to report directly to Admiral Nimitz, our skipper talked about the great party he was going to give on arrival with the *sake* sent him by the Japanese skipper. Shortly after we got to Guam, the two temporarily assigned Japanese-language officers took off, and with them the *sake*. Their memory was not honored on our ship.

Now to find TF 38, which we knew to be cruising somewhere off the coast of Japan. The war was drawing rapidly to a close, although we were not then aware of it. TF 38 was launching almost daily air strikes against Japan. Speculation was rife as to when we would land on the Japanese coast. With Iwo Jima and Okinawa secured, Japan had to be next. I was beginning to get nervous; I had been at sea far too long. I had put in and been accepted for the DD gunnery officer's rotation program that sent a veteran gunnery officer back to the States for a month of leave, followed by a month of schooling in which he would be updated on all the new procedures and improvements that had been developed while he had been at sea. After that, he was to go back to the fleet and serve as a liaison between the naval technical staff and the destroyer gunnery officers in order to indoctrinate them with the new procedures. The forces afloat were inundated with books, manuals, periodicals, and sundry navy publications describing these improvements, but the officers didn't have much patience with the technicians in Washington, who were not dealing with the enemy on a day-to-day basis. Consequently, much of this material ended up underneath bunks instead of being implemented, even though it contained genuine improvements. The navy was not unaware of this problem, and so they used the experienced officer who went through the gunnery officer's rotation program as an ambassador of goodwill to his contemporaries. He could explain the problems to the officers at sea in their language and overcome their reluctance to adopt new procedures. After that the rotating officer would be ordered to new construction, because ships were always being built, and he would help put a new ship in commission as gunnery officer.

To me this program was like a prospect of heaven, and just as distant. The war seemed endless. A Comdespac dispatch to the *Murray* in June stated that my orders would issue when the skipper reported my relief qualified. I went to Captain de Vos to get his approval, but he said, "Well, you're qualified for this, but I can't approve your leaving until your relief"—my assistant gunnery officer—"is qualified to take over." My relief was a Naval Academy graduate, Walter Helm— "Junior," we called him. He was perfectly well qualified, but the Captain was reluctant to say so, and he never did. As it turned out, the Captain himself was detached long before I was.

We reported back to TF 38 about mid-July. All that summer until the end of the war, this force continued to pound Japanese homeland airfields and shipping on a near-daily basis, withdrawing occasionally to refuel and replenish supplies. On the night of July 30-31, all aboard the *Murray* had a good case of jitters, for our squadron made a complete circuit of Suruga Wan, a bay which lies just south of Tokyo Bay. This would be comparable to a sweep of Long Island Sound, or perhaps Massachusetts Bay. Had the night been clear, Mount Fuji would have been plainly visible. Fortunately it was not. There were no regrets. An aluminum plant at Shimizu was bombarded as the squadron passed by. Morison comments that "this did not accomplish much because production at Shimizu industrial plants had already fallen to almost zero owing to lack of raw materials; and the railroad yards were not hit."

Then the atomic bomb was dropped. It came as a complete surprise. When I heard about it, I felt tremendously relieved. I didn't know what an atomic bomb was, but when I learned that it was likely to bring the war to a conclusion, I thought it was wonderful. Looking back, I have some second thoughts, but I don't think my second thoughts now are really pertinent to what happened then. By August 1945, anything that was going to shorten the war was a good thing in my book. We had been out there for so long, and I thought that if the war didn't end soon, our luck was finally going to run out. We had escaped from our sweep of Suruga Wan because it was a foggy night, but how much longer could we engage in raids like that without getting badly hit? I am sure that if we'd had to invade the Japanese mainland, the casualties would have been immense, and the Japanese would have resisted vigorously in defense of their homeland. It's true that we might not have had to drop the atomic bomb if we could have modified our demand for unconditional surrender. To surrender unconditionally is a frightening concept, and nobody wants to do it. The Japanese didn't want to without knowing what was going to happen to their emperor. We know

Lieutenant William S. Beinecke.

now that some people in the Japanese government were sending out feelers to try to arrange a negotiated peace. But I was only a lieutenant out on a ship at sea, and I didn't know anything about that then. What little I know about it now is based on the reading that I have done since. But hell's bells, we all remembered Pearl Harbor. We heard nothing except how brutal and ruthless the Japanese were, and we were continually reminded about the rape of Nanking and other Japanese atrocities. Even today, I have mixed emotions about the Japanese. It is difficult for me to reconcile the cruel, rapacious, and unfeeling way they conducted themselves in war with the way we see them now as global tourists and successful businessmen, always bowing, always polite. And Japan today is a very peaceful nation, speaking forcefully in the cause of international peace. It's a paradox.

After the bombs were dropped, TF 38 kept to sea, maintaining pressure. The war ended on August 15, 1945. Then came one of the craziest performances imaginable. No troops were available for a landing. There were believed to be several million men under arms on the

Japanese home islands. Admiral Halsey began to make preparations to land. Each ship was directed to organize a constituent element for part of the small landing force. A table of organization was provided. The total number of marines in the TF was toted up. Whatever it came to, there were miserably few. None of us had the faintest idea how to maneuver troops on land in an enemy-infested area. The obsolete landing-force manual was dug out of the filing cabinet. On the carrier flight decks, groups of bluejackets could be seen going through the motions of close-order drill. The little detachment of about thirty men under my command hardly had room for a left face, right face, about face on our restricted decks.

One day during this period, one of the gunner's mates appeared on the bridge and said he wanted a word with me. We stepped off to one side, out of earshot of the captain, to talk things over. He asserted that the bayonets did not fit the rifles, and held up one of each. This seemed incredible. I refused to believe him and tried to put them together myself. He was right. Clearly etched into the steel of the bayonet was "Lee Enfield 1918," and on the rifle, "Smith Corona 1942." Fortunately the landing-force preparation did not develop into anything more serious. The fleet continued to stay at sea through August and well into September. Troop-laden transports eventually appeared on the scene. The surrender ceremony was held, and the occupation of Japan was undertaken by those who knew what they were doing. Certain ships, including the *Murray*, kept at sea during the balance of August. During the September 2 surrender ceremonies on the *Missouri*, our carriers supplied continuous air cover, and of course the destroyers screened them. Not long after the ceremonies, my aunt Emmy Lou arrived in Japan in the company of her husband, Paul Liston, who was in the army of occupation. Emmy Lou's first marriage to Bliss Woodward had ended in 1935 and she had married Paul. He had been a well-known football player at West Point, and after a stint in the army he had served as assistant coach to Lou Little at Columbia, doing scouting for Columbia on the side while working for a bank in New York. He went back into the army when the war came along, and was in Japan with Emmy Lou for some time.

One of the *Murray*'s highlights during this neither-war-nor-peace period was, on August 27, to accept the surrender of one of the newer and larger Japanese submarines, which had a small hangar on deck that was large enough to accommodate a small patrol plane. This sub had been engaged in carrying supplies to some of the bypassed Japanese islands. Our boarding party stayed aboard and in command for a day or two, then turned the A-14 over to a crew of experienced submarine sailors at the entrance to Tokyo Bay (see Appendix). Japanese officers' swords and dirks, fans, prints, and other souvenirs were all turned over to the submariners, who promised to send them on to us. I never saw any souvenirs myself and long regretted what I thought was our naïveté, but I recently learned that some souvenirs were indeed turned over to the *Murray*'s prize crew.

A few days later, the *Randolph*, one of the carriers in our group, turned into the wind to recover aircraft. The *Murray*, the nearest destroyer, was directed to serve as plane guard. The *Randolph* was on course 090, due east. After a couple of days, the realization dawned on us that she was not turning around. We were on our way home!

By the end of the war, I was the third most senior officer aboard the *Murray*. As a matter of fact, I was by that time the oldest officer on board, even older than the skipper. Our new Captain, Frederick Malcomb Radel, was in the class of '39 of the Naval Academy, so I was three years his senior in age, though of course I was junior to him in rank. The next step up for me would have been to be promoted to executive officer, and I had in a way been preparing myself for that job. One of the responsibilities of the executive officer was to be the navigator, but because I had been forced to take the engineering course on the *Prairie State*, I had never taken the course in navigation given to the deck officers. So on the voyage across the Pacific in the summer of '44, I thought it was about time that I knew something about navigation. I got out the books, and I plotted the ship's course on my own. I'd get up every morning and shoot the stars with the navigator. Later, I'd shoot the sun with a sextant. I liked to see how close I was able to put the ship's position to where it actually was. But although I was preparing myself for the executive officer's job, in the end I was not selected. The post went to my friend Scott Martin, who had been away from the *Murray* for a year serving as squadron communications officer aboard the *John Rodgers*, the flagship of our squadron. Had I been selected instead, I might have stayed on board the *Murray* and ridden it back home to the East Coast, but I had no intention of pursuing a naval career. I was far from home and my young family, and I had now been on active service in the navy for forty-eight months, with very long absences away from civilization. The last thing I wanted to do was continue to be on active service in the navy. Instead, I decided to leave the *Murray* and the navy when we reached Hawaii.

I was entitled to make that decision because I had enough points to do so. The point system was interesting. The whole nation had been mobilized for the war, with millions of men and women under arms, and when the war ended, the military had to develop a system to achieve an orderly demobilization. I wanted to get out, and I was not alone. When the *Murray* came back to Pearl Harbor in late September 1945, we found out how reserve officers could be detached and returned to civilian life if they had a certain number of points. I don't remember the magic number, but you earned so many points for the time you served aboard ship at sea, and there were other considerations. When you had the requisite number of points, you were eligible to apply to be detached from your duty station and processed for return to civilian life. I had sufficient points, so I went to the captain and asked him if he would approve my request to be detached. He had no choice but to approve it, but he advised me that if I would put off my request, I could go all the way to Philadelphia, because the *Murray* was now scheduled to go there to take part in the Navy Day celebration on October 27, the birthday of Theodore Roosevelt. In retrospect, as I look back on what I had to deal with to get myself home to New Jersey, I would have been much more sensible had I accepted his invitation and stayed with the ship to Philadelphia. I ended up beating the ship home by two or three weeks, so I wouldn't have gotten back quite as soon as I did, but the living would have been more comfortable.

I was in due course detached, and that meant removing myself and all my belongings from the *Murray*, which had been my home for thirty months—two and half years. The navy was very kind. The carpenter aboard the *Murray* made me a great big box, I put all my stuff in it and stenciled on my name and address, and the navy shipped it from Pearl Harbor to my home in Madison. Eventually it arrived there, and Betty and I unloaded all of this accumulation of two and half years and decided what to keep and what to throw out. The box contained mostly my uniforms and my personal papers. I don't think I had any souvenirs. I had a lot of letters.

And so I left the *Murray*. I felt elated, simply elated. I was still in the navy, so I had to have orders to move from one place to another. I got orders from the captain to report for separation to the naval headquarters at 90 Church Street in New York City, which was the nearest place to my home. I was now in Pearl Harbor. I was a long way from New York. There was no easy way to get across the Pacific to California. I took my suitcase, which contained only a few shirts and a uniform, and moved into a BOQ. Every morning I went to an office, along with all the other officers who were trying to get home to be separated, and the clerks would put the names of the lucky winners up on a pole. When you eventually made your way through the throng up to the pole and found that your name was not on it, you went back to play tennis with some of the other young men, or to go swimming, or both. I passed a week that way and finally got transportation on the new cruiser *Vincennes*. (The earlier cruiser *Vincennes* had been lost in August 1942 at Guadalcanal in an action with the Japanese.) Among the twenty or thirty other passengers aboard the *Vincennes*, I met a young lieutenant named John Roper, who was also headed for New York. He was a native of North Carolina and said he was a nephew of Secretary of State James F. Byrnes. We got a hotel room together when we arrived in San Francisco, but then we were faced with the problem of finding transportation to New York. All the trains and planes were operated by the military. There was no room on the troop trains headed east, and you couldn't get on an airplane unless you were a VIP of some kind with special priority. Finally I went to Elmo Pearson, the S&H vice president in San Francisco. He had a small car that he had made available to me when I was there in November 1944, and now he was gracious enough to let John Roper and me drive it back east. I telephoned Betty in Stamford, told her that I was on my way home, and asked her to meet me at my family's home in Madison, which was an hour or two west of Stamford. She thought that was a good idea, and she called my parents at their home in Great Barrington to tell them I was on my way.

John Roper and I drove across the United States almost nonstop, and we did it in about three days. We didn't really know our way, but we just followed Route 30 across the country. There was little traffic on the road. No cars had been produced during the war, and it was quite a while before the backlog of demand for new cars was taken up. Fortunately, the gasoline rationing was over by that time. Mr. Pearson's car was a coupe, with no backseat, and curling up and going to sleep in the front seat was difficult, so at one point somewhere in Iowa we holed up in a motel and slept for five or six hours. But the rest of the time we drove. We both wanted to get home. We got to Pittsburgh early on the morning of our third day. Men were walking across the bridge into the city, going to work in their nice, starched white shirts, and here we were dirty and decrepit, worn out from our long drive. We drove on the Pennsylvania Turnpike, which was my first experience on a modern divided highway, and crossed the Delaware River into New Jersey. "Now, John," I said, "we'll soon be at my home and I want you to meet my wife and my parents and stay to dinner." "Well, Bill," he answered, "that's very nice, but I want to get to New York to see *my* wife."

Late in the afternoon, we got to my parents' place, and I ran up and banged on the door. I had just driven across the country, I hadn't shaved in days, and I looked pretty awful. The butler came to the door, and he just looked at me. I said I wanted to come in, and he asked, "Who are you?" I explained that this was my home. He said, "Well, I've been here two years, and I've never seen you before." I convinced him in very short order that this was where I belonged, and then I added that my friend and I would like to have a drink. He replied, "Mrs. Beinecke locked all the liquor cabinets when she went up to the country." My parents had gone to Great Barrington for the weekend, and neither they nor Betty had expected us to drive day and night and get home that quickly. John said to me that he thought he'd wash up a little, and if I didn't mind, he'd like to take the car and go on to New York and see his wife, and we would meet later at the separation center in navy headquarters in New York. And that's what happened. Later in the day, Betty and my parents arrived, and we had a wonderful family reunion.

John and I met up several days later at naval headquarters, and he told me about his return home. He said, "I drove into New York and up Third Avenue, and I turned right onto my street in the East 70s, and there were workmen demolishing my apartment building." "Holy mackerel," I said, "where was your wife?" "Well, I went up to the corner and bought a newspaper, and I said to the newspaper man, 'I'm John Roper, and I've just returned home.' 'Oh yes,' he said, 'your wife said that if you turned up, you should know that she moved out to Long Island.'" He finally did find her, and everything was all right. A month or two later, my mother had an ear operation to try to improve her hearing, and the superintending nurse in the hospital came to see her and said, "My goodness, Mrs. Beinecke, you have a very unusual name. My husband traveled across the country with a man by that name when he came back from the war." Of course my mother realized immediately that this was the wife of John Roper. They embraced and had a nice conversation.

I finally went on inactive duty. I had been in the navy longer than I had been at Yale. I regard my navy service as one of the most important experiences in my life. It was burned into me in a way that I can never forget. I came away with a sense of loyalty to my colleagues and comrades and a realization that you can overcome fatigue and carry on to achieve results that you never thought you could. I took away a sense of duty and even honor, a sense of how to measure up to responsibility. It's interesting to remember just how much responsibility was given to very young and inexperienced people. I think that military training is a wonderful experience for a young person. Some of my memories are of moments of terror, such as the time at Aitape when the Japanese plane came out of nowhere and its flares lit up the ship. Neither can I forget the morning when the *Murray* was bombed. And many of my memories are of interesting moments, as when we exploded the surface mine; indeed, the whole experience of being in the South Pacific is such a memory. The *Murray* had many adventures, enough to qualify anyone

Lieutenant Commander William S. Beinecke, 1945. Eleven battle stars on his Pacific ribbon.

who rode her from commissioning to the war's end to wear eleven battle stars on a Pacific ribbon.

The main thing I got out of my naval service, though, was the close associations and the deep friendships with the people who served with me. Forty years later, I was selected to organize a 1984 reunion of the *Murray's* officers. It took a good year of preparation, from spring 1983 until we pulled it off in June 1984. Of the thirty-five or thirty-six officers who had been attached to the ship during her war cruise, twenty-nine were still extant. It was the devil of a time to locate them. The navy was not much help—their address files were way out of date. Using those shipmates I had kept up with as a nucleus, I sent off periodic bulletins reporting who had been found, who was still missing, where so-and-so was last heard of or from. The best sources, it turned out, were college alumni record offices. In the end, all twenty-nine were located. Twenty-three turned up, some with spouses. Since I had been the one to organize the reunion, I chose to hold it at a Cape Cod inn five miles from our home in Chatham. They came from all over the country: Jim Boyd and Marshall Cleland from California, Bill Dozier from Texas, Bill Hunzelman from Iowa, Walter Williamson from Florida, Bob White from New Hampshire, Frank Barcus and Sidney Legg from Indiana.... While it was a little awkward for the first ten minutes, the years soon fell away. We had a superb two days retelling old sea stories and reliving old memories, such as the time we intercepted the *Takasago Maru* or the time we shot ourselves with our own torpedo. Bill Speck worked up a first-class ship's history based on the ship's logs, which he pored over in the reading room of the National Archives.

One of the high points of the reunion was my court-martial for "conduct unbecoming" before a real-life San Diego judge, Smythe Campbell, and a former South Carolina prosecuting attorney, Phil Wilmeth. Witnesses produced the forty-year-old directive, somewhat flimsy but still legible, from the stuffy old admiral who had expressed dismay at the behavior of some "tin horn drunks" at the Efate officers' club. The mock court-martial concluded by awarding Betty a Purple Heart for being married to me. And for me, conviction and then a plaque bearing a small model of a Fletcher-class destroyer together with the words "WELL DONE, MURRAY REUNION, CAPE COD, 1984." Needless to say, it touched a warm spot.

CHAPTER TEN

Return from the War and the Creation of a Law Firm, 1945–1951

uring the war, all employers had been required by law to hold the places of their employees who had gone into the armed forces, and after the war they had to give those veterans their jobs back. I knew that I could return to my job at the law firm of Chadbourne, Wallace, Parke & Whiteside after my separation from the navy, but I didn't want to do that immediately. I had been away for four long years. I had a child I hardly knew and a wife I didn't know well enough. We decided to go up to the Laurentian Mountains in Canada to spend some time together. We drove up in October 1945 and rented a house for the winter in a little French village called Saint Sauveur des Monts, in the foothills of the Laurentians. It was a tiny house with a coal-fired furnace in the basement, and a Frenchman would come by periodically to tend and refuel the furnace. Other than that, we were pretty much by ourselves. Betty and I went skiing a lot, and I gradually let go of the war. I stopped groping for a handhold as I walked around, and I stopped feeling the ship rolling as I slept. From time to time I dreamed that the Japanese were coming, and I perspired so heavily in my sleep that when I woke the bed was soaking wet, even though it was twenty degrees below zero outside. After four years in the war, it took a while to get that heightened awareness out of my system.

We flew back to Madison for Christmas with my parents, then returned to Saint Sauveur until spring. In late March, we left Canada and drove back to our apartment on Strawberry Hill Avenue in Stamford. I returned to work at Chadbourne, Wallace, Parke & Whiteside in April 1946. I was reemployed at a higher salary than my former $1,800 a year, but it was not enough for a married man with a wife and child, and it became even less sufficient when our second child, John, was born in the fall of 1946. I was fortunate that my father had made some additional funds available to me, which enabled us to make ends meet.

I took the train to New York every weekday for a year, but the commute from Stamford all the way down to lower Broadway was really too much, and Betty and I decided we'd give New York a try. It was very difficult to get into apartments in New York after the war. Luckily, the Manufacturers Trust Company controlled an apartment building at 155 East 72nd Street, and since my uncle Ed was on the Manufacturers board, he managed to squeeze my family and my cousin Edwin, Jr., into the building. Eddie's apartment was on a different elevator bank, so we saw him frequently but not all the time; it was rather like living in two different entryways in the same residential college. The apartment into which Betty, Rick, John and I moved in 1947 was quite lovely. It was a duplex apartment, on two floors. On the lower floor, it had a living room, a dining room, and a small bedroom for Nancy, our live-in maid. A staircase led up to three more rooms upstairs.

We continued to return to Stamford at regular intervals, and we also made regular visits to see my parents in Madison and my brother, Dick, and his wife, Doris, in Basking Ridge, New Jersey. After Dick had been hit with malaria in the war and spent almost a year in Australia, he was returned to the naval air base at Weymouth, Massachusetts, just

Richard Sperry Beinecke,
c. 1955

Doris Adeline Kelle Beinecke

south of Boston, and was on limited duty there for the duration of the conflict. His rank was private first class in the United States Marine Corps, and that was his rank and rate all during his service. He met Doris in Weymouth and was married there in July 1945. The navy continued to fight in the Pacific until August 1945, so I couldn't attend their wedding. Shortly afterward, Dick was mustered out of the marines on a medical discharge. For a few years after the war, he returned to the dairy business with Alan Day, and he and Doris lived in a small house in Basking Ridge. They held a surprise party there in November 1947 to celebrate my parents' thirty-fifth wedding anniversary. I remember well how my mother thought that she and Dad and Betty and I were just going over to Dick's house for a little family celebration, and how very moved she was to open the door and see the many friends and relatives of hers from such a long time ago who had gathered for the event. In the mid-1940s, my parents bought a lovely home, Tredinnock, in Great Barrington, Massachusetts, in the heart of the Berkshires. There was a great shift in emphasis away from our Madison house after that, and the Madison house was donated to Drew University in 1949.

Every weekday morning during that first year in New York, I rode the Third Avenue El down to Hanover Square, then walked a couple blocks to Chadbourne, Wallace, Parke & Whiteside at 25 Broadway,

Fritz and Carrie's home, Tredinnock, Great Barrington, Massachusetts, as seen from the lower garden.

where I shared an office with a couple of people whose names I don't remember. The firm had been required to hold the jobs of its returning veterans, but it had also hired a complement of new lawyers during the war and immediately afterwards in order to remain at full strength, so we were working in quite crowded conditions. One of the men hired after I had left was Frank Moon, who later had a career with W. R. Grace & Company, and another was Thibaut de Saint Phalle, who was another Columbia Law graduate. Indeed, Thibaut had roomed with my friend John Bainbridge at Columbia, along with Richard Keresey and John Touhey. They were all members of Kent Moot Court, my court, and were in the class of 1941, one class behind me.

It became clear to me that Chadbourne was overpopulated, and there were more lawyers on the premises than could usefully be employed. I worked at the few assignments I was given and tried to ripen my litigation skills, but some of my tasks were make-work jobs, and I got fed up because I wasn't sufficiently occupied. I found out that lawyers from the city's law firms were needed at the New York Legal Aid Society to augment its full-time staff. Chadbourne was delighted to have me volunteer for that work, because it meant one less body around the overcrowded offices. The New York Legal Aid Society, which provided legal assistance to the indigent, was headquartered at 100 Centre Street. I was assigned to the litigation section of the criminal law wing of the society, and I worked there for several months. I picked up a lot of litigation experience in the beginning stages of the criminal-law process, and while I was not involved in any actual trials, I handled a lot of arraignments and pleas and the like. I thought it was thrilling. The clients, who were mostly criminals, did not appeal to me, but I was absorbed by the whole experience of being in court every day, learning about the courts, and getting an active understanding of what went on there. At the same time, I wondered seriously whether I should return to Chadbourne after I finished the volunteer work. I scouted around for other employment, and I received an offer from the major firm of Simpson, Thacher & Bartlett, where my good friend Cyrus Vance served for a long time as senior partner. I didn't communicate that information to Chadbourne right away, but I probably would have joined Simpson, Thacher & Bartlett if events had transpired differently.

Then one day in May 1948, I got a call from Jim Casey, my friend from Columbia Law School days. He had also served on destroyers in the far Pacific during the war, and we had shared a beer on the desolate isle of Feitabul at Ulithi in the Carolines in 1945. In the spring of 1948, Jim was working with the New York law firm of Breed, Abbott & Morgan. We met for lunch at a downtown branch of the now-defunct New York restaurant chain called the Exchange Buffet. The food was served cafeteria-style; it was inexpensive and pretty good, and you paid for it on the honor system. That is, you saw how much a particular item cost, and then when you went to pay, you told the cashier how much you owed. That may be why the Exchange Buffet went out of business. Over lunch that day, Jim Casey told me that he and a young lawyer at Cravath, Swaine & Moore named Paul Chase, whom I hardly knew at all, had been talking about starting up a law firm. Jim wondered if I would be interested in joining them. I thought about it, Jim and I met for lunch a couple more times at the Exchange Buffet to talk it over, and finally I decided that I ought to take the plunge. I was at a turning point in my life, and I think Jim saw that I was willing to take a bold and potentially risky step. And so the law firm of Casey, Beinecke & Chase was born in the Exchange Buffet restaurant, and we went into business in June 1948. I was only thirty-four years old, Jim was a year younger than I was, and Paul Chase had only just turned thirty. None of us knew anything about how to start a law firm, or how to organize it, or how much initial capital we had to have. And since we didn't realize that we were too young and innocent and powerless to compete in the rough-and-tumble world of New York law, we managed to create a successful law firm.

Jim Casey had been captain of the basketball team at Columbia College, and he was a tall, driving, and ambitious man. I think it had been his goal to have his own law firm ever since he entered Columbia Law School. Paul Chase had been in the illustrious Yale College class of '39 and had gone to the University of Virginia Law School before his wartime service. Jim and Paul had become good friends in the two or three immediate postwar years, and the decision to form the law firm had grown out of their conversations during that time. Jim thought I could contribute something to the firm and perhaps provide some balance between Paul and himself, so he asked me to join. It must have been Jim's persuasiveness that swung Paul into leaving Cravath, for Paul had a good and very time-consuming job there. Because Paul had important work to finish at Cravath, it was some weeks before he actually joined Jim and me in the practice.

Jim and I sublet a one-room office downtown from a man named Parnell Calahan, an office that we shared with a Cuban businessman of some sort. When Paul joined us, we moved to a space at 37 Wall Street, along with two secretaries, a man and a woman whom Paul had persuaded to follow him from Cravath. Wall Street was a prestigious address, but number 37 wasn't much of a building, and the rents were quite low. It didn't require much initial capital to set up Casey, Beinecke & Chase. Law firms in those days did not need a lot of equipment beyond space, office supplies and law books. We were really providing time and service, and we needed only enough capital to pay rent, salaries, and expenses. I don't know how much money each of the partners had to pay in to get our firm started, but I don't suppose that any of us put up more than a couple of thousand dollars. We bought secondhand furniture, and Jim found a law firm up on 42nd Street that was going out of business and was willing to sell its set of *New York Reports* for a relatively low price; we needed them in order to look up the New York law. I hired the Congo Trucking Company (which wasn't anything more than two men and a truck) to move those reports to Wall Street. One night when the traffic was light, we drove the books downtown and wrestled them up to our office. And then we were in business.

It was the responsibility of Paul and Jim to represent companies in corporate law, which was the more lucrative part of our business. One of Jim's clients was a subsidiary of Pan American Airlines, and operated the hotels that Pan Am had all around the world. That was the beginning of the Intercontinental hotel chain. Paul, because of his relationship with Cravath, was able to bring in work from his former employer, often surplus work that Cravath was good enough to hand on to us. I ended up bringing in rather a lot of business from The Sperry and Hutchinson Company, but that was not something I had anticipated. My initial responsibilities were to do what litigation the firm had and to serve as office manager. We were building the firm from the ground up. I devoted some intense study to the business management of law firms, and I gave a lot of attention to giving our firm the proper organization.

There were considerable similarities between putting a navy destroyer into commission, as I had done with the USS *Murray* in 1943, and creating a law firm five years later. There were dissimilarities too, of course. Casey, Beinecke & Chase had only the three of us, plus our office staff, whereas there were over three hundred people on the multimillion-dollar destroyer. The navy also had reams of navalese and instructions and procedures and duties that had been defined over several hundred years, while our law firm lacked both established order and established procedures. For example, it never occurred to us that we should have a holiday policy. In our first year of existence, naturally we took the Fourth of July and Labor Day off, but when Columbus Day rolled around and one of our employees suggested that it might be an appropriate day to stay home, it suddenly dawned on us that we needed to establish a holiday policy. Businesses have to have those sorts of procedures, and I knew a lot less about those things then than I know now. But what little insight I had into running a business I owed to what I had learned in helping to launch the *Murray*, and I was grateful for that experience.

There were considerable challenges to running our own firm, as well as some advantages. We had to be able to meet the payroll. We had to be alert to the possibility of new business and try to figure out ways of getting it. Jim Casey was especially good at that. And because there were so few of us, we had to be more versatile and less specialized, more able to do more different things in the law, and sometimes we were as much lobbyists as lawyers. I found myself doing everything from contracts to wills to corporate work, as well as the litigation and office management that were my primary responsibilities. The man Paul Chase had brought over with him as a secretary was now our office manager. This was an aid to me, for while I continued to supervise in the role of managing partner, I was freed somewhat from the day-to-day management chores and was able to devote more time to the practice of law.

We had one dreadful experience early on that reflected our youth, innocence, and lack of experience. As all law firms do, we had clients' funds in a special account. That was money we didn't own, that we were in charge of looking after. Since we were a fledgling law firm, there wasn't much money in the account, but it was important to safeguard those funds if we were to develop relationships and understandings with our present and future clients. Unknown to us at the time, our office manager, who had come with Paul Chase from Cravath, Swaine & Moore, was forging Paul's signature on checks drawn on that account. I don't think all the money went into his pocket. I suspect that he spent a lot of it at the racetrack and always hoped that someday he would make so much on a bet that he would be able to put what he had taken back in the account without any of us being the wiser. But, as is often the case, the deeper the hole, the deeper he fell. We didn't have the financial controls that we ought to have had. Every month we relied on our office manager's report, which showed how much money he claimed was in the bank, and we didn't look at the bank statement, which would have told us how much money was actually there. We had faith and confidence in this man. Indeed, we thought he was a very reliable fellow because he would always get to work so early to examine the mail.

As it happened, I went into the office one Saturday morning and opened the mail myself, and I noticed a great discrepancy between the amount of money shown on the bank statement and the amount our office manager had reported to us. That was a shock and a severe blow. I had considerable difficulty convincing Jim Casey what had happened. He was aghast at the thought that anybody could have been taking this money. Of course, we had to make good the clients' account with our own money. We met the problem, but it wasn't easy. We soon implemented the financial controls we ought to have had from the beginning, but that was one instance where we learned it the hard way, a very hard way indeed.

I handled several interesting pieces of litigation for the firm. One case involved a group of Harvard alumni who were working in lower Manhattan and wanted to have a place where they could eat inexpensively during the day. They formed an organization called the Downtown Harvard Lunch Club and contracted out with a local Italian restaurant operator for their lunchtime meals. One day they went to the restaurant and found that the doors had been locked. The man was losing money on the lunches and thought his only recourse was to shut down the restaurant. This didn't please the members of the Downtown Harvard Lunch Club, so they decided to sue him, and we got the case. I thought it was a little amusing that although a lot of these members were Harvard Law School graduates and up-and-coming lawyers for important New York firms, they designated a Columbia Law School graduate from a three-man firm to sue on their behalf.

We won the suit, but it was something of a Pyrrhic victory. There are two basic types of breach of contract suits. In the first, the lawyer argues that his client has suffered damages as a result of the breach and puts forward a monetary claim for them; if the jury or the court agrees, it renders a judgment for some amount. The other type of suit happens if the contracting parties have already set the breach of contract damages at a certain figure, called "liquidated damages" or the "preset damage figure." There was such a provision between the Downtown Harvard Lunch Club and the restaurant proprietor, so while we didn't have much difficulty establishing that the restaurateur had breached the contract, the "liquidated damages" were set at an amount that was much less than the club thought it was entitled to. I tried to urge the court that the club should receive more money than this preset amount, but I was caught in a dilemma, which the judge pointed out. He said, "You can't have it both ways. You can either accept the liquidated damages that are set in the contract or you can give up the liquidated damages and take your chances with a jury." I considered the situation from a prospective juror's point of view. On one side was a humble Italian restaurant owner who claimed to be losing money through this lunchtime arrangement. On the other was the Downtown *HARVARD* Lunch Club. What a name! Juries not infrequently side with the poor against the rich. Whom would they be likely to side with in this case? The club members could not have been in a worse position if they had called themselves the Wealthy Lawyers' Lunch Club. I decided to settle for the liquidated damages, and I'm afraid that was the end of the Downtown Harvard Lunch Club.

Betty and I and our family spent only a year at our New York apartment on East 72nd Street. Both Betty and I longed for a little more greenery and space of our own, and we used to take Sunday drives out to New Jersey, sometimes to visit my parents in Madison but more often simply to drive around and have a look at the area. (It was on one of those Sunday drives, while we crossed the river on the ferryboat to Yonkers, that I felt a pain in my stomach that turned out to be appendicitis.) But the decisive factor that led Betty and me to move was that the New York life wasn't right for parents with young children. Summit appealed to us, both because it was a very pleasant place and because it was in easy commuting reach of Wall Street. And so in the summer of

1948, we closed on a house at 156 Beechwood Road in Summit, and we moved there in the fall. That was the house in which our children spent most of their earliest years, and our youngest child, Frances, was born there on August 2, 1949.

I had no expectation when we formed Casey, Beinecke & Chase that I would be doing any substantial work for The Sperry and Hutchinson Company. S&H was a Beinecke family concern, but I hadn't had any real experience with it at all. So I was quite surprised when, in the late summer of 1948, my father and my uncle Edwin asked me to attend the annual meeting of the American Bar Association in Seattle, along with Charles Wesley Dunn, who had been doing the legislative work for S&H. They told me that S&H had some important problems in that part of the country, and they suggested that I help Mr. Dunn with the problem in any way I could. Here was an opportunity to further my law business and help out the business interests of my father and Uncle Edwin. I leapt at the chance.

The counsel for The Sperry and Hutchinson Company was a firm called McNamara & Seymour. It was a small but solid firm headed by Stuart McNamara, who was a friend and contemporary of my uncle Ed's. McNamara had been either United States attorney or assistant United States attorney, and he was a well-respected lawyer. Seymour was very active in the patriotic organization called the Sons of the Revolution. But the person who actually worked on S&H issues in that firm was a trial lawyer named Charles Greene Smith, a distinguished man in his midseventies. S&H did not have an in-house lawyer. I believe that before World War I, they'd had a general counsel named John Hall Jones, but the company had shrunk in the twenties, so there was no need to have a lawyer on the premises. When the company started to reemerge after the Depression, it began to use the services of McNamara & Seymour. Charles Wesley Dunn was the legislative counsel to S&H, and he retained counsel around the country to fend off adverse legislation affecting the trading stamp business. One such piece of hostile legislation had come forward in Washington State, which was why my father and Uncle Edwin suggested that I go to Seattle.

I went to the law library and spent many hours poring over the relevant laws and regulations. Charles Greene Smith had amassed a personal library of the legal decisions pertaining to trading stamps. He had a summary of the principal precedents in a big notebook that he usually kept on his desk, and he would refer to these authorities in preparing a brief. The trouble was, they had been copied and recopied so many times that errors had crept in during the transcription process, and because he was fairly elderly by this point, he no longer went back to the library to check his references against the original sources. I found a number of these mistakes and worked with Mr. Smith to correct them, and he was very appreciative of my doing that as a young lawyer.

I learned that trading stamps in Washington State had long been subject to strict and onerous regulations, almost to a prohibitive degree. While the trading stamp business was lawful in the state, trading stamps had to be redeemed solely for cash. The merchandise redemption system that was the backbone of our business was illegal. Further regulation seemed gratuitous; even most of the people who didn't like the stamp business seemed willing to let it be. But a few die-hard opponents had the brilliant idea of trying to persuade the state attorney general to declare that trading stamps were "evidences of indebtedness" and thus securities within the meaning of the "blue sky" laws of the state. Securities are today regulated by the Securities Exchange Commission, which grew out of legislation passed during the New Deal. The states had their own devices to regulate the sale of stock, however, which had preceded the SEC and continued on the books after the SEC had been established. In former times, crooked speculators would issue securities that didn't have any substance to them—that were backed by nothing but the blue sky—so the state created regulatory laws called blue sky laws to eliminate the issue of fraudulent securities. If trading stamps were deemed securities, then every little filling station and store that issued a trading stamp would be, by law, an issuer of securities and would therefore have to abide by complex securities regulations and file complicated reports on their securities transactions. That would have put trading stamps out of business in Washington, which of course was the goal of S&H's opponents. I prepared a voluminous file of material from the collective opinions of other state attorneys general and other cases on the subject, and went out to Washington.

I had spent so much time going over this material that when I arrived and met with Mr. Dunn and the Spokane lawyer he had retained, it turned out that I knew more than anybody else on the subject. This was a very fortunate thing for me; it meant that in my first exposure to the senior people in the business, especially on the legal side, I made a good initial impression. Paul Graves, the Spokane lawyer who would represent us in the state, said that with the information I had brought along with me, he felt that he could obtain a meeting with the attorney general and present our case but that we would have to wait a week or so before we could get on with the next stage of the matter. In 1948, you couldn't just jump into a jet and go back to the East Coast. There was air transportation, but it was still relatively slow. Mr. Dunn suggested that we go salmon fishing while we waited for our case to develop, and so we took a little plane up to Campbell River on Vancouver Island, a hundred and fifty miles or so northwest of the city of Vancouver, across the bay. Much of Vancouver Island is taken up by Strathcona National Park. Strathcona Hall is one of the principal buildings of Yale; both the park and the hall were named for the same Lord Strathcona. We had a fine time fishing for salmon.

Charles Wesley Dunn and I, dining by ourselves for several nights in our hotel, noted from afar the liveliness and conviviality of four attractive young couples who were also up on a fishing expedition. One evening as we were leaving the dining room, I overheard them lamenting that they had run out of whisky. I was able to plug that hole. They introduced themselves as Clarence (Bunny) and Betty Ambrose, Bob and Grace Isaacson, Howie and Polly Richmond, and Ned and Kayla Skinner. They were all about my age, all from Seattle, and we had similar backgrounds. It turned out that they were good friends as well of my Andover classmate James Tate Mason and my Yale classmate Stewart Ballinger, a native of Seattle. From that beginning grew a friendship that lasted for quite a few years.

When Charles Wesley Dunn and I returned to Washington, I thought it would be a good idea for Betty to join me out there. We had just completed our move from New York City to Summit, and Sarah, our third child, had been born on June 21. This seemed like a good chance for Betty to get some kind of a vacation and for us to take a little trip around the West after I finished my work in Washington. I told this to Mr. Dunn, and he said it was such a good idea he'd invite his own wife. Betty and Mrs. Dunn came out to Washington on the same plane from New York. Charles Wesley Dunn—I could never bring myself to call him anything but Mr. Dunn—was a very nice man, though a very stern and proper one, but he was a whole generation ahead of me. He was the same age as my uncle Ed, born in 1886. He had graduated from Princeton about 1907 or so, and gone on to law school at Harvard or New York University. When he told his wife, Alice, that Mrs. Beinecke was coming out on the plane with her, Mrs. Dunn assumed that it was to be some senior Mrs. Beinecke. It never dawned on her that this young lady, who was twenty-eight years old at the time, was Mrs. Beinecke. So they both disembarked in Spokane after that very long trip without once having recognized each other on the airplane.

The S&H case in Washington was an important piece of work, and I was in over my head with these very senior lawyers. I was working around the clock, and I was experiencing a lot of tension and anxiety. When Betty arrived in Spokane, Paul Graves had a very nice dinner party at his home for us, together with Mr. and Mrs. Dunn and perhaps a few other guests. I was sitting next to the hostess, and suddenly I felt uncomfortable and started to perspire. I excused myself from the table, and as I was leaving the dining room, I collapsed. Of course, everybody thought that I had some physical ailment, a heart attack or something, and they were very upset, but I think I fainted simply because I was overcome by stress. A lawyer's job is often very stressful. Many times during those years, my stomach was tied up in tight knots of anxiety. I'm not sure that I could have made a long-term career in the more high-tension aspects of the legal profession.

Our host arranged for us to go out to Grand Coulee Dam on the Columbia River, about ninety miles east of Spokane. It's a massive dam and lake, and it supplies irrigation and power all through that part of the Northwest. Betty and I also rented a car and drove out to Mount Hood in Oregon, where we stayed at the aptly named Timberline Lodge. Although it was not long after the summer, there was already snow at that altitude. After a few days of traveling around western Oregon, we took a plane and went home.

When Mr. Dunn and I had returned from salmon fishing in Campbell River, Mr. Graves had told us that he had met with Smith Troy, the state attorney general, and had convinced him that our position was the right one. The attorney general therefore had to issue an opinion to the effect that trading stamps were not securities within the meaning of the blue sky laws of the state of Washington. In order to do that, he had to buttress his opinion with the proper citations and references. Mr. Graves, through Mr. Dunn, invited me to prepare a draft of the opinion that would ultimately be issued by the attorney general of the State of Washington. When I returned to New York, I submitted my draft of what I considered to be the proper position to Mr. Dunn, who passed it along to the State of Washington, and the attorney general issued it without changing a word! So his opinion, which is now on the books, is the opinion I wrote. But our troubles in that part of the country were far from over.

In the autumn of 1948, shortly after my return from Washington, I decided that since I now owned property with trees I ought to do some tree work. I didn't understand how to do tree work, and I shouldn't have done it. I fell out of the top of a tree, although fortunately I didn't fall together with the part of the tree that I was amputating. When I hit the ground, I severely dislocated my right foot, so that where the top of my foot should have been, I saw the bottom of my foot looking up at me. There wasn't much of a bone fracture, but my foot was extremely painful. In order to return it to its proper position, it had to be pulled down and turned and pushed back into place, then splinted up. That meant that I was on crutches for all of that fall of '48. I was lucky to have a very good friend named Alan Schmitz, who was in the business of printing materials for lawyers, mostly in New York. He lived near us in Summit, and for the month after my accident, he was kind enough to pick me up at my home, drive me into New York, and drive me home at the end of the day. I was very much indebted to him.

While I was in this crippled condition, late in the fall of 1948, my uncle Ed asked me to go down to Fort Worth to do some work with George Sirback, the S&H vice president down there. We negotiated the purchase of a building that for a while became the S&H warehouse and headquarters in Fort Worth—but only for a while, because the business grew so fast that in a few years we had to move out to a larger warehouse in the area. I accomplished that mission, and I think that, too, helped give my father and my uncle some confidence in me as a lawyer.

Trading stamps are collected in books, and the completed books are presented at redemption centers and exchanged for what in the early days were called "premiums." That became a word we didn't want to use, so in my time they were called "merchandise," and they have more recently been called "gifts." But it's all more or less the same thing. Trading stamps that are redeemable for gifts or merchandise are much more attractive to the consumer than those that are redeemable for cash. If you go out and present a book of stamps and you get $2.00 in cash for it, that's very nice, but it's not as nice as if you take five or ten books of stamps and bring home an iron or a tennis racket or a washing machine or something of that sort. The trading stamp business flourished where stamps could be redeemed for merchandise, but certain places restricted the business so that stamps could be redeemed only for cash.

In Oregon, there was nothing to hamper or hinder the way the stamp business was done, and stamps were particularly effective there. Roberts Brothers, a small department store in Portland, was one of our success stories. It had not been able to compete with the major store in the city until it became our customer, and then the popularity of stamps helped send its sales through the roof. The corporation commissioner of the state of Oregon was a man named Hudson. He had heard about the effort in Washington State to have stamps declared securities and therefore subject to regulation under the blue sky laws. He thought this was a fine idea. The fact that the attorney general of Washington had delivered an opinion that stamps were not securities didn't bother him. After all, it was only the opinion of the attorney general of Washington, which had some force within that state but which certainly was not binding in Oregon and didn't have the force of a judicial decision. So Hudson declared stamps securities within the meaning of the blue sky laws of Oregon, effectively making it impossible for S&H to operate in that state. This time it wasn't a matter of getting a favorable opinion from the attorney general, as we had in the state of Washington. It was necessary to mount a lawsuit to enjoin the commissioner from taking such a step, and to have the courts decide that trading stamps were not securities under the law.

The name of the suit was *Sperry and Hutchinson v. Hudson*. It is still the leading case on the subject. No other such case ever came along, I think because by the time it was finally disposed of, everybody thought Mr. Hudson's action was silly. But we did have to pursue this suit in Oregon in 1949, a year after we had received the opinion from the attorney general of the state of Washington, and so I spent a lot of time over the next many months familiarizing myself with the state of Oregon. We retained Rupert Bullivant, a diligent lawyer in Portland, to represent us. The case went all the way to the Oregon Supreme Court, and it was ultimately decided in favor of the S&H position. That took care of that particular problem, but it was clear that S&H's legal and legislative difficulties were just beginning.

When The Sperry and Hutchinson Company had been a small business struggling to survive the Depression and the war, there had been few legal challenges to the trading stamp business. The growth of this troublesome legislation was a backhanded tribute to the company's amazing postwar success. By 1951, S&H was still a small company, relative to what it would later become, but its growth was nothing short of phenomenal, and it lacked the administrative and in-house legal capacity to deal with that growth and the challenges to its dominance. S&H needed a general counsel, and it wanted a young man who could deal with the heavy demands of travel and activity that the job would surely entail. I was asked to become S&H's general counsel by my father and Uncle Ed late in 1951. It didn't hurt at all that I was a Beinecke, of course, but I got the position more because I knew as much as anyone about the legal difficulties that S&H was faced with, because my father and uncle had reason to be impressed with my past legal performance, and because I possessed the resilience of youth that would be required for the job. I took the position, even though it meant breaking up my law partnership, both out of familial obligation and out of a real excitement and anticipation for the opportunities and challenges that I knew would lie ahead.

Our law firm had been successful. We didn't get rich at it, but we established that we could do it. Our business was expanding. We needed more manpower, and we employed a young lawyer named Ed Madden as an associate in the firm. My cousin, friend, and law school classmate Connie Mittendorf had joined the firm as a partner in 1950, so that for the last year we were together, we were in effect Casey, Beinecke, Chase & Mittendorf. Jim Casey brought in his friend Samuel Morse Lane to take over my role in the firm. Sam was a graduate of Harvard College and Harvard Law School and had been a superb litigation lawyer at the New York firm of Baldwin, Todd & Lefferts. When I left the firm on December 31, 1951, I quite literally passed on my responsibilities to Sam Lane. Sam came into my office, and we circled around the desk so that Sam was sitting in my chair and I was sitting across from him. I took out the various folders of the cases that were still unfinished, and I said, "Here, Sam, I pass these on to you," and I handed them across the desk. Sam accepted them, we shook hands, and I left. Betty and I went away to Barbados for a month, and I began work as general counsel at S&H on February 1, 1952.

From the original firm of Casey, Beinecke & Chase, two firms emerged. One was the direct lineal descendant, you might say, which became Casey, Lane & Mittendorf and still exists today as Lane & Mittendorf. Charles Greene Smith effectively retired, and while I was general counsel, S&H's outside litigation was handled by Sam Lane at Casey, Lane & Mittendorf. We did a lot of work together in the following years. Paul Chase, on the other hand, joined forces with his former Cravath colleague Dick Olwine, who was crippled from a youthful bout with polio but was a very energetic and hard-working lawyer, and another lawyer named Connelly. Together, they formed a firm called Olwine, Connelly, & Chase. That firm was very successful for about forty years, upgrading from one building to another, until they ended up at a prestigious address on Park Avenue with a prohibitively high rent. When they lost some important clients, they were unable to pay it. Their landlord didn't show them any mercy, so they had to liquidate the business. Some of the lawyers retired, others went to other firms, and some of the more senior members like Paul Chase joined existing firms as counsel.

CHAPTER ELEVEN

General Counsel for The Sperry and Hutchinson Company, 1952–1956

he Sperry and Hutchinson Company, the nation's first independent trading stamp company, was founded in Michigan in
1896 by my great-uncle Thomas Sperry, who was then a traveling salesman for the Howard Cutlery Company. Trading
stamps had long been used as a discount for customers when they paid
their bills on time or in cash. In America in the nineteenth century,
credit at the retail level was widespread, which meant that the retailer's
working capital was frequently under serious strain. In many rural
areas, bills weren't paid until the crops came in, and in urban areas,
wages were lower and more irregular than today, and credit collections
more difficult. Trading stamps helped the retailer out because they
accelerated payment of bills. This freed his capital, reduced his book-
keeping expenses, and minimized the impact of bad debt losses.
Stamps quickly paid for themselves on that account alone. Stamps also
were a promotional tool and a means of enlarging sales.

Until 1896, however, trading stamps were used only by individual
merchants. Each store issued its own stamps and allowed only its own
stamps to be redeemed for merchandise or other premiums. It was the
stroke of genius of Thomas Sperry and his partner, Shelly B. Hutchinson of Baltimore, to conceive of an independent company that would
issue a universal trading stamp. The stamps would be offered by a large
number of noncompeting stores in each community and could be
redeemed for a wide variety of merchandise provided by the trading
stamp company at its redemption stores. My great-uncle Thomas
started the business as a partnership with Hutchinson, and in 1896 it
began by marketing the soon-to-be-famous S&H Green Stamps to
retailers in Jackson, Michigan. Trading stamps were issued to shoppers
at a rate of one stamp for every ten cents of purchases. Customers
pasted the stamps into books that S&H provided, with twelve hundred

stamps per book. When the customers had filled a book or more, they could exchange their books for merchandise—called "premiums" in the early days—at the Company's redemption centers. Merchants paid for the stamps up front and at that time were charged by the stamp.

The Sperry and Hutchinson Company was an almost immediate success, not only because of the strength of the idea but also because it was promoted with vigor and ingenuity. S&H from the beginning had attractive catalogues (with full-color spreads as early as 1910), first-rate redemption stores, and high-quality merchandise that people wanted. The trading stamp was such an effective incentive-promotional device that the merchants who employed stamps quickly enjoyed a positive effect on their business. Hutchinson and my great-uncle Thomas soon went in search of a larger field for their enterprise. They incorporated the business in 1900 and moved its headquarters to New York City. Not long after S&H was incorporated, Shelly Hutchinson sold his share of the Company to my grandfather, William Miller Sperry, and the Company became a Sperry family enterprise. But my grandfather's share wasn't quite a half interest; it was a little more than 49 percent, and just over 50 percent was held by Thomas Sperry. So Thomas had sole control of S&H, even though each brother owned about half of it. Consumer acceptance of the trading stamp concept gradually spread through the East, and within the next few years, trading stamps were adopted by retailers throughout the United States.

The Company experienced gradual but somewhat uneven growth under my grandfather and great-uncle. Prior to World War I, S&H's biggest customer was the A&P supermarket chain—ironic considering that A&P became one of our most obdurate opponents in the 1950s. S&H's primary market in those days, however, was big department stores, such as the Houghton & Dutton store in Boston that my father headed during the Depression. The larger purchases that customers made in department stores allowed them to fill their books more quickly and to see the results of their purchases that much faster. The American trading stamp business experienced its first boom about 1914, when industry volume reached an estimated $25 million. Not surprisingly, the stamp industry also experienced its first rash of antistamp laws and legal cases then as well. The disruptions of World War I ended the nascent boom.

The early success of S&H had enabled my grandfather and my great-uncle Tom to move to Cranford, New Jersey, where they built their large and beautiful homes. While I grew up in Cranford, I never went inside Thomas Sperry's house, for reasons having to do with business relationships among my Sperry relatives. Thomas Sperry had died in 1913 from ptomaine poisoning contracted on a return trip from Europe; he was only fifty years old. He left some of his stock in S&H to his widow, my great-aunt Kate Sperry, and some in trust for his children. I believe he left the shares in trust in such a way that Aunt Kate, through voting her children's shares as well as her own, had the controlling interest in the Company. She remarried, to a man named Goodrich whom I never knew, and the two of them lived on in the Sperry home in Cranford behind the big iron fence. Mrs. Goodrich exercised the power of her controlling interest in The Sperry and Hutchinson Company to make life difficult for my grandfather. I don't know all the circumstances of the matter, but I know that my grandfather was an officer at one of the banks in Cranford in which Mrs. Goodrich also had the controlling interest, and she used her financial interest in that bank in a way that was extremely disagreeable to my grandfather; perhaps she had him removed as president or something equally unseemly.

The fallout from these disagreements was so intense that I remember my father one year sending back a Christmas card from the Goodriches, saying that their Christmas card was not welcome in our house. I was very young when all of that happened, but I learned about it much later when I asked my father about his recollections of those years. So the relationship between the widow of Thomas Sperry and William Sperry and his family was anything but warm. Consequently any socialization between the two branches of the family was cut off, and that was unfortunate. That rift in the family didn't carry on to the next generation, and my brother, Richard, and I, as we grew up, were very friendly with the grandchildren of Thomas Sperry. Thomas Sperry's oldest child, his daughter Katherine, married my uncle Walter Beinecke, with the unusual result that their two children, Walter Beinecke, Jr. and Betsy Beinecke, were my first cousins on the Beinecke side and my second cousins on the Sperry side. We were once very close. Now a rift has opened up between us, for reasons related to the same business after two generations, and we have grown apart again.

In January 1918, after my father and Uncle Walter married into the Sperry family, my grandfather William Sperry sold his interest in S&H to my uncle Edwin, though the money for the purchase was supplied in equal amounts by my father, Edwin, and Walter. While Edwin was the nominal buyer, they worked it out so that each of the three brothers had an equal interest. Edwin went on the board of the Company in 1918, followed by my father in 1920 and Uncle Walter in 1922.

Edwin J., Frederick W., and Walter Beinecke, c. 1955.

Curiously, the first relative from my father's side to go on the S&H board was my father's cousin, George Mittendorf. He had helped defend William Miller Sperry in a lawsuit brought against him by S&H's co-creator, Shelly Hutchinson, some time after Hutchinson had sold his half-interest in S&H to my grandfather. George Mittendorf's law firm was also counsel for the bank named as trustee under the will of

Thomas Sperry, and George Mittendorf became a member of the board of S&H in his representative capacity.

The majority interest in S&H, in the form of Thomas Sperry's shares, passed in part to his widow, Mrs. Goodrich, and in part to the four trusts set up for the benefit of each of his four children. His oldest child, Katherine, had married Walter Beinecke. Under the terms of the trust, when she reached her thirtieth birthday in 1923, her interest matured in a way that permitted her to vote her shares. This interest, plus the William M. Sperry shares now held in the name of Edwin Beinecke, constituted a majority interest in S&H. This interest was sufficient to initiate a petition to the equity court in New Jersey that supervised the management of the estate, asking that all the S&H shares of the estate of Thomas Sperry be sold. The chancellor of the equity court granted the petition, and arranged that the shares be sold at an auction in a courtroom in Jersey City. The Beinecke brothers knew that they didn't have enough money to make a winning bid, so my father's old boss at the Studebaker Corporation, Albert Erskine, introduced them to the investment banking firm of Goldman Sachs, which made available a credit line of a million dollars. At the auction, Goldman Sachs's representative, Clarence Dauphinot, made the bids on behalf of the Beinecke brothers. Aunt Katie wanted her siblings to get a satisfactory price for their shares, so Uncle Ed had promised her he would purchase the shares for not less than a certain amount. When the bidding began slowing down before that price was reached, Uncle Ed communicated to Dauphinot that he ought to jump to the set price; he did, and the auction was over. When someone later asked Dauphinot why he made such a surprising leap to end the bidding, he replied, "Because I was in a hurry to get back to New York." With that purchase, the three Beinecke brothers had acquired the remaining shares of the Company, and by January 1, 1924, they had become the sole owners of S&H.

I don't believe they ever considered changing The Sperry and Hutchinson Company name, which was fairly well established by that point. At the time they acquired it, however, S&H was a small company, insignificant when compared with the Beinecke brothers' other business activities. My father's automobile business in Newark was one of the most successful Studebaker distributors in the country. Uncle Walter was treasurer of John C. Paige and Company, an insurance brokerage, and became president of the later incorporated company in 1926. And even by the early 1920s, Uncle Edwin was a power in the New York business and industrial community and was probably the most prominent and influential of the three brothers. He had left Yale in 1905 to work as a timekeeper with the George A. Fuller Construction Company, which was then building The Plaza Hotel. He rose to become head of that company. He was president and chairman of the board of the U.S. Realty and Improvement Company, owner of The Plaza Hotel in later years. The Beinecke brothers had many irons in the fire, and S&H was by no means the most important. Uncle Ed's Fuller Construction Company office was located in the famed Flatiron Building at Fifth Avenue and 23rd Street, conveniently close to The Sperry and Hutchinson Company headquarters at 114 Fifth Avenue. He became president of S&H in 1923. Day-to-day operations were run by the executive vice president, Vernon C. Brown, who later was made president. My father and Uncle Walter both became vice presidents of the company in 1927, but it was not until 1938, when S&H was making its slow recovery from the Depression, that my father joined it on a full-time basis.

Frank Rossi, who was my chief operating officer when I was chief executive officer, joined S&H in 1938 as well, having worked for several years at Hurdman and Cranstoun, S&H's accounting firm. As comptroller, he had what was considered a large department, consisting of all of seven people. The other principal officers, besides V. C. Brown, included Walter Eckert, the treasurer; Joseph (Joe) Peters, the head of the merchandise division; and George Schirer, who was in charge of sales. S&H was a small, close-knit, and rather sleepy company. Total sales during the 1930s amounted to only about $3 million annually and dropped to $1 million at the nadir of the Depression. Business remained at a low ebb during World War II, when merchandise was scarce, and retailers, when they had any goods to sell, had no need for promotional devices to attract customers. At the close of World War II, S&H sales were about $5.5 million. In the next few years, though, S&H began to expand at such a tremendous pace that the trading stamp industry has to be ranked among the greatest business successes of the twentieth century.

It's difficult to say precisely why trading stamp sales soared after the war, but it's possible to pinpoint some of the causes. Economically and psychologically, trading stamps were a good fit for America in the 1950s. The system made sound economic sense. Trading stamps were then and remained one of the few promotions that rewarded customers in direct proportion to the size of their purchases. It was a cash transaction where there was a direct relationship between what you spent and what you got. It wasn't like a sweepstakes, where you put down money hoping you would be the lucky one in a million. Stamps were something substantial that, like money, could be used to purchase goods. The trading stamp system was a fair one. From the consumer's point of view, it was a simple and systematic way of acquiring household articles.

Part of what made S&H so successful after World War II was that it benefited from the pent-up demand that had accumulated during the war, when there was rationing and little production for civilian use. The gifts that S&H offered were, at least in the late 1940s, things that people wanted and were unable to get in stores during the war years: irons, lamps, small household appliances, and so on. Even in the 1950s, households were still catching up with the deferred consumption of the war years. And the merchandise we were able to offer by that time was of the highest quality, from top-notch brand-name firms like Sunbeam and General Electric. In the 1950s, after fifteen years of Depression and wartime privation, Americans were looking for stability and security. Postwar prosperity, the move to the suburbs, and the baby boom were the hallmarks of the era. For millions of 1950s housewives, trading stamps were "woman's money," her currency, sometimes called "egg money." (In agricultural societies, the farmer's wife could keep the money she made from the sale of eggs.) For women, trading stamps provided a kind of freedom; they gave women power. Stamps were a form of savings, which was important to young families in the early 1950s who were looking to the future. Finally, there was something new, fresh, and intriguing about trading stamps. Even though they represented an old concept, they seemed new at the time, and it was an era that prized novelty.

I never thought that the reason behind the success of trading stamps was that people wanted something for nothing. I always thought they were looking for something instead of nothing, some extra value that would not be found elsewhere. I had no truck with the economists' argument that competition ought to be confined solely to price. Human nature doesn't work that way, and the idea of attracting customers with "something extra" has a long and honorable history. Purchasers of ladies' cosmetic articles in ancient Rome, for example, were given free trinkets of extraordinary value, such as the gold-mounted tooth of a Hyrcanian wolf or other magical charms guaranteed to help a woman win the heart of her secret love. Athenian idol manufacturers offered special free premiums—incense, lamps, and drinking cups—to their customers. Grecian garment makers gave special ornaments to purchasers who spent above a certain amount. And I saw for myself that this practice was still alive and well in that part of the world when I visited the Cairo bazaars with my parents in 1937 and we were always offered a cup of coffee to drink with the proprietor before getting down to business. In this country, you could point to the traditions of the baker's dozen, the free peppermint stick offered to a customer's boy or girl, the complimentary coffeepot and cracker barrel in the rural general store, and the lagniappe in New Orleans. S&H Green Stamps stood firmly in that tradition of a patronage dividend, of offering something instead of nothing.

In a way, S&H was dealing with matters of human psychology. A filled book of stamps was usually worth two dollars in cash, but because S&H bought merchandise in bulk and distributed it efficiently, it could deliver a value of three dollars (or more) in merchandise for each filled book of stamps—so the customer was better off exchanging the stamps for merchandise. More than that, the people who redeemed their stamps for our goods enjoyed getting those tangible proofs of their savings and thrift. If a woman exchanged a book of stamps for two dollars, the money would go into her pocketbook and be spent along with her other cash. There was no "remembrance value," as we used to call it, in the redemption of stamps for cash. But the goods that people acquired through stamps were long-lasting and often provided daily reminders of the benefits of saving trading stamps. In states like Washington and Wisconsin, which required that stamps be exchanged only for cash, trading stamps did not have the same appeal as in the other states.

I don't think my father and his brothers had any idea how big S&H would become, but they did sense something of its potential. As the Company grew, they became more involved, and made changes in S&H's operations that helped accelerate its growth. In particular, Uncle Edwin and my father began to light a fire under the sales staff and to provide them with the organization they needed to increase S&H's accounts exponentially.

The twelve hundred stamps in a book cost the merchant on the average about $2.70, or about two percent of the sales on which stamps were given. That meant that trading stamps were initially a hard sell, because many merchants would argue that their profit margins were only two percent or even less, so how could they afford stamps? Our salesmen had to convince them that using stamps would increase their volume, which would allow them to manage their costs without raising prices. If, instead of paying for stamps, a retailer decided to take the two percent of annual sales that stamps would cost and apply that money toward price cuts, the reduction would be imperceptible and have little influence on his sales. And our salesmen like Elmo Pearson, Walter Whitnack, and George Sirback did a fantastic job of pointing out that customers preferred stamps, because they offered extra gifts customers often would be reluctant to buy with cash. Customers began flocking to stores that offered trading stamps. That made stamps a major weapon in the period of increased retail competition following World War II.

My father and Uncle Ed, with Frank Rossi's assistance, also oversaw a drastic improvement in the Company's way of handling the merchandise used for redemption. Before 1950, many manufacturers wouldn't sell us their merchandise, since S&H was considered a weak link in the distribution chain. The merchandise division lacked larger ambitions; Frank Rossi remembered that Joe Peters became highly excited when he was first able to list a Big Ben alarm clock in the S&H catalogue. Even when the Company purchased the goods, the manufacturer often failed to deliver on the date promised or our men failed to pick up at the location where the goods had been delivered.

S&H had a large number of redemption locations. They ranged from nothing more than a counter at a department store to freestanding stores of as much as three thousand square feet. S&H used to order merchandise for its redemption facilities directly from the manufacturers, but often the merchandise didn't arrive in sufficient quantities and many items would be out of stock. We'd have to tell customers, "I'm sorry, we haven't got those catalogue items." That wasn't good for business. Because the Company lacked warehousing facilities, when we ran out of a certain item, let's say toasters, we would use the storage facilities in back of a redemption store to house the new toasters ordered. Then this particular redemption store would serve as the toaster warehousing unit for the other stores in the general area. The whole system was overseen by a handful of merchandise managers in New York, each of whom was expected to keep track of the perpetual inventory of a number of stores. But as the business began to grow and expand, this proved inadequate and the system began to become overburdened and break down.

To solve the problem, we had to build a series of distribution centers. Our first warehouse was constructed in Fort Worth, Texas, and I had gone out to talk with George Sirback about it in my legal counsel days. Then S&H acquired another, smallish warehouse in Hillside, New Jersey; it had once been part of my cousin Bud's automobile distributorship. Eventually we had ten highly organized, state-of-the art warehouses in various parts of the country, including Boston, Atlanta, Chicago, Fort Worth, Los Angeles, San Francisco, and Portland. The first generation of distribution centers quickly became outmoded as S&H did its imitation of Jack's magic beanstalk. George Sirback's headquarters were remodeled and expanded several times, and the relatively small warehouse in Hillside was replaced by a mammoth and modern warehouse in Edison, New Jersey, near Metuchen. The merchandise purchased from the manufacturer was delivered directly to the distribution centers, each of which was responsible for a certain number of redemption stores, servicing them through a trucking system we rented. For the first time, the merchandise was regularly making it from the manufacturer into our redemption stores, and we therefore had far fewer out-of-stock items. It was always a fight to keep items from running out of stock in that business, and there was never a 100 percent success rate. Still, we improved the situation a great deal. Our relations with our suppliers changed as they began to notice that they were selling a great deal of merchandise to us. Far from S&H's having to struggle to be able to offer their products, most of the brand-name merchandisers were now competing to list their items in our catalogue.

The major development that affected the growth of Sperry and Hutchinson was the revolution in the food business during the early 1950s, when supermarkets truly became super. The postwar years saw an enormous increase in the number of large self-service stores that sold food and other items in high volume for cheaper prices. More and more, the level of competition became supermarket against supermarket, with consumers finding little difference among such stores in terms of price. Supermarkets began to battle for customers by relying on nonprice incentives, such as convenient location, high quality and service, air conditioning, wider aisles, and ample parking, until the competition had leveled off in those categories as well. Then along came trading stamps.

The trading stamp business took off in the early 1950s. No one could get enough of them. Trading stamps were such an effective promotional tool that some of our experiences in those days sound like fiction. Our first supermarket account was with a store in Texas, which had been signed up by our sales vice president, George Sirback. The supermarket was looking for a way to shift some of its business from the weekends, which were its busiest time. Since most merchants needed extra personnel on weekends, if some of their business could be shifted to the middle of the week, they would lower their expenses on a total basis. So Sirback urged his Texas accounts to give double stamps on Wednesdays, and it changed the character of their business. From attracting very few customers on Wednesdays, the stores started attracting almost all their customers on Wednesdays. It was unbelievable.

Another classic example was our interaction with Thorofare Markets, Inc., of Pittsburgh, a well-managed though relatively small local chain. We believed Thorofare could use our service effectively but encountered a certain skepticism. So we said, "Give us your toughest market, your biggest problem store, your real dog." The test store was located in Clarksburg, West Virginia. It was barely holding its own, with gross weekly sales of $11,000, and all prior efforts to increase volume had failed. We introduced stamps there in March 1953. Within three weeks, sales rose to $31,000, an increase of 182 percent. Four months later, the store was doing $42,000 per week, up 282 percent.

It was incredible but true, and the pattern repeated itself all over the United States. S&H stamps sparked unprecedented growth at Eberhard's, a local chain in Grand Rapids, Michigan. In an amazingly short time, the chain went from a small enterprise struggling desperately to stay out of the red to a solidly profitable organization. The head of the chain couldn't get over it. He made speeches to retail and business groups and praised stamps to anyone who would listen. George Schirer, for many years our chief operating officer, occasionally referred to him as our best salesman. More and more chains across the country were going to stamps, and the number of customers using trading stamps was exploding. Within a few years, according to Department of Agriculture estimates, more than half of all American households would be saving trading stamps, and growth continued to climb. For many years S&H had been effectively the only trading stamp business in America. It soon became no secret that stamps were a powerful way to attract customers. There were local trading stamp companies like Yellow Stamp in cities such as Pittsburgh and Saint Louis, "captive" stamp brands like Top Value (which was wholly owned by the Kroger's food chain), and companies like Gold Bond that sprang up in imitation of S&H to do business on our exclusions. But we remained the only national trading stamp company, the only one that did business from Maine to California. S&H was always number one, and the Green Stamp was considered the Tiffany of the stamp business.

Part of what made S&H special was that we served what we called a "family" of retailers: a limited number of noncompeting merchants in any given area, each of whom had an exclusive contract for S&H Green Stamps. Each of the merchants had the benefits of our trading stamps, yet the customers could get their stamps from the butcher, the baker, the candlestick maker—wherever they shopped. Each participating supermarket, drugstore, and department store helped share the cost of the joint promotion and helped strengthen the pulling power of the stamps for others—and, in the end, for itself. Our system of exclusive franchises conferred the unique S&H advantage on all those cooperating merchants inside the program, and the essence of a successful promotional tool is that you are offering something no one else has. But this necessarily required more retailers to be at all times outside the program than in, which stirred up resentment on the part of the majority of merchants who didn't have Green Stamps.

Trading stamps were not magic in and of themselves. They were a powerful promotional tool in the hands of the merchant who knew how to use them as an "extra" to supplement competitively low prices, quality products, good service, effective advertising, and other fundamentals of retailing. We always told our customers that neither stamps nor any other promotional tool could compensate for poor management or the failure to be competitive in the basics of store merchandising. Trading stamps, like other promotional devices, attracted customers who regarded a participating store as approximately equal to alternative stores in overall attractiveness. The stamps really had to be something extra, and if they were, they could be a tremendous edge. One man who knew this very well was a shrewd and successful businessman who owned a thriving independent department store in Chicago. He used to say, "I'd gladly pay ten cents a head for each customer I can draw off the street—just to get her inside my store." He had two main drawing cards: our trading stamps and a huge aquarium that cost him $250,000 a year to maintain. One day the biggest department store chain in the Midwest made him an attractive offer for the store, and he sold it. The big chain was fanatically antistamp. Its first action was to drop stamps. Its second was to dispose of the expensive aquarium. And its final action was to get rid of the store, after trying unsuccessfully to make a go of it.

Trading stamps were most valuable for those merchants who had large additional sales potential and who had enough slack in their operations to absorb substantial gains in volume with little change in operating cost. That meant, in practice, that S&H was almost always a champion of the underdog. If you took a situation where two stores were competing in the same market, with the large store drawing ninety percent of the customers and the small store only ten percent, the small fellow obviously had the far greater potential for increasing his business. The number one store in a community didn't need a champion; it was its own champion. Trading stamps gave the underdog the opportunity to compete. One key example of that was the Roberts Brothers department store in Portland, Oregon. It had been driven to the verge of extinction by the local giant, Maier and Frank. With the aid of stamps, it was able not only to survive but to thrive. Another example was George Jenkins, who started the Publix chain of supermarkets in Florida. For many years George was our biggest and most loyal customer, and he used trading stamps to help make his chain number one in Florida. The news got around to other upstart entrepreneurs, who concluded, "S&H must be the best." But by turning the tables in this way, trading stamps incurred the wrath of the largest and most powerful merchants in each community where they were used. We were stirring up a hornet's nest of opposition.

My father often said of S&H that "the virulence of the opposition is the measure of our success." In the early years after World War II, we had been a small company. Because of our modest size, we excited no interest in academic circles, and not much in the press either, except for occasional local news that was generally hostile. But in the period before World War I, when S&H had experienced its first boom, there had been a moderate-sized flood of hostile legislation against trading stamps from merchants who were threatened by the new promotional device. In fact, part of my work in the late 1940s had involved attempting with Charles Wesley Dunn to get those old restrictive laws off the books. We persuaded the legislature in North Dakota, for example, to pass corrective legislation repealing one of those laws. As S&H became more successful in the early 1950s, history repeated itself. As merchants who were not part of our franchising system lost market share to those who offered stamps, every once in a while some of them would run to their government representatives to try to put us out of business, rather than compete in the marketplace as business proprietors are supposed to do under our free enterprise system. More restrictive laws were passed, and legal challenges were mounted by our disgruntled competitors.

My uncle Edwin asked me to join S&H as general counsel in 1952, not only to deal with all the legal issues that any successful company encounters but to spearhead the counterattack. I had no sense that I would ever eventually become head of the Company. I didn't even think about it. I was fascinated by trading stamp law, which was so interesting and fiendishly complex. So even though I felt some twinges about leaving the law firm I had helped to found, I was excited by the prospect of working for S&H. My responsibilities as general counsel were defined by myself, my father and my uncle, and the shifting legal and legislative problems S&H encountered in the 1950s. I took minutes at the annual stockholders' meeting, amended S&H's charters and bylaws, and did considerable legal work for family members. I was supposed to be the problem solver for anything that seemed to have a legal angle. To some extent I took over work that had long been carried out elsewhere in the Company. The merchandising department, for example, had always negotiated the leases for the redemption stores, but as soon as there was a lawyer on site, all of that sort of thing would be sent over to the legal department. I was the sole lawyer in the Company when I came aboard, but not long after I hired an assistant, David Maclay, who had graduated from Williams College and Yale Law School. I hired Jim Mills, another Yale Law graduate, the year after that. The volume of legal work we encountered quickly became excessive, and it was my responsibility to build up a fair-sized legal department, with several other lawyers. We also continued to send a lot of business to my old law firm, which was now Casey, Lane & Mittendorf. Sam Lane was our principal contact there, along with Fred Collins, a Harvard Law graduate who had followed Sam from Baldwin, Todd & Lefferts.

I took the train every weekday morning from New Jersey to the S&H office in Manhattan. When I joined S&H in 1952, its headquarters was on lower Fifth Avenue at number 114, at the corner of 17th Street. The Sperry and Hutchinson Company had a long history of serving department stores (the principal outlets for S&H Green Stamps before World War II), and most New York City department stores were down on the Lady's Mile in the neighborhood of Sixth Avenue and 23rd Street. One of the cornerstones of that commercial district was the Siegel-Cooper department store on Sixth Avenue and 18th Street, whose fountain had been as famous a rendezvous point for my parent's generation as the Biltmore clock was for mine: "Meet me at the Fountain" was a common phrase in the first two decades of the twentieth century in New York City. Siegel-Cooper was among the most important customers of S&H, and that was why our company had located its headquarters in that vicinity and was still there in 1952, even though by then Siegel-Cooper had long since gone out of business.

When I first arrived at S&H as general counsel, the Company employed only seventy or eighty people in its New York office and everything was on one floor. Everyone knew everyone else there, and relations were harmonious and even intimate; it was like a family. Chances are that S&H had fewer than a hundred redemption stores then. That's just a guess, but it was a reliable rule of thumb that there were roughly as many employees in the S&H headquarters in New York as there were redemption stores out in the field. The Company headquarters at 114 Fifth Avenue was a small and friendly place in those days, without much red tape or formality. With the explosive boom of the 1950s, S&H began to grow like Topsy. We expanded to several floors, then had to break through the walls to take some space in the adjacent building at 110 Fifth Avenue. The floors of the two buildings were not at the same level, so you had to go up and down two or three steps to get from one address to the next. The stairs and corridors began to be filled with the continuous bustle and hurry of a growing staff, many of whom I no longer recognized. Eventually S&H had over eight hundred redemption centers and over eight hundred employees in our Manhattan headquarters, and we had to move to a new office building farther uptown at the corner of Madison Avenue and 43rd Street, which became known as the S&H Building.

I got considerable insight into the working relationships between my father and his brothers, Edwin and Walter Beinecke. The three were very different people, yet they formed a cohesive team. Uncle Walter, who served as executive vice president and chairman of the finance committee, was a people person. He could walk within a twenty-block radius of his New York apartment or office and talk with policemen, cab drivers, the doormen, and his neighbors. He knew them all by name, and they knew him. He was a terrific salesman because he liked people, and selling came naturally to him. He was a skilled athlete and an enviably good golfer; his hole in one on Pine Valley's third hole was an achievement that would make any golfer happy. He had a brilliant mathematical mind. As a young man, Uncle Walter and my grandfather Beinecke would play chess in their heads, even though a game sometimes took them weeks to complete. And as one of the world's greatest contract bridge players, he had actually served on the committee that established the official rules of the game.

My uncle Edwin—who was called E. J. within S&H, just as my father was called F. W.—was the businessman's ideal of a successful businessman. He was decisive, bright, quick, tough, determined, and indomitable. He served as president of S&H until 1952, chairman of the board until 1960, and simply chairman from 1960 to 1966, when the title was retired when he did. Uncle Edwin was involved in a wide variety of business activities, all of them successful. He was one of the early directors of the Conrad Hilton Hotels and a director of the Hogan Company (the parent company of Tiffany's, Bergdorf Goodman, and other retail giants), Curtis-Wright (the aircraft engine company), and over a dozen other boards. He was president of U.S. Realty & Improvement Company, one of the outstanding companies operating buildings in New

York and other large cities throughout the nation. He was chairman of the board of the Fuller Construction Company, which had built not only The Plaza Hotel but also Quonset Point, the major naval base on the East Coast, and the airfield at Gander, Newfoundland, a city that served as America's "back door" to Scotland during World War II.

My father, who was named president of S&H in 1952 and chairman of the executive committee in 1953, was the only one of the trio with any technical skills or aspirations. He was also the abstract philosopher of the group. Although his demeanor was more professorial and even artistic than the stereotypical businessman's, few college professors (and few businessmen, for that matter) could have built the country's second-largest Studebaker distributorship, as he had done back in the 1920s.

All three brothers believed that a major factor in their business success was the solidarity between them. They were also convinced that there wasn't any room for company politics at S&H, even when it became a corporate giant. In their business dealings, they always presented a united front. They would go into a room and talk through their disagreements. They had a rule that as long as any one of the three still wanted to talk, the other two had to remain in the room. If one of the brothers disagreed with the others, couldn't persuade them, and had been given as much time as he wanted to present his argument, he had to accept their view. When the three of them came out of the room, whatever differences there had been, they were in total unity and unanimity.

Two of my cousins from the second generation of Beineckes preceded me at S&H. Edwin Beinecke, Jr., had been the first to come aboard. Eddie's problem was that he wanted more than anything else in the world to be like his father. Unfortunately, he arrived at S&H with no experience; he had attended Brown University and served in the army field artillery during the war, but he didn't have any independent business or legal or other training to draw upon. When Eddie started having responsibilities of his own at S&H, he was placed in an impossible situation, and he struck out. His father placed enormous expectations on him, and since both of them were strong personalities, it was an extremely difficult and tense relationship for all concerned. Eddie was farmed out to the Patent Scaffolding Company (for which I had once served as an impromptu vice president) and rejoined S&H several years later.

Walter Beinecke, Jr., had also come before me at S&H. Bud had attended the St. George's School in Newport, Rhode Island, and served in the merchant marine. After World War II, he worked for the American Tobacco Company before making a short-lived venture into the automobile business with the Kaiser-Frazer Automobile Company. That company was founded in the immediate postwar years by Henry Kaiser, who had achieved great fame by manufacturing supply ships very rapidly for use by the navy and merchant marine during the war, and James W. Frazer, who had been an automobile company executive before the war. Then as now, the major American automobile companies were the Big Three: General Motors, Ford, and Chrysler. But it was thought by some people that following the war, when the market for automobiles was terrific because no cars had been produced for four years, another company could rise and join the ranks of the major manufacturers. That was the dream that brought the Kaiser-Frazer Automobile Company into being. My uncle Walter Beinecke, although he was in the insurance business, knew some of the people involved and was invited to become a member of the Kaiser-Frazer board. He accepted, and it seemed to him and his son that this was a golden opportunity for Bud to get in on the ground floor with an important distributorship for Kaiser-Frazer automobiles. In an odd coincidence, he established his business at 1015 Broad Street in Newark, the very same place where my father had had his Studebaker business in the 1920s.

All went well for a short time, but then the competition of the more experienced automobile companies proved too much and the Kaiser-Frazer company failed. Around 1950, Bud called me at my office at Casey, Beinecke & Chase to ask if I could act as a lawyer in connection with closing down his business, and I did. His action was very timely, because he managed to get out while there was still some substance to the parent company. It wanted to protect the market for its cars, so it agreed to take back all its unsold cars at an agreed-upon price. As the representative of Bud's company, I participated in drawing up a long and complicated legal agreement with the parent company's lawyers. Kaiser-Frazer was represented by Willkie, Farr & Gallagher, as that well-known firm had come to be called since Wendell Willkie, the Republican candidate for president of the United States in 1940, had come aboard. In order to reach a deal, we had to move quickly, and so we worked all night long until the agreement was signed in one of the major New York hotels by the appropriate officer of the Kaiser-Frazer Company. I returned home to Summit and went to bed for several hours, and came downstairs just as our local minister called on us. He must have wondered what kind of young man I was to be having my breakfast at one o'clock on a weekday afternoon.

Although Walter Beinecke, Jr.'s venture with the Kaiser-Frazer Automobile Company was a mixed success, it had some positive results. It taught me that Bud Beinecke, in deciding to shut down his business in a timely fashion, had good judgment. And when he subsequently went to work for S&H, he brought with him a group of young executives who had worked for him at his Kaiser-Frazer distributorship and did yeoman service for S&H over the years. One of them was Joseph Oros, who became the first of our Washington representatives. I don't think "lobbyist" is the right word to describe his position, because a lobbyist is a person who seeks either to prevent legislation or cause it to be enacted, and our representatives in Washington were not so engaged. We did employ lobbyists in most of the state capitals, but the task of our Washington representative was more to keep us informed and apprised of developments that might affect the Company and to get to know the agencies and find out where we should go if we needed to file a brief or pursue a particular procedure. Bud also brought over from Kaiser-Frazer a salesman named John Beinert, who eventually became one of the vice presidents in charge of S&H business in California and the West, an accountant named Robert Patterson, and a few other young men of considerable ability. Bud served as a sort of assistant to Uncle Edwin and was involved in the elaborate system of merchandise distribution that evolved during the Company's period of explosive growth. He had a flair for design, working with the architects to create the major warehouses.

In 1950, Bud suggested that he and I create trusts for our children for the specific purpose of acquiring some of the S&H common shares from our respective parents. It was a good time for Betty and me to do so, since all four of our children had been born, and our youngest child, Frances, was not quite a year old. Our S&H lawyers Frank Lavery and George Doner always referred to these trusts as "the bootstrap trusts," a reference to the fairy tale in which the protagonist lifts himself up by his own bootstraps. The trusts were given this whimsical designation because they started out with a nominal sum and, through a complicated process of borrowing and buying, actually "bootstrapped" themselves into a fine financial package. It was an exercise that required a thorough understanding of tax law, good financial planning, a certain amount of financial legerdemain, and even some ability to foretell the future. The reason this last quality was required is that tax law is not an eternal base of solid bedrock but a mass of shifting sands blown by social and political winds. When we were attempting to build an enduring support for our children's future, we had to take into account not only what was taxable in 1950 but what might be taxable in years to come.

The story of the trusts' creation requires a backward glance at the history of the stock of The Sperry and Hutchinson Company. When Edwin, Fritz, and Walter Beinecke acquired the Company in the early 1920s, there were only 10,000 shares of stock. Each of the brothers and each of their wives owned one-sixth of the stock, or 1,666 shares. Since the total added up to 9,996, the odd four shares were used for director's qualifying shares or some such technical purpose. As the American economy painfully clawed its way up from the Depression, S&H began to recover financially and the senior Beineckes decided to bring the next generation into the ownership of the Company. In 1941, Dick and I received 500 shares of S&H, as did our cousins Bud and Betsy. Our cousins Edwin, Jr., and Sylvia were married by that time, and their spouses were taken into account in the gift of stock; Ed was given 400 shares and his then-wife, Margaret, received 100, and Sylvia was given 400 shares while her husband, Dr. John Robinson, received 100 shares.

I don't know what the tax implications of the gift may have been, since I was away in the navy at the time. I was glad to get the shares and particularly the modest dividend income, for it was a welcome addition to the pittance the navy was paying me. When Ed's wife, Margaret, died in 1949, an estate tax return had to be filed for her S&H shares. Because the Company was still privately held in its entirety, however, there was no market and hence no price for Margaret's shares. A value was put on the shares by calculating a multiple of the average earnings per share for a period of years, possibly the preceding ten years. The IRS accepted this formula. This enabled us for the first time to have a value for the S&H shares.

According to my cousin Walter, Jr., his father had been seeking ways to pass along S&H stock to the succeeding generations of Beineckes. It was of course very important in the settlement of Margaret's estate for the value of S&H shares to be as low as the Internal Revenue Service would accept as reasonable. The lower the rate the IRS would accept, the lower the tax. At the time of Margaret's death in 1949, or at least by the time the trusts were created the next year, her shares were more numerous than the hundred shares she had originally been given. The stock had been modestly split by that point, perhaps by as much as 10 to 1 or more, which also meant that there were then sufficient shares to enable some to be distributed. That facilitated the transfer of an ownership participation to different family members.

The establishment of a low value for the S&H stock meant that the younger generation could acquire stock from the older Beineckes at a price we could manage. We were now planning a sale of stock from the senior Beineckes to trusts for the benefit of the new younger generation. We were confronted by two potential tax problems unrelated to each other. In the case of the sale, we wanted to make sure that the stock was sold at a price low enough that we would be able to buy it and yet high enough that the IRS would not challenge the sale and rule that it was partially a gift, with a resulting gift tax. Then there was the matter of the income received by the trusts. We had the legal obligation to support our children. With that thought in mind, we were concerned lest the income received by the trusts be attributed to us, thus subjecting us to increased income tax liability. In the event, neither of these dread eventualities occurred.

The low value assigned to the stock for estate tax purposes, however, was a potential obstacle to such a transfer from older to younger generations. It was feared that since the price assigned to the stock was so low, the IRS might rule that the sale was partially a gift. The risk would have been accentuated, we thought, if I were to act as the trustee for my children's trusts and Bud for his. Moreover, we believed that if Walter and Katherine Beinecke had sold their stock to Walter Jr.'s children's trusts or if my parents had sold their stock to my children's trusts, and if then the IRS had ruled that the transaction was taxable, the transfer might turn out to be taxable to Bud and me as the parental trustees. On the other hand, if the stock was passed to a third party as trustee for the same children, the trust rather than the parents would be more likely to be the taxpayer. Consequently, seeking to minimize the risk of added income tax liability and the risk of potential gift tax implications, we devised a plan whereby I served as the trustee for Bud's children and Bud for mine.

The only fly in the ointment was that I didn't have any capital to speak of in 1950. Betty and I created four trusts, one for each of our children. Betty was the settlor (that is, the creator) of the trusts, and initially funded them very modestly, to the tune of about $1,000 for each one. By that time we had a value for S&H shares—a different value from that used in the settlement of Margaret's estate, but a value reached by the application of the same formula. The trusts then contracted with my parents to purchase a certain number of shares of S&H common stock from them at that price. The trusts had no means, however, of paying for those shares. Instead, each trust borrowed from the Manufacturers Trust Company a sum sufficient for a down payment, pledging the shares of S&H stock as collateral. My parents were given promissory notes representing the remaining balance.

The trusts of course were obligated to pay off the bank loan and the promissory notes held by my parents, as well as the interest periodically due on each. In the 1950s, S&H was becoming larger and more profitable each year, so the dividends that the trusts received were sufficient to enable the gradual repayment of the Manufacturers Trust loan, after taking into account the income tax due on the dividends. Eventually the promissory notes held by my parents were paid off as well. The trusts then owned the shares of S&H stock free and clear of any obligation. They were not required to pay anything out of their dividends except income tax. There were no other expenditures because the beneficiaries of the trust, namely, our four children, had all their expenses taken care of by Betty and me.

Later, after Bud had left S&H and we were not as close as we had been, we ceased to be the trustees for each other's children. I asked Bob Dunn, then general counsel of S&H, to act as trustee for my children. Subsequently I became the trustee. Now that Rick, Sarah, John, and Frances are grown and have offspring of their own, although I am still (as of 1999) the trustee for the trusts for my children, that is a responsibility I will soon pass along to someone else. Each trust now has quite a substantial value, which is an excellent result when you reflect that each started with nothing. These trusts have proven to be of great benefit to our children, and I take some pride in their creation. They are an example of what a little hard thinking, careful planning, and attention to detail can accomplish.

In my early years at S&H, I was completely absorbed with dealing with the legal and legislative firestorm that the Company had to deal with in the early 1950s. In the spring of 1952, the operator of a Sioux City, Iowa, food chain, way off in the northwestern corner of the state, had enjoyed such success with S&H Green Stamps that his competitor rushed down to Des Moines to try to put a stop to it. This man persuaded his friend Leo Hoegh, the attorney general, to dust off an old anti–trading stamp statute and apply it to S&H Green Stamps. The news was reported on the local radio, and the result was pandemonium. Crowds of people (mostly women), terrified that their stamps would soon be worthless, lined up at the six or eight redemption stores throughout Iowa, in much the way that fearful depositors make runs on weakened banks. The panic lasted for several days, and S&H met the demand by running trucks full of merchandise night and day from warehouses in Fort Worth and Chicago.

Sam Lane and I turned up the next day in the attorney general's office armed with the applicable legal and legislative history. There had been a regulatory law passed in Minnesota back in 1910 that imposed great restrictions on the trading stamp business, and the adjacent state of Iowa had enacted an identical law immediately afterwards. That law, which was right there in the collected statutes of the state of Iowa, was the law that Leo Hoegh sought to invoke in 1952. What he did not know, however, was that the Minnesota law had been immediately challenged and held by the Supreme Court of Minnesota to be invalid and an unconstitutional violation of due process. A county judge in Ottumwa, Iowa, a city in the southeastern part of the state, had been persuaded by the ruling of the Minnesota Supreme Court and had made a ruling in 1912 that held the Iowa law unconstitutional as well. His decision had never been appealed. That meant it had never gone on to the state supreme court in Iowa as it had in Minnesota, and so there was no published record of the opinion. But I had a copy of it in our files, and S&H had been doing business in Iowa ever since 1912 on the basis of the decision by that Ottumwa judge. Sam and I reported all of this to Attorney General Hoegh. "What's that to me?" he responded. "I'm going to have the county attorneys in all the ninety-nine counties of the great state of Iowa file criminal informations against you, your company, your employees, and your customers. I'm going to do to you what I did to the whores and the gamblers. I'm going to run you out of the state." It was very dramatic. Every now and then, even today, when I pull up alongside a car with Iowa license plates I'll lean out and shout, "How's everything in all the ninety-nine counties of the great state of Iowa?" Needless to say, I stayed in Des Moines and retained local counsel. We got a temporary restraining order preventing Leo Hoegh from putting us out of business right away.

I did a lot of research in the state law library, located right in the capitol building in Des Moines. Our local counsel, Frederic M. Miller, the diligent and careful lawyer preparing the brief, wanted to get all the background he could on how successful S&H had been not only in holding restrictive laws unconstitutional but also in getting legislatures to repeal restrictive legislation. I remembered that we had received a favorable legislative action in Louisiana back in 1928, and so I was hunting through the law library looking for the published record of the legislative session for that year. I found the *State of Louisiana Acts and Resolves* for 1928, a thick volume, and skimmed through the index. Nothing. There was a thinner book next to the *Acts and Resolves*, which turned out to be a record of the "First Extra Session of the Louisiana

Legislature for 1928." It contained about a dozen pieces of legislation, but nothing relating to S&H. There was an even thinner volume on the shelf, a record of the "Second Extra Session of the Louisiana Legislature for 1928," which contained only three or four acts and resolves, none of them what I was looking for. There's something the matter here, I thought. Then I noticed a paper-thin booklet lying flat atop the other books on the shelf. I pulled it out and discovered that it was a record of the "Third Extra Session of the Louisiana Legislature for 1928." It contained exactly one act, the one repealing the restrictive trading stamp law that had been put through a dozen or so years earlier. I figured that back in 1928, some influential lobbyist through some means had persuaded the Louisiana governor to call a third extra session of the legislature. It probably met for all of ten minutes one morning and passed that piece of corrective legislation. I occasionally had to do that sort of library detective work when I was general counsel. Nowadays the compilation of those collective statutes is done much more efficiently and they are available on-line, but we didn't have that electronic luxury nearly fifty years ago.

We took the case to trial and won an up-to-date holding that the old anti-stamp law was still unconstitutional. The Iowa Supreme Court ultimately affirmed the holding, continued the injunction, and the old restrictive law was stricken from the books. The much-maligned Ottumwa judge of long ago was right all along. It came out, oddly enough, that both Leo Hoegh's wife and his daughter collected S&H Green Stamps, but that didn't make much difference to the attorney general. He went on to become director of civil defense or some other job at that level in the state and eventually became governor of Iowa.

I spent most of that long, hot summer in Iowa, but it was more interesting than you might expect. I was working with a number of S&H witnesses and other personnel besides Sam Lane in Des Moines, and at the end of the day we would sometimes go out for a beer. We noticed that one bar in town had all the business while the others were starving. Was the booming bar offering S&H Green Stamps? No, its patronage dividend came in the attractive form of a particularly well-endowed barmaid outfitted in a rather low-cut bodice. She had the ability to stand behind the bar, place two beer glasses on either side of her chest (her term), and, taking a beer bottle in either hand, fill both glasses without spilling a drop. So famous did she become that a picture demonstrating her beer-glass-filling ability was featured that summer in the *New York Daily News*.

I didn't spend the whole time I was in Iowa in Des Moines. One weekend Sam and I went to Storm Lake, up the road a little way from Sioux City, where our Iowa problem had originated. We played golf and visited my late friend and *Murray* shipmate Bill Hunzelman, a highly regarded accountant and at that time head of the Iowa Society of CPAs. I also discovered the little-known fact that although Council Bluffs, Iowa and Omaha, Nebraska are separated by the Missouri River, because the river moves around a bit, there's a tiny portion of Iowa that is actually on the west side of the Missouri River just outside Omaha.

The Iowa case was a great victory, but unfortunately it proved to be only the first of a number of problems. Up until the early 1950s, S&H had always been identified with the small independent merchant. The two developments that changed that were the aforementioned super-market revolution and the coming to maturity of the service station industry. The corporate methods of gasoline distribution had come a long way since my boyhood days in Cranford, when we bought gas from the local hardware store owner, who would hand-crank as many gallons as you ordered out of a little fuel tank on wheels. Filling stations, like supermarkets, had sprung up everywhere to compete for the patronage of families who moved to the suburbs after World War II. Like the supermarkets, a number of the filling stations offered Green Stamps as an incentive. By the mid-1950s it was even harder to differentiate between service stations than between supermarkets in terms of quality, convenience, price, and so forth. All the service stations were selling a uniform product at a uniform price. Gasoline was so completely fungi-ble, in fact, that it was not unusual for one oil company's service station to borrow gas from a competitor when its tanks ran low. At that level of parity, introducing S&H Green Stamps at one service station would push it immediately to the head of the pack.

The growth in the number of gas stations offering S&H stamps had a synergistic effect. When people could get stamps by filling their tanks, stamps became more popular at supermarkets as well. And those gas stations were like billboards all across America, with big signs out front reminding people that they should get Green Stamps at the supermar-ket and the drugstore, too. Terrific publicity! The effort to sell the S&H stamp service to regional supermarkets soon became no effort at all. The regional supermarket chains were simply jumping out of their skins to get trading stamps, and they wanted ours. Once we began to serve the regional chains, their success with stamps was so quick that the national chains felt the competition immediately. Until our tremen-dous experiences with regional outfits like Thorofare began, we were of little interest to the national supermarket operators. Up until that point, they had always had things pretty much their way. But when stamps began to be used widely in the highly competitive supermarket business, the national chains began losing so much business to the upstarts that they had to take notice.

The national supermarket operators considered a number of responses. Once we were approached by some representatives from one of the largest chains. They had made exhaustive studies of the value of trading stamps and saw stamps as a powerful competitive tool. They came to us, they said, because S&H was number one in the field and they wanted to use our stamps. We weighed their offer carefully, but we had to turn it down. If we had sought to serve this organization, we would have had to provide our stamp service to all or most of its stores. This would have meant conflicts with some of our existing franchised accounts. It was our policy never to cancel a smaller account in favor of a larger one. We believed in repaying loyalty with loyalty. As a result of our decision, the chain helped institute a very successful trading stamp company that became one of our leading competitors. A number of trading stamp companies—such as Curt Carlson's Gold Bond company, and Top Value, Blue Chip, and Plaid—came into being in that way, to do business on our exclusions or to be the wholly owned captive brand of a particular national chain.

But some of the chains took another approach. One day late in December 1954, just a few days before Christmas, we had a very special visitor at our New York office. It was Lingan Warren, chairman of the enormous Safeway supermarket organization, the second-largest food chain in the United States. He was the power in Safeway, though it was nominally headed by Robert Magowan, the son-in-law of Charles Merrill of Merrill Lynch, which had a substantial interest in the company. My father, my uncle Ed, and I gathered in my father's office to meet Mr. Warren. He had not come to wish us a Merry Christmas. He came quickly to the point: we were to stop providing our trading stamp service to his competitors or he would ruin us. What he meant, of course, was that our trading stamps were so effective for Safeway's competitors that the company thought it important that Lingan Warren come all the way from California to New York to deliver his ultimatum. He added that he knew that S&H's Achilles' heel was its reserve for unredeemed stamps, and he would have it declared "public domain" unless we complied with his directive. This, he must have assumed, would be a death blow to our company. And well it could have been, for there was no "kitty" of windfall profit in our bank account. So those were Mr. Warren's grim alternatives: either S&H would get out of the food business or we would face ruin! My uncle Ed was a soft-spoken man, known for his self-composure. He quietly informed Mr. Warren that we had other ideas. I still remember the look on Lingan Warren's face. There was nothing in it of the Yuletide spirit. He left our office with one purpose in mind: to destroy The Sperry and Hutchinson Company and eliminate trading stamps from the marketplace.

We soon found that Lingan Warren was true to his word. Within a month of his visit, the Company was named a defendant in a suit in which the state of New Jersey sought, under its abandoned property, or "escheat," laws, to claim the value of the Green Stamps that had gone unredeemed since S&H's incorporation in 1900. "Escheat" technically refers only to real property, when a particular piece of real property for which no owner can be found goes to the state. The concept comes out of English common law. When a vassal who had been granted land by the king failed to produce a male heir, that land escheated back to the crown. Trading stamps, like money or shares of stock in General Motors, do not escheat, because they are not land and the crown isn't there to get them, but similar laws apply to abandoned property. S&H was a New Jersey corporation, so the suit laid claim to all unredeemed stamps, whether issued in New Jersey or not. The amount claimed exceeded the total net worth of the Company!

I went down to Trenton with two or three other lawyers to ascertain from the attorney general just why the state had started this malicious suit against us. Among other things, I wanted to know why, without so much as a previous visit, a phone call, or a letter from the attorney general's office, we were suddenly summoned to court. We were a good corporate citizen, and it was astonishing that as a good citizen we would be treated like this in our home state. We also felt it would be of interest to the attorney general to know that the Newark law firm of Carpenter, Bennett & Morrissey, which was representing his office in the case, also represented the very same Safeway chain whose head honcho had paid us the threatening call. The New Jersey escheat statute would award part of the recovery to the informant who turned it up, so the private counsel stood to make a bundle. One of the aspects of the case that especially infuriated me was that the private counsel, Elmer J. Bennett, lived just down the block from my house in Summit and passed the plate in the church I attended! We felt, too, that the attorney general should be apprised of the effect that this suit was having on us in far-off places and of the likelihood of other states jumping on the bandwagon with their own escheat suits against S&H if the New Jersey suit proceeded any further. For example, it had by then been seriously asserted in Montana's legislature that the state of New Jersey had already collected $500 million from The Sperry and Hutchinson Company.

The attorney general, Grover Richman, said that he was shocked, shocked to learn all of this. He explained that he had been called into the governor's office one day and found the governor with two attorneys from Carpenter, Bennett. The attorneys suggested that an escheat case against S&H—to be carried out at the taxpayer's expense, of course—would be an excellent way for the state to realize some millions of dollars. They further suggested that one of their attorneys be appointed escheator and that their law firm be designated as special counsel.

Now all the facts were in the open, and the real motives behind the case exposed. But because of the publicity the case had already received, the attorney general believed it was too late to withdraw it. So it ran its expensive course through the courts.

The suit was ridiculous. Lingan Warren, not knowing our business, either believed or had been led to believe that S&H's economic survival hinged on issuing many more Green Stamps than we would ever be required to redeem for our merchandise. Many people thought that stamps that were never presented for redemption were a great source of profit to the Company. Indeed, in the early 1920s the Internal Revenue Service had taken the position that the value of unredeemed trading stamps should be considered a taxable profit for the trading stamp company. S&H researched the matter, and in study after complicated study we found that the actual redemption rate was extremely high, something like 95 percent. Some stamps were destroyed or lost, and I'm sure that there are still a few neglected Green Stamps that survive today, hidden away in desk drawers or the glove compartments of junked automobiles. But trading stamps had a very high redemption rate—unlike supermarket coupons, which have always had a high *non* redemption rate. Coupons just floated around. You didn't feel that you had actually parted with something to get that coupon. Stamps were a medium of exchange, like money. Some money gets lost, but most money doesn't. Most money is saved to be spent. The same was true of S&H Green Stamps. People collected stamps carefully with their purchases, saved them, and used them. Every once in a while, some older stamps would show up, just as dollar bills from previous years surface now and then. But there was no huge treasure trove of old unredeemed stamps. If there had been any backlog earlier, the Depression had taken care of that. In those hard times, people were desperate for any source of cash or merchandise they could find, and they were not about to let their stamps languish in the attic.

In fact, S&H operations for each year were based on projections for high redemptions. To the extent that a small number of stamps did go unredeemed, we spent more on service to customers and merchandise values to customers. We always took the position that we spent 100 percent of our revenues providing services and merchandise for the benefit of the 95 percent of the stamps that were redeemed. And if we could build better value in the minds and pocketbooks of the people who saved our stamps, that would make them more loyal stamp savers and customers. There was no pile of windfall profits, and it would in any case have been impossible to enjoy windfall profits in an industry as competitive as the trading stamp industry became. S&H's battle with the Internal Revenue Service was never tried in the courts. S&H claimed a higher redemption rate, the IRS a lower. The result was a compromise, and both sides accepted that eventually 95 percent of all stamps issued would be presented for redemption, and 5 percent would not. The Company filed its income statement on the basis of that agreement from the time it was made, and it was still doing so when I left in 1980.

Mr. Warren was a determined man. Shortly after his visit and the initiation of the New Jersey escheat suit, double-page Safeway advertisements began to appear in scores of large dailies in the West, the area where Safeway was dominant. These were followed by an unprecedented amount of anti-stamp publicity in all media: newspapers, radio, television, magazines. The ads made the baseless charge that stamps raised the price of food. The entire trading stamp concept was branded as a deception, a something-for-nothing scam. We were charged with hoodwinking the housewife, with making inordinate profits, with redeeming only 40 percent of the stamps issued. Our enemies' publicity showed little or no regard for accuracy. It was clear that professional, resourceful, and utterly amoral people were responsible for this attack.

It quickly became apparent that the widespread impact of Safeway's campaign was really a prelude to something far more serious—the introduction of a whole flood of anti-trading stamp legislation all over the country. Bills were introduced in state after state. Almost all of them were similar; many were identical, word for word. It seems fair to assume that many of them had some common origin. In 1955, fifty anti-trading stamp bills were introduced in twenty-five states. Powerful lobbying forces and the almighty dollar were brought to bear in the effort to have trading stamps banned. In practically every state capital, we were denounced as a "foreign corporation" that was draining millions of dollars from local merchants and consumers. Charges that were cunning, ingenious, and in most cases preposterous were hurled at us from all directions. Every imaginable legal and propaganda resource was mustered against us.

We were not babes in the woods. Over the years, there had been a number of anti-stamp bills introduced into the legislatures of the land, and I had dealt with such efforts in places like North Dakota, Maine, Ohio, Maryland, and Texas. But those cases were isolated and usually easy to contain. It was entirely different when anti-stamp bills across the country were coordinated by one large and powerful company, concealed behind a variety of fronts, that was bent on destroying us. I was astonished how much clout a company like Safeway had in the world of business, how dangerous it could be, and how ruthless it really was. Those of us at S&H used to call Safeway "the octopus," and its anti-stamp efforts revealed the company's many tentacles, its incredible reach, tenacious grip, and horrible strength. The legal battle with our opponents that stretched over the next several years was not only immensely time-consuming and costly but exhausting, nerve-wracking, and sometimes agonizing. It was war.

Everyone at S&H had decided, from the moment that Lingan Warren left our offices on that eventful day in December 1954, that we would roll up our sleeves to do whatever might prove necessary to protect our business. The spirit of self-protection was strong in all of us. And as honorable people, we really had no choice about what we had to do. We had contractual obligations with a great many fine merchants across the nation—people who had strengthened their businesses through the use of our promotional service. And in the process of protecting ourselves, we were also protecting some fundamental American rights. In addition to our own right to do business in a free society, there was the right of the customer to seek the best possible value, including trading stamps or anything else. There was the right of the retailer to use, or not use, any legitimate promotional tool he wished in order to win customers from his competitors. That's the American way. It takes a great deal of presumption to tamper with rights as basic as these.

There was another factor, too, the most vital of all, which Mr. Warren had neglected to consider. If he had forces on his side capable of putting us out of business, we had even more powerful allies of our own. We had the consumers. Most people liked the extra value of trading stamps, and to an ever-increasing degree consumers were voting for them—by patronizing those stores where stamps were given.

The pattern of opposition to competitive effectiveness was not new. Years ago when the large department store came into being, a great ruckus was raised by local merchants. They organized into militant groups and called upon their legislators to help squelch what they referred to as a "frightening menace." But the department store concept survived, and for a very good reason: housewives liked department stores and patronized them. The same story was repeated when mail-order houses started to make their impact on the marketplace. Legislators were flooded with appeals to ban their operation. Some merchant groups organized "catalogue bonfire parties" and offered ten cents for every catalogue brought in for destruction. Next it was the turn of the food chain store. Again, groups were formed to destroy this newest alleged "threat to the economy." And the same pattern was manifest in the attempt to kill trading stamps. As my uncle Edwin observed, whenever a competitive activity is successfully launched, a storm of protest arises from the vested interests on the receiving end of the competition, and every effort is made to destroy the new or better way of doing things. It's ironic, given this history, that some of the large food chains were our most bitter opponents. But if the trading stamp concept would survive, it would be because the customer liked stamps, just as she had come to like department stores, mail-order houses, and food chains. When prudent consumers decide collectively that they want something, they usually get it.

It was also claimed that trading stamps violated the fair-trade laws, which permitted the manufacturer to control the minimum price at which his product would be sold at retail. Let's say you were a manufacturer of toothpaste, and you wanted your toothpaste to sell for no less than a dollar a tube. The fair-trade laws permitted you to put that minimum retail price on your product, and the druggist who sold that toothpaste for less than a dollar was breaking state law. The retail drug manufacturers were the most stalwart defenders of the laws. But those laws had nothing to do with fair trade. They were called fair-trade laws so that state legislators could justify them to their constituents—who is against fair trade?—but all they amounted to was an anticompetitive price-fixing measure. State after state across America enacted these laws; it's strange to think of the reach and breadth they had in those years. As far as trading stamps were concerned, the argument against them was that by issuing stamps, the merchant was in effect reducing the price of the product, and so was in violation of the fair-trade laws. Meanwhile, others were accusing stamps of driving prices up, a charge that was eventually put to rest by the US Department of Agriculture. So while one group was charging that stamps *cut* prices, another was contending that stamps *raised* prices. It was like something out of an absurd French farce.

It was suggested to the press that trading stamps cut advertising revenue, when all evidence proved that, to the contrary, trading stamps actually stimulated advertising. Various retail trade associations heard the insinuation that stamps represented an unfair form of competition to the detriment of most association members. Consumers' groups were told not only that stamps raised prices but that they were a nuisance and the people who saved them were fools. We heard a lot of stories about women who gathered up their stamps and left their change on the counter, and the like. It was charged that we were unfair to labor, unfair to farmers, unfair to small business, unfair to just about anyone the anti-stamp propagandists could conjure up, from the sons of the Napa Valley grape pickers to the Daughters of the American Revolution.

There were bills to tax stamp-giving stores at punitive rates. There were bills imposing prohibitive taxes against stamp companies. There were bills applying gambling regulations to trading stamps, bills forbidding the issuance of stamps with specific products ranging from eggs to gasoline, bills denying the right of stamp companies to offer exclusive franchises, and bills forbidding the issuance of stamps with fair-trade items. In Orlando, Florida, in 1955, a city ordinance was adopted requiring that the face of each stamp—an area about the size of a thumbnail—be imprinted with the name of our company, the address of our company, the name of the Florida merchant issuing our stamps, his address, and the information that the stamps would be redeemable in cash.

S&H in 1955 was not geared to respond to a legal and legislative attack of the magnitude of the Safeway blitzkrieg. Fortunately we had the counsel of that tough and wily old bird Charles Wesley Dunn, who had been working in the area of legislative uproars for years. We fought the battle during that legislative session on a catch-as-catch-can basis, with all the vigor we could muster. We couldn't go around to the state capitals and just buttonhole legislators by ourselves. We didn't have the local knowledge, and state legislators were acutely averse to what they thought of as carpetbag easterners coming in dressed in their velvet-collared chesterfield coats and telling the locals what to do. Under Charles Wesley Dunn's guidance, we quickly developed a nationwide organization of lawyers and lobbyists. We utilized experienced lobbyists where we had them, we hired new lobbyists where we had to, and we turned out rebuttal material as quickly as we could to meet the thrust of the attack. S&H offered generous fees and paid its bills on time, so our business was almost always welcome.

We retained two kinds of lawyers all over the country: practicing lawyers and political lawyer-lobbyists. Some of them performed in both roles, but most of the political lawyers were really lobbyists. Our lobbyist in Utah, for example, Calvin Rawlings, had an active law practice, but he was more of a political lawyer than he was a practicing lawyer. When we had a legal problem in Utah, he'd participate in it, but he wouldn't be the man who would do the grunt work, the researcher or writer of briefs. There were capable people in his office who could do that, and usually those of us from New York had all the cases at our fingertips anyway. Cal became a good friend, and when over the years adverse or hostile legislation was introduced into the Utah legislature, he dealt with it summarily. If we'd had a Calvin Rawlings in every state, we would have had considerably less legislative trouble than we had. Lobbying was a tricky business. In some of the Deep South states at that time, it involved passing brown paper bags full of money over the transoms of hotel room doors while the legislature was in session. My assistant Dave Maclay was flabbergasted when one of our lobbyists in the South told him that we would lose if we didn't bribe, but S&H never stooped to those sorts of practices.

Not all the state legislatures met every year; some of them met only every other year. That meant that our opponents couldn't introduce hostile bills in all forty-eight states at once, but they managed half that number in the 1955 legislative session, and most of the rest in the subsequent years. I spent so much time on the telephone during this period that I developed two cauliflower ears. And I traveled so much, visiting so many state capitals, that I often say that I am the only person beyond the eighth grade who can name all the state capitals with no difficulty. I know, for example, that Pierre, South Dakota is pronounced "Peer" and that the head of the gavel in Augusta, Maine, is about the size of a small keg. I know which states Salem, Frankfort, and Carson City are the capitals of. I dealt with important lawsuits from Montana to New Jersey, from Idaho to Florida. When all this adverse legislation erupted in 1955, my parents happened to be away on an extensive cruise around the Mediterranean. I used to send my father cabled reports at least three times a week, bearing messages like "Arizona sick, Alabama very sick, Georgia getting better, Tennessee practically dying, Michigan all well." My father, having stacked these together, would cable back questions about the states I had omitted: "Minnesota still sick or dead?" The radio operators who received these messages probably thought we were a pair of spies.

In those days before commercial jets, I usually flew in DC-8's, but I also spent a good deal of time on trains. I was in a train wreck once in Sand Point, Idaho. I was coming back from Oregon on the Great Northern Line, when our engine hit a rock slide and rolled into the Kootenai River. We were twenty-two hours late getting into Minneapolis. It was different traveling around the United States in those days. It was a much less homogeneous country. There were fewer national chains, fewer companies like McDonald's and Howard Johnson's, and more regional differences and regional peculiarities.

At one point we had some adverse legislation coming up for debate in Maine, and I wanted to be on the scene in the hope we could keep the hostile forces from enacting it. One local businessman stood up before the members of the legislature and told them he was from a little town in Maine and had created a small trading stamp business that served just a few stores in that town. Although the proposed anti-stamp bill had really been designed to drive the big stamp companies like S&H out of the state, if it was enacted, it was going to put his little stamp company out of business as well. Of course, we were delighted to see a hometown businessman addressing other Maine folks about what they might be doing to him. He said to the legislators, "You've got to consider that I'm a Mainer. If I were one of these big stamp company fellows, I wouldn't be here, I'd be down in Florida. And my face wouldn't be this color"—he tipped his head over to reveal his pale pate—"I would have a beautiful tan!" That produced a lot of smiles and a lot of "no" votes, and the anti-stamp legislation went down to defeat.

That was the story in most of the state legislatures that year. When the dust had cleared and we toted it all up, our enemies had succeeded in passing two of the fifty bills introduced. One, in North Dakota, imposed a prohibitive license tax. In 1956, Dwight D. Eisenhower carried North Dakota with a landslide 156,766 votes—and 159,801 citizens voted in favor of trading stamps in a referendum repealing the restrictive legislation of the previous year. The other bill was a minor regulatory act in Utah that, to my knowledge, was never enforced. I found that, by and large, the state legislators were men of common sense. The majority of them were not seduced by the arguments and cash of our opponents. They saw the move to pass punitive legislation of this sort as an unhealthy effort to transfer the problems of the marketplace into legislative halls. But there would always be a few politicians willing and eager to accept the bait dangled by our enemies in their various guises, so we knew that the next legislative session would bring more of the same.

The attacks of our opponents not only stimulated state legislation but also instigated probes at the federal level. One was a Federal Trade Commission inquiry, begun in July 1955, that scrutinized and turned upside down all our files, records, and correspondence. Another was a House Agriculture Committee investigation that proceeded through traveling committee hearings in different parts of the country. At one such meeting in the old Customs House in New York City, the anti-stamp counsel righteously quoted the opinion of a distinguished federal court that, because of an excessive number of middlemen, prices to consumers were ballooning and that much of this was caused by trading stamps. I rose to my feet and asked the chairman if the counsel would mind telling the committee when this comment was made. When he finally muttered, "1910," he was practically laughed out of the hearing room. The hearings petered out, and my recollection is that they never even produced a report.

When we went to court to contest hostile legal action, we had to skate around a very difficult constitutional law problem. Back in 1915, the state of Florida had passed a statute that imposed a prohibitive tax on trading stamps, coupons, and other promotional incentives. The statute was then challenged as a violation of the federal Constitution. The law was appealed right up to the Supreme Court of the United States, and in 1916 the Court held in *Rast v. Van Deman & Lewis*—always referred to by us as the Rast case—that the Florida legislature was acting within its constitutional boundaries by enacting this regulatory law. Worse than the mere fact of losing the case was the language that the Supreme Court's opinion used to describe the stamp business. Those nine old men decided that stamps "tempt by a promise of a value greater than that article and apparently not represented in its price, and it hence may be thought that thus by an appeal to cupidity lure to improvidence." That opinion always drove us crazy. And of course every time we went into a courtroom, this antique language would be trotted out and thrown in our faces. The curious thing was that the restrictive statute which had provoked the case had been repealed by the Florida legislature. So even though the law was gone and S&H had been free to do business in Florida for many years, the opinion remained out there to plague us.

We couldn't afford to go back into the federal courts to try to get the law reversed, because if we had failed and the Supreme Court had affirmed its earlier ruling, there would have been instant nationwide repercussions. That would have been taking an all-or-nothing risk. Had we lost, we would have been faced with a modern, up-to-date

Supreme Court ruling that anti-stamp legislation was acceptable. I think everybody understood that we were better off not to try to reverse the Supreme Court case. We had to live with it, and that opinion is still on the books and remains the federal constitutional law regarding trading stamps. But we were able to nibble away at the law by attacking it piecemeal, on a state-by-state basis. We argued time and again that the anti-stamp state statutes were in violation of the states' constitutions, and as we carried the day on the state level, the 1916 federal case became less relevant. We were dealing with a difficult but challenging problem over a widely varied legal patchwork, and it was quite an education.

Charles Greene Smith and I took to the courts to argue against the claim that trading stamps violated the fair-trade laws. We developed the position that the use of trading stamps did not constitute a price cut. It was a discount for cash, and it compared with the two percent that wholesalers often took off when their bills were paid within ten days. That argument was accepted in law courts in most of the states where such cases went to trial. We lost only one of those fair-trade cases, but it happened right in our own backyard in New York. We won our case at the trial stage in the Bronx. Another case was heard by a New York judge named Ferdinand Pecora. He had been quite well known back in the 1930s, when he was a practicing lawyer and served as special counsel for the Senate Banking Committee during the Roosevelt era. (At a famous hearing of the committee, J. P. Morgan was testifying when somebody hoping to embarrass him had a dwarf go up and sit on his lap.) After all the testimony was in, the case before Justice Pecora was pending for many months, and we naturally wondered what had happened. It turned out that the papers relating to the case had been lost, until one of Pecora's clerks finally found them on a chair in his office underneath a pile of file folders. We might have done better if those papers had not been found, because Pecora's decision went against us. So now we had a decision against us and a decision for us. The problem was that the decision for us was without much of an opinion, whereas the decision against us was supported by Pecora's rather lengthy one. The appellate division reversed the ruling of Justice Pecora, but the other side took the case to the court of appeals, the highest court in the state of New York. Under the rules that then applied, you could not appeal as a matter of right in a civil case if you had a unanimous affirmance by the appellate division. You had to get leave to appeal by petitioning the court of appeals. But if the affirmance was a reversal or if there was disagreement between one lower court and another, you could appeal, and that's what happened in this case. We eventually lost by a shocking five-to-two vote in the court of appeals, and that was the only fair-trade case we ever lost. It was a major blow to me, since I was so sure that we were right and since we had already won so many similar cases. The episode drove home to me that litigation is inherently a high-risk activity and you should never be complacent when you enter a courtroom.

Hanging over us throughout all these legislative and legal battles was the New Jersey escheat case. We retained the Newark law firm of Stryker, Tams & Horner to represent us. Sam Lane and I collaborated with a lawyer from that firm, Josiah Stryker, a stern and unbending man. Sometime between the trial and the final appeal, Stryker voluntarily withdrew from the case. Don Kipp, from the firm of Pitney, Hardin & Kipp, became the New Jersey counsel for the company in this litigation. I also received some useful advice from my friend Howard Clark, the chairman of American Express, who had dealt with a similar claim in the state of New York with respect to traveler's checks.

I worked closely with Sam Lane, and each encounter only increased my respect for him. Sam was a quintessential Yankee from Quincy, Massachusetts. His collar was always half turned-up, his hair always needed to be cut or combed or both, and despite having made a lot of money in the law business, he looked as if he bought his suits in secondhand stores. He was also one of the best litigators I've ever known. He was a spellbinding speaker, a clear thinker, and a prodigious worker. His sincerity and his convincing arguments made it difficult for any judge or jury to resist his presentations. My associate Fred Collins said that when he was still at Casey, Lane & Mittendorf before coming to S&H, Sam used to ask him into his office and present a problem. Fred would listen and say, "Sam, I can't give you an answer now. I've got to go into my own office to think about it, because as long as I'm in here with you, I'm going to agree with you." We were counting on Sam's persuasiveness in the New Jersey escheat case.

Suffice it to say that our case was bitterly contested. We won it three times. The first victory came when the trial judge dismissed the case, ruling that trading stamps did not qualify as abandoned property. Then the three-judge appellate division unanimously held the claim to be worthless. Finally the case came up before the New Jersey Supreme Court. Sam Lane knew every twist and turn of the case but, being Sam, he gave it the most careful preparation, including a dress rehearsal. He rented the auditorium at the Bar Association on 44th Street and asked three prominent trial lawyers in New York to act as judges while he argued the case. Sam didn't merely invite those lawyers there, he actually paid them a fee and sent them copies of the briefs so that they would do their homework and be prepared. I was in attendance in the Bar Association auditorium, which resembles a courtroom with a large raised bench at the front where the judges sit. The three lawyers Sam had hired sat up there and put him through his paces, asking pertinent questions and challenging his arguments and so forth. Sam was superb, giving quite a performance. He did the same thing a few days later at the real event in Trenton, where he argued the final appeal, joined by Don Kipp. All seven judges of the New Jersey Supreme Court unanimously affirmed the judgments of the lower courts, thus throwing this outrageous case out for good. Eleven judges had considered the case on the merits—one judge at the trial stage, three judges at the appellate stage, and seven in the supreme court—and we did not lose a judge. It takes but a moment to retell it, but that escheat case lasted five years and cost approximately a million dollars, a good many sleepless nights, and the life of one lawyer who died of a perforated ulcer during the proceedings.

At the conclusion of each stage, I called on the attorney general, and once even on the governor, Robert Meyner, in an effort to persuade them not to press on with this costly and time-consuming litigation. The governor's only comment: "We might be criticized." Needless to say, I never had much affection for him. And after all, Robert Meyner had allowed this particular snowball to start rolling down the mountain at the importuning of Safeway's lawyers, without so much as inviting the defendant company's representatives in for a talk. I confess I was pleased to see the ignominious collapse of his Presidential balloon at the 1960 Democratic Convention.

The year 1955 had been our baptism by legislative fire. Although 1956 was an off year for most state legislatures, it was not for our commercial opponents. They made the most of even their limited opportunities for legislative harassment and succeeded in introducing fifteen hostile bills in eight different states. We emerged, however, with only superficial scratches. But with federal agencies under pressure to scrutinize our operations, and with 1957, another "on" year coming up, it was increasingly obvious that the Company might very well be in for a battle for its life.

CHAPTER TWELVE

General Counsel for
The Sperry and Hutchinson
Company, 1956–1960

he struggle in which S&H had been engaged was making clear
to some of us that the long-range survival of an American business does not depend on successful sales and service alone. We
had always had a top-quality reputation among our customers. We had always run a good business. We had always been appreciated by our suppliers and the merchants who used our service. For
years, we believed that these things were enough. Our attitude was that
what we did was our own business. We were content with our achievement in supplying a useful service to our customers, and we felt that
this, in the long run, was all that mattered. We reasoned that since we
sold stamps to a particular merchant on an exclusionary basis, we were
necessarily going to make enemies of the more numerous group of
merchants who were left out, and so there wasn't anything to be gained
in talking to people who were already dead set against us. We didn't
often respond to inquiries from the press—sometimes we would simply
hang up the phone when they called—and we certainly didn't volunteer any information.

As a business enterprise, we were successful. Our growing numbers
of customers, even in the midst of the legislative and legal onslaught,
confirmed that. We were, in fact, under increasing attack precisely
because we *were* successful. But the public generally knew so little about
us that it had no basis for questioning or doubting even the most
extreme and irresponsible charges against us. The events of 1954 and
1955 had a tremendous impact on S&H's destiny and reshaped some of
our previous firm opinions. The massive legislative attacks of those
years showed us that while sales and service must, of course, be main-

tained at a high level, it is also fundamentally important to see to it that you receive some understanding among the people whom you affect or who can affect you—and when you have grown to a certain size, that means a lot more people than just direct business contacts.

To ready ourselves for new attacks, therefore, we decided to reexamine our policies, particularly our communications efforts. The self-analysis to which we subjected S&H late in 1956 revealed a number of things. On the basis of its size, it was clear that the Company would receive increased attention. It had, after all, become a large company by that time, with total sales of well over $100 million, serving some seventy thousand outlets across the nation. And the fact that the Company was serving large food chains increased manyfold the number of people affected one way or another. Indeed, as one of my colleagues said at the time, "Although S&H is privately owned, in all other respects it is a public company." As such, we had become obliged by our scope of operations, our leadership position, and our responsibilities to an increasing number of accounts and employees to keep the public more fully informed of our objectives and our actions. It was manifest that the Company would have to adjust to living in the public view, and abandon forever our patiently held hope that sound performance alone would speak for itself.

It happened that Uncle Ed, through one of his outside connections, knew T. J. Ross, the head of the T. J. Ross & Associates public relations consulting firm. The founding partner in that firm had been Ivy Lee, the man who had polished the image of John D. Rockefeller by advising him to give out dimes and directing him toward other worthy acts of philanthropy. That effort had almost completely dispelled the bad repute in which Rockefeller had been held, and when he died he was thought of as a kindly and generous man, not the rapacious robber baron of old. T. J. Ross had been a junior partner to Ivy Lee and took over the firm when Lee died. Ross came over to talk with my father and me during this time of reassessment, and he brought with him a consultant in his firm named Bill Gaskill. Bill subsequently became a close associate and a great friend, and an important influence on S&H. He was a pugnacious New Jersey Irishman who had dropped out of high school to become a reporter for the Trenton *Telegraph* and had actually done some prizefighting in his youth. He went back to high school when he was twenty-eight, then continued on to Rutgers University, and later, when he was the senior partner of the Ross firm, became chairman of the Rutgers board of trustees. Bill was absolutely convinced that both personal and corporate behavior should be founded on integrity, that you should never mislead people, and that problems should be met head-on, promptly and honestly.

At this meeting in 1956, Ross and Gaskill emphasized that the only thing most people knew about S&H was what others wrote and said. Since most of the information—or misinformation—being circulated in the media sprang from sources that had been stung by trading stamp competition, we should take the initiative to counteract it. Their opinion was that not only did we have nothing to hide, we were performing a positive role in the American economy. They were preaching to the converted there. My father and I believed that each day our system of free enterprise was moving in the direction of greater efficiency in the distribution of goods, increased savings for the consumer, and constantly improving values in return for dollars spent. It was a working principle at S&H to participate as fully as we could in attaining these objectives.

My father raised the idea of employing someone of the caliber of Jim Farley—a well-respected, nationally known figure with lots of political connections—to be a spokesman for the Company and help us with our interactions with the outside world. Both Ross and Gaskill disagreed vehemently. "No," T. J. Ross said to my father, "that's not what you should do. The best people to go into the public halls, to go into the legislatures, to go on radio, and to meet with the consumers are yourselves." Bill Gaskill continued, "After all, nobody knows this subject better than you. You work at it every day. You're the people who should go out and talk about it and answer questions about it. If you can't go, then the next-best person to go is someone in your employ who is close to you—not a high-profile outsider and not a P.R. man hired to deliver the message for you."

Having reviewed S&H's long-standing policy of silence, our newly emerging role as a public corporation, the mounting problems at federal and state levels, and our conviction that we were engaged in a perfectly sound business, we decided to encourage public scrutiny of the trading stamp business for the first time. We decided to cooperate with the press, to answer their questions, and to take information to them without waiting for queries. We would expand the production and distribution of booklets, leaflets, speech reprints, and other materials to help acquaint the public with our business. We would encourage marketing students, economists, and others to investigate all aspects of our business. We would cooperate with all federal probes. The more the public and all interested groups knew about us and understood our motivations, we hoped, the broader our support would be.

Finally, we decided to put down for our own guidance what we thought to be the key facts about our business. We would try to make them known to the public through the media and by sending people like yours truly out on the stump to give speeches and answer questions. We held it to be a self-evident truth that a trading stamp company was a legitimate business. We didn't ask anyone to like us or to like trading stamps, but we did insist that a free-enterprise system allows a company to offer its services freely, and protects the right of any customer or merchant to accept or reject such services. We knew that the controversy over trading stamps was fundamentally a struggle between business competitors and, as such, belonged in the marketplace, not in legislative halls or in the courts. We believed that since trading stamps were primarily a promotional tool, an attack on stamps was essentially an attack on the concept of all promotions; in a sense, it was an attack on the economic system itself, because the distribution side of our economy depends heavily on effective advertising and promotion techniques. We emphasized that S&H, while it was a successful operation, made no more than a modest profit. Our profits for most of the 1950s ranged between five and six percent on net sales after taxes. We had a much higher redemption rate than many had believed. We made every effort to encourage maximum redemption, and it was in our own best interest to do so. The housewife became an enthusiastic stamp saver only after she had redeemed her stamps for merchandise that would be valued and remembered. Without enthusiastic stamp savers, we wouldn't have had a business.

Having set down these factors, we prepared to carry the fight to the public. In order better to understand and articulate the impact of trading stamps on consumers, merchants, and the economy as a whole, we hired Eugene Beem, a business economist of unusual talent. He had made exhaustive studies of the trading stamp business as a professor at the University of California at Berkeley and had scared the bejeezus out of Frank Rossi and me when he came to visit us at 114 Fifth Avenue when he was doing his research. In those days we were very suspicious of outsiders, and we politely stonewalled Gene. When he saw we were not going to answer his questions, he asked us to tell him whether his figures were at least in the ballpark. We agreed and then squirmed in our chairs as he gave us his estimates for our buying rate, gross profit, profits after tax, rate of redemption, approximate "float," and so on. Not only was Gene in the ballpark, he knew what the home plate umpire had had for dinner the night before. In the late 1950s I sat down with Frank Rossi, who was then vice president in charge of merchandise distribution for the stamp division, and we decided that we needed someone to help us develop the data and theories supporting trading stamps. We immediately thought of Gene, and he came to work for us in January 1958. In some ways he understood the dynamics and psychology of stamp saving better than we did ourselves. We counted on Gene to help us combat more effectively the emotional and quasi-economic charges that would be raised against us. He mapped out areas of Company activity requiring research. He retained outside organizations such as Louis Harris & Associates (later pollsters for President John F. Kennedy), Benson & Benson of Princeton, and a Harvard Business School group. We also turned to the universities for a series of basic research projects that would contribute to a better understanding of trading stamps. At the same time, we enlisted a national network of persons trained in public information work, whom we knew we would need as members of our fire brigade for the 1957 legislative season.

And what a nightmarish season it was! An even hundred bills were introduced in some thirty-five states. At least thirteen of the bills enjoyed the dubious respectability of saying what they meant: with no attempt to cloak their wolfish appetites in sheeplike garb, they called for the outright prohibition of trading stamps. All the anti-stamp bills shared the single goal of crippling the trading stamp business, yet they were paraded through the legislative halls in the wildest imaginable array of noble disguises, waving the flags and pennants of the public interest. When the motley assemblage had strutted and fretted their hour upon the stage, only two bills had been passed that affected us in any way. Of particular significance was the one in Tennessee that, among other things, imposed a prohibitive tax on stamp-using merchants. A storm of consumer protest followed, with *Life* magazine covering the story. Although the legislators were persuaded that the elimination of trading stamps was vaguely related to the public welfare, the courts did not share this view. The law was promptly held unconstitutional by the Tennessee Supreme Court in July of that same year. It never became effective.

The other state that passed anti-stamp legislation that session was Kansas. The state had long had a restrictive law on its books, similar to the one in Washington, that permitted a stamp company to do business if the stamps were redeemed for cash. But the law had a quirk that stipulated that if the stamps were exchanged for goods, wares, or merchandise, a license fee would be imposed, which would very quickly amount to a lot of money. That was a serious restriction, and we knew that the opposition in the state of Kansas was pretty strenuous, so we chose not to do business in Kansas at all, not even to redeem stamps for cash. One day the man who was in charge of sales for our Company got a call from the vice president out in that part of the country. The midwestern vice president said he had a terrible problem, because the Kroger Company (a large grocery chain dominant in the midwestern states just as Safeway was dominant in the West) had just started issuing trading stamps in Kansas. Kroger had once been rabidly anti-stamp, but after trying every promotional and cost-cutting trick in the book and still losing sales to stamp stores, it signed up with a minor competitor to create the Top Value line of trading stamps. S&H was going to lose its prominent position in the Midwest if we didn't respond to this challenge, our vice president lamented, and what was he going to do? I authorized him to allow the use of stamps in Kansas, but only if they were redeemed for cash. Within forty-eight hours, I got a telephone call from the assistant attorney general of Kansas. He said, "You owe the state of Kansas $100,000, and I'm going to send you a bill for that right away." Sam Lane and I went out to Topeka, the capital, bringing along a copy of the law and its application to trading stamps. The assistant attorney general of Kansas turned out to be a nice young man about my age. I persuaded him that we were right on the law and that it was as clear as the nose on his face that we could do business for cash. Our problem was solved in this one encounter, and we left without even meeting the young man's boss, the attorney general of the state. Not long after I returned to New York, I heard from the assistant attorney general confirming that he accepted our point of view as correct, and asking if I would give him a job! I had no job to offer, but the encounter turned out to have been more pleasant than I had anticipated.

The Kroger people had been led down the primrose path by a former governor of Kansas, who told them, "Sure you can trade stamps for merchandise in Kansas. Just you leave it to me, I can fix anything." So they started doing business in Kansas in the traditional way, redeeming their stamps for merchandise, and they got nabbed for a substantial amount of money, something like $100,000. That was a very large sum for those days, and you couldn't pay that kind of money in licensing fees and operate a profitable stamp business. Kroger soon switched its business over to redeeming stamps for cash only. Then at the 1957 session of the Kansas legislature, the lawmakers passed a flat prohibition on trading stamps. They forbade stamp companies of any kind to do business in the state of Kansas, the only such blanket prohibition ever passed by a state legislature. I deplored that action, because I really didn't want there to be any state where we could not do business as a matter of law. Even though we never had a presence in Kansas, I had always taken the position that we didn't do business there because we chose not to. We knew the anti-stamp climate in the state. When we were forced to go into Kansas to meet the challenge that the Kroger Company and its Top Value stamps had laid down, the end result was that nobody at all could do business in Kansas.

While we met with a few losses here and there during the 1957 legislative session, we also managed to repeal some old restrictive laws. For example, there was a law in place in the District of Columbia that had been passed in 1870 during the brief period when the District had home rule, with its own legislative assembly. The law was not aimed specifically at trading stamps, which didn't exist, but stamps fell under the language of promotional devices prohibited by the law. I thought it was a shame that S&H couldn't do business in our nation's capital, and we worked for and won a repeal of the law by an act of Congress.

Meanwhile, the federal investigative probes ground onward. For more than two years, the Federal Trade Commission had been sifting through our records. With our wholehearted cooperation, it made a thorough study of our operations, our pricing policies, and our contracts. This was by far the most searching investigation of a trading stamp company ever conducted. The outcome was highly gratifying. Normally it is the commission's custom, following an investigation of this type, either to file a complaint or to do nothing. Instead, on October 3, 1957, the FTC took the unprecedented action of issuing a press release, which began: "The Federal Trade Commission announced today that it did not consider trading stamp plans in themselves to be an unfair method of competition under the laws it administers, and concluded not to issue any complaints at this time prohibiting the use of trading stamps."

So it went, case after case, probe after probe, charge after charge. The facts were laid on the table. Legislators and investigators who looked at the facts were usually quick to recognize that the fuss represented an attempt by commercial interests to achieve favorable legislation as a relief from a competitive situation. One by one the charges were made, met, and exposed as distorted or ludicrous.

A pet notion was that consumers lose when stamps are introduced because they force prices to go up. The US Department of Agriculture made an exhaustive study of this charge. Relying on US Bureau of Labor Statistics data, the Department traced the price trends of supermarkets before and after their introduction of stamps in twenty-one cities. These were compared with those of supermarkets that made no use of stamps over the period of the investigation, November 1953 to March 1957. In very nearly half the cases, the prices of supermarkets that adopted stamps either remained the same or fell, compared with those of stores that did not use this type of promotion. When the entire group of stamp-using stores was considered, a small price gap of about six-tenths of one percent opened up in favor of those not using stamps. The Agriculture Department pointed out, however, that "the difference in price trends observed in this study may have been caused in part by non-stamp stores lowering food prices to meet the competition of stores adding trading stamps." We took this finding as evidence that, as usual, some stores were responding to competition from trading stamps by reducing prices, so all consumers gained. The department went on to point out that the merchandise value of redeemed stamps was several times greater than the minor price differential between the stamp and nonstamp groups. The department concluded: "It would appear that, on the average in the twenty-one cities studied, consumers who save and redeem stamps can more than recoup the relative price difference between stamp and non-stamp stores."

The Agriculture Department's studies confirmed what we at S&H already knew from years of experience. There was no evidence that stamps necessarily brought about an increase in prices. The cost of trading stamps, if they were properly used, was offset by increased volume. In fact, the sum of all studies, including those carried out by S&H, academic researchers, and government probes such as the Agriculture Department's, suggested that the competitive impact of trading stamps was to bring about a *downward* pressure on price structures.

Although 1957 was a totally disruptive legislative nightmare and a serious financial drain, I believe S&H gained from the experience. We learned what an invaluable asset competent research can be. We learned, as Bill Gaskill had told us repeatedly, that if a corporation is solidly operated, the more information the public has about it, the more favorably it will be regarded. Even more important, we learned to appreciate fully the critical role played by the consumer in the economy of the nation. We learned in North Dakota, New Jersey, Oklahoma, Tennessee—all across the country—that where any "vested interest" group had the temerity to attempt to deprive the customer of her rightful freedom of choice, she could be counted on to strike back. With our help, seventy-five thousand women in Nashville organized themselves in one week to oppose the anti-stamp lobby. Women filled the house galleries during hearings. They flooded lawmakers with mail protesting anti-stamp legislation. One group filled clothes baskets with pro-trading stamp postcards and presented them personally to legislators. The sponsor of an anti-stamp bill in Colorado was forced to withdraw his support when his stamp-saving mother publicly threatened to campaign against his reelection!

My friend Peter Cooper, who joined S&H as a young lawyer in 1960, has reminded me that the reason the vast majority of anti-stamp bills didn't pass was that "we were right on the law and we were right on the facts." Peter used to say to legislators, "You don't have to like trading stamps. All you have to do is recognize that they are part of the fabric of the American system. Leave the regulation of stamps to the marketplace." A lot of free-enterprise-minded legislators were convinced by that argument. To the more judicially oriented legislators, Pete would say, "You know, this move to outlaw stamps is an unconstitutional and discriminatory exercise—it's really an illegal use of police power!—and therefore you shouldn't pass an unconstitutional law." That was also an effective argument. Then there was the type of legislator who didn't care one way or another about stamps but would vote whichever way his local people told him to. In those cases, we would demonstrate that many of the legislator's constituents were in fact vitally interested in trading stamps. Our employees helped rally housewives who collected stamps, and made sure the legislator heard from them. We'd have merchants who were issuing stamps contact the legislator, and we'd have S&H employees who worked at local redemption centers contact him. We'd get the banks that handled our local affairs to protest the bill, we'd urge the landlords whose property we rented would get on the phones, and we'd enlist the support of the railroad and trucking companies we patronized. We'd make sure that the major manufacturers who sold us merchandise for our redemption centers spoke to the legislators and let them know what they thought about anti-stamp legislation. I went around the country to get the word out, and so did just about everyone else in the Company, from the executives down to the office boys. We visited with newspaper and magazine editors to tell the story of stamps and accepted invitations to talk on the radio, on TV, and to live audiences. Many of our middle-management people crowded years of experience into a span of months. We emerged battle-weary and scarred, but in the process we developed a strong, flexible, loyal, and superior organization.

In 1957 anti-trading stamp legislation effectively crested. The attacks did not cease—there were a number of hostile bills in 1959, and I remember a particularly vicious piece of legislation passed in Montana in 1961—but there were nowhere near as many wildfires to put out as in the banner years of 1955 and 1957. Safeway's lobbying and its legislative and legal attacks had been costing them dearly as well, without significant success. In the end, Lingan Warren spent so much of Safeway's money trying to kill S&H, and failing to do so, that his own people threw him out. So you might say that Lingan Warren, by attempting to put us out of business, ended up putting himself out of business. Safeway finally extended an olive branch of sorts in the early 1960s. Winthrop Lenz, a neighbor of mine in Summit who was a senior officer in Merrill Lynch and also a good friend, engineered a meeting in New York. Merrill Lynch had ties to Safeway, and this meeting in effect brought the war to an end. S&H never capitulated or kowtowed to Safeway or any other national chain. In fact, the chains' attitude in the 1960s was, "If you can't beat 'em, join 'em." Kroger had created the Top Value trading stamps. A&P's president, though he had called stamps "a drag on civilization," finally gave in and went to Plaid Stamps, which had been created by a certain E. F. McDonald. And eventually Safeway signed up with Blue Chip, a trading stamp company jointly owned by the most powerful food chains in California.

With the legal and legislative battles effectively turning in our favor, all of us at S&H moved into the 1960s confident in the worth of our service and the value of trading stamps. Still, I often wondered how much *greater* value the consumer might have received if, during the 1950s, all the millions of dollars and all the human energy employed in trying to stop trading stamps had been diverted into competing more effectively against them—in the marketplace. It's still something to think about.

The period of massive legislative and legal attacks on trading stamps had some personal costs to me, principally stress and the amount of time my work took me away from my home and family. The stress became so extreme that I began smoking cigarettes again, after years of not having smoked at all. Betty smoked occasionally in those days, and one Saturday morning as we were having breakfast, I asked for one of her cigarettes and began to smoke it. "Why are you smoking that?" she wanted to know, and I replied, "Oh, you know, I've got all these problems with what's going on with S&H." "That's crazy," she said, "you haven't smoked for years." Betty ground her cigarette out and said to me, "I'll tell you what I'll do. I'll bet you fifty dollars that I don't smoke before you do." I put my cigarette out and said, "The bet is on." That was over forty-five years ago, and it was the last time but once that I've ever touched a cigarette. The exception was in the 1970s, when Betty and I visited my aging aunt Katherine Sperry Beinecke at her winter home in Palm Beach. Aunt Katie was the widow of my uncle Walter, and she smoked until the day she died. Her hand shook so that she couldn't get the flame of her lighter to ignite her cigarette. I offered to hold her lighter, but she said, "Don't do that. Take this cigarette in your mouth and light it properly." I lit the cigarette, took two puffs to get it going, and handed it back to her. I declared how dreadful the cigarette tasted, and Betty and I agreed that the incident was not within the parameters of our bet.

While that period of massive legislative and legal attacks brought a lot of stress and strain, there were some great personal benefits as well. I learned a lot about our country. I got to know many fascinating, personable people, like the exceedingly colorful Cal Rawlings of Utah and Ed Clark of Texas, and many of them became good friends. I gained valuable experience and more confidence in myself and my abilities. It's difficult for me to evaluate my own skills as a lawyer, but I was good at what I did. Columbia Law School had taught me always to be prepared. When I went to Washington State to do battle with the blue sky laws, I was so well prepared that I knew more about the issue than even the people on the scene. I remember that when I went down to Roanoke to handle a fair-trade law problem, our Virginia counsel, Frank Rogers, was quite impressed with the thoroughness of the outlines I sent him. (Frank later went to Moscow as the lawyer for the U-2 pilot, Gary Powers.) Looking back many years later, I'd say that I was a good lawyer because I was prepared and I did the job that I was supposed to do. If, through the turmoil and expense of the hostile legislation and litigation, S&H had become wiser and more mature, so too perhaps had I. But I had no leisure for such thoughts at the time, when I was caught up in the whirlwind.

During the years of crisis, I was also adjusting to life in a new home and settling into my role as a father of four. We had lived at 156 Beechwood Road in Summit since 1948. It was a lovely house, and we'd had several wonderful years there. By 1954, though, we had all four children, things were looking a little better for me financially, and we thought about moving to a bigger house. One day I was driving around Summit with Betty and through the trees we glimpsed a large, beautiful house at 20 Prospect Hill Avenue. We looked at each other and said, "Gee, wonder if that house will ever go on the market?" We asked one of the real estate agents in Summit to keep an eye on it and let us know if it ever came up for sale. Then in May 1954, when we were down at The Homestead, a resort hotel in Virginia, where we had gone for two or three springs for trout fishing and a little golf, we got a message from

20 Prospect Hill Avenue in the spring.

the agent. The house was going on the market the following day. Were we still interested? We were, and within a short time we acquired the house. It had belonged to a man named Broadbeck, the American head of the Swiss pharmaceutical company Ciba, located in Summit. Broadbeck had been accused, perhaps falsely, of being a Peeping Tom; whether the accusation was true or not, he received adverse publicity in the local paper, and I think he was eager to leave Summit. We paid around $80,000 for the house, almost four times as much as we had paid for the Beechwood Road house. We had sold our old house at a substantial appreciation, however, and the proceeds from the sale, together with a mortgage loan, allowed us to purchase our new home. I have never liked debt, so I paid that mortgage off as quickly as I could.

Prospect Hill Avenue was an oval-shaped street running around a parklike residential area. Our house was at the south end of the oval, and the house of our escheat case adversary Elmer J. Bennett was at the opposite end. We were on a high bluff at the summit of Summit. The view to the east looked across Newark to the distant spires of the Empire State Building and the Chrysler Building in Manhattan. The Lackawanna Railroad trains would chug their way up the hillside just below, rounding the big curve that would take them into the station in

Summit. The railroad that we saw from the top of the hill had a long run from Hoboken through the Oranges, slowly ascending through Maplewood until it hit the abrupt slope below the spot where our house would eventually be built. The summit of that slope was the highest point on the railroad line—hence the name of the town. In the early days of the railroad, when trains were hauled by coal-fired steam engines, those engines had to huff and puff there, waiting for their water to be replenished from the tanks, before continuing west through Chatham and Madison to Morristown and on to the end of the line.

Summit was a relatively young town compared with some of the adjacent towns. To the west was New Providence and to the east Springfield, both farming towns, set on a low-lying plain. For that reason, both had long histories and had played a role in the Revolutionary War. Summit, because of its height and inaccessibility, didn't have any colonial history, and thus retained its arboreal cover long after most of the trees in the surrounding towns had been cut down. Many times I flew low over Summit coming into Newark Airport, and all I could see below was a lovely sea of trees. On our property at 20 Prospect Hill Avenue were two wide, spreading white oaks that had been young in the colonial era and so were called Washington oaks. (There's another Washington oak in the cemetery at Basking Ridge, New Jersey, and one standing in the middle of Prospect Street in Madison, to which it is alleged Washington once tied his horse.) The house had originally been called "Twin Oaks" in honor of the two massive trees that stood there. The name still remained on one of the gateposts by the garage, but we never referred to the house as such. People who were impressed with that sort of thing, though, used to address cards and letters to us at "Twin Oaks."

The house was a magnificent three-story structure with an attached garage, sited on a broad three-acre expanse of land. It had been built in the early 1920s by Spencer Weed, creator of the Grand Union food chain; a prominent businessman during the twenties and thirties, he was a friend of my father's. The house had a grand living room and a charming sun porch. Over time, we made substantial improvements. When we bought the house from Mr. Broadbeck, we found that every interior door in the house had deadbolts high above the doorknobs, and the top panels of two of the upstairs doors had been removed and replaced by panes of glass. These modifications, which Broadbeck had presumably implemented for the safety and surveillance of his young son, seemed strange to us, so we employed a carpenter to remove all the hardware and restore the doors. We hired Yasua Matsui, the resident architect at S&H, to remodel the library. He was Japanese and had done some work for the George A. Fuller Company. In 1942, at a time when the US government was interning other Japanese-Americans in prison camps, my uncle Ed had hired Matsui and given him a permanent office at S&H. That's another example of the kind of man Uncle Ed was. Matsui was a talented and gifted architect, and he did a lot of personal work for my uncle as well, playing a major role in the design of Uncle Ed's absolutely beautiful home in Greenwich, Connecticut. We renovated our heating system and a few years later built an addition to the garage. We also added a tennis court on the north side of the house, adjacent to the great lawn, and on the southwest side we created a swimming pool beneath the outspread branches of one of the Washington oaks. The pool was heated so we could use it from early spring until midfall.

We lived at 20 Prospect Hill Avenue for twenty-five years, from 1954 to 1979. We had a wonderful family experience in that home. There was land and space for our children to grow up in, and many other children lived in the area. Our nearby neighbor Bill Simon, for one, who later became secretary of the Treasury, had seven children, and it seemed there was always some sort of youthful game or pursuit or festivity taking place in our yard. Every year we had a Christmas Eve party, to which we invited all our friends and neighbors. We served eggnog in the dining room, and all the neighborhood children were thrilled to watch the little toy skiers whooshing down the miniature ski slide we had bought at F.A.O. Schwarz and rigged on the banister. Those were warm and festive occasions.

The 1950s were busy in terms not only of involvement in business, but also of raising a family. Our four children were all different and all special in their own unique ways. They were born within six years of one another and they were always very close, though they're even closer today as adults. Rick, our eldest, was five years old when we moved to Summit in 1948—he's the only one of the children who has memories of our apartment in New York—and he was eleven years old when we moved to 20 Prospect Hill Avenue in 1954. Frances, our youngest, was born in Summit, and was only five when we relocated.

All four children went to elementary school at the Summit public schools. Rick was the first of our children to go to private school, and he began as a day student at Pingry. Rick liked Pingry, but he was not enthusiastic about it. He got off to a slow start. Until he went to Andover, in his late teens, he spent his summers at camps that focused on learning processes and academic instruction, and he took extra time during the school year doing extension classes and receiving tutorial help. Rick had less free time than the other children, therefore, but they always looked up to him.

John also went to Pingry, entering at a younger age than Rick had, and he liked it more than his older brother had. John was a big success there, beginning with his first year, when he won the award for the most-improved student. That early triumph may have had some less positive side effects. John was bright and quick, but soon discovered that he could get by doing the minimum. John went steadily along. He was the leader of his group of friends in Summit. He was always a terrific athlete, and Betty and I both remember that one time when he was young, after he had been taken to a football game at Princeton, he played a close and hard-fought football contest on the front lawn— against himself! When he was about fifteen, in the late 1950s, John went away to boarding school at Westminster, a year or so after Rick had enrolled at Andover.

When Rick and John were each about eight years old, I enrolled them in the Indian Guides, a group sponsored by the YMCA that was a bit junior to the Cub Scouts. Each troop had from eight to ten boys in it, and they were all good friends. No boy was allowed to attend a meeting without his father, and vice versa. This was a good rule, for it meant that no father could say to his son, "You go, I'm too busy." Fathers had to make the effort. One boy in John's troop, Jimmy Lathrop, lost his father in an accident, and thereafter my friend Dick Moser acted as a surrogate father to Jimmy and always accompanied him to the meetings.

Sarah and Frances were toddlers in the early 1950s, and they were only eleven and ten respectively when the decade came to a close. Even at that young age, though, their distinctive personalities had begun to emerge. Sarah was an enormously outgoing person. She could pick up friends anywhere, and attracted a vast constellation of them in Summit and on the Cape. She was an extrovert like John, and I used to joke that it was as though she exuded pheromones that could draw people for miles around. Frances was more reserved. She had fewer acquaintances, but made extraordinarily deep and lasting friendships. Some of her friends even today are people she has been close to almost all her life. As the youngest child, Frances sometimes felt put upon by her older siblings. While all the children went their various ways, Frances in particular forged her own path. From early on, she was a great reader, and she has always been interested in nature and the outdoors. Both

Sarah and Frances went to the Kent Place School in Summit as day students when they were young, and they both liked it.

We all had some marvelous times together, not only at home in Summit but also on our family excursions. I tried to spend as much time as possible with my children, both because I wanted to and because I had seen far too many examples of lawyers and businessmen who had let their dedication to their work make them poor fathers. We took lots of family expeditions around New Jersey, mostly weekend drives out to the state parks to go hiking and picnicking. We went skiing together for many years, and as the children grew older, we traveled to a great number of prospective schools and colleges. I took my sons on a June trout-fishing trip to some lakes north of Quebec when each got to be eleven or twelve. We went with my friend Hugo Meyer and his sons, who were about the same age, and our guides there loaded us into canoes and paddled us over to the cabins where we spent four or five days. It was a good place to take children fishing, because there were lots of trout biting all the time and there wasn't much of the Zen-like contemplation between infrequent bites that mature fisherfolk enjoy but children do not. When Frances was about seventeen or eighteen, I took her to a different and highly touted trout fishing camp elsewhere in the Province of Quebec. George Lindsay, who was taking her out at the time, also went along, as did Marvin Speir, the son of my longtime friend Dean Speir.

For two summers, our whole family went to White Grass, a marvelous ranch in Moose, Wyoming, near Jackson Hole. One night out there I got into an all-night poker game, and as I was headed for bed along about 7 AM, I was intercepted by the early-rising members of my family. All of them had the view that our morning ride should go on as usual and that it would be good discipline for the old man! One year when we were in Wyoming, the children had to set aside an hour every morning for summer reading. I wanted to be part of the deal and so subjected myself to Thackeray's *Vanity Fair*. In retrospect, I don't know who suffered the most.

Aside from the trips west, summers during the fifties were spent principally on Cape Cod, where we rented houses in and around Orleans. We had stayed at my parents' place in Great Barrington for two summers in the late forties, but it had really become too much for them to have so many young children around, so Betty and I decided to summer on Cape Cod instead. In 1950, our first year on the Cape, we rented a house in Eastham, and the next year we rented a small cottage in East Orleans. Then in 1952 and for the next several years we rented the Thompson House, a large and lovely home overlooking the harbor on the bluff in East Orleans. We didn't do much on the Cape besides spend time with the children, take them to the beach, and go fishing with them. There was enormous pleasure in those simple activities. Betty and the children would go up to the Cape for most of the season, and I'd join them during my vacations or commute up from New York on free weekends.

S&H continued to be privately owned in its entirety by the Beinecke family throughout the 1950s. As the size and scale of the company grew, so too did the value of the shares and dividends held by my father, his brothers, myself, and other members of the family. By the late fifties, when I had been a paid employee of S&H for several years, I was reasonably well off, but I was by no means a person who didn't have to count his pennies. Our lifestyle was comfortable but not lavish. Betty and I had to budget our affairs carefully to be able to afford summer vacations in those years. We made some trips and excursions every now and then. In 1949, about a month after Frances's birth, Betty and I had gone to Nantucket and then up to New Hampshire for a few days to view the fall colors. In 1954, we flew to Rome and drove to Florence once we had succeeded in renting a car—a much more complicated business then than it is now. That was Betty's first trip to Europe, and my first since the war. In 1955, tired out from the legislative onslaught, we went to Hawaii. We stayed in the Royal Hawaiian Hotel on Oahu for a week, then went to Hana Maui on the island of Maui at the recommendation of Bill Gaskill, who had lived in Hawaii before going to New York to join T. J. Ross & Associates.

Then in 1959, Betty and I took a short cruise with my parents aboard the *Coronia*, one of the star cruise ships of the Cunard Line. My parents were on an around-the-world cruise at the time, and we had gone to San Francisco to see my father, who had taken ill in the Philippine Sea. Fortunately he had recovered by the time we arrived, we had a nice visit, and we joined my parents on the short cruise to Acapulco. They continued on back to New York via the Panama Canal. Betty and I didn't have the time to stay on for the duration of the cruise, but we wouldn't have been able to return with my parents aboard the *Coronia* in any case because of the Smith Act, which sought to protect American maritime commerce by prohibiting travel between two American ports on a foreign-flag vessel. Instead, Betty and I took a night bus to Mexico City arriving on May 1, in time for the socialistic celebration of the international workers' labor day. That was the first time I had been to Mexico City since my visit there in 1939 (as well as the last time I've been back), and our return trip from Mexico City to New York was the first time I had ever flown on a jet.

One of my principal social outlets in those years was the Beacon Hill Club. I helped bring it into being in 1954. The man who'd had the original dream for the club was a Summit pediatrician named Pat Maroney. He had come up with the idea after wandering around Cape Cod in the early 1950s and seeing Strong Island (in Pleasant Bay, facing our present Chatham home). He thought it would be a great place for a community club. When that idea proved impractical, he began to look closer to home. The plan was for a group of people we knew in Summit to acquire the large, old-fashioned Bassett estate and recreate it as a nice family club where people could meet, socialize, and play practically every sport except golf. It took a lot of doing to get the club off the ground. The original board included Pat and me and our friends H. Stanley Krusen, Alan Schmitz, Jack Mackie, Harold Graves, Win Lenz, Hugo Meyer, and Bill Poten. The nine of us met in one another's living rooms every Sunday afternoon all through the winter of 1954, making plans and trying to solicit subscriptions from other potential members. We had to get authorization from the city of Summit, and we had difficulty collecting subscriptions until we actually had something to collect for. Eventually I took a chance and loaned the incipient club enough money to pay off its initial bills. The Summit city authorities soon gave their approval, my loan was quickly repaid, and the club became an immediate success. Once it got going, it had a hockey rink, bowling alleys, a swimming pool, tennis courts, a snack bar, and a fine dining room and other public rooms. The Beacon Hill Club has now been there for nearly fifty years, and to the young people who use the club and whose children play on the club's hockey team and so forth, it looks as if the club has always been there. But I was present at the creation, so to speak, and the club was something I got a good deal of enjoyment from in those days.

My parents' lifestyle did not change drastically during this period. In 1949, they had generously given their home in Madison to Drew University. They moved to the cooperative apartment in New York they had acquired some time before, and spent more time in Great Barrington, Massachusetts. Their home there, Tredinnock, was a lovely country house but not really elaborate considering that my father was now quite successful and well off. But then, I don't think my father was ever really able to think of himself as a rich man. He found S&H's tremendous expansion exciting and stimulating but, being older and having seen both boom and bust before, he viewed his good fortune with a philosopher's eye. He appreciated the rewards of S&H's success. He appreciated even more what those rewards enabled him to accomplish.

My father did not abandon his many hobbies. They at that time included model-railroad building and still and motion picture photography. His hobbies were a necessary part of his life; that was the nature of the man. He began to develop an interest in Western Americana about the time he decided to terminate his interest in the Copper Gate dairy farm in Basking Ridge. My father had acquired the farm for the sake of my brother, after Dick had left college and gone to work in the dairy business with my boyhood friend Alan Day. Dick returned to Copper Gate Farm after war service with the marines and continued to work on the farm in partnership with Alan Day for several years. Then he acquired a place in Florida, where he became an enthusiastic deep-sea fisherman and caught a record 535-pound blue marlin. Eventually he decided that he preferred to work for S&H rather than continue with the dairy business, so he was hired on as regional man for S&H in Florida. He had an office in the Palm Beach redemption store and traveled up and down the state carrying out his responsibilities.

My father continued to provide financial backing for the Copper Gate Farm, and I remember the close attention he paid to the bloodlines of his cows. For a while he lived and breathed Guernseys. He concentrated on breeding show animals and strove for records. Then in 1949, his interest suddenly waned. Partly that was because Dick had not taken the interest in the dairy business that my father had hoped, but it was also because most of Dad's hobbies would go through a cycle. When he had learned all he could, the cycle would end and he would move on. My father terminated his participation in the farm and transferred its ownership to Alan Day, a generous act because Alan would never have been able to afford it on his own. And then my father began casting around for a new interest.

My uncle Ed wasn't as much of a hobbyist as my father. He did have some major interests outside of business, ranging from his exquisite collection of fourteenth- and fifteenth-century German glass to the overwhelming horticultural display of narcissuses, dogwoods, azaleas, and rhododendrons that bloomed every spring at his home in Greenwich, Connecticut. For as long as I can remember, Uncle Ed had also collected the works of Robert Louis Stevenson, including letters, manuscripts, first editions, and so forth. Uncle Edwin was the head of the Yale Library Associates, not only because of his undergraduate connection with Yale but because he was a scholar himself. His Stevenson collection became famous in bibliographic circles as the outstanding example of how deeply a scholar or collector could explore a figure of the past. Uncle Ed and Aunt Linda even named their home "Skerryvore," after Stevenson's home in Bournemouth, England. (Stevenson's home had in turn been named for the famous Skerryvore lighthouse in Scotland built by Stevenson's uncle, the renowned lighthouse designer and engineer Alan Stevenson.)

My father had always taken a tremendous interest in books, had long been interested in the West, and had read widely and collected books on a modest scale. But I think the influence of Uncle Ed's interest in Stevenson, together with my father's interest in hobbies and in books generally, and perhaps the experiences of his brother Ben Beinecke in Montana, led my father to cross the threshold from casual reader and collector of Western Americana to serious collector and scholar. By the early 1950s, he had settled on the fields of major interest to him, the Plains and Rockies region and the Spanish Southwest. While he was very much interested in the Mexican War and the settlement of Texas, he was also interested in Lewis and Clark's explorations of the American West and many other related subjects. He assiduously built one of the three or four outstanding collections of Western Americana, including maps, manuscripts, and books. Indeed, the citation of my father's 1959 Yale Medal observed that he was so enthusiastic a bibliophile that, even in his business office, booksellers and collectors received his undivided attention and appreciation. (I always felt that this was a bit overblown even for a Yale Medal citation.) For several years, he would make photographic reproductions of certain items in his Western Americana collection, assemble them in little booklets, and send them to friends as unique Christmas cards. My father's friend Herman W. Liebert (also nicknamed Fritz), who was a librarian at Yale during the 1950s and eventually became the first librarian of the Beinecke Library, suggested that my father was attracted to Western Americana for two reasons. First, the opening and settlement of the West spoke to him because it was an act of synthesis and completion, a building toward order. Second, he felt the opening up of the West put the men who settled it face-to-face with insurmountable problems and enormous struggles. My father could understand and appreciate that. He greatly admired the courage and vision that went into the building of the West.

Through their book collecting, my father and uncle became friendly with James Babb, then the chief librarian of Yale University. One day Babb received a phone call from A. Whitney Griswold, then president of Yale, instructing him to report immediately to the president's office. When he arrived in some trepidation, President Griswold handed him a note that read: "We consider it disgraceful that your librarian has never been to Europe. Enclosed please find a check for a European trip for him and his wife." The note was signed by E. J. and F. W. Beinecke. Jim Babb encouraged my father and uncle to get on with their collections, provided them with expert assistance, and urged them to think about Yale when they ultimately had to dispose of their collections. Babb was very ambitious, and when he realized that these two men were genuinely interested in library work and the many rare and irreplaceable books in Yale's collections, he drew their attention to the deficiencies of Yale's rare book room. Yale's collections were inadequately housed on the first floor of Sterling Memorial Library, on the Wall Street side, across from the law school. The room lacked the thermostatic and ambient controls that old books need if they are to resist humidity and keep from disintegrating.

Both my father and Uncle Ed were eager to do something meaningful for Yale. They had both had warm and valuable experiences there, and their loyalty to Yale and their classes was at a high point. So Jim Babb, Fritz Beinecke, and Ed Beinecke put their heads together. Not only would my father and uncle donate their entire collections, two of the finest of their kind, to Yale. They would also create a new rare book and manuscript library, large enough to house all of Yale's collections. It would be financed by the Beinecke brothers and their families. My uncle Walter had died in 1958 at the age of seventy. He'd had cancer and had been incapacitated for a few years before he died, although until his death he had continued to be a director of S&H, while my father was president and chairman of the executive committee and my uncle Ed was chairman of the board. My father and Uncle Edwin wanted to include their brother Walter in this benefaction, and they did, together with their wives and Walter's widow. They were able to obtain a prime location for the new library at the corner of High and Wall Streets, adjacent to the law school and the Freshman Commons, in the area then known as the Hewitt Quadrangle. The library would eventually replace a row of old redbrick houses along High Street. One of them had housed the office of the dean of freshmen, where I paid a visit once or twice in my first year at Yale. The dean in 1932 was Percy Walden, who had been one of my father's engineering professors when he had been a Yale student in the class of 1909S; in those days, some of the Yale professors and administrators seemed practically eternal.

While my father and uncle were having their conversations about the new library with James Babb and other Yale officials, the New

Jersey escheat case continued to hang over our heads. The lawsuit dragged on from 1955 to 1960 and was the thing that preoccupied me more than anything else. I was very much concerned with anything that would have an adverse effect on the case. Rightly or wrongly, I thought that the announcement of the donation of the Beinecke Library to Yale should be soft-pedaled while the case was going on. I worried that it would be bad public relations and that some judge might react negatively if he got wind of it. Would he take it amiss if the owners of the Green Stamp business were giving this tremendous benefaction to Yale at the same time they were resisting paying over the value of unredeemed stamps to the state of New Jersey? I don't think I put it quite that explicitly, but I did suggest to my father and uncle that they slow down the rate at which this gift was moving toward the university. I lost that argument, though our debate was never heated. Uncle Edwin said to me, "We are old men, and we want to enjoy this while we are still able to." They wanted to have the benefaction take place and be realized so they could experience the fulfillment of the gift during their lifetimes.

My grandfather Bernhard Beinecke had not been associated with a great single act of philanthropy on anywhere near the scale of the Beinecke Library gift to Yale. But while he hadn't built buildings or endowed chairs or things of that sort, he had responded to the needs of the poor and to individual requests. My father and uncles were brought up in a family of means. They were accustomed to living well, and they were used to the responsibilities of wealth. The Depression had knocked them down for several years, but they had recovered their positions by the late 1930s. When the 1950s brought financial success beyond their wildest expectations, they didn't indulge in the sort of conspicuous consumption that gave yuppies a bad name in the 1980s. They were too conscious of their families to waste their money on flashiness or dissipation. They were secure in their positions, they knew who they were, and they didn't need to impress anybody. Betty and I have tried to keep to that standard in our turn; we could maintain a much splashier lifestyle than we do. My father and his brothers genuinely believed that their good fortune obliged them to carry out the obligations and responsibilities that go with financial success. In my father's case, it was only the deed of giving the library to Yale that mattered, not the applause. My uncle Ed might have taken a greater satisfaction than my father did from the name recognition that the Beinecke Library afforded the family. Edwin Beinecke was more of a public person than my father; they were different types of men.

Topping off the steel ceremony at the Beinecke Rare Book and Manuscript Library, 1962. Left to right: workman (unidentified); James T. Babb, Yale Librarian; Frederick W. Beinecke; A. Whitney Griswold, Yale University President; Edwin J. Beinecke; Rick Beinecke.

Some of the money used to build the library came from the Beinecke family through an innovative act of financial planning. My cousin Walter Beinecke, Jr., was an able and imaginative member of the Short Hills Country Day School board of trustees. He helped the school acquire a new football field by creating a short-term charitable trust holding a certain amount of his S&H stock. By alienating the shares and arranging for the trust to pay all the income to the school, he avoided the income's being taxed to him during the life of the trust. This rather brilliant device was applied to the creation of the Beinecke Library and helped substantially in solving the funding problem. A certain amount of Beinecke family stock was put into a three-year trust. The dividend income paid to the trust was then paid over to Yale and used for the library building costs, and at the end of the three-year period the stocks reverted to the Beinecke family. Additional contributions came from the Beinecke Foundation (which my father and his two brothers had created) and individual donations from my father and Uncle Edwin, their wives, Uncle Walter's widow, and other members of the Beinecke family, including my brother, me, and my cousins Sylvia, Edwin Jr., Bud (Walter Jr.), and Betsy.

The gift of the Beinecke Rare Book and Manuscript Library to Yale University was announced in 1960, and the topping off the steel ceremony took place early in the fall of 1962. I have a terrific photo of my son Rick, then a freshman at Yale, at the ceremony together with his grandfather and great-uncle Edwin, along with Whit Griswold and Jim Babb. The building was completed and donated to Yale in 1963. At the dedication ceremony, Uncle Edwin handed a symbolic key to the library over to Yale's provost Kingman Brewster, who accepted it on behalf of Griswold (who was too ill to attend) and the university. Even at the time the Beinecke Library was recognized as one of the world's most significant libraries for rare books and manuscripts, and its donation, design, and reputation have been more and more widely praised as the years have gone by. The building was designed by Gordon Bunshaft, a prodigiously talented young architect from the firm of Skidmore, Owings & Merrill. I remember going with my father and Uncle Ed to the firm's work area in Weehawken, New Jersey, back in the late fifties to see a model of the design taking shape. Anthony Hobson, in *Great Libraries*, called the Beinecke Library "the most imaginative construction of its kind for at least two centuries," and added, "This is a library of all the virtues, luxurious for readers, administratively convenient and with an exhibition hall of a brilliance that has had no parallel since central European baroque." It is the largest building in the world devoted entirely to rare books and manuscripts, and houses more than a quarter of a million volumes and a million manuscripts. The area facing the library is now universally known as Beinecke Plaza, and I'd be amazed if one Yale undergraduate in five hundred is aware that it used to be called the Hewitt Quadrangle.

There's a persistent undergraduate rumor that the Beinecke Library was supposed to be built of green onyx in tribute to S&H Green Stamps. That's strictly a myth, but not without its tiny grain of verisimilitude. It is true that the library was principally financed by contributions from the Beinecke Foundation, which had been formed by Edwin, Fritz, and Walter Beinecke in 1944 to provide support for the charitable organizations in which they had an interest, and of course the foundation received its income from S&H. The library was also supported by short-term income-producing trusts funded with S&H shares and by direct gifts from members of the Beinecke family, whose means derived in large part from S&H. It is also true that Gordon Bunshaft had, from the beginning, wanted to bring luminescence to the interior of the library by building the outside walls of translucent stone, and one of the materials he experimented with was onyx, of a kind that was quarried in Algeria. The idea of using onyx foundered when doubts were raised as to whether the quarry could supply sufficient stone for the building design and whether Algeria would remain intact and politically quiescent long enough for the stone to be quarried. Instead the building was constructed of translucent, gray-veined Vermont Danby marble, framed by Vermont Woodbury granite. That was a happy decision, both because of the intrinsic beauty of the stone and because it was a domestic product.

My father and Uncle Edwin anticipated that the Beinecke Library would make available to scholars and other researchers one of the world's great collections of rare books and manuscripts and would also attract other bibliophiles to donate their collections to Yale, and indeed it has. The library has fully lived up to my father's hopes. He put those hopes into words that are now engraved on the plaque at the entrance: "May this library, given to Yale University by Edwin John Beinecke, Frederick William Beinecke and Walter Beinecke, three Yale men, stand as a symbol of the loyalty and devotion of three brothers, and serve as a source of learning and as an inspiration to all who enter." The building has also provided a spectacular setting for many university functions and is the climax and terminus point of tours of the university campus. It's one of the brightest jewels in Yale's crown.

CHAPTER THIRTEEN

President of The Sperry and Hutchinson Company in the Early to Mid-1960s

I had been made a vice president of The Sperry and Hutchinson Company in April 1954 and was elected to the board of directors in November 1955. As the 1950s drew to a close, I had been working more and more on the business end of S&H as well as the legal end. Uncle Edwin was chairman of the board, and my father had been president of S&H until 1953, when he became chairman of the executive committee and George Schirer was made president. Because the business was owned and organized as a stockholding corporation, it had to have these formal titles and positions, but in actuality it was run more like a partnership between my father and my uncle Edwin. The partnership was so seamless that it was difficult to say how my father and uncle divided up their responsibilities. In 1960, my father was seventy-three and my Uncle Edwin was seventy-four. Uncle Ed had suffered a severe heart attack and perhaps a partial stroke when he was abroad in Paris sometime in the late fifties—worrisome for him, and more worrisome for us. With the help of his secretary, he continued to attend to all of his business responsibilities. He would always be present at ceremonial functions like the directors' meetings or the big dinner at "21" that we used to put on for our major executives around the country, but he had stopped coming to the office on a regular basis. My father was more frequently around S&H headquarters, but by then he was concentrating on plans for the Beinecke Library and his Western Americana bequest.

By 1960, I had already been acting as head of S&H in some respects for a year or so. The two principal figures in the Company had become disengaged from the business, although I continued to go to my father and Uncle Edwin for advice on the really tough questions.

Many issues that would normally have gone to the president also came to my desk, because George Schirer's function in the Company was not so much to be president as to continue to be the general sales manager he had been before he was promoted. He was an able sales manager, but he didn't deal with the financial, distributive, legal, and policy aspects of the business. I suppose this was not unusual in a family company. Someone had to take care of those functions, and Mr. Schirer was content to let me step into the vacuum and deal with the day-to-day issues involved in running the Company.

At the directors' meeting in June 1960, my father and Uncle Edwin asked me to become president of The Sperry and Hutchinson Company. The presidency wasn't anything I had been expecting or angling for, but it was a great thrill when I was offered the position. I'm sure the offer came about in large part because my father and Uncle Ed had been impressed with my performance and abilities as general counsel during the years when the Company had faced down the legal and legislative assaults of our enemies. I had worked closely with my father and uncle during that time. That made it a more natural transition when I took over some of their responsibilities as they grew older and gradually began to move away from the business. The strength and stability of my marriage, and the love and respect that everyone had for Betty, may also have been a point in my favor.

My cousins Edwin Beinecke, Jr., and Walter Beinecke, Jr., were disappointed. Each wished that the presidency had gone to him instead. Eddie was less disappointed. I think he recognized that I was fit for the job and that he would be better off in a junior position within the Company, and he did indeed stay with S&H for the rest of his life. Bud, on the other hand, resented my promotion considerably. He had also been elected to the S&H board of directors in 1955, had become a vice president not long afterward, and had done a fine job working on the merchandise distribution system and warehouse design. Bud felt that he was the businessman, I was the lawyer, and so therefore he should be the president of the business. Walter Beinecke, Jr., was and remains a complicated character. He is an individual possessed of great but often erratic and undisciplined talents and energies. He and I were in some ways the most able of our generation of Beineckes, and there had always been an element of rivalry in our relationship. We were not particularly alike as individuals, but we shared certain interests and perceptions. Not long after I became president, he left S&H to head up his own operations, including the campaign of Sherburne Associates to rebuild the rundown waterfront of the Nantucket harbor and preserve its historical character against commercial exploitation. Bud ran his operation with a steely disregard for the opposition. That made him quite unpopular in certain circles, but he and his associates did succeed in rejuvenating the island. Bud has performed valiant efforts for historical and environmental preservation. And though he never graduated from college, he served as an able and effective trustee for Hamilton College in Clinton, New York.

By the early 1960s, S&H was no longer the small and rather sleepy company it had been at the start of the 1950s. Our industry was on the threshold of becoming a billion-dollar business. S&H had expanded to the point that it was entering the ranks of the *Fortune* 500 companies. The company's growth during the 1960s was as amazing as it had been during the 1950s. By 1962, we employed over seven thousand people throughout the country. A 1963 Benson & Benson survey disclosed that S&H trading stamps were being saved in some thirty million US households, or 55 percent of the total. By the end of the decade, more than 80 percent of American households collected stamps. S&H alone had more than seventy-five thouand loyal stamp-giving outlets, and we actually issued more stamps than the United States Post Office.

Bill Beinecke and Fritz Beinecke at the latter's 75th birthday, Morris County Golf Club, 1962.

Richard S. Beinecke and Frederick W. Beinecke, 1962.

Most of S&H's profits at that time came from what the merchants paid us for the use of our stamps. The merchants weren't simply buying a piece of paper with mucilage on the back that we got from our stamp supplier in Scranton, Pennsylvania; they were buying an item that had value packed into it. Once the stamp was in the customer's hands, S&H made money in the same way that Macy's or Gimbel's made money. The stamp company was buying its merchandise in bulk from the manufacturers and putting it on sale at a markup in the redemption stores. Instead of getting money from the people who redeemed the stamps, though, our Company was getting it from the merchants, who, in turn, got their money from the customers who received the stamps.

Trading stamps, like currency, are a medium of exchange that allows the holder to settle a future claim, but stamps have a much lower turnover rate than cash. Although we had a high redemption rate—95 percent and more—it took even the most assiduous shoppers several months to fill a book. The float, which was the lag from the time a stamp was issued until the time it was presented for redemption, was money that could be invested by the Company. Trading stamps worked much like traveler's checks in this regard. When the American Express Company sells you a ten-dollar traveler's check, it gets money from you and holds it until you cash your check. The length of time that your ten dollars is in the hands of the company is the float. When you multiply that by all the millions of traveler's checks that are in circulation at any given time, you can see that the American Express Company has a substantial float, which is money that they can invest. While American Express is not willing to divulge its daily statistics, it's well known that the ratio of uncashed traveler's checks to total checks issued peaks during those times of year when people set off on vacations, around Christmas, Easter, and summertime. Trading stamp redemption operated along a different dynamic, because selling the use of our stamps to a merchant wasn't strictly a financial transaction, it was a merchandising transaction. Still, we had an enormous amount of liquidity, and a substantial portfolio of assets invested in securities. We purposely ran the business along conservative financial lines and carried huge reserves to back our stamps so that we always had sufficient liquid assets when stamps were presented for redemption. That was one of the major differences between our company and the fly-by-night trading stamp operations. We also used the float to operate our merchandise redemption stores and buy merchandise to put into them.

One thing that contributed vastly to the profit of the company was our purchasing power. There were more than two thousand high-quality items available in our illustrated S&H Ideabook catalogues, over thirty million of which were published yearly by the late 1960s. The most popular merchandise items were, in order, soft goods (such as sheets, pillowcases, bedspreads, and blankets), furniture, appliances, housewares, outdoor accessories, and sporting goods; together they accounted for more than 60 percent of all redemptions. Our many warehouses acted as supply depots for our eight hundred redemption centers, conveniently located for shoppers so as to encourage high redemption. Through our warehouses, redemption stores, and mail services, we annually distributed over a million lamps, clocks, wallets and billfolds, towels, garden tools, luggage, cookingware, and so on.

As I often used to say, trading stamps allowed people to save as they spent. There was only one thing a consumer could do with her stamps. She couldn't, in a weak moment, shake them out of the piggy bank and fritter them away. Stamp saving thus became a relatively painless process of saving for the desirable things consumers wanted but ordinarily wouldn't (or couldn't) go out and buy. The child's rocker that we offered in our catalogue, redeemable for one-and-a-half books in the early sixties, was a good example. It was a useful addition to any home with children, yet many families were reluctant to lay out cash for what might be construed as a luxury item. But it was an important number in our catalogue. In 1962, we distributed 184,000 of them.

These were extra sales, ones that ordinarily would not have occurred without trading stamps. Some merchants used to complain that merchandise distributed through redemption stores deprived them of sales. Such complaints all but vanished when it was documented that the redemption process actually stimulated a great deal of new buying. My son Rick once saved enough trading stamps—Green Stamps, naturally—for an Eastman Kodak motion picture camera, but no sooner had he picked the camera up at the redemption store than he had to have a projector, screen, film, and carrying case, all purchased from a local merchant. The pattern applied to a host of products, with the local retailer reaping the benefit of follow-up buying to complete sets, provide accessories, match luggage, and so on.

We played a small but significant role in helping stimulate America's production and employment and to expand the distribution of the nation's goods. Through the course of stocking our warehouses and redemption centers, we became one of America's biggest single customers for small appliances. By 1961, trading stamp companies added about 14 percent to the total distribution of heating pads in the United States, about 8 percent to the distribution of toasters, and about 4 percent to the distribution of electric coffee makers. We were frequently the largest purchaser of a particular company's product. S&H's impact was felt on entire industries; the development of RCA's market for consumer electronics, for example, was given a tremendous boost by the vast numbers of clocks, transistor radios and record players acquired in the 1950s and 1960s through stamp programs. We could point to a host of other products that developed into major sources of manufacturing income as a result of our catalogue distribution, ranging from pinking shears to card tables to room dividers. Manufacturers fell all over themselves in their desire to get their products into our catalogue, which would instantly give them thirty million prospective customers.

By the mid-1960s, S&H's revenue per thousand stamps roughly matched what its operating costs had been a decade earlier. Had we not succeeded in sharpening our operations and reducing costs, we would soon have been ranked among the country's largest nonprofit institutions. One of the triumphs of those years was the superb performance of our operating people in overcoming the demands imposed by rising costs and rapid growth. S&H's explosive development was potentially a double-edged sword. The enormous multiplication in our sales over a brief span of time brought on a staggering volume of problems that had to be overcome if S&H hoped to retain its service reputation. We succeeded by vastly expanding our inventories, by building new warehouses (which were almost immediately enlarged), and by constructing, relocating, stocking, and staffing hundreds of new redemption centers. During one year we opened an average of one redemption center every four days! We launched a national advertising campaign. We revamped our entire internal organization, overhauling our salary and sales compensation systems and expanding our recruiting and training programs. And we installed a multimillion-dollar data processing center and telecommunications system, honing our operating efficiency through technical improvements and a close scrutiny of costs. We were among the first companies in the country to employ computers to meet business needs. We had enormous data-punch-card-operated computers with external drives, positioned in a room with windows along the length of one wall so visitors could admire our marvelous new machines at work. Now, of course, all the tasks of inventory control, payroll, and so forth that required a room-sized computer in the early sixties can be done on a lap-top computer the size of a book. I even took a computer course offered to chief executives by IBM in the sixties and spent several days at an office building in New York with nine or ten other would-be techies learning the prehistoric computer languages and rudiments of programming.

While it was essential to S&H's viability that it become more efficient, there were limits to the drive for efficiency. We had to be loyal to our customers. I once received a letter from a woman down in Georgia who had spent a year and a half accumulating twenty-five books of stamps to buy an item in the S&H redemption store in her town as a wedding present for her best friend. When she had pasted the last stamp in her twenty-fifth book and gone to the redemption store, she found that the new catalogue had come out and the price of the item had gone up to thirty books of stamps. The wedding was the next week, and what was she going to do? I called up the manager of the woman's local redemption store and explained the situation. "Oh, yes," the manager said, "that nice lady was in the store just the other day. Too bad she doesn't have enough stamps anymore now that the price has changed." I replied, "Well, as far as I'm concerned, the price hasn't changed." The store manager was shocked. "How can you do that, Mr. Beinecke?" she asked. I could do it because I was the boss, and I assured the manager that her accounts would be straightened out by our accounting department. But the important thing was that by bending our rules a little bit to be loyal to a customer who had been loyal to us, we were creating immense goodwill. I got the nicest letter from the woman I had helped, and I added more to our reputation by giving away the equivalent of fifteen dollars than if I had spent thousands of dollars on advertising.

My desire to make S&H more efficient sometimes involved going against the pattern my father and Uncle Ed had laid down. When I joined the Company, a number of our most important customers were still department stores, including Vandiver's in Tulsa, Brown's in Oklahoma City, Gold's in Lincoln, Nebraska, and major stores in Pacific Grove and San Bernardino in California. My uncle Ed had thought it would be a good idea for S&H to acquire department stores to serve as an anchor for our stamps in the areas where the stores were located. The Company bought up the Hens & Kelly department store in Buffalo, several stores in Michigan including Wurzburg's in Grand Rapids and Arbaugh's in Lansing, and another in Salt Lake City, Utah. I had been part of the S&H team that bought Arbaugh's and had participated in the legal work in connection with the acquisition and purchase of all the shares from surviving members of the Arbaugh family. By the time I was president of S&H, though, I had begun to wonder whether these department stores were really pulling their weight. Many of these stores, it seemed to me, were not profitable enterprises in and of themselves, and since the 1950s the importance of department stores to S&H had been eclipsed by supermarkets and filling stations. It wasn't my style as president simply to dump the stores based on my own suspicions. I appointed a study group, including several accountants and financial analysts, to determine whether department stores were in fact an economic asset or an economic liability to the Company. The group gave consideration to the financial aspects of all the stores we owned and concluded that S&H would indeed be well advised to clean up its balance sheet and dispose of those stores, not in a distress sale but in an orderly manner over time. I regard those decisions to streamline the Company and make it more efficient as among the most significant business decisions I made, but I tried not to act on something as important as disposing of the stores without consulting widely and attempting to reach thoughtful understanding and consensus.

My desire to have a higher level of advice and consultation led me to make major alterations in the role and composition of the board of directors. We'd had a board all along, but the Company was run by the people who owned it and the board was essentially superfluous. The board existed to satisfy the requirements of the law under which corporations were regulated and to ratify certain formalities that needed board approval: the execution of a lease, the purchase of real estate, and things of that sort. The board kept minutes of its decisions, but since the Company was private, so too were our minutes and financial information. The board members in my father and uncle's day were their friends and family, who were occasionally useful to the chief officers in terms of advice and approval but who didn't govern the Company in any meaningful sense. My cousins Ed and Bud and I had become members of the S&H board in 1954, and over time we were joined there by my brother and other relatives. By the end of the 1950s, there were nine Beineckes on the board of directors. I began to feel that the board was becoming inbred and was not keeping up with the changes in the Company's growth and importance. What had worked for my father and his brothers in their day would not work for my cousins and me in ours.

I wanted board members to be useful counselors who could advise and support me in certain difficult business decisions that I could see would have to be made. I brought in Charles Phillips, the president of Bates College in Lewiston, Maine, who was also a well-known economist and the author of several books on marketing; Robert Austin, a professor at the Harvard Business School; John McGillicuddy, the chairman of Manufacturers Hanover, the bank on whose board I served; George Zipf, whom I got to know during his service on the board; Charles Laing, vice president of the Prudential Insurance Company; and John T. Connor, then head of Merck, who served until he was named secretary of commerce during Lyndon Johnson's administration. These outside directors provided a necessary balance to the family members on the S&H board. Any company that has that kind of family dominance ought to have a balanced board, with outside directors who can bring objectivity and flexibility to the enterprise.

The job of recruiting members of a board is typically the responsibility of the chief executive officer, and I was careful about how we dealt with compensating our directors. Directorships, unlike trusteeships, are usually paid positions. Certainly directors deserve to be adequately compensated for their time. You don't want them to feel underpaid or, worse, that they are providing a pro bono service to a purely for-profit company. On the other hand, it is the obligation of the CEO to see that a director's compensation is not overstated. It should not be so large or play such an important part in the director's yearly income that it causes him or her to lose objectivity about the company's performance; otherwise a situation can easily develop where the director relies so much on the compensation, together with whatever perks are offered, that he or she becomes a captive of that CEO. Not only has this phenomenon occurred in the past, it continues to happen, and it's a regular issue of discussion in the public media that report on business matters. I firmly believe it is the duty of a responsible CEO to prevent such a situation by ensuring that a director's compensation is reasonable but not overstated, but it's a difficult balancing act.

Neither should directors be either secretly compensated or compensated out of balance with respect to other members of the board. Some companies will offer additional compensation to a director if, for example, he serves as chairman of a certain committee. That's fine, provided it's not secret. But I have heard that Gerald Ford was lured to a particular board with the promise of a payment grossly out of proportion to that of the other directors. Certainly no one would deny that it is highly prestigious to have a former president of the United States as a member of your board, but if this story is true, it places Ford in a difficult position with respect to his brethren on the board.

The board members I had recruited to S&H played an increasingly important role over the years, and eventually proved helpful in extricating S&H from its first business loss in many years. Trading stamps had been so successful in the United States that it seemed to me that S&H could be equally successful elsewhere in the industrialized world. In the early 1960s, I designated a small group headed by Emil Corona to take the trading stamp business to Europe. Corona's group established itself in London, and we launched S&H Pink Stamps in Britain. We couldn't use Green Stamps, because an English entrepreneur had already copied us by establishing Green Shield Stamps in that country. I went over to England in November 1963 to take a look at our operation and deliver a speech on trading stamps to the London Economic Society. I got a great roar of laughter and applause out of the audience when I said, "I'll concede that the right to issue trading stamps was not specifically granted by the Magna Carta." That became the *New York Times*'s "quote of the day."

In making the decision to start the European operation, I'd had to buck the opposition of my father and Uncle Edwin. S&H had unsuccessfully tried to establish itself in Europe in the long-ago days before World War I, and the elder statesmen of the Company clearly recalled that episode and worried that history would repeat itself. It turned out that they were right, but I thought we were matched with different times and conditions and could now succeed in Europe. I thought the prestige and know-how of S&H would enable us to overcome the local competition and the opposition of the large food chains like

Sainsbury's. This did not prove to be the case. The S&H name meant little in England, the Green Shield Stamp entrepreneur had stolen a march on us, and Lord Sainsbury and his colleagues proved to be formidable opponents. Neither did Emil Corona succeed in establishing S&H in Belgium, France, or Spain although, oddly enough, trading stamps were a big hit on the little island republic of Malta. Our European operation continued to lose money, and eventually I had to send our accountant, Robert Patterson, over to London to pay off the obligations of the S&H Pink Stamp Company, repatriate our people, and shut the operation down at a considerable loss. Eventually we sold our assets there for one pound and other considerations. Somewhere in my collection, I have that one-pound note in a frame, along with the language that finalized that melancholy transaction. Looking back, I see that it was a mistake on my part to have pushed so strongly for the European venture, although the lens of hindsight is always sharp and clear. The experience humbled us a bit and gave us a better sense of our limitations. That was probably healthy. Despite the European example, I continue to believe that we made a mistake by not taking the trading stamp business to Japan. A Japanese entrepreneur sought us out in New York during this period and proposed a partnership. We turned him down, but I think we could have made a success of it. He was a man of vision and ability, and Japan had a more receptive climate for trading stamps than Europe.

At about the time we were launching the British operation, I concluded, after much discussion with members of the board of directors, that The Sperry and Hutchinson Company should branch out and diversify. I had no notion that the stamp business was on its way down. The trading stamp boom continued throughout the sixties and seemed likely to last forever. But I did sense that growth in the stamp business inevitably had to taper off or continue at a shallower slope. We still did robust trade through the supermarkets, but after the boom of the fifties and the rise of trading stamp companies that did business on our exclusions, it was apparent that eventually we would reach a saturation point. Consequently, it seemed to me that we had to find other ways to grow.

We also had quite a lot of money, measured by the standards of that time, from the portfolio that we reserved for unredeemed stamps. That reserve continued to grow, and I felt we could make better use of our enormous liquidity from the float. I didn't want to use too much of it. I was quite conservative in that regard, and I'm still conservative in the way I manage my own finances. But the salient fact was that we had all our eggs in the trading stamp basket, and that was no longer growing as it once had. We had great liquidity, and the idea of diversifying, to spread ourselves over a wider area financially and commercially, seemed both practical and sensible to me as insurance against the future. I was seconded in this conviction by my sharp and able executive vice president, Frank Rossi, and I asked him to form a committee consisting of himself and two outside directors to suggest directions that the Company might take. I wanted Chuck Phillips to be on the committee, for not only was he an expert on marketing and economics, he was a good, thoughtful man who was quite rightly asked to serve on the boards of many distinguished companies. I also thought Bob Austin would be a big asset, bringing the expertise of the Harvard Business School to our deliberations. For a number of years, Rossi, Phillips, and Austin met periodically and weighed the available options. Their deliberations were crucial in our determining to begin a program of diversification.

I asked Jim Mills, who had done a superb job as my successor as general counsel, to be in charge of diversification and deciding which companies S&H should acquire. He became the vice president in charge of diversification, and Fred Collins took his place as general counsel. Jim had to learn his job on the job, so to speak. He had to learn about companies, about how to employ outside consultants and advisers, and about all the rest of it. It was difficult, complicated work, particularly since my father and Uncle Edwin were not as enthusiastic about the diversification program as I was. They were not opposed to it, and they gave it their reserved blessing though it wasn't a decision they would have made themselves. But I was the man they had put in charge of running the Company, and they believed in me and supported me, just as I never second-guessed Jim Mills once I had put him in charge of diversification. Jim came up with the recommendations, and we would take them to the board for approval. I didn't play a direct role in that process, though I had conceived it and set it in motion; I didn't believe in micromanagement.

It was the view of Rossi, Phillips, and Austin that we should not embark on activities that were so technical as to be beyond our general expertise. We were skilled in financial management and merchandising, and since we distributed so many consumer goods to housewives through our redemption store program, it made sense to stick to those categories. Therefore, we concentrated on developing incentive promotions for retailers, bankers, and major business firms and on acquiring companies which dealt with furnishings and insurance and financial services.

Our first acquisition, in 1967, was Bigelow-Sanford, the oldest and one of the nation's largest carpet companies. Bigelow-Sanford's wares were widely distributed, and the company had a reputation for quality and innovation, and that was exactly what we were looking for. One of the most beneficial outcomes of that acquisition was that it introduced me to Lowell Weicker, who had been head of Bigelow-Sanford since the mid-1950s. Lowell had graduated from Yale in 1926 and had become president of E. A. Squibb & Sons by the time the United States entered World War II. He served on General Spaatz's staff in the US Strategic Air Forces in Europe and was awarded military decorations that ranged from the US Legion of Merit to the British OBE to the French Croix de Guerre. In the early 1950s he held a high position in the NATO command and was instrumental in bringing the European Union into being. He returned to the United States to become head of Bigelow-Sanford, and after S&H's acquisition of the company, Lowell joined our board in February 1967. With his wealth of knowledge, service, and ability, Lowell was incredibly important to me as a source of experience and counsel and became a close and valued friend as well. He provided thoughtful assistance in good times and staunch support in bad times. I also got to know his son, Lowell Jr., who became a US senator and later governor of Connecticut. He was a thinking person's politician.

Over the next several years, S&H expanded its furniture holdings substantially, ultimately becoming one of the largest producers of furniture and carpet in the United States. We looked forward to acquiring companies that manufactured furnishings for the home and office, and it was our long-term objective to produce or market virtually everything that could be found in the home and office, be it a lamp, chair, drape, carpet, table, cabinet, or what have you. Our first venture into insurance was the California firm of Bayly, Martin & Fay, a commercial insurance brokerage and one of the few major insurance brokers in the United States. We were looking for sturdy, substantial businesses with potential for growth. Naturally, not every acquisition proved a bonanza, but we had good and sometimes enviable success, and our acquisitions added value to the Company.

We were not necessarily looking for businesses that made products that might end up in the S&H Ideabooks and warehouses. We were so large in terms of the number of household items we purchased for our redemption stores that to some extent we could make or break a supplier. It seemed unwise to me to acquire a company that sold a substantial amount of merchandise to us. We wanted to offer merchandise of such high quality that its manufacturers could stand on their own feet whether or not we purchased from them. So if we were to acquire, let's say, a toaster-making company, and then stocked the company's toasters in our redemption stores, there was a danger that our subsidiary company might rely too much on the parent market and lose its competitive thrust.

In retrospect, I think it would have been wonderful for us to have gone into the rapidly moving technology market. We had the assets to do so, and it might have made sense, given that we were one of the first companies to apply computer methods to our business. We also missed out on a superb opportunity to acquire a substantial interest in the American Express Company at a very low price. American Express had run into an extremely difficult situation when, through a complicated financial transaction, it incurred a tremendous loss on a vegetable oil in some New Jersey storage tanks. The stock price of American Express dropped sharply, and my friend Sidney Weinberg of Goldman Sachs asked me whether S&H would be interested in acquiring a major share in American Express at a fire-sale price from an entity down in Tennessee. Jim Mills and I talked it over. We both concluded that because of the scandal that had infected American Express and the great loss it had recently taken, the whole idea of American Express would be in bad odor with my uncle Ed, and so we said, "No, thank you" to Sidney Weinberg. I wish we had at least run it by Uncle Ed, because that deal would have secured us a substantial interest in American Express, and, considering the storming success of American Express in subsequent years, it would have given us a tremendous leg up for the future. That was one of the ones that got away.

At the same time that we were mapping out the diversification of S&H, I was planning the most momentous decision of my presidency, the decision to take S&H public. In a way, the decision had been taking shape for a long time. We had recognized, during our battle with Safeway and other opponents, that S&H was already a quasi-public entity, even though it was privately owned. The decision to take the Company public was the logical next step and would be the culmination of S&H's becoming increasingly responsive and responsible to the public. Another consideration was that in the generation before me, the Company had been owned essentially by the three brothers, with their wives. They were very close, they saw things on the same level, and they were profoundly interested in the Company. By the time I became president in 1960, there were not just the cousins of my generation but our descendants as well. There began to be a multiplicity of people who had some kind of family interest in the Company, and not all of them could work for the Company. The S&H shares weren't bought or sold, and nobody knew exactly what their value was. The shareholders were, in a sense, locked in with an illiquid resource. By going public and creating a market for the S&H shares, we were able to establish the value of the shares by having them publicly traded. That also enabled family members, if they wished, to capitalize on their property, to realize that value and turn the shares of stock into more liquid resources. Finally, by making S&H a public company, we were in a better position to pursue the diversification goals we had set up.

It would have been possible to take the Company public by encouraging another company to acquire S&H. But I never considered that a real possibility. I thought S&H was a wonderful company with a bright future, and I believed it would continue to grow and prosper. There were tentative feelers from other companies interested in acquiring S&H, but we had no interest in pursuing them.

By the time S&H went public in 1966, the total number of shares had increased from 10,000 to five million, following a series of stock splits necessitated by the growth of the Company. The shares had been split five hundred to one even before 1966. At the time of the initial public offering, there were already five million shares in existence, and my original holding of 500 shares had grown to 250,000 shares. We had split the stock in order to make it easier to distribute within the family; establishing trusts for children and grandchildren is much easier if there are five million shares as opposed to 10,000.

The initial public offering was spearheaded by Goldman Sachs. Each of the stockholders participated. I remember trying to get everyone to participate equally, taking an identical percentage of our holdings, so that when we went public we would end up in the same position with respect to one another. Each stockholder contributed ten percent of his or her holding toward that initial public offering, and of course they received the money when their shares were sold for the IPO price. Sidney Weinberg led me through the tortuous pathway that led to the final fruition of the initial public offering. On his advice, it was a two-for-one split, doubling the total capitalization of five million to ten million, of which one million shares were then offered to the public. One million shares was a respectable number and enabled us to set the price of the Company's common stock at $33. If our total number of shares had been one million instead of ten million, the stock price would have been prohibitive—around $330. Had we remained at five million, it would have been $66. By doubling our five million, we were able to set a price that encouraged trading. It was a great day in 1966 when my son

John and I went on the floor of the New York Stock Exchange with Sidney Weinberg and saw our "SNH" symbol flash across the board for the first time.

There were clear benefits that went along with "listing," as it is referred to on Wall Street. As we had anticipated, it was now possible for S&H's shareholders to evaluate the worth of their personal holdings. Previously we had been forced to rely on an inexact formula of estimation, combining the earnings of a share during the course of a year with a certain multiple—say, ten or twelve. This method provided an approximation of the share's worth, but it wasn't entirely accurate. We had a much more realistic sense of our holdings once the shares were thrown into the lion's den of the New York Stock Exchange and unsentimental traders were setting a definite value on them. Another advantage of the listing was that a company that had met the strict requirements of the world's most important stock exchange had taken an important step toward assuring greater public confidence in its business and its product—or, in our case, in its service. And if a corporation is judged by the company it keeps, well, we were among the mere thirteen hundred major corporations listed on the Big Board.

Our listing presented a problem, however, to *Fortune* magazine. In a fall 1966 issue, the magazine's editorial column posed the rhetorical question: "What's Big, Green and Hard to Classify?" *Fortune* observed that S&H's sales in 1965 were $331 million, profits were $22 million, and assets at year-end were $303 million. "The figures are impressive," *Fortune* agreed, yet it turned out that the Company still didn't qualify for any of the *Fortune* 500 lists. The problem, as the editors saw it, lay in the peculiar nature of the trading stamp business. They considered classifying S&H as an industrial company. After all, we had a product (i.e. the stamps) that we sold to a not-inconsiderable number of customers (i.e., the retailers). Had S&H been so considered, it would have ranked 209th on the list of industrials, just behind Merck. But *Fortune* had determined that in order to be included among the industrials, a company had to derive at least half of its revenues from manufacturing or mining. Neither was much of an S&H specialty. But perhaps S&H could be classified as a merchandising company; by 1965, we were buying goods from a vast number of suppliers and distributing the goods through about eight hundred fifty of our own outlets. But *Fortune* objected that "S&H is primarily selling a *service*, not merchandise, and comparisons between its own sales and those of, say, Macy's would be wildly misleading." The editorial concluded by saying that *Fortune* had no category for S&H. This special treatment at the magazine's hands, in my opinion, was better for us than being quietly inserted into one of *Fortune*'s lists without any comment.

We had never been more optimistic and confident about the future of The Sperry and Hutchinson Company. We were totally aware that henceforth we would be operating in full public view—in fact, under public *scrutiny*. One effect of taking S&H public was, as I have suggested, that it made us more responsible. I don't want to give the impression that we had been irresponsible in the past, but when you constantly have to report publicly on what you're doing and when all your financial figures are public, you become extremely conscious of every decision—and you become more responsible. It's a consequence of being more open. We now had a responsibility to allow the public shareholders some representation in the governance of the Company. That didn't change the responsibilities of the board—the responsibility was always there—but it changed the way the board went about discharging that responsibility. And it really changed the way I, as chief executive, dealt with the board. Now that the Company was publicly held, I had to report periodically to the board, along with the other officers, on how we were running the Company. We had to obtain board authorization for certain major activities, such as selling off the different department stores and pursuing and implementing the diversification program.

We were not blind to the danger that often accompanies the fast growth of a company, namely, the risk of becoming institutionally paralyzed. But we were determined to maintain what George Schirer, Walter Whitnack, Frank Rossi, and others used to call "the romance of S&H," that difficult-to-define attribute behind all our success. I thought of it as attitude or "corporate chemistry"—that vital something that is the hallmark of a personal company that cares.

As head of the Company, I tried to combine tradition and innovation in our approach to the business. We continued to rely on the trading stamp program but attempted to develop it in new ways. An S&H division had been created earlier in the decade to develop incentive programs for retailers, bankers, and major business firms. For example, "S&H Motivation," founded in 1963, came up with programs to increase the productivity, efficiency, and morale of employees, improve customer service, and stimulate the movement of products and services through marketing channels. Companies that ranged from makers of business machinery to agricultural producers could get more out of their employees by dangling merchandise and exotic travel packages in front of them. Banks and savings and loan companies used our stamps to attract new depositors and stimulate loans. Employers used them as a recruiting aid in a tight labor market. By 1966, we were the third-largest operator in the incentive industry, and number one in the stamp incentive field. Not long after, we adopted a prize point system, which rewarded a salesperson's performance with merchandise from a special incentive catalogue.

S&H's advertising program in the 1960s included our sponsorship of several television celebrities, particularly Perry Como, Danny Kaye, and Dinah Shore. I met all of them, though I wouldn't claim to know them well. I knew Como the least well, and I found him a strange guy. One time when we were driving around L.A. in his car, he ran out of gas as we were cruising down Wilshire Boulevard and just managed to glide the car into a gas station. The man at the pump jumped up and down when he saw us, crying, "Perry Como! Perry Como!" It was rather odd, and I wondered if it was some sort of contrived Hollywoodism.

John Beinert, our California operations head, knew Danny Kaye, and John said to me, "When you come to town, let's see Danny at his home." So we went over to Kaye's house, and he cooked us a magnificent Chinese dinner. He had several Chinese helpers doing the chopping, but he put the ingredients in the wok and cooked them up. John and I were sitting in a booth in the kitchen, and Kaye sent over a variety of dishes: beef, pork, prawns, vegetables, and so on. He didn't sit down to eat with us, but as soon as one dish had been served, the next would be chopped and prepared. Immediately after John and I had finished eating, Kaye announced, "That Barbra Streisand is on TV, and I have to see her." And so we all went into his den and watched Streisand perform. I saw Danny Kaye almost twenty years later when I was in Jackson Hole with Betty, Frances, and our granddaughter Carrie, on a trip Betty had won as a door prize at a New York Philharmonic benefit. Kaye was staying in a house nearby with a few of his friends, and I got to say hello to him. He was cordial and claimed to remember very well the time I was over at his house, but I wondered whether he was merely being polite. I didn't realize at the time that he was already suffering from the illness he died from not long after.

I got to know Dinah Shore somewhat better. After her show stopped being sponsored by Chevrolet, in those days of single-sponsor television, we picked up her sponsorship for about six years. She was slightly past the zenith of her career by that point, but still very popular. Dinah was an extremely attractive and warm person, and I was fond of her. At one point in the early 1960s, we were having some anti-stamp political trouble in Tennessee, and Senator Estes Kefauver decided it would be a good idea to persuade us to bring Dinah Shore to sing at the Ramp Festival in East Tennessee. A wild onion grows in that part of Tennessee that's called a ramp, and each spring a Ramp Festival is held outside Newport, near the North Carolina border, at which the locals harvest and cook the onions. They set up booths and have entertainers, like at a big country fair. Dinah Shore was extremely popular in Tennessee, since it was her home state. So we persuaded her to sing at the Ramp Festival, and S&H picked up the bill. I went along with Betty, Sarah, and Frances. Dinah got out of her plane in Knoxville, where she was met by a phalanx of photographers and a limousine that took her the hour or so drive to the festival. It did not have much in the way of dressing rooms for the stars, but Dinah was always a trouper. She went behind a chair, changed into something flimsy, walked carefully across a cow pasture in her bright green shoes, and got up on the stage and belted out her songs. Afterward, Betty and the girls went back to the airport, and I got into a car with Dinah, Senator Kefauver, and the governor of Tennessee. Off we went to Chattanooga, where Dinah was scheduled to give another performance. Senator Kefauver was sitting next to Dinah, and he drawled, "You must be t'ahd, honey. You rest yore li'l head on my shouldah." She did not! Dinah eventually retired. While she spent some time in New York, she was essentially a Californian. A well-known LPGA golf tournament in the West is named after her. She died a few years ago.

Despite the Company's great success and my promotion to president, our lifestyle in Summit remained more or less what it had been in previous years. We joined several golf clubs, and Betty and I belonged to the Summit Dancing Class, better known as the "Old Folks." The group was not, in fact, comprised of old folks, nor was it a dancing class! Most of the members were in their forties and fifties—old perhaps in comparison with our teenage children, but not really all that old. The group was a social organization that sponsored about three or four parties a year, when we would get into our evening clothes and dance at the local clubs. It was a pleasant group of friends.

For several years during the 1960s, I was a member of the Monday Night Club, a sort of men's literary club in Summit that is still going strong after more than a hundred years. It met once a month, from September through May. Each meeting was a black-tie dinner held at a member's home, and the responsibility of hosting the dinner rotated through the club's fifteen or sixteen members. It was an exclusive club. We wouldn't get up and leave the room if it was mentioned in public, but it was not considered proper to refer to the Monday Night Club out

Betty and Bill Beinecke while visiting Libby and Bob Porter in South Harpswell,
Maine, early 1960s.

loud in the presence of others. My friend Win Lenz (of Merrill Lynch)
was an ardent Monday Nighter, and other members included Bob
Porter (head of the Chemical Fund), Toni Knoppers (president of
Merck), Fred Palmer (in the public relations business), Jack Connor
(one-time Secretary of Commerce), Wally Wilkinson (of Allegheny
Power), and three prominent lawyers, Bill Vanderbilt, Jim Burke, and
Ted Kenyon. Each meeting was devoted to a discussion of a paper by
one of the members of the club; the duty of writing and presenting a
paper also rotated through the membership.

I have a 1982 book listing the programs of all of the papers ever
written for the Monday Night Club up to that time. The secretary of the
club was Fred Palmer, and his minutes commenting on the paper presented at the previous meeting were a treat. In my time, the fashion was
to have the title of one's paper shroud the nature of the subject matter. I
remember that Ted Kenyon, a leading New York patent attorney,
wrote a marvelous piece entitled "The Greatest Sight in Nature." It
turned out to be about a steam locomotive zooming through a winter's
night in Vermont, the white hills lit by the red glow of the firebox. I
wrote two papers for the club. My first was entitled "Of Some Americans
and Some Russians." It was not about the Cold War but about the American landings at Archangel and Vladivostok in Russia in 1918, during

the Bolshevik Revolution and the Russian civil war; I leaned heavily on George Kennan's accounts. My second piece was "Christmas at Funafuti," about my wartime experiences in the Pacific. I thoroughly enjoyed my membership in the club, but I was too busy with S&H to devote the requisite amount of time to putting together my pieces. I found the research a burden, and so I let my membership lapse.

For two or three years in the 1960s, I was a member of the Black River Fishing Club. It's on a stretch of the Black River, a rapidly flowing stream near Pottersville, New Jersey. Our club leased a portion of the stream and periodically stocked its waters with trout. It was a treat to be on hand when the truck from the hatchery turned up, laden with keeper-size trout. I eventually resigned from the club because I couldn't find time for both trout fishing and golf.

I also belonged to the Scorpions, a bridge club whose membership was composed of men from Summit and Short Hills. We met for bridge every month. I've played it since I was at Andover, and I'm a decent player. I'm not a life master, and I don't have the patience to study the game and memorize all the different conventions, but I'm better than average. I have good card sense and, particularly in the 1960s, I had a lot of practice. I played bridge nearly every weekday on my way home from work. I was a member of a club car on what was originally the Delaware, Lackawanna & Western Railroad. There were three club cars on the D, L & W: one on the line to Bernardsville and Peapack and two on the main line to Summit and Morristown. On the main line, you belonged either to the Summit or the Morristown Club Car, but you could ride on either one. The club cars left Summit at 8:07 and 8:36 each weekday morning and returned from Hoboken at 5:15 and 5:54. The members of my club car were all professionals or CEOs and included my lawyer friend Jim Burke and my friend Bob Baldwin, who was head of Morgan Stanley. It was a good set of associations. I had actually inherited my father's spot in the club car, but since he lived in Madison, he belonged to the Morristown Club Car. It didn't make much of a difference to me, since memberships in the Morristown and Summit Club Cars were interchangeable, but in due course I was officially transferred to membership in the Summit Club Car.

Our automobiles did get a little fancier with my various promotions, I suppose. During my last year of law school, my father had been kind enough to give me a Mercury sedan, and that remained our family car during the war years. Indeed, we continued to drive it for some time after the war ended because new cars simply weren't available. The odometer failed at around eighty thousand miles, but we must have put another fifty or sixty thousand miles on it before exchanging it for a Buick. After the Buick, we had a series of station wagons in the 1950s, the better to ferry young children around to all their activities. Finally, in 1959, I purchased my first Mercedes-Benz. I bought it from the same dealership in Elizabeth, New Jersey, I patronized for new cars and servicing for nearly forty years. My first Mercedes was a little roadster runabout known as a "190." The advertising campaign for the car was extremely effective and I had high hopes, but the fact is that the 190 was somewhat underpowered. Though the company had equipped it with a supercharger, it didn't really meet the Mercedes-Benz standards and never lived up to the advertising claims.

In the years since that initial disappointment, we've had a succession of quite good Mercedes-Benz cars. In 1961, when Betty and I took our four young children to Europe, we purchased a car known as the "300 automatic" from the Mercedes-Benz dealer in Elizabeth and took possession of it in Heidelberg, Germany. The six of us, with all our luggage, squeezed into what was really a five-passenger car and drove from Heidelberg to a little town just southeast of Munich. Fortunately the Mercedes was a beautiful, roomy car and also boasted an automatic transmission—still something of a novelty in the United States in the early 1960s.

There was more to that 1961 trip to Germany than simply picking up a new Mercedes, of course. That was the first time Betty and I had taken the children to Europe, and we had an enjoyable family vacation. My cousin Berni Weickert was no longer living in Germany, having emigrated to the United States with his wife, Alex, in the mid-1950s, but he was a native German and knew the country well indeed. On his advice, we stayed at a hotel in Prien, a little Bavarian town on the Chiemsee. During our two or three weeks there, I chartered an eighteen-foot sailboat, and we had fun taking it out on the water. Not far from our hotel, on an island in the the lake, was the Schloss Herrenchiemsee, one of King Ludwig's elaborate castles. We attended several glorious summer evening concerts there, when the entire castle was illuminated by candlelight. My cousin Putti, who lived near Leipzig, drove over with her husband and teenage daughter Barbara in their little East German Trabant automobile. They stayed in a small B&B nearby, and we had a nice weekend together. That was the last time such easy interaction was possible, for the Communists built the barrier between East and West Germany that very summer, just a few weeks after our visit.

We returned to the States and took the new Mercedes with us. That car had the strangest way of starting. The key turned on the ignition, but in order to start the engine, it was necessary to lift the gear shift lever as well. The Germans presumably were used to this peculiarity, and I soon grew accustomed to it, but I encountered problems back in this country whenever I took the car to a parking garage or any place that featured valet parking. I would say to the attendant, "Now, this car is difficult to start, perhaps I could explain it to you—" only to be cut off quite rudely, as though I had insulted the man. He would growl something along the lines of, "I know all about cars, thank you very much," and I had no choice but to step aside and watch him hopelessly attempt to start the car. After a few minutes, I would approach him and say, "Perhaps I'd better show you how to do it." Usually the response was a snarl mingled with profanity to the effect that the car was broken and in need of repair. After a few years of this, we traded the car in for a later model, built for the American market, that had a more sensible way of starting. I always liked that strange-starting Mercedes, though. It was painted a deep tan and was a high-quality car both in appearance and handling. I've only seen three other cars here in the States that started in the same manner, and one of them, curiously enough, belonged to my Summit friend Harvey Mole.

One autumn day in the late 1950s, a man named Charlie Wells came to see me at my office in New York. He wanted to interest me in a piece of property that was up for sale. I was extremely busy then, and I said as politely as I could manage that I had too much going on at the moment to discuss a real estate project. "But it's on Cape Cod," Charlie protested. I thought that perhaps the best way to get rid of him might be simply to let him make his sales pitch, so I impatiently agreed to look at the map he had brought with him. I had absolutely no inclination to buy anything Charlie was selling, but when I looked at the map I nearly fell out of my chair! I saw then that the property for sale was along my favorite stretch of Pleasant Bay, right at the edge of the Eastward Ho! Country Club in Chatham, where I had played golf only the week before. "My God," I said to Charlie, "this is the one and only piece of land I might be interested in buying." "That's why I'm here," he replied. Charlie explained that Eastward Ho! was then in straitened circumstances and was asking $75,000 for the approximately thirty acres, including the pond, the tract now known as Fox Run. Charlie had put up $25,000 for the property, had convinced his nephew, George Cutting, to do the same, and needed another partner to provide the final $25,000. I agreed to do so, and we purchased the property through the

BCW Trust (from our initials); it was a form of business organization called a Massachusetts trust, a business animal peculiar to Massachusetts. Charlie Wells, as operating head of the trust, employed landscapers to clean out the underbrush and hired a private contractor to put in the roads and mark out the property into one-acre lots. As a condition of my participation, I was given my choice of three lots, and I selected the beautiful two-lot site overlooking the water on which our house now stands and the wooded inland lot separating us from our nearest neighbor. After the land was sold off, we liquidated the business enterprise and conveyed the pond, the common lands, and the private roads to the newly created Fox Run Property Owners Association, the organization that continues today to take care of those properties.

Construction on our new house began in the fall of 1961, and it was furnished and ready for occupancy by the summer of 1962. Our house at Fox Run overlooks Pleasant Bay, with a splendid view to nearby Strong Island. While the view has remained the same over the years, we remodeled the house considerably in 1992. When the house was constructed in 1961-62, it was built to an extremely tight budget. We have since added a library (where once a large rhododendron held sway) and an entranceway and have enlarged the master bedroom, replacing its rather skimpy bathroom with a large and somewhat sumptuous new bathroom. The remodeling actually cost more than three times what it cost us to build the house in the first place, though of course the dollar is worth less now than in 1962. But at that time I wasn't so well off that I didn't have to scrimp and save, and for thirty years ours was simply a modest family summer home. Fox Run is appropriately named, and we really do see foxes on the property from time to time. We also share the property with several raccoons and excessive numbers of rabbits, along with a vast, chattering profusion of birds of all varieties.

Our summers on the Cape were very simple when our children were young: swimming, fishing, tooling around on the beach in an old Jeep, and messing around in boats. In the early 1960s, as the children became teenagers, these simple pleasures weren't quite enough; they wanted to be out in the social whirl of the Cape with other kids their age. I found it rather ironic that I had built the house in Chatham so that all of us could spend more time together, and yet the children only wanted to be out with their friends! John and Sarah in particular felt there was too little activity around the house, but we were reluctant to turn them loose.

Our main shared activity was at the Chatham Beach Club, which featured swimming and tennis; John excelled at tennis. It was five miles from our house, and even there John and Sarah were always up to one thing after another. One time I was in my boat down near the beach club, and as I was out in the middle of the channel crossing the harbor to the Outer Beach, I saw the heads of two people swimming across the inlet—a rather risky thing to do, since the inlet was at least a quarter mile wide and there were fishing boats crossing back and forth. I thought I'd swing across the inlet to make sure the swimmers were okay and ask them if the water was cold. As I drew alongside, one of the heads called out, "Hi, Dad! Give us a ride!" Sure enough, it was Sarah and a friend. I was sufficiently steamed that I wasn't about to give them a ride, but I did follow them back to the harbor to make sure they made it safely. Of course, I knew Sarah probably made that swim every day when I wasn't around to catch her at it.

The tides of adolescent rebellion that became famous in the late sixties were already flowing by the early sixties. We had the usual tumultuous times that all parents experience when their offspring reach the noisy, active, feckless teenage years, all of which was height-ened by the turbulence of the decade. There were the normal struggles over curfews and the like. One evening when my late friend and class-mate Wid Cates was spending a weekend with us at the Cape, Sarah and Frances paused on their way out to ask, "Dad, what time do we have to be in tonight?" I suggested that, for the sake of novelty, they negotiate their curfew with Mr. Cates. Wid said, "Come back any damn time you wish," and the girls zipped out the door before I had a chance to inter-vene!

One summer, Betty and I decided that there was too much teenage hanging-around going on at the Cape, and we closed the house after less than a month and returned to Summit. That produced some grum-bling, to put it mildly. The children thought we had gone bonkers. While we continued to go back to Chatham every summer, that's when we began to do much more travel as a family during the summers, which was more satisfactory than having the children bum around the Cape for three months. We also thought that when John turned six-teen, he should have some summer employment in order to prepare himself better for college. One of my fellow directors of Manufacturers Hanover, who was CEO of a major paper company, helped me secure a summer job for John at a paper mill in Millinocket, Maine. He roomed with a local family and did various jobs for the company, including using a hand-operated counter to count logs in the mill yard. At first John resented being removed from Chatham and his friends, but he made new friends in Maine and became quite involved in his job, so it turned out to be a worthwhile and productive summer for him. It was important for him to have work experience in his background when he applied for admission to Yale. I think his Maine experience was also useful to him when he worked one summer at Goldman Sachs and another at Merrill Lynch during his college summers. Of course, my daughters still tease me about my sending John into "exile" in the Maine woods.

Rick spent less time at the Cape than the other children did, being preoccupied with his various summer educational enrichment programs. One year in the late 1950s, he went to summer school at Phillips Academy in Andover and absolutely fell in love with the place. At Andover that summer, he finally saw the value of learning—the experience was like a curtain going up. His awakening came late, but when he "came to" after years of plodding along, it was almost instantaneous. Now he's quite an intellectual, but he was seventeen or eighteen years old before that happened. Once Rick took off, he remained on a steady course and gained his self-confidence. He transferred from Pingry and repeated his junior year at Andover. He graduated from Andover in 1962 and enrolled at Yale in the fall, graduating in 1966. Rick had a successful career at Yale and also had a good time there. He was a member of Calhoun College, played intramural soccer and squash, and was a member of the Zeta Psi fraternity. He became interested in architecture, design, and art history at Yale, and majored in history of art. John graduated from Westminster in 1965 and went to Yale that fall, so he and Rick overlapped at Yale for a year. While Rick has been loyal to Yale, his primary involvement has been with Andover, which was the school that really did the most for him. I had served briefly as an Andover alumni trustee, along with George Bush in his pre-presidential days. Andover picked Rick as a charter trustee several years after I had gone off the board. Rick chaired the Investment Committee and has served as treasurer of Andover, during which time his leadership has enabled the school to increase its endowment sixfold.

Sarah's popularity only increased as she moved further into her teenage years, and she began to attract particular attention from boys her age. I used to enjoy teasing the boys who would call our house around the clock asking for Sarah. I'd pick up the phone and hear, "Is Sarah there?" "Yes!" I would reply with great enthusiasm. Then there would be silence until the young man figured out that he had to ask, "May I speak to her, please?" When a boy would arrive on our doorstep looking for Sarah, I'd ask, "What's your name?" "John," would come the muffled reply. "John what?" I'd ask. "Just John." I'm not sure why there was this insistence on keeping on a first-name basis, because when I would ask the boy, "Do you have any parents?" he'd reply, "Oh yes, Mr. and Mrs. So-and-So in Short Hills," or wherever he lived. Sarah went away to Dana Hall, a girls' school where she made some wonderful friends whom she continues to see even now. Sarah was not an enthusiastic student in those days, though she has since become one. It has turned out that Sarah has had a lifelong involvement with Dana Hall. She has been one of the more active trustees for several years and played a vigorous role in the school's capital fund drive. She was invited to chair the board but turned the offer down in view of her wide involvement in other activities. After Sarah graduated from Dana Hall in 1966, she spent a wonderful summer in Bergen, a fishing town on Norway's southwest coast. She lived with a Norwegian family, an arrangement that was organized by the Experiment in International Living, the very popular program run out of the Putney School in Vermont. It was a terrific experience.

Frances attended the Ethel Walker School, a girls' school in Simsbury, Connecticut. Though both the Westminster School and Ethel Walker's were in Simsbury, there had been little interaction between the students of the two schools when I had attended Westminster. In fact, the Ethel Walker girls were forbidden to talk to us Westminster boys. So it was interesting to be able to see Ethel Walker's from a parent's perspective. Frances liked the school well enough and made some great friends there, including the well-known actress Sigourney Weaver. But she and her friends are loyal to one another, not to the school. They were displeased with the change of administration and direction that happened after they left. Frances has always gone along a straight line. She makes up her mind and accomplishes whatever she sets out to do. When she was about fourteen years old, she decided that she wanted to go to a summer program in Europe. On her own, she went through various brochures and picked a program in Switzerland that advertised summer activity on Lake Geneva. Even at that time, Frances was determined to show us that she was able to make her own decisions. Unfortunately, while the activities were fairly well run by the nuns of whatever order administered the program, it was full of wealthy kids from all over the world whose parents apparently didn't want them around. Within forty-eight hours, Frances called up wanting to come home. We agreed, but she decided otherwise and stayed on, and eventually enjoyed her summer very much. She met one tremendous girl from Sweden, Christina Rydorff, who became one of her closest friends.

I suppose it's a cultural stereotype that businessmen love golf, but I have to admit that my promotion to president of S&H coincided with an increasing love of the game! Perhaps it was because the children were older and so, for the first time in a long while, I had the opportunity and inclination to become truly enamored of golf. While I had played even as an undergraduate and had been a member of both the Morris County Golf Club and the Baltusrol Golf Club in the fifties, it wasn't until the sixties that there was time for more than an occasional weekend round. My partner and I were the runners-up in the 1951 Morris County "Weekend of Golf," but I think that had less to do with my own performance than with the skills of my partner in the event, Howard Clark. Howard, who was later CEO of American Express, was an outstanding businessman, an excellent tennis player, and—luckily for me—a most skillful golfer. I myself was not a serious golfer then.

Mine was a case of ever-increasing interest in the game. The first golf club in New Jersey to which Betty and I belonged, the Morris County Golf Club, was really a country club, offering tennis and swimming as well as golf. Baltusrol, which we joined in 1958, was a golf club, period. The final stage in the evolution of my interest came when we built our house on Cape Cod in the early sixties, adjacent to the Eastward Ho! golf course. It was then that the bug really bit, and I've been addicted ever since. At last count, I've played over four hundred golf courses, from New Jersey to Singapore. I've played courses as far north as Royal Dornoch in Scotland and as far south as Christchurch, New Zealand. It's hard for me to list my favorites, because courses are like symphonies, and how can you compare them? I've kept a book of old scorecards, and one that I remember particularly well was a 75 at Eastward Ho! Bob Mustard, my companion that day, later presented me with a little statue of a golfer to commemorate the occasion, with the date and score engraved on the pedestal. These things mean a lot to golfers.

Betty is a golfer as well, and a good one. Her first exposure to the game came in 1949, during a trip to Nantucket we took after Frances was born. Betty took a number of lessons from the golf pro at Sankaty. Later, she was taught by Walter Kozak at the Morris County Golf Club and played there nearly every Tuesday, Ladies' Day. When we joined Baltusrol, which was much closer to our home, Betty took lessons from Johnny Farrell, a United States Open champion who was the club's pro. He was not only a great player but a talented teacher, and Betty's golf game improved immensely.

In 1965, Betty and I took the children on another family vacation to Europe, this time to Austria, and we stayed at a marvelous small inn called Schloss Fuschl, in the Salzkammergut, not far from Salzburg. There were trout streams nearby, the wonders of Salzburg were down the road, and the inn even had its own golf course. The first hole was on a sort of hill, so high above the starting level that when I teed off for the first time, I could only just see that my ball had landed on the green, though clearly to the right of the pin. John, who was not yet nineteen, shot next. His ball appeared to be heading straight for the flag, but from our perspective it was impossible to follow its trajectory. We hiked up to the green, and I found my ball more or less where I expected to find it, but John's ball was nowhere in sight. We searched around for a while and eventually thought to look in the hole. There it was—a hole in one! It was a thrilling moment. We turned our cards in at the pro shop, obtained the proper signatures attesting to the score, and the spectacular shot was made official. The next day, Frances and I went trout fishing while Betty and John played another round. Midway through the course they were invited to "play through" by another group of golfers, and no sooner had Betty hit her shot than the Austrians began yelling, "Eins! Eins!", which of course is the German word for "one." And sure enough, she'd done it! When they came to pick us up at the end of the afternoon, John thrust his head out of the car and said, "Dad, you won't believe what happened on the golf course today." I said, "Don't tell me you made another hole in one." "No, I didn't," John replied, "but Mother did!" Needless to say, two holes in one in two days by two different members of the same family is extremely unusual. Although Betty's triumph came on a different hole than John's, I wondered if the people in the pro shop thought we were a bunch of frauds when the name Beinecke appeared on the hole in one scorecard once again! I've been playing this game since 1925, and until quite recently John's was one of the few holes in one I'd ever witnessed. It is a rarity.

My growing interest in golf prompted the realization that the Yale golf course was in desperate need of an irrigation system. From a design standpoint, the course was wonderful, but it was in poor physical condition since it relied exclusively upon "natural irrigation"—i.e., whatever rain happened to fall. In 1966, I approached Yale's president, Kingman Brewster, with the offer of a grant to the university for the course. Kingman, who was acutely conscious of tensions in town-gown relations at the time, felt it would be unseemly to announce that a major gift to the university was going to be used to improve the golf course. He tried to convince me to divert the money to some academic purpose. I pointed out that the Beinecke Library, which seemed to me to be serving a very good academic purpose, had only recently been dedicated. I now wanted to do something to please myself, namely, to underwrite this watering system. Kingman eventually consented and the irrigation system was created.

When the grant was made, I hoped that improvements to the golf course would bring the alumni into closer contact with it (and Yale, of course), and I believe that this hope has been realized. The original irrigation system I put in wore out after thirty years and was replaced without assistance from me. Funds were raised to finance it. Our Prospect Hill Foundation financed the splendid new clubhouse, which is called the Prospect Hill Golf House. I think there are now indications that enough alumni are interested in the future of the course to underwrite other such improvements. Nonetheless, Yale golf has had a difficult time of it over the years. Once upon a time, the golf course (like the rest of the Yale plant) was exempt from taxation. But New Haven kept gazing with yearning eyes at the university, wanting to extract more revenue and threatening to put some or all of Yale on its tax rolls. Yale entered into negotiations with the city and eventually capitulated to some of its demands. The university agreed to pay taxes on the golf course in exchange for certain concessions by the city, such as closing portions of High Street and Wall Street in order to unify the central campus.

I wanted to give Betty an Impressionist painting as a present for our twenty-fifth wedding anniversary in May 1966, but I really knew little about Impressionism or art in general. I went to Fred Palmer, the secretary of the Monday Night Club and a fellow member of my club car, for advice. He gave me the address of a gallery in Manhattan. When I went there the next day, I asked to see an Impressionist painting of a rainy day in Paris. Something like fifty pictures of Paris under the weather were trotted out, and I was overwhelmed. Back I went to Fred. "Oh," he said, "that was just your indoctrination. Now here's the name of the dealer you really want to go to. He's reliable. You can use my name." I went to the dealer's gallery in a brownstone quite far uptown between Broadway and Riverside Drive. The townhouse was crowded with stunning authentic Impressionist paintings, almost all for sale. I bought the Pissarro that now hangs over the fireplace in our apartment in New York. I was somewhat bemused when I realized that I paid more for it than I'd paid for our home!

The night of our twenty-fifth anniversary coincided with a long-planned dinner we'd been invited to at the home of John D. Rockefeller

III, which stemmed from his interest and mine in Lincoln Center. Betty and I decided that we ought to go to the dinner. Somehow the Rockefellers caught wind of the fact that it was our anniversary, and they even found out that I was going to give Betty a Pissarro. After dinner, the men and women separated, in the old-fashioned way, with the men going off for brandy and cigars. Blanchette, Mrs. Rockefeller, was showing Betty around the apartment, dropping subtle hints: "Do you like Pissarro? Here's one—and here's another! This one is even better than the last two. . . ." As we were on our way home, Betty told me wonderingly that after dinner, Blanchette Rockefeller had pointed out to her a number of genuine Pissarros. I had previously arranged to have our Pissarro placed on an easel under a spotlight in our living room while Betty and I were out at the dinner. When we returned home, as we were entering the driveway Betty looked at the house and exclaimed, "Something's the matter! The wrong lights are on." Well, it all came right in the end. Betty walked into the living room, and there was the painting. She *was* surprised!

Our twenty-fifth wedding anniversary was one of the high points of 1966, but there were low moments as well. My father suffered a serious stroke in August of that year. Though for several years thereafter he remained functional and in possession of all his faculties, he was never quite the same. Only a couple of months prior to the stroke, Rick and I had accompanied my father on one of the last ventures in which he was able to participate actively. He had decided to make a substantial gift to

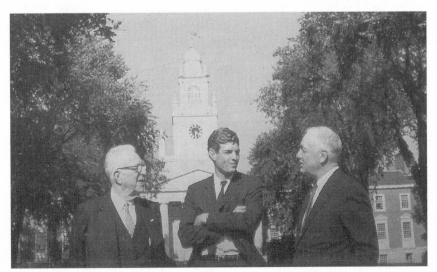

Frederick W. Beinecke, Rick Beinecke, and William S. Beinecke at Andover, 1966.

Andover, and the three of us went there to walk around the grounds and discuss how the money might be applied. Rick had just graduated from Yale. Fred Stott took a photograph of my father, my oldest son, and me in front of Samuel Phillips Hall on the Andover campus. That's a picture that means a lot to me. Afterwards, I drove Dad across the state to his home in Great Barrington. We didn't talk about anything in particular on the ride back, but I'd give almost anything to have another conversation like that with him again.

On November 7, 1966, my brother, Richard, died of Hodgkin's disease, a form of cancer of the blood. He was only forty-nine years old, and it was a terrible thing. He had been diagnosed with the disease five years earlier, around the time when we had been scheduled to go down to Skytop in Pennsylvania for Thanksgiving. Our small family group (six in all) did go, but my parents elected to stay in New York with Dick and his wife, Doris. I tried to see him as often as I could after that. His disease grew progressively worse, and he no longer came up to the small and attractive house that he and Doris had in the Dennis area on Cape Cod. They remained in their home in Palm Beach, on the northern end of town just before the Palm Beach inlet. Dick lived in Florida largely because of his love of deep-sea fishing, and he was at one point the president of the Sailfish Club in Palm Beach. The record 535-pound blue marlin he caught was exhibited in the Florida Building at the New York World's Fair and was eventually hung over the bar in the Sailfish Club, because there wasn't room enough for it in Dick and Doris's house. I went down to see my brother in the fall of 1966, about a month before he died. That was a deeply sad occasion, as was his funeral in Palm Beach. But he suffered so long, with such a cruel illness, that in some ways it was better that he was released at last. I took some comfort in thinking of him as he was before he was ill and of the many good times we had together. I still think about him a lot. While his life was much too short, it was a good one and he left many good memories.

And then in early 1967, I lost my friend and colleague Sam Lane through a strange and awful disaster. You'd think, to talk to Sam, that he was a quiet and unassuming man, but beneath the placid surface was an ego and ambition of iron. He liked to take risks, to gamble against fate and the elements. He bought an antique forty-foot sloop and, in early February 1967, told his family and a few friends that he was going to sail it single-handed to Bermuda. He planned to meet up with his four children, who would be on spring vacation by the time he arrived, and then sail with them to the Caribbean. His wife and I and just about everyone who knew about this cockeyed plan all pleaded with him to

Dick and Bill Beinecke on Dick's boat, Palm Beach, Florida, c. 1960.

abandon it. Sam was still in his fifties, and Casey, Lane & Mittendorf was booming. He had too much going for him to risk it all on this sort of gamble. But he was firmly the individualist, the lone eagle, full of determination and free will. "It's my life," he said. Several of his friends thought seriously about asking the Coast Guard to prevent him from making his insane trip, but that was impossible and he never would have forgiven us for trying to interfere.

Peter Cooper was the last person to talk to Sam, just before he set sail from Buzzard's Bay on February 22, 1967. Peter telephoned Sam and tried to persuade him to abandon or at least postpone the trip, but nothing could change Sam's mind. "It was a relatively short conversation," Peter said recently, "but I was so horrified by what happened that I've remembered it all through these years." Sam was only a few days out when he was overtaken by a fierce blizzard. My son Rick had sailed to Bermuda the previous summer with Fred Collins and George Dixon, and I knew enough to know that solo sailing on the Atlantic in midwinter is an appallingly dangerous activity. The slightest injury, even something as minor as a sprained wrist, can mean death. Two weeks after his departure, Sam hadn't been spotted since the blizzard, and his wife asked that the Coast Guard conduct a search for his boat. A large-scale, intensive search was begun on March 10 and completed eleven days later. I twice visited the Coast Guard Search and Rescue Center on Governor's Island during that period and was impressed with the high quality of personnel, the professional way they went about their tasks, and the courtesy with which I was received. But no trace of Sam or his boat was ever found.

While the promotion to president and later chairman and CEO of S&H did not significantly affect my family's Summit lifestyle, it definitely produced some changes in my executive life. Some of these were minor. For example, one of my colleagues at S&H convinced me to have a personalized license plate bearing the initials "WSB" made for the Company car. After about a year of driving around with that plate, I decided that it was too damn conspicuous, so I canceled it and returned to a sensible, conventional license plate. Other changes were more substantial. I was honored with invitations to join the boards of several corporations, and I accepted a few with pride. Through these directorships, I formed contacts with other CEOs, many of whom I subsequently encountered at California's Bohemian Grove encampment and many of whose services I drew upon in later years as chairman of the Central Park Conservancy. I was also asked to attend a number of important conferences. One that comes to mind was a luncheon for CEOs at the Federal Reserve Bank in New York City. You do get a clearer understanding of the American economic picture when you talk it over with the head of the Fed and a number of the country's sharpest CEOs.

Since the 1950s, I had been a director of the Home Insurance Company, a New Jersey-based insurance company. Its president during most of that time was a man named Kenneth Black. The role of the directors was quite limited, however, and my involvement was not substantial. Prior to becoming president of S&H, I had also been a director of the Harlem Savings Bank, an old and respected name among the savings banks of New York. The Beinecke family's long-time ally and associate Lou Crandall, the head of the Fuller Construction Company, was also on the board. The Harlem Savings Bank, which in the early sixties had half a dozen or so offices, was headquartered at 125th Street and Lexington Avenue. It was a mutual, which meant that the depositors owned the bank, and the board met to endorse the work of the president and his officers. Its business wasn't all that profound, consisting mainly of receiving deposits and making mortgage loans. The responsibilities of the directors were not particularly onerous, either; one of my more vivid recollections of that association was the golf outing of the board and a few officers. I do remember that Edward Pierce, the president of bank, was troubled by the economic and social deterioration of the Harlem area after World War II. He wondered whether the bank's headquarters should remain there and indeed whether the name itself had become a liability. The bank was established when Harlem had been a largely white and upper-middle-class area, and while the bank welcomed the patronage of the blacks who had come to dominate the community by the 1950s, Harlem by itself was too economically depressed to support the bank. The headquarters were eventually moved out of Harlem. The bank itself, after several mergers, is now the Apple Bank for Savings, playing on the New York nickname "The Big Apple." My directorship with the Harlem Savings Bank was not a difficult or consuming responsibility, but I'm glad I did it. It was an interesting relationship, and it broadened my associations.

In 1962, several years after I had become a director of the Harlem Savings Bank, I became the first outside director of the newly created Manufacturers Hanover bank. Manufacturers Hanover was brought into existence by a merger of two quite different banks, the Manufacturers Trust Company and the Hanover Bank. The Hanover was a patrician bank, while Manufacturers Trust was regarded as a hoi polloi one. Manufacturers Trust had a great many branch offices, while the Hanover Bank had only a main office uptown and a Wall Street office. Manufacturers Trust wasn't exactly a blue-collar organization, but it was definitely more oriented toward all the people. The Hanover Bank served mainly the affluent upper crust. There were those at Hanover who looked down their noses at Manufacturers Trust, or perhaps it would be more accurate to say that they took off their pince-nez and looked sideways. Assessing the merger from outside, I think it was a good union because it brought together different organizations serving different markets. The Hanover Bank did well to rid itself of some of its aristocratic airs, and Manufacturers Trust benefited from the larger depositors who were brought into the new organization.

The Manufacturers Hanover bank had a distant Beinecke connection. The Manufacturers Trust Company had been created in the 1920s through the merger of several New York banks. One of them was the Commonwealth Bank (originally the Germania Bank), which had been started early in the century by my grandfather Bernhard Beinecke and several of his partners. Because of this family connection, my uncle Edwin J. Beinecke became one of the original members of the Manufacturers Trust Company board. By the time of the merger with the Hanover, Uncle Ed was seventy-six and one of the older members of the Manufacturers Trust Company board, and consequently he was not included in the group of directors that was carried over.

In order to make the board function effectively, it was organized into committees: the Audit Committee, the Compensation Committee, and the Loan Committee (which was probably the most important). As a director, you would serve on different committees, sometimes serving two terms on one committee, but usually rotating around in sequence. I was diligent in my work as a director, but it was not particularly taxing. The bank was well-run, and the officers were on the job. We were fortunate not to have to deal with any big rifts in the management; the job of a director can become very difficult when the directors have to decide, for example, whether to fire the head of a company. During my eighteen years on the board, fortunately, the bank's management was getting along and making progress.

I served as a director of Manufacturers Hanover until I stepped down as head of S&H. The bank wanted active heads of companies on its board, and its bylaws had a provision to that effect. If a former CEO stayed on the board after he had ceased to be actively involved in his company, his successor could not be put on the board and would likely be invited to join the board of a competing bank and put his business into the competitor's bank. During the 1980s, Manufacturers Hanover and the Chemical Bank merged, and this large bank in turn merged with Chase Manhattan to create the giant known as the Chase Manhattan Bank.

As a director, my greatest involvement was with the boards of the Manufacturers Hanover Corporation, the Texas Gulf Sulphur Company, and the Consolidated Edison Corporation. My membership on the Texas Gulf Sulphur board came about in an interesting way. In the

1960s, Texas Gulf Sulphur was using a sulfur mining technique in which a pipe—actually three pipes within a larger, single pipe—was lowered vertically into the ground. One of the inner pipes served as a shaft through which extremely hot, pressurized water was pumped into the sulfur deposit. The water melted the sulfur, and the sulfur (suspended in steam) was channeled into the outer pipes and forced to the surface. The sulfur was then condensed, dried, and shipped to its destination. This was not a particularly revolutionary procedure; the processes involved were covered in my high school chemistry class, and I am aware of at least one other competing company that was utilizing the same method. But from that activity, Texas Gulf expanded its mining operation and eventually discovered a fabulous deposit of nonferrous metal in Ontario. The company set up an open-pit mine on the site of the deposit, with terraces extending from the rim to the bottom. Clearly this discovery was going to have a positive effect on the stock price of Texas Gulf Sulphur, and insiders were not supposed to trade stock until news of the mine was made official. But some mishap occurred in handling the information, the leak was made public, and the company got into a very difficult situation with the SEC. One of the directors of Texas Gulf Sulphur was Thomas Lamont, a famous Harvard figure, senior partner of J. P. Morgan & Company, and a prominent man in the business world. (His son Lansing Lamont is the author of some highly readable books and a good friend of mine. He and I went together to the North Pole—or very nearly—in 1980.) Texas Gulf Sulphur came into a great deal of criticism and scrutiny as a result of the leak, and Thomas Lamont was seriously embarrassed by the situation. He decided that the board needed a fresh perspective and that directors with no prior knowledge or experience in the mining industry would provide an objective view. And so he recruited me to the board, along with Bob Smiley, who was then chairman of the R. H. Macy Company.

I certainly qualified as someone who didn't know anything about the mining industry. Yet perhaps my ignorance was precisely why my years on the Texas Gulf Sulphur board were so interesting. As the company expanded its mining interests, eventually moving as far afield as iron mining in western Australia, I was exposed to business activities I'd never heard of and was able to travel to places I otherwise never would have visited. Because I knew nothing about the mining industry upon joining the board, I made sure that I always did my homework and was scrupulously conscientious in fulfilling my responsibilities. The directorship was really a broadening experience, and the company treated me wonderfully well. Texas Gulf Sulphur owned a lodge on some forest land in Pennsylvania, and one time when Betty and I were en route to Toledo to play golf with some friends, we had dinner there. On another occasion I was invited as a member of the board to visit the celebrated Ontario mine. We traveled in the company's Lear jet. Rick had just returned from Vietnam and I wanted to spend time with him. Fortunately there was ample room in the plane, and I invited him to come along with us. When my father's stroke in 1966 made commercial air transportation too difficult for him, the company flew my father and mother back and forth to their apartment in Palm Beach on one of the several high-speed jet planes the company owned. Naturally, I was billed for these trips and I always reimbursed the company, but it was a great help and a real load off my mind, because I was concerned about my parents traveling at that age.

I eventually terminated my relationship with Texas Gulf Sulphur in order to become a trustee of the Consolidated Edison board. When I was asked to join the Con Edison board, I had a difficult time deciding whether I should leave Texas Gulf, the company that had been so good to me and had so much to offer. I couldn't serve on both boards, because there simply wasn't time. I was still a director of Manufacturers Hanover, and of course I was extremely busy at S&H. The Texas Gulf board generally met in New York, but the annual meeting was held in Texas because the company was incorporated there, and those trips took up more time than I had imagined. I knew it was (and still is) considered bad form to resign from one business board to join that of a more prestigious corporation. The business community does not look favorably on a person who abandons a small company board the minute an offer from, say, General Motors or AT&T materializes. I don't think it really can be said that the Consolidated Edison board was more prestigious than the Texas Gulf board. That was not a factor in my decision, and the issue was something that I gave careful consideration at the time and have thought about a great deal ever since. My decision to resign from the Texas Gulf board ultimately hinged on the fact that the Consolidated Edison responsibility carried with it an important element of public service. Texas Gulf Sulphur was an important private business activity—important not only in terms of prestige but in providing the nation with the raw materials necessary for industry—but it was strictly a private, for-profit business. Consolidated Edison, on the other hand, was one of the country's major power companies. Living in the New York area, I felt that in becoming a trustee on the Consolidated Edison board, I would be engaged in what you might say was a quasi-public service. (Usually, the word "trustee" has the connotation of a fiduciary relationship, that is, of somebody's looking after a trust, but it just happens to be the old-fashioned term Con Edison uses to characterize people who are, in fact, directors.) At any rate, I didn't want to give the impression that I was exchanging my previous directorship for a more "important" position or one that offered better compensation.

Consolidated Edison, like the Texas Gulf Sulphur Company when I first joined its board, was a company suffering from a crisis of public confidence after the great New York City blackout of 1965. I had been in Manhattan at the time of that first blackout, which struck just as I was heading home from work. In order to get back to Summit each day, I had to walk from the S&H offices to 42nd Street and 6th Avenue, take the 6th Avenue subway line to 33rd and 6th, ascend from the subway, and descend into the PATH terminal for the train to New Jersey. On this particular evening, I had emerged from the subway, was standing on the platform, and was just about to board the train when the lights went out. It was pitch black, so dark that you couldn't see your hand in front of your face. Initially everyone on the platform assumed that something had gone wrong with the PATH system, but as we groped our way out into the streets we discovered that all of New York City's lights were out, and the only illumination came from the passing beams of automobile headlights. Aside from that, Manhattan was as dark as the Black Forest at midnight.

I headed for a phone booth to call Betty and let her know I was all right, but a lot of other people had been struck with similar ideas, so I had to wait my turn. Ahead of me in line were three young women, all of them completely at sea. They knew how to board the subway line leading from their homes in farthest Brooklyn and they knew how to retrace their steps at the end of the workday, but beyond that they were utterly lost. I overheard one of these young ladies, who couldn't have been more than twenty, talking to her father, and it was clear that she was terrified. She knew where she was but had no idea what to do or where to go because her ability to navigate her way around New York's streets went no further than getting on the subway. I'm sure that would be equally true of a lot of people who work in Manhattan today. I tried to reassure her that everything would be all right, and I gathered that her father told her to stay where she was.

I finally reached Betty and told her I would try to make my way to my parents' home at 888 Park Avenue, on the corner of 78th Street. As I was walking in that direction, I decided to stop in at the Union League

Club on the corner of Park Avenue and 37th Street, where I was a member. The club was handling the situation with tremendous aplomb, with meals served by uniformed waiters as was customary. I sat down to an excellent dinner—by candlelight, needless to say. I telephoned my parents from the club, and of course they agreed to put me up for the night. I went outside and found a taxi, and on the drive uptown to my parents' apartment I was pleased to see that New Yorkers had taken it upon themselves to restore discipline and order. Since all the traffic lights were out, volunteers stood at the corners directing traffic so that cars wouldn't batter into one another at the intersections. Everybody was most cooperative, and the spectacle was really quite impressive. I arrived at my parents' building in due course. The elevator was not working, and I have to say that the most painful part of the blackout for me was the climb up the eleven flights of stairs to my parents' apartment.

The 1965 blackout predated my participation with Consolidated Edison, but I was on the board during the second New York City blackout, in 1977, and that was a real disaster for Con Edison. The second blackout took place after lightning struck the high-voltage lines in Westchester County, causing the whole system to go down. Fortunately I was not in New York at the time. Betty and I were spending the night at the home of my friend Brad Wiley in Rhode Island; Brad was then chairman of John Wiley & Sons book publishing firm, and he and his wife, Esto, used to be across-the-street neighbors of ours in Summit. New Yorkers did not behave so magnanimously in this second blackout. There was a problem with looting, and Consolidated Edison got the wrong end of some of the resulting damage suits, the claim being that Consolidated Edison had failed to prevent the loss of electricity that led to the pillaging. We managed to sort out most of the claims and appeal the most egregious ones, but that was a learning experience for everyone on the Con Edison board.

I found being a board member of an operating company more interesting and challenging than sitting on a bank board. In my experiences on the boards of Texas Gulf and Consolidated Edison, I saw how those companies ran, and the directors had to pay close attention to the business of the companies. Charles Luce, the head of Con Edison during my time on the board, once paid me quite a compliment. He told me that he remembered my inserting a well-placed cautionary note into one of the board's discussions. In Chuck's opinion, my remarks saved the company from taking a course that subsequent events proved would have had serious adverse financial consequences. A director of a business enterprise really can have an impact.

My work and the associations I made through S&H broadened my understanding of the national and international economic picture. I learned a great deal about America largely by making good friends among the lawyers, lobbyists, and other people whom I met in the different states. Our lawyer in Arizona, for example, was a man named Louis McClennen. In 1962, during the first summer Betty and I spent in Chatham, Peter Cooper came out to the Cape and told me that some important legal problems had arisen in Arizona. He suggested that I discuss them with McClennen. We met in New York, and there I discovered that Louis had spent every summer since he was a boy in Chatham, just across the bay from our house. Louis's father had been a prominent Boston lawyer with a summer home in Chatham, and Louis's brother Allen has lived in Chatham all these years. At the golf club to which I belong, the Allen McClennen Award is given each year to the member or couple who have done something wonderful for the club, and in 1996 the award was presented by Allen himself to our neighbors and good friends Barbara and Bob Mustard. Louis decided to follow his father into the law. Rather than return to Boston, he joined a firm in Arizona after falling in love with the area during his wartime service there. We've been good friends ever since that S&H business brought us together. Louis was our principal guide to the political scene in Arizona. Texas, on the other hand, is so big that we retained several lawyers. One was a man named "Tiny" Gooch. He had been a football player at the University of Texas and stood about 6'6", with hands as big as hams—hence the nickname. He was our lawyer in Fort Worth, where we were involved in legal issues having to do with land acquisition for our regional distribution center there.

And then there was Ed Clark, lawyer and lobbyist par excellence. When Ed first came to the attention of S&H, he was a lawyer in Austin, the capital of Texas, and we retained him to keep on top of any hostile legislation that might be introduced there. Ed Clark was an extraordinary man. He was a friend and confidant of his fellow Texan, Lyndon Johnson, and during Johnson's presidency Ed served as a trustee for the blind trust that holds a president's assets during his term of office in order to prevent any conflict of interest. President Johnson respected and honored Ed and appointed him ambassador to Australia, where Ed left behind a record of accomplishment that may well be unrivaled in the annals of American diplomacy. The official residence of the US ambassador to Australia is in the capital city of Canberra, but Ed felt that the American ambassador should travel the country and make his presence felt all over. And so Ed went almost literally everywhere in Australia. He went to the cities, the coastal towns, the little remote villages, and the outback settlements that weren't even villages. He was known far and wide, all over Australia. He returned to the States when his term came to an end, but when he revisited Australia a year or two later with his lovely wife, Ann, the headline of Sydney's principal newspaper read: "ED IS BACK!" It's almost inconceivable that a foreign ambassador could be so generally known and loved that the media could mention him by his first name only, but that tells you a lot about Ed Clark.

Ed and I became good friends right from the time when I first visited him in Austin while I was still general counsel of S&H. Jim Mills and I made a last-minute discovery that we had some business to do in Austin, and it was only the day before our departure that we called Ed and asked him if he was free for lunch. Ed Clark, in his outgoing, expansive, and—I have to say it—Texan way, said, "Sure, let's meet. I'll invite a few friends over." When we arrived at the hotel where the luncheon was to be held, we discovered that the "few friends" who were to join us were all the judges sitting on the federal court in that part of Texas, most of the judges on the Texas Supreme Court, several chairmen of consequential committees in the Texas legislature, and even the governor! And all these people had come at a day's notice at Ed's request to meet the so-called important people from New York. I've never seen anything like it. It could only happen in Texas. I was amazed at Ed Clark's ability to turn out so many high-ranking, busy people at such short notice, and I've never forgotten it.

I don't know how it came to pass, but at some point Ed decided that I deserved an honorary degree. Because he was Ed Clark, on October 24, 1967, I was privileged to receive an honorary LL.D. degree from Southwestern University in Georgetown, Texas, not far from Austin, along with Lady Bird Johnson and W. Grogan Lord, who was president of the Texas Capital Corporation and treasurer of the university's board of trustees. Mrs. Johnson was given a doctorate of humanities, and we had a pleasant conversation in which she was absolutely charming, as she had been on a previous occasion when I had spoken with her. The ceremony also marked the opening of the Edward A. Clark Collection of Texana; Ed was a great collector of Texas-related memorabilia and historical artifacts, and had donated his collection to the university. Betty was with me when I received my degree, and much to my delight our daughter Sarah came down from Colorado College,

Southwestern University honorary degree ceremonies, October 24, 1967. Left to right: Ed Clark, William S. Beinecke, Lady Bird (Mrs. Lyndon Johnson), Durwood Fleming (president of the university), and W. Grogan Lord.

where she was then a sophomore, to attend the ceremony. My friend John O'Boyle, brother-in-law of my dear friend John T. Connor, also came over from Dallas to attend the ceremony, for which I was pleased and grateful. At the reception for the honorees that was held afterwards, the S&H executive in that particular part of Texas was greeted at the door by Sarah, and much to her amusement he mistook her for Luci Johnson, the daughter of the president. All in all, it was a lovely day and a memorable event.

One more thing I owe to Ed Clark is the friendship I formed with Sam Winters, who was one of Ed's law partners and is still practicing law in Austin. Sam and I discovered that we had a lot in common, including our service on destroyers in World War II. I think of my friendship with Sam as another of Ed Clark's gifts to me.

As I have mentioned before, I became great friends with Calvin Rawlings, S&H's main lawyer in Utah. Betty and I were extremely close to Cal and Ruth Rawlings, who was a wonderful lady, and they once invited us to accompany them to Las Vegas on a tour of its shows and casinos. The fifth member of the party was the former owner of Salt Lake City's principal television station, a certain Mr. Fox. He had built up his business himself, and it was so successful that he had shortly before sold it to one of the networks for $7 million. Mr. Fox was an inveterate gambler, well known in the casinos we visited. When we entered, he was welcomed enthusiastically and escorted to a seat at his favorite craps table, where he would bet many thousands of dollars on each roll of the dice. Some time after our visit, I learned that Mr. Fox had lost all the money he'd realized from the sale of his business and ended up working as an assistant in his wife's dress shop in Salt Lake City. It was tragic, but unfortunately I suspect that stories like that are not unusual. The proliferation of gambling houses around the country seems to be making the casinos rich and other people poor. I'm lucky that I was never bitten by the gambling bug. It seems to me that the odds are pretty much against you, and what's the use of pouring money out when you know where it's going to end up?

Cal Rawlings also provided me with some interesting insights into the American political scene. Throughout the 1960s, S&H was keeping close ties with the political world, contributing financial support to various political campaigns during that decade, as it had done throughout the 1950s. I honestly can't recall whether the Company made direct contributions or whether it was a case of personal donations from family members; I suspect the latter. Of course, the fact that we retained political lawyers in a number of places may be considered an indirect form of corporate contribution. Most of our energy was focused on the state level, because the litigation in which we were then entangled really involved state and not federal laws. But through our constant need to have the best representation possible in all different states, we often ended up with contacts whose political aspirations led them to desire more than mere local or state recognition or who had connections with others who later moved up to important roles on the national scene.

One of S&H's most politically well-connected contacts, of course, was Calvin Rawlings. Cal was an ardent Democrat but he was also an aficionado of the good life; as he once put it to me while we were taking a drive in the Company limousine, "I don't want to be a Republican. I just want to live like one!" Betty and I accompanied Cal to the 1964 Democratic National Convention in Atlantic City. He was not only head of the Utah delegation but chairman of the entire Western Conference, which comprised delegates from several western states. Cal was an extremely influential political figure in the West, and he knew everybody and everybody knew him. It soon became clear that when you went to the convention with him you were "THE GUEST OF CALVIN

RAWLINGS!" in big neon capital letters. Nondelegates are not normally allowed to enter the convention hall, but he led us in and seated us right down on the floor with the Utah delegation.

After the nomination of Lyndon Johnson had been wrapped up and all the states had voted on it, it was announced that Bobby Kennedy, brother of the late martyred president, was in the hall and would address the delegates. The response to this announcement was incredible. Bear in mind that the convention took place in July 1964, only eight months after that fateful day in Dallas. Jack Kennedy's assassination was still sharp in everyone's memory, and the country was still mourning his loss. A silence fell over the hall as a film about Jack Kennedy's life was shown. When Bobby Kennedy rose to speak, there was an absolute, unrestrained outpouring of emotion. It was an intense, palpable feeling. The applause, the yelling for "Bobby!" was like the roar of a cresting wave, but it went on and on without subsiding. Luckily for Johnson, his nomination was secured before the late president's brother appeared on the rostrum, because the emotional response to Bobby Kennedy in that hall was so great that it felt like he might have run off with the nomination by acclamation.

Betty and I were strolling along the Atlantic City boardwalk with Cal and Ruth one afternoon when we ran into the famous James Farley, postmaster general during Franklin D. Roosevelt's administration and an important Democratic political figure since the 1930s. I had never met Mr. Farley, but because Cal knew everybody, of course he knew Jim Farley, and I was glad to make his acquaintance. For quite a few years thereafter, I would run into him almost every time I went to the Waldorf-Astoria Hotel barbershop to get my hair cut; I think it was a ritual with him to go there every morning for a shave.

Partly through my association with lobbyists like Calvin Rawlings and Ed Clark and partly because I was heading a major American corporation during the 1960s, Betty and I were invited to the White House on several occasions and I attended a number of business functions there. I recall only one visit during John F. Kennedy's presidency. In 1962 or early 1963, a group of businessmen, myself included, were summoned to the White House for an important announcement to be delivered by President Kennedy in the Rose Garden at ten o'clock in the morning. Now, when one gets an invitation to the White House, it's kind of a command performance. But it so happened that I had a long-standing engagement in Lewiston, Maine, the night before the scheduled announcement. As much as I wanted to hear Mr. Kennedy, it was absolutely essential that I attend this other meeting, an affair of some significance in terms of The Sperry and Hutchinson Company's future. I managed to do both, although it took some maneuvering. I chartered a small plane to take me from Lewiston to Washington, leaving Lewiston in the evening and arriving in Washington in the wee hours. After a very short night, I went to the White House and presented myself at the southwest gate, where I was able to produce sufficient identification to get by security. I must say, I don't think the security was as intense then as it is now. Of course, it became tighter and tighter after Kennedy's assassination, and even more so after the attempted assassination of Ronald Reagan. At any rate, I made my way to the Rose Garden and arrived just in time to hear the president's remarks and shake his hand. That was my only meeting with Jack Kennedy, and my first encounter with a United States president.

Like most people who were around in 1963, I remember exactly where I was when I heard that President Kennedy had been shot. Like the day when Lindbergh crossed the Atlantic and the day Japan bombed Pearl Harbor, Kennedy's assassination was one of the events that are burned into the memory of everyone who lived through them; no one will ever forget where they were when they heard the news. On the afternoon of November 22, 1963, I was at S&H headquarters in my office entertaining two or three guests, and we were all seated at a little table while the German man who was working for us as a steward served lunch. He left the room for a moment, and when he came back he leaned over and quietly told me that the president had been shot. New York was in shock that day. The whole city was affected. You could see it in everyone's face—people were quiet, stunned. Betty and I were scheduled to host a business dinner party that night at The Plaza Hotel, and despite the assassination, we felt obliged to see it through. We had originally planned to hold the dinner in the Persian Room, a popular place to entertain in New York. It featured fine music, dancing, and good meals. But the joyous, noisy, celebratory activities of the Persian Room would have been totally unacceptable that night, and indeed the Persian Room closed its doors in mourning, as did other usually festive public places in New York City and across the land. We held a quiet dinner and attended to our business matters in an upstairs room provided by the hotel. The mood was subdued, and the terrible event hung over us.

I had first met Kennedy's successor, Lyndon Johnson, years before, when he was the Democratic leader in the Senate. Our encounter took place in his Washington office, and I particularly remember a sculptor being present in one corner of the office, quietly modeling a bust of

Johnson while the senator was speaking to me or haranguing someone on the phone. Not long after that, I was introduced to Mrs. Johnson, who had accompanied her husband to a Democratic Party event in Washington. Like most people who've ever met her, I thought she was charming. I've always admired the active role she played in encouraging the planting of wildflowers across the country. I had the opportunity to visit the Johnson ranch in Fredericksburg, Texas, in the spring of 1993, when the hillsides were alive with bluebonnets and other wildflowers—a glorious sight. Mrs. Johnson had led the effort to encourage people in that part of Texas—and elsewhere—to plant, and look after, those wonderful flowers.

I was at the peak of my business career in the years of Johnson's presidency. By virtue of my position, I was invited to dinners and special events at the White House, and had occasion to meet with Johnson more than a few times. In person he was immensely tall, with a commanding presence. Yet while I knew him as well as I knew any other president, with the possible exception of Nixon, I never got over the impression that there was something strange about him. I can't be more specific than that; he was just strange. One time when I met him, he shook my hand and held onto it for what seemed like a full minute, not saying anything, just looking down at me and swaying gently back and forth. Nonetheless, I voted for Johnson in his 1964 campaign against Barry Goldwater. If I had it to do over again, I think I would have voted for Goldwater, because he was an amazing man. He was highly regarded by his senatorial colleagues, but for some reason the press branded him as a rabid, Louis XIV-type conservative, which he really was not. In 1964, I believed Goldwater was a greater warmonger than Johnson, and of course it was Johnson who wound up leading us further and deeper into the Vietnam quagmire—though to give Johnson his due, the nation wanted to go. It's difficult to say whether Goldwater, who certainly was making some extreme statements, would have reacted any differently.

My first dinner at the Johnson White House was strictly business. The audience was composed mainly of representatives from various corporations, and Johnson was on hand to answer questions. Each table was asked to designate a speaker to represent it in addressing the president with its concerns or requests. Our chosen speaker was Alex Heard, then president of Vanderbilt University, and our table was pleased at how skillfully and articulately he phrased our questions. The second Johnson dinner was a state dinner, a very formal affair. It was given in honor of the Australian head of state, Harold Edward Holt (who not long afterward drowned while swimming off the Australian coast). Through our friendship with Ed Clark, Betty and I received an invitation. I'd been to the White House several times by that point but, my goodness, how often does one get invited to a state dinner there? As you would expect, we were highly excited. We normally took the shuttle when we went to Washington, but this time we decided to reserve seats on an airline. We got our reserved seats all right, but when we arrived in Washington we discovered that one of our suitcases was missing. Fortunately it was mine, so it was just a matter of renting evening clothes for the night. Later, standing in the receiving line to shake hands with the president, who should be standing next to me but the chairman of the board of the very airline that had failed to deliver my bag! I took the opportunity to complain, naturally, but the bag, which had visited Atlanta and Chattanooga by then, eventually found its way back to our hotel and was there waiting for us by the end of the evening. That dinner was a lot of fun, with music and dancing and more. Mrs. Johnson was there, and the president of course was the host. Protocol required everyone to remain at the festivities until the president himself had retired, but Johnson was dancing with all the ladies and enjoying himself immensely, which made it a long evening!

In 1966, Betty and I attended an afternoon tea at the White House at Mrs. Johnson's invitation, an event that actually grew out of a connection between Jackie Kennedy and The Sperry and Hutchinson Company. During her husband's term, while Mrs. Kennedy was upgrading the White House art and furnishings, she realized that the White House library was a meager, third-rate collection, comprised mostly of old census reports and other musty tomes. She felt that the White House library did not contain a single book that anyone would want to take down off a shelf, and she wanted to create a first-class collection stocked with readable works by American authors. She asked that a committee be formed to compile a list of more appropriate works, and James Babb, Yale's librarian, was made the chairman of that committee. With Mrs. Kennedy as the guiding force, the plan for the library began to take shape. Book selections were made, books were acquired (most were gifts from publishers), the downstairs area that was to house the library was fixed up, and bookplates were ordered. But the project abruptly stopped when President Kennedy was assassinated, and it was not completed until several years into the presidency of Lyndon Johnson. When it was finally finished, Mrs. Johnson invited all the people who'd had anything to do with the creation of the collection to the White House for tea. The book that listed the contents of the

White House's new library, entitled *The White House Library: A Short List*, was financed by The S&H Foundation, so Betty and I were there to represent S&H—a happy and pleasant occasion!

An aside: Jim Babb didn't think that "The S&H Foundation" was a sufficiently dignified name to appear on the flyleaf of this book, and insisted it be changed to "The Sperry and Hutchinson Foundation." Alas, there is no Sperry and Hutchinson Foundation. While our business's full name was indeed The Sperry and Hutchinson Company, it was popularly known as S&H, and when we created the foundation, we decided upon this shorter and more familiar designation. "The Sperry and Hutchinson Foundation" was what appeared on the flyleaf of the book, but it never existed!

My earliest encounter with Richard Nixon took place in the 1950s, during his first term as vice president. We were having our usual difficulties in Washington, and our S&H representative there felt it would be a good idea for me to go down and shake hands with Mr. Nixon. As presiding officer of the Senate, the vice president has an office in the Senate part of the Capitol, and I met him there. It was St. Patrick's Day, and he was wearing a green tie to honor the occasion. After that first

William S. Beinecke and Richard M. Nixon, c. 1958.

meeting, our paths crossed perhaps half a dozen times, both before and after his presidency.

Following his unsuccessful run for governor of California, after which he famously told the press, "You won't have Dick Nixon to kick around anymore," Nixon returned to private life, and was practicing law at the New York firm of Mudge, Stern & Rose in the early 1960s. By that point, S&H was a good-sized company, and we were punching doorways through the walls of our office at 114 Fifth Avenue so we could spill over to the building next door. Mr. Nixon and one of his law partners paid a visit to our offices, and I remember leading them on a tour through the punched-in walls, up and down between the buildings. It was kind of funny. I introduced Mr. Nixon to several of our employees, and he made a favorable impression. Even during his legal years, he was still a very famous man in this country, since he had been vice president for eight years under Eisenhower. He was at that time very much a lawyer on the make. It was obviously his intent to impress his partners and attract business to the firm, and I'm sure that he would have done so if he had stayed.

Several years into Nixon's first term in office, Betty and I attended a White House musical recital. Beverly Sills was the featured performer. It was held in the State Dining Room and was a highly elaborate affair. In the midst of this, in the State Dining Room of the White House, a congressman from Florida dropped the cigarette he had been smoking and ground it into the carpet with his foot! Well, I looked at him, and I looked at the cigarette on the floor, and I said something to the effect that this was the White House and not a public railroad station, whereupon he bent down and retrieved the butt. I still find it difficult to believe that any man—a congressman, no less!—would do such a thing.

One of the perks that went with being the head of S&H was that I was granted the use of the company limousine. Our driver, Jim McTernan, had heard about one of my White House visits, and since he had long wished to visit the president's home, he volunteered his services as driver if I was ever invited again. Later in Nixon's administration, just such an opportunity arose. Twenty businessmen were invited to the White House for a conference, ostensibly to acquaint the administration with what we believed were the important economic factors in the country. (When we arrived, we discovered that in fact we had been invited for the opposite purpose, which was for *them* to tell *us* what the important economic factors were.) I told Jim that I had been invited to the White House and that while I didn't feel like riding down to Washington in a car, if he didn't mind the drive he could meet me at the airport. We arranged for Jim to leave a day early, and planned to meet at the airport and drive to the White House together.

The conference was held in the Roosevelt Room of the West Wing of the White House. Nixon was on the West Coast in San Clemente, so Pete Flanigan acted as host. Pete Flanigan was the son of Hap Flanigan, chairman of Manufacturers Hanover and the man who had invited me to join that company's board. Pete was a prominent figure in the political world, and he was very close to Nixon in those days. By the end of the conference, the weather had turned rainy and unpleasant, so I asked Jim to drive the car right up to the door when it was time to pick me up. As I was leaving, Pete noticed the New York license plates and said, "Bill, you didn't drive all the way down from New York to come to this meeting, did you?" I told him about Jim McTernan and how much he had wished to see the White House. "Bring him in," Pete said, "and we'll show him around." Jim was the picture of excitement.

The first room we visited happened to be one that I remembered contained chairs made by Gunlocke, one of our subsidiaries. I mentioned this to Pete Flanigan and turned a chair upside down to confirm that the manufacturer's name was in fact the same, whereupon I was accosted by security guards who demanded to know what I was doing. Pete assured them that everything was all right and that I was the man who made these chairs. Unfortunately, when I turned the chair upside down I was embarrassed to discover that it was made not by Gunlocke but by our principal competitor! In fairness, the room had indeed contained Gunlocke chairs during Johnson's administration. (Johnson's people had told us that we could not make any mention of this fact in our advertising, so instead our salesmen carried postcards of the White House room and its chairs to show to prospective buyers.) What I didn't know, however, was that when the cabinet members of an outgoing administration leave office, they pay a nominal fee and take the chairs with them, so when Nixon and the Republicans came in, it was necessary to buy new chairs. The new administration had a new interior decorator, and they wound up buying chairs from a different company. Anyway, regardless of the embarrassment I may have suffered, Jim McTernan enjoyed his White House visit immensely.

Some years after Nixon had left the White House in disgrace, he was the guest speaker at a luncheon I attended sponsored by Morgan Stanley, one of New York's important investment banking houses. Morgan Stanley was headed by Bob Baldwin during the time that I was CEO of S&H. Every year Bob would host an extremely lavish and tasty Christmas luncheon for fifty or sixty prominent New York businessmen, many of them clients of Morgan Stanley. Bob made it a point to have a distinguished political or military figure as the honored guest. One year it was the chief of naval operations, for example, and this particular year it was Richard Nixon. Before lunch, everyone gathered in a meeting room for drinks and hors d'oeuvres. We then filed into Morgan Stanley's private dining room to hear Nixon speak. We were seated at six or seven tables, with perhaps seven or eight people to a table. Nixon was in the process of rehabilitating himself, making a comeback of sorts through his political writings. He delivered a truly remarkable address, very thoughtful and clear. I was struck by how knowledgeable he was and how intently interested in United States foreign affairs. He gave one of the most fascinating and comprehensive discussions of the relationship between this country and the Soviet Union that I've ever heard.

Indeed, Nixon was an incredible public speaker. A year or two before he died, he gave a lakeside talk at the Bohemian Grove, which has become legendary. It was said to have been one of the best lakeside talks ever. He was a member of Cave Man, my camp, and the camp hosted a luncheon for him. Unfortunately, that year I couldn't get there early enough to hear Nixon; my son-in-law Paul Elston (my guest that year) and I arrived two or three days after he left. But from what I heard, invitations were much sought after and the event was very well attended. Nixon left an excellent impression at the Bohemian Grove that summer. In some respects, it was his last hurrah.

CHAPTER FOURTEEN

Chairman and CEO of The Sperry and Hutchinson Company in the Late 1960s

The late 1960s were exciting and unsettling years in American history, years of change and turmoil. I had close and constant personal connections to the debates over the unrest of the younger generation and the war in Vietnam. At one point during the 1960s I was the father of four teenagers, and later my son Rick would be a combat soldier in Vietnam. But the late 1960s were also busy and eventful years in terms of the business at S&H and my experiences during that period.

I had been CEO of The Sperry and Hutchinson Company since June 1962, and I became chairman of the board in January 1966. But neither date really sticks in my mind, because I had been de facto chairman and CEO for several years before formally assuming those positions, even while I continued to be president of the Company. I took on more roles within the Company because of my responsibilities as president, because of my family position, and also because the senior Beineckes began to bow out of the picture operationally as they became older. I'd defer to them and consult with them, but the daily activities of the Company were left to me. Even though my uncle Ed was the titular CEO of S&H, his near-total absence and my father's other involvements meant I was in effect the chairman and CEO. The president of a company is supposed to be the chief operating officer, carrying out the business activities of the firm. The chief executive officer must give shape to the enterprise and direct day-to-day operations, and the chairman of the board should work with and cultivate the board if it is to serve the company well. The line between president and CEO is not always easy to define, and sometimes their relations need to be clarified either by the board or by an outside consultant—in our case by our principal outside consultant, the firm of Cresap, McCormick & Padgett.

Even after I was named chairman of the board, I continued to use only the title of president until March 1967, when I thought Frank Rossi should be made president of the Company. Even though he was the longtime senior executive vice president of S&H, Rossi was really the chief operating officer, and we had divided the top responsibilities between us for some time. We complemented each other quite well. Frank was excellent at making S&H's day-to-day operating decisions, he knew the Company inside and out, he had superb organizational skills and a finely tuned mathematical mind. I had the legal and inter-personal skills, and we had a good working relationship. As our chief S&H economist, Gene Beem, commented, "Bill Beinecke's energies were focused on creating the corporate culture, being a spokesman for S&H, and giving strategic direction to the Company. He delegated much of the responsibility for running the business to Frank Rossi and then Frank's successors." As I wrote to my uncle Edwin, Frank's promotion would also have a good effect within the Company, because it would demonstrate that you didn't have to bear the name Beinecke to get to the top. After Frank became president, I shifted over to using the title chairman of the board and continued as chief executive officer, and thereafter we were set up on a much better framework organizationally.

A large part of my goal in creating the overall corporate culture of S&H was to try to convert a colorful but rather undisciplined outfit into a professional organization. By the time I became chairman, many of the old guard salesmen—men like George Schirer (whom I succeeded as president), Herb Newman, Elmo Pearson, George Sirback, and Walter Whitnack—were passing from the scene. Many of them had been with the Company since it was very small. As Jim Mills recalls, those old salesmen "were marvelous, just marvelous. I always thought of them as bandits, not in the sense that they stole money, but just that they had their own colorful, semi-lawless, Wild West culture." By the late 1960s, however, the Company had revenues of more than half a billion dollars annually. It had grown and diversified enormously, and needed a new kind of professional management. As the old salesmen retired, I replaced them with younger, more professional managers, most of them with advanced degrees. I hired George Dixon, a graduate of Harvard Business School, as chief of finance, and brought in men of the caliber of Jim Mills and Fred Collins. There were still plenty of salesmen in the top ranks, notably Jackson Smith, who was a dynamo but was also more comfortable than the older salesmen had been in the more structured and less freewheeling organization that S&H became as it grew. He was as rough and ready as the older generation of salesmen, but while none of them had been to college, Jackson Smith was a graduate of Georgia Tech.

Even so, when the old characters retired, we sent them off in style. When George Sirback reached retirement age, we gave him a sendoff at the "21" Club, up in the Hunt Room with its animal trophies. Because he was head of the southwestern region, we had all the guests remove the bow ties from their tuxedos and replaced them with cowboy-type bolo string ties, and everyone donned ten-gallon hats. As chairman of the program, instead of rapping a gavel to get everyone's attention, I fired off blanks from a six-shooter! We had a lot of good times at S&H, even in our more professional era.

In November 1966, the undersecretary of the navy invited me and about ten other people to take a VIP cruise aboard the carrier USS *Enterprise* from the Naval Air Station at Alameda, California, to the Pacific Fleet Headquarters in Pearl Harbor. I was happy to receive the invitation, not only because it was a chance to revisit my old naval haunts but because I wanted to hear from the top military brass about the war in Vietnam. By then the war had begun to dominate the headlines and to provoke antiwar demonstrations on college campuses across the land. It was an interesting trip. My traveling companions included Gus Levy, who was then the senior partner at Goldman Sachs, and K. J. Luke, who was head of the Hawaii National Bank, a bank catering to the Chinese population of the islands. We were addressed by some impressive military personnel, including General Victor Krulak, commander of the Fleet Marine Forces in the Pacific, whose explanations of why we were winning the war in Vietnam were particularly convincing. I was also pleased to become friends with K. J. Luke, who was quite a character. His parents were Chinese immigrants, and he had held a wartime job as a steward in the officers' club at Pearl Harbor. K. J. had the prescience to realize that the unutilized land that then separated Pearl Harbor from downtown Honolulu would someday be developed, and he bought up as much of it as he could after the close of the war. When the former wasteland was bought up and converted to industrial use, K. J. became a wealthy man.

I wanted to learn more about the United States effort in Vietnam because Rick was at the Marine Corps Officer Candidate School in Quantico, Virginia, preparing to fight in Vietnam. In 1966, when he had graduated from Yale, Rick decided to volunteer, along with a large group of his classmates. After spending the summer sailing to Bermuda and vacationing in Jackson Hole, Wyoming, he reported to the Marine Corps OCS at Quantico in October. We attended his commissioning ceremony there in November. In June 1967, after completing the Marine Corps Basic School in Quantico, he left for Vietnam, where he served with the First Battalion, First Marines, First Marine Division.

At the time I approved of the American intervention in South Vietnam. I believed that this nation was engaged in a terrible struggle against Communism and had embarked upon the proper course in entering the war. As it happened, Betty's uncle was the famous Presbyterian leader the Reverend Dr. Eugene Carson Blake, who had married Betty's aunt Valina Gillespie. He was the stated clerk (i.e., the chief executive officer) of the United Presbyterian Church in the USA; among ourselves we occasionally referred to him as the "pope" of the Presbyterians. The leader of the National Council of Churches, he later became the head of the World Council of Churches. He was a wonderful man, and a big man in all senses of the word; he had played football as an undergraduate at Princeton. He had the ear of presidents and statesmen, as well as of the general public, and was an early and outspoken opponent of the Vietnam war. This was a matter on which we respectfully but firmly disagreed, and I wrote to Gene in 1967 that "I am satisfied that our commitment in South Vietnam was properly and honorably given, and that in the long view of humanity, the United States is pursuing the correct policy." I have since reassessed my view, and regard the US involvement in Vietnam as having been ill-advised. In the late 1960s, however, I believed in the war, and I'm still proud of Rick for deciding to enlist. Betty was more dubious about the value of the American intervention, but she, too, was proud of Rick's decision. We both knew what it meant for the nation to be at war, and we believed that military service was the right thing to do.

Of course we were concerned for Rick's safety and welfare, as any parents would be with a son in the military in a wartime situation. I remember having an unsettling conversation on this subject with my friend Bob Baldwin, then head of Morgan Stanley. Bob and I would often meet on the train. Bob had been in Washington, D.C., as secretary of the navy, and by this time was back in New York at Morgan Stanley. One day he said to me, "Bill, I have very good connections in Washington. Don't you worry. I know about your son out there in Vietnam, and when *it* happens, I'll let you know." Well, with Lieutenant Rick Beinecke then in the Marine Corps in an exposed position, I didn't think that this was a very kind thing for him to say—but one has to know

Bob Baldwin to understand that he didn't mean it the way it sounded. When I later mentioned the comment to some of his friends, they all said, "Isn't that just like Bob?"

Rick became eligible for some well-deserved R&R after six months in an advanced position in Vietnam, and Betty and I flew to New Zealand, hoping to rendezvous with him in Sydney, Australia, in February 1968. Rick's leave seemed perfectly timed to coincide with my January 1968 visit to the South Pole—surely one of my life's most memorable and exhilarating experiences. After I had returned from Antarctica to New Zealand, Betty and I were able to meet up with my goddaughter Penny Bull Davies and her husband, Peter, and my parents, who were cruising the South Pacific aboard a large passenger liner, the *Kungsholm*.

I became particularly anxious to see Rick when, by chance and serendipity, Betty and I met R. W. "Johnny" Apple, Jr., and his then wife, Edie, as we were all attempting an arduous trek along the Tasman Glacier. They were on their way home to New York after three years in Saigon, where Johnnie had been chief of the *New York Times* bureau and Edie had served in the Saigon embassy, one of two women in the US Foreign Service there. Her arm and face bore scars testifying to the 1965 bombing of the embassy. When we were safely back in our hotel that evening, Betty and I dined with the Apples and asked them many questions about Vietnam. Their appraisal of the situation was discouraging and even alarming. Johnnie's business was to study and analyze the Vietnam situation. He thought the US position there was terrible— untenable and likely to degenerate further. He felt that the country's policy in Vietnam was being dictated by men whose mentalities were frozen in World War II and who did not understand the contemporary situation in South Asia. Nonetheless, he agreed that our commitment there meant that we couldn't pull out, but he felt that a compromise was all that could be hoped for. It was a pessimistic assessment, and one that made us more eager than ever to join up with our son in Sydney. After a few years, Johnny and Edie grew apart and eventually separated permanently. Johnny remarried. He and his second wife Betsey are good friends of ours.

Betty and I traveled to various towns and cities in New Zealand, including Queenstown, Te Anau, Wellington, Hamilton, and Ngaruawahia. All were enjoyable visits, but colored somewhat by the bad news filtering in about the situation in Vietnam and the American stock market decline. In Paihia, I was reunited with my old friend John Bull at his home on the beautiful subtropical Bay of Islands. He was just as lively, just as curious, and just as interested in everything as when I had first encountered him and Bill Rathbone aboard a Canadian Pacific train to Vancouver way back in 1936. When Betty and I arrived in Auckland in early February 1968, we received word from Rick in Hue, South Vietnam, telling us he had been promoted to acting commanding officer (or CO) of his company. We proceeded on to Australia with great excitement.

Alas, we reached Sydney only to learn that Rick had canceled his leave. He had voluntarily postponed the R&R to which he was entitled because of the seriousness of the North Vietnamese Tet Offensive then under way, and because of his new role as CO of his company. Naturally, we were terribly disappointed, and also quite worried. The Vietnamese Communists, on January 31, 1968, had launched a massive attack to coincide with Tet, the lunar new year, a Vietnamese national holiday. Tens of thousands of enemy troops invaded more than a hundred South Vietnamese cities and towns, and Vietcong commandos even stormed the American embassy in Saigon and killed American soldiers there before they were repulsed. There was particularly fierce hand-to-hand, door-to-door fighting between American marines and Communist forces in Hue, which was especially frightening to Betty and me, since we knew that Rick was in combat in the area and in an exposed position. Rick and I have discussed his service in Vietnam a little in subsequent years, but he has never said much of anything about his experience in the Tet Offensive; I think it must have been grim.

For his service in the face of that attack, Rick was awarded a Bronze Star with a combat V, the same award granted to me for service in World War II. The award states that "As a platoon Commander with Company D, First Lieutenant Beinecke distinguished himself by his exemplary and highly professional performance of duty. . . . Reassigned as Commanding Officer at the beginning of the enemy's Tet Offensive, he successfully coordinated the defense of four bridges located on vital National Route One, despite numerous hostile attacks. Personally leading a force composed of Marines and Popular Forces units and Civilian Irregular Defense Groups, his superior tactical skill and leadership were responsible for routing a main force Viet Cong unit from Phu Bai Village." Although the Tet Offensive decimated the Vietcong and cost the North Vietnamese heavy casualties, many commentators interpreted it as an American defeat. Certainly it dealt a major blow to the credibility of the Johnson administration. Johnson and his spokesmen had been proclaiming that victory was at hand, but Tet helped turn American public opinion against the war.

I heard little further news of Rick until the summer of 1968, during my first visit ever to the Bohemian Grove. I was the guest of Randy Crossley, whom I'd seen again during my 1966 trip to Hawaii on the carrier *Enterprise*. On that visit, Gus Levy and I had been grateful guests at a splendid Thanksgiving dinner at Randy's beautiful home near Diamond Head. Randy was a prominent man in Hawaii. He had run for governor of Hawaii in the early 1960s, but since he had campaigned as a Republican in that solidly Democratic state, his electoral run was unsuccessful. His wife, Florence Pepperdine Crossley, was the daughter of the man who founded Pepperdine University. For some years, Randy Crossley had been inviting me to join him at the annual summer encampment in the Bohemian Grove at his camp, Midway. I did not know much, if anything, about the Bohemian Grove. Moreover, I'd been too busy to take him up on his offer. I had heard a little bit about it from my Uncle Ed, who had been out there a few times in the early 1960s. It wasn't until I went myself in the summer of 1968 as Randy's guest that I realized how interesting that gathering of prominent and talented men truly is. I later became a member of the Bohemian Club and returned to the Grove each summer for many years.

One day during that first visit, I came back to Randy's camp after a stroll and walked up the steps onto what is known as "The Platform," where everyone sits around and has drinks. A bulletin board was set up, leaning against a big redwood, and there in the middle I saw the characteristic yellow paper of a Western Union telegram. People of my generation could always identify one, even from a distance, especially those of us who had been through World War II and had relied on telegrams for the communication of important information. I walked up to the board to find out whom the telegram was for and found that it was addressed to me. I opened the envelope and saw this message: "Lieutenant Beinecke is home."

Until that moment, as far as I was aware Rick was still in Vietnam. Now I knew that he had served his thirteen months and made his way back home. The Bohemian Grove is very busy during weekends, but on weekdays it is relatively quiet. On that particular weekday afternoon, there was no one but me in the Midway campsite. I started walking down what's called River Road by myself en route to dinner when along came a group of three or four men heading in the same direction. I said to one of them, "Do you realize that I'm the happiest man out of all the two thousand people in this place tonight?" (This was a bit of an exaggeration, since the encampment may reach two thousand people on weekends, but it was a moment of high excitement.) The man I'd addressed didn't know me and I didn't know him, but he looked at me and replied, "That's quite a claim." "Yes," I said, "and I can support it." I pulled out the telegram and showed it to them, and the men read it and said, "You're right," and enthusiastically clapped me on the shoulder. Even today, I still get a little emotional when I think about it.

The late 1960s was a time of great change, and few people emerged from the decade untouched by the confusion and excitement of those years. My family was no exception. Rick had his experiences in Vietnam. Frances was at Yale during the most intense period of student protests there. John and Sarah, too, were affected by the events and movements of the time, while we older goats were looking out on the campuses and wondering what had happened to the placid world we had known. "What's the matter with the younger generation?" we asked each other. "Why do they act this way? Don't they know they don't know anything? Don't they know that they are supposed to receive all wisdom from us?" And so on and so on.

John graduated from Westminster in 1965 and entered Yale in the fall. He had a good time there and acquired the social graces. He majored in political science, played some intramural soccer, and was a member of the Fence Club. He was in Berkeley College and shared a suite there with friends who were Orthodox Jews from New York; he had to open the door for them on the Sabbath. John traveled in a much faster social set than Rick had, which may have had something to do with the changes at Yale in the late 1960s as well as with John's personality. In the fall of 1967, for example, John and some of his friends went from a hockey game at Madison Square Garden to a white tie and tails debutante ball at The Plaza Hotel. They arrived in a pink limousine driven by a real live Playboy bunny. In his senior year, John was part of a group that lived off campus in a rented house in Branford. He met his first wife there, Lynn Hutchings, who was then an undergraduate at Briarcliff College. John had some awful experiences at Yale as well. One of his friends took his own life, and another friend was killed in an auto accident while driving back to his house in East Haven. It was quite sobering. John graduated from Yale in 1969, at a somber ceremony in which his classmate Mac Thompson addressed the crowd about the need to halt the conflict in Vietnam. John had warned us that he was missing some credits and so would not be receiving his degree at the ceremony. But when he opened up the black folder that he presumed would be empty, there was his degree! John chose not to take advantage of this clerical error, however, and took classes that summer to earn the credits he needed.

At some point during his teenage years, John adopted the view shared by so many of his contemporaries that the war in Vietnam was not a good thing and certainly was not something in which he should get involved. There was a massive shift in undergraduate opinion about the war between the time Rick graduated in 1966 and the time John graduated in 1969. John and I have never discussed this, but our opinions about the war were much closer by the time he graduated from what they had been when he entered. After graduation, John spent a couple of years teaching at the Browning School, a boys' school in New York City. I don't think he had any great urge to be a schoolteacher, but teaching was one way to avoid the draft. Whatever his motivation for taking the job, though, he was a very popular teacher. The students appreciated his wit and personality, and a lot of the boys idolized his sporting prowess and quick mind.

To a greater degree than those of my other children, Sarah's outlook and activities were influenced by the anti-establishment leanings of the late 1960s. There was a widespread feeling of unrest among young people. It was a period of great emotional seizure, the violent reaction of the baby-boom generation against a society that they thought had no regard for the moral issues of the era. Sarah graduated from Dana Hall in 1966 and enrolled at Colorado College in Colorado Springs, the only school she wanted to attend. Colorado College was a major countercultural center in the late 1960s, but there were few places that weren't influenced by countercultural ideas in those years. Sarah was caught up in the movement around her, and was both thrilled and overwhelmed by it. She was also terribly upset when a favorite art teacher was killed in a drunken driving accident. It was too much of a burden. She was an extremely sensitive person, and it just got to her. It was hard on us, too. We felt like she was slipping away from us.

I flew out to see Sarah in April 1967, and we went exploring in Indian country in New Mexico. Colorado was quite far away, however, and we didn't see her anywhere near as often as we would have liked. We knew something was amiss when she came home in the summer of 1967. Sarah was and is a marvelously warm human being, and ordinarily when she would come home she would transform the house into a vibrant and exciting place. But now she was not her usual exuberant self. She was not bubbling over with excitement about her first year at school. Some of the sparkle came back later that summer when Betty and I spent a month with her and Frances in Hawaii, but her troubles were waiting for her when she returned to college. She stayed at Colorado College only until Christmas of 1967, then left for San Francisco, where she enrolled at the Art Institute. While at Colorado College, Sarah had fallen in love with a young man named Reid Will Smith. It was an unstable combination, but there was nothing to be done about it. She left San Francisco to return to Colorado Springs to be near Reid, who had been drafted into the United States Army. We didn't fight her. We felt that we had to be supportive, or we would alienate her forever. Sarah and I wrote each other very long letters during that period, and although I was concerned about her, in some ways that brought us closer together.

Frances had graduated from the Ethel Walker School in 1967. After spending several years in the backwoods of Simsbury, she was determined that after she left Ethel Walker's she would get out of the boondocks and go to a big city university, so she enrolled at the University of Pennsylvania. Philadelphia was perhaps too much of a big-city environment; when she entered Penn there was a great outcry because a man running a shop in the vicinity of the campus was molesting children. Franny hadn't spent any time in a city, and she found it rather a shock. She didn't like Penn much, and for the first year or so she kept leaving town to go up to Boston, where her boyfriend was an undergraduate at Harvard. But it was at Penn that Frances also got to know Sarah Bates, who is still one of her best friends in the world.

In the spring of 1969, Yale announced that it would admit women as undergraduates for the first time in the institution's 268-year history. Without our knowledge, Frances applied to Yale as a transfer and got in. She just announced it to us one day. Of course I was very pleased! Frances enjoyed Yale tremendously. She was a member of Ezra Stiles College, a member of the Elizabethan Club, and took part in a number of dramatic activities. She majored in history and was a fine student. She really couldn't get enough of Yale's academic offerings, and she received a terrific education. Frances will remain a student all her life.

Yale, like most other universities across the country, was caught up in the political strife of the late 1960s and early 1970s. A number of potentially perilous situations arose during the two years Frances was a student there, most notably the May Day demonstration of 1970. We invited her home to get her out of the fray, and she did agree to come for part of the weekend. All in all, however, Yale's student protests and uprisings were contained more effectively than similar ones elsewhere. After all, these were the years of the commotion at San Francisco State, the blowup at Columbia, the Kent State shootings, and that frightening building takeover at Cornell, with students toting rifles and bandoliers.

It was a rough and dangerous time. Yale was extremely fortunate to have Kingman Brewster as president. Those were difficult years for a man in that spot, but Kingman was amazing. If Harvard, Cornell, Columbia, and other universities had had a man like Kingman at the helm, I believe they could have avoided the disastrous outcomes of that period.

During Frances's years at Yale, there was a lot in the news about the Patty Hearst kidnapping. I was concerned that anyone with the last name Beinecke might be a likely target on a campus where the Beinecke Library was such a prominent landmark, so I asked Louis Cappiello, then the head of the Yale Campus Police, to keep his eye on Frances. I don't know whether he put any more of a security watch on her than he did on any other Yale student, but I found it reassuring to have spoken to him.

In the late 1960s, my friend Hugo Meyer asked me to deliver the commencement speech at Union College in Cranford, New Jersey. I agreed, and I jokingly told him that my topic was going to be "Why We're All So Mad at Society." It was an offhand comment but unfortunately one that was taken seriously, as I discovered upon being introduced to the audience at the graduation ceremony! I did my best to point out that the late 1960s were not the first time that our nation's colleges and universities had been involved in such difficulties. President James Perkins of Cornell, at the height of the crisis at his school in April 1969, pointed out that way back in the 1850s, college enrollment fell off because the academic offerings were not, to use a modern phrase, "relevant." From that discontent came changes that made the schools relevant to their times once again. I expressed the hope that out of the current unrest would come a restructuring that would make our own colleges and universities more responsive to the day's issues. But I also flatly stated my opinion that student protest could be pushed too far, reminding the students that campus unrest might become so acute as to provoke violent repressive reaction. I quoted my friend John Gardner's 1969 speech at Harvard, in which he pointed out that for some dissenters, the call for the destruction of the system was merely taking a position, while for others it was a deadly serious objective. Gardner had cautioned his listeners to remember that "when a social system is destroyed, the resulting chaos is supremely antagonistic to *any* organized purposes, including the purposes of those who initiated the destruction." He added, "Those who would destroy the system also fail to understand that periods of chaos are followed by periods of iron rule." It was apocalyptic talk, but such were the times.

The theme of my speech was that the Vietnam war—and the militant and vocal reactions it inspired on college campuses—would, like the American, French, and Russian Revolutions, someday come to an end. After it was over, the world would be different. Whether it would be better was a different question. The answer to that question, I suggested, depended on whether students could resist the urge to polarize, to divide campus activists on the one hand from those responsible for college and university management on the other. Because the war would pass, it was important to look beyond it, and beyond the anger and turmoil it engendered, by seeking constructive change that would outlast all of these things.

Were the events at the universities in the late 1960s part of a reconstructive process? In some cases, yes. The dialogue in which Kingman Brewster and a few other university administrators engaged with student challengers was not provoked by fear of the number or power of the dissenters but reflected the university's ability to weigh the merits of expressed grievances, even in a highly confused and emotional situation. With some exceptions, the changes sought were long past due. University administrators and faculty for the most part recognized this and took steps accordingly. It was this flexibility, I told the students, that was capable of assuring productive changes and helping us avoid dangerous either-or scenarios.

I thought I gave a pretty good graduation talk, but in looking at the students I learned something about commencement addresses. The students out there are intent solely upon one thing, their graduation, and what is said to them by the graduation speaker doesn't make any difference. For a year or two after the Union College speech, I received requests from colleges all over the country asking me to address their graduating seniors. I guess the colleges were having a devil of a time getting commencement speakers in that era, because some of them even offered me honorariums. I didn't accept any of the invitations, however. The only reason I had agreed to the Union College speech was because Hugo Meyer was a member of the board of that college and it was in my old hometown.

Sarah was married early in the summer of 1969. The ceremony took place in the Central Presbyterian Church near our home in Summit, and the reception was held in a tent on our back lawn. John was married a month after Sarah's wedding, at his bride's girlhood home in West Hartford, Connecticut. Both were delightful family occasions. In July, in between the two weddings, I took Frances out to Long Lake in the Adirondacks to visit my friend and Yale classmate Jonathan

Family photo, Summit, New Jersey, 1969. Left to right: John, Rick, Frances, Bill, Betty, and Sarah Beinecke

Pine. I had been visiting Jonnie at his "camp" (as Adirondack summer homes are called) since 1938. By 1969, Jonnie's camp was somewhat less primitive than it had been in the 1930s; that is to say, it still didn't have electricity, but it did have running water and he had installed an indoor flush toilet to complement the outside privy. As Frances and I were sitting on the Pines' porch, Jonnie pointed to a spot across the lake and said, "See that land around Buck Mountain? It's for sale. Would you like to join a group to keep it out of the hands of developers?" Frances and I investigated, and it turned out that a wonderful tract of Adirondack wilderness was indeed available. I made an offer which was immediately accepted. The tract after a survey turned out to be a little over 3,000 acres. I soon transferred the ownership to my children, and they own it jointly through a corporation called Langley Park, named after their great-great-grandmother, Susan Butler Langley. Our children have managed the property well. And also through the Langley Park entity, they now own in common our Cape Cod house, which we conveyed to them some years ago.

I hoped that by owning the Long Lake property in common and by working out among themselves how it was to be shared and used, they would be brought closer together, and they were. Frances has made the most extensive use of it. She and Rick built a lean-to, to use the Adirondacks term for any sort of shelter, from primitive to very comfortable. When Charlie Farr, a leading citizen of Long Lake who had first escorted Frances and me around the property, was taken to see it, he whistled and said, "That sure is a lean-to!"—high praise from an Adirondacks old-timer. The Long Lake camp is Frances's paradise. She loves it there and knows all the trails and peaks for miles around. The camp has come a long way since the days of the lean-to. Frances and her husband, Paul, have a lovely main house there now, and several boats, including a gem of an electric boat that is used for quiet sunset cruises around that end of the lake. In 1999, they added a superb guest house so that they now have the ability to put up their family and many friends, something they very much enjoy doing. In August 1999, the family gathered there to help Frances celebrate her fiftieth birthday, a gala occasion for all who attended. While I was there, I was glad to see again an old photograph in Frances's camp showing my father and his brothers Edwin and Walter when they were little boys, together with their older brother Ben and some of his contemporaries, all gathered at a campsite on Long Lake approximately a hundred years ago.

The late 1960s are memorable in American history for their dark events, including the assassinations of Martin Luther King, Jr., and Bobby Kennedy, the riots at the 1968 Democratic Party convention in Chicago, and of course the shadows cast by the war in Vietnam. On the other hand, they were very good years for The Sperry and Hutchinson Company. More supermarkets were using our stamps than ever before and consumer attitudes had never been more favorable; more than four out of five households saved trading stamps. Although competing stamp companies were flooding the market, it was encouraging to note that more people preferred S&H stamps than all six of the next most successful stamps combined.

The S&H Green Stamp service continued to be the most profitable entity of the Company. By the end of the 1960s, Green Stamp sales had grown to $341 million. Domestic stamp service revenue was booming as a result of increases in the use of stamps by both new and existing accounts. The list of varied accounts ranged from the countrywide program for National Car Rental to such newer uses as fueling stations for private and industrial aircraft, bowling lanes and truck stops, not to mention the traditional mainstays like supermarkets, service stations, and pharmacies. Thousands of charitable organizations throughout the country collected our stamps for worthwhile causes like kidney machines for hospitals and Braille readers for libraries, and some civic groups even used Green Stamps to acquire airplanes and zoo animals! The Company issued more than thirty million Ideabook catalogues each year, one of the largest commercial printing orders in the United

States. S&H's 1969 Christmas catalogue for the armed forces in Vietnam and Thailand also brought a good response.

We were holding our own in sales to supermarkets—by far the greatest source of revenue in our stamp operation—despite a proliferation of food discounters. The discounting trend did not seem a source of concern. After all, supermarkets had been the original "discounters" in their day, providing lower prices through volume purchases. When they became well established, supermarkets sought new means to gain distinctiveness and loyal patronage. We believed that trading stamps were still the best method of achieving those goals, and were confident that when discounters had saturated the marketplace, they too would turn to a trading stamp promotion.

We did have a continuing problem in the 1960s with the Blue Chip stamp program, the creation of Safeway, Albertson's, and other major supermarkets in California. The Blue Chip venture, like Gold Strike in Utah and several others around the country, was a nonfranchised stamp program. It was essentially a collusive effort to drive independent trading stamp companies out of business by making nonexclusive stamp plans available to everyone, at a cost lower than that offered by independent companies like S&H. Blue Chip never worked out quite the way its planners intended. By making stamps so widely available in California, Blue Chip created truly remarkable consumer acceptance for the stamp idea. The effect of those large food chains moving to stamps after decades of opposition was to make consumer acceptance and enthusiasm for stamps grow stronger with each passing year. And though Blue Chip was widely available, the value of its program was so thinly spread among so many competitors that none of them secured a perceptible gain. Nonetheless, it was an anticompetitive device intended to damage S&H, as we eventually proved in a successful antitrust case. We retained our number one position, and moved from strength to strength.

S&H's expansion during the 1960s helped drive up our net earnings per share and increased our stock prices as well. In late 1969, S&H purchased a fifty-acre industrial site outside Atlanta, Georgia, where we built a warehouse to replace the one that was serving about a hundred redemption centers in the region. Like our warehouse in Chicago, it was extremely modern and relied on state-of-the-art technology. The Southeast was one of our most rapidly growing marketing areas and the hub of our Bonus Gifts incentive program. We were experimenting with direct-mail marketing, a venture that appeared to hold promise for the future. By 1970 we had substantially reduced operating losses in the United Kingdom, and soon would discontinue the small, unprofitable operation on the Continent. The interior-furnishings group had weathered 1969's economic slowdown. Our two major subsidiaries outside the furnishings group, the State National Bank of Connecticut and the Hens & Kelly department store, were doing well and adding to S&H earnings. Despite the turbulence of the late 1960s, then, we had performed extremely well and looked forward to the 1970s with much optimism. But that decade would bring more challenges than we had anticipated.

CHAPTER FIFTEEN

The Sperry and Hutchinson Company in the 1970s, Retirement, and the Creation of Antaeus Enterprises

he 1970s were turbulent years for The Sperry and Hutchinson Company. It was the most difficult period of the Company's existence since the Depression of the 1930s. After the disastrous oil embargo of 1973–74, the bottom fell out of the trading stamp business, and the Company was afflicted by the difficulties that beset the rest of the national economy. We recovered and even prospered by the end of the decade, largely because S&H had diversified and in effect remade itself as a conglomerate company. But it was a challenge to keep the Company together through the changes of the 1970s.

There were hints of the economic turmoil to come as the decade began. America's long postwar boom was coming to an end, and the stock market was beginning to sputter. Even so, it seemed in 1970 that the decade's main problems would continue to be political. The war in Vietnam continued and even widened after Nixon sent US troops into Cambodia in May 1970. Thousands of demonstrators descended on Yale for the May Day weekend to protest the trial of Black Panther leader Bobby Seale. Yale emerged unscathed from that terribly dangerous situation, due largely to the skillful crisis management of its president, Kingman Brewster. Other universities were not so fortunate. On May 4, four students were shot to death by National Guardsmen at Kent State University in Ohio. That tragic event, combined with outrage at the US intervention in Cambodia, led to student strikes and demonstrations all over the country, some of them peaceful, others not. Earlier that spring, Rick, who had returned from combat in Vietnam, went to Washington, D.C. to participate in a peace march protesting our involvement in the war in Southeast Asia. Frances, who was in New

Haven for part of the May Day weekend, went down to Washington with a number of Yale students to call on members of Congress to talk about the war. Divisions in American society cut more deeply than they had since the Civil War, and it seemed as though the country might actually be on the verge of disintegration. And yet the political polarization of May 1970 was the crest of the wave. By the time Frances graduated from Yale in June 1971, the campus mood had shifted from protest to what my friend Kingman Brewster called "eerie tranquillity," and the national mood was something close to exhaustion.

The problems I had to deal with in the early 1970s were more personal than political. My uncle Edwin Beinecke died in January 1970, not long after his eighty-fourth birthday. He really had not been well since he'd had an attack of ill health in Paris in the late 1950s, after which he had come into his office at S&H only sporadically, principally for directors' meetings. And in the late 1960s, his health had deteriorated further when he suffered a stroke one day while he was having lunch with me in the S&H officers' dining room. It was just before a meeting of the board of directors. We had been conversing when all of a sudden he stopped in midsentence and became motionless, the fork in his hand frozen halfway between the plate and his mouth. He continued to look right at me with his bright blue eyes, but it was as though he had turned to a statue. I realized that something had overtaken him, though I didn't know what. I asked somebody to call 911 and asked somebody else to clear the main dining room so my uncle could be carried out. Someone then had the good sense to suggest that I get a private ambulance service to take my uncle up to the Columbia-Presbyterian Hospital, where he was known and could get a private room, rather than have him taken to the city hospital by the 911 people. That was good thinking. When the emergency team arrived, they ascertained that Uncle Edwin had suffered a stroke, and the doctor gave him medication to bring down his blood pressure. An attendant took a reading on his blood pressure and said, "It just dropped sixty points." And then Uncle Edwin, whom everybody had thought was on the verge of death, opened one eye, looked at the doctor, and said, "Sell!" My uncle was a great man. I rode in the ambulance with him to the hospital, and I asked Tom McCarthy if he would preside at the directors' meeting in my absence. That was one of only two directors' meetings I missed in all the years I served at S&H; the other was the time I went to the South Pole.

Uncle Edwin survived the stroke, although in a much-weakened condition. His mind remained steady, but he lacked the strength to read or make extended conversation. His death in January 1970 was not unexpected, but it was still a blow. I'd had my disagreements with my uncle, and there is no doubt that his conservatism and his reluctance to relinquish the reins made my job as head of S&H more difficult and cost the Company some opportunities. But I had also relied heavily on his wisdom and long experience.

And then my father died in July 1971. He had not been the same after he'd had a stroke in 1966, and while he remained functional and lucid for a time, he wasn't really himself after that, particularly in his last two or three years. But I was very close to my father, and I felt his loss keenly. When I got the call telling me that my father was failing fast, I was with Betty and my friend Hugo Meyer and his wife, Liza, on a salmon fishing expedition on Anticosti Island in Canada. We were deep in the woods, and it was not an easy task to get to my parents' home in Great Barrington, Massachusetts. Betty and I ended up taking a truck down a long dirt road to Anticosti's little airport and then chartering a small plane. By the time we arrived in Great Barrington, my father had already died, and I had to comfort my mother as best I could and assist her as much as possible with the funeral arrangements.

My father's memorial service was held at Great Barrington. I was one of several speakers. I recited the poem "Abou Ben Adhem" by Leigh Hunt, an English poet of the first half of the nineteenth century. In the poem, Abou Ben Adhem awakes one night to see an angel writing in a book of gold "the names of those who love the Lord." Ben Adhem asks, "Is mine one?" and is told, "Nay, not so." He responds, "I pray thee, then,/ Write me as one that loves his fellow men." The poem concludes: "The angel wrote, and vanished. The next night/ It came again with a great wakening light,/ And showed the names whom love of God had blest,/ And lo! Ben Adhem's name led all the rest." Fritz Liebert, the first head of the Beinecke Library, later remonstrated with me for quoting a lesser poet like Leigh Hunt, but the poem seems to me a perfect description of my father. In time, I got over my grief, mostly because I knew my father would have wanted me to. But I think of him often, and there have been occasions in the years since his death when I would have liked his guidance. It's not that I necessarily find myself saying, "I wish I could take this question to my father," but when I'm trying to make a decision, I find it helpful to imagine how he would have reacted to the problem and dealt with the situation. And I think the technological advances of the past twenty-five years would have fascinated him.

My father's death marked the passing of the last of the three brothers who assumed leadership of The Sperry and Hutchinson Company in the 1920s and oversaw its phenomenal growth. When Frank Rossi retired in 1971, the Company lost another link to the past. I promoted Fred Collins to replace Rossi as president and chief operating officer. Fred had been associated with S&H since 1953, when he was an attorney with Casey, Lane & Mittendorf, my old law firm. He joined the Company in 1965 as vice president of the legal and public affairs division. I liked Fred, and I respected him for his incisive mind and his integrity. He also had a certain inflexibility that sometimes proved a liability when S&H's fortunes took a turn for the worse.

The Company's revenues declined in 1970, for the first time in eight years. The drop was not major, but it did reflect the economic downturn that was becoming evident in the rest of the country. More worrisome was the falling off of trading stamp revenue from its all-time high in 1969. There were several factors behind the decline of trading stamps in the 1970s. In the first place, part of what had made S&H so successful after World War II was that it benefited from the pent-up demand that had accumulated during the war, when there was rationing and little production for civilian use. The merchandise that S&H offered were things that people wanted and were unable to buy during the war years: irons, lamps, and small household appliances. Even in the 1950s, households were still catching up with the deferred consumption of the war years. People who had been through the Depression and the war were more willing to wait before making their purchases, to put aside instant gratification and save for the future. After incomes rose during the boom of the 1950s and 1960s, people became less willing to go through the inconvenience of saving stamps and making the trip to the redemption center. Their time horizons shortened. It was just a lot easier to go right out and buy whatever it was they wanted. You could see that happening even in the 1960s.

A second factor in the decline of trading stamps was inflation, which accelerated in the 1960s and 1970s. Inflation caused increased price sensitivity. There was more price awareness, and retailers became more savvy in making a two or three percent price reduction in a few high-volume grocery items look like more. Some supermarkets dropped trading stamps to be better able to meet the competition of the food discounters. The 1960s also saw the rise of the "closed-door" discount store, where customers had to become "members" in order to make purchases. That arrangement came into being to get around the fair-trade laws that set fixed prices for particular commodities. The discounters sold items at a lower markup than the fair-trade laws stipulated, so that an item such as an electric mixer that sold for a fair-trade price of eighteen dollars would be available for fourteen dollars at a discount store. That practice paved the way for closed-door discounters like Price Club and Sam's and for non-membership stores like Kmart and Wal-Mart as well. Because the fair-trade laws had been used as a club with which to attack trading stamps, S&H was opposed to them. I believed in the arguments I made against those laws as the Company's general counsel, and I still believe they amounted to an anticompetitive, price-fixing restraint of trade. Ironically, though, the fair-trade laws also worked to S&H's benefit. They helped keep up the prices of things like small appliances, and so they made the gifts in the S&H catalogue more valuable. The attractiveness of our redemption center merchandise fell when those products became available at the lower-markup discount outlets.

Then in October 1973, the Arab oil-producing nations imposed a total ban on oil exports to the United States. In part this was retaliation for American support of Israel in the Arab-Israeli war and in part it was a strategy by the Organization of Petroleum Exporting Countries (OPEC) cartel to raise oil prices. It was not long before the energy crisis hit home in America, and the result was skyrocketing gasoline prices and long lines at the pump, when there was any gas at all to be had. Peter Cooper remembers sitting in the office of Gene Beem, our staff economist, toying with worst-case scenarios. Gasoline had been selling at thirty cents a gallon, and Peter asked Gene how high he thought the price might go. Gene thought that ultimately it might exceed a dollar a gallon. Everyone thought he must be kidding. But his prediction came true, and the result was the loss of almost all our service station accounts.

For reasons that remained unclear to me, many US oil companies had long been opposed to Green Stamps as a promotional device. Perhaps it was because we were never the client of a particular oil company but instead contracted with local filling stations. When we were dealing with supermarkets, the hostility of the chains that found themselves excluded from our stamp program was more than offset by the enthusiastic support of participating merchants. But in the case of the service stations, the hostility was widespread and originated in high places in the oil industry. Years before, when I was still general counsel, the situation was unpleasant enough that one S&H lawyer who also represented an oil company resigned because he felt that in representing both companies he was placed in a conflict of interest situation. (At the urging of Charles Wesley Dunn, I flew out to see him in California in an effort to convince him otherwise but my mission proved fruitless—and exhausting in those pre-jet days.) Nonetheless, we continued to enjoy a good relationship with the filling stations and their representatives. While contracting with supermarket chain A meant we would not contract with supermarket chain B, the filling stations were individually signed by traveling salesmen. This contributed to the good business relationship that existed until OPEC began imposing its oil embargo.

The immediate effect of the embargo was that filling stations no longer needed stamps to draw customers. The demand for gas was greater than the supply, and cars were lining up around the block. Filling stations could charge as much as they wanted for gas, when they could meet customer demand at all; why should they pay for trading stamps? Some of them still regarded stamps as a helpful sales device, but many more threw stamps out the window. In the years immediately before the oil crisis, service stations had represented a quarter of our stamp revenues and much of the Company's most profitable high-markup, low-volume business. Almost overnight, we lost nearly a hundred million dollars of service station revenues. And when the gas stations stopped offering stamps, trading stamps also became a lot less important at the supermarkets. S&H continued to sell millions of dollars of Green Stamps throughout the 1970s, and we regained a few service station accounts after the oil embargo was lifted in March 1974, but the bloom was off the rose. It was the beginning of the long decline of the Green Stamp, and of every other kind of trading stamp as well. I'm almost glad that my father and Uncle Edwin weren't around to see it, because they believed so deeply in the value of trading stamps. There was nothing that anyone could do to offset the decline. And, to make matters worse, in May 1974, Jackson Smith, the president of our Green Stamp division and perhaps our most able salesman, died suddenly at a tragically young age.

The year 1974 was the most difficult one the Company had weathered since the Depression. The full impact of the energy crisis hit our trading stamp operations, and other aspects of our business were also severely affected by the oil embargo. Our furnishings division, for example, sustained rapid cost increases in petroleum-based synthetics and other raw materials, which led to the furnishing industry's worst recession in forty years. And all our operations were affected by the terrible recession, the phenomenon known as "stagflation" (a combination of inflation and stagnant economic growth), and the decline of the stock market that went on day after day, like Chinese water torture.

Our Company's fortunes began to improve slowly in the latter half of 1975, though our profits were offset by the $8 million we paid to our competitor Curtis Carlson to settle the lawsuit he had brought against us back in 1972. It was a sorrowful story. Carlson, who was a very able man, had created the Gold Bond Stamp Company, based in Minneapolis. It brought a private antitrust suit under the Sherman Act against The Sperry and Hutchinson Company. Gold Bond was not really a serious competitor of S&H and had never bothered us much. It was like a gnat: annoying and distracting, but not dangerous. Gold Bond did indeed have difficulty competing against S&H in the open marketplace, but that was because they were not in our class, not because we had done anything illegal.

Unfortunately, Carlson was able to achieve, through the legal process, the success against S&H that had eluded him in business competition. His opening came with a decision against us by the Federal Trade Commission in 1972. The FTC had been engaged in proceedings against S&H since 1962. We won the case at the hearing examiner level, and the US Supreme Court agreed that S&H did not illegally restrain competition. In 1972, however, the full commission of the FTC found that certain of S&H's practices were anticompetitive. The practices cited were minor details that were easily corrected, so the finding did not constitute a major loss for the Company. But it raised the issue of unfair competitive practices, and suddenly we found ourselves surrounded by antitrust sharks. The shark representing Gold Bond was one of the better ones. He came into S&H and began a long, exhaustive discovery proceeding, turning over everything he could find. It was customary for each major S&H account to cut its own deal, and the Gold Bond shark uncovered deals with some of the major customers that perhaps were not as upright as they should have been.

More's the pity, Curt Carlson's lawsuit was placed in the federal district court in Minneapolis. Carlson wanted something on the order of $20 million compensation for the alleged harm done to his trading stamp company by our alleged anticompetitive actions. Under the terms of the particular provision of the antitrust law that Carlson had invoked against us, if the jury found for the plaintiff, the damages were tripled. (We knew all about that triple damages provision, because we had ourselves used it in our antitrust suit against the Blue Chip stamp company.) So I was looking at a potential $60 million suit that would be played out in Carlson's backyard, with sympathetic jurors responsive to the hometown boy's desire to reach into the deep pockets of a big national company. In addition, the Gold Bond shark had dug up dirt on the sexual indiscretions of certain S&H salespeople, information that might have done some damage to the Company's reputation if it became public. So I decided to settle the case. I flew out to Chicago, a neutral location, and Carlson came down from Minneapolis to have lunch in my hotel room. He was pleasant enough but absolutely unbudgeable. So in 1975, we settled the suit for $8 million, at a net cost of $3.9 million. Carlson subsequently created the Radisson Hotel chain, and every time I pass one of his hotels, I think, I know where the seed money for that hotel chain came from.

I don't want to convey the impression that the 1970s were years of unrelieved, gloomy financial crisis for S&H, because they were not. My work never ceased to be busy, hectic, and fun. The Company had record breaking years in 1970, 1971, and 1972, as it did after 1976. Its total revenues were just over $500 million in 1970, and by the end of the decade they would approach $1 billion. Despite the economic difficulties of the era, we had reached about the 300 mark in the *Fortune* 500 list by the end of the 1970s. We never stopped paying a dividend to our stockholders. And even in the less prosperous years, particularly 1973-76, the Company became stronger. We engaged in much more systematic strategic planning than we had before, we asked ourselves harder questions, and we got rid of units that were not performing. Turbulent times provide the true test of an executive's ability to make tough decisions, and I think we came through that test fairly well.

The decline of trading stamps vindicated the decision to diversify the Company that had been taken back in the 1960s. S&H would have collapsed in the mid-1970s if it still had rested entirely on the trading stamp business. The subsidiaries we had acquired, particularly the State National Bank and the Bayly, Martin & Fay insurance brokerage, proved to be our salvation during the hard times. In the tough years between 1973 and 1976, the State National Bank provided about twenty percent of the Company's earnings during seven consecutive quarters. It was a first-class financial institution run by first-class people. Bayly, Martin & Fay also held strong. Insurance companies do well in difficult economic times because people can't stop insuring their investments, no matter what the economic climate. And by 1977, the furnishings division had grown to be our largest division, and it experienced some banner years in the late 1970s. There was also great camaraderie at S&H. Our people liked one another and worked well together. I continued to hold golf outings for the Company's executives at the Morris County Golf Club. Those events were marked by great fun, friendship, and a few happy, silly antics, like the time someone teed up a fake golf ball made out of soap for John Beinert and it exploded when he hit it off the tee! That spirit of fun and friendship added immeasurably to the cohesiveness and effectiveness of the operation.

The 1970s were also rather happy years for our family. Rick had intended to be an architect, but the experience of Vietnam caused him to reevaluate his plans and he decided to become a lawyer. He enrolled at the University of Virginia Law School, graduated in 1972, passed the New York Bar, and, after a month spent hiking in Afghanistan, started work with the New York law firm of Hughes, Hubbard & Reed. The firm put him on a sequestered investigation of Weis Securities, a brokerage house that had gone bankrupt. Rick was basically locked up with the papers for a year, and really couldn't stand it; he felt he was in purgatory. So he resigned and went to work for the South Street Seaport, where he contributed greatly to that institution's early years. One tremendous benefit of Rick's time at Hughes, Hubbard & Reed was that there he met Candace Krugman, who later became his wife. Rick joined S&H in 1974 and quickly proceeded to put his legal training and experience with the South Street Seaport to good use. S&H also sent Rick to the Harvard Business School's Program for Management Development, a thirteen-week course for business professionals. It certainly added a special extra dimension to my experience at S&H to know that Rick was part of the Company and was taking on greater executive responsibilities.

In the early 1970s, after a few years of teaching, John wanted to follow his heart's desire by going into the wine business, since he was (and still is) highly knowledgeable on the subject. Unfortunately, none of the wine importers and distributors were willing to hire him without experience. It was the old chicken-and-egg conundrum: John felt that his future was in this line of work, but couldn't get a job. So, in a move that I thought demonstrated great resourcefulness and audacity, he and his then wife, Lynn, left New York and went to France for a year. John lived in the small town of Talence and studied oenology at the University of Bordeaux, acquiring a working knowledge of French in the process. It was a risky move, but one that paid off. When he returned to New York, he found a job working for Schieffelin & Company, one of the major importers of wine and spirits. He was very successful there and ultimately became the national sales manager. There, too, he met Gaily Wurtzel, the most attractive young woman who became his wife. This was a special dividend not unlike the marital bonus Rick derived from his days at Hughes, Hubbard & Reed! Schieffelin also sent John to the Harvard Business School PMD program, two years after Rick had graduated from it. Both of them found the program a valuable experience.

After Sarah's husband, Reid, finished his army service in Germany in 1971, they moved to Santa Cruz, California, and took classes at the university there. Then they returned to Colorado Springs, where Reid reenrolled at Colorado College. Our first grandchild, Jesse, was born there in February 1972—a thrilling event! We flew out to be with them not long afterwards. In the spring of 1973, after Reid graduated from Colorado College, the family moved to Stuart Island, part of the San Juan island group that lies north of Seattle and a bit northeast of the Canadian city of Victoria. Sarah and Reid and some of their friends wanted to live simply and close to nature, a plan that caused her parents some trepidation. There were no ferry services to Stuart Island, conditions were rather primitive, and the only time we would hear from Sarah was when she went to buy supplies on an adjacent island and would call us from a telephone in a bar. Frances visited Stuart Island to see her sister and came back with tales of harvesting vegetables and waking up at dawn to milk the goats. That worried Betty as she envisioned her beautiful daughter as a horny-handed pioneer woman. But Sarah's experience helped me appreciate the positive side of alternative lifestyles and journeys off the beaten track. The San Juan islands are fantastically beautiful. Sarah still has a house on Stuart Island, part of which is built into a cave—and it's a great deal more comfortable than it sounds.

Sarah and Reid separated in 1974 and were divorced the next year, after which she lived in Seattle for a year taking care of Jesse. Then Craig Richardson reappeared in her life. They had been friends at Colorado College, and he was at her wedding in 1969; in fact, there's a photo of Sarah sitting on Craig's lap at that event. She moved back East with Craig, and they lived as caretakers at "Seafair," a rambling, run-down Newport, Rhode Island "cottage" on the seaside. They were married in 1978 and built a house for themselves in Saunderstown, Rhode Island. Craig has been wonderful for Sarah, and they make a good match. They now live on Jamestown Island, overlooking Newport Harbor. There at Beavertail they built their second Rhode Island home, a beautiful idyllic place that bears all the creative earmarks of Craig the artist. Sarah has her horses there too, and her gardens are truly a work of beauty. Altogether they have a lovely way of life. In recent years, Sarah has become involved in a number of Rhode Island charitable, educational, and environmental activities. One such activity was the effort to preserve Block Island. The experience of living on Narragansett Bay, I am sure, inspired Sarah to do volunteer work for Save the Bay, Rhode Island's outstanding environmental organization.

It is devoted to cleaning up Narragansett Bay and making it more livable and enjoyable. She did a fabulous job there, becoming president of the organization and of course getting to know all the Rhode Island politicians. More recently still, she returned to college at Brown University and got her B.A. degree in 1997 at age forty-nine—quite an accomplishment!

Frances graduated from Yale in 1971. She and her friend Lucie Sides went on safari in Africa with Betty and me that summer. She then returned to New Haven to take more classes at Yale and figure out what she wanted to do next. Finally she applied to the Yale School of Forestry and Environmental Studies, where her friend Sarah Bates from Penn was enrolled. It was a sensible decision; Frances, like her sister, Sarah, had always been interested in nature and the environment. In the summers while she was studying at the forestry school, she worked for the Natural Resources Defense Council, a legal outfit that fights for environmental causes. She spent her first summer with NRDC examining how to develop a land use plan for the Catskills. The NRDC spotted her talents and has hung onto her. In 1998, she became executive director of the organization, while the long-time executive director, John Adams, became president. He is almost always out on the road, so Frances in effect runs the operation. They have made the NRDC an extremely successful organization. Frances's job has called for great knowledge, commitment, and patience; lawyers and scientists can be very difficult people to deal with.

I continued to make trips big and small, for business and pleasure, throughout the 1970s. In most years, Betty and I took a January break in Eleuthera, visited my mother in Florida in early spring, and spent time on Cape Cod in the summer. We traveled to see our children when they were away from New York, as for example when Sarah was in Germany and on the West Coast. Betty and I made more extended trips, such as our visits to East Africa in 1971, to South America in 1975, to Australia, the Philippines, and Hong Kong in 1977, and to China in 1978.

Rick married Candace Krugman in October 1976. Their wedding turned out to be the last family event that my mother attended. By 1977, my mother was eighty-six years old. She was in command of her faculties, but physically she was showing signs of running down. Nonetheless, she still maintained her three lovely homes: her country home, Tredinnock, in Great Barrington and her apartments in New York City and Palm Beach. Frances was engaged to be married to Paul Elston in June, and she wanted to have the ceremony outdoors in my mother's garden at Great Barrington. Betty, Frances, and I, together with Paul and his parents, all went up to Great Barrington in March 1977 to make wedding plans. We walked around in the garden through the newfallen snow, mapping out where the members of the wedding party would stand and where we would put the improvised altar. I went into the house and telephoned my mother in Palm Beach to tell her about our ideas. My mother asked some questions, made some helpful suggestions, and said she was looking forward to the wedding with much enthusiasm. That was the last time I spoke with her.

I spent the night at a motel not far from Great Barrington, and in the morning the manager said that I had a phone call. It was from Mrs. Pease, the woman who was my mother's secretary and helper. She told me that my mother had died during the night, in her home and in her sleep—which is really the best that anyone can hope for. But I didn't expect to lose my mother so soon and so suddenly. As I was on my way back to New York, I stopped in (as previously arranged) to see Marian Wright Edelman, who was on the Yale Corporation with me at the time and with her husband had rented a house nearby in Chatham, New York. She was the first person outside my family whom I told about my mother's death, and I remember her warm, sympathetic response and embrace on that sad occasion. I went down to Florida to make arrangements with the undertaker, and Betty supervised the difficult tasks of putting my mother's possessions in order. The memorial service was at the Central Presbyterian Church in Summit. I said a few things, and each of the children participated. We interred my mother's ashes next to my father's in the Fairview Cemetery in Westfield, New Jersey, just across the road from where my Sperry grandparents are buried. It is a beautiful sylvan spot and a peaceful place. Frances and Paul Elston were married in my mother's garden in Great Barrington in June, as planned. I felt—everyone felt—that my mother was there in spirit.

By the mid-1970s, the era of anti-trading stamp legislation was drawing to a close. Such activity had already tailed off from its peak in the 1950s and early 1960s, partly because the uniqueness of The Sperry and Hutchinson Company had been diluted by the proliferation of competing stamp companies in the late 1960s and early 1970s. Stamp companies had cropped up all over, and merchants who felt left out in the cold by S&H now could turn to King Korn or Plaid Stamps or Gold Bond or dozens of other companies. The competition adversely affected S&H's profit margins but also diminished the intensity of feeling against our company. The more important factor, however, was that as the 1970s progressed, the stamp industry was declining. S&H, as the strongest of the stamp companies, was the most resistant to the fall-off, but by the mid-1970s we were no longer experiencing even modest growth. As my father used to say, "The virulence of the opposition is the measure of our success." With the entire industry sagging, the competitiveness that had spurred hostile legislation vanished; trading stamps were no longer perceived as a threat.

Despite the falloff in anti-stamp legislation, we retained the services of an S&H lobbyist in Washington throughout the 1970s. Joe Oros had retired for health reasons. He was succeeded by Ed Hynes, previously my personal assistant at S&H, who had helped me with speechwriting and various office responsibilities. Ed was thoughtful, kind, intelligent, responsive, loyal, and extremely helpful. He remained with us until we sold the Company in 1981 and is still a good friend of mine. He is now active in a Catholic organization, Morality in Media, here in New York City. Ed's office in Washington, D.C., was in the Pennsylvania Building, not far from the US Treasury. It happened to be a convenient spot for observing the activities of Pennsylvania Avenue, and I watched Gerald Ford's inaugural parade from that vantage point in 1974. Four years later, I enjoyed drinks and a buffet luncheon with Ed and George Dixon (a former S&H financial vice president who went on to become undersecretary of the Treasury) as Jimmy Carter's inaugural parade proceeded down the same route.

In April of 1977, Fred Collins was approaching sixty-two and I was just about to turn sixty-three. At the annual board of directors meeting, I proposed a new organizational structure at the top of the business that would allow us to manage S&H more effectively and pave the way for a smooth management transition when it came time for our retirements. We recommended that the Company designate two executive vice presidents, Jim Mills and Jim Kelly, in order to lighten the load on Fred's shoulders. I wanted Jim Mills to succeed Fred Collins as president in the fall of 1978, and Jim's new position would give Fred and me an opportunity to observe his performance at close range for a year and a half before he assumed the president's post. Jim would continue as general manager of the furnishings division, our largest division in both sales and earnings. While Fred and I would still have access to all the staff officers as needed, Jim Kelly would represent the two of us in the administration of corporate work.

Some members of the board had reservations about Jim Mills's succeeding Fred as president, but I had faith in Jim. He had the essential qualities of breadth of view, comprehension of the whole company, and a sense of how it fit into the evolving social scene of American society in the last quarter of the twentieth century. He was broadly educated. He knew the entire company. He knew the stamp business, having come to it as my assistant when I was general counsel and having assisted me when I was racing around the country dealing with myriad litigations and putting out legislative fires. By 1976, he had been given the responsibility to run a number of these companies: first Bigelow-Sanford and then all the companies in the furnishings division.

I had never made a secret of my desire that my son Rick would someday become president of S&H. Both Fred and I believed that he had the right stuff and would make an able and effective executive head. I believed that when Fred and I had retired—or earlier, if for some reason we both became incapacitated—the board could safely entrust the enterprise to Rick. In fairness to Rick, however, I didn't want to plunge him into too much responsibility too quickly. I believed that he should be given time to get there. I had not the slightest doubt that he could do the job, but I wanted him to have the chance to get some more seasoning. In 1977, Rick was sent to Wayland, New York, to take charge of the Gunlocke Company. The move caused his wife, Candace, some unhappiness since she was on track to become a partner at Hughes, Hubbard & Reed—and indeed, she is now senior partner and head of the firm. So she had to stay in Manhattan and see Rick on weekends. But it was essential for Rick to have the opportunity to be the head of a company and really to have the responsibility of running it. He was in charge of Gunlocke for a long and difficult year, but the experience truly demonstrated his ability to run a large corporate enterprise. When he returned to S&H, he assumed responsibility for the headquarters staff activities of the furnishings division.

In the late 1970s, all three branches of the Beinecke family were still represented on the S&H board of directors. Nonetheless, the family was no longer one unified family, as it had been in my father's time, but three distinctly different families. The stock ownership, as well as participation in the Company's affairs, varied substantially between the three branches, in part due to widening interests and career concepts among family members but also due to the diffusion resulting from the sale of different quantities of stock by different family units. Each of the three families continued to have a substantial interest in S&H. My cousins Betsy, Sylvia, and Ed were very large stockholders, and it was my view that until the eventual disposition of their stock became known, it was best for the ownership posture of the Company to continue in the three-family form.

Unfortunately, my relations with the family members on the S&H board of directors deteriorated as the trading stamp business ran into difficulties and as John R. Robinson (Sylvia's son) and Mickey Michel (Betsy's son-in-law) joined the board. Jim Mills correctly observed that "the S&H board of directors was hamstrung by its inside, so-called family members, who were critical and generally negative. The board meetings were rarely constructive because the family members on the board had adopted the attitude, 'If Bill Beinecke's for it, we're against it.' The family bloc never had any specific suggestions as to what should be done differently; their contributions were limited to a kind of carping negativism. It was one of the unpleasant things Bill had to deal with." The problem worsened when it became evident that Sid Bass, a Texan with very deep pockets, had managed to accumulate a significant portion of S&H stock.

In early 1973, I had received a letter from Richard Rainwater, the investment manager at Bass Brothers Enterprises in Fort Worth, Texas. Rainwater congratulated me on S&H's strong performance in 1972 and hoped I would keep up the good work. I thanked him for his compliment, but in hindsight, that was the moment when S&H became a "project" of the Bass family. They concluded that S&H stock was badly undervalued—which was true—and began buying as much of it as they could get their hands on. The Bass family's wealth rested on their oil and gas holdings, which then were parlayed into many millions (even billions) of dollars through Rainwater's canny investments. Perry Richardson Bass was in the class of 1937 at Yale, a year below me, but I had not known him as an undergraduate. His sons also attended Yale, and that perhaps inclined me to respond favorably at first when I learned sometime in 1975 that Sid Richardson Bass was quietly buying up shares of S&H. In fact, Fred Collins and I thought that Sid Bass might be a positive addition to our board of directors. As we learned more about the Bass brothers' investment policy, however, we began to reconsider. The Bass family had a track record of buying up companies whose stock was undervalued, stimulating a transaction (such as forcing a sale), and making a killing. With regard to S&H, however, Sid Bass did not initially express any desire to have a seat on our board, nor did he attempt to exercise any influence on S&H policy. But he continued to acquire shares and acquire shares and acquire shares until it became a matter of some concern to us that this very wealthy Texan had such a large interest in the Company. I met Sid Bass in February 1977, in connection with the capital fund campaign for Yale, with which we were both involved. He seemed a polite and personable fellow, but it was unnerving to know that his investment in S&H was approaching my own.

Finally, in August 1979, I decided that I had to meet with Sid Bass to plumb his intentions. He cordially agreed to meet at my office in New York. I told him that it was the conclusion of the directors that the Bass brothers' purchase of large amounts of S&H stock was not in the best interest of the Company or its shareholders. The sizable holdings of Bass Brothers Enterprises, combined with those of Beinecke family members, meant that there were comparatively few shares of S&H stock in public circulation; that helped to depress the stock's value further. Sid Bass, far from agreeing to desist from his purchases of S&H stock, inquired whether there might be any members of the Beinecke family who would be willing to sell their shares to Bass Brothers Enterprises. He specifically mentioned a conversation he'd had with Mickey Michel about acquiring the holdings of my cousin Betsy and those in her mother's estate. But he also emphasized his favorable assessment of the Company and its potential and his interest in actively working with the management to improve its value. It was a rather unsettling conversation. Not long afterward, the members of the Beinecke family met in my cousin Ed's apartment in the Carlyle Hotel to discuss the Bass situation. My cousin Betsy seemed to speak for all of us when she said, "As long as we all stick together, we'll have nothing to fear."

I retired as chairman and CEO of The Sperry and Hutchinson Company on January 30, 1980. I was almost sixty-six years old. I had done my work at S&H, and had been in charge for long enough. It was a disappointment that trading stamps had declined, but I thought I had started the Company in the right direction in terms of diversification and took some satisfaction in the fact that S&H's revenues had increased from about $100 million when I became president to almost $1 billion when I retired. In hindsight, it would have been wonderful if I could have detected the coming electronic revolution and put a few million dollars into Microsoft, but hindsight is 20/20—and most of the electronics companies that started up around the same time as Microsoft have long since gone broke. When I retired, Rick became president and Jim Mills became chairman and CEO, and I felt good about leaving the Company in their very capable hands. Three months later, I was on my North Pole journey, fulfilling a long-held dream.

Back in New York, however, the Beinecke family solidarity was shattered when Betsy made an arrangement to sell both her interest and the S&H shares held by her mother's estate to none other than Sid Bass himself, giving him a large enough interest in the Company to require immediate action on our part. I'm a great believer in what is known as the law of unintended consequences. Betsy's decision to sell her interest to Sid Bass seemed like a disaster, but it may have saved us from later heartbreak. Her actions prompted our decision to sell The Sperry and Hutchinson Company. In light of what happened to the stamp industry in the 1980s, this was the best thing we could have done. Had matters continued apace, and had circumstances not forced us to sell, I suspect that the Beinecke family would have continued to own S&H on down through its decline.

To be honest, if I had been the S&H decision-maker at that time, I probably wouldn't have agreed to the sale. I had spent so many years developing the Company and had such great confidence in it that I was inclined to view the downturn in sales as a temporary setback and the Sid Bass situation as a not-insuperable obstacle. I had more than a disinterested business feeling toward S&H; there was a nostalgic family tie that may have prevented me from viewing the developments of the late 1970s and early 1980s in a cold-blooded, objective manner. But, fortunately for me and my family and the others involved, I was no longer running the business. Rick and Fred Collins (who became CEO after Jim Mills resigned and went on to serve as CEO of The Conference Board) were the decision-makers for The Sperry and Hutchinson Company.

In the years since 1981, it has occasionally been tempting to wonder what might have happened if we had not sold the Company. Many bright playwrights and fiction writers have approached historical events from the perspective of "What would have happened if such-and-such decision had gone the other way? What would have happened if Lincoln had not been assassinated in 1865? What would have happened if Archduke Francis Ferdinand had not been assassinated in Sarajevo in 1914?" But the reality of life is that you are stuck with what you have. Lincoln *was* assassinated, as was the archduke, and the rest is history. In life, as in chess, you can't retract a move once you've taken your finger off the piece. You may be forced into making a decision by circumstances beyond your control or you may make that decision after carefully viewing the conditions of a given situation. But regardless, the rest of the game unfolds from that point, and you can't undo what has been done. And in life, unlike in chess, you can't replay the game. So once the decision was made to sell S&H, I resisted the urge to look back and think, "What if...?"

We retained the investment firm of Goldman Sachs to find what is known as a "white knight," a company willing to buy S&H. Goldman Sachs located the Baldwin-United Corporation of Cincinnati, and we commenced negotiations. I had kept my entire holding up until then. My parents had given me my first five hundred shares in S&H back in 1941, and because I believed in S&H and had witnessed so many years of the Company's growth, I had never seen any reason to sell. We joined forces with Edwin Beinecke, Jr.'s branch of the family, whose interest was represented by John R. Robinson. Pooling our resources, we sold our entire interest in S&H to Baldwin-United, following its agreement to acquire S&H through a merger on January 30, 1981. In the ten-year interval between the first oil embargo and the sale of S&H, the share price had declined to the point where it was no longer up in the fifty-dollar range but closer to the initial public offering price. Despite this, through our negotiated agreement, we were able to sell to Baldwin-United at a very favorable price, considerably above that which Sid Bass had paid Betsy for her shares. In retrospect, Sid Bass never had an interest in running or owning S&H but was simply looking for a way to make money. His strategy had been to buy S&H shares at a respectable average price, purchasing on the margin and averaging his purchases. To the stock acquired in this fashion, he added Betsy's shares, also purchased at a good price near his average. He also sold his interest in the Company to Baldwin-United in advance of the corporate merger transaction.

Thanks to the hard-nosed stance taken by Rick, who was involved in all the negotiations, we received cash for our interest in S&H. Again, my faith in the Company prevented me from seeing the need for this. In my trusting way, I would have accepted stock in a tax-free, stock-for-stock trade, but he said, "No, Dad, we are taking cash." How wise he was! Within a couple years of assuming control of S&H, Baldwin-United went into a Chapter 11 bankruptcy proceeding. I don't believe it was the purchase of S&H that did them in. It was, rather, another of its highly ambitious acquisitions of the early 1980s: an insurance company dealing in single-premium deferred annuities that was burdened by obligations that Baldwin-United was not able to handle. S&H had, through the years, carefully husbanded a large portfolio that we administered quite conservatively, using that asset to further the growth of the other businesses we had acquired. It is my understanding that when Baldwin-United came into possession of S&H, it used up the entire reserve. Its eyes were too big for its stomach, as it were. Meanwhile, we had our money in hand, paid off the capital gains tax, and have been very fortunate since then.

The worst part about the way S&H came to an end was that it ruined my relationship with my cousin Betsy. Of all my relations on the

Beinecke side, she was the person closest to me. She was simply a marvelous person: a terrific athlete, wonderful company, full of personality and ability. And she was so close to Betty—they were kindred spirits. So when Betsy, my dear beloved cousin, sold out to Sid Bass without so much as telling me, it left a deep wound. We didn't even see her for ten years after the sale, though we have seen her recently. To make matters worse, the actions of Betsy, my favorite relative, forced Rick and me into an alliance with John Robinson, who had been the single most unhelpful family member on the S&H board of directors. Being forced into an alliance with him was rather a bitter pill to swallow.

Of course I was dismayed that S&H was no longer in our family. The Company was a legacy from the past and was practically synonymous with the Beinecke name. Running that enterprise was a wonderful source of gratification to me. Often, in dreams, I return to the board room of the S&H Building, with its paneled walls and long, gleaming table. The camaraderie and team spirit of S&H were impossible to duplicate, and I miss a lot of the people I worked with in those days. At least we managed to hammer out an extremely generous severance policy for our employees when the merger with Baldwin-United went through. Still, the sale of S&H meant that at last I was no longer harnessed to my cousins, and they to me. Everybody went their own way. I think that was a good thing; it freed us all. I was free, with Betty, to do the things we wanted to do. And ever since 1981, we have done what we've wanted to do. I haven't been hampered by any business responsibilities, and I've had the liberty to work on various forms of public service, philanthropic activities, and my definition of the good life.

Rick was deeply disappointed when S&H had to be sold. The tremendous success he has achieved since 1981 attests, I am sure, to the great leadership he would have exercised at S&H had things turned out differently. But Antaeus Enterprises, the company that emerged from the sale of our S&H holdings, has also been a splendid opportunity for Rick and for John too. Antaeus is a personal holding company that I created in 1975, when it was known as the FWB Corporation. It was able to preserve, for the benefit of our four children and their heirs, a substantial amount of S&H share value. In a way, it had some of the bootstrap aspects of the 1950 trusts.

The S&H stock price varied widely in the first half of the 1970s. From a high of $45/share at the time of my father's death in 1971, it had sunk to a low of $11/share in 1975. By utilizing the marital deduction, my father had been able to leave to my mother a substantial number (350,000) of S&H shares without incurring any estate tax. This meant that she had locked in a high basis of $45/share for those shares; the basis, in tax law, means the price at which stock is acquired.

Ed Beimfohr, a lawyer at Casey, Lane & Mittendorf, the firm representing S&H, came to me and explained that if my mother were to transfer those shares to a personal holding company, the high basis could be preserved and subsequent sales of those shares would avoid any capital gains tax. Acting on this advice, we formed a personal holding company. Its common shares had but a nominal value and were purchased by four trusts, one for each of our children. Preferred shares were issued and transferred to my mother in exchange for her S&H shares, reflecting the market price, then around $11/share. In this way, the high tax basis of the S&H shares was carried over to the holding company. Subsequently, my mother gave twenty-five percent of those preferred shares to trusts for the benefit of her grandchildren (my four children) and left the balance by will to the Prospect Hill Foundation. At the time of my mother's death in 1977, the S&H stock price had recovered a bit to $16/share. This increment in value now accrued to the common stock of the holding company. When The Sperry and Hutchinson Company was sold to Baldwin-United in 1981 at a price of $36/share, that increase in price also was absorbed in the higher tax basis, so a substantial value had successfully been preserved without incurring a capital gains tax. In fact, even after the sale of S&H, Antaeus continued to experience a number of years of capital appreciation free of capital gains tax before the high basis advantage was completely absorbed. Later on, Antaeus redeemed the shares of preferred stock held by the Prospect Hill Foundation and the trusts of my four children. Since that time, Rick and John have given this enterprise excellent leadership and have managed this investment vehicle very well indeed.

Throughout those years we were most fortunate in having sound legal advice. I mentioned Ed Beimfohr. Much of the later planning involving a number of family trusts was based on the excellent advice received from William Jordan, also one of the partners of Casey, Lane & Mittendorf. He later became a member of the well-known firm of Cadwalader, Wickersham & Taft.

I renamed the FWB Corporation in 1981. I didn't want it to have the family name. I did some searching and hit upon Antaeus, the legendary son of Gaea and Poseidon. He was noted as a wrestler who could not be overthrown so long as his feet were planted firmly on the ground. It seemed to be a good symbol for a company that was owned one hundred percent by my children; so I renamed the company and it has been known as Antaeus Enterprises ever since. The company has operated successfully and has earned considerable profits for many years now, so that the value of the Antaeus common stock has increased substantially.

Rick was principally responsible for setting up Antaeus Enterprises as a physical entity when Antaeus became the recipient of the proceeds from the sale of my mother's S&H shares to Baldwin-United. John joined Antaeus in 1982. Rick is the president of the company and John the vice president, but they are essentially partners; the titles simply reflect the corporate form of organization. Rick and John, together with Robert L. Bael (until his death in 1997) and other advisors, have augmented the original capital significantly; it has appreciated greatly under their direction. They have succeeded because they are thorough, bright, careful, and considerate on behalf of everyone who has entrusted them with the management of their assets. I believe that one of its most successful ventures has been Catalina Marketing Corporation, a company that—ironically, given the history of S&H in the supermarket wars—deals in supermarket coupons. I don't focus much on the business affairs of Antaeus. I leave that to my sons. I attend board meetings four times a year, but I don't participate in the investment decisions Antaeus makes, and no one asks me to. Antaeus was for more than a dozen years in the Graybar Building at 420 Lexington Avenue but recently moved to more spacious and well-appointed quarters at 99 Park Avenue. I have an office there, and the secretarial assistance they provide me is helpful. When I am there I mainly handle personal chores. But I sometimes like to go just to see Rick and John at work and to reflect that all's well that ends well.

CHAPTER SIXTEEN

Philanthropic Activities and a Touch of Social Philosophy

*I*am not sure that I can adequately explain why I have been an active philanthropist for most of my adult life. After all, giving money to support the causes and organizations that I believe in is one of my life's highest enjoyments. Those who do not understand that philanthropy is a joy and a pleasure should try it sometime! Certainly I have been influenced by the example of giving set for me by my parents and other family members, and there are elements of my background and education and religious tradition that may explain it as well. But it is impossible to separate the act of philanthropy from the causes that have drawn my most active interest and concern.

I had made an assortment of charitable contributions each year since I had graduated from law school, but they were nothing extraordinary: contributions to the Yale and Columbia alumni appeals, donations to the Legal Aid Society and the Salvation Army, gifts to the *New York Herald Tribune* Fresh Air Fund, and so forth. My first significant philanthropic act, I believe, was to establish a scholarship for minority students at the Yale Law School. Sometime in the late 1950s, I was invited to attend a Yale Law School conference on how to improve relations between the races. I ended up in a small discussion group in the school's lounge. One of the people in the group, a black professor from Georgia, said, "You know, it's very difficult for two people of different races even to sit down and have a meal together. They both feel awkward. Perhaps it's too much to expect a black man and a white man to be able to have dinner together; maybe they ought to settle for light conversation over a cup of coffee. From this little acorn, an oak tree might grow."

It seems almost incredible today to think that the races were so far apart that you had to take such a gingerly approach even to having a conversation. But looking back at my own experience, I can understand why. There was little contact between the races in those days. It wasn't intentional; that was just the way it was. The only contact I had with black people was when a porter would carry my bags. We didn't have any equal relationships at all. I knew that wasn't right. So when I went back home, I thought, "Well, maybe I should do something." I'd had exactly one black classmate at Columbia Law School. His name was William Fillmor Wood, and he had gone on to become a judge in Plainfield, New Jersey. Betty and I decided to invite him and his wife over to have dinner with us at our home in Summit, and they accepted. We had to think hard about which of our friends from Summit to invite. In the event, we invited Jim and Muriel Burke and Jim and Jane Heekin, the couple who lived next door. It all came off very well. Judge Wood's wife's name was Sarah Frances—an easy name for me to remember! And the judge and I spent more time discussing legal issues and the quality of the dinner than we did ways to uplift race relations. In hindsight, that dinner seems sort of touching and naive, but it's a measure of how far race relations have moved since those days. Many people think that relations between blacks and whites are deplorable today, and there is some truth to that, but I also have to say that some real progress has been made.

From that beginning, I increasingly came to feel that I should do something to give substance to my belief that more should be done to give blacks equal opportunities for professional development. And so I established the William S. Beinecke Yale Law School scholarship for minority students. Every year I would take the recipients of the scholarship to lunch at Mory's, and that led to some interesting conversations and new insights for me. My theory was that educating greater numbers of black professional leaders would have a ripple effect. I believe it has.

I was interested in the civil rights movement, but it was something I followed in the newspapers, not something in which I participated actively. Still, you didn't have to go on a protest march or sit in at a lunch counter to make a positive contribution to the movement, particularly if you were in a position of executive responsibility. As I began to think more about these matters, I called my personnel executive, Pat McGee, into my office one day and asked, "Why don't we have any black people here working for us?" I wasn't accusing him of anything. I didn't feel that S&H was a racist environment. But it wasn't until the civil rights movement came along that I began to wonder if it really was a natural and normal state of affairs that the S&H staff was lily-white. That was the benefit of the protest movements of that era; they pointed out that most people took the status quo for granted and never questioned it. And so Pat and I began to explore that condition—because we weren't yet prepared to say that it was a problem. We learned that whenever we would tell our employment agency that we had an opening for a certain position, the agency would automatically screen out all black applicants. That seemed ridiculous. This was years before the commissions on fair employment practices and the laws against racial discrimination in hiring came into existence. I just thought, Here we are in a city with two million potential black employees, and this whole vast section of the labor market is being denied to us. That simply didn't make sense. So we began to employ black people, not for humanitarian reasons but because it seemed to be a more realistic and hard-headed capitalist way to go about business.

Of course, we found then that if you hired someone from an all-black environment in Harlem or Bedford-Stuyvesant, you couldn't simply plop that person down in the predominantly white environment of S&H. We had to take steps to enable the new employee to make the transition. One of the best decisions we made in the 1960s was to hire a wonderful black woman named Dolly Christian as an employment specialist and personnel manager. Her job really was to be a counselor, adviser, and integrator for the blacks whom we employed. Later on, she became our director of civic affairs. In that capacity, she was responsible for our affirmative action program (when that became required by law), directed the Company's participation in civic and community affairs, and administered S&H's corporate charitable contributions program. Because we had taken an early lead, S&H was spared some of the racial tensions that affected other companies during the late 1960s and early 1970s. We also gained considerable recognition for the role we had played in making it possible for minority people to work in our Company. Dolly Christian won widespread admiration for her work at S&H, and after the merger with Baldwin-United, she went on to a top position at IBM.

S&H also formed direct and active associations with minority organizations, at a time when visible support of such groups was sometimes controversial. We had excellent relations of mutual cooperation and respect with the National Urban League, the NAACP, the Council of Concerned Black Executives, the Interracial Council for Business Opportunities, the United Negro College Fund, and many more. Our association with these organizations often went well beyond financial support. Our employees served as officers, assisted in committee work, and generally gave of their time and themselves. We considered these efforts a very good investment, not only for our company but in the world around us. I tried to set a good example myself. For example, I was a member of the national businessmen's committee of A Better Chance, Inc., a program that sought out talented minority youngsters and paid for them to go to some of the best preparatory schools in the country. ABC was an organization that truly changed lives. I was at my most effective with that organization when I was a trustee of Phillips Academy.

My closest association was with the Opportunities Industrialization Centers (OIC), an organization that on the one hand provided training for people who didn't have jobs or much education and on the other hand worked with industry to make sure that appropriate jobs existed. It was an excellent concept. The OIC grew to national reach after it was started in an old Philadelphia jailhouse in 1964 by the remarkable Reverend Leon H. Sullivan, the head of Zion Baptist Church in Philadelphia and a highly energetic and moral man. I got to know him well, and I respected him tremendously. On one occasion I suggested to Bob Stephens, the minister at our Central Presbyterian Church in Summit, that Leon would make an excellent guest speaker and might shake up that comfortable congregation in a positive way. Bob agreed enthusiastically and asked Leon to come preach at the morning service. I invited Dolly Christian and several other S&H employees and associates to come out to Summit for the service. Afterward, we had a luncheon at our house, to which we invited several of our Summit neighbors, including Jack and Mary Connor. Jack and Leon knew each other because they served together on the General Motors board. As a director, Leon pushed for GM to perform in a socially responsible way. He articulated the Sullivan Principles, which addressed the manner in which business should be conducted in South Africa, particularly with respect to black employees. I ran into Leon and his right-hand man, quite by accident, in the Sandton Towers Hotel lobby in Johannesburg, South Africa, in 1997. The date was March 28, Good Friday. Leon invited us to come hear him preach in Soweto on Easter Sunday. We couldn't go, for our golfing group soon departed on schedule for Victoria Falls. I'm sure we missed an inspiring Easter Sunday celebration.

I also got to know Leon through summers on Cape Cod, because he had a summer home in Harwich, not far from Chatham, and he came over to see us several times. He and his wife, Grace, were in attendance when Betty and I celebrated our forty-ninth ("ringing in the fiftieth") wedding anniversary, at which Leon delivered the invocation. And when Leon and Grace celebrated their fiftieth wedding anniversary in Harwich a few years ago, Betty and I were both enthusiastic participants in the celebrations.

I personally worked with the OIC on the National Industrial Advisory Council, and I was greatly honored to receive the OIC Pathfinder Award in 1972. Even after I had to resign from the Advisory Council because of the press of my other responsibilities, it continued to meet in the S&H board room. I supported programs like those of ABC and the OIC because I believed that as more blacks were able to hold their heads up in an economic sense, the strains on the society would be eased. I think that has proven to be the case. My association with Leon Sullivan and many other blacks of outstanding leadership ability and character also broadened and educated me and enabled me to function as a more effective citizen in my own segment of society.

Leon Sullivan, William S. Beinecke, and J. Paul Austin, chairman of Coca Cola, on the occasion of the presentation of the OIC Pathfinder Award to William S. Beinecke, Washington, D.C., 1972.

S&H, particularly after it went public, was one of the nation's most socially responsible corporate citizens. Some of our actions came at Bill Gaskill's suggestion and grew from the strategy he laid out when he first met with us. We had not by any means been a heedless, self-interested company prior to that meeting, but we were too small to have much of an effect on anything. When S&H was continually the target of vicious attacks from our enemies, we became unusually sensitive to public perceptions and we tried to live up to the responsible image we wished to project. There was an element of self-interest in some of our good works, but there's such a thing as enlightened self-interest. And it was very much in the Beinecke family tradition to treat employees like family, rather than hard-heartedly showing them the door when their time was up.

As an example, consider the case of Bede Ullman Welker. Her father was the vice president and general manager of Houghton & Dutton, the Boston department store my father had managed during the Depression years. When he died, my father placed Mrs. Ullman on the S&H pension list as a direct pensioner. When a pension fund was established in 1952, she became one of the beneficiaries of it, even though she had never been directly employed by S&H. When she died, either my father or I extended the benefit so that it applied to the Ullmans' daughter, Bede. A few years ago when the folks now running S&H examined their pension lists, they discovered Bede on the list and cut her off. It seemed to me that the compassionate thing to do was for Antaeus to pick up the obligation, and Rick agreed. My father had a long, appreciative memory when it came to S&H's employees and their families, and I tried to follow his example. Unions never made a big impact at S&H, not because the Beinecke family frowned on unions but because the unions offered employees few benefits that they didn't already enjoy. Employees were treated well and generously, and we tried to look after everyone, though of course that became more difficult when the Company became larger.

S&H didn't just preach corporate social responsibility, we practiced it. I believed, as my father and uncles had before me, that it was our responsibility to give something back to the system from which we had prospered. The law allows a company to give away up to five percent of its pretax income a year and have it considered deductible. It's a high figure and few companies have ever reached it. S&H did, repeatedly. It was one of the few companies that gave up to the limit. The principal vehicle of our corporate philanthropy was the S&H Foundation, which was established in 1962. Each year, the Company made a contribution to the S&H Foundation—usually about a million dollars, depending on how successful a year it had been. The foundation ultimately made about $13.5 million in charitable grants between 1963 and 1981. The S&H Foundation was not anywhere near the size of some of the larger corporate foundations, but our managers did an excellent job of targeting S&H interests while creating a broad, diversified program, and the foundation was greatly respected despite its relatively small size.

One of the S&H Foundation's most famous projects, known throughout the academic world, was the Lectureship Program. Every year, we made awards to colleges and universities across the country to bring in really exciting speakers to lecture on the hot topics of the day. Inevitably, these lectures were very well attended. Not only were faculty and students present, but because we insisted that the lectures be open to the public, members of the local community were there as well. The grants were available to any college or university, but we stressed geographical distribution, to make sure that the lectures weren't all in the Northeast or California but were spread across the country. Newspapers often wrote articles about the speeches, which was very good publicity for S&H. One feature of this lectureship program was that it served as enrichment for many smaller colleges. Yale, Harvard, Wisconsin, Stanford, and the like have many ways of bringing talented speakers to their campuses and thus offer their students a wide spectrum of viewpoints, information, and inspirations. Many smaller, financially less well-endowed schools frequently offer not much more than the established curriculum. Our lectureship program helped bridge this gap.

Another successful endeavor—and one that was extremely popular within the ranks at S&H—gave four-year college scholarships to children of employees. Unfortunately, the Internal Revenue Service audited our program and issued new national guidelines limiting scholarships to one-quarter of applicants. We had been giving scholarships to a lot more than twenty-five percent of our applicants, so the new number constituted a significant reduction. The "twenty-five percent rule" came about as a direct result of our audit but applied to all corporate scholarship programs in the country. Still, the Employees' Children Scholarship Program remained successful even after we'd been forced to cut back on the number of scholarships we gave out. Every year, whoever was president of the Company would invite the local winners and their families to a luncheon at corporate headquarters. Photos of the winners, with a little write-up under each picture, appeared in the Company magazine.

The Merchants Scholarship Program, which was phased out by 1978 or so, was similar in concept to the Employees' Children Scholarship Program, but the awards were given to children whose parents were involved in retail businesses that used Green Stamps. We gave out a lot of those scholarships. Matching Grants was another very generous program in which the foundation matched or doubled employee gifts to educational institutions. For example, if an employee made a donation between $5 and $100, the foundation would give double that amount. On gifts exceeding $100, up to a maximum of $1,000, the S&H Foundation would give double the first $100 and match the remainder dollar for dollar.

S&H was extremely loyal in its support of a number of groups. Distributive Education Clubs of America was an organization that was very close to the foundation's heart. We worked very closely with the Girls Club of America over the years. 4-H programs were also strongly supported. We had a 4-H Home Environment Scholarship Program that honored the winners at the various 4-H fairs. If you had the cow that gave the most milk, you got a little 4-H pin and a grant; if you decorated a room through the 4-H program and your room was judged to be the best-decorated room at the fair, you got a little pin and a grant; and so forth. S&H was very involved in 4-H because, to a degree, the organization was related to the stamp business. While Green Stamps sold all over the country, they were particularly successful in the Midwest, the heartland of America, where 4-H clubs are so popular. Frankly, supporting 4-H was a way to get young people familiar with the name "S&H," in the hopes that when they got a little older they would welcome the opportunity to collect Green Stamps.

The Edwin, Frederick, and Walter Beinecke Memorial Fund Scholarship Program was established in 1971 as an endowed scholarship program for young men and women of exceptional abilities. It commemorates the three brothers—my father and my two uncles—whose many years of S&H leadership helped shape the character of the Company. My uncle Walter had died of cancer in 1958, when he was seventy years old. My uncle Ed died in 1970, and my father in 1971. When my father died, I was chairman of S&H, and I suggested to the S&H board of directors that we establish a scholarship program in memory of these three gentlemen who had such an influence in the growth and history of The Sperry and Hutchinson Company. Our board member Polly Bunting (former president of Radcliffe College) was very helpful to us in giving direction and form to this program. It was she who suggested making awards to distinguished students in their last year of college to encourage them to go on to graduate study. The result was the Edwin, Frederick, and Walter Beinecke Memorial Fund Scholarship Program. It covers a student's senior year of college and the first two years of graduate school. The Beinecke Brothers Memorial Scholars are chosen on the basis of their ability to be innovative, thoughtful, and original in pursuing their subjects of interest. (I thought it particularly appropriate that a scholarship with an emphasis on creativity and originality be set up in memory of my father.) Financial need is also taken into consideration in making the awards. It's a useful program, and one we're extremely proud of.

As of 1999, the program (now administered by The Sperry Fund) has over sixty Beinecke Scholars enrolled in first-class universities. Since some students have deferred acceptance of their awards to take advantage of other scholarships (such as the Marshall) or job opportunities, we actually have seventy-five students "in the pipeline," so to speak. There is also a special African Scholars Program, operating in collaboration with the Wildlife Conservation Society, that brings scholars annually from Africa to the United States for graduate study in conservation or wildlife biology. A few years ago we had a dinner at the River Club in New York for past and present Beinecke Scholars, an enthusiastic gathering of some exceptional people.

The highest order of business is to operate successfully—that is, profitably. No employee ever thanked his company for going bankrupt. So a CEO's principal activity is to make sure that the business is profitable and that all available resources are utilized in bringing this to pass—for example, by employing the latest technology. It is also true that the responsibility of the board of directors is to represent the shareholders. But it is not the directors' job to focus on the bottom line and nothing else. I always felt that when people preached the "bottom line only" philosophy, their rationale was that it is not the responsibility of the company to look after the environment or to interest itself in social concerns; it is the government's problem. I don't buy that view. I think that being a leader in the business community requires an awareness of the company's role in society. The larger the company, the more important the role and, as I see it, the greater the opportunity to influence society in a positive way. Even back in the early 1970s, corporations were being called on to make decisions that would have seemed incredible five years before. Some of the greatest corporations, organizations that had created hundreds of thousands of jobs, poured millions into the economy and still more millions into every conceivable kind of good work, were coming under attack for not meeting the test of corporate responsibility. They were being asked to make decisions on pollution even if they were not creating any; on minority employment, even if they had fine records in this area; on consumers' rights, even if they had devoted themselves to improved consumer awareness.

I saw this as a healthy thing. It was, at its very best, a reaffirmation of our belief in the human heart and, at the least, a response to a plea that the business community somehow attack and help solve some of mankind's problems. The 1960s produced a demand for change, reaching all the way from a reexamination of the human spirit to a restructuring of the corporate establishment to something as simple as the office routine: what people could wear, say, and do. One of the salutary side effects of the political disturbances of the 1960s was that more people were impelled to take a closer look at ethical issues that had not received much consideration in more placid times. That attitude persisted into the 1970s. I remember that in 1970 I spent a long time wrestling with my conscience on the question of whether S&H Green Stamps ought to be given for purchases of cigarettes. S&H had long refused to give stamps for alcohol purchases, on the grounds that it was in neither the Company's interest nor society's to subsidize alcohol consumption. Now in 1970, the question was whether we could, with integrity, offer our services to the promotion of cigarettes, a product that we knew to be harmful. Finally I decided that Green Stamps did not have much effect in determining whether or not people smoked, or how much (though stamps could affect which brand they smoked); that a decision to sever ourselves from cigarette purchases would not result in a wholly favorable public relations response; and that if we cut our ties to the tobacco industry, we would lose substantial business to our competitors, who had no such inhibitions. So I concluded that we ought to continue to serve the cigarette manufacturers. I was not sure the decision was the right one, and it cost me some sleepless nights. Of course, in 1970 much less was known about the long-term harmful effects of smoking and the difficulties of overcoming the addiction, cigarette manufacturers still enjoyed public approbation, and smoking was much more visible and accepted than is the case in the late '90s. I'd like to think that if I knew then what I know now, I might have made a different decision.

There are times when one can increase the profits of the company in a way that might not be good for the nation in the long run, one which might have adverse environmental or social consequences. It becomes necessary to balance company interests with the role that company plays in society. As CEO of S&H, I was particularly concerned about the environment. In my view, it was not enough for business to respond to laws requiring it to stop polluting. Business must clean up after itself. And then it must take steps to see that what has been made clean stays clean. This is an enormous task. S&H itself was responsible for pollution in some of its manufacturing subsidiaries. I was very firm in my insistence that steps be taken to stop the problem, even if the need to keep the environment clean threatened a portion of our profits. I appointed my assistant, Ed Hynes, to a newly created position of director of environmental and urban affairs, and he was very effective in that role.

The subject of corporate responsibility reminds me of a conversation I had with Tom McCarthy many years ago. Tom was of the generation before mine, a friend of my father's. He was the head of Austin Nichols, the liquor company that distributed Wild Turkey bourbon. I was telling Tom about my difficulties in persuading the company to adopt a certain course, and he said, "Well, Bill, what you have to do is remember that you put your hand on the shoulder of the elephant and then you lean. You lean, and you lean, and you lean, and after a while maybe the elephant turns a little bit to the right." He didn't mean that in an ideological sense; his point was that if you push hard enough for a long enough time, you might be able to exert an influence on the direction of this particular behemoth. I think that this example is analogous to the role of a corporation in society as a whole. While always remaining conscious of the bottom line, a corporation should strive to move in the direction of effecting societal change and improvement.

But I think businessmen like Tom McCarthy were the exception rather than the rule. In my thirty-odd years in business, few things surprised and disappointed me more than the attitude many businessmen had about the world beyond their businesses and their careers. It was hard to say which was greater—their ignorance or their indifference. Even men of the highest capacity would, without regret, limit themselves to a two-course curriculum: they majored in bottom line and minored in golf.

This phenomenon continues among all too many businessmen today. It is, first of all, a disservice to themselves. It limits their imaginations and can turn them into terrible bores. It is also a disservice to their companies. The events of the day—even minor and remote ones—can come to have devastating effects on corporate earnings. What does it say about the alertness and sophistication of the American business community that, in industry after industry, it is being proved that foreign companies understand and serve the American market better than American companies do? But the greatest disservice is to America itself.

Our business leaders are among the ablest, most energetic citizens we have. We can use their brains and drive in every important thing that needs doing. The lack of interest of some, their nonparticipation, their narrowness mean that the United States is a less successful, less rewarding, less happy country than it can be and should be—for us and for them, too.

I increasingly came to feel that the narrowness of many executives stemmed from the business-focused educations they had received in college. And so I held a regular series of lunches and meetings for our executives, where I would bring in an interesting and diverse group of speakers. The speakers, all of whom received an honorarium, included my journalist friend R. W. Apple, Jr., Beatrice Tinsley (a professor of astronomy at Yale), Bob Henry (my Yale classmate and a skilled Arabic speaker who was the government relations adviser for Aramco), and Clarence Walton, who had been dean of the School of General Studies at Columbia University during the troubles of 1968 and was a remarkable scholar and a tough little guy. (He went on to become president of Catholic University in Washington, D.C., and it was thanks to his good offices that I received an honorary LL.D. degree from that institution.) I hoped that discussions of this sort would give our executives information and perspective on contemporary events but also would help them develop the breadth and open-mindedness that are necessary for effective business leaders.

When The Sperry and Hutchinson Company was sold to Baldwin-United, no mention was made in the negotiations about the S&H Foundation; no one crossed that threshold. But not long afterwards, someone in the new Baldwin-operated S&H remembered the S&H Foundation and said, "Ho! We should have it!" Rick and I disagreed. The foundation was not included in the negotiations for the sale of S&H. If it had been, some consideration for its assets would have been included in the purchase price. The S&H Foundation's board of directors said, "We are independent, and will remain so." Baldwin-United had hoped to put a majority of new directors on the board, but the members of the foundation said, "No. We'll refuse to elect them." This was a legally correct stance. Fred Collins, who had continued on at S&H under the auspices of Baldwin-United, took the position of his new employers. A lawsuit was brought. The plaintiffs were Fred Collins (suing individually and as a member of the S&H Foundation), the S&H Company, the S&H Group, and the Baldwin-United Company. Rick and I were defendants, as was my cousin Ed, and the S&H Foundation itself was named as a defendant.

The suit sought to remove us as directors and install representatives of Baldwin-United in our place. The plaintiffs' legal representative, Harold "Ace" Tyler (who had been a prominent US district court judge), argued that all the money in the S&H Foundation came from the Company, that the foundation was there to serve the Company, and that therefore the foundation should stay with the Company. Our counsel, Dan Pollack, pointed out that according to law a foundation is a separate legal entity. It has its own board of directors and is governed solely by that board. As long as the board members don't misuse the foundation's assets or engage in acts that are "unfair, oppressive, or manifestly detrimental to the [foundation's] interest," they have the right to make whatever decision they want. As an independent corporation, the S&H Foundation had the right to make up its own mind. The suit dragged on for several years through various appellate stages, until finally in 1986 the New York State Court of Appeals ruled unanimously in favor of the foundation's remaining apart from Baldwin-United. As a matter of fact, it was unanimous all the way. The trial judge held for us and the Appellate Division unanimously affirmed. We didn't lose a judge. The S&H Foundation has since been renamed The Sperry Fund and is currently administered by my sons Rick and John, myself, and two outside directors. The investment policies of The Sperry Fund have been very successful. In the case of the Beinecke Memorial Scholarships, that has enabled us to increase not only the amount of money given but also the number of scholarship awards made each year.

Besides my work at S&H, my public activity took several forms. I was actively but indirectly involved in politics. I'm a Republican by affiliation, though I deplore the extreme right wing of the Republican Party. I'm a moderate-to-liberal Republican, of much the same sort as my fellow Yale Corporation members William Scranton and John Chafee. So, too, was my father. He was an FDR supporter, which was at that time somewhat unusual among businessmen, and he had a forward-looking and progressive philosophy about the social structure and economics of the land. His brothers Edwin and Walter were more conservative, but my father was a liberal businessman. "Liberal" is a tainted word now, and I am sorry to see the way it has come to be used as an epithet. In my father's day, a liberal was a person who believed in civil rights and civil liberties, a position that was well within the mainstream and deeply rooted in the American tradition. "Liberal" was a respected term, and indeed there were liberals in both parties. I contributed to and campaigned for George Bush, who was a liberal Republican until he became Ronald Reagan's vice president; it was Bush, ironically, who in his 1988 campaign against Mike Dukakis caused the word "liberal" to fall into disrepute. Now you can't find anyone in the Republican Party who would say, "Yes, I am a liberal." The politically correct term for liberal now is "moderate." But I was a supporter of quite a few "moderate," or "liberal," politicians.

As I have said, I always regarded my trusteeship at Consolidated Edison as a sort of public service. To be sure, there were fees, but no one on Chuck Luce's board served for money. That was just as well since no amount of money would have compensated for the aggravations to which we were subject. Describing those travails in a letter to the *New York Times* in 1974, I observed that service on the Consolidated Edison board "adds nothing to my purse, shortens my life, disturbs my equilibrium, and confirms my view that Sisyphus had nothing on Charles Luce."

I was also directly involved in many other public service activities. I was a trustee of Roosevelt Hospital (New York's oldest voluntary non-profit hospital) and the Committee for Economic Development in Washington, D.C. (a sort of think tank devoted to analyzing controversial economic and social problems), and played a role in numerous other organizations. I went on the board of the New York Botanical Garden in the 1970s, when the garden was an undiscovered treasure; it has since achieved a gratifying boom in popularity. I was on the board of the American Museum of Natural History, where we used to take our children for Saturday morning programs. Gardner Stout, a loyal Yale man, was the chairman, and I had such a good time on the board that I really should have joined it ten years earlier. The American Museum of Natural History is another institution that you appreciate more each time you go there. In March 1973, my friend John Lindsay was mayor of New York, and he arranged a public relations initiative to show people how well the city was being run. He set up a day trip that included a tour of a new sewage disposal plant, the downtown police headquarters, and City Hall and ended with a party at the Museum of Natural History, held in the Akeley African Hall. It featured the Harlem Girls' Choir and fashion models parading around the benches at the edges of the hall. It was really quite a party!

One of my first major philanthropic ventures was the donation I made, together with my mother, of the William Miller Sperry Observatory to Union Junior College in Cranford, New Jersey. It's a gift that still means a great deal to me, both because it was collaboration with my mother and because it is the most significant contribution honoring the Sperry side of my family. Union College in the early 1960s was hoping to construct an observatory because they had forged a partnership with Amateur Astronomers, Inc. (AAI), an eager bunch of astronomy enthusiasts from northern New Jersey. My good friend Hugo Meyer, who was vice chairman and later chairman of the college's board of trustees, knew that I was looking for an appropriate way to memorialize my grandfather William Sperry. He suggested the possibility of donating the observatory while we were on a trout-fishing expedition in Canada with our boys in the summer of 1963. The idea appealed to me, though I knew little about Union College or astronomy (a subject that I pursued in earnest only in my later years). I talked it over with my mother after I returned to the States. We decided that the proposed observatory on the Cranford campus would be an appropriate way to recognize her father, my grandfather, since it would be located in his home town, almost within sight of his burial site in Fairview Cemetery, adjacent to the campus. We agreed to finance the William Miller Sperry Observatory with a gift of just over $100,000. The story has it that my mother added the caveat that the facility had to include a small kitchen, since she allegedly felt that men and women viewing the heavens late at night in wintry weather should have a place to get hot chocolate or coffee. The gift, announced publicly in February 1964, was the largest the college had ever received. My mother and I attended the groundbreaking ceremonies in November 1965, and were both present at the dedication in May 1967. The invocation on that occasion was delivered by my mother's cousin, William Butler Sperry, a distinguished Episcopalian clergyman. We had invited many members of the extended Sperry clan to the dedication, and after the ceremonies Betty and I held a memorable luncheon for that large family gathering at our home in Summit.

The observatory has been—if you'll pardon the pun—a stellar success. It has made a significant contribution to the activities of both Union College and AAI, and has made the wonder and excitement of sophisticated astronomy accessible to thousands of people in the area around Cranford. As the *New York Times* wrote in an article about the facility in 1972, "it is rare that ordinary people can take a peep at the stars through telescopes in an observatory." I am glad that my grandfather has been memorialized in this way, and I have retained an interest in the observatory. I gave a speech at the May 1992 ceremony to commemorate its silver anniversary—and my eleven-year-old granddaughter Carrie, her large hat tilting in the breeze, stole the show!

I have also made charitable and philanthropic contributions through the Prospect Hill Foundation, which I established when I became president of S&H in 1960. I didn't want to name the foundation after myself, so I named it after the street where we lived. One important feature of a personal foundation is that it allows you to take your time about making charitable contributions. When you make charitable donations out of your own personal income, you have to do so in a certain calendar year or tax year. By having a foundation, you can time the payouts over a longer period. Initially I funded it by making over the maximum charitable contribution of my income to the foundation. In 1983, the Prospect Hill Foundation merged with the Frederick W. Beinecke Fund, which had been established by the will of my father and was later augmented by the will of my mother. As of 1998, the foundation was worth about $65 million. In the more than thirty-five years of its existence, it has disbursed about $37 million for charitable purposes. The total charitable giving of our family foundations (including the Frederick W. Beinecke Fund and The Sperry Fund) was just under $46 million as of the end of 1998.

The Prospect Hill Foundation has been a very useful way of having our children join us in charitable activities. We invited them onto the board when they were rather young; I would guess that Rick has been on the board since he was about thirty-five years old. It's a family activity in which we all participate, and we all respect one another's views. The foundation has a broad range of philanthropic interests in a few well-defined fields. One large and fairly traditional category is the support of artistic, cultural, and educational institutions. Most of the educational institutions that receive our support are those we've attended. This has led to a philosophical disagreement with my children, because of course they're now being solicited for support from the institutions that their children attend. I have a feeling that that's too much proliferation in this category.

From the time I created the foundation, I saw three problems towering above all others on the troubled world scene. These problems continue and will continue, I am sure, into the next millennium. One is the need to curb the alarming growth of the world's population, with its dangerous potential for generating strife over inadequate resources. Another is the need to increase the supply and broaden the distribution of food throughout the world, so that an adequate diet is available to even the least favored of humanity. And a third is the need to limit, reduce, and in time end the arms race, which now endangers life as we know it on this planet—and ultimately persuade all nations to renounce armed warfare as a means of settling their differences. Accordingly, the Prospect Hill Foundation has concentrated on the areas of population, environmental conservation, and nuclear weapons control.

My concern with the population explosion predated the creation of the Prospect Hill Foundation. At some point in the late 1950s, I was invited to attend a forum at the Harvard Club of New York about the population problem. I think I was invited because the Beinecke Foundation had made a small contribution to support Planned Parenthood. Later I met with Don Strauss, who had been one of the sponsors of the forum. I remember saying, "Don, I have a problem with this. I understand the issues. But I'm the president of a company that distributes its trading stamps to people, and the more people the better. When I was recently in California, one of the men driving me around said, 'See this citrus grove? This is going to go soon and be replaced by houses, and they'll all be filled with savers of S&H Green Stamps.' I'm told by the people in my company that the increasing population and the growth of cities are good for business, and yet you're telling me the opposite." So Don sent me some economic material that laid out in plain terms the difficulties that even the developed countries would have down the road if population growth continued to outstrip resources.

From that beginning, I have gone on to support (mainly through the Prospect Hill Foundation) efforts at population control. The operation of economic and social factors has brought down the population rate in Europe, and even the United States's population growth is the result not of natural growth or of high fertility rates but of immigration (legal and illegal) and of the enormous baby-boomer cohort's having children; the latter phenomenon will slowly level off. The population still grows at an explosive rate in much of the Third World, but the good news is that fertility rates are going down everywhere, even in these populous countries. I think the efforts of the people we make grants to is having a slow but definite effect. I am confident that eventually the population will level off—at too high a number, but the sooner we get to the level-off point, the better off we'll be.

I believe that the population problem, the nutrition problem, and the armament problem are interrelated. If we do not solve them, the age of civilized man may turn out to be relatively short. If we do solve them, the future is beyond my twentieth-century imagination. In order to get to the limitless future promised by science fiction writers and utopians, however, mankind must cope with the immediate present. And I think that's the best explanation for why I have carried out my philanthropic activities over the years.

CHAPTER SEVENTEEN

The Pingry School and the
Story of Its Move

mong my eleemosynary activities over the years, I have
served as an elected alumni trustee of Andover and as a
trustee of the Kent Place School in Summit, but I've had a
much larger involvement as a trustee of the Pingry School
in New Jersey. I have served Pingry for over forty-five years, first as an
active trustee and more recently as an honorary one. For me, the most
exciting feature of that long service was the part I was able to play in
moving the school from its Hillside campus to a beautiful new, spacious
site in Bernards Township, some twenty miles to the west. There are
only a few times over the course of a lifetime that you are given an
opportunity to do something really significant, something with an
effect beyond your immediate circle, something that can fairly be said
to have made the world a better place. In bringing the school to its current home in Martinsville, New Jersey—where, I am convinced, it will
flourish as never before, for the everlasting benefit of all connected
with it—I was offered such an opportunity.

The Pingry School was founded in Elizabeth, New Jersey, in 1861
by the Reverend John Francis Pingry, a Dartmouth man, an honorary
Princeton Ph.D., and a Presbyterian (although not above filling in at a
Dutch Reformed service when needed). In 1892, a new and larger
building was built on newly acquired land. In the early 1920s, just
before my arrival as a student, the school received a gymnasium, pool,
and locker room. Since 1892, Pingry has twice relocated: in 1954, from
the Elizabeth campus to a building in neighboring Hillside, and in
1983, from Hillside to its present location in Martinsville, the move I
initiated. Over the years, the institution has undergone many other
changes as well, notably the shift from the sole owner-proprietorship of
Dr. Pingry to today's not-for-profit institution governed by a board of
trustees.

After attending first through third grades at the Grant School in Cranford, I entered Pingry in the fall of 1923, and thanks to what was evidently excellent preparation at my public elementary school, I skipped fourth grade and went immediately into the fifth grade class. I attended Pingry for fifth and sixth grades, and had a marvelous elementary school education there. The facilities were far superior to any I had experienced before, the teachers proved able and dedicated, and I made a lot of friends. When my family moved from Cranford to Madison in 1925, I continued at Pingry for another year. The long commute to Pingry from our new home was too arduous for a small boy, and I was enrolled at the Madison Academy in the fall of 1926.

For many years thereafter I didn't think much about Pingry. Then one day in the mid-1950s, I took Rick, then about ten, down to Hillside for a look at the new school under construction. I was impressed. The new Pingry had everything anyone could want in a school. I even found an old friend of years gone by who was also looking around that day: Charlie Atwater '31, who, it turned out, had become Otho Vars's successor as head of the junior school. Well, the decision was made, and Rick went to Pingry shortly after it was opened for business in the Hillside location. He was soon followed by his brother John.

In 1955, I was asked to become a member of the board of trustees at the Pingry School. I accepted and have been an enthusiastic participant in the life of Pingry every since. The board had three giants in those days. The first was the chairman, Conover English, whom I always called *Mister* English. He had been instrumental in raising the funds that made it possible for Pingry to leave its old, worn-out facilities at Parker Road and build the fine, new school on North Avenue in Hillside, a mile or so away. Then there was Chester Smith, who succeeded Mr. English as chairman, and the late and incomparable Robert Wade Parsons, who subsequently became both president *and* chairman of the Pingry trustees. I was happy to sit at the feet of those great men and, as a new trustee should, listen much and say little in order to understand not just the workings of the institution and the problems before it but the flavor and character of the place, all so that I might do my bit to keep Pingry headed in the right direction. I'm a slow study, so that took me about fifteen years. Then one day at Christmastime 1969, I went to see Bob Parsons, who lived near us in Summit, and handed him a very hot potato.

I said that I thought Pingry was in a deteriorating position over there in Hillside and that the students and parents whose support the school would need in the future were steadily gravitating westward to less-congested parts of New Jersey. Elizabeth, the city adjoining Hill-side, was not going to supply the caliber of student Pingry needed, and not many Pingry prospects were going to be found in the city of Newark, the Newark Meadows, or the New York Harbor. By remaining in Hillside, we therefore were eliminating as potential students everybody in a 180-degree arc around the school. The school was separated from the towns that could provide these students—Summit, Short Hills, some of the Oranges, and the areas surrounding Bernardsville—by several miles of tortuous, congested highways, amounting essentially to an industrial moat. It was clear to me that if Pingry stayed in its current location, it would lose its ability to attract the best students in the face of competition from better-situated schools, Newark Academy being the prime example. That school had recently relocated its entire plant to the country. It was no longer anywhere near Newark but was nestled in a beautiful spot in Livingston, New Jersey. Many of the boys who might have gone to Pingry were choosing Newark Academy instead because it was closer and the location was so ideal. We had long been in possession of a competitive edge over Newark Academy, or so we thought. Now we were at a disadvantage, and the gap could only widen. It would lead to other difficulties as well, such as a reduced ability to recruit first-class faculty and ultimately to finance what we were doing. When that happened, no one could predict what course Pingry would take. Vail Dean, which was once a very good girls' school in Elizabeth, was barely creeping along by 1970 and eventually had to close its doors. I did not want to see that fate befall Pingry.

Bob Parsons was the board's elder statesman, and that was why I went to him with my idea for relocating Pingry. But I did so very nervously, because less than twenty years earlier, he had been in the thick of the move to the *Hillside* campus. He had experienced all the difficulties and headaches involved in such a project: acquiring the land, planning the new construction, selling the old plant, reconciling the many different points of view, and, most importantly, finding the money to pay for it all. He had reason to send me packing. Not only was the North Avenue school in excellent physical condition, it had even been given four add-ons since the new building had been started, including a swimming pool while the building was under construction, a second gym (1957), a science wing (1960), and a first-class library (1966). (My cousin Kim Whitehead, who was a prominent Pingry alumnus, had been the speaker chosen to deliver the dedicatory remarks for the 1957 addition, and he had done a very good job.) And here I had the temerity to suggest to Bob Parsons that all his excellent work should be set aside! I was suggesting that Pingry should start over again, that we should junk his enterprise—or sell it if we could—and move the school to an as-yet-undetermined new location. I had no idea how Bob would react to my proposal.

Nonetheless, the thought of Pingry's land-buying fund galvanized me into action. The purpose of this fund, unstated publicly but known to Bob, me, and a few others, was someday to be able to purchase a plot of land for the Hillside campus that would provide a necessary addition to playing fields no longer adequate for the fine athletic program laid out by Pingry's athletic director (familiarly known as Mr. Les). The property the trustees had in mind was almost directly across from the school but separated from Pingry by the Elizabeth River. It was thought that a connection between the two playing fields could be made by obtaining an easement from the Union County Park Commission and constructing a bridge spanning the Elizabeth River. This plan troubled me. Pingry's Hillside location was in no way going to improve. If we went to the trouble of laying out a substantial bit of dough to buy land, fixing it up, and building a bridge, I could see that Pingry would be locking itself into the Hillside location for good.

I arrived at Bob's home accompanied by Rick, who was home on vacation from Virginia Law School. I had armed myself with a New Jersey road map that showed the intersection of Interstates 287 and 78. Reminding Bob that many of the cities of Europe had prospered at the intersections of two main highways, I presented my view that Pingry ought to move out to the neighborhood of that important junction. So situated, it would be able to attract students from a 360-degree circle rather than from a semicircle. To my amazement, Bob took my point immediately and even proposed that we go out together to look at some possible sites. Later that winter, Bob and I drove out into the countryside near Bernardsville, Basking Ridge, and Martinsville, searching for the right site. We saw some fine land, but we couldn't agree on any particular piece.

My proposal to move the school was presented to the Pingry board of trustees some time thereafter. Bob was no longer an active member of the board, and the response that greeted our proposal was not particularly enthusiastic. The board was divided on the question of whether the school faced a deteriorating situation. Many members felt that since the Hillside plant was excellent and the school's reputation superb, Pingry's quality education, faculty, and student body were enough; the school could continue to hold its dominant place in north central New Jersey right where it was. You could see them thinking, *We* don't have to follow Newark Academy's example in relocating, because we're Pingry. We're better. On the other hand, several board members shared my view that it was in Pingry's interest to move. It was along in there that I came to an important conclusion of my own. I realized that a large deliberative body like the Pingry board of trustees would have great difficulty *making* such a decision. It was sort of a chicken-and-egg problem they were facing. Should they decide to move and then look for a site? Or vice versa?

So I pushed for a consulting committee, which ended up consisting of prominent educators led by Larry Springer, our esteemed headmaster emeritus, flanked by Mrs. James Holec, principal-elect of the Girls' School of the Westminster Schools in Atlanta, Georgia; Miss Margaret Johnson, principal of the Girls' School at Milton Academy; and Mr. Henry Scattergood, principal emeritus of Germantown Friends School. The committee's task was to examine two major questions, for both Pingry and Kent Place, a neighboring girls' school. The first was what the best form of education would be for the two schools and whether a union of those two already strong schools would result in a program of even greater excellence. The second was whether, regardless of the question of union, either school should move to a new location. The committee finally decided in February 1971 that Kent Place and Pingry ought to come together in a coordinated relationship and that Pingry should not remain in the deteriorating situation in Elizabeth. The committee also stressed the obligation of independent schools to have a broad socioeconomic base—that is, to continue to enroll scholarship students—and to make opportunities available for all students to work in social agencies and tutorial programs that could acquaint them with urban problems. Finally, the committee urged both schools to have assurance of adequate financing before combining forces.

While this was going on, to spare the trustees the agony of forcing them to decide about the move, I invited them to look for suitable land while they were in the process of making up their collective mind. If such a piece was found, I told them, I would buy it and assume the downside risk but would sell it to Pingry if they did decide to move. Not long after, I was vacationing in Cotton Bay on Eleuthera in the Bahamas when I received a visit from Dick Mixer, a surveyor and Pingry trustee who had flown down to tell me that he had an option on a wonderful piece of property in Bernards Township of Martinsville, New Jersey. After examining the map and listening to his description, I said, "That's fine with me. If that's the property Pingry wants to buy, I'll buy it." And that is exactly what happened. The tract I purchased, known as the Loft property, was about ninety-four acres. Later, following the board's decision, the school bought for its own account two adjacent tracts, including the seventy-two-acre Denton property and the sixteen-acre Ferrovechio property along one of the borders of my tract, which had the effect of straightening out the boundary.

The land was purchased, but the journey had just begun. The vicissitudes of the next twenty-one years—which is how long it took for the move to be effected—were many. Fortunately, I was not alone in pursuing the goal of a new campus for Pingry. The duke of Wellington, commenting on the great victory of the British forces at Waterloo, once declared that "I don't think it would have happened if I had not been there." Most historians agree with him. However, there were many movers and shakers who were instrumental in bringing about Pingry's exodus from the Hillside location to the promised land of Bernards Township. Much honor is due to all, but particularly to a sort of rump committee that remained in more or less continuous session throughout the ordeal that followed the purchase of the property. Bob Parsons was a key member, of course. He was joined by Joe Engel, David Baldwin, Mac Bristol, Harry Hoyt, and Fred Bartenstein, who had to untangle many of the details. The headmaster, Scotty Cunningham, was also there every step of the way.

In their exodus from the land of Egypt, the children of Israel had to overcome plague and pestilence, the vengeance of Pharaoh, and the barrier of the Red Sea. We in our exodus would have to overcome the demands and the obstacles put in our way by the city of Elizabeth, the county of Union, the township of Hillside, and the state of New Jersey. We even had our Red Sea: the Somerset-Raritan Valley Sewerage Authority. Also the waste-disposal pharaohs of Warren Township, Bernards Township, the town of Martinsville, and the Middlebrook Trunk, none of whom could seem to agree about anything except the desirability of blocking Pingry's progress to our Promised Land. Mac Bristol, of the Bristol-Myers Company, one of the most modest and yet determined men I know, led the trustees in the early going, partly by setting a good example with his own generosity and inspiring others to follow his lead.

In December 1971, some ten months after receiving the Consulting Committee's report, Pingry and Kent Place agreed to affiliate. We at Pingry had thought that since coeducation was inevitable, the Kent Place School might be interested in merging, joining with us in establishing a new boys-*and*-girls' school on the fine tract we had found out in Bernards Township. But though the idea got off the ground, it didn't fly for long. The affiliation came to an end in 1973 because Kent Place decided it was in their best interest to remain where they were. Fortunately, Pingry had better success at enticing the neighboring Short Hills Country Day School to merge. Short Hills Country Day was a basic feeder school for Pingry, so a Pingry-SHCD merger came about naturally, strengthened both schools, and has proved highly successful. Among its other merits, it enabled Pingry to go coeducational across the board in the fall of 1974. Pingry thus became a two-campus school. The junior school occupies the old SHCD campus in Short Hills while the upper school continues on the new Martinsville campus.

Then the real problems began. Sooner or later every prolonged effort hits a trough. The original thrust and enthusiasm have faded away, no light has yet appeared at the end of the tunnel, and it is not even clear how long the tunnel may be. It was the misfortune of Harry Hoyt, then chairman of the board, to be our foreman for this graveyard shift. Disposing of the North Avenue plant was turning out to be a much more difficult task than we had anticipated. Initially, all had gone well. We had put together a handsome brochure and in January 1976 entered into a firm contract to sell the property to the state of New Jersey for $5 million. The state intended to use the property as a school for handicapped children. This was a sensible idea, since the state had insufficient facilities and had to export handicapped boys and girls to be educated in New York and Pennsylvania, at considerable per capita expense. The state could not pay us, however, without a recommendation from the governor to the legislature that the purchase money be appropriated, and that recommendation was never made. After a long wait, the school canceled the contract early in 1977.

One factor that contributed greatly to the stalling on the part of the legislature was the way Pingry was regarded by parts of its local community. Pingry was (and I dare say still is) resented in certain quarters as a seat of privilege. Some people therefore opposed the move because they felt the State was being hornswoggled into bailing out this rich boys' school. Others opposed the move because they wanted a fine school to remain in an area that might change for the worse with its departure. Though small in number, these opponents managed to heat up a vigorous anti-Pingry campaign. Articles reporting the controversy appeared in the newspapers. The result was that the state officials simply would not move. I remember one occasion down in Princeton at a New Jersey Historical Society dinner, when I tried to engage the governor on this issue over a drink. I had hoped that the combination of tradition and alcohol might render him mellow, but as soon as I uttered the word "Pingry," His Excellency picked up his glass and walked away. So we were left with our property, a determination to move, and not enough money. What then?

We had naturally looked to the city of Hillside, because the existing campus would have made a perfect high school. In 1978, the Hillside Board of Education offered $3 million for the property but withdrew the bid a short time later. Either they didn't have the money or they decided that they didn't need the plant. Meanwhile, the projected cost of the new building in Bernards Township had gone up by more than $6 million as a result of inflation. Total construction costs, originally estimated at around $10 million, ultimately came to over $18 million. So there were many occasions when our little band had reason to feel discouraged, and some of those who watched us flailing around had reason to say that Pingry, having made one big mistake in trying to move, was about to make an even bigger mistake in not being able to. That's when Joe Engel was at his best, providing not only the encouraging words that kept the rest of us going but also the vital green transfusions necessary to sustain the effort.

By this time, Harry Hoyt had broken his pick, if not his heart. He also had a business to run, so he turned the tiller over to Fred Bartenstein. But he stayed with the team, and I never saw him look so happy as on the day when he saw the first steel girders going up on the new site. Back in the late 1970s and early 1980s, the site was presenting what appeared to be insuperable obstacles. Mostly they had to do with toilets and plumbing. On a farm of many acres, to take a shower or flush a toilet is a minor matter, ecologically speaking, as even the most extreme environmentalist would acknowledge. But replace the farmhouse with a school of 750 to 1,000 souls, and the consequences of showers and flushings become of immediate concern. There was a need to construct an on-site disposal facility, without which we could not get a building permit. Unfortunately, Bernards Township ordinances prohibited us from erecting a permanent facility. We therefore arranged to tap into the nearby Warren Township Sewerage System (which we had helped to fund). To do so we had to obtain State Department of Environmental Protection approval for an expansion of the Warren system, a long and frustrating procedure. At the same time, we found ourselves up against the Bernards Township Planning Board, the Bernards Township Sewerage Authority, the Bernards Township Engineering Department, the Bernards Township Board of Health, the Warren Township Sewerage Authority, the Somerset-Raritan Valley Sewerage Authority, the Bridgewater Township Planning Board, the Somerset

County Planning Board—the list could go on and on. Even after we received Department of Environmental Protection approval, Warren Township refused to let us tap into its system without a recompensating flow from Bernards Township. Bernards Township saw no need for recompensation. We were left without a sewerage system.

The prospect of dealing with all those bodies—not to mention the difficulty of meeting their infinitude of requirements—intimidated even Fred Bartenstein, who had been president before becoming chairman of the board. And who can blame him? Naturally he looked for an alternative solution, which is why, one snowy day, Fred, Joe Engel, and I found ourselves tramping over the Schiff estate, a piece of property out at Mendham. It had been used for Boy Scout work but was not a camp—or, you might say, it was *more* than a camp. It consisted of a number of buildings and quite a lot of land, some of it already converted to playing-fields. The buildings had been used for classrooms and as a national training center for scoutmasters and were readily adaptable for school use. But the site was not as attractive as Bernards Township, the roads in would have been more difficult for buses, and adapting the buildings was not as desirable as building a completely new plant. Nevertheless, we began to negotiate. We wanted to keep two options open so we could go whichever way circumstances dictated. But this luxury was soon denied us by a third party. AT&T bought the Schiff property. They didn't *have* to negotiate; they just up and bought it. So that put us right back where we'd been, facing the twin problems of resolving the Bernards Township difficulties and selling the Hillside property.

As to the former, there was nothing left but to grit our teeth, go hat in hand to all those boards and authorities, and somehow satisfy them. Fred Bartenstein did exactly that, along with much else relating to architects, engineers, and loan officers of banks. He descended on those municipal monsters like a latter-day Saint George, dispatching some with shafts of legal brilliance and disarming others with the courtliness and the soft accents of his Virginia upbringing. Fred and I have been friends for a long, long time. We met on one of the old Washington-bound Pennsylvania Railroad trains back in the days when Fred was a lawyer working for Merck and I was the same for The Sperry and Hutchinson Company. We were both engaged in necessary but vexatious dealings with the government, so we both needed to know our way around Washington. To that end we one day boarded the train for the annual New Jersey Congressional Day, as it was known. The train was packed with local politicians—mayors, county supervisors, and such—

bent on lobbying their US representatives and senators for federal favors. Also aboard were most of those same representatives and senators, who had come up from the capital especially to ride back with all the hometown big shots, pressing flesh all the way. My respect for Fred Bartenstein began on that journey. Politicians at a big dinner or fundraising party will work the room, and that day I saw Fred work the train—but he didn't glad-hand. In his quiet, unassuming way he seemed to know exactly which elected officials he should speak to or make appointments with, what to say to each, and, most important, how to terminate a conversation gracefully and move on. It was an object lesson in both determination and finesse.

Warren Township eventually dropped its demands for a recompensating flow but insisted that we tap into the Middlebrook Trunk of the Somerset-Raritan regional system, then under construction, as soon as it was finished. We agreed to this condition, in the meantime planning and making the formal arrangements for our own setup in order to obtain the building permit. Eventually, through federal funding, the Somerset-Raritan regional system was enlarged, and we tied into it. And now at the new Pingry campus, you may shower, you may bathe, you may flush, you may gargle, you may do the dishes—and environmentally, ecologically, and legally not a dog will bark.

In 1980, the asking price for the Hillside plant was reduced to $4,250,000. Back in the late 1960s, Pingry had established a land-buying fund in its hopes of adding playing fields across the Elizabeth River. The Elizabeth River isn't much of a river; I always thought of it as more of a sewer. But it does manage to flow, running through a brick-lined channel into and through the city of Elizabeth. Immediately across the river, more or less facing the intersection of North Avenue and Morris Avenue, is the Kean Mansion, where John Jay was married. Morris Avenue existed as far back as the eighteenth century, when it was known as the Morris Turnpike and ran from Elizabeth to Morristown. The Kean Mansion is a historic relic dating to those times. It was originally the home of a prominent New Jersey family, but now the house and grounds are preserved by the state. When I was a boy, the Kean dairy farm was still in operation across Morris Avenue from the mansion, a beautiful farm complete with modern barns. It was the type of facility that could not run without the funding of an extremely wealthy family, so when the dairy farm closed its doors it became the site of Kean College, one of New Jersey's four-year, state-run schools.

By the 1970s, Kean College, our neighbor across Morris Avenue, was coming to the realization that our plant was the answer to some of its expansion needs. Pingry still had an option to buy the land across the Elizabeth River, but by that time the school had committed itself to a new location for the school and I had already purchased the land at Bernards Township. Kean College could use an additional education building, surely, and the Pingry plant was now available at an attractive price. The college was interested, and we began negotiations. David Baldwin, besides working effectively with architects and engineers, knew real estate values, and he gave vital assistance to Fred Bartenstein in handling these negotiations. Unfortunately, Kean was an arm of the state of New Jersey. The state kept haggling for an even lower price, and in the end Pingry was forced to sell at the near distress figure of $3.9 million. To add insult to injury, a catch was inserted into the contract stating that if Pingry had not vacated the premises by the end of 1983, a charge of $75,000 a month for the first three months and $100,000 per month thereafter would be exacted by the state. Pingry had to accept the terms, but it was not a happy moment. The problem then became one of getting the state to implement its agreement and pay for the school. I believe that it required an act of the legislature to collect the funds that the state had agreed to pay. I can't tell you how worrisome all of that was, particularly given my past experiences with the New Jersey State administration. In the end, the state finally coughed up the money. It was not nearly enough to pay for the new plant, but it was helpful. Pingry then embarked on a major fund-raising effort, and took out a mortgage of $7 million to cover the cost of building the new school.

On a cold day in April 1982, we all went out to the site of the new school and performed a simple groundbreaking ceremony, in which a shovelful of sod was lifted from the field. In June of that year, Pingry signed a contract with the Torcon construction company; it agreed to erect the new plant at a price not to exceed $16,995,200. Once construction began, Fred Bartenstein quickly shed his Saint George armor to reveal that underneath he wore an acrobat's costume. He proceeded to juggle the project's financing so dexterously and to keep the hundreds of change orders in the air so adroitly that the show opened on time and on budget in September 1983. I also worked intimately with Mac Bristol in effecting the move.

Nearly all the building work was completed by the time of the school's formal dedication in May 1984. The total cost had come to $23 million, but the end result was well worth it. What many had feared might be a flop ended up as "My Fair Pingry." Pingry's new home was favorably commented on in several architectural publications. The new

*Groundbreaking ceremony, April 1982. Left to right: Fred Bartenstein,
Dave Wilson, Bill Beinecke, Scotty Cunningham, and Mac Bristol.*

campus was dedicated to Fred Bartenstein, pale recognition for all he
did to bring the Pingry of today into being. Four successful years of
operation later, we held a great dinner party to celebrate the discharge
of the mortgage.

Although the school was still indebted to me for the cost of the
land, I encouraged the trustees to defer payment until such time as a
proper endowment for the school could be established. I had purchased the Loft property in the 1970s and, as I had promised, sold it to
Pingry at cost. When work began on the new plant in 1982, I had not yet
received any payment from Pingry but had instead accepted a non-
interest-bearing promissory note in exchange for the land. I intended
to have that note discharged upon my death. Some years before, I had
established what is known as a unitrust, a trust from which I would
receive income during my lifetime but the principal of which would go
to Pingry upon my death. I was confident that the principal of the trust
would be more than enough to cover the cost of the land, thus ensuring
that when I died and the note was being held on my estate, Pingry
would be in a position to pay my estate what it was owed. That was the
plan. Well, a few years ago, I decided that I didn't want that to happen. I
thought, Why not give the note back to Pingry either in one chunk or in

segments? This would absolve all of Pingry's debts and would allow me to take a tax deduction each year until the note was discharged. And so, in 1991, I canceled the debt of $525,000. In return, Pingry surprised me with a big party at Baltusrol. That was an occasion to remember. It had been a twenty-one-year journey, but at long last the school was paid for, the mortgage was discharged, and Pingry held the land free and clear.

Through Pingry, I was able to make a difference. Not alone, as I have explained. Not as a pioneer, either. Earlier friends of Pingry went through many of the same trials as we did—in 1892, when a new building and land cost $24,000, and in the early 1920s, when a new gymnasium, pool and locker room cost $34,000. Those sums are small potatoes today but certainly weren't then. And neither was I the workman who finished the job, nor would I want to be. As long as there is a Pingry, there will be a need to make Pingry better—and the people and the means to do so will surely appear, as in our time and in the past. For now, it's a great satisfaction for me and the rest of our little group to see Pingry in good hands, in a wonderful new plant and location, and continuing as a first-class academic institution. John Hanly, who served as headmaster for more than a dozen years until arranging to step down in the year 2000, was a truly remarkable headmaster who well positioned this fine school for a leadership role in the next century.

CHAPTER EIGHTEEN

The Yale Corporation and the School of Management

For many years after I graduated from Yale in 1936, I had little connection with the affairs of my alma mater, largely because I wasn't asked to play a more active role. To be sure, I attended my class reunions and dinners. At the class of 1936's twenty-fifth reunion in 1961, I ran the class raffle, which was more complicated than one would imagine, and also more humorous; the event ended with the loud lamentations of the man who had won a nanny goat and newborn kids (donated by a Vermont classmate) but wasn't allowed to take them back to Chicago in his wealthy host's private airplane. I was tangentially involved with the negotiations that led to the donation of the Beinecke Rare Book and Manuscript Library to Yale, and in 1960, I'd seen to it that the Beinecke Foundation gave money to the Yale Law School to augment the William S. Beinecke Scholarship Fund I had previously established to help finance the education of promising African-American law students.

My first direct involvement with Yale's affairs as an alumnus, however, came in the early 1960s when my classmate S. Dillon Ripley asked me to become a member of the University Council Committee on the Peabody Museum of Natural History. The Peabody Museum has impressive collections in fields ranging from anthropology to zoology, but it's best known to thousands of starry-eyed young boys and girls for its dinosaur skeletons and other fossil remains. Dillon, who was then running the museum and would soon become general secretary of the Smithsonian, was aware that I didn't know the difference between a pterodactyl and a tyrannosaurus. But he also knew, or suspected, that I had a deep and abiding love for Yale that needed to be fulfilled somehow. From that involvement came my second major gift to Yale, a freight elevator to the Peabody that is large enough to transport dinosaurs or parts thereof. Through the same connections, I helped Yale acquire Horse Island, one of the largest of the Thimble Islands group off the Connecticut coast, to be cordoned off from public intrusion as an environmental research station.

By 1963, I was a full-fledged member of the University Council, and in 1967 I was named to the Council's Executive Committee. The University Council is a useful body for Yale in several ways. It's a means of getting alumni interested in the university and keeping them interested, particularly alumni who might not otherwise be actively participating in university affairs. And it's a way for alumni and outside experts, through the University Council committees, to visit and examine parts of the university (like the library or various professional schools) and get a feeling about how they're going about their work. These committees can then report that information (together with any recommendations) to the president. Some of these reports have had a significant effect on certain directions that the university has taken; the School of Organization and Management at Yale, with which I have been heavily involved for several decades, owes its original conception to the thoughts expressed in a University Council Committee on the Graduate School more than thirty-five years ago.

My connection with the University Council led to another commitment: in 1969, Yale's president, Kingman Brewster, invited me to have dinner with him and his lieutenant Howard Phelan in New York. In the course of the dinner Kingman asked me to become the head of the university's Development Board. The board was then composed of 157 prominent Yale alumni and was chiefly responsible for helping the university raise money from its alumni. I accepted, and in December 1969 succeeded DeWitt Peterkin as chairman. I saw quite a lot of Kingman Brewster after that, and I always had a high regard for him. He was a very warm and exciting fellow to be with. He was full of ideas. He would sit down and have a drink and visit with you the same as anybody would, but he didn't really enjoy just sitting around and talking about nothing. Trivia didn't seem to satisfy him. When you were with Kingman, it wasn't long before you were examining some important question and he was asking you your views on it. He had a questing mind. He was always interested in what people thought and felt but had his own firm, well-developed ideas about some of the problems that troubled society. He sometimes fell back on a convoluted and lawyerly syntax, and fairly early in his incumbency I went to him and said, "Look, you have got to stop making those polysyllabic speeches and make speeches that even I can understand." Far from being offended, he was delighted to have what he called "a candid coach and critic," and for years afterward he used to call me "Coach."

Yale's relations with its alumni were in a parlous state when I became chairman of the Development Board, mainly because so many alumni were so damned mad at students everywhere at that time. Student unrest, fueled by the war in Vietnam, was sweeping across American college campuses in the late 1960s. The established institutions of society—the presidency, the armed forces, university administrations, the corporate world—were being stigmatized as self-serving oppressors deserving of almost any outrage that could be perpetrated against them. Yale students contributed their share to the tumult. The demonstration on the New Haven Green in May 1970, with the National Guardsmen waiting in the wings, could easily have turned into a bloodbath, as a similar demonstration did at Kent State University a few days later. But despite some extreme and dangerous provocations, Yale was *not* torn apart by violence as were Columbia, Harvard, Cornell, and so many other universities. Even today, I can close my eyes and see a photograph of a Cornell student standing on a platform brandishing an assault rifle, with a bandolier of cartridges around his shoulder. It's a terrifying image, the sort of thing you'd expect to see in revolutionary Cuba, not in an American university. The fabric of Yale was stretched in those years, but it did not break— for which one man above all was responsible. With almost unerring insight, President Brewster made masterly use of his powers of persuasion so that common sense, decency toward others, and regard for the university prevailed—at Yale, at any rate—over the powerful forces of disruption then at large. Kingman was sensitive to the issues, sensitive to the voices of the undergraduates, and sensitive to their concern about the involvement of our country in Vietnam. He listened to them. No one has ever done more for Yale than Kingman Brewster did then.

Of course, at the time of the May Day demonstration, Kingman made that statement—which has been both misquoted and misunderstood—in which he said that he was skeptical whether a black revolutionary could get a fair trial anywhere in the United States. He did *not* say that a black revolutionary could not get a fair trial, he said that he doubted whether one could; that's an important difference in connotation. But his statement was misinterpreted by people who were far from New Haven, and by some who were not so far but who were not as sensitive to the issues as Kingman was. In my opinion, that statement went a long way toward defusing the situation. But it was misread and misconstrued at the time, and consequently there was a division among the alumni respecting the president of the university.

Coupled with this problem was an admissions policy that, in the opinion of some, was not sensitive enough to the sons of alumni (in that era before coeducation) who were seeking admission to Yale. Brewster's dean of admissions, "Inky" Clark, changed the composition of the Yale undergraduate body from one largely made up of prep school graduates to one in which there were more graduates of public high school and in which a greater effort had been made to achieve ethnic diversity. Yale for the first time admitted women as undergraduates in the fall of 1969, and my daughter Frances was one of that group of pioneers. These admissions policies caused a lot of distress and concern on the part of the more conservative alumni. Brewster and Clark also instituted a need-blind admissions policy, which required strong financial undergirding. And in order for Yale to have the resources to implement these policies, it had to go to those very same disgruntled alumni and ask them to give the university the money that would enable it to move in directions they didn't like. It was an anomalous situation. But in the last third of the twentieth century, for an American university college *not* to have moved in those directions wouldn't have been in keeping with the spirit of the times. If the changes Yale made during the 1960s had not happened, Yale would not now be in the forefront of American education, nor would it be as highly regarded as it is today. And I think that we can thank Kingman Brewster for his foresight, and also for his courage, in that respect.

At the same time that I was trying to mediate between Yale and its alumni as chairman of the Development Board, I was also helping to push forward plans that would eventually result in the creation of the Yale School of Organization and Management. Since the mid-1950s, a growing number of alumni had felt that Yale should give serious thought to establishing, as we called it, a "business school." For me and many others, this conviction was a product of personal experience. Following the outbreak of World War II, we had witnessed a swift evolution in the structure of US business and industry. The norm was no longer single-product enterprises under the leadership and control of founding entrepreneurs or single families; now it was public ownership, diversified product lines, and institutionalization that created a growing need for the organizational and operating techniques customarily referred to as "modern management." We believed that this trend would continue to surge for years to come, as indeed it has. We felt that Yale could and should play a direct role in shaping a development of such obvious importance to the capitalistic system and our national life. We were confident that Yale, being Yale, could make a uniquely valuable contribution to the education of managers, just as the Yale Schools of Medicine, Law, and Divinity had done for many generations of doctors, lawyers, and ministers. We constituted not an organized movement of alumni but a diffused body of opinion that hoped to bring about constructive action in what it saw as Yale's best interests. Our view of those interests was not universally shared, however—the leading dissenter being Yale's president during the 1950s and early 1960s, A. Whitney Griswold.

If ever a man was a darling of the gods, that man was Whitney Griswold. He had been my favorite teacher as an undergraduate, a man who made American history live and breathe. He possessed an intellect both powerful and supple. In character and convictions, he was determined, forthright, and confident. And yet these intimidating virtues were balanced by an effervescent personal charm. His smile was warm and engaging. His conversation sparkled with wit and good humor. He loved to sing songs and play the banjo. President Griswold was dedicated, heart and soul, to academic humanism and to Yale. In his view, the purpose of an education—especially a Yale education—was to strengthen one's powers of thought and instill a knowledge and appreciation of civilization and civilized values. In this he saw no place for what he sometimes referred to as "a trade school for businessmen."

Furthermore, President Griswold could count on some powerful allies. At the time, the Yale Corporation included among its sixteen members the heads of three of the country's most important companies: Irving Olds of United States Steel, Brewster Jennings of Mobil Oil, and Juan Trippe of Pan American. They were all firmly in his corner, along with two of Yale's greatest past and potential benefactors: John Hay Whitney, also a trustee, and President Griswold's Yale College classmate Paul Mellon. It is a comment on President Griswold's powers of leadership that these five tycoons—who collectively commanded the loyalty of millions of employees and shareholders, not to mention billions of dollars in assets—were in educational matters proud to be commanded by him.

A man must be appraised in the context of his times. Whitney Griswold graduated from Yale College in the fateful year of 1929. His studies in the Graduate School, his acceptance into Yale's history department, his steady climb up the faculty ladder until his appointment, in 1949, as Yale's sixteenth president took place in a period of economic depression, followed by wartime and postwar economic turmoil. For two decades, American institutions of higher education, Yale included, had to live on continually short rations. With that background, it was inevitable that President Griswold viewed Yale's finances as what we today would call a zero-sum game. That is, any funds required for new educational programs would have to be withdrawn from current programs. He set forth his priorities clearly. Yale's strength, glory, and mission as a university were bound up in the liberal humanities. Having been underfunded for years, they must be given their full due, with no diversions or sideshows.

President Griswold died well before his time, at age fifty-six. He was succeeded by Kingman Brewster, whom he had persuaded three years earlier to leave the faculty of Harvard Law School and accept appointment as university provost, Yale's second-ranking officer. The two men, though separated in age by twelve years, had much in common. They were at one in their devotion to Yale and its continuing improvement. They shared a liking for sailing and summers on Martha's Vineyard. But there were differences, too, the most important being that President Brewster was a strong academic expansionist. He wanted not just a better Yale but a bigger, more diverse, more universal Yale as well. And he is not to be faulted in this. A great university is poorly served by a leader who looks at the place as Theodore Roosevelt looked at the Grand Canyon, saying, "Leave it alone. You cannot improve upon it."

Furthermore, the times favored expansion. When President Brewster took office in 1963, the country had been blessed with prosperity for nearly fifteen years. Gifts to Yale from alumni were increasing sharply. Foundation giving was moving into high gear. This rising tide was soon to become a flood with the huge new federal subsidies to higher education—especially to leading research universities like Yale—resulting from the Great Society legislation of the Johnson administration. From every corner of the university came proposals for the disposition of this largesse. But the new president had his priorities, too. The humanities had had their day under his predecessor. President Brewster—trained in the law, skilled in journalism, and with a gift for advocacy and debate—was interested in government, economics, and the development of public policy. He sought a greater role for Yale in helping make our system work better.

In Brewster's early annual reports one can find phrases on the order of "Yale needs to do more in the social sciences" and references to Yale's mission of educating future leaders in, among other fields, management. You will look in vain, however, for the word "business."

President Brewster's interest was not confined to the private, profit-making sector but included the not-for-profit and public sectors as well. His real focus was on institutions, especially the large, bureaucratic organizations that increasingly dominate American society: *Fortune* 500 corporations, of course, but also federal regulatory agencies, municipal school systems, hospitals, universities, centers for the arts, and so on. Though their goals differ, large institutions of every kind are much alike in their need for capable and far-seeing management. It is important to society that this need be met—and an opportunity and an obligation for Yale to educate men and women to meet it. Thus ran President Brewster's reasoning.

Nevertheless, those of us who wanted a business school at Yale appreciated the difference in his outlook from what President Griswold's had been, and felt that at last we were getting somewhere. Furthermore, this time *we* had an important ally. John Perry Miller, long a professor of economics at Yale and in the mid-1960s dean of the Graduate School, had come to believe as we did. As a hard-working and effective fund-raiser for a variety of academic programs, Professor Miller was personally acquainted with many Yale alumni who occupied important positions in American business. He recognized the great value to Yale of their efforts, influence, and financial support. The Yale experience of business leaders of the 1950s and 1960s almost always had been as undergraduates. But Professor Miller was convinced that by the mid-1980s and certainly afterward, a preponderance of American business leaders would hold advanced degrees. He believed it essential for many reasons, including future Yale fund-raising, that a body of loyal alumni should exist who had earned those advanced degrees at Yale. I myself felt that without a school of business, Yale was a truncated university and as such couldn't fully compete with its venerable elder brother on the Charles River. I also knew that the Harvard Business School had built up a very loyal alumni body of its own, and that in turn financially benefited Harvard substantially. Many of these people had had no Harvard connection at all until they went to the Business School, and many of them had attended institutions as undergraduates to which they had no great sense of loyalty: small, undistinguished colleges or state universities that were so large that their students were lost in the process. But when they got to the Business School, they became Harvard men and Harvard women. That has been a very positive force for Harvard in the world, because so many of the people who graduated from the Harvard Business School have gone on to take important roles in business and other management activities.

The Brewster–Miller approach was to appoint a sequence of committees on the social sciences at Yale: first a University Council committee composed mostly of alumni, then a faculty committee, and finally a parallel faculty *and* alumni Committee on the Operational Uses of the Social Sciences, on which I had the honor to serve, to implement the recommendations of the first two committees. These bodies concluded that for proper teaching and study of the management of institutions (whether public, private, or not-for-profit), several academic disciplines would have to be involved. For example, to understand the workings of a big-city school system would require specialized knowledge from such varied departments as economics, government, administrative sciences, and sociology. Public health might also have a contribution to make, and perhaps even psychology as well. But there was no way under the departmental system prevailing in the Yale Faculty of the Arts and Sciences for such a diverse group of specialists to be gathered together on the kind of formal and continuing basis necessary to attract students and generate useful results.

The solution, as the committee I served on recommended, was to create such a forum, and this was done. It was called the Institution for Social and Policy Studies. John Perry Miller moved from his post as dean of the Graduate School to become the first director of the ISPS. It was in the beginning to be a house with three wings, so to speak: urban studies, education studies, and management studies. For each wing, faculty members were to be borrowed from their regular academic departments for part-time teaching and study. Other specialists would be brought to Yale from the outside as adjunct professors with term appointments. A degree program would be set up and graduate students would be encouraged to apply. The studies themselves would be in no sense theoretical but would deal with existing conditions and institutions. This emphasis would, we hoped, counter the excessively theoretical orientation of many of Yale's social science departments, which were not attuned to the world of affairs and had no interest in preparing students for operational careers. One of the first study programs set up was a nondegree program for potential superintendents of large city school systems.

The ISPS was an innovative idea at a time when academic innovation was much in fashion. It went well from the start. At the outset, however, only two wings of the house were occupied: urban studies and education studies. Management studies was delayed because a proper assortment of faculty could not be recruited in time. For me and many others, this was a keen disappointment. It was our hope and belief that the management studies wing of ISPS, if it proved successful, could within a couple of years be separated from the other two and set up on its own as the "business school" we had so long wanted. Now we would have to wait before the stepping-stone would be in place.

As we waited, our disappointment deepened. It was feared that in the antiestablishment context of the late 1960s, the implementation of the management studies program would be branded as proof that Yale had become the lackey of corporate America. So once again we had to wait for a couple of years until the political winds had shifted. Meanwhile the ISPS had developed its own style and way of doing things. Its approach to urban and education studies was specific and concentrated, tightly confined to the problems being studied. Its orientation was toward ad hoc academic study rather than career preparation. Consequently, John Perry Miller and his associates at ISPS had concluded that a program for the education of managers, if it was to be successful, should be organized as an independent school with its own dean and faculty rather than as a degree program with ISPS. Otherwise, they feared, the best faculty and students would not be attracted. The stepping-stone having thus crumbled, the choice lay between crossing the stream without it or not crossing the stream at all. John Perry Miller remained firm in his conviction that a full-fledged "school" should be established, but with no faculty, no financing, not even any housing, the long-sought goal remained remote. As the boom times and expansionist outlook of the 1960s faded into the distance, the prospect of *ever* reaching it became more bleak with each passing month.

I like those movies where the Indians have the wagon train surrounded and the settlers are about to be massacred, when suddenly the United States Cavalry appears on the crest of a hill, the bugle sounds the charge, and the day is saved. Nothing so spectacular as that saved our day. In fact, it was a commonplace thing. An elderly gentleman died. He was my father, Frederick William Beinecke, of the class of 1909S. He loved Yale and, with his brothers, Edwin and Walter, had over the years shared his good fortune with Yale. He had helped finance the ISPS because of where he and I hoped it was heading. In his will Yale was named heir to one-quarter of his estate. At his death, several previously established trusts also went to Yale. That occurred in 1971. It took well over a year for everything to be sorted out, by which time it was clear that quite a tidy sum was involved. Not enough to endow a new school, not enough to make it financially independent, but enough to get a school started.

Meanwhile, the Yale Corporation had undergone some changes. In 1971, at the very time of Frances's graduation from Yale College, I was asked to become a successor trustee of the Yale Corporation. The formal announcement was made at my thirty-fifth reunion. I was not the first of our class to serve on the Corporation; Jonathan Brewster Bingham was elected to fill an unexpired alumni trustee term in 1949 and was on the board for two years. But I remember well, and with some emotion, the loud cheer that erupted in Woolsey Hall when Kingman Brewster announced my election.

I'd had no indication that Kingman was thinking of inviting me to be a member of the Corporation, but I had hoped in the bottom of my heart that it might happen. In the late 1960s, I had turned down invitations to join other college boards, determined to keep myself free just in case Yale came calling. One day in 1967, I received a call from Bob Baldwin, the head of Morgan Stanley, who was then in Washington. "Bill," he yelled in his emphatic and outgoing way, "has the president called you yet?" I replied, "What president?" "What president?! For God's sake, Bill, there's only one president!" I was still puzzled. Bob explained that President Lyndon Johnson wanted to appoint me to the board of visitors of the United States Naval Academy. I told Bob that I would have to think about it. Only a few days before, Grayson Kirk, the president of Columbia University, had invited me to serve on his institution's board of trustees. While Kirk's invitation was a wonderful honor, I knew that if I accepted I would never be offered a seat on the Yale Corporation—or if I was, I wouldn't be able to accept it, because I certainly couldn't serve on both the Yale and the Columbia boards. I had asked Grayson Kirk to give me the weekend to mull it over, and while I was doing so, in came this call from Bob Baldwin!

Bob informed me that I had better think the matter over fast because the president was ready to announce the appointment to the press. That decided me. "If I have to think about it that fast, Bob, the answer is, 'No, thank you, I cannot accept.'" He agreed to tell the president. It's a darn good thing that Johnson never called me himself, because you can't very well say no to the president of the United States. Only a few minutes after I'd hung up the phone, however, it rang again. It was Bob: "Bill, it's too late!" "What do you mean?" "It's too late," Bob repeated, "the president has already released news of your appointment to the press." "He can't have!" "He has!" The next morning I woke up and read in the *New York Times* that I had just been designated a member of the United States Naval Academy board of visitors. I thought, "This is terrible. I hope Grayson Kirk doesn't see this, because he'll take it as a personal affront." Indeed, I decided right then that I'd better seize time by the forelock and mention this item to Kirk just in case he should be inspired to a particularly thorough perusal of the *Times* that Saturday morning. It's a good thing I called him, because he had in fact already seen the announcement. I said something to the effect of, "Well, you know how enthusiastic the president gets sometimes. His excitement carried him away and he announced the appointment to the press before consulting me." I assured Kirk that I had not accepted the invitation and that I was not going to be a member of the Naval Academy board of visitors. He was very polite and gracious in accepting my apology, as he was a few days later when I told him I couldn't accept his invitation to serve on the Columbia University board of trustees. I got to know Grayson Kirk better a few years later, when we both served on the board of Consolidated Edison. He was kind of a stuffed shirt, and he had a terrible time with the Columbia riots of 1968, but he was an intelligent man and I always liked him.

I was one of four new members named to the Yale Corporation in 1971. The other successor trustees were Hanna Holborn Gray (later provost and president of Yale, and subsequently president of the University of Chicago) and Lance Liebman (later dean of the Columbia Law School). Marian Wright Edelman, longtime head of the Children's Defense Fund, was elected as an alumni trustee. The four of us formed a little group; we called ourselves "The Freshman Class." I quickly decided that it had been worth it to hold myself open for Yale. The Yale Corporation was one of the warmest fellowships and collegial groups I've ever participated in. Over the years, I've been on lots of committees and business and eleemosynary boards, but I've never had an experience like that one. You inevitably develop intimate friendships with other members of the Corporation while serving on the board. I became close friends not only with my fellow freshmen but with such outstanding individuals as Cyrus Vance, Bill Bundy, Strobe Talbott, John Chafee, John Danforth, Irwin Miller, Caryl Haskins, Bill Scranton, Leon Higginbotham, Jake Madden, Barbara Preiskel, and Maxine Singer. I became particularly good friends with J. Richardson Dilworth. Dick and I had known each other for years, but not well. For most of my time on the Corporation, Dick was the senior fellow, the nearest thing the Yale Corporation has to a chairman. Dick was a model of wise and informed leadership, and any chair of any organization would do well to look to his example. In such a gemütlich atmosphere as the Yale Corporation, all votes are usually unanimous, and only every once in a while is there a division. I was interested to find that on those very few occasions, the division was never the same. People voted their individual consciences, and there was never a bloc that voted in accordance with any preordained shibboleth.

When I joined the Corporation in 1971, Yale was still in a state of some turmoil, though we certainly didn't expect any more events as serious and even terrifying as the May Day demonstrations of 1970. But if it was not a time of unrest, it was at least a time of serious questioning by the students of the day, who wondered whether the people who were supposed to be guiding their education were doing it in a sensible or correct manner. They were a questioning crowd, the undergraduates of the early 1970s. I used to encounter them quite frequently at the student-fellow meetings arranged by the university. Quite often one or two of the fellows of the Corporation would go to a residential college and have breakfast in the master's house with twenty or so students. I also made it an annual event to organize a luncheon at Mory's or the Graduate Club for students whom I either knew or had some connection with, including the children or grandchildren of friends and the minority students who held the Beinecke fellowships at the Law School. I'd invite maybe eighteen or nineteen young people, ranging from freshmen to advanced graduate students. Those occasions gave me a good opportunity to listen to the students on an informal, unstructured basis.

The early 1970s were a difficult time for Yale financially, but the crisis wouldn't have been all that severe if Yale hadn't been seeking to do more than it had money for. Kingman Brewster was very ambitious for Yale and sought to involve the university in a multiplicity of things, all of which strained the budget—both the operating budget and the endowment, to the extent that spending from the endowment can be considered part of the budget. Yale had a deficit during all eleven years I served on the Corporation, and the university has only recently got its annual accounts in balance. The financial problems came about because of Kingman's ambitions for the university on the one hand and rising inflation on the other. Costs were going up faster than our income, so that even if we maintained the educational services at a level, they were costing us more money than we were taking in. That's one reason tuition went up at such an alarming rate. As for operating the plant, we had to face the rising cost of petroleum, brought about by the oil embargo of the early 1970s, and Yale was largely dependent on petroleum to run its power plant. Yale needed to work harder at achieving economies in operating its plant—buildings would remain overheated all the time—and to employ tighter management in its financial controls. Alumni contributions may have declined in the 1970s because there was the feeling by a large number of people in the financial world that Yale was not managing its endowment very well. I was one of the Corporation members urging a more conservative policy on spending unrealized capital gains from the endowment, and we did fix spending at a much more conservative level. As a consequence of that change, and as a result of good financial management and investment strategy, the Yale endowment has done extremely well for the last decade.

The economic tribulations of the 1970s were particularly hard on Kingman Brewster, since he was temperamentally suited to preside over a university that was expanding rather than contracting. There were many other unpleasantries of the early 1970s that would have caused a lesser man not to enjoy the job of the Yale presidency—not only May Day 1970 but also the 1971 labor strike, when the Brewsters' yard at Hillhouse Avenue was trashed. But Kingman's brilliance and high spirits overrode those things, so that he always appeared to be full of enthusiasm and good spirits and dedicated to moving Yale forward.

In the spring of 1973, with President Brewster in the chair, with John Perry Miller impatiently waiting in the wings, with Fritz Beinecke's bounty in the bank, and with many hundreds and even thousands of Yale alumni hoping for a yea vote, I had the honor of moving the Corporation's establishment of a Yale School of Organization and Management, and the satisfaction of having the motion carry. John Perry Miller, in his personal memoir, *Creating Academic Settings*, gave me more credit than I deserve for this development; the school's creation was the work of many hands over many years. In any event, the cake came out of the oven just in time. Within weeks of the vote, war broke out in the Middle East, to be followed by the Arab oil boycott, the ascendancy of OPEC, and a long run of heavy economic weather. The effects of all this on Yale's budget and Yale's endowment were so serious that the status quo ante was not restored until well into the 1980s. There is no doubt in my mind that if the vote to establish the School of Organization and Management had been delayed for another six months, the decision would have gone the other way. As the duke of Wellington said of the battle of Waterloo, "It was a damned near-run thing."

Kingman, being Kingman, had supported the proposed school all along, but as a Yale man he didn't want it to be simply a carbon copy of the Harvard Business School. He was the one who decided that it should be a school of organization and management instead of just a business school. It was also Kingman, with his Anglophilic propensities, who suggesting replacing the word "School" in SOM's title with the

European term "Faculty," so that Yale's new creature would bear the mysterious name "Faculty of Organization and Management." He assured the members of the Corporation that "Faculty" was a very respected term abroad. When Kingman forwarded this suggestion, I found myself in a bind. On the one hand, the president of the university is the president, and when he makes a recommendation to the Corporation on an academic matter, he carries all the weight of the academy with him. On the other hand, I was convinced that this "Faculty" business simply would not fly. Nobody would understand what it meant. It was difficult enough to launch a new educational unit within a university without complicating matters by giving it a name no one would understand.

In the presence of our colleagues on the Corporation, I objected, as mildly as possible, to the proposed designation and suggested we stick with the dull but functional "School." The Corporation, by a

Yale Corporation, December 16, 1978. Seated, left to right: Lance Liebman, Bishop Paul Moore, J. Richard Dilworth, A. Bartlett Giamatti, William P. Bundy, William S. Beinecke, Senator John Danforth. Standing, left to right: Joseph H. Williams, Bayless Manning, Maxine Singer, John B. Madden, David Grimes, Strobe Talbott, Barbara Preiskell, Gilbert Grosvenor.

divided vote, declined to accept the president's recommendation. I am convinced that this was a very good thing in retrospect. One of the people who had voted the other way later confessed, "I voted with Kingman because I felt that in academic matters, one has to support the president. But you know, Bill, now I think you were right." The vote made it clear that the Corporation was not just the president's rubber stamp, as many had charged it was. On another occasion I had made a record of the votes, pro and con, for one of the other rare issues that had divided the Corporation, the decision to drop the coeducation ratio that had limited women to forty percent of the undergraduate body. I compared that list with the tally of the people who had voted in favor of the "School" of Management versus those who had voted in favor of a "Faculty." The results were revealing: there was no uniformity between the two lists. The votes were completely different. This indicated to me that the members of the Corporation came to each individual issue and voted their own consciences.

It was decided that graduates of the Yale School of Organization and Management would receive a MPPM degree—Master of Public and Private Management—rather than the traditional MBA. I felt this decision was just another attempt to differentiate SOM's program from Harvard's, and I didn't think it was a good idea. Although some students maintained that the degree's initials stood for "More Power, Prestige, and Money," the MPPM was not a generally understood degree in the way that an MBA was, and I foresaw that it could create problems for graduates in search of first-time employment. Fortunately, Yale has had good students in the program who have been able to overcome the difficulty of explaining to potential employers what their degree stands for. The counterargument was that once the students *had* that first job and had proven their worth, their employers wouldn't care about the initials on the degree—and five or six years down the road, SOM graduates might take pride in this degree with the strange name and lord it over Harvard graduates with their less exotic MBAs. Over the years, however, it turned out that the degree remained more a curiosity than a virtue. In 1998, the school—now called simply the Yale School of Management—finally adopted the MBA. I think the change is a sign of strength, since there's no longer any worry that SOM is a Harvard imitator. In the future, Yale's graduates should have an easier time getting that first job with an MBA.

We had come up with a name for the school and had decided upon a degree, but much more had to be done before the school was ready to admit its first students. In fact, the next three years brought greater obstacles than had yet presented themselves. The major reason for the delay was that Kingman wanted to appoint a dean who would really launch the school, somebody who would be a kind of entrepreneur. He could have put his hand on some academic who was prominent on the faculty of Harvard, Columbia, Stanford, or some other business school, but he wanted to wait until he had found the right person. I think it was a wise decision. When he chose a dean, he reached into the Corporation itself and asked Bill Donaldson (who used to sit next to me at Corporation meetings) if he would take on the task. Bill was a Wall Street financier rather than an academic, but he was an entrepreneur. He had a lot of energy, and he launched the school and got it going. I remember stopping in to see him in the early days of summer when they were processing the applicants for the school's first class. He had set up camp in one of the buildings on Hillhouse Avenue that are now part of SOM. He showed me the students' folders and told me how thrilled he was by the quality of the applicants for this first class.

Yale's School of Organization and Management was launched in 1976, and graduated its first class in 1978. The class was small compared with those of today, but the graduates took a certain amount of pride in the fact that they were the school's "charter class." I was asked to deliver a speech to the members of that first class at their fifth reunion in 1983, which I did, and I've gotten to know some of SOM's graduates rather well. In the years that have followed, I've kept up with the school's activities and watched its struggle to define itself. In the relatively short period of its existence, it has had eight different deans, with an average tenure of only two years. That suggests that SOM has had a hard time finding its niche in the world, but I would prefer to say that the school has experienced growing pains. Overall, though, I am very pleased with the direction it has taken. It has gone far in fulfilling its purpose of bringing the same kind of excellence that characterizes a Yale College education to the instruction and training of the country's and the world's future managers. Those managers of tomorrow include not only men and women whose destination is private enterprise but managers at all levels of government (people with whom private enterprise increasingly must deal and who frequently are found wanting), as well as in the third sector. This last group includes those partly private, partly public institutions that embody so much of the quality of American life, such as hospitals, universities, museums, and the like. I think that what makes the school distinctive is this larger mission of educating managers to serve our society's system, not simply as it has been but as it is becoming.

The creation of a business school at Yale (even if it wasn't referred to as such) was the fulfillment of a long-held dream by many alumni. Other initiatives were under way in the 1970s that also aimed to heal the strains in the Yale family brought about by the pressures of the 1960s. Kingman was very concerned about Yale's frayed ties to its alumni and caused a commission to be set up under the chairmanship of Martin Dwyer that studied all aspects of alumni relations. From this commission came the Association of Yale Alumni, designed to unify the many disparate bodies that once represented the alumni and make them more effective. There are semiannual AYA meetings at Yale, with representation from all the various Yale constituencies across the country. As intended, the AYA has been a very positive factor, both in keeping the alumni informed and in soothing the hurt feelings of the 1960s. To my mind, the creation of the AYA is the best evidence of Kingman Brewster's sensitivity toward the alumni.

Another major way of reaching out to the alumni was The Campaign for Yale, a major capital-fund drive launched in 1974 that was also intended to strengthen Yale's relations with its alumni. Private higher education in America was then in a state of crisis. Whereas ten years earlier Yale's cup had runneth over in terms of government contributions and foundation assistance, the 1970s were a time of reduced government support for research, scholarships, and loans and of ever smaller and more restricted grants from foundations. First-class education is extraordinarily labor-intensive, and the effects of rising inflation had been devastating. With competition among all universities, private and public, growing more intensive, Yale initiated the drive not for any great expansion of its academic programs and physical plant but simply so that the university might be able to carry on with what it had been doing.

I was on the Corporation committee chaired by William McChesney Martin (then head of the Federal Reserve) that was charged with looking into Yale's capital needs. While it was clear that Yale could effectively put to work at least a billion dollars, we knew that there was no way such a sum could be raised. We eventually recommended a goal of $370 million. That was the largest campaign ever undertaken by an American university up to that point. In fact, though, we knew that Yale actually needed more than $400 million but were so shy of that first digit that we thought the best way to avoid scaring people would be to ask for something in the $300 million range—sort of like a $9.95 price. We thought that would sit better with the alumni and with the people who were charged with the task of soliciting all that money. Of the $370 million,

$65 million was to come from foundations and corporations, but for the remaining $305 million we were dependent on the generosity of individuals, mostly alumni. With that decision made, I returned to my job in New York, where I was visited by an unexpected delegation of Yale types. They told me that since I had played such a major part in the recommendation to raise $370 million, the least I could do was to serve as chairman of the National Leadership Gifts Committee that would concentrate its efforts on a thousand or so of Yale's largest donors. I asked how much this committee had to raise and was told the answer: $165 million. After a dash of cold water brought me to, I went to work.

It didn't take long for me to discover that raising large sums of money is an arduous task. Compared with the $1.5 billion that Yale raised in its most recent campaign, $370 million seems like a pittance. But you have to adjust for inflation and the unpropitious financial climate of the mid-1970s. I kept looking enviously at the Harvard Business School alumni roster and thinking, "Yale should have something like that." I was called upon to speechify in New Haven, Minneapolis, and even Hong Kong, where I was attending a Manufacturers Hanover directors' meeting. Those outreach missions, and many others like them, were useful not only in raising money for Yale but also, like the AYA, in dissipating the legacy of hurt feelings and misunderstandings of the 1960s. The Campaign for Yale wound up going over the top, continuing even after Kingman Brewster left Yale. When we finally closed the books, the Leadership Gifts Committee had exceeded its goal of $165 million by $8 million. At some point, George Bush was brought in as co-chairman, although he didn't play a very active role and was essentially a titular head; he was involved in the CIA or the UN at the time. The man who truly provided the leadership for the campaign was my good friend Ed Swensen, then head of a Miami bank.

Needless to say, the Beinecke family was active in The Campaign for Yale, just as we have tried over the years to make a significant contribution to Yale, through the Beinecke Library, the School of Organization and Management, and several other means. While the donations of my father's estate had gotten the ball rolling for the School of Organization and Management, my uncle Edwin provided further financial support for the school with the creation of the William S. Beinecke Chair of Management. Shortly before his death in 1970, my uncle told me that he was earmarking a certain portion of his estate for Yale University, and the two of us discussed the general direction in which that funding should go. I remember so well my uncle Ed's saying to me,

"What's that thing you're interested in up at Yale?" Management studies, I told him. The almost immediate result was his creation of a chair
in management studies in my name at ISPS. What a man! Because the
Center for Management Studies never really got off the ground, the
William S. Beinecke Chair (along with the ISPS's Department of Indus-
trial Administration) was absorbed by SOM with its founding in 1976.
There is also a second Beinecke chair at SOM, the Edwin J. Beinecke
Chair of Econometrics. I don't know whether E. J. funded it himself or
whether it was funded by his estate. My father also established the Fred-
erick W. Beinecke Chair in Economics, which is within the College of
Arts and Sciences and is held today by Yale's current president, Rick
Levin. I admit I was pleased to see President Levin continue on as the
Frederick W. Beinecke professor even after he was named Yale's chief
administrator. And in May of 1996, I established the Frederick W.
Beinecke Chair in Engineering. Engineering at Yale has had some ups
and downs. At various points in the university's history the department
has languished, but at present it's on the upswing. It has a superb dean
in Allan Bromley, and the administration has been making efforts to
strengthen Yale's engineering activities. I heard about these efforts and
realized that my family had never really done anything in this area
despite the fact that my father had graduated summa cum laude with a
Sigma Xi key (the scientific equivalent of Phi Beta Kappa) in civil engineering from Yale's Sheffield Scientific School. I thought it would be
appropriate for me to honor his memory by doing something that
would benefit engineering at Yale. When in May 1996 the university
announced the creation of the Frederick W. Beinecke Chair in Engineering at a celebration held at the Beinecke Library, President Levin,
Dean Bromley, and I all spoke briefly. The chair is not limited to a specific branch or specialty within the field of engineering—Yale no
longer offers civil engineering, my father's area of study—but can be
for any engineering discipline, as designated by the president and the
Corporation.

The principal benefaction to Yale of my father, my uncles, and
their wives was, of course, the Beinecke Rare Book and Manuscript
Library. It has been a constant source of inspiration and interest. A
couple of my cousins have retained that bibliophilic interest; Bud
Beinecke collected an impressive amount of material dealing with
James Barrie and the Lesser Antilles, and his sister Betsy Shirley
amassed one of the great collections of children's literature. I'm not a
book collector, but I have kept in touch with the librarians at the
Beinecke Library and have tried to keep a watchful eye on its financial

welfare. I've looked to Yale's nonacademic needs, too, as when, in 1966, I proposed giving Yale a certain sum to provide a watering system for the Yale Golf Course. As I said before, Kingman counterproposed that I give the donation to some other, more academic purpose, but eventually he graciously, and gratefully, acquiesced. A few winters ago, I saw one of my Columbia Law School friends down in Florida, not long after Lee Bass had rescinded his $20 million gift to Yale for the study of Western civilization. My friend needled me about the situation, saying, "Bill, this is nothing new. I remember when you wanted to install a watering system on the golf course, and that president you had up there then, Brewster Somebody, said he was going to use the money for a chair in Sanskrit. You told him you would take the money back." It's true that Kingman had misgivings about the public impact of a golf course irrigation system in the mid-1960s, and he also had his own ideas about Yale's funding priorities. But it's entirely right and proper for the president of a university to jockey with potential donors to get the most money under the most favorable terms possible, just as it's right and proper for the donor to negotiate the best use of his or her gift. And there were two other not-insignificant differences between my situation and Lee Bass's: my donation wasn't anywhere near the $20 million range and there was no way I could take the money back, since I hadn't parted with it yet. I subsequently made a number of other improvements at the Yale golf course, including the installation of golf carts and golf cart paths and, more recently, the building of its handsome clubhouse.

At various points throughout the long course of The Campaign for Yale, I worked with Acting President Hannah Gray and President Bart Giamatti. The Corporation later voted to change Hannah Gray's designation from acting president to president, so that in the long line of Yale presidents, she is number eighteen. I supported that decision; although she was president of Yale only for a year, she did a fine job, and she became an excellent president of the University of Chicago. I served for five years on the Corporation when Bart Giamatti was president, and I always had the highest regard, respect, and affection for him. He brought life, wit, vivacity, and energy to our collegial group. If Kingman's focus was on the modernization of the university, Bart's main emphasis was more academic, more like Griswold's. He was a great intellect; he could spin golden paragraphs in the air. I had retired from the Corporation before his troubles with the labor strike of 1984 and the student protests over university investments connected with South Africa. Those problems seemed to bother him more than similar

Bill Beinecke and Bart Giamatti, c. 1982.

problems had bothered Brewster, but I don't know whether that was because Kingman was inwardly tougher or because Bart was more sensitive. In hindsight, Bart probably should not have left Yale to become president of the National League and then commissioner of Major League Baseball; all the turmoil surrounding Pete Rose's expulsion from baseball undoubtedly hastened Bart's premature death.

One of the more important issues I played a direct role in during Giamatti's presidency was the disposition of the Seven Springs conference center. Seven Springs Farm in Tarrytown, New York, was the summer home of Eugene Meyer, the noted financier. He had made a fortune in Wall Street just before World War I, and during the war he assisted Woodrow Wilson with the bond issues that were used to finance the war. After the war he was the chief administrator with the Farm Loan Bank, and while I was in college he was the head of the Federal Reserve. Meyer had four children, one of whom, Eugene Jr., was a class or two behind me at Yale, and we lived for a year in the same entry in Berkeley College. Meyer's daughter Katherine married Philip Graham, and today she is the very same Katherine Graham who owns the *Washington Post* and *Newsweek* magazine. When Meyer died, his heirs decided to do something with the Seven Springs estate. I believe they had in mind the example of Arden House, farther to the north near the Hudson River. It had once belonged to Averell Harriman and had been given to Columbia University for use as a conference center. The Meyer heirs wanted to make a similar arrangement. It is possible that they turned to Yale because Agnes Meyer, Eugene's widow, was a great admirer of Kingman Brewster. A legal document was drawn up to convert Seven Springs into a site for academic (nonbusiness) conferences and to support its operation and maintenance with an endowment of several million dollars. Yale was not to own Seven Springs outright, but it was to be responsible for its management, and Kingman's classmate Joseph Greene was put in charge of scheduling its programs. As a final inducement to Yale, the conversion document stipulated that if Seven Springs ceased to operate as an academic convention center, the property would go to Yale.

On the surface, it was a fine arrangement. Unfortunately, Seven Springs operated at a substantial deficit each year and drew down the endowment that had been set up to support its operations. I watched this go on for several years and realized that if the endowment was drained, Yale would be blamed by the Meyer heirs and was bound to look bad in the public eye. Finally I brought up the subject in a Corporation meeting. My fellow trustee Jake Madden (who had an acute financial mind) got the point immediately and spoke in support of reevaluating our advisory relationship with the conference center. A committee was convened, and we examined Yale's position carefully. We concluded that it was in the university's best interest to withdraw from Seven Springs altogether and to renounce the contingency by which the property would fall into Yale's hands; that had always been a highly remote possibility in any case. And so Yale and Seven Springs went their separate ways. I still feel we made a wise decision, though it's always difficult to determine whether preventive action of this sort would have averted major disaster or only mild embarrassment.

I ceased being a member of the Yale Corporation in 1982, when I turned sixty-eight. It had been agreed that my term of service to the Corporation would be twelve years or until I reached retirement age, whichever came first, so I ended up serving eleven years of the successor trustee's twelve-year term. Once upon a time, successor trustees served for life, and since some of them had lingered on past the point of decrepitude, a mandatory retirement age of sixty-eight was adopted. It's advisable for organizations to mandate a retirement age, but many people now stay healthy and spry well into their "golden years," and sixty-eight seems a bit of a premature cutoff. The mandatory retirement age for Corporation members has since been extended to seventy years, which I look upon as a good thing.

Some time after my retirement from the Yale Corporation, I was invited to become a member of SOM's advisory board. I think it would have been inappropriate for me to have been serving on both organizations at the same time, and I guess others felt the same way because the invitation wasn't extended until after my involvement with the Corporation ceased. The invitation came from Bill Donaldson's successor as dean, Burton Malkiel, a former Princeton economics professor. I was fairly religious in my attendance at meetings. "Advisory" is a rather strange term for the board, because while it may advise, it really does whatever the dean of SOM wants it to do. With Dean Malkiel, we seemed to do more listening than advising. However, Malkiel was responsible for putting into effect a very good idea. That was to have members of the advisory board interact with SOM's students. The night before a meeting, we would dine with the students in Donaldson Commons, and it gave us a better sense of what the students were like and what their concerns were.

While Burt Malkiel's replacement was being sought, a man named Geoff Hazard, a professor at the Law School, served briefly as acting dean. During his tenure, the Richard and Doris Beinecke Courtyard was dedicated in a ceremony presided over by President Bart Giamatti. The courtyard is situated on Sachem Street between Hillhouse and Prospect, behind SOM, and the names of the benefactors are engraved on the wall to commemorate the donation of the wall and the trees that are planted within the courtyard. My brother's widow and I had decided that the courtyard would be an appropriate way to do something in his memory. I could not persuade Doris to come all the way up from Florida to New Haven for the ceremony, but I sent her the photograph of Bart and me along the wall.

Hazard was followed by Michael Levine, who had come to SOM from the airline industry and served a short time as dean during Benno Schmidt's presidency. Later still was Paul McAvoy, whose attitude toward the advisory board was quite similar to what Malkiel's had been. There was very little interaction between the board and McAvoy, who spent the meetings telling us what he thought about the way the school was going and about the relation of the school to the university. John Macomber was then chairman of the advisory board, and he took the position that it should *advise* and should interact with the dean in the matter of academic activities. Macomber was strongly opposed to the idea of the board's being used as a fund-raising arm of the school. If he hadn't been so outspoken in his disapproval, it's likely that the board would have been asked to undertake some fund-raising responsibility for the school. I'm not sure now as I look back that that would have been a wholly bad idea.

After McAvoy, SOM had a first-class acting dean by the name of Stan Garstka. He was a very thoughtful, quiet person who did an exceptional job of interacting with the advisory board. Under Garstka, we were asked to deliberate SOM matters much more than we had been under his predecessors. He gave the school good leadership and remains a member of the faculty. In November 1995, the current dean, Jeffrey Garten, joined SOM. He terminated the existing advisory board and a year later recruited a brand-new one, consisting of people he knows who are very prominent in the world. I think he did a very sensible thing. He asked me to serve on the new board, and while I initially felt my membership would be inappropriate—I'm over eighty, after all—he persuaded me and I accepted on the condition that I would function as a kind of emeritus member. Our first meeting was held in February 1997.

In 1986, Yale awarded me an honorary LL.D. The citation read: "Businessman and benefactor, your company, schools, and communities have been nourished by your wise and devoted service to them. Under your leadership, New York's Central Park has been restored as a public space of beauty and vibrancy, and museums, gardens, and libraries have benefited from your determination for their betterment. Yale, your *alma mater*, takes great pleasure in conferring upon you the degree of Doctor of Laws." Needless to say, I was delighted beyond words. The award was also somewhat ironic, because during my eleven-year tenure on the Corporation I had scoffed at the concept of the honorary degree, pointing out with scorn that distinguished but not well-known academics were easily chosen while outstanding businessmen of remarkable ability got short shrift. William McChesney Martin to some extent shared these views. And then there I was on the honorands' platform... It was a great moment.

And then in the spring of 1999 came another marvelous event. Rick, Sarah, John, and Frances had come to me several months earlier and told me that they wished to honor Betty and me with major philanthropic donations to institutions of our choice. I immediately told my children that the contribution that would mean the most to me would be a professorial chair in my name in the Yale School of Management. And so on April 28, 1999, I went up to Yale for the presentation of the second William S. Beinecke Chair in Management Studies at SOM. I

Yale 1936 classmates in September 1993. Left to right: A. R. Richard Pinkham, Oliver O. Jensen, Ogden W. Sutro, John W. Barclay, and William S. Beinecke.

spent the day at Yale meeting with members of the administration and faculty and students in SOM, and that evening there was a gala dinner in my honor at the president's house at 43 Hillhouse Avenue. All four of my children and all but one of my grandchildren were there, as were President Levin and his wife, Jane, my classmate Oliver Jensen, and other friends from the Yale family. President Levin thanked my children handsomely on Yale's behalf, and my son Rick gave a moving and eloquent speech. It was an occasion of great magnificence and an act of great munificence on my children's part. Betty spent more time thinking about where her benefaction should go than I did. After examining all the pros and cons very carefully, she has decided to have this gift go to the New York Philharmonic Orchestra, because of her involvement as a member of the board and her longtime interest in music. The gift will endow the Principal Associate Concertmaster chair. There will be a special event at Avery Fisher Hall in December 1999 celebrating that wonderful act of generosity by our children. Needless to say, we will all be there.

By any measure, my involvement in the affairs of Yale University has been among the most satisfying and exhilarating of my experiences over the past fifty years. And it's an involvement that has continued into the next generation, for in addition to my children's donation of the SOM chair in my name, Frances was elected to the Corporation as an alumni trustee in 1995. Betty and I were thrilled when we heard the news, and I've marched side by side with my daughter in the academic procession in recent commencements. On the first of those occasions, someone told me that it was the first time in the history of the university that two generations of the same family had served on the Corporation. I have a feeling that some others—Timothy Dwight the Elder and Younger? Hiram and Jack Bingham?—must have preceded us. I do know, however, that this is the first time in the nearly 300-year history of Yale that there has been a father and daughter combination on the Corporation. Frances makes up her own mind on the things she has to do about Yale. She doesn't always clue me in on all the activities of the Corporation, nor is there any reason she should. We share Yale opinions and experiences, but I don't look at Yale through her eyes. In the end, however, we both agree that Yale is a great international university, and we are proud to give it our continued support and loyalty.

CHAPTER NINETEEN

The Central Park Conservancy, 1980–1986

*O*n 1979, Betty and I left Summit, New Jersey, where we had lived for thirty-one years, and moved to a penthouse apartment near Fifth Avenue in New York City. The apartment has splendid views over Central Park, and it became our practice to go for a walk in this new front yard every now and then. But we were disturbed, even shocked, at the increasing evidence of what I would call "neglected maintenance." As New York City had plunged into fiscal crisis in the 1970s and as the city administration had cut the budget for the Parks Department, Central Park had deteriorated. When Betty and I went wandering through the park, we found litter strewn about everywhere, weeds cropping up at every step, graffiti scrawled on the rocks and walkways, and the shrubbery ill-kempt and in certain spots badly overgrown. Either the benches were broken or their wooden slats had rotted, exposing the rusting skeletons of their metal supports. Nor did the park feel like a place where two people like ourselves, who were getting on in years, could feel safe going for a stroll. It bothered us to see the park in this sad state of disrepair and decay, but we weren't sure what to do about it.

Then in the early spring of 1980, there was a heartening development. We started noticing signs posted in various places announcing the formation of a task force dedicated to the preservation and rehabilitation of Central Park and inviting those interested to participate. We made inquiries and were directed to Elizabeth Barlow Rogers, better known as Betsy, a remarkable woman whom the city had recently appointed Central Park administrator. She was a Wellesley graduate who had earned a master's degree in city planning at Yale and had written about Frederick Law Olmsted, the landscape architect who, together with Calvert Vaux, had designed Central Park in the 1860s. Betsy invited Betty and me on an hour-long tour of the park in our own area, from 79th Street south. She, too, was appalled at the park's dilapidated condition but was convinced that a new infusion of private support could help reverse the decline. As we walked along the overgrown and vandalized pathways, she spoke of the proposed new public-private partnership to rejuvenate the park that she hoped to build with the assistance of independent funding.

Not long after, in June 1980, I was invited to meet with Betsy and Gordon Davis, an able and articulate lawyer who was then parks commissioner. They handed me a pile of documentation, which was essentially a paper concept of what would become the Central Park Conservancy. The Conservancy was still in the planning stage. It had been incorporated under the authorizing statutes of the state of New York, but nothing further had been done. Betsy and Gordon asked if I would be willing to serve as chairman of the group. I had only recently retired from the chairmanship of S&H and had just turned sixty-six, so I wasn't sure that I was ready to undertake a project of such magnitude. I asked them to give me some time to make a decision. That summer, Betty and I went on a cruise along the waterways of southeastern Alaska with Rick, Candace, and Bill Dewind, a New York lawyer who later became chairman of the Natural Resources Defense Council and served with me on the board of the Hudson River Foundation. While on the cruise, I thought over the offer to become chairman of the Central Park Conservancy and decided to accept.

I took the job because the dangerous and degenerating state of the park was a matter of great concern to Betty and me. It wasn't a question of the view from our window. Central Park makes an immense and immeasurable contribution to the quality of life of every New Yorker and visitor to the city. I can't conceive of the city without the park. That stretch of pastoral landscape between 59th and 110th Street, in the midst of the world's busiest metropolis, should delight the eye and refresh the spirit of everyone who encounters it. The blight that afflicted that green and scenic space in the early 1980s was a tangible drain on New York's inhabitants and the city's reputation and fortune, whether or not it appeared on any financial statement. I hoped that by chairing the Central Park Conservancy I could further my interests in the environment and urban affairs, harness private resources for the public good (as I had tried to do at S&H), and contribute to the well-being of the city that had meant so much to me and my family for many years. And there was, of course, a family connection to the park itself. My father had bicycled through Central Park on his way to school around the turn of the century, and at the southeast entrance to the park my grandfather Bernhard Beinecke had built The Plaza Hotel, looking out over Grand Army Plaza to the Pond, the Zoo, and the Mall beyond.

Just before I accepted the job as chairman of the Central Park Conservancy, there had been a great deal of controversy over the "appropriate" uses of the park. The internationally known artist Christo had wanted to make Central Park the stage for one of his spectacular art exhibits. Christo specialized in outdoor art installations that played off of their settings, like the twenty-four-mile-long "fence" he had already put up in rural western California and the wrapping of the Reichstag in Berlin that he would later undertake in the 1990s. He wanted to try something similar in Central Park. He proposed erecting thousands of metal gateways along the park's pathways that people could walk under. Each gateway would be draped in brightly colored synthetic cloth that would wave and flutter in the breeze for that distinctive Christo effect. Gordon Davis, the parks commissioner, rejected the application and wrote a very thoughtful opinion stating the reasons he thought the work inappropriate for Central Park. The gist of his argument was that much of the park's charm is that it's a quiet refuge where New Yorkers can escape the noise and chaos of their city.

Although many disagreed with Davis's decision, I was favorably impressed by his thinking. By the early 1980s, the park's naturalistic and pastoral qualities—its greenery, trees, flowers, meadows, woodlands, and streams—had been overshadowed by concerts and celebrations and almost every outdoor sport except golf. All manner of groups seemed to feel they had a right to use the park for any sort of activity they wanted, regardless of disturbance to others and wear and tear on the park itself. And many of the large-scale public activities were quite harmful to the park; a great deal of shrubbery was damaged during a raucous Diana Ross concert in the summer of 1983. I wasn't about to try to return the park to its nineteenth-century state as a leafy bower where ladies and gentlemen could promenade and decorously ride bicycles. You can't turn back the clock, and it made sense that the park's uses be commensurate with the state of modern society. I'm all in favor of people enjoying and using Manhattan's natural resource in myriad ways, whether it be jogging, rollerblading, concerts, ball games, croquet championships, or lawn bowling. But the serenity and quiet shouldn't have to be completely destroyed to make that possible. Central Park should remain at least in part as a scenic retreat where a lone wanderer can sit in a shady, secluded spot or where a family can sit down to a peaceful picnic on untrampled grass. I believe that there have to be limits and a balance between competing claims if the park is to be protected for the public, and I was very encouraged to see that Gordon Davis and I were thinking along the same lines.

Betsy and Gordon had put forward the offer of the chairmanship, but my formal appointment came from Mayor Ed Koch. Before I knew what was happening to me, I found myself with an awesome title and not much else. Betsy and I realized that if the Central Park Conservancy was to be a success, we needed a strong board, with names that people in our city would recognize. Then we had to figure out how to recruit distinguished, highly sought-after people to serve on the board of an organization that existed only on a piece of paper in Betsy's desk. We set about identifying people whom we thought would give this fledgling organization some éclat and élan, and then through the fall of 1980 we recruited and recruited and recruited. I was assigned the task of enlisting the support of the CEOs of major corporations. I spent a lot of time on the phone, either trying to convince these CEOs to join our board or soliciting funds from the corporations with which they were affiliated. One time Betsy and I were escorting Howard Clark, chairman and CEO of American Express, across the Sheep Meadow. It was clear that it had been a long time since he had walked in the park, if indeed he ever had. He was visibly apprehensive, and about halfway across the Meadow, he turned to Betsy and asked whether she was armed: "Where's your gat?"

I was not the first member of the Yale class of 1936 to have become deeply involved with Central Park. My classmate August Heckscher was named parks commissioner in 1967, during John Lindsay's administration, and served until 1972. He and I discussed the park, but only casually. His years as parks commissioner were quite successful—the financial woes didn't begin until Abe Beame's mayoral administration—but he had to deal with the political turmoil of the 1960s. In the obituary of August Heckscher that appeared in the *New York Times* in April 1997, the current deputy parks commissioner, Alan M. Moss, recalled that once while Heckscher was commissioner, "There was a Black Panther encampment at 125th Street, in an empty lot, and the Panthers had run up their flag on a city flagpole" nearby after taking down the United States flag. Mayor Lindsay wanted the Black Panther flag taken down, but the police commissioner was reluctant to act. As a result, according to Mr. Moss, "Augie took a group of us and we went up there, and Augie went by himself to the flagpole and he took the flag down, and then a group of blacks approached him. The Parks Department feared a confrontation, but the blacks said, 'May we please have our flag?' and Augie said, 'Certainly. Please don't put it up again.'" August Heckscher was a courageous man. I'm grateful that in the 1980s we didn't have those kinds of political challenges on top of the financial problems we were dealing with.

I spent the fall of 1980 organizing the group, recruiting board members, planning fund-raising activities, establishing various committees, and generally trying to breathe life into this new creature and get it on its feet. Mayor Koch officially announced the formation of the Central Park Conservancy in December 1980, and before the year was out we had our first meeting of the board. It consisted of thirty private citizens, most of them active or retired banking and corporate executives, and six "public" trustees, including three of Mayor Koch's appointees (of whom I was one) and three city officials serving ex officio. In the *New York Times* article on Koch's announcement, I was quoted as saying that the organization's goals were "to assist in the physical restoration of the park and to bring about improvements in its maintenance and security." The *Times*, in an appreciative editorial, also noted that the Conservancy "would, in effect, constitute a board of trustees" for the park, along the lines of a museum or orchestra board. It would raise money and serve as "a continuing society of protectors," offering "the judgment and taste without which new investment would make Central Park worse, not better."

The relationship we maintained with the city of New York was a friendly but wary partnership between the private and public sectors. The care and maintenance of Central Park, as with other parks in New York, is provided for in the city's parks budget. And three trustees of the organization, including myself, had been appointed by the mayor. On the other hand, the amount of money we were receiving from the city was insufficient for our purposes, and we were worried that as we raised funds from the private sector, the city would siphon out the difference from its budget or even reduce its contribution altogether, so that the amount spent on the park would remain the same. Clearly we didn't want this to happen.

My position on the matter was that we should arrange an agreement with the city guaranteeing that the city's support would not fall off even if we were successful in procuring incremental funds from the private sector. I paid a visit to Mayor Koch and discussed the situation. I told him that the Conservancy simply could not replace the job of basic maintenance that was done by civil service workers, nor could it fund all the capital construction needed to restore the park to first-class condition. We could, however, supply some valuable "extras" like more tree care, design and planning consultants, repair of certain deteriorated structures, relandscaping of some areas, and programming and operating facilities like the Dairy. The mayor said that he saw my point. He later sent me a letter stating that the city would not make disproportionate cuts in the amount it contributed to the maintenance of Central Park in the event that we were able to get additional money from outside sources. If the city budget for parks went down, we would share the pain but we wouldn't be penalized because of successful fund-raising. The mayor anticipated, however, that the city administration would honor this agreement "given the present outlook," an escape clause that unfortunately meant his assurance was not binding. I am told by Betsy Barlow Rogers's successor, Karen Putnam, that in recent years the Central Park Conservancy has had to shoulder an increasing portion of Central Park's expenditures, as the city has been forced by circumstances to reduce its budget and the Conservancy has grown ever more successful. And in February 1998, the city and the Central Park Conservancy entered into a contract whereby the Conservancy has emerged as the manager of the park, even getting city funds and a percentage of the revenues from concessionaires to assist it in this process. This arrangement is based on a formula in which the Conservancy must raise X dollars to get Y city funds. On February 11, Mayor Giuliani signed the contract at a ceremony at the Arsenal.

Much of the Conservancy's success was due to the redoubtable Betsy Barlow Rogers, who accomplished great things through her mixture of charm, intellect, executive ability, and capacity for hands-on work. Betsy oversaw a talented team of landscape architects who for several years studied all aspects of the park and came up with a master plan, "Rebuilding Central Park," that called for spending $150 million to renovate the park over a ten- to fifteen-year period. By 1990, the Central Park Conservancy had raised more than $65 million toward that goal and, according to the *New York Times*, was providing half the park's annual operating budget, half the funds for capital improvements, nearly half the 234-person staff, and almost all the recreational programming.

The results of our efforts are observed by Roy Rosenzweig and Elizabeth Blackmar in their recently published history of Central Park, *The Park and the People*. "By the end of the 1980s," they write, "with the infusion of conservancy money, Central Park looked startlingly different from its appearance just a decade earlier: visitors stretched out on a lush, green Sheep Meadow, now guarded by a fence and by rules against loud noises and active sports; schoolchildren learned about the environment in a graffiti-free Belvedere Castle; skaters glided across

Karen Putnam, Ira Millstein, William S. Beinecke, and Betsy Barlow Rogers at the dedication and reopening of the Great Lawn, Central Park, October 10, 1997.

the [restored] ice-skating rink; tourists picked up information about the park's past and present at a refurbished Dairy; fashion photographers posed their models against the backdrop of a lovingly restored Bethesda Terrace; wedding couples took their vows in a replanted Conservatory Garden; New Yorkers who could afford it dined on the terrace of the renovated Loeb Boathouse." It was deeply satisfying to have been part of that renewal.

My chairmanship lasted a little over five years. When I turned seventy, I felt I'd reached the appropriate age for retirement and asked the board members to begin looking for a successor. I believed, and I still believe, that it is important that the chairmanship of the organization change periodically. When I became chairman in the summer of 1980, I had only recently retired as chairman and chief executive officer of a major corporation with headquarters in New York City. I was on the board of one of the city's largest banks and had a good networking relationship with other CEOs in New York. These connections were important, because support for an organization like the Central Park Conservancy really comes from the CEOs and their influential role in the city's financial structure. Although the organization receives a lot of personal support from private individuals—the Ladies Committee, for example, holds an annual luncheon that raises a great deal of money—it's important to have the interest of as many CEOs as you can. With each year that elapsed after my retirement, my networking role diminished because the people I knew in the business world were retiring and being replaced by people I did not know. This was another reason I put forth my offer of resignation. But the board members insisted that I was "a very *young* seventy," and asked me to stay on for another year. I consented, with the understanding that during that time they would find someone to replace me as chairman.

As it turned out, I found my own successor, a man named Jim Evans, who was just then stepping down from the chairmanship of Union Pacific. He was ideal for the new role because he was in a very important networking position. In fact, because of the diversity and importance of the outside boards he'd served on, he was in a much better position than I'd ever been in. Jim was chairman for six years and then turned the job over to Ira Millstein, who has also proved excellent in the networking role. It was good to have those two fellows succeed me, because they made me look good! They built and they built, and they kept saying out loud that they had a terrific foundation upon which to build. That, of course, made me feel great. So the momentum that we developed continued right along.

I was grateful that my chairmanship terminated when it did. It was a tiring job, and it took a lot out of me. There was never a day when I was in New York during that entire period that I did not devote some time and energy to the affairs of the Conservancy: telephoning, calling on prospective donors, signing and indeed composing and writing endless letters, conferring with staff, attending committee meetings, and continuing actively to recruit strong and effective new trustees. I am very pleased to have played a role in the revival of Central Park through my work with the Conservancy and, looking back, I feel that I did a job I could be proud of as chairman. At the conclusion of my services, the organization presented me with an old security from the Central Park Improvement Fund stock of 1887. I had it framed and it now hangs in our apartment.

Almost twenty years later, Betty and I are still taking walks through Central Park. The places we visit most frequently are those within easy walking distance from our apartment. Our window looks out over the East Drive and Cedar Hill. In the distance beyond Cedar Hill, visible in winter, is *Still Hunt*, the statue of a crouched mountain lion. It is of particular interest to me, for I contributed to the endowment for its permanent maintenance. The good idea of procuring such endowments (probably Betsy Barlow Rogers's) has provided for the maintenance of many statues and other objects in the park. Betty and I usually walk through the Cedar Hill area in the direction of the Belvedere and the Great Lawn. The one exception that takes us farther afield is the Conservatory Garden, a beautifully maintained park-within-a-park on 104th Street, just off Fifth Avenue. The garden is surrounded by a fence. The entrance gates on Fifth Avenue are over a hundred years old and originally belonged to the Vanderbilt mansion. The gates, which at one point were in danger of being thrown into an ironworker's furnace and melted down, were preserved and have recently been refurbished and rehung. The garden itself is an absolute gem. It's alive with chrysanthemums in the fall and with daffodils in the spring, and all summer long it's ablaze with summer flowers. It is a lovely, pleasant, and peaceful place, with a couple of fountains sending sprays into the air. Many newlyweds use the park for their wedding photos, and almost every weekend in good weather you'll see pictures being taken of a bride and groom and their wedding party. It's wonderful that the park is used and appreciated, and I hope it will continue to be for many generations to come.

CHAPTER TWENTY

The Hudson River Foundation, 1980–1996

For sixteen years, from 1980 to 1996, I served as chairman of the Hudson River Foundation, one of the two most important leadership roles of my retirement years. Because 1980 was also the year I became actively involved in the Central Park Conservancy, for a period of six years I was chairing both organizations at once. Fortunately, I had recently retired from S&H and had no business responsibilities impinging on me.

In 1980, I was approached by John Adams, the head of the Natural Resources Defense Council (NRDC), who asked if I'd be willing to chair the Hudson River Foundation. I knew little about the new organization, but as a trustee of the Consolidated Edison Corporation I was quite familiar with the events that had led to its formation. The power company had been the prime mover in an ill-fated venture that ultimately resulted in the establishment of the Hudson River Fund, the original source of funding for the Hudson River Foundation.

In the early 1960s, Consolidated Edison had joined with several other companies and formed a consortium to build a pumped storage hydroelectric plant at Storm King Mountain, fifty miles north of Manhattan on the Hudson River near Cornwall. The plant, to be located at the base of the mountain, would have been the largest of its kind in the world. Each day during off-peak hours, when electricity consumption was at a minimum, the surplus electricity generated would be used to operate large electric pumps that would suck up millions of gallons of river water and pump it through a very long tunnel up to a storage reservoir. During peak hours, when the regular powerhouses couldn't produce enough electricity to meet the demand, the water would be released. Those millions of gallons of water would pour down the mountain, turning the turbines and generating millions of kilowatts of hydropower before flowing back into the Hudson. The

485

pumped storage method has been successfully implemented elsewhere. I am aware of one such plant on the Delaware River, and there are several others as well.

But the proposed Storm King project met with such violent opposition that it never advanced beyond the initial planning phase. Groups such as the Scenic Hudson Preservation Conference and the Natural Resources Defense Council objected to the proposed plant on environmental and aesthetic grounds. They argued that it would deface Storm King Mountain, that the enormous, unsightly high-tension towers would scar the surrounding hills, and that the pristine scenery and ecosystem of the Hudson Highlands would be marred by further development. Groups like the Hudson River Fishermen, Inc., feared that the storage plant would heat up the Hudson, much to the detriment of the river's fish and the dismay of the men who liked to catch them. This concern was without basis, as it turned out, but it drew attention to the fact that the Consolidated Edison nuclear power plant on the opposite bank of the river at Indian Point, fifteen miles south of Storm King, was discharging heated water into the Hudson. The resulting publicity, and the hearings before the Federal Power Commission and various public agencies, were all quite damaging for Con Edison. There was a major backlash against the company and its "Dig We Must" slogan. The folksinger Pete Seeger got into the act, elevating the project to a national conservation issue. One of the government regulatory agencies that conducted hearings into the matter of the river's temperature suggested that Consolidated Edison be required to erect cooling towers at the nuclear power sites. The prospect of enormous, vapor-streaming cooling towers lining the scenic Hudson River generated a lot of heated debate—no pun intended—particularly since there was no guarantee that the cooling towers would accomplish the purpose for which they were intended.

As a result of the controversy, a very complicated lawsuit was brought against Consolidated Edison and the other power companies to deny them the right to erect the pumped storage power plant at Storm King. The case dragged on for several years but was eventually settled out of court. Russell Train, a well-known public figure, served as the mediator who brought together the opposing factions in the public utilities camp and the environmentalist camp. Out of the litigation came a settlement agreement whereby the consortium agreed to give up the Storm King project, establish a fish hatchery for striped bass, and put up $12 million to establish the Hudson River Fund, to be administered by the Hudson River Foundation for Science and

Research. The money would be used to make grants to scientists studying various aspects of the Hudson estuary. As a concession by the environmentalists, the requirement that Consolidated Edison construct several costly cooling towers was dropped.

The Hudson River Foundation that the settlement agreement provided for was created under the law of the state of New York. Each of the various entities that had participated in the lawsuit—among them the Natural Resources Defense Council, the Environmental Protection Agency, the state of New York, Consolidated Edison, Scenic Hudson, Hudson River Fishermen—was permitted to designate a person to serve as a director of the foundation. I believe there were eleven directors in all. It was then necessary to find a person acceptable to both the public utilities and the environmental groups who would chair the organization. At that time, I was still on the board of Consolidated Edison, so clearly I was an acceptable candidate from the power company's point of view. Yet while I am sympathetic to the realities of the business world, I'm also concerned about environmental issues. I don't know how it was that my name came to appear on the environmentalists' list of prospective candidates, but I suspect that I was suggested by someone from the NRDC, an organization in which my daughter Frances has played a significant role for many years and of which she is now the executive director. Perhaps it was felt that because I had a foot in both camps, I would be able to preside over a group of people coming from widely disparate points of view, or maybe it was just thought that I was innocuous. I personally thought the invitation was more than a little flattering, for it represented a consensus between the utilities and the environmentalists—one of the first things they had agreed on in a number of years.

I accepted the position and in 1981 became the first chairman of the Hudson River Foundation. The board met quarterly. Ross Sandler, one of the lawyers for the NRDC who had brought the lawsuit against Consolidated Edison (and now a professor at New York Law School), was named executive director. He eventually left to become head of the New York City Department of Transportation under Ed Koch and later assisted me in convincing the city to make the street crossing near the Yale Club safer. His successor, the current executive director of the Hudson River Foundation, was a man named Clay Hiles, a Yale alumnus from the class of '69 and a graduate of Columbia Law School. Bill Dewind, a member of the board of the Hudson River Foundation and later the chairman of the board of trustees of the NRDC, was named chairman of the investment committee. When Bill stepped down, he was succeeded by Charles Luce, who was the chairman of the board of Consolidated Edison during my time as a trustee. Chuck Luce—no relation to Henry Luce, as far as I know—was a Wisconsin native who received his undergraduate and law degrees from the University of Wisconsin and for many years practiced law in Walla Walla, Washington on the West Coast. He subsequently directed the large government power project at the Bonneville Dam and, after that, became undersecretary of the Interior during the Lyndon Johnson administration. Consolidated Edison hired Chuck as CEO at a time when they were experiencing many difficulties, and the company performed very well under his leadership. My friend Wilson Newman, formerly chairman of Dun & Bradstreet and then a member of the Consolidated Edison board, had much to do with bringing Chuck Luce from Washington to head that company. Chuck was presiding over Consolidated Edison at the time of the settlement that resulted in the formation of the Hudson River Foundation. Though I was no longer on the Consolidated Edison board when he joined the board of the foundation, we greatly enjoyed becoming colleagues again, and Chuck did a superb job as chairman of the investment committee.

When John Adams had asked me to serve as chairman of the Hudson River Foundation, I assumed that the board was to be responsible for processing applications for grants submitted by scientists to conduct research in the Hudson estuary. The foundation's original charter, however, assigned the grant-making responsibility to an advisory panel of scientists, a provision that represented a substantial departure from a foundation's standard organizational structure: the panel was going to be doing the work the board was supposed to be doing. I expressed some skepticism about that arrangement to John Adams and was told that the advisory panel was something "brand new" and "unique," an "innovative" advancement in the way a foundation was to be organized and to act. I found the idea puzzling, but I swallowed my doubts. Suffice it to say that the advisory panel just plain didn't work. I never attended its meetings, but all the reports I received from the executive directors suggested that the panel was ineffective. The scientists argued and debated and fought and had extreme difficulty achieving results. It took several years for the realization to dawn, but it eventually became clear that the panel would have to be abolished. Clay Hiles recommended replacing it with a program committee consisting of members of the board, a proposal I enthusiastically endorsed.

Unfortunately, getting rid of the panel required amending the original provision to set up the foundation. While the settlement agree-

ment stated that it was possible to amend anything in the original provision, it also stipulated that any change had to be approved by every
one of the parties involved. By the late 1980s, all but one of the parties
had agreed to the change. The lone holdout was the Hudson River
Fishermen, an organization headed by John Cronin, the Hudson's
riverkeeper, in collaboration with Bob Boyle, a writer on fishing and
the Hudson who was one of the environmental leaders most active in
the fight against the pumped storage plant at Storm King.

Bob Boyle is quite a character, but he can be shifty and difficult to
deal with. At one point I went up to see him in his hometown of Garrison, New York, and we went to lunch at an attractive riverside inn called
The Bird and Bottle, on Route 9 across the river from West Point. We
had a nice time, but I didn't get Bob's agreement. In December 1989, I
had lunch with Bob again, this time in New York City. We didn't meet at
the Sky Club, where I would have normally hosted such a luncheon, but
at a place called The Board Room, a now-defunct men's luncheon club
that was up on the top floor of one of the midtown bank buildings on
the west side of Park Avenue. I had the document to amend the settlement agreement out on the table, but Bob hemmed and hawed and
said that he couldn't sign it without getting the approval of the board of
directors of the Hudson River Fishermen. I promised that the foundation wouldn't take any action until he was able to get the approval of his
organization, but he still wouldn't go along. As I was sitting there wondering what next, it so happened that into the dining room walked my
friend Ed Beimfohr, a lawyer at Lane & Mittendorf. I had a bright idea.
I went over to Ed and asked him to join Bob and me at our table for a
minute. I told Bob that my friend Ed was a lawyer and assured him that
if he would just affix his signature to the document, the Lane &
Mittendorf firm would hold it in escrow until he agreed to authorize its
release to me. Bob thought that was an inspired improvisation on my
part, but he still wouldn't sign. As Ed was about to go back to his table,
he asked, "What are you fellows up to, anyway?" This was not too many
months after the fall of the Berlin Wall, and Bob, who has a puckish
sense of humor, replied, "We're just now putting together the corporation that's going to take over Eastern Europe." Ed managed to keep a
straight face.

In the spring of 1990, with the tedious process of amending the set-
tlement agreement still unresolved, I went down to Guatemala with
Betty, Frances, Sarah, Coco Eiseman, the executive director of the
Prospect Hill Foundation, and her husband Michael Altschuler. The
Prospect Hill Foundation had been making substantial grants to fund

activities in population control. Given the foundation's finite assets, we had determined to limit our international activities to the Western Hemisphere. We supplied a substantial amount of money to agencies working on population control in Latin America, and Coco Eiseman thought it would be a good idea for us to visit Guatemala and learn for ourselves what happens out in the field. We were there for about ten days, equipped with a car and driver and a very knowledgeable interpreter, who enabled us to carry on conversations with the Guatemalans who operated the clinics and related agencies that we helped support. That was a useful and instructive trip.

While we were in Guatemala, however, I had numerous lengthy telephone conversations with Clay Hiles, the executive director of the Hudson River Foundation, about the continuing effort to procure the remaining signatures to amend the foundation's settlement agreement. When I arrived back in the States, we decided that we'd gone about as far as we could in our friendly persuasion of Messrs. Boyle and Cronin. We finally mounted a lawsuit against the Hudson River Fishermen, on the grounds that by refusing to sign the amendment that all the other parties had agreed to, the group was unreasonably withholding its consent. We retained Dan Pollack, a very effective litigator whom I'd had some experience with in the lawsuit over the S&H Foundation. Sometime before the summer of 1990, Mr. Boyle and his organization capitulated and signed the amendment, and we finally achieved our objective of getting rid of the panel. We compromised by expanding the board; Bob Boyle became a member of the board, with a term of ten or eleven years. We had long been willing to expand the board, so I can't explain why the Hudson River Fishermen were so intransigent in their refusal to amend the settlement agreement. I think that through years and years of activism and opposition, Bob Boyle and his companions had become paranoid and almost physically averse to compromise, even when it was in the best interest of the river they wanted to protect.

At any rate, the replacement of the panel with the program committee was a substantial change in the way the Hudson River Foundation functioned and made it much easier to process the grants. The program committee was first chaired by Saul Levin, a professor of marine biology who was then at Cornell and is now at Princeton. While the foundation had supported valuable scientific research in the Hudson estuary during the decade of the panel's operation, the grant-giving procedure moved much more expeditiously under the program committee. I'm not a scientist, of course, but I quickly learned how complicated the problems that face the Hudson River really are, and how difficult it is to study any one aspect of the river environment in isolation. A scientist's application for a grant to study the life cycle of the striped bass, for example, can't be limited to the bass alone. Such a study would need to take into account the levels of oxygen and other compounds in the river water, the temperature and flow of the river, the complicated organisms that inhabit the benthic layer (the ooze at the bottom of the river), and so forth. I believe that the scientific panel had been hampered in its operation in part by turf wars among scientists who specialized in these different areas of the marine environment. The process works much more smoothly today, and over $18 million of scientific research on the Hudson has been carried out under the foundation's auspices.

Another reason the Hudson River Foundation's research-granting process is more effective today is because there is more money to be spent. The Hudson River Fund has grown substantially from its original donation, thanks in large part to the leadership of the two chairmen of the foundation's investment committee, Bill Dewind and Chuck Luce. The $12 million originally put up by Consolidated Edison et al. has more than doubled, and after two augmentations, the fund's total has grown to more than $37 million—and this after sixteen years of giving away grants that now approach $2 million annually.

In recent years, two additional settlements have resulted in funds that are separate entities designated for different purposes but are administered, looked after, and invested by the Hudson River Foundation. The first, the Hudson River Improvement Fund, came about as a result of alleged malfeasance by the Exxon Corporation. Exxon had been bringing oil to New York from Aruba or some other country in the Caribbean, unloading the oil, loading the empty tankers with water from the Hudson, and carrying it back to the Caribbean, where fresh water is in short supply. While in a strict legal sense there was nothing to prevent the company from considering the Hudson's water free for the taking, many environmental groups felt that it was wrong for Exxon to withdraw water from the Hudson. A lawsuit was filed, and the eventual settlement required Exxon to stop removing water from the Hudson and to put up $1.5 million for the purpose of financing improvements along the banks of the river. That money was received by the state of New York and then passed on to the Hudson River Foundation by Governor Mario Cuomo. Being a politician, the governor decided to hand it over to the foundation at a big public presentation and picture-taking ceremony in the middle of the Tappan Zee Bridge, complete with a check blown up to the size of a bathtowel. The money has been used to clean up the shorelines, to remove rotting piers and wrecked hulks and burnt-out automobile carcasses and other debris, to construct boat ramps, to improve access to the river, to restore many of the old lighthouses located on little rocky islets in the Hudson, and to fund other riparian improvements. The grants are overseen by a special committee, one member of which is nominated by the Hudson River Foundation.

The other fund, more recently acquired, was the result of a $5 million judgment against Consolidated Edison and is to be spent completely—it can't be used as an endowment—in the Con Edison service area in New York City and Westchester County. Like the Hudson River Improvement Fund, it is administered by and yet is distinct from the Hudson River Foundation. At the time of my retirement in September 1996, the decision as to how this money was to be allocated had not yet been agreed upon.

Across from Storm King Mountain, in the little town of Cold Spring, is Gardner Point, a very attractive piece of land that juts out into the Hudson. There one finds the Dockside Restaurant and its parking lot, fringed by some worn-out, broken-down docks that remain from an old and disused marina. Ten or a dozen years ago, John Adams argued that the point had considerable environmental value and ought to be purchased by the Hudson River Foundation in order to save the land from falling into the hands of rapacious commercial developers. The foundation entered into a strange rental agreement with a person who may or may not have been the owner of the property, and eventually it acquired the land. The Dockside Restaurant continued to operate, though the management changed hands, and it paid the foundation a reasonable rent for use of the property. After several years of this arrangement, Chuck Luce and I and a few others on the board came to the conclusion that this property was not doing the Hudson River Foundation any good. Neither were we supposed to be in the land preservation and acquisition business; our mission was to fund scientific research. And as chairman, I thought it unwise to have a large chunk of our limited assets tied up in a piece of real estate rather than in more productive investments. On the other hand, it was difficult to deaccession the property, because we really could sell it only to conservation-minded individuals or organizations. I pushed hard to bring about a resolution, together with Clay Hiles and our general counsel, and the issue occupied a deplorably large amount of time in our board meetings. Finally, we entered into negotiations with the Open Space

Institute, an organization dedicated (as its name suggests) to preserving open undeveloped lands, wilderness areas, and the like; it is principally supported by the Lila Acheson Wallace Fund. Early in 1999, the matter was finally resolved and the title passed to the Open Space Institute. The successful conclusion to this long, drawn-out negotiation, I feel, finally closed the circle of my stewardship over the enterprise.

While public-service organizations like the Hudson River Foundation often labor in obscurity, the foundation in recent years has received gratifying public recognition of its labors. The splendid two-part article about the Hudson's revival that appeared in the *New York Times* in June 1996, followed by a fine laudatory editorial on June 16, was a milestone of sorts. I saw evidence of the Hudson's revival myself several years ago when I spent a day on the river with Clay Hiles, the foundation's executive director. We cruised around Rhinebeck, had lunch at a waterside restaurant in Kingston, and looked at a disused lighthouse that, with assistance from the Hudson River Improvement Fund, was being restored and converted into a bed and breakfast. We saw fishermen catching sturgeon, some of which were as big as a young woman.

I'm proud that the Hudson is recovering from its blighted state, in part due to the efforts of our foundation. There's considerable room for improvement, and although the levels of PCBs, dioxins, and other chemical poisons have been considerably lowered, Hudson River striped bass, crabs, eels, and some other seafood are still considered dangerous to eat. But I have hope for the future. Maybe someday the river will once again be as fresh and clean as it was when my father and his brothers used to swim and fish in it during their golden boyhood summers at Oscawanna, my grandfather Beinecke's house on the Hudson. In the meantime, my successor as chairman of the Hudson River Foundation is Ned Ames, an able and knowledgeable man, who has the assistance of a dedicated board. Ned is also several years my junior, which is a fine thing, and I feel that the foundation, and the Hudson, are in good hands.

CHAPTER TWENTY-ONE

Notes from My Trip Logs

started keeping logs of my trips in 1968, when I made my journey to the South Pole. The spur was provided by my late Yale classmate Wid Cates, who at that time was the scribe in charge of our class notes. When Wid heard that I was going to the South Pole, he asked me to keep a record of my trip so that he could have some material to include in his column on the doings of the class of '36 in the back of the *Yale Alumni Magazine*. Had it not been for Wid's pressing me, I never would have undertaken the effort of keeping a trip log, so I am very much in his debt. At first I thought of it as a chore, but I soon found myself becoming interested in my note taking, and I have kept travel journals ever since. I think the act of keeping track of where I have been and what I have learned has made me a better traveler and observer. Sights, encounters, impressions, and information that otherwise would blend and blur together have become better and more accurately implanted in my memory. And many of the trips I have made have been truly educational, in the best sense of the word.

A few years ago my children celebrated my birthday by having my trip logs collected and bound in leather. They add up to six large volumes, a sizable collection of impressions! Sometimes my friends and visitors leaf through segments of the volumes, and I often refer back to them myself, but it would require considerable endurance for anyone to sit down and read my journals from cover to cover. And yet my travels have been a very important part of my life for the past thirty years. What follows, then, are brief excerpts from my journals and recollections. They at least give a glimpse of the journeys I have made and the world as I have found it.

In January 1968 I was invited by the US State Department to participate in a VIP trip to "see what we are doing in Antarctica." The invitation came about through my political contacts, and in particular through my friendship with Ed Clark, who had been a guest on an earlier expedition. The State Department had wanted to do something for Ed, as the friend of President Lyndon Johnson and ambassador to Australia, so they invited him to visit the navy base at McMurdo Sound, Antarctica. He accepted, he went, and he enjoyed. From there, it was just a matter of Ed's suggesting to the State Department that they extend the invitation to Mr. Beinecke, which they did. I jumped at the chance. We were to approach Antarctica via New Zealand, where a United States support base was located in the city of Christchurch. From there, it was a straight shot south about twenty-four hundred miles to the military base at McMurdo Sound, where the Ross Sea and Ross Ice Shelf meet.

The adventure began with a short detour to Tahiti—it conformed perfectly to the image of the South Seas I had long ago formed in my mind—and then to Christchurch, where I was met by Rear Admiral Lloyd "Doc" Abbot, who was to oversee the Antarctic expedition, and two of his staff. The expedition was part of what was known as Operation Deep Freeze, the support activity for the various scientific programs on the Antarctic continent. (In 1968, the scientific work undertaken in Antarctica was substantially performed by university-accredited civilian scientists, with the Navy providing logistical support. I am not sure whether this division still obtains in 1999.) Our gear was issued shortly before we were to depart. To be fully prepared, I made a crucial last-minute purchase at the Navy Exchange store: a penguin tie bar. On the evening before departure, I played golf at Russley, near the Christchurch airport, a course notable for being the southernmost point I've ever played a round!

The next morning, at 0830, we set out for McMurdo Sound. This large indentation is located on the New Zealand side of the great white continent and thus makes the Pole a little more accessible. Scott and Shackleton established their bases in this area. We arrived at Williams Field, Antarctica, after a seven-and-a-half hour flight from Christchurch in a C-130 Hercules. The first glimpse of the Antarctic continent was breathtaking. As we flew over the Ross Sea, a dozen whales cavorted in the waters below. On our left rose Mount Erebus, an active volcano that looms over the military base. With its plume of white smoke curling up out of a stark white cone, Erebus is truly one of the rare sights of the earth. On all sides, as we descended, high mountains dominated the view, gleaming white and scattered with rocky outcroppings.

The plane landed on skis. Expecting to be met by a blast of cold air, I exited the plane heavily bundled in long johns and a jacket, with multiple layers in between. Truth is stranger than fiction—the weather in Antarctica was a balmy 30 degrees, warmer by far than New York had been when I left it. It quickly became clear, however, that in the Antarctic, the slightest breeze is a cold one. I was thankful for my "Bunny Boots," eight-inch-high white rubber boots that kept my feet nice and warm.

Several small buses were on hand to meet us, and we climbed aboard, bumping our way over the icy road leading to the McMurdo Sound military base. En route, we passed the New Zealand base, Scott Station, and were delighted to glimpse a herd of seals basking on an ice shelf. In 1968, the McMurdo settlement consisted mainly of Quonset huts, supplemented by a few larger, more permanent structures. With a population of almost a thousand, McMurdo stood like a sentinel at the edge of the huge continent. I was told that the logistical problems facing the station were immense. Supplies originating in Davisville, Rhode Island, had to be carried by ship through the Panama Canal and across the Pacific. Oil arrived by chartered tanker from New Zealand and Australia.

Shortly after our arrival, we were informed that the first Antarctic tourist ship ever, the *Magga Dan*, was stranded in the channel with engine trouble. Because the *Magga Dan* couldn't move, she was blocking the path of a ship carrying supplies to the station and consequently making herself rather unpopular with the McMurdo community. The ship's maiden voyage from Christchurch to McMurdo apparently cost each of her passengers six thousand dollars. There was widespread puzzlement as to what the tourists were getting out of the trip, as there were no facilities at McMurdo to house, feed, or transport them.

The "Ross Hilton," our so-called hotel at the McMurdo base, was a Quonset hut attached to the officers' club. Each of the nine members of our party had his own "room," a curtained-off cubicle containing a chair, a bed, some hooks, a shelf, and a standard navy aluminum locker. After getting settled, I ventured into the bar for a before-dinner beer. In keeping with the "truth is stranger than fiction" theme of this day, the first people I encountered in the Antarctic bar were two pure-blooded Hawaiians! After dinner, we took an extensive sightseeing walk. Several members of our party climbed seven hundred feet up to the top of Observation Hill. I turned back when I was about a third of the way up, but even from this vantage point the view was spectacular, and I successfully completed the climb a few days later. The landscape defied description. There was not a tree, not a bush to be seen. From the edge of the sea, the white, mountainous terrain sprawled outward, broken only by fragments of rock and the dusty dirt of the settlement. As I perched atop a chunk of timber overlooking the settlement, with some 5.5 million square miles of ice and mountains and a continent two-thirds the size of North America laid out before me, I experienced a weighty obligation to say something profound. I did not rise to the occasion, but it's the realization that counts!

The next day, we toured McMurdo's offerings, from its chapel to its nuclear power plant, from the biological lab to Scott's hut. McMurdo Station, Williams Field, and Scott Station are all within ten miles of one another on Ross Island. The island, halfway up the Ross Sea on the western shore, is home to Erebus and another great mountain, Terror. To the south lies the Ross Ice Shelf. Scott's hut, one of three Antarctic huts erected by the explorer, has been partially restored. It was the base for his first Antarctic expedition, in the years 1902–04. To see that hut still standing (although dwarfed by an enormous fuel tank), and to retrace the route Scott followed as he set out for the Pole made his story seem both more real and more unreal.

On the morning of January 26, we took a massive C-130 to the South Pole. As he had on our trip from Christchurch, the admiral asked me to watch the landing from the cockpit. Wearing headphones that connected me to the controller at the Pole station, I mentally coached the plane in, from 26,000 feet to our touchdown at 10,500 feet. There were course changes and altitude directions all the way, but no traffic information! The trip was an easy one, of little more than two hours' duration. Compare that with Amundsen's record trip or Scott's heroic but tragic one, or even that of Byrd, who didn't land but had to jettison some of his survival equipment to gain sufficient altitude.

There was little to see as the plane prepared for landing. No mountains were in sight; the Pole is located on a plateau 11,000 feet in elevation, 9,000 of which is ice. We disembarked about a hundred feet from the Pole itself. The temperature, reported as –18 degrees Fahrenheit, seemed much colder due to the breeze. From an aesthetic perspective, the South Pole has very little to offer. Protruding from the snow were a number of radio masts. A shelter built over a flight of stairs, not unlike a subway entrance in New York City and not much larger than an outhouse, stood at the top of a slight incline; from its roof flew a US flag, the admiral's flag, and a state flag. The stairs led to the Pole Station, a multichambered underground camp. Nearby stood a Quonset hut, some oil drums, and a few heavy-wheeled vehicles like bulldozers. That was all.

We hiked until we reached the hallowed spot where a stone tablet and a ten-inch silvery globe atop a staff mark the official site of the South Pole. An American flag flew overhead. A signpost, some feet away, listed the distances from the Pole to Chicago, Boston, and other locations, including some fairly small American hometowns. We all had our pictures taken and I diligently walked around the Pole. This effort may have been fruitless, for it seems there is some dispute as to the exact location of the Pole. The latest computation has it fixed a thousand yards from where I stood, but the Norwegians refer to that site as "the American Pole" and have established one of their own. Further complicating matters is the fact that besides the Geographic Pole and the Norwegians' "P.R. Pole," there are three other poles, with locations equally difficult to pinpoint: the Pole of Inaccessibility, the Magnetic Pole, and the Geomagnetic Pole. Some of this confusion arises from the fact that while the Pole is a fixed geographic location, the buildings and other structures are built on the ice, which is imperceptibly but constantly in very slow motion.

When the picture-taking session was completed, we returned to the "subway" stair shelter and descended into the Pole Station. Although annual precipitation at the Pole amounts to only three inches of snow—a third of an inch of water, as little as falls in a desert—the wind causes the snow to accumulate. The original, aboveground Pole Station had been buried so often beneath snow drifts that it was deemed necessary to move the operation below the snow level. Each chamber of the station was a separate building, but all were equipped with electricity, water, and heat and connected to one another by a series of unheated tunnels—and I do mean *unheated*! At either end of the complex, huge ramps extended upwards into the outside world, large enough to admit tractors and trucks bearing loads of freight.

The first chamber we entered was "Club 90," a fairly large common room with comfortable chairs, a pool table, a bar, a tiny Navy Exchange store, and a post office. We mailed postcards before repairing to the mess hall, where the luncheon consisted of steak, salad, lima beans, potatoes, three kinds of Kool-Aid, coffee, milk, tea, chocolate ice cream with chocolate sauce, and of course the ever-present vitamin pill that all hands are cautioned to take at the rate of one a day. The meal was followed by a tour of the station. The Pole Station included living quarters, a maintenance shop, a sick bay, and a first-class radio station with unlimited communication range. I declined the opportunity to join the 200 Club; membership is earned by sitting in a hot room and then run-

Rear Admiral Lloyd "Doc" Abbot and William S. Beinecke at the South Pole,
January 1968.

ning around the outside of the compound au naturel. The difference in temperature: two hundred degrees.

After lunch, another photo session was held, this time featuring Brian Lochore kicking a rugby football over the Pole. Brian was a modest, unassuming, very gentlemanly twenty-seven-year-old who also happened to be the national hero of New Zealand. He was the captain of the All Blacks, the great New Zealand rugby football team that had recently returned from a triumphant tour abroad. Brian was a little shy about the kicking assignment but was prodded into action by our lieutenant, who reminded him that numerous New Zealand newspapers were eagerly awaiting the prints.

Visiting the South Pole, even as a pampered passenger, is a unique experience that cannot be replicated. Nonetheless, for me the most interesting part of the Antarctic experience was the chopper flights on the days that followed. First on the agenda was Cape Royds, home to the southernmost penguin rookery in the world and the site of Shackleton's hut, the base from which that explorer achieved his "farthest south": 88•23' S, which works out to ninety-seven miles from the South Pole. Like Scott's hut at McMurdo, this hut had been partially restored. Many of Shackleton's stores were still there, unopened and in good shape: bacon, mutton, beef, table salt, parsnips, and many cans and boxes with labels rendered illegible by the passage of time. Returning from the penguin rookery to the chopper, I must have disturbed a skua nesting place, for a pair of them suddenly dive-bombed me. The attack was prolonged and vigorous, worse than a tern ambush on Cape Cod. I grabbed a stick to ward them off, at the same time urging a New Zealander companion to capture the performance on film. Unfortunately, the shutter of my camera was frozen, so documentary evidence of the battle was lost to posterity.

From Cape Royds, we traveled to Cape Evans, where the last of the three huts that served as bases for Scott and Shackleton is located. It was from Cape Evans that Scott set off on his 1911–12 expedition to the South Pole. Again, we found a quantity of unopened provisions. There were even some old pony droppings adorning the ice, preserved in deep-freeze all these years, along with several bales of hay in a remarkably good state of preservation. Scattered outside the hut were the bones of what looked like ponies and dogs. On the "front porch" reposed a carcass clearly recognizable as a dog, still in possession of all of its teeth and a bit of skin and hair as well. There were no penguins here, but I did have my first and only close encounter with an Antarctic seal, a lone, sickly, snuffling specimen with a very runny nose.

Our last few days in Antarctica were divided between Williams Field, Scott Base, and McMurdo Station. Williams Field lies about ten miles south of the McMurdo town, so far out on the shelf ice that from the crest of the road behind McMurdo its camp buildings are barely discernible specks in the distance. The camp consisted of several rows of extremely low-lying buildings, Quonset or Janeway-type in appearance. The walls of these buildings were nothing more than fabric zipped over insulation material. If the fabric were to tear, the whole building would fill with snow.

Scott Base, the New Zealand station, is just over the hill from McMurdo. Unlike the US bases, which are maintained by the military, it is wholly manned and staffed by research scientists. Nearby great masses of seals were sunning themselves on the floe, periodically disappearing and reappearing through holes in the ice. Two teams of huskies were staked in the snow outside the base, each dog chained just far enough from the others to prevent attacks. These dogs lived out in the snow the year round. The New Zealanders took them for a run every day, and the first half mile was a mad rush as the dogs burned off their pent-up energy.

For several years after my return from Antarctica, it was my privilege to recommend to the State Department people who I thought might benefit from the South Pole experience. I had thoroughly enjoyed my trip to the Pole, but I thought the criteria for selecting members of the VIP expeditions ought to be modified to include more American leaders. There was nothing wrong with bringing along a famous rugby player or the chief justice of the New Zealand Supreme Court, but it seemed to me that the invitations should be issued to Americans who were in a position to spread the word about the scientific work being done there, with logistics provided by the US Department of Defense. When I mentioned my opinion to Doc Abbot, he handed me a pad and told me to write down what I thought the criteria should be. He looked at what I'd written and said, "That's fine. Do you think you could identify people who meet those qualifications?" For two or three years thereafter, I nominated people who were leaders in the business and academic communities or who had some other sphere of influence, including Kingman Brewster of Yale, Thomas J. Watson, Jr., of IBM, Toni Knoppers of the Merck Corporation, and George Dixon, the former undersecretary of the Treasury and head of one of Minnesota's major banks. All my nominees were people of that quality. Kingman Brewster was dealing with a lot of angry alumni in the late 1960s when he was invited to go to Antarctica, and he declined. His response to the invitation was typical Kingman: "Maybe a lot of people would be pleased if I went down to Antarctica and never came back!" I also nominated Wilson Newman, then chairman of Dun & Bradstreet. His autobiography, *For What Do We Labor?*, includes a photo of him at the South Pole.

In September 1969, Betty and I took a cruise through the Aegean aboard the *North Star,* the beautiful yacht of my fellow S&H board member Lowell Weicker. Accompanied by our friends Bee and Don Kipp and Beryl and Ben Moyer, we had eighteen days of idyllic travel through Homer's "wine-dark sea." Each day brought a new experience, a new and different island, a glorious Grecian or Roman archaeological site, or some delectable Mediterranean dish prepared by the ship's cook. One of my most vivid recollections of that trip, however, is of the second night we spent in Greece, even before our cruise began. We had flown to Athens from New York and devoted two days to explorations of the archaeological treasures of Athens and Delphi. There is much to see at both sites, and by the end of the second day Betty and I were look-ing forward to a quiet evening of rest and relaxation. Beryl and Ben Moyer felt the same—we were not scheduled to meet up with the Kipps until our arrival at Samos. Upon returning to the hotel in Athens, how-ever, we found three messages awaiting us from Spyros Metaxa, of the Metaxa brandy family. At his urging, we met him in the Hilton's Pan Bar, and from there he whisked us off to a shoreside restaurant where we feasted on lobster, mullet, and flounder. This seemed, at least to me, to be ample Sunday evening entertainment, but Spyros insisted on one more stop, a place where we'd be able to "hear some nice Greek music and see some pretty Greek girls." He assured us that we would be back at our hotel in half an hour. In our innocence, we agreed.

Over the course of the next many hours, we learned that there was much truth in Ben Moyer's claim that "the Greeks have more fun than anybody." When we arrived at the establishment to which we had been lured, the dance floor was empty. One lone, long-haired girl was sing-ing. A count of the house, including our party of five, might have toted up to twenty. I put this low attendance down to the slowness of Sunday evenings; the correct reason was that midnight is far too early for the Greeks. Hardly had the first of several bottles of whisky arrived, and ice and glasses had been placed before us, when—bang! crash!—a glass shattered on the terrazzo floor at the singer's feet. This was startling, to say the least, but even more startling when we realized that the glass thrower was our host, Spyros. He explained, "We used to do this all the time, but the police don't allow it anymore." This didn't seem to deter him, for as the evening progressed at least three dozen glasses followed the first, plus an assortment of crockery, bottles, ashtrays, and silver.

When the first glass fragments flew across the floor, the singer looked up with what can only be described as a "Now there's a man who really appreciates my singing" expression on her face. The establishment's response was equally interesting. A waiter armed with a broom appeared in no time at all. While he swept the shards into a corner, another waiter tended to Spyros, setting a glass in front of him, placing a lump of ice in it, and refilling it with whisky—in short, setting the stage for a repeat performance. Meanwhile, a middle-aged woman was wandering the floor, selling bunches of balloons (about eight to a bunch), each balloon tied closely to the next like a cluster of grapes. While these balloons occasionally made their way to the center of the dance floor before being punctured—principally by our host, who was busy throwing cigarettes, knives, forks, and ice at them—more often they hardly made it from one end of the table to the next before the entire bunch was cigarette-popped.

The singer, a tall, sexy, miniskirted blonde, gravitated toward our table, there to remain for the rest of the evening. She received the most attention from Spyros. Whether this was because Ben and I were inhibited by the presence of our wives, by our own inhibited natures, by our limited grasp of the Greek language (this may not have mattered much; she said "darling" very well), or some combination thereof is ground for speculation. In any event, when Spyros's signing of the check in the middle of one of her songs seemed to suggest our imminent departure, she indicated her displeasure by shifting the performance to the table top, planting herself firmly between Betty and Beryl while pouring the contents of a new bottle of J&B whisky all over the splintered glassware and assorted crockery shards, flinging the empty bottle to the floor in conclusion. Spyros's reaction was to throw all the glasses remaining on the table, and everything else available, down among the rivulets of whisky. As he did so, he commented, "It's good for the business"—he being the Greek J&B distributor.

I was so engrossed with the entertainment at our own table that I didn't notice the crowd slowly filling up the two rings of tables enclosing the dance floor. The activity onstage and on the dance floor increased, although the accordion player appeared to be conducting a business conference all evening with the nonmusician who came to sit next to him. Another singer appeared, along with several male dancers who danced in trousers, neckties, and shirtsleeves; whether they were guests or professional entertainers is uncertain. The proprietor, who played the bouzouki (a more than adequately amplified string instrument), kept wandering through the commotion, singing all the while. When we ran out of steam and made our departure around 3 AM, the party was still going full speed. Thus ended our "Quiet Sunday Evening in Athens." I thought to myself, "If that's Sunday night, what do the Greeks do on Saturday nights?"

In the fall of 1971, Betty and I took Frances and her friend Lucie Sides on a safari expedition through Kenya and Tanzania to view and photograph the profusion of wild creatures there. My parents had been to various ports of call in Africa on some of their cruises, and my mother had been to a game preserve in Africa in the 1950s. She was so impressed that she urged Betty and me to see Africa while it was still somewhat unmodernized and there was wildlife in abundance. That was a persuasive argument for me, because of my long-standing concern about overpopulation in Africa and elsewhere; increasing population pressures mean more and more land converted to agriculture, until wildlife is confined to land areas that cannot support them. And of course Frances was excited about the trip, because of her special interest in nature and the environment. She had graduated from Yale College in June, and in a little more than a year would decide to enroll at the Yale School of Forestry.

We experienced a wide variety of environments in East Africa, from the bustle of the Kenyan capital city of Nairobi to the placid fishing villages of Pemba Channel to the vast expanses of the Masai Mara and other national parks. We identified dozens of species of wildlife and saw many of them in greater numbers than we could count. One two-day segment of our adventure epitomized the journey for me. I awoke in the Lake Manyara National Park in a residence tent—a rather luxurious tent, with beds with sheets and blankets, an oriental rug on the floor, camp chairs, washstands, a small table, and a little room in back for the compact tin trunks into which we packed our gear. Other tents nearby housed Frances and Lucie, our professional hunter guide, Robin Francis Smith (no longer referred to as a "white hunter"), and a staff consisting of a head boy, a cook, a lorry driver, a gun bearer, two porters, and three mess tent men. We left camp at 7:30 A.M. and drove over atrociously rutted roads to the Ngorongoro Crater. As we drove around the rim of the crater, we were completely overwhelmed by the wild variety of birdlife—a symphony of flashing color—and thousands upon thousands of zebras, wildebeests, and gazelles, living side by side as in some primeval Garden of Eden. In the late morning, we came across a royal black-maned lion, head high, sitting in the shade by a stream. Nearby, barely visible, was a lioness. We realized it was mating season when the young gentleman roused himself, stood proudly before us for a moment or two, then ambled over to the lioness and mounted her. We passed elephants, baboons, giraffes, buffalo, and, in the distance, a rhinoceros, all coming and going as they pleased and as nature moved them. "The placidity of it all," I wrote in my journal, "is what is most impressive to me. Here is nature in balance, in harmony with itself. All is peaceful. It really makes a profound impression on one's innermost processes." Not that nature was always peaceful and well behaved—as we were eating lunch, the piece of cold chicken that Fran was eating was grabbed right out of her hand by one of the dozen yellow-billed kites swooping all about us, and part of our guide's lunch was stolen by the vervet monkeys that came begging and scrounging around our car.

The next day we drove to the Olduvai Gorge, where the famed anthropologists Louis and Mary Leakey made their remarkable discoveries of early man dating back 1.75 million years. We also visited a Masai village, a primitive collection of huts surrounded by thornbush fencing. The village contained a number of children, one man, and a group of four or five women working on some hides spread on the ground; the men and boys were off with the cattle. The villagers were covered with flies and looked sickly; syphilis and glaucoma are widespread among the Masai. Our guide obtained permission for us to go inside one of the huts where the Masai sleep with their calves to protect them from hyenas and marauding lions. I went inside and sat on a little stool beside a cooking pot simmering above a fire. It was dark and as hot as a sauna, and smelled distinctly of the cow dung that had been plastered onto sticks to form the hut. Later that evening we camped under a clump of trees on the shore of Lake Lagaja, a short distance from the Serengeti Plain. We were the only people present on that long, sandy flat which ran two or three hundred yards downhill to the soda (or salt) lake. At cocktail time, the great bright disk of the moon began to show through the acacia trees at the edge of the plain. As we watched, the moon rose through the branches. The rising moon, the utter stillness, the vastness of the empty plain, and the mountains ascending in the distance are a powerful memory of Africa.

Betty and Bill Beinecke in the Serengeti, February 1995.

Betty and I returned to the States in late October, but Frances and Lucie stayed for several weeks to pursue further African adventures. They traveled by bus to Rwanda, where they met Rosamund Carr, the cousin of our neighbor across the street in Summit, the publisher W. Bradford Wiley. Ros had taken up residence in the country that used to be known as "the Switzerland of Africa," and had a lovely home where she operated a flower farm with her husband. Frances has been a great friend of the actress Sigourney Weaver ever since they were classmates at the Ethel Walker School, and so when Sigourney went to Rwanda to film *Gorillas in the Mist*, about Diane Fossey, she visited Ros Carr and induced her to play a role in the film. When Rwanda erupted in civil war and mobs rampaged through her house, Ros escaped to the United States. But Rwanda was her home, and she returned there. As of 1999, now in her late eighties, she is still there, looking after approximately fifty children uprooted by war.

In September 1974, Betty and I were in Italy and paid a visit to Admiral Means Johnston, who was then the commander of NATO's southern forces. We knew the admiral because his wife, Hope, had grown up with Betty in Stamford, Connecticut. I had first met Admiral Johnston in 1966, when he was the commanding officer of the Newport Naval Base and we were assigned to the same committee in the Global Strategy Discussions that are held each year at the Naval War College. In 1974, the admiral's NATO residence was the Villa Nike in Naples, a commanding spot on the hills above the harbor. We arrived in time for an elaborate dinner party given by Mrs. Johnston in honor of the secretary of the navy, William Middendorf, who was over there inspecting the naval facilities.

The next day we accompanied Admiral Johnston and his wife down to the harbor, where there were two Japanese training vessels in port. Protocol required the admiral to greet them. The newly commissioned Japanese officers on board were clean-cut, nice-looking young fellows. I was also quite impressed by their fluency in the English language, though of course part of their training is to learn English. And yet I felt a little awkward. It was almost thirty years after the end of the Second World War, but that conflict was still very green in my memory. It felt strange to step on board a Japanese ship. Even though the crew had laid out a lovely buffet and were making every effort to entertain their guests, it still made me uncomfortable to look at the stern of the ship and see the flag of the rising sun. I think Admiral Johnston felt the same way; he was in the class of 1939 at the Naval Academy and was also a World War II veteran.

Both of us were introduced to the man in command of the training cruise, a Japanese admiral about our age. I asked him where his training cruise had gone thus far. "First stop, Pearl Harbor!" he exclaimed. I must say I was somewhat taken aback. When we returned to the Villa Nike, the admiral and I went into his study, and he said, "Bill, let's have a drink." "I sure could use one," I replied. I asked him, "What did you think when that Japanese admiral said, 'First stop, Pearl Harbor'?" "Well," Admiral Johnston answered, "he might have been there before."

In late 1974, I received a brochure from the American Museum of Natural History. The brochure described a cruise that would take place under the museum's auspices, retracing Darwin's voyage to explore the flora and fauna of the South American coast aboard the H.M.S. *Beagle*. Never having taken a guided educational trip of this sort, I looked over the brochure and thought, This is an absolute must. I told Betty that I had to go on this trip, and she too became excited by the brochure and decided to come along. We recruited our Summit friends Jo and Dick Kixmiller and set forth on our adventure in February 1975.

After stopping in Lima, we flew to Santiago and then to Punta Arenas in the Strait of Magellan. There we were met by the M/S *Lindblad Explorer*, a 250-foot, 2,325-ton ship. We joined roughly fifty passengers and a group of staff professionals from the museum on this exciting odyssey. The number of experts and specialists involved in the endeavor was astonishing, with fields ranging from archaeology to zoology and much in between. All of them were ready and eager to answer whatever questions we might have, whether on ornithology or botany or marine biology. The astronomer aboard was actually the director of the American Museum of Natural History, Dr. Thomas D. Nicholson, who then wrote the "Celestial Events" column each month in *Natural History* Magazine. The celebrated alpinist Eric Shipton, who at the time had been on more Everest expeditions than anyone else and had taken Edmund Hillary on his first visit to Mount Everest, was part of the group, too. Also aboard was Walter Berlet, a professional motion picture photographer who was making a nature film of the journey, and Russ Kinne, a professional still photographer.

Even though the group was comprised largely of tourists, the cruise was a research expedition and there were moments of real exploring; our pass through the Channel of Mountains, for example, had been previously unattempted by a large vessel. Certainly the non-specialists on board were among the very few tourist-type visitors ever to visit many of the places along the route. We were able to go ashore in Zodiacs, sturdy rubber-floated dinghies with outboard motors.

The first leg of our journey took us from Punta Arenas west along the Magellan Strait to Puerto Natales, passing through the famous Kirke Narrows. My friend Russell Bennett, who was also along on this trip, wrote that "these waters—channels, fjords, passages—are the most intricate navigable waters of the world. Suffice it to say that there are two passages through Tierra del Fuego running from Atlantic to Pacific: Magellan Passage to the north and Beagle Channel to the south. We were in each at various times. The scenery is almost beyond description for grandeur and magnitude." The scenery was indeed solemn and splendid, with great towering, cathedral-like glaciers and the spiky, crenellated peaks of the various mountain ranges. Though it was the height of summer in the Southern Hemisphere, there was rain and squalls and even an occasional flurry. And the wind was omnipresent, ranging from brisk to furious. The weather did not stop us from visiting many sites along Darwin's route as well as those of Magellan and Drake. Our days were filled with lectures by the specialists on board; readings from Darwin; shipboard and on-land sightings of elephant seals, right whales, sea lions, and guanaco; visits to archaeological digs; guided shore excursions; nature films and various films about trips to strange parts of the earth. The M/S *Lindblad Explorer* was a perfectly conceived vessel for the sort of out-of-the-way cruising we were doing, with adequate power, shallow draft, and every navigational aid imaginable.

After a stop at Basket Island (where the Alacaluf Indians stole one of the *Beagle*'s boats), we entered the open sea and sailed down past the grim and inimitable silhouette of Cape Horn. Rounding the cape, we headed for the Falkland Islands. From an ornithological point of view, this part of the world is a paradise. Although as a birder I must be classed as a rank amateur, I was soon able to identify a great many species, including indigenous ones like the elegant crested tinamou and the rhea, the South American ostrich. West Point Island, at the northwestern edge of the Falklands, featured a marvelous bird sanctuary that included a colony of penguins. These were mostly rockhopper penguins, but we saw many Magellanic penguins, too. They are slightly larger and were slaughtered by the hundreds of thousands in the nineteenth century by the Spaniards and colonists, who boiled them down for oil. Albatrosses were nesting right beside the rockhopper penguins. Our guides warned us to maintain a respectful distance between ourselves and the young albatrosses. It seems the bird's one and only defensive mechanism is projectile vomiting. When a human approaches too close, it begins to open and close its mouth rapidly, emitting an ominous "tok-tok" noise indicative of its intention to vomit in one's direction. We were told that albatrosses are very accurate up to four feet and likely to hit at six. The vomit is a nasty, smelly, oily substance that has a tendency to linger in one's clothing for some time.

I had become interested in the controversy surrounding the Falkland Islands. The Falklands are a crown colony, but Britain's title has been—and still is—contested by the Argentines, who call them the Islas Malvinas. I had read a book on the dispute by my old Columbia Law professor Julius Goebel, Jr., called *The Struggle for the Falkland Islands*. It was nearly impossible to read—I think it might have been his doctoral dissertation—but I was able to deduce that the events that led up to the dispute took place between the 1760s and the 1830s and that since then the matter had been frozen in status quo. On our last evening at sea, I gave a talk on the dispute and fielded questions. My basic conclusion was, as I wrote in my journal, that "the rival claims for the Falklands, even to those of us who know about them at home, seem trivial and unimportant." But the British and Argentines took the dispute seriously enough to go to war over it in 1982, with the loss of several hundred lives. Needless to say, I followed the developments of the war with great interest. I thought that the Argentines made a great mistake in going to war. In 1975, it was apparent that the whole infrastructure of the Falklands (such as it was) was oriented toward Argentina. Although the nearest Argentine city, Comodoro Rivadavia, was six to seven hundred miles away, that was still much, much closer than Britain. There was only one ship a year from Britain. Children attended elementary school in the islands, but went to Argentina when they got older. People who were ill went there for treatment. It was quite clear that the Falklands were an expense to the British, and since the age of coaling stations had passed, they had no economic or strategic value. The tendency was toward phased control of the islands by Argentina, and that most likely would have happened if the Argentines had waited instead of getting all hot in their pants.

After several more stops at some amazing penguin rookeries, we made the Valdez Peninsula, which juts out seventy miles into the Atlantic Ocean and is home to great numbers of wildlife, including many playful porpoises that leaped and splashed about our boat, to the great delight of both passengers and porpoises. From the peninsula we sailed to Mar del Plata, the coastal resort for Buenos Aires, and from there returned home to New York. The *Lindblad Explorer* cruise was a spectacular education and turned out to be the first of several guided tours of this sort that Betty and I have taken in recent years.

In May 1977, the Manufacturers Hanover Company arranged for the members of the board of directors and their spouses to be flown to Asia so that we could attend meetings in Manila and Hong Kong. It was a phenomenal experience. Betty and I traveled to Hawaii, New Zealand, and Australia en route to Manila, though an air traffic controllers' strike stranded us in Sydney for a week, forcing us to drop our plan to visit Bali. We were able to visit my Yale classmate Jim Castle in Hawaii—someone I hadn't seen since I passed through Honolulu on my way around the world in the summer of 1936—and my old friend John Bull and his wife, Mary, in New Zealand, along with their daughter (my goddaughter), Penny Davies, and her husband, Peter. We also saw Elizabeth Rathbone, though her husband, Bill, had died in the years since my previous visit in 1968 and Elizabeth had suffered a couple of strokes. We experienced a superior mixture of business and pleasure in magnificent Manila and throbbing, humming, bustling Hong Kong. The Manufacturers Hanover meetings were perfectly planned and executed, with meticulous organization of transportation, accommodations, dinners, guest lists, and so forth in countries where the protocol and customs were different. Throughout the trip, we had carefully prepared and well-put-together briefings on the countries of the "great arc of Asia," plus presentations on the Manufacturers Hanover Company's involvement in those countries and projections of the bank's plans. We returned to London as the guests of Ren and Nancy McPherson aboard the Dana Corporation's G-2 Gulfstream jet, touching down at Kuala Lumpur, Bombay, Tehran, Munich, and finally London. Betty and I celebrated both my sixty-third birthday and our thirty-sixth wedding anniversary along the way. And we went around the world in twenty-five days—with apologies to Phileas Fogg, who made it in seventy-nine days! It really was a trip that had a little bit of everything. I even gave a short talk on the Campaign for Yale at a dinner of the Yale Club of Hong Kong.

One of the most interesting aspects of the trip however, was the chance to see at close range the dictator of the Philippines, Ferdinand Marcos, and his wife, Imelda. There was little hint then of the unrest that would topple the Marcoses in 1986, but there were straws in the wind, and some of them were perceptible to us even when we were experiencing hospitality like no other I've ever experienced. Manila was a city I would have liked under almost any circumstances, with its crumbling stone walls and the broad, sweeping bay—so evocative, for an American, of Dewey's stirring victory over the Spanish fleet and his immortal words, "You may fire when you are ready, Gridley." As it was, we lived like nabobs during our three days in Manila. We stayed at one of the world's finest hotels—certainly one of the best I've ever stayed in. We were overwhelmed with presents: magnificent baskets of fruit, fresh flowers every day, a beautiful Philippine hardwood box, some mint-condition coins from the head of the Central Bank, and assorted mementos from the president and his wife. We had a police escort everywhere we went, complete with flashing lights and the blaring of sirens. And we were the recipients of a full-scale charm offensive from the president and Mrs. Marcos.

At 7:30 A.M. on the first day of our visit, we were picked up at our hotel and transported to the presidential yacht, the *Ang Pangulo*. We spent the entire day in the company of the president and Mrs. Marcos. We went for lunch to the Marcos's country home on Bataan, where we were surrounded with music and entertained by lovely Filipino dancers. The hospitality continued with evening dinner at the Malacañang Palace with the First Couple. Mrs. Marcos herself escorted us through the sumptuous rooms of the palace. The next day, the president escorted us, by bus and helicopter, to Bataan and the ruins of Corregidor—names that had special significance for a person who had spent over two years in the Pacific war and participated in the Philippine liberation at Leyte Gulf. And that afternoon, Jim Finley, Charles J. "Chuck" Pilliod, Jr., and I played golf with President Marcos at the Wack Wack golf course.

Meeting the Marcoses gave me a lot of strange and conflicting reactions. They really were a charming couple—and I even discovered that Imelda Marcos was a good friend of *my* great friend Thibaut de Saint Phalle. Ferdinand Marcos was an undeniably impressive person. His golf handicap, I noticed, was an incredible seven. I wrote in my journal that the president, though he was about to turn sixty, "has the figure of a young man and is almost a professional athlete in the way he takes care of himself. I saw him water-ski and play golf and can attest to his athletic ability. I was told he plays pelota daily as well as other sports. He seems tireless. He has the courtesy of one who has absolute power: always asking you to go first, being extremely solicitous of all your wants..." I spoke to him at some length about my war experiences in the Pacific, and he knew something of the war himself; he had escaped three times from the Japanese, the first time from the Bataan Death March. I noticed that he taped his ankles while water-skiing, and asked him why. "Another memento from our friends the Japanese," he replied. "They hung me up by the heels for twenty-four hours and my ankles have been weak ever since."

And yet... The country had been under martial law since it was imposed by edict in 1972. "Martial law is something that is foreign to us," I recorded in my journal. "It doesn't seem right somehow." We were told that martial law had helped rescue the nation from turmoil, that stability had been achieved, that land reform and other reforms were being undertaken, and that some kind of family planning was being put forward to slow the population growth in a country where the median age was seventeen. "It seems peaceful now, and the people contented," I wrote. "At least that is the impression one gets in Manila, yet we know there is a rebellion of some kind among the Moros on Mindanao and, at the moment, there is an uneasy cease-fire; in the north, too, I understand all is not quiet." The *New York Times* was banned in Manila, and the press, while not controlled, was "guided." When I put the question of succession to the US chargé d'affaires, the answer seemed to be that the president had placed some names in a safe somewhere and, in the event of his death, these names would constitute a committee to see to the succession. "In the thirties, it was said of Mussolini, 'He made the trains run on time,'" I wrote. "I'm left with a large question mark. Personally, Marcos is a charming man. His lifestyle has all the trappings of an emperor's. I know it is said that the best form of government is a benevolent dictatorship. But the adjective is all-important."

All my life I have been interested in the polar regions of the world. I had visited the South Pole in 1968, an exhilarating experience, and so I required no persuasion when the opportunity to visit the North Pole came along a dozen years later. Some people who were putting together an expedition, knowing of my interest in the Arctic and Antarctic, asked me to go along. This was an extraordinary trip, too. The group consisted of (a) several ham radio operators who wanted to talk to their friends from "farthest north"; (b) six skydivers, marvelous young athletes, who wanted to jump on the Pole; (c) an ABC camera crew who were there to film the skydivers for *Wide World of Sports*; and (d) me and two friends, George Dixon and Lansing Lamont, whom I'd recruited for the expedition. George was formerly financial vice president of S&H, and Lansing was a writer from New York. The mission of (d) was to help share the cost.

I retired as chairman of the board and chief executive officer of S&H on April 24, 1980, and set forth for the North Pole on April 25. Our group came together in Edmonton, Alberta, and left the next day for Resolute Bay in the Northwest Territories. We spent a couple of days there working out the logistics of the clothing, food, and fuel supplies we would need, then boarded a Twin Otter airplane and headed north. We were soon far above the tree line. All the seas and lakes over which we passed were frozen, and the treeless land was covered with snow and ice. The vast expanse of white presented an awesome, mystical, beautiful landscape.

We landed at Lake Hazen, some six hundred miles south of the Pole, and spent several days there in a Quonset hut-type lodge. We were so far north that there was absolutely no difference between night and day. The sun maintained a constant altitude of about 30 degrees, making a complete circle in the sky in a twenty-four-hour period. It took a while to get used to. Here the small group of skydivers made their first jump. They were diligent, well trained, and highly disciplined. Their leader, a young man in his late thirties, had some thirty-six hours of free-fall time—not bad when you realize that the maximum free-fall time in any one jump is about thirty seconds. The skydivers stepped out of the Twin Otter at 7,500 feet and landed on Lake Hazen. Their multicolored canopies floated gracefully above the frigid white landscape. One skydiver had put down his red shirt as his target and, to my surprise, he landed precisely on the spot.

Our small party set out for the Pole on May 1. We didn't quite make it. The far northern cap of the earth was simply fogged in, making it impossible to land. We had to turn back at 88°N, about ninety-six miles from the Pole. The Twin Otter could not carry sufficient fuel in its tanks to make the round trip, and although the accompanying DC-3 carried reserve fuel in its drums, no fueling in flight was possible. This meant that we had to turn around while we were still within range of our base.

Not long after the turnaround, someone spotted a frozen patch of open water called a "lead," and a landing was made at 84°N. There, with the assistance of Harvard man Lansing Lamont, I planted the Yale flag high on a pressure ridge overlooking our landing site, and many pictures were taken, including one of the S&H flag that I had also brought with me. The planes were refueled under the supervision of an able female flight engineer. She did most of the work—rolling the drums down a ramp, hand cranking the fuel into the tanks. Our skydivers

At the northernmost redemption center, 84°N, 70°W, in 1980.

changed into their gear, went up in the Otter, and jumped out as the cameras rolled. It gave us all a thrill to see them drifting down in the sparkling sunshine, some of them streaming smoke from little canisters attached to their shoes—vivid streaks of color and motion against a brilliant blue sky above the frozen white ocean. Beautiful and impressive! To celebrate the whole event, especially the successful skydive, we spread a red tablecloth on the frozen ocean and all hands enjoyed champagne and caviar.

The first time one of the jumpers landed smack on his target at Lake Hazen, I thought it was luck, but when he did the same thing up near the North Pole, I figured he knew what he was up to. He repeated the feat yet again when the skydivers made a third and final jump at Grise Fiord, the northernmost inhabited community in North America, en route back to civilization. The Eskimos who lived in the village regarded the tumbling parachutes with great wonder and surprise; I have photos of Eskimos photographing skydivers.

The expedition had been an exciting and successful failure—failure in that we did not set foot on the frozen Arctic Ocean at exactly 90•N, success in that we ventured far into the North, a region that is not known by many. It was an experience from which I learned much and that I will treasure.

For years I had been yearning to go back to the South Pacific islands where I served aboard the *Murray* in World War II. In February 1983, I persuaded Betty to accompany me on a month-and-a-half revisit of the old battlegrounds. My sentimental journey began on the island of Efate in the New Hebrides (now an independent nation called Vanuatu). We met up with my old shipmate Jim Boyd and his wife, Phyllis, and my goddaughter Penny Bull Davies and her husband, Peter. We cruised on a chartered yacht for ten days, starting from Port-Vila on Efate and going round the island to Havannah harbor (where the *Murray* had put in several times thirty-nine years earlier), then working our way up to Espiritu Santo. The familiar elements of the South Pacific came flooding back: the heat and humidity, the blazing sunlight, the clear water, the marvelous multicolored fish darting every which way through the lacy convoluted shapes of the live coral, the brilliant spangles of the southern constellations sparkling against the black night skies. The islands we visited were so quiet and placid and seemingly deserted that it was hard to grasp that the wartime United States military population of Espiritu Santo exceeded the 1983 population of the whole Vanuatu group. It was strange to remember the vast anchorage at Santo, once so full of ships, and then to see it with hardly any vessels present. At the time of our visit, the prime minister had flown up from Vila (the Vanuatu capital) to fete the new mayor of Santo at an outdoor buffet in the back garden of our hotel. All hotel guests (about seven) were included. Vanuatu, though a member of the United Nations, does not maintain a mission in New York. Consequently, it was represented by a lawyer with an office in the city on 145th Street. He was in Santo visiting his client while we there. I had a couple of beers with him.

Penny and Peter Davies had to return home to New Zealand, a two-day journey—further confirmation of how very remote we were in that part of the world. The Boyds and Beineckes went on by air to the Solomons, landing first at Guadalcanal. We toured Henderson Field and the other famous battlefields and chartered a plane for a good two-hour look around. We saw the rusting remains of Japanese and American ships resting on the ocean's floor and crossed Iron Bottom Bay to fly above Tulagi, site of the officers' club where I celebrated my thirtieth birthday. I was impressed anew at the size and ruggedness of Guadalcanal, which made one appreciate all the more how brutal it must have been for the troops who fought on the ground there. Jim and Phyllis returned to the States, but Betty and I flew up "The Slot" via commercial Solomon Airways to Gizo, near Kolombaranga. While there, we went out to look over and snorkel at Plum Pudding Island, famous as the place where John F. Kennedy and the ten or eleven other survivors of PT 109 took refuge after their boat was sliced in two by a Japanese destroyer. From there we flew to Rabaul (where the *Murray* was part of the screen for a carrier strike in November 1943) and then to Lae in New Guinea.

The war obviously was a constant backdrop to our travels through the South Pacific, and war relics were everywhere. Wherever we went snorkeling, we had an excellent chance of coming across some rusty old wreck, American or Japanese insignia clearly visible through the gin-clear waters. If we had wanted to do some aqualung diving in the Santo harbor, we could have gone eighty feet down to visit the transport *President Coolidge*, sunk by one of our own mines as she was entering port; you can swim in and out of the hold and see jeeps lined up in good order, and cases and cases of supplies. On all the islands you saw remnants of military supplies, from the fences made from the metal mats used to surface airstrips to the homes and buildings set up in rusting, corroded Quonset huts. But while reminders of the war were everywhere at hand, they did not dominate, and what was around was rusting, falling apart, and usually out of the way. The battlefields were not maintained, and the jungle had reclaimed many sites, such as the great airstrip on Guadalcanal. The forty years that had passed since the war's end were a long time for most of the islands' inhabitants, particularly since most of the population was very young. For them World War II was a legendary history from olden times. The moment I told anyone on the islands that I had been there during the war with the Japanese, their eyes would light up and they would smile excitedly and sometimes ask, "How was the fight?" One young lady I met in the post office in Santo made me write down my name and address and told all the other customers about me, because I was the first person she had ever met from the war.

But the war and its legacy also fit in with my other main impression of the South Pacific revisited: the often-startling juxtaposition of the primitive and the modern. As we cruised through Vanuatu on our chartered yacht, we were approached by natives in outrigger dugout canoes, hollowed out by hand and secured with vines; but elsewhere we encountered fiberglass canoes propelled by powerful Yamaha outboard motors. In parts of Malaita in the Solomon Islands, some people still used bead money, and barter was everywhere a common medium of exchange; but some of the most primitive peoples would several times a year come out of the bush to board modern airplanes that would take them to dancing and singing competitions on nearby islands. At Port Moresby on New Guinea, natives in traditional dress would jostle islanders in shorts, but sometimes you would see men in grass skirts and bark belts who were also wearing Western-style shirts or even jackets. Perhaps most dramatically, when Betty and I flew into the New Guinea highlands in a chartered helicopter, we visited an immense gold dredge, as large as an apartment building lying on its side, that had been flown in piecemeal in the 1930s and assembled on-site. Several of these monsters now sit abandoned in those isolated interior valleys, and the old hulk that Betty and I saw served as a home to a number of Melanesians—a particularly poignant blending of Stone Age culture with modern industrial development.

My return trip to the South Pacific gave me perspective on the places where I'd had some of my most formative experiences, and taught me a lot about that little-known corner of the world. When I returned to the States, my friend Charley Woolsey was lamenting that he lacked responses to his requests for material for his Andover class notes. I sent him my South Pacific log. His problem was solved, for one issue anyway.

Betty and I have taken many other trips, too many to recount here. Some of the standouts included a trip to China in 1978 (also sponsored by the American Museum of Natural History); a trip to India in 1985 following the New York Philharmonic (one of Betty's major interests), on which we met Indira Gandhi about a month before her assassination; and another around-the world trip in 1995, again with the American Museum of Natural History, to critical points of biodiversity around the globe, including Belize, Guatemala, Brazil, Easter Island, New Guinea, Malaysia, China, Mongolia, Burma, Madagascar, and Tanzania. And we have continued our travels: to South Africa on a golfing trip in 1997, to Greece and Turkey in 1998, and most recently to the Galápagos in 1999.

I am fortunate that I've been financially able to make these journeys, but of course there are many people who are financially able to travel and do not. That's too bad; travel is a splendid antidote to narrowness. Through my travels, I have increasingly come to appreciate what good fortune it is to be an American, and to see how we appear in the eyes of other nations. Too often we do seem narrow and self-oriented and insufficiently aware of how our actions affect people across the globe. I have learned that wherever you are in the world, the United States looms as the most important nation, just as the president is the most important man in the world. As an Englishman once said to me in Barbados, "The president of the United States is the emperor of the world." When you listen to the local radio of countries across the globe, the president of the United States is being listened to, quoted, analyzed, and pondered, almost regardless of the issue. He turns out to be the world's greatest authority on the widest variety of subjects. This fact makes it all the more important, I feel, that the president be a man of character as well as power, a man of morality as well as might.

To repeat myself yet again, all these trips have been a real education. There is no substitute for seeing, experiencing, and being in a place. You have to visit the Orient to understand the reality behind the cliché about "masses of humanity," to truly sense it. When you read that one-quarter of the population of the world is Chinese, it doesn't mean anything; it just doesn't sink in until you go there and see it and feel it. Travel has been perception and instruction and revelation all in one, and I hope that Betty and I can continue our education for some time to come.

CHAPTER TWENTY-TWO

Later Life

When Betty and I sold our house on Prospect Hill Avenue in Summit and moved to an apartment in Manhattan in 1979, a year before I retired from S&H, many of our friends assumed I was looking to shorten my commute. Evidently they had no understanding of the real power structure in our family. The truth was that I loved our Prospect Hill Avenue house and would have been content even to have moved to a smaller house in Summit. But by that time the management of the Prospect Hill Avenue home was more than Betty wanted to handle. We were both getting on in years, and it wasn't fair to ask her to maintain a big house on three acres and the lawn and shrubs and garden that went along with it. Betty was also quite active in New York affairs and events, and her own commuting time could be quite substantial. Since my assumption of the chairmanship of S&H, we'd had the use of a midtown Manhattan apartment that was one of the perquisites of the job. I had so many things with business overtones to do in New York that it was good to have a place to stay in the city when various functions went too late. But I would soon be retiring, and we would have to give up the apartment. So we made the mutual decision to sell our house in New Jersey and move to our present apartment on East 79th Street. It's much simpler to maintain, and our lifestyle in New York makes it much easier for us to travel; we don't have to get a housesitter or take other elaborate actions.

And yet I still consider myself a New Jerseyan at heart, and even after our move to Manhattan, I remain vigilant in helping to protect the Garden State's good name and reputation. Back in 1974, I had noticed that the eighth edition of Merriam-Webster's *Collegiate Dictionary*, in a run-on entry next to the state listing, identified a resident of New Jersey only by the spiteful term "New Jerseyite," with its suggestion of "termite." I wrote to the editor deploring the pejorative term, and observed further that "New Jerseyan" was the preferred usage and

521

was so employed throughout the state. I received a cordial response claiming that "New Jerseyite" had wide currency, but I was assured that my comments would be considered in the production of a new edition. And so I was most disturbed when, in 1986, I noticed that the ninth edition of the *Collegiate Dictionary* continued to identify a resident of New Jersey only as a "New Jerseyite." I dug out my correspondence and wrote to the editor, Frederick Mish. I enclosed examples of the usage of "New Jerseyan" in no less an authority than the *New York Times*. I compared "New Jerseyite" to the offensive term "Chinaman," knowing that would get their attention—and it did! They didn't remove the term "New Jerseyite," which they claimed was well established in use, but they did make a plate change to add the proper term. I feel that I have won a great moral and diplomatic victory on behalf of all the state's residents and offspring in achieving this official recognition of our proper appellation. And although I could not remove "New Jerseyite," at least "New Jerseyan" appears first alphabetically. I sent a copy of my correspondence to the New Jersey governor, Tom Kean, and received a letter from him congratulating me on my persistence.

The Yale Club of New York City is located at 50 Vanderbilt Avenue, on the corner at 44th Street by Grand Central Station. It used to be an extremely perilous intersection. The crossing was marked only by two ill-defined white lines. Taxis, automobiles, and trucks came roaring down Vanderbilt, horns blaring. When I used to go to the Yale Club in those days, I often had to leap for my life as I attempted to cross the street. I had long predicted that an accident would happen there, and indeed one day in September 1984 I arrived at the intersection just after a pedestrian had been struck by a speeding taxi and had to be taken away in an ambulance. This incident impelled me to write to the mayor, Ed Koch, pleading that the city mark the crosswalk more distinctly and perhaps even station an officer at the intersection once in a while to persuade motor vehicles to pause occasionally and let a pedestrian cross the street. I sent my letter off, received a polite acknowledgment from one of Koch's assistants, and heard nothing further. One day I went to a reception celebrating the restoration of Gracie Mansion and mentioned my concern about the Vanderbilt crossing to the Koch assistant who had responded to my letter. I was assured that the matter would soon be taken care of. Nothing happened. Then in 1988 my friend Ross Sandler, the original executive director of the Hudson River Foundation, became commissioner of transportation. I mentioned to him my long-standing concern about the Vanderbilt crossing, and this time something was done. Bold white cross marks were painted on the pavement, which slowed the traffic somewhat and made crossing much easier. Then in 1991, the city repaved Vanderbilt Avenue, obliterating the cross marks. I despaired. But the city administration must be something like those large, slow-reacting dinosaurs that were constructed so that a sensation in their feet would eventually reach their brains, perhaps after being routed through sub-brains in their tails. A few years ago, the city finally erected stop signs at the corner of Vanderbilt and 44th Street. All this has happened since I began my crusade to make it a less perilous crossing. Some people have since referred to that intersection by the Yale Club as "Beinecke Crossing." I like to think that I have helped make that place safe not only for Yalies but for all New York pedestrians.

Though it may not be a matter of international or even local significance, the game of golf has been significant to me, particularly as I have gotten older. It has kept me in fairly good physical shape, and because the game is so complex, it has kept my mind active as well. Golf has helped me stay in touch with many of my contemporaries and has introduced me to many more.

I became a member of the US Seniors Golf Association in 1970, and it has been one of my life's sustaining enjoyments ever since. On turning eighty, I became an emeritus member. That means that I pay no dues but still am eligible to play in the events. When the association was founded, it was national in name only; its membership was effectively limited to the East Coast. With the development of jet travel it truly became a national organization and has turned out to be almost too popular. When I joined, the criteria for membership were fairly simple: a candidate had to be over fifty-five years of age, a gentleman, a member of a golf club, and in possession of a reasonable golf game. At that time, almost all qualified people were admitted. Today, there is room enough to admit but a fraction of the many well-qualified applicants. The admissions limitation is based on the widespread feeling that the championship played in June each year should be able to accommodate members without a waiting list; that sets an automatic restriction on the number of members. The US Seniors Championship is played at Apawamis in Rye and at Round Hill in Greenwich. Those members who are on the older side play their thirty-six-hole tournament at Blind Brook in Purchase, New York, but join up with the other members for the awards dinner at Apawamis. I was elated, playing in the national championship in June 1998, to finish as runner-up in my class. I was awarded a nice silver medal, which is proudly on display in my New York apartment. It was the first time I'd ever won anything in the national championship, though I've been playing in it for over twenty-five years.

Besides the national championship, there are satellite tournaments that are just for fun. The oldest of the satellite tournaments is at Ekwanok in Vermont. It goes back to 1962, and Betty and I have played in that tournament twenty to twenty-five times, and we have also played many times in the one at Kittansett not far from our Chatham home in September. (In the US Seniors events, you don't play with your wife except on the day before a tournament's official start; the day before is either a practice round or a mixed event.) There are now about a dozen of these satellite tournaments played from January to November from the Bahamas north to Massachusetts and west to California. These tournaments have a nice tradition of awarding crockery to the winners in different categories. We have a few of the glass and crystal plates that used to be awarded at some of those earlier tournaments, and on the third floor apartment that we keep in New York are a couple of pewter plates that I won at one or two of the very early satellite events at Ekwanok. Nowadays each member of the winning team of each flight is

"The Golfers." Left to right: Harold Goodbody, Johnny Farrell (former U.S. Open champion), Jack Connor, and Bill Beinecke at Chatham, Massachusetts, c. 1975.

awarded a Lenox china dinner plate bearing the USSGA insignia. The runners-up get smaller plates, as do the winners of the beaten division. I have a nice collection of crockery from the tournaments I have played in over the years. One year I had won one of the smaller plates, but for some reason I failed to go up to the head table to collect my prize when announced. When I spoke to the chairman after the dinner, he said that my plate had been locked up in a safe but that he would send it to me. And then he simply put the plate in an envelope and dropped it in the mail! It arrived at our home in Florida, broken only into three or four pieces rather than a hundred, fortunately, so Betty glued it together. We have our smaller-sized tournament plates displayed on little stands in the second bedroom, and if you stand far across the room, you can't see the cracks in that particular one. But every once in a while our cleaning woman dusts it back into three pieces.

Besides the US Seniors, I was a member for a while of the New Jersey Seniors Golf Association but resigned when we moved to New York City. When I was about sixty years old and in a joining mood, I joined the American Seniors, the New England Seniors, and the International Seniors, but soon resigned because I didn't play in them enough or didn't play in them at all. I have been a more active member of the Bay State Seniors in Massachusetts, and I play in one or two of their events each year. That organization has an interesting summer tradition of playing team matches against the seniors of every other New England state. Over the years I've played against all the New England states, not only at home in Massachusetts but also in all the foreign climes.

For the last several years, I've been an active participant in another golfing group called the Three Score and Ten. You have to be at least seventy years old to be a member, and the symbol for membership is LXX, which is displayed on a little badge that goes on your lapel. I've been a member since they invited me to join when I became seventy, and I played in their tournament for fourteen straight years through 1997. I've served on the board for a number of years, and I was president from 1993 to 1995. I worked hard at that job, and tried to help the organization. It had direction, but it needed to improve its finances. Dues were set at the ridiculously low level of twenty-five dollars per annum. We had only one paid employee in the more than thirty-year history of our organization: Mildred McIntosh, our executive secretary, who just recently retired. Dues had never been increased, nor had the twenty-five dollar initiation fee. I was concerned that we were not going to be able to meet our obligations, so I persuaded the board to recommend to the membership that we increase both the dues and the initiation fee. That decision, plus a few other things I attended to, left the organization in better financial shape. Each president has to do his own bit to push the organization along, and I did mine. The Three Score and Ten tournament is always played in mid-October in North Carolina down at Pine Needles, not far from Pinehurst. I have many friends who are members, and many of them go down to the tournament with their wives. It makes a very pleasant week. Betty and I are not sure whether we will go again, however, since the tournament date falls so close to the time when we come back from Cape Cod. And I'm reaching an age where I'd better not participate all that much in golf tournaments.

Every golfer has a few scores of which he or she is unbearably proud. I will tell anyone who'll listen about the time I shot 75 at Eastward Ho! and the day I bettered my age—77—on May 12, 1993, at the Baltusrol Upper Course. On July 17, 1998, I made my first hole in one. Lightning struck that day on hole 8 at the Kingsway golf course on Cape Cod! It was unbelievable; I had been playing golf for over seventy years without a hole in one and was convinced that I would never make one. Prior to that day, I had only *seen* three holes in one, the first of which was John's first shot at Schloss Fuschl in 1965; I missed seeing Betty's the next day. And my hole in one was the first in the family since Betty's!

I also take great pleasure in the memory of the incredible win that Richard McLaren and I achieved at the 1997 Eastward Ho! annual member-guest tournament. Dick, who is a Yale man as well as a fellow member of my Cape Cod bridge club, is by far the stronger golfer. It was his strength and skill that carried us to, and through, the tie-breaking shootout on the eighteenth hole. We won when I sunk a long, curling putt in front of the entire gallery. Was I nervous! But I made myself oblivious to everything, and my putt was both lucky and good. The next thing I knew, a great cheer arose from the clubhouse as the ball went in the hole. A miracle! I have a big hunk of Polish crystal as a souvenir of that happy day, and a nice picture, courtesy of my friend Dean Speir, depicting Bobby Jones making his famous putt on the seventy-second hole at Winged Foot in 1929. The painting is entitled *Golf's Greatest Putt*, but the shot was really golf's second-greatest putt, as my friends tell me! That's the beauty of golf—you never know when you might make the shot of a lifetime.

With my seventy-fifth birthday looming in May 1989, I asked myself how best I could, with my family, celebrate that event. I remembered the example of my late friend Ted Kenyon. He was a great fan of

trains—he had written that memorable Monday Night Club paper entitled "The Greatest Sight in Nature," about a coal-fired steam train passing through the Vermont hills on a winter's night. He had also chartered a car on a Canadian railroad and taken three generations of his
family across Canada. Determined to do something similar, I chartered
two old traditional private rail cars, which would be attached to the rear
of three different Amtrak trains: the first journeying from Los Angeles
to Seattle, the second from Seattle to Salt Lake City, and the third from
Salt Lake City to Chicago. Thus our whole family could ride together,
in sybaritic comfort, through some of the country's most glorious scenery. And the trip would include not just Betty and me and our children
but their children as well. Because our route was fixed and our minute-
by-minute, mile-by-mile timetable set in advance, friends and family
could meet up with the train and get on and off as their schedule
allowed.

The two cars, the Yerba Buena and the Bella Vista, were up to the
high standard of my expectations. All the rooms were duly marked with
the occupants' names, and even the big round illuminated drumhead
(or bull's-eye) hanging on the back of the observation platform at the
end of the last car was perfect: concentric circles of red, white, and blue,
inscribed with the initials WSB and the number 75. We departed Los
Angeles's glowing old Spanish-style railroad station on June 17, and
traveled along the sea to Santa Barbara, with lovely views along the
coast and occasional glimpses of surfers riding the waves of the blue
Pacific. We then turned inland through lush, fertile agricultural valleys
and the spectacular, heavily forested mountains of northern California
and the Cascades in Oregon and Washington. From Seattle we
returned south to Portland, turned east, and headed through more
splendid scenery along the Columbia River and through southern
Idaho to Salt Lake City. The all-day ride from Salt Lake City to Denver,
crossing the Rockies, was truly spectacular.

All my children and grandchildren were aboard the whole way
through to Denver, with John and his family continuing on to our terminus at Chicago. A lot of my old friends came along for part of the
ride: Marshall Cleland, Jim and Phyllis Boyd, Scott Martin, Bill and
Marge Hunzelman. Jack and Jane Sylvester and Stew and Wade
Ballinger joined us for dinner while the cars were detached in the Seattle railroad station. Some of Sarah's friends, with their children, also
came aboard. We were well fed and taken care of, and there were some
stopovers along the way for walking and sailing and riding and golf. On
board there were movies on the VCR, the children put on plays and

Frances, John, Sarah, and Rick Beinecke at John's fiftieth birthday party, 1996.

magic shows, and of course there was plenty of time to hang about on the open rear viewing platform, just enjoying the wonders of the western part of the good old USA. We arrived in Chicago after a week on the road, having had a euphoric and successful time. It was quite a way to celebrate three-quarters of a century!

Betty and I were married on May 24, 1941, which meant that our fiftieth wedding anniversary would be in 1991. But instead we decided to celebrate our fiftieth anniversary a year early, in 1990; we called the event "Ringing in the Fiftieth." There was a very good reason for this preemptive celebration. We were afraid that some of those we very much wanted to have with us on the occasion might not make it if we waited another year—and our precaution proved justified. In the event, we held the celebration on May 17, 1990, a week ahead of the actual date, and we were rewarded with a very good turnout. Some 140 of our dearest friends made the trek into New York to join us at the Yale Club. We had music, of course, from that old Yale perennial Ben Cutler, and some additional entertainment in the form of a wandering magician. Among the guests were three people who had actually been in the wedding when Betty and I tied the knot all those years before. Thirteen of my Yale classmates were in attendance, along with a scattering of cousins. Our good friend the Reverend Leon Sullivan (of Sullivan Principles fame) gave the invocation. We were very proud to be able to introduce our grandchildren to our friends. Many of our grandchildren were quite young at that time, and the littlest ones came early and went home before dinner was served. After dinner came the toasts and some dancing. All in all, it turned out to be a most successful celebration of half a century of an excellent marriage.

In the time since my retirement, my year has developed a sort of rhythm that suits Betty and me extremely well. January usually finds us in our New York apartment on the Upper East Side, with its sunny yellow living room, its plant-filled terraces, and its all-important proximity to children and grandchildren. Upstairs in my penthouse study, amidst Betty's collection of elephant figurines, I look out on a sweeping view that includes Central Park, the Chrysler Building, and the Empire State Building. For many years, at the end of January we had our family reunion at Skytop, an all-inclusive resort in Pennsylvania. It's in the Poconos, the beautiful low-lying hills that are only an hour and a half from New York City. Skytop offers a wide variety of diversions, including snowy lakeside walks, skating, skiing and tobogganing, massage rooms, a small gymnasium, billiards, miniature golf, and a rain-or-shine outdoor cookout on Saturdays. Its main attraction for us, though, was that it brought us all together without the need for drudgery and responsibility on the part of a host or hostess. It gave the grandchildren an opportunity to get to know one another better and helped keep us a cohesive family unit. We never quite assembled every one of our children, their spouses, and their children at Skytop on any one occasion, but all of them came at some point over the dozen or so years we were together there.

Betty and I spend February until early April in the small apartment in Delray Beach, Florida, that we have owned since 1984. I like to be able to swim and golf and read in the pleasant Florida warmth and sunshine and to wait out the worst of the northeastern winter. I know a lot of people down there, including my good friends Harry Stimpson and Dick Keresey, and I have made a lot of new friends there as well. Betty and I belong to the Gulf Stream Club, the Ocean Club, and the Little Club. I play golf or hit some balls at the Gulf Stream Club just about every day that we're in Florida, and I play some bridge on Mondays. Some winters I also attend a Gulf Stream Club bridge class that is conducted by a professional; it runs for five or six sessions and helps to sharpen one's game considerably. Once in a while I fiddle around with the Questar telescope I inherited from my father. It has frustrated me. I like to look at the planets, the moons of Jupiter, Saturn and its rings, and the phases of Venus, but I find it confounding to try to locate more

The ladies in my life. Left to right, Candace Beinecke, Carrie Elston, Frances Elston, Elizabeth Beinecke, Sarah Richardson, Gaily Beinecke. Seated, Elizabeth Elston, Mary Elston.

elusive celestial bodies. My Yale classmate Ted Woolsey recommended a book on using a telescope. While I can understand some of the instructions reasonably well, putting them into practice is about as easy as relying on an auto mechanic's manual to change the rings in your car. I get more vicarious satisfaction out of reading *Sky and Telescope Magazine.*

Betty and I come back up to New York in April, and in June we go out to Chatham and the Cape. We have an active life on Cape Cod, much of which revolves around golf at Eastward Ho! and social functions with our friends. I start every morning by going out to the flagpole and raising the American flag and one of the state flags, though on the Fourth of July I fly just the American flag. I usually put the state flags up in alphabetical order, but when visitors come, I almost invariably raise their state flag (or that of a state associated with them) in their honor. I like to take a brisk morning swim in Pleasant Bay, and on the days when I don't play a full round of golf, I get some afternoon exercise by smacking a few old balls off the bluff out into the bay. I play bridge as part of a group known as the Circulating Library, playing each Thursday in our

The men in my life. Left to right, Paul J. Elston, Frederick W. Beinecke,
Jacob S. Beinecke, Benjamin B. Beinecke, William S. Beinecke, John B. Beinecke,
Craig Richardson, Jesse Smith. In front, William Barrett Beinecke.

members' homes and rotating around the list. The club got its name
when the handful of original members would play their games in the
libraries of their homes. There are about thirty of us today, and we're
all at about the same level of skill, so our games are competitive and
fun. Since 1989 I have flown out every July to the annual encampment
at the Bohemian Grove, and I have usually brought along as a guest one
of my sons or sons-in-law to take part in the festivities and fellowship.
After the 1998 Bohemian Grove encampment, I reached the conclusion that now, in my eighty-fifth year, it was time that I put that behind
me. I had been there many times since first going as Randy Crossley's
guest in 1968. Also I thought leaving Betty alone in midsummer was
rather unfair. Consequently in early 1999 I applied for a change of
status. I am now an inactive member, sort of an emeritus classification.
On Sunday, May 9, 1999, while on a California trip, I took Betty up to
the Grove for a picnic and a look around. I was able to show her Cave
Man, Midway, the Great Stage, and many other points of interest. We
had a wonderful day.

In late September Betty and I close up the Cape house and return to New York, where we celebrate Thanksgiving and Christmas with our children. And come the new year, the whole cycle begins again.

I've been very fortunate to make it to my eighties in as good shape as I am. Of course, this doesn't stop me from complaining about the infirmities and indignities of old age. I have arthritis in my hands and various aches and pains elsewhere, and I have lost a lot of my upper-body strength; I especially notice that when I'm driving a golf ball. I also don't hear as well as I used to, and that drives my poor wife crazy. But I also spend a lot of time trying to look after my friends and contemporaries who have suffered debilitating mental and/or physical ailments, and I know that I'm really very lucky. I try to keep myself mentally as well as physically active. I read as much as I have time to, and I listen occasionally to Books on Tape. In the years since I turned seventy-five, the personal computer has transformed my life. The ease of composition and editing that it makes possible has been a boon and a blessing. I find it difficult to write now, particularly as my handwriting has grown more atrocious every year, but the computer has enabled me to keep up a wide correspondence, to write memoranda on a number of subjects, and to add to my travel logs. In recent years, I have tried (without much success) to surf the Net on my laptop computer, and I make extensive use of the wonderful device of E-mail to communicate instantaneously with lots of people.

One of the things that has pleased me most in my later years is to see how well all my children get along with one another. I suppose there's always rivalry between and among siblings, but the congeniality, conviviality, and collegiality that has always existed among our four children is remarkable. I think it's largely attributable to the influence their mother had upon them over the years—the influence of her compassion and leadership, and everything that flows from those qualities. And our children get along even better now than they did when they were younger. The younger children have always looked up to Rick, and they still do. Over the years, Betty has worried about money's giving rise to sibling jealousy—not an unreasonable fear given some of the rifts that have occurred in the extended Beinecke family in the past. But our children seem determined not to let that happen. They really trust one another, and that's a source of great joy to me.

And of course my grandchildren are a constant delight. They call me Opa, the German term for grandpa, just as my children used to call my father Opa. My mother didn't want to be called Grandma; our children called her Cacky, which was one child's mispronunciation of

Carrie. Betty didn't want to be called Grandma either, and so our grandchildren adopted her schoolgirl nickname, Gilleps.

Our oldest grandchild is Sarah's boy, Jesse William Smith. Sarah took Jesse's upbringing and education very much to heart. She enrolled him at Proctor Academy, which she chose because it offered a continuous, steady, and highly personalized education; he needed that kind of setting after having attended school on both coasts during his formative years. Proctor Academy was a wonderful place for him, and Sarah eventually became a trustee of the school. As I write this now in mid-1999, Jesse is taking sculpture classes in New York, and not long ago he assisted his stepfather, Craig Richardson, in film production. He and Annice Kenan of North Carolina, a lovely girl, were married in the Breakers Hotel in Palm Beach in June 1999. Jesse is growing up to be a fine young man.

Our next-oldest grandchild is Rick and Candace's older son, Jacob Sperry Beinecke, better known as Jake. He's a very serious, very mature person, who graduated from Trinity School and has reached his sophomore year at Columbia. As of 1999 he is working in the ski country in Telluride, Colorado, and is planning to resume his studies at Columbia University in January 2000. His younger brother, Benjamin, better known as Ben, turned sixteen in August 1999. He also attended Trinity, is as self-composed as his brother, and is already only an inch shorter than his father—and Rick is six foot two! Ben recently decided to follow his father, grandfather, and great-grandfather to Andover and entered in the fall of 1999. His decision is a great joy to Rick, who has faithfully served that school for twenty years as a dedicated, hard-working trustee.

Frances's oldest daughter, Carrie Sperry Elston, was born on Christmas Eve, 1980. Very artistic and very into dance, she developed into a master of choreography at the Fieldston School in Riverdale. Her hair has recently been bright red but changes according to her moods; I eagerly await the next color! It goes without saying that I am delighted that she is now enrolled in the Yale College class of 2003. She is the fourteenth member of my family to attend Yale in the direct line starting with my uncle Ben in the class of 1898S. Her younger sisters are twins, Mary Beinecke Elston and Elizabeth Beinecke Elston. They turned fifteen in December 1998 and are both enrolled at the Fieldston School, where they are both doing very well. Mary is musical and something of a prodigy at flute and piano, and Lizzie loves horses, is a good rider, and has champion potential.

Our youngest grandchild, born in 1988, is John and Gaily's son, William Barrett Beinecke, known as Barrett. He is a student at the

The grandchildren: Standing in front: W. Barrett Beinecke. In the rear, left to right: Jacob Beinecke, Jesse Smith, Benjamin Beinecke, Mary Elston, Elizabeth Elston, Carrie Elston.

Rudolph Steiner School, right next door to our apartment on East 79th Street. Barrett is artistic, beautifully mannered, and such a golfer! He knows the game inside and out, and is obsessed with it. I long ago had to learn to adjust to having my son outgolf his old man—John has an eight handicap and is a very good player—but John may someday have the same humbling experience. Over the years I have enjoyed reading to my grandsons. I have read *The Three Musketeers* to Jake, *Kidnapped* to Ben, and *Huckleberry Finn* and *Black Beauty* to Barrett.

My grandchildren are the main reason I first sat down to write this memoir. There are so many things I don't know about my own grandfathers, so many things I would have liked to have asked them! I hope that through this memoir, my grandchildren can know me better than I knew my forebears. When I am with my grandchildren, I think about the world they will inherit and the future they will live in. Will they be as nostalgic about automobiles and airplanes as I am about the bygone age of railroads and ferryboats? Will they experience another depression, another world war? Will they see the trading stamp rise again?

Bill and Betty Beinecke.

Will they know the answers to the problems that have perplexed me, from overpopulation to the environment to nuclear war? Will they see humanity plant a colony on Mars and other planets of our solar system? Will they witness new technologies that may in some strange, dreamlike science-fiction future allow humanity to export new settlements to planets elsewhere in the galaxy? And when they are my age, will they sit and tell their grandchildren about their own lives, their times, their ancestors? A family passes down many inheritances. Money is certainly a nice thing to inherit, but it can be lost, as my family lost most of our money in the Depression. It's more important to inherit a sense of who you are and where you come from. I hope that's something that my children's children, and their children's children, will never lose.

Appendix

$\mathcal{T}$he first entry in this appendix gives William Sperry Beinecke's genealogy. Names and relationships discussed in the early chapters of this book can be confusing. It is hoped that this chart will help to make clear some of those relationships.

The *Murray*'s wartime movements may be difficult to follow if the reader is not familiar with her operational area. The map on pages 540–541 shows the locations of places mentioned in the text

The two final entries reproduce extracts from the ship's reports for *U.S.S.Murray* on the occasions of the boarding of the Japanese hospital ship *Takasago Maru* on July 3–5, 1945, and the surrender of the Japanese submarine A-14 on August 27, 1945. The reader should keep in mind that these reports were typed aboard a pitching and heaving destroyer amid the pressures and confusions of wartime, and so naturally contain a few typographical errors.

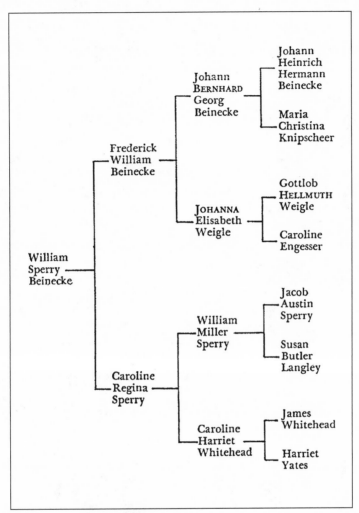

Ancestry of William Sperry Beinecke (compiled by Paul W. Prindle).

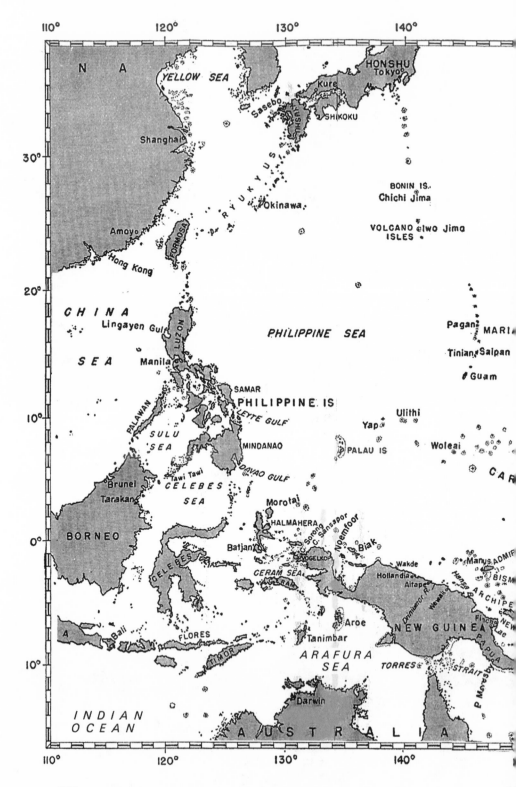

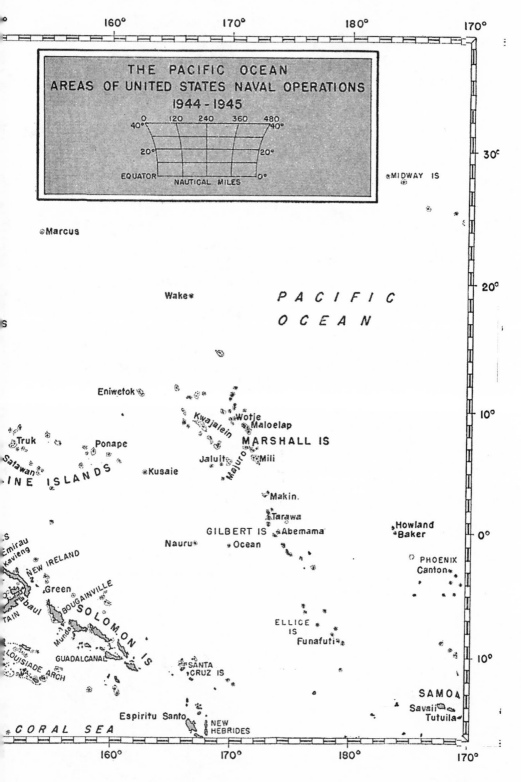

THE PACIFIC OCEAN
AREAS OF UNITED STATES NAVAL OPERATIONS
1944 - 1945

NAUTICAL MILES

Marcus

Wake

PACIFIC

OCEAN

MIDWAY IS

Eniwetok

Kwajalein   Wotje
            Maloelap

Truk   Ponape   MARSHALL IS

Salawan   Jaluit   Mili
                Majuro
        Kusaie

INE ISLANDS

Makin.

Tarawa

GILBERT IS   Abemama

Nauru   Ocean   Howland
                Baker

Emirau
Kavieng   PHOENIX
NEW IRELAND   Canton

Green   BOUGAINVILLE

baul   SOLOMON IS
TAIN

Munda   ELLICE
GUADALCANAL   IS
                Funafuti

LOUISIADE ARCH   SANTA
                CRUZ IS

                            SAMOA
Espiritu Santo   NEW   Savaii
                HEBRIDES   Tutuila

CORAL SEA

Report of the Boarding of Japanese Hospital Ship
Takasago Maru by crew of the USS *Murray*, July 3–5, 1945

```
A16-3/
Serial 006397
```

SECRET

                                    1st Endorsement on
                                    Co, USS MURRAY Secret
                                    Ltr. DD576/A16-3 of
                                    6 July 1945

From: Commander in Chief, U.S. Pacific Fleet
To: Commander in Chief, United States Fleet.

Subject: Boarding of Japanese Hospital Ship "TAKASAGO MARU" on July 3-
                5, 1945.

Reference: (b) CinCPac Adv. Hq. dispatch 120745 of July 1945.

     1.   Forwarded.

     2.   Orders to the MURRAY are contained in reference (a).   After
the second boarding, all U.S. submarines were informed of the prospective
movements of the TAKASAGO MARU and were ordered to permit her to pass.   The
Commander THIRD Fleet was informed, and authorized to divert the ship as
necessary to maintain his security.   Subsequent sightings and boarding are
described in reference (b).   This ship was recently sighted in YOKOSUKA by
planes of Task Force 38.

Copy to:
     ComDesPac (complete)

DD576/A16-3
Serial 00263   U.S.S. MURRAY (DD576)   c/o Fleet Post Office
                                                     San Francisco, Calif.,
                                                     6 July 1945

<u>SECRET</u>

From: The Commanding Officer
To: The Commander in Chief, U.S. Fleet
Via: The Commander in Chief, Pacific Fleet

Subject: Boarding of Japanese Hospital Ship TAKASAGO MARU on July 3-
            5, 1945.

Reference: (a) CinCPac Secret dispatch 020021 of July 1945

Enclosure: (A) Boarding Officer's Report on Boarding July 3, 1945
            (B) Boarding Officer's Report on Boarding July 5, 1945
            (C) Medical Officer's Report on Boarding July 3-5, 1945
            (D) Supply Officer's Report on Boarding July 3-5, 1945

PART I   (All times zone minus twelve East Longitude Date).

            In compliance with reference (a) and subsequent dispatches
the Japanese Hospital Ship TAKASAGO MARU was twice stopped and boarded at
sea as follows:

            On July 3, 1945 in Latitude 23-56N, Longitude 164-48E.
            On July 5, 1945 in Latitude 20-03N, Longitude 166-09E.

In neither boarding was any violation of international conventions
detected. Appropriate entries to this effect ere entered in the vessel's
log and she was permitted to continue her voyage on both occasions.

PART II   A brief summary of conditions found follows:

            (a) At 1930, July 3, 1945 the TAKASAGO MARU was directed to stop
for investigation in the position given above. The vessel immediately
complied. At this time the vessel carried no patients. Her crew consisted
of 157 men, all civilians except for navy boat crews and communication
personnel. A naval medical staff of 189 members was attached to the
vessel. Her captain gave her destination as Wake Island to evacuate the
sick and wounded. The vessel was half sand ballasted and carried no
provisions or stores that would indicate any violation of her status as a
hospital ship was contemplated. At the time rations carried were estimated
to be sufficient for 1500 men for one month (this was later revised based
on computations for U.S. Navy requirements as sufficient for 2000 men for
one month). The utmost cooperation was met during the search.

            (b) At 1858, July 5, 1945 after departing from Wake Island, the
TAKASAGO MARU was again boarded. There was no discernible difference in
the conditions regarding stores previously noted. About 974 bona fide
hospital patients had been embarked since the last inspection. This

DD576/A16-3
Serial 00263   U.S.S. MURRAY (DD576)

                                                        6 July 1945

SECRET

Subject: Boarding of Japanese Hospital Ship TAKASAGO MARU on July 3-
                5, 1945.
----

figure, 974, was supplied by the TAKASAGO MARU.   At the time the medical
staff was still busy arranging for these patients.   The MURRAY's medical
officer estimated, by rough count, that about 1050 patients were embarked.
of these patients it is estimated ten to fifteen percent could not survive
the voyage, twenty five per cent might be restored to duty in sixty days,
fourteen men were wounded, and fifteen per cent were believed to be
suffering from tuberculosis.   There were no Allied personnel.   In view of
the foregoing, the vessel was permitted to continue her voyage.

                B. Performance of Own Personnel.

                The   stern formal. dignity with which the boarding party
conducted the boardings and searches was impressive.   Especially tall and
military disciplined men were selected for this duty.

                                                P. L. de VOS

Copy to:
        CominCh (direct)
        CinCPac (Direct)
        ComDesPac via CinCPac

DD576/A16-3
Serial 00263   U.S.S. MURRAY (DD576)

                 6 July 1945

SECRET

Subject: Boarding of Japanese Hospital Ship TAKASAGO MARU on July 3-5, 1945

PART II   Chronological Account of Events.

         On the night of July 1, 1945 MURRAY was directed to get underway on one hours notice after 2200. Fueled to capacity.

0800 - July 2, 1945 Lieutenant F.B. Huggins, S(I), USNR and Lt(jg) R.P. Brown, S(I) USNR reported on board as interpreters.

0812 - Underway. Based on two sighting reports set course and speed to be on station on 200 mile circle north of Wake Island two hours prior to earliest possible arrival of hospital ship.

1010 - Heard plane 16X026 repeatedly attempt to establish communication (Plane used superseded voice call). This plane could be heard loud and clear but was unable to hear MURRAY. It was quite certain his receiver did not operate properly. However, the alert pilot of plane 14X was able to relay a fragment of a sighting report made at 1000.

1041 - Plane 14X relayed 1000 sighting report made by 16X026. Position: Latitude 25-27N, Longitude 163-00E; course 150 degrees T, speed 12 knots. Set course to intercept at speed 20 knots.

1240 - Plane 14X relayed second 1000 sighting report. Latitude 25-26N, Longitude 164-23E, course 160 degrees T, speed 12 knots. This position appeared more probably and course was altered to intercept.

1442 - Increased speed to 30 knots to intercept prior to nightfall.

1600 - An unidentified aircraft was reported approaching from directly astern. No IFF indications were observed nor were communications established until the plane was within gun range (It was not believed that there were any aircraft on Wake Island but under the circumstances it was not prudent for a plane to make such an approach without being postively identified).

1805 - Plane identified as 23X.

1845 - Plane 23X reported position of hospital ship as Latitude 23-35N, Longitude 165-00E.

1849 - Sighted round spherical black object equipped with spikes (believed to be a mine) dead ahead. Avoided. Tactical situation did not permit stopping to sink it.

Serial 00263   U.S.S. MURRAY (DD576)

                                        6 July 1945

SECRET

Subject: Boarding of Japanese Hospital Ship TAKASAGO MARU on July 3-5, 1945

1856 - Made radar contact on surface target dead ahead, range 35000
         yards. Went to general quarters and called away boarding party.

1912 - Directed hospital ship to stop, lie to, not to transmit by radio,
         and receive boarding party. Vessel promptly complied. Ship
         identified as TAKASAGO MARU.

2255 - Completed inspection. Since no violations of international
         conventions could be found, vessel was permitted to continue
         voyage.

2300 - Cleared area. Tracked at radar ranges from 39,000 to 42,000
         yards.

0720 - July 5, 1945 Japanese Hospital Ship TAKASAGO MARU hove to about
         one mile west of Wake Island. Continued surveillance at radar
         ranges from 38,000 to 42,000 yards. Observed myrids of birds well
         out to sea suggesting island might be unhealthy for them.
         TAKASAGO MARU kept station from 1000 to 3000 yards west of Wake
         Island.

1600 - TAKASAGO MARU underway belching heavy black smoke. Course 330
         degrees T, speed 15 knots. Maneuvered outside of visual range to
         take station 42,000 yards ahead.

1738 - Increased speed to 28 knots.

1814 - Went to general quarters; called away boarding party and began
         closing TAKASAGO MARU.

1852 - Stopped and boarded vessel.

2142 - Investigation completed. Since no violatons were discovered,
         vessel was directed to proceed.

0000 - 6 July. Set course at 20 knots to Eniwetok.

PART IV and V - Not applicable.

PART VI   Special Comments.

         A.   Communications

         It has been the experience of this ship that very often
aircraft (and even large ships at times) due to their altitude can often be
heard at far greater distances than the aircraft can hear a destroyer.
While in this case the failure of plane 16X026 to transmit his contact
report directly to MURRAY might be attributed to his faulty receiver, it is
considered the report should have been broadcast. Apparently this aircraft
was successfully communicating with his base. Attempts to discover what
frequency of the series was in use by "listening in" were unsuccessful.

Report of the Boarding and Surrender of Japanese Submarine A-14, to USS *Murray* August 27, 1945

CONFIDENTIAL   U.S.S. MURRAY (DD576)
DD576/A16-3
Serial 0333   c/o Fleet Post Ofice
                                               San Francisco, Calif.
                                               6 September 1945

From: The Commanding Officer
To: The Commander in Chief, U.S. Fleet
Via: (1) The Commander Destroyer Squadron TWENTY-FIVE
               (2) The Commander Task Group 38.1(ComCarDiv 3)
               (3) The Commander Task Force 38 (CSCTFPac)
               (4) The Commander THIRD Fleet
               (5) The Commander in Chief, Pacific Fleet.

Subject: Action Report for period 15 August - 2 September 1945

Reference: (a) PacFlt Conf. Ltr. 1CL-45
               (b) Com3rdFlt dispatch of September 1945

Enclosure: (A) Boarding Officer's report of boarding and surrender of
                   Japanese Submarine A-14.

PARTS I and II
               Omitted in accordance with reference (a) and instruction of
               Commander Destroyer Squadron TWENTY-FIVE

PART III   Chronological account. All navigational positions herein are
               expressed in North Latitude and East Longitude.   All times,
               except date-time groups of dispatches are zone time Item(-9),
               and all dates are East Longitude. All bearings are true.

        A.   The period covered by this report was without incident until
               27 August 1945 when the Japanese Submarine A-14 surrendered
               to a boarding party from MURRAY under the   following
               circumstances:

                              27 August 1945

    1110   While steaming in the screen of Task Group 38.1 received
               orders to form Task unit 38.1.12 with DASHIELL,   OTC,
               Commanding Officer MURRAY, for the purpose of investigating a
               Japanese Submarine reported by aircraft of the Task Group on
               the surface 18 mils to westward.

    1130   Made radar contact bearing 286 degrees T distant 24,000
               yards. Went to General Quarters and set condition Affirm.

    1137   Sighted submarine, fully surfaced and flying black flag.
               Commenced   high speed approach,   ziz-zagging   radically.
               Submarine on a North Westerly course.   Requested permission
               of Commander Task Group 38.1 to board. Permission not
               granted at this time.

U.S.S. MURRAY (DD576)
DD576/A16-3
Serial 0333   6 September 1945

Subject: Action Report for period 15 August - 2 September 1945

1217   On orders of Commander Task Group 38.1 directed submarine to
           take   course 180 degrees, at 12 knots, using international
           code of signals.   Submarine complied.   Efforts to reconcile
           her   appearance   and   call   with   available   information
           unsuccessful.

1239   Directed by Commander Task Group 38.1 to board submarine and
           to ascertain her fuel endurance.   Ordered sub to heave to.
           Position 37 degrees - 33'N, 144 degrees - 43'E.

1302   Boarding party of 4 officers and 12 men left ship (Lt. Comdr.
           F.M. RADER, USN, PCO* MURRAY, in charge). This party was made
           up partly of members of a party which had previously boarded
           the   Jap   hospital   ship TAKASAGO MARU and   partly from the
           ship's   regularly assigned boarding party.   The latter group
           was organized with a view to the possible capture of an enemy
           DD or similar vessel and some reorganization was necessary in
           order to meet the demands of submarine operation.

1311   Boarding party aboard submarine. Reported submarine had fuel
           for 800 miles at 12 knots. Sub identified as A-14.

1334   Hoisted U.S. colors on sub.

1352   Received   orders   from   Commander Task Group   38.1 to   leave
           boarding party on the submarine and to escort her to Sagami
           Wan.

1358   Search of submarine reported completed, and no explosives,
           Arms, charts or documents discovered except for 8 swords and
           10 dirks belonging to the Japanese officers.   These were
           surrendered to Lt. Comdr. RADEL on demand and with the
           request that they be returned.   These sidearms were sent to
           MURRAY, and transferred to the custody of Commander Escort
           Division 32 when MURRAY was relieved by BANGUST (DE739).
           This course was adapted in view of a broadcast originating
           on MISSOURI which suggested that surrendered side arms would
           be returned to their owners by Commander Third Fleet.

1430   Dispatched boat to A-14 with stores and replacement personnel
           in view of change in nature of mission.

    *PCO = Prospective Commanding Officer.

CONFIDENTIAL   U.S.S. MURRAY (DD576)
DD576/A16-3
Serial 0333   6 September 1945

Subject: Action Report for period 15 August - 2 September 1945

1500   Underway for Sagami Wan on course 230 degrees at 12 knots,
            MURRAY taking station on port beam of sub, DASHIELL on
            starboard beam.   On being informed of the destination, the
            Japanese Commanding Officer protested that he had been
            proceeding to OMINATO on order of his "highest Commander", a
            fact known to "your Commander, MacArthur". He was informed
            that his orders no longer held good and that he, his officers
            and his men were Prisoners of War.

1555   Detached DASHIELL on orders of Commander Task Group 38.1.

0125   Made contact with WEAVER (DE471) who reported she was
            searching for a Jap Sub in the custody of a U.S. DD. It was
            determined that she was referring to another boat, which has
            surrendered to BLUE(DD-387).   Shortly after these orders
            were received for the MURRAY to rendevous with Commander
            Escort Division 32 in BANGUST(DE739) and transfer the A-14
            to prize crew from the DE.

0540   Changed course to 215 degrees.

1400   After considerable communication difficulty extending over a
            period of several hours, the position of BANGUST was
            determined and course was changed to 003 degrees, speed 13
            in order to effect rendevous.

1610   Sighted BANGUST bearing 000 degrees, distance 8 miles.

1630   Ordered A-14 to heave to.   Directed BANGUST to close and
            effect transfer of boarding party.   Swords and dirks of Jap
            Officers transferred to Commander Escort Division 32 for
            safe keeping.

1710   Transfer completed.   Directed Commander Escort Division 32
            to proceed as previously directed.   MURRAY proceeding on
            course 055 degrees at 25 knots to rejoin Task Group 38.1.
            The report of the Officer in Charge of the boarding party
            covering the inspection and surrender of as well as the
            passage to rendevous with BANGUST is included as enclosure
            (A) of this report.

                            29 August 1945

0045   Effected rendevous with Task Group 38.1.

1500   Lt. Comdr. F.M. RADEL relieved Comdr. P.L. de VOS.

<u>CONFIDENTIAL</u>   U.S.S. MURRAY (DD576)
DD576/A16-3
Serial 0333   6 September 1945

Subject: Action Report for period 15 August - 2 September 1945
----

30 August 1945

1804   In company with McKEE formed Task Unit 38.1.14, OTC McKEE,
            with mission escorting LEXINGTON(CV16) to rendevous with
            Task Group 38.3 to South West of Miyake Shima.

31 August 1945

0655   Effected rendevous with Task Group 38.3.

1820   Task Unit 38.1.14 dissolved. MURRAY assigned Task Unit
            30.18.42 for onward routing to Task Group 30.8 and thence
            to Task Group 38.1.

2 September 1945

0625   Effected rendevous with Task Group 30.8.

1815   Detached from Task Group 30.8 with orders to proceed and
            rejoin Task Group 38.1.

2400   Rejoined Task Group 38.1.

PARTS IV, V and VI - No Comment.

PART VII   Performance of personnel was at all times of the highest
                caliber. It is particularly worthy of mention that only 2
                men of the MURRAY's boarding party, an Electrician Master
                first class and a Chief Commissary Steward, had had any
                previous submarine experience and that only the Chief
                Commissary Steward had had actual submarine duty.
                Notwithstanding this, all hands showed intelligence and
                resourcefulness in taking hold of an unfamiliar situation,
                and did the job in the best tradition of the service. Men
                of this caliber require no assistance in the carrying out of
                such as mission.

                                                        F.M. RADEL

Copy to:
    CominCh (Airmail)
    CinCPac (3 copies)
    ComDesPac

Index